Progress and Poverty

AN ECONOMIC AND SOCIAL HISTORY OF BRITAIN 1700–1850

M. J. Daunton

OXFORD UNIVERSITY PRESS

1995

Oxford University Press, Walton Street, Oxford OX2 6DP

Oxford New York
Athens Auckland Bangkok Bombay
Calcutta Cape Town Dar es Salaam Delhi
Florence Hong Kong Istanbul Karachi
Kuala Lumpur Madras Madrid Melbourne
Mexico City Nairobi Paris Singapore
Taipei Tokyo Toronto
and associated companies in
Berlin Ibadan

Oxford is a trade mark of Oxford University Press

Published in the United States
by Oxford University Press, New York

British Library Cataloguing in Publication Data
Data available

Library of Congress Cataloging in Publication Data
Daunton, M. J. (Martin J.)
Progress and poverty : an economic and social history of Britain, 1700–1850 / M. J. Daunton
p. cm.
Includes bibliographical references (p.)
1. Great Britain—Economic conditions—18th century. 2. Great Britain—Economic
conditions—19th century. 3. Great Britain—Social conditions—18th century. 4. Great
Britain—Social
conditions—19th century. I. Title.
HC254.5.D23 1995
330.941—dc20 94–46403
ISBN 0–19–822282–3
ISBN 0–19–822281–5 (pbk)

Typeset by Create Publishing Services Ltd.
Printed in Great Britain by
Bookcraft Ltd., Midsomer Norton, Avon.

To Claire

ACKNOWLEDGEMENTS

I WAS first approached by Ivon Asquith and Robert Faber to write an economic and social history of Britain during an international conference on Jeremy Bentham at University College London; whether the result has been for the greatest happiness of the greatest number I leave for others to assess. The sufferings of the author have certainly been reduced by the support of the Press, both from Robert Faber and his successor as history editor, Tony Morris. When the initial one-volume survey of the period from 1700 to 1914 grew too large, we agreed that I should produce two volumes, the first on the period from 1700 to 1850, followed by a second from 1850 to 1939 which will appear in the near future. The starting-point of my survey is the performance of the economy, but the aim has been to integrate social and political history into the analysis in a way which will, I hope, make the more technical writings of economic historians accessible to a wider audience, while at the same time adopting a critical stance on the underlying assumptions of some of the recent work of economic historians. Obviously, I am dependent on the work of a large number of other scholars which is recorded in the guide to further reading. The footnotes could have become excessively long, and I have tried to exercise as much restraint as possible: references are supplied to direct quotations, statistics, and controversial interpretations.

I would like to thank the following for permission to reproduce maps and figures: J. Thirsk and the Economic History Society for a map of agrarian regions from *England's Agricultural Regions and Agrarian History, 1500–1750*; B. R. Mitchell and Cambridge University Press for data on wheat prices and price indices from *British Historical Statistics*; J. A. Yelling and Macmillan for maps of the Vernon estate and enclosure from *Common Field and Enclosure in England, 1450–1850* (1977); J. R. Wordie for figures on rent on the Leveson-Gower estate from *Research in Economic History*, 6 (1981); A. R. H. Baker, R. A. Butlin, and Cambridge University Press for maps of common fields at Cuxham, open fields at Holkham, and infield–outfield at Westertown from *Studies of Field Systems in the British Isles* (1973); J. Langton, R. J. Morris, and Routledge for maps of parliamentary enclosure, employment in textile factories, distribution of steam engines, production of pig iron, regional coal output, inland navigation, railways, agricultural labour, and paupers from *Atlas of Industrialising Britain* (1986); R. V. Jackson and

Blackwell's for statistics on industrial output from *Economic History Review*, 2nd series 45 (1992); R. A. Dodghson, R. A. Butlin, and Academic Press for a map of textile specializations from *An Historical Geography of England and Wales* (2nd edition, 1990); P. Hudson, A. J. Randall, and Cambridge University Press for a diagram of the organization of the woollen cloth industry in P. Hudson (ed.), *Regions and Industries: A Perspective on the Industrial Revolution in Britain* (1988); the Oxford University Press for a map of coalfields and index of coal prices from M. W. Flinn, *History of the British Coal Industry*, ii: *1700–1830: The Industrial Revolution* (1984) and diagrams of steam engines from C. Singer et al., *A History of Technology*, iv: *The Industrial Revolution c. 1750–1850* (1958); P. Hudson and Cambridge University Press for diagrams of the credit matrix from *The Genesis of Industrial Capital: A Study of the West Riding Wool Textile Industry, c. 1759–1850* (1986); G. Turnbull and the Economic History Society for maps of canals from *Economic History Review*, 2nd series 40 (1987); G. Jackson and Manchester University Press for a map from D. H. Aldcroft and M. J. Freeman (eds.), *Transport in the Industrial Revolution* (1983); E. Pawson and Academic Press for maps of the turnpike system, travel times, and a graph of transport developments from *Transport and Economy: The Turnpike Roads of Eighteenth-Century Britain* (1977); P. K. O'Brien and Longmans for data from *English Historical Review*, 100 (1985); E. A. Wrigley, R. S. Schofield, and Cambridge University Press for population data from *The Population History of England, 1541–1871* (1981); and J. Landers for data on London demography from *Population Studies*, 41 (1967).

During the lengthy gestation of this first volume, I benefited from the advice and criticism of Julian Hoppit, who was always able to see a way through my difficulties; and I gained considerably from the regular seminars at the Institute of Historical Research and particularly from the remarks of the Director, Patrick O'Brien. At University College, the secretarial support of Nazneen Razwi was invaluable. Indeed, her assistance during the final stages of preparing the manuscript when I was a visiting fellow at the Australian National University was absolutely crucial. At the Press, Anna Illingworth, Milica Djuradjević, and Jackie Pritchard dealt with my long and long-distance manuscript with great speed and efficiency. Above all, Claire tolerated me during the writing of this book, when any country walk might become a study of field systems, an excuse to reflect on lead mining in the Pennines, or to consider the cloth industry in the Cotswolds. Her critical reading of drafts made it a better book, and rescued me from at least some of my details.

M.J.D.

Canberra
September 1994

CONTENTS

LIST OF FIGURES

LIST OF TABLES

STATISTICAL APPENDIX

1 Population

(*a*) Quinquennial totals of births and deaths, England, 1650–1654 to 1845–1849

(*b*) Quinquennial English population totals and annual growth rates, 1651–1851

(*c*) Gross reproduction rate and life expectancy at birth, England, 1651–1851

(*d*) Proportion of people never marrying per 1,000 aged 40–44, England, 1651–1851

(*e*) London Bills of Mortality: annual averages of recorded events per decade

2 Prices

(*a*) Price of wheat, in shillings per Winchester quarter, at Winchester College, 1690–1817

(*b*) Average price of domestic wheat per imperial quarter, England and Wales, 1771–1850

(*c*) Schumpeter–Gilboy price index, 1696–1823: consumers' goods

(*d*) Gayer–Rostow–Schwartz index of British commodity prices (domestic and imported), 1790–1850

(*e*) Index of coal prices, England, 1700–1830

(*f*) Terms of trade between agriculture and industry, 1690–1820

3 Output

(*a*) Trade in wheat and wheaten flour, Great Britain, 1697–1842: net import and net export

(*b*) Coal output, Britain, 1700 to 1850–1854

(*c*) Pig iron output, 1720–1724 to 1850

CHAPTER I

Introduction: The Possibilities of Growth

Adam Smith, in book i of *The Wealth of Nations* (1776), pondered 'the Causes of Improvement in the Productive Powers of Labour', and he was clear that he had the answer: 'The greatest improvement in the productive powers of labour, and the greater part of the skill, dexterity, and judgment with which it is any where directed, or applied, seem to have been the effects of the division of labour.'[1] He illustrated his argument with the famous example of the pin trade. A single workman could scarcely make one pin a day and certainly no more than twenty; division of tasks between specialized workers, each undertaking a distinct part of the process, permitted ten men to make 4,800 pins each a day, or an increase of at least 240-fold in labour productivity. The division of labour was clear in the pin trade, for relatively few workers were needed and they were gathered together in a single workshop; trades which employed a large number of workers 'to supply the great wants of the great body of the people' were more dispersed, and division was less obvious to the casual observer. But it was, argued Smith, at the heart of the process of growth and led to similar gains in productivity to those in the pin trade:

The division of labour ... occasions, in every art, a proportionable increase of the productive powers of labour. The separation of different trades and employments from one another, seems to have taken place, in consequence of this advantage. This separation too is generally carried furthest in those countries which enjoy the highest degree of industry and improvement; what is the work of one man in a rude state of society, being generally that of several in an improved one. In every improved society, the farmer is generally nothing but a farmer; the manufacturer, nothing but a manufacturer. The labour too which is necessary to produce any one complete manufacture, is almost always divided among a great number of hands. How many different trades are employed in each branch of the linen and woollen manufactures, from the growers of the flax and the wool, to the bleachers and smoothers of the linen, or to the dyers and dressers of the cloth![2]

The division of labour, Smith argued, increased productivity by workers' attaining greater dexterity in one particular task; by saving time which was otherwise lost in switching from one task to another; and in the development of specialized tools or machines.

Smith was describing a process of growth based upon *specialization*, which had certainly gone a long way in Britain by 1776. It was typified by the woollen coat of a labourer. The cloth was the product of the shepherd who tended the sheep and cut the wool, the sorter and comber who prepared it for the scribbler, spinner, dyer, weaver, fuller, and dresser; merchants and carriers transported materials from one group of workers to another, and brought dyestuffs from across the world; shipbuilders, sailors, sail- and rope-makers were needed to provide the vessels; the shepherd's shears depended upon the efforts of miners in winning iron ore which was processed in furnaces, forges, and smithies fuelled by charcoal and built from bricks. The same specialization applied to every item of the labourer's dress, food, and furnishings, from his shoes to his linen shirt, knives and forks, and beer. The division of labour, and the possibilities of growth by specialization, were, Smith believed, limited by the extent of the market, for concentration on the production of a highly specialized commodity was only possible when the level of demand justified workers devoting their whole time to the task, and when they were able to obtain other commodities from specialized workers. The extent of the market depended in turn upon the availability and cost of transport, and the development of a monetary system which freed trade from the constraints of barter. Consequently, a major element in the development of the British economy in the eighteenth century was the extension of the market in order to realize the potentialities of specialization. An area could only concentrate on the production of a commodity when the transport system permitted goods to be exchanged, which entailed a considerable investment in improved roads, rivers, canals, harbours, wharfs, docks, and railways. This rested upon innovation in the capital market to raise the necessary funds, which far exceeded the capabilities of a single individual or partnership. Merchants were needed to mediate between specialist producers, and to provide links with consumers; credit was necessary to facilitate the trade. The cost of transactions was reduced, and the tyranny of distance overcome.

Yet specialization did not lead, in Smith's account, to exponential growth or permit an escape from restraints on the standard of living. Smith was inclined to see a limit to the growth of the economy as well as prospects of improved productivity through the extension of the division of labour. The 'great commerce' of a society, he believed, was

carried on between the inhabitants of the towns and those of the country. It consists in the exchange of rude for manufactured produce ... The country supplies the town with the means of subsistence, and the materials of manufacture. The town repays this supply by sending back a part of the manufactured produce to the inhabitants of the country.[3]

The productivity of land set limits to the growth of the economy, for it provided food to the urban work-force and raw materials for processing in industry. He also believed that the growth of population was likely to place pressure upon the means of subsistence: 'As men, like all other animals, naturally multiply in proportion to the means of their subsistence, food is always, more or less, in demand.'[4] There were tight restraints on the possibilities of growth: despite the progress which had undoubtedly occurred, poverty remained an ever-present reality.

Smith assumed that investment passed through stages, and would eventually fall away as the rate of return declined. Investment would initially take place in agriculture, which offered the greatest benefit to society, for it enlarged the productive base for the whole economy and earned the highest rate of return. A surplus of food was, according to Smith, the motive power for the development of the economy. An inland area with abundant food had difficulties in selling its crops abroad because of limits to transport, but the availability of cheap food would attract workmen to process the raw materials produced by the land, which gave farmers a higher income and supplied them with goods to purchase. The fertility of the land encouraged manufacturers to settle in the area; subsequently, the manufactures encouraged farmers to improve their land. The quality of the manufactures improved, and higher-value commodities were able to bear the costs of transport to distant markets: surplus corn which could not be sent overseas could support workers who made high-value commodities for export. 'In this manner have grown up naturally, and as it were of their own accord, the manufactures of Leeds, Halifax, Sheffield, Birmingham and Wolverhampton. Such manufactures are the offspring of agriculture.'[5] Yet the process of growth could not continue indefinitely, for Smith assumed that the opportunities for investment in agriculture would be exhausted. Attention would turn to industry, until opportunities for profitable investment were in turn exhausted, and attention shifted to commerce, initially at home and at length in international trade. Holland had already reached this last stage by 1776, and England was following close behind. The exhaustion of opportunities for investment would, Smith argued, be reflected in a decline in the level of profit and the rate of interest. In Holland, the government could already borrow at 2 per cent and a businessman with good credit at 3 per cent; in England, the rate was 4 per cent and in Scotland and France still higher. The lower the rate of interest, the closer the country was approaching to a 'stationary state', the point at which it 'had acquired that full complement of riches which the nature of its soil and climate, and its situation with respect to other countries, allowed it to acquire; which could, therefore, advance no further, and which was not going backwards'.[6] Not only profits but also wages would be low: the population would be as large as the land could maintain and capital employ, so that competition for work would reduce wages to the bare minimum needed to keep them alive.

The analysis of the balance between land and population was taken further by T. R. Malthus in his *Essay on Population* of 1798. He assumed that population had a capacity to increase at a faster rate than the supply of food. The population would, unless checked by the exercise of prudence and restraint, double every twenty-five years in a geometric ratio from 1 to 2, 4, 8, 16, 32, and so on. Malthus feared that any increase in the food supply would 'by no means be obtained with the same facility':

When acre has been added to acre till all the fertile land is occupied, the yearly increase of food must depend upon the amelioration of the land already in possession. This is a stream which, from the nature of all soils, instead of increasing, must be gradually diminishing... The improvement of the barren parts would be a work of time and labour; and it must be evident to those who have the slightest acquaintance with agricultural subjects that, in proportion as cultivation extended, the additions that could yearly be made to the former average produce must be gradually and regularly diminishing.[7]

Although agricultural output might possibly double in the first twenty-five years, it 'would be contrary to all our knowledge of the properties of land' to expect the same rate of increase in the next twenty-five years. The output of agricultural produce could not, Malthus felt, expand faster than an arithmetic ratio of 1, 2, 3, 4, 5, 6, and so on. There was a constant dread that population could outstrip food supplies, with the result that prices would rise because of increased demand, wages fall because of the glut of labour, and the standard of living decline to subsistence level.

Malthus believed that the prospects of long-term economic growth were bleak, and restraints were inescapable; the only choice was whether population and resources would be balanced by 'positive checks' of famine and death or 'preventive checks' on procreation. 'Positive checks' were

every cause... which in any degree contributes to shorten the natural duration of human life. Under this head therefore may be enumerated, all unwholesome occupations, severe labour and exposure to the seasons, extreme poverty, bad nursing of children, great towns, excesses of all kinds, the whole train of common diseases and epidemics, wars, pestilence, plague, and famine.[8]

A larger population, more densely settled on the land or herded together in towns, was more prone to the spread of disease, especially when a deterioration in diet weakened resistance, and the water supply was contaminated. The second method of adjustment was through 'preventive checks', which could be the product either of vice or of moral restraint. Malthus sternly denounced controls on fertility produced by 'promiscuous intercourse, unnatural passions, violations of the marriage bed, and improper arts to conceal the consequences of irregular connexions'.[9] Prostitution, homosexuality, coitus interruptus, and abortion were anathema to Malthus, who believed that population should be regulated by the 'moral restraint' of celibacy and delaying marriage, based upon rational calculation and a desire to maintain status and respectability. A man contemplating marriage would, said Malthus, consider whether his present possessions and earnings could support children:

Will he not lower his rank in life, and be obliged to give up in great measure his former society? Does any mode of employment present itself by which he may reasonably hope to maintain a family? Will he not at any rate subject himself to greater difficulties, and more severe labour, than in his single state? Will he not be unable to transmit to his children the same advantages of education and improvement that he had himself possessed? Does he even feel secure that, should he have a large family, his utmost exertions can save them from rags, and squalid poverty, and their consequent degradation in the community?[10]

Malthus believed that most people did indeed make these rational calculations, so that English population growth was regulated by the age of marriage and the proportion of the population marrying. The preventive check was, he felt, apparent in all ranks of society. Men of 'liberal education' who had just enough money to associate with gentlemen feared a descent in the social scale; farmers' and tradesmen's sons needed to acquire a farm or business to support a family; servants would have to leave their positions on marriage; and labouring men were reluctant to share their pittance between four or five when it was barely enough for one. His chief fear was that the labourers' 'prudential restraint' and 'love of independence' were being threatened by the provision of poor relief linked to the number of children, which lessened the need to control family size. However, Malthus felt that English society in general exercised restraint and carefully assessed marriage in order to maintain social position and comfort. By these means, it was possible to preserve a precarious prosperity, and handicap the hare of population in its race with the tortoise of production.

The underlying assumption in Malthus's analysis of British society was that a collapse of the standard of living was held at bay through the prudence of the people; he did not foresee the possibility that the economy could escape from strict bounds and move to a higher level of prosperity. His emphasis was on a *cycle* in the balance between food supply and population, rather than long-term growth. If agriculture could feed a population of 11 million, an increase to 11½ million would reduce the living conditions of the poor as food prices rose and wages fell. A labourer would consequently have to undertake more work in order to maintain the same standard of life:

During this season of distress, the discouragements to marriage and the difficulty of rearing a family are so great, that population is nearly at a stand. In the meantime, the cheapness of labour, the plenty of labourers, and the necessity of an increased industry among them, encourage cultivators to employ more labour upon their land, to turn up fresh soil, and to manure and improve more completely what is already in tillage, till ultimately the means of subsistence may become in the same proportion to the population as at the period from which we set out. The situation of the labourer being then again tolerably comfortable, the restraints to population are in some degree loosened; and, after a short period, the same retrograde and progressive movements, with respect to happiness, are repeated.[11]

Malthus assumed that a continued improvement in the standard of living was impossible: any increase in real wages soon produced an increase in population and deterioration in real incomes. Britain was able to escape the worst consequences of population's ability to outstrip the supply of food only because prudential restraints upon marriage prevented the balance between population and the means of subsistence from moving too far out of line. The balance of population and resources in eighteenth- and early nineteenth-century Britain was relatively favourable and the process of adjustment reasonably painless, depending upon conscious actions rather than natural disasters of famine and disease such as in the Black Death of the early fourteenth century.

Malthus's main concern was the operation of the demographic system; Ricardo in *The Principles of Political Economy and Taxation* of 1817 concentrated on the distribution of wealth. At the heart of Ricardo's analysis was the concept of 'economic rent', a term with a more precise meaning than the everyday sense of the sum paid by a farmer to his landlord for use of land. The growth of population resulted in the extension of cultivation onto marginal land, and more labour and capital were needed to obtain a smaller output from each additional acre. Prices rose to a level sufficient for farmers on marginal land to obtain a normal level of profits, with the consequence that the profit on better land increased. This high level of profit was not retained by farmers, for they competed for access to superior land, so forcing up the level of rent paid to landowners. 'Economic' or Ricardian rent was the difference between the amount of rent farmers paid to their landlords on marginal land, and the premium which farmers were willing to pay for superior land. Farmers' profits on the superior land would decline to the normal level received by farmers of marginal land, so that any gains from the use of superior land were taken by landowners, who appropriated the difference in output between the two areas as 'economic rent'. Not only did the shift to marginal land allow landowners to take a larger share of the national income; it also meant that more labour was required to produce each addition to agricultural output. Wages would absorb a greater proportion of what remained after the payment of rent, so that less was available for profits. There would also be an increase in the price of agricultural produce, so that it would 'exchange for more hats, cloth, shoes, etc., etc., in the production of which no such additional quantity of labour is required'.[12] Food and raw material prices would increase relative to industrial prices, and more and more industrial goods would be needed in exchange for a given quantity of food and raw materials. Wages would fall to subsistence level; profit in industry would decline to the level obtained by marginal agricultural land; and growth would stop with the onset of the 'stationary state'. Any expansion of the economy would, according to Ricardo, simply allow landowners to increase their economic rent. 'The interest of the landlord', Ricardo concluded, 'is always opposed to that of the consumer and manufacturer.'[13]

Smith, Malthus, and Ricardo feared that the natural fertility of the population always had the potential to outstrip the land's capacity to produce food, which would cause dearth and a collapse in real wages. It was possible to make some gains, by developing the division of labour and carrying specialization to a higher point by extending the market with better systems of distribution and currency. But they did not hold out much hope of a major breakthrough in production that would permit continuing improvement in the standard of living. Their analyses assumed that the long-run equilibrium of the economy rested upon a balance between labour and land, and they did not expect that the application of capital and technology would permit a higher level of productivity and prosperity for the bulk of the population. The curse of declining marginal returns could not be escaped: growth was *asymptotic*, falling away to zero, rather than *exponential*, accelerating over time.[14]

The classical economists were perceptive contemporary observers of the British economy at the end of the eighteenth and start of the nineteenth centuries, and their analyses suggest a number of questions which provide the agenda for this book. The first and most obvious issue is: were they accurately describing the mechanisms by which the economy was brought into equilibrium; and at what point did the mechanisms change? A major task for the historian of Britain between the late seventeenth and early nineteenth centuries is to establish whether Malthus was accurately describing a shifting balance between population and land, which was corrected through changes in the age of marriage rather than by adjustments in fertility within marriage or by changes in mortality. What needs to be established is whether Britain did experience a cycle on the lines predicted by Malthus and Ricardo. If they were right, a favourable balance between population and land led to low food prices and high real wages; early marriage was encouraged, which led to a rapid growth in population; wages fell as a result of an over-stocked labour market, and food prices rose as the marginal productivity of agriculture fell; landowners reaped the benefit of higher rents and real wages deteriorated; eventually, the fall in real wages led to a delay in marriages, and the balance between land and labour was restored. Unfortunately, it is extremely difficult to test this model for the seventeenth and eighteenth centuries before the introduction of the census and other statistical series, and much attention will necessarily be paid to the difficult task of compiling reasonable estimates from recalcitrant sources. A strong case can certainly be made for the existence of a Malthusian or Ricardian cycle in Britain. But, at some point, there was a change in mechanisms which established the long-run equilibrium of the economy: a Malthusian balance between population and land gave way to capital and technology as the crucial variables, which allowed an increase in the level of productivity and an increase in per capita incomes. The restraints of the Malthusian economy were released, and growth became cumulative. When did this change occur, and how much impact did it have by 1850? At what point was there a noticeable increase in the level of fixed capital formation, and in the application of powered machinery to production? When did the relationship between population movements and real wages change, so that an increase in population did not threaten a collapse in the standard of living, and an increase in the standard of living did not stimulate a rise in fertility? At some point, the *modus operandi* of the British economy underwent a major transformation.

The views of the classical economists started to change from the 1820s and 1830s as they combined Smith's emphasis upon the division of labour with a new stress upon investment in fixed capital in machinery, which meant that Ricardo's theory of rent and Malthus's law of population started to appear irrelevant. Ricardo himself argued that further growth was possible, provided that food and raw materials could be imported from abroad in return for manufactures. His model was, to some extent, a 'methodological fiction'[15] which was based on the current assumptions of government policy, that agriculture should be protected by import duties and trade restricted. The 'stationary state' was a 'useful device for frightening the friends of protection',[16] and he argued that its onset could at least be delayed by removing import and export duties on raw materials and manufactures. Here he departed from Malthus, who was a staunch protectionist on the grounds that it was crucial to maintain self-sufficiency in food. Ricardo disagreed. 'While trade is free, and corn cheap', he commented in 1820, 'profits will not fall however great be the accumulation of capital.'[17] He had greater optimism about the prospects of growth *provided that free trade was introduced*, and he was willing to accept that growth could derive from investment in fixed capital. Ricardo argued that the accumulation of capital *without technical change* required a wider margin of cultivation which would lead to declining marginal returns and a collapse of profits. However, capital accumulation *with technical change* removed the need to extend the margin of cultivation and avoided declining marginal returns. Ricardo could therefore be understood as warning politicians that an expansion of population and capital *without international trade and technical improvement* would soon lead to falling rates of profit and a stationary state. Nevertheless, it would be difficult to convert Ricardo from a gloomy prophet of declining marginal returns and the stationary state into an apostle of growth. His economic analysis rested upon what he called 'natural tendencies', and the opening of the economy to free trade did not make a fundamental change in the growth process: there was simply a shift to new areas of cultivation where decreasing marginal returns were not yet apparent. He remained sceptical about the possibility of permanent gains in the standard of living. Cheap food imports would allow profits to be maintained by reducing the subsistence cost of workers and cutting the share of wages, rather than allowing a permanent gain in prosperity. Similarly, the accumulation of capital in machinery would maintain the level of profit through a reduction of wages. He also continued to accept Malthus's assumption that any increase in real wages would continue to produce higher population growth and an erosion of gains in the standard of living, rather than producing a change in expectations which would lead wage-earners to purchase more commodities instead of contracting early marriages. Although Ricardo was starting to feel his way towards a change in the long-run equilibrium of the economy, he still based his analysis upon the tendency of profits to fall and a stationary state to emerge.

By the 1830s, there was more confidence that capital and machinery offered an escape. Nassau Senior, for example, stressed the increasing returns to labour from the application of fixed capital to large-scale production and technological improvement, primarily by subordinating workers to control by capitalists rather than through the application of a centralized source of power. Senior's optimism that population growth would not necessarily threaten immiseration marked a shift in attitudes to the poor law. Malthus contended that relief of the poor was a delusion, for it allowed couples to marry and have children, which simply intensified poverty. Senior was more sanguine that an increased population could be employed at a higher level of productivity and wages.[18] In the 1840s the attention of economists shifted from the accumulation of fixed capital in machinery to the application of inanimate power and particularly steam. Clearly, these changes in the perceptions of economists from Malthus to Senior are important for an understanding of policy debates over the poor law and protection. But how far do they also reflect changes in the behaviour of the economy? Were they correct in ignoring or minimizing the application of machinery and centralized power until the second quarter of the nineteenth century?

The debate over changes in the long-run equilibrium of the economy is related to a second issue: the *chronology* of growth. The classical economists assumed that growth was hitting the barriers of possibility at the end of the eighteenth and start of the nineteenth centuries. Population growth, they feared, was placing pressure on resources, profits were falling, and the standard of living was eroded. There is little sign in the writings of the classical economists that an industrial revolution was in progress and it could be argued that Smith, Malthus, and Ricardo were simply mistaken, ignoring changes which were transforming the British economy and removing the fetters on growth. At no point did Smith consider the impact of steam power or the application of coal to industrial processes. His fellow Scot James Watt had patented a major improvement to the steam engine in 1769; and, within a short distance of Smith's study in Edinburgh, coal was being exploited by the Prestonpans vitriol-works and the Carron ironworks which were established in 1749 and 1759. Was Smith an academic whose vision was limited by the library and lecture theatre, oblivious of the endeavours of engineers and entrepreneurs in transforming the economy?

The dominant view amongst economic historians in the 1960s was that the classical economists had indeed mistaken the chronology of growth, ignoring major economic changes which were transforming Britain as they wrote. Towards the end of the eighteenth century, so these historians argued, an agricultural revolution was raising yields by the adoption of new rotations, improved breeds, and the enclosure of the open fields; a 'wave of gadgets'[19] swept across England as steam power and machinery were applied to production; and the rate of growth of the economy accelerated. Sceptics who contended that the standard of living was falling around the turn of the eighteenth and nineteenth centuries, or that the rural poor were being dispossessed by enclosure and the erosion of their traditional rights of gleaning or grazing, were dismissed by optimists who argued that economic change was for the best in the best of all possible worlds, leading to efficiency rather than immiseration, and allowing an acceleration of growth from which the majority of the population benefited.

There was, argued W. W. Rostow, a 'take-off' into self-sustained growth between 1783 and 1802: the British economy, like an accelerating aircraft escaping the pull of gravity, made a decisive break with 'the habits and institutions, the values and vested interests of the traditional society'. The process was, he suggested, driven by a 'leading sector', an industry with a particularly rapid rate of growth which could push the whole economy forward: in the case of Britain, it was cotton, with its new spinning-machines and factories. 'Compound interest', claimed Rostow, 'gets built into the society's structure.'[20] The pioneering national income estimates of Deane and Cole appeared to confirm his chronology. There were, according to their figures, 'few signs of growth in the economy as a whole' between 1700 and the 1740s, when real national output and output per head both grew by 0.3 per cent per annum. Between 1745 and 1785, they estimated that real national output grew more rapidly, by 0.9 per cent per annum, but growth in output per head still remained at 0.3 per cent per annum. The breakthrough, on their statistics, came in the 1780s and 1790s, when real national output grew by 1.8 per cent per annum, pulling ahead of population growth so that output per head grew by 0.9 per cent per annum.[21] Clearly, this interpretation and these estimates suggested a different chronology of growth from that of the classical economists, and Smith, Malthus, and Ricardo simply appeared to have missed a spurt in the rate of growth at the very time they were stressing the limits to growth.

The reputation of the classical economists as observers of the contemporary scene was rescued in the 1980s, when many historians came to the conclusion that they had a firm grasp of the chronology and possibilities of growth in Britain. The 'new' econometric historians started to subject existing interpretations to scrutiny, using explicit economic theory and statistical techniques. The figures of national income and output were reworked, to suggest that there was no acceleration of growth in output and no surge in income per capita at the end of the eighteenth century.[22] Attention turned to the explanation of Britain's slow rate of growth, rather than a search for the origins of the 'first industrial revolution'. Britain, it was argued, could not grow rapidly until the termination of the French revolutionary and Napoleonic wars in 1815, for the massive cost of public finance 'crowded out' investment in industry, and forced industrialists to develop production technologies which saved capital and relied upon labour-intensive production.[23] The emphasis upon a leading sector of mechanized, centralized production in factories gave way to a stress upon the high proportion of workers employed in 'traditional' hand labour with limited prospects of improved productivity. The concept of 'social saving' was used in order to measure the impact of the steam engine on the economy, and it was found that it made little difference until the second quarter of the nineteenth century.[24] Doubts were expressed whether enclosure and the 'agricultural revolution' were means of achieving higher productivity, or a means by which landowners increased rents as Ricardo suggested. British aristocrats were, on this view, not heroic 'improvers' who spread prosperity amongst a grateful tenantry: they were the parasitical beneficiaries of an economy tending towards a 'stationary state'.[25]

Above all, E. A. Wrigley argued that the classical economists had a firm grasp of the possibilities of growth within an *advanced organic economy*. Smith and Ricardo were, he suggests, largely correct: land was the source of food, energy, construction materials, and raw materials for industry. The economy described by Smith, Malthus, and Ricardo was based upon textiles produced from animal and vegetable fibres, leather from animal hides, wood for fuel and building. Industrial growth would place increased demands on the land to provide fodder for horses or wood for building, domestic fuel, and charcoal, and a ceiling of output would soon be reached. The energy needs of the economy were largely supplied by a *flow* from food crops and wood, supplemented by water and wind power, which could not easily be increased. Any temptation to cut more wood than the annual growth would run into problems as reserves were exhausted; the use of more land to grow vegetable raw materials would collide with demands for food. The possibilities of growth in an organic economy were therefore limited, until restraints were removed by the injection of massive amounts of mineral fuel, which did not come until the nineteenth century.[26]

By down-playing the pace of growth at the end of the eighteenth century, the chronology of economic development could be shifted in one of two directions. On the one hand, the emphasis could be pushed ahead to the second or even third quarter of the nineteenth century, viewing the preceding two centuries as a period of slow growth in which the economy was not 'pervasively innovative'. Rather, 'the period of rapid productivity growth was a relatively brief mid-nineteenth-century phenomenon'.[27] On this view, the pace of *growth* was slow, but the economy underwent a major *structural* transformation in the later seventeenth and eighteenth centuries as a result of the release of people from the land into industry, services, and towns. Rapid structural change did not, according to the proponents of this interpretation, produce an acceleration in productivity growth or output, for it is assumed that workers moved from an efficient agricultural sector into 'traditional' labour-intensive, low-productivity trades and services rather than into high-productivity 'modernized' industries using factories and steam power which only became significant in the mid-nineteenth century. It could, on the other hand, be argued that the chronology should be adjusted in order to emphasize the achievements of the British economy in the later seventeenth and early eighteenth centuries. The ability of agriculture to release labour into industry and services would suggest that there were significant gains in agricultural productivity and output in the late seventeenth and early eighteenth centuries which enabled more people to move into non-agricultural pursuits. Could this argument be pushed a stage further, to suggest that there were gains in efficiency outside agriculture and that economic growth at the end of the seventeenth and opening of the eighteenth centuries was a more general phenomenon? Here the issue of chronology moves into another area of controversy: the nature of the growth *process*.

The 'new' econometric historians assume that growth took place as the result of the emergence of capital-intensive factories with powered machinery and the application of large quantities of mineral fuel to escape from the constraints of an organic economy. They minimize the possibilities of growth in so-called 'traditional' industries and services, and their estimates of national income growth crucially assume that little or no gain in productivity was possible in these sectors. However, the division between low-productivity 'traditional' handicraft industries and high-productivity 'modern' industries has been challenged, on the grounds that it takes for granted a model of economic growth which stresses the virtues of mass production. Perhaps growth could be based upon an alternative path of 'flexible specialization'.[28] Smith had pointed to the gains from the division of labour in the production of pins, which were a simple, standardized item where the possibilities of growth through specialization were soon reached. There were, however, other cases in which workshop or domestic production provided continued possibilities of growth, by allowing producers to respond swiftly to changing markets and fashions, whether for cutlery, tableware, buckles, or furniture. The distinction between 'traditional' hand production and 'modern' factories rests upon the belief that powered machinery allowed gains in productivity, but an increase in the quantity of goods produced is only part of the picture. Hand production permitted innovation in commodities and their design, and could add more value to materials. Further, historians who have analysed the social organization of production in particular localities rather than constructing macroeconomic aggregates have found that the organization of handicraft production was undergoing major changes.[29] By a close analysis of the organization of domestic outwork in textiles or the small metal trades, they have charted significant shifts in the relationship between stages of production, between workers and employers, between merchants and producers, with continuing adjustments in the design of hand tools which permitted gains in productivity. Further, the so-called 'modern' sectors were not rigidly separated from 'traditional' handicraft producers, for centralized factories or plant often provided raw materials or 'intermediate' goods to be transformed into final consumer goods; and powered machinery was often utilized in one stage of an industry which otherwise remained 'traditional'. A clear distinction between two sectors obscures the gradual transformation of the so-called traditional sectors by their own internal dynamic, as they accumulated capital for investment in factories, adopted powered machines in order to escape particular bottle-necks, and utilized different production methods to cater for particular markets. Rather than stressing a division between one group of industries with limited prospects of improvement in productivity and another group which escaped from the fetters of traditional technology, they should be seen as part of a single process of growth. There would, it is true, be considerable variation in the capacity of different trades and regions to transform, for the organization of the industry might ease or hinder the emergence of centralized factory production, depending on who accumulated capital, or how new machines affected social relationships. This is to point to a third issue in the analysis of the British economy from the late seventeenth to the mid-nineteenth centuries: should it be understood by a close analysis of regional economies rather than by a reliance upon macroeconomic aggregates?

The suggestion of the 'new' economic historians that economic growth in the eighteenth century was slow, and that the breakthrough to a new rate of growth was delayed until the nineteenth century, assumes that an integrated national market already existed by 1700. Neo-classical economics, which provides the framework for their analysis, takes the existence of a market for granted, with perfect competition, an absence of transaction costs, a freedom from uncertainty, and stability of economic institutions. In fact, the gradual emergence of an integrated market economy could be the crucial determinant of the chronology and pace of growth within a 'Malthusian' economy.[30] The emergence of an integrated market economy needs to be carefully measured and dated rather than assumed, for the prospects of growth in the late seventeenth and eighteenth centuries would be greater if an integrated market was still in process of creation. New economic historians who simply assume that the economy was integrated by 1700 miss a major source of growth which could be much more significant than large-scale investment in production. The development of an integrated economy would, as Adam Smith stressed, lead to specialization and the division of labour. Clearly, there were more severe limits on growth if each region in the country was obliged to grow its own grain in order to be certain of supplies, despite poor climatic conditions or soil types. There were greater possibilities of gains in productivity within the limits of an 'organic' economy if regions were confident that they could abandon self-sufficiency and concentrate on the agricultural or industrial goods to which they were most suited. Integration of the economy could also contribute to growth through the reduction in 'transaction costs' and uncertainty. Even if there were no major changes in the cost of production or in technology, there could still be significant reductions in the costs of information, credit, transport, and merchanting, which formed a high proportion of total costs.

Any understanding of the development of the British economy between the late seventeenth century and early nineteenth century must rest upon a careful measurement of the integration of the economy, the extent of specialization, the containment of uncertainty, the level of competition, and movements in trans-action costs. These were complex historical phenomena. The reduction in freight costs entailed a series of technical improvements in the design of ships and road vehicles, and the emergence of engineering skills in the construction of harbours, waterways, bridges, and roads. New forms of organization were needed in order to raise considerable sums of money for investment in projects such as docks and canals, and to manage the ventures. The development of specialist ship brokers provided a more active market in freights which could speed the turn-round of vessels and allow them to be more fully utilized; and the emergence of marine insurance reduced risks. The growth of an integrated economy rested upon the endeavours of merchants and bankers, and the enterprise of hawkers and shopkeepers. It involved the extension of a monetized economy to areas such as the Highlands of Scotland where the clan system still survived, and the replacement of payment in kind and 'entitlements' by a money wage.

An emphasis upon the creation of an integrated market, patterns of special-ization, and reduction in transaction costs affects the way in which the economic and social history of Britain between 1700 and 1850 should be written. Much of the work of the 'new' econometric historians deals with national aggregates, measuring the gross national product and testing relations between national population trends and wages. But is this approach satisfactory? There is a danger of combining very different patterns of behaviour in a number of distinct groups or regions in order to produce a single aggregate which fails to describe the experience of any single class or area. A fall in real wages might produce a delay in the age of marriage amongst artisans or smallholders who needed to accumulate assets to start a business or buy livestock; but if the prospects of even attaining independence were reduced, they might decide to marry early. Similarly, the impact of price changes varied between regions. In an area with customary tenure or long leases, the advantage of higher prices for agricultural commodities was taken by the tenants, who did not need to pay higher rents; in areas with short leases, the landowners would be able to increase rents. Landowners who were not able to appropriate the profits from high prices would seek to overturn customary tenures and long leases, which might well depend upon their ability to convince the courts or to obtain an act of parliament. Market forces were, in other words, mediated through the legal and political system, and involved issues of power and social conflict. Diversity was not removed by the process of integration, for it permitted a greater degree of specialization in a single com-modity which was exchanged for other goods. One region might shift to pastoralism, where small farms were more likely to persist, with a more egalitarian social structure and a survival of annual labour contracts to provide a steady supply of labour; a second region might concentrate on arable farming, with larger farms, a highly seasonal pattern of employment, and a reliance on short contracts of employment; a third region might rely on rural industry. Each region would have its own distinctive social structure, which shaped the response to changes in prices or wages. The emergence of an integrated national economy meant that signals were transmitted to all regions, but their response differed.

The creation of an integrated, market economy was also a political phenomenon: the state and public policy need to be fully incorporated into the economic and social history of Britain. The role of politics in market integration is most obvious in the case of Scotland: in 1707 the two kingdoms of England and Scotland were united, although they still maintained their distinctive banking systems, poor laws, and legal codes which provided different frameworks for the operation of market mechanisms. The operation of markets is not the abstraction of neo-classical economic theory, for it involves issues of power and policy. Changes in the law relating to bankruptcy, the security of loans, banking, and limited liability affected the organization of commerce and credit, the cost of transactions, and the level of uncertainty. The mobility of labour was influenced by the nature of the poor law, which could work in opposite directions. On the one hand, Malthus feared that it could interfere with the mobility of labour, for parishes tried to limit the right of labourers to settle in order to guard against potential claims for relief. On the other hand, the fact that the English poor law gave an absolute right to relief could offer security for men and women to migrate in the knowledge that their welfare did not depend upon their family of origin. In Scotland, there was no such absolute right and social policy might therefore have a different impact on the labour market. Above all, the assumption that wages and prices were determined by the unfettered operation of the market, which is taken as axiomatic by neo-classical theory, was itself the subject of dispute in the eighteenth century. It begs the whole issue of the proper basis of public policy which was at the heart of British history. The emergence of a market economy was, in the opinion of some historians, the result of a legal transformation which destroyed a 'moral economy' of fair prices and just wages, and the rights of workers to perquisites and access to land in the form of 'contingent property rights' of gleaning, grazing a few animals, collecting wood. The substitution of 'political economy', they argue, imposed stricter work discipline by criminalizing perquisites and eroding contingent property rights. Custom, they argue, was replaced by contract.[31] Should developments in the law be interpreted as part of the imposition of capitalist property relations, and the subordination of workers to the discipline of a monetized economy? Or could the legal system provide a resource for them to delay the transformation of the economy?

This raises the issue of whether the state was an active agent in the transformation of the British economy, or whether it was at best indifferent and at worst a barrier to change. The contention of Adam Smith was that the mass of trade regulation and protection which survived until the 1840s was harmful. The market could be limited by protection of domestic production and limits on imports of food which, he argued, led to inefficiencies. Scotland could, he remarked, produce wine from grapes grown in heated glasshouses, if the level of duties on imported French wine were sufficiently high. The result would be inefficiency: cheaper and better wine could be obtained from France, and it would be preferable for Scotland to concentrate on producing goods for which its resources were more suitable. A free market would lead to the benefits of comparative advantage, extending the market and reducing costs. Was Smith's condemnation of the system of protection correct? It was argued by economists in Germany and the USA in the nineteenth century that protection was needed in order to develop new industries in order to meet competition from British goods. Could it be that British governments had successfully used protection in order to foster British industries in the eighteenth century, allowing them to capture markets at home and overseas? Investment in the navy and imperialism could secure markets, which allowed industrialists and merchants to increase their production and efficiency, and make it feasible at a later date to support a policy of free trade, in the knowledge that there was little to fear from potential rivals. Perhaps Smith's criticism of protection as a hindrance to comparative advantage and the creation of an integrated international market was mistaken: protection might have fostered growth and contributed to British dominance of international trade which subsequently permitted the imposition of free trade from a position of power. Or was investment in war and imperialism a policy designed to assist an alliance of 'moneyed' interests, who provided the state with loans, and aristocrats who obtained profitable opportunities in public service, at the expense of the productive classes who paid high taxes? Such criticisms inspired the 'country' critics of the eighteenth century and the radical attack on government policy in the early nineteenth century. It connected with protection for agriculture, which was criticized by free traders as a policy designed by selfish landowners in order to maintain their rent levels at the expense of the rest of society. But was this the intention of the government? Malthus certainly remained sceptical of the virtues of free trade, for he felt that it was not prudent to rely upon imports of food; a disruption of supplies, or the erosion of a surplus in the producing country as a result of population growth, would create a serious crisis at home. Consequently, he was an advocate of a balanced domestic

economy rather than extreme specialization, stressing the need for self-sufficiency in food. Arguably, the government was showing a sensible concern for the
prosperity of the British economy in maintaining protection for agriculture until
1846, rather than pursuing the narrow interests of landowners. Such debates
were at the heart of British politics during the eighteenth and early nineteenth
centuries.

New economic historians do, it is true, often test the impact of policies
adopted by parliament, inquiring whether a duty did in fact lead to a misallocation of resources, or a payment in aid of wages did stimulate population
growth. Although their findings are often interesting, they do not explain why
the measures were implemented nor do they consider what they indicate about
the nature of the British state. The question arises of who was shaping policy, in
whose interests. To some historians, the British state in the eighteenth century
was dominated by a small oligarchy of landowners who wielded electoral
influence over constituencies, which did not have an active role in the shaping of
policy. Such an approach at first sight meshes with the work of economic
historians who indicate the emergence of a more concentrated pattern of
landownership and the decline of small proprietors or 'yeomen'. The emphasis
on the limits to growth in eighteenth-century Britain has also been seized upon
by critics of Marxist interpretations which stress the emergence of class conflict.
Marginalizing the impact of steam engines and factories seemed to preclude the
emergence of a factory proletariat and class conflict on the lines proposed by
Marx and Engels, and one historian has gone so far as to argue that eighteenth-
century England should be viewed as a stable *ancien régime* in which patriarchal
relations survived within family-based workshops, and society was tied together
by the acceptance of a divinely ordained social order.[32]

In fact, the reinterpretation of British economic growth should be seen as a
challenge to notions of oligarchic stability or the survival of an *ancien régime*. A
slow rate of growth was allied to a major structural shift in the population from
the land to industry, services, and towns. The result was the emergence of a
larger and more influential commercial and industrial middle class, which could
challenge the existing basis of political power. Close analysis of the political life of
constituencies has indicated that the 'middling sort' were far from being the
manipulated puppets of a small landed élite, and politics was a matter of
negotiation rather than a one-sided wielding of influence. A new range of public
institutions was set up, from charities to turnpike trusts, which extended the
boundaries of civil society; and parliament passed a mass of legislation at the
behest of local interests. Indeed, it could be argued that the British state of the
eighteenth century was characterized less by a closed, oligarchic structure, than
by its accessibility to a wide range of influences. The increase in the scale of

industrial activity could, even in the absence of factories and mechanization, create tensions within industries based on workshops or domestic production, upsetting the existing social organization of work through the need for stricter controls over labour or an intensification of competition. There is, after all, no reason why factory workers rather than artisans or rural cottages should be at the forefront of social protest and conflict. On the contrary, it might well be artisans, with a sense of property in their skill as 'honourable' trades, who were most able to organize in protest against a deterioration in their position. Similarly, the new economic historians have provided support for critics of enclosure as a device for 'class robbery' which removed the rights of small farmers and shifted income to landlords, and have challenged the apologists of rural change who stressed efficiency and productivity gains. Further, the emphasis upon the slow rate of economic growth gives more support to those who argue that the standard of living was eroded in the late eighteenth and early nineteenth centuries, and that the industrial revolution led to hardship and misery rather than improvement. Far from supporting the notion that eighteenth-century Britain was a stable, patriarchal *ancien régime* which was innocent of social conflict, the thrust of recent work on the slow rate of growth could support an interpretation which stresses social tension.

Application of these themes and approaches starts with the agricultural basis of the economy, which was so important to Smith, Malthus, and Ricardo. Was it really the case that British agriculture was facing declining marginal returns by the end of the eighteenth century, with a rise in prices and rent, which led to a redistribution of income in favour of landowners? Clearly, the first task must be to establish the chronology of agricultural output and yields in Britain from the late seventeenth century.

NOTES

1. Adam Smith, *An Inquiry into the Nature and Causes of the Wealth of Nations* (1776), ed. E. Cannan (1904; repr. New York, 1937), 3 (book i, ch. i).
2. Ibid. 5–6 (book i, ch. i).
3. Ibid. 356 (book iii, ch. i).
4. Ibid. 146 (book i, ch. xi).
5. Ibid. 383 (book ii, ch. v).
6. Ibid. 94 (book i, ch. ix).
7. T. R. Malthus, *An Essay on the Principle of Population* (1803 edn.), ed. with variora by Patricia James (Cambridge, 1989), i. 13, 14.
8. Ibid. 18.
9. Ibid.
10. Ibid. 17.

11. Ibid. 20.
12. D. Ricardo, *The Works and Correspondence of David Ricardo*, ed. P. Sraffa, i: *On the Principles of Political Economy and Taxation* (Cambridge, 1951), 74.
13. Ibid. 335.
14. These are the terms used by E. A. Wrigley, *Continuity, Chance and Change: The Character of the Industrial Revolution in England* (Cambridge, 1988), 48.
15. M. Blaug, *Ricardian Economics: An Historical Study* (New Haven, Conn., 1958), 31–2.
16. Ibid.
17. Quoted in M. Berg, *The Machinery Question and the Making of Political Economy, 1815–48* (Cambridge, 1980), 48.
18. See Ch. 19, pp. 492–3, for the implications for the poor law.
19. The phrase is in T. S. Ashton, *The Industrial Revolution, 1760–1830* (1948), 58.
20. W. W. Rostow, *The Stages of Economic Growth: A Non-Communist Manifesto* (Cambridge, 1960), 36.
21. P. Deane and W. A. Cole, *British Economic Growth, 1688–1959* (Cambridge, 1969), 80, 280.
22. N. F. R. Crafts, *British Economic Growth during the Industrial Revolution* (Oxford, 1985) and, for an overview minimizing the role of industry in Britain's economy, C. H. Lee, *The British Economy since 1700: A Macroeconomic Perspective* (Cambridge, 1986).
23. J. G. Williamson, 'Why was British Growth so Slow during the Industrial Revolution?', *Journal of Economic History*, 44 (1984).
24. G. N. von Tunzelmann, *Steam Power and British Industrialisation to 1860* (Oxford, 1978).
25. P. K. O'Brien, 'Agriculture and the Home Market for English Industry, 1660–1820', *English Historical Review*, 100 (1985); R. C. Allen, *Enclosure and the Yeoman: The Agricultural Development of the South Midlands, 1450–1850* (Oxford, 1992).
26. Wrigley, *Continuity, Chance and Change*; and *People, Cities and Wealth: The Transformation of Traditional Society* (Oxford, 1987).
27. Crafts, *British Economic Growth*, 87.
28. C. Sabel and J. Zeitlin, 'Historical Alternatives to Mass Production: Politics, Markets and Technology in Nineteenth-Century Industrialisation', *Past and Present*, 108 (1985); M. Berg, *The Age of Manufactures: Industry, Innovation and Work in Britain, 1700–1820* (Oxford, 1985).
29. e.g. M. Berg, P. Hudson, and M. Sonenscher (eds.), *Manufacture in Town and Country before the Factory* (Cambridge, 1983).
30. J. Hoppit, 'Understanding the Industrial Revolution', *Historical Journal*, 30 (1987); D. C. North, *Structure and Change in Economic History* (New York, 1981).
31. This approach is above all associated with E. P. Thompson: see his collected essays in *Customs in Common* (1991).
32. L. Namier, *The Structure of Politics at the Accession of George III* (2nd edn., 1957); J. C. D. Clark, *English Society 1688–1832: Ideology, Social Structure and Political Practice during the Ancien Regime* (Cambridge, 1985).

FURTHER READING

Allen, R. C., *Enclosure and the Yeoman: The Agricultural Development of the South Midlands, 1450–1850* (Oxford, 1992).

Ashton, T. S., *The Industrial Revolution, 1760–1830* (1948).

Berg, M., *The Machinery Question and the Making of Political Economy, 1815–48* (Cambridge, 1980).

—— *The Age of Manufactures: Industry, Innovation and Work in Britain, 1700–1820* (Oxford, 1985).

—— Hudson, P., and Sonenscher, M. (eds.), *Manufacture in Town and Country before the Factory* (Cambridge, 1983).

Blaug, M., *Ricardian Economics: A Historical Study* (New Haven, Conn., 1958).

Clark, J. C. D., *English Society, 1688–1832: Ideology, Social Structure and Political Practice during the Ancien Regime* (Cambridge, 1985).

Crafts, N. F. R., *British Economic Growth during the Industrial Revolution* (Oxford, 1985).

Deane, P., and Cole, W. A., *British Economic Growth, 1688–1959* (Cambridge, 1962).

Harley, C. K., 'British Industrialisation before 1841: Evidence of Slower Growth during the Industrial Revolution', *Journal of Economic History*, 42 (1982).

Hoffmann, W.-G., *British Industry, 1700–1950* (1955).

Hoppit, J., 'Understanding the Industrial Revolution', *Historical Journal*, 30 (1987).

Hudson, P., *The Genesis of Industrial Capital: A Study of the West Riding Wool Textile Industry, c. 1750–1850* (Cambridge, 1986).

Langford, P., *Public Life and the Propertied Englishman, 1689–1798* (Oxford, 1991).

Lee, C. H., *The British Economy since 1700: A Macroeconomic Perspective* (Cambridge, 1986).

Malthus, T. R., *An Essay on the Principle of Population* (1803 edn.), ed. with variora by Patricia James (Cambridge, 1989).

Namier, L., *The Structure of Politics at the Accession of George III* (2nd edn. 1957).

North, D. C., *Structure and Change in Economic History* (New York, 1981).

O'Brien, P. K., 'Agriculture and the Home Market for English Industry, 1660–1820', *English Historical Review*, 100 (1985).

O'Gorman, F., *Voters, Patrons and Parties: The Unreformed Electoral System of Hanoverian England, 1734–1832* (Oxford, 1989).

Ricardo, D., *On the Principles of Political Economy and Taxation* (1817), ed. P. Sraffa (Cambridge, 1951).

Rostow, W. W., *The Stages of Economic Growth: A Non-Communist Manifesto* (Cambridge, 1960).

Sabel, C., and Zeitlin, J., 'Historical Alternatives to Mass Production: Politics, Markets and Technology in Nineteenth-Century Industrialisation', *Past and Present*, 108 (1985).

Smith, A., *An Inquiry into the Nature and Causes of the Wealth of Nations* (1776), ed. E. Cannon (1904; repr. in 1 vol. New York, 1937).

Thompson, E. P., *Customs in Common* (1991).

von Tunzelmann, G. N., *Steam Power and British Industrialisation to 1860* (Oxford, 1978).

Williamson, J. G., 'Why was British Growth so Slow during the Industrial Revolution?', *Journal of Economic History*, 44 (1984).

Wrigley, E. A., *Continuity, Chance and Change: The Character of the Industrial Revolution in England* (Cambridge, 1988).

——*People, Cities and Wealth: The Transformation of Traditional Society* (Oxford, 1987).

PART I

....

Agriculture and Rural Society

....

CHAPTER 2

Agricultural Production:
The Limits of Growth?

In 1842, on the death of Thomas Coke, the second earl of Leicester, his tenants erected a monument to celebrate his encouragement of agricultural 'improvement'. A column was surmounted by a sheaf of wheat and flanked by a massive cow, plump sheep, and modern plough; the frieze around the base showed Coke passing on his advice to a prosperous and grateful tenantry. The monument symbolizes one view of the process and chronology of agricultural growth: a 'modernizing' landowner swept away ignorance, breaking the shackles of tradition, and allowing yields and output to rise at the close of the eighteenth century. But should the monument be read instead as an exercise in deference and self-justification? The analysis of Malthus and Ricardo would suggest a different interpretation: by the end of the eighteenth century, growth of output could only be achieved at the expense of decreasing marginal returns, and prices and rents rose as population growth outstripped the capacity of the land to provide food. Perhaps the monument, on the hill above Coke's lavish Palladian house, symbolized Ricardian rent rather than an agricultural revolution, marking the increased power and wealth of great landowners at the expense both of consumers who paid more for their food and of farmers who paid more for the use of land. Were Malthus and Ricardo correct in their belief that the limits of agricultural production were being reached at the end of the eighteenth century, creating pressure on wages and profit, redistributing income to landowners, and threatening the onset of a 'stationary state'? If they were correct, and growth of output and productivity were faltering at the end of the eighteenth century, could it be that the growth of agriculture in the later seventeenth and early eighteenth centuries was rapid, and that it took place without the intervention of 'improvers' such as Coke?

Measuring Agricultural Output

The dearth of reliable data makes it difficult to measure agricultural output and the productivity of land and labour. The goods produced by farmers were, of course, highly diverse and the composition shifted over the period. The most important crops were cereals: barley was converted into malt in large maltings and brewed into beer or distilled into whisky; oats became less important as a source of food for humans and remained important as animal feed; and wheat was increasingly the staple for bread, as well as being converted into gin. The importance of these grains changed relative to each other, and as a proportion of total agricultural production. When grain prices were low and real wages high, consumers were likely to consume more meat and dairy products, and farmers had every incentive to shift to pastoral agriculture, rearing and fattening livestock or producing dairy products. In addition, there was a plethora of specialist commodities, from the farmers of Norfolk who reared turkeys, to the producers of hay around London for the horses of the metropolis, the hop-growers of Kent who catered for brewers in a large part of the country, and the market gardeners who supplied vegetables and fruit. Of course, agriculture was not simply providing food for humans and animals, for it was also the major source of industrial raw materials. Arable farmers grew flax for the linen and sailcloth industries; and straw was woven into hats and matting. Sheep provided wool for spinning and weaving; and cattle were sources of hides for the leather industry and bones for boiling into glue. The marshes and fens supplied reeds for thatching cottages, and willow for making baskets. Woodland was 'coppiced' by periodically cutting trees to produce new growth, and catered for a huge range of industries: large oak timbers were used for shipbuilding and construction; wagons and carts were assembled in the workshops of wheelwrights and coach-builders; carpenters and joiners made doors, panelling, and furniture; coopers produced a constant flow of barrels and casks to contain a wide range of goods; wood was burned in domestic hearths, and converted into charcoal for specialist industrial uses. There are obvious difficulties in measuring output in all these sectors, and estimating the changing composition of production.

Different parts of the country had their own specialisms, depending on the constraints of soil and climate. At the crudest level, there was a distinction between the highlands of the north and west, and the lowlands of the south and east. In the highlands, heavy rainfall and poor soils made it difficult to grow cereals, which led to dependence on grass and pastoralism on the fells and moorlands of the Pennines, Lake District, and north York moors in the north of England, on Dartmoor, Exmoor, and Bodmin Moor in the West Country; and in large parts of Wales and Scotland. The major occupation was livestock-rearing, with the cultivation of hay in the valleys for winter feed and 'lesser' cereals such as oats for subsistence. Cattle and sheep were kept in the valleys during the winter, and turned on to the moors in the summer for common grazing; they were sold to farmers in the lowlands for fattening. Some upland areas had significant industry, complementing stock-rearing which did not require large amounts of labour: they developed industrial by-employment such as knitting in the Yorkshire Dales or weaving in parts of the Lake District; the Peak District of Derbyshire and the Pennines in Co. Durham were mined for lead and copper; Dartmoor was quarried for granite; and they attracted mill-owners in their search for increasingly valuable water power (see Fig. 2.1).

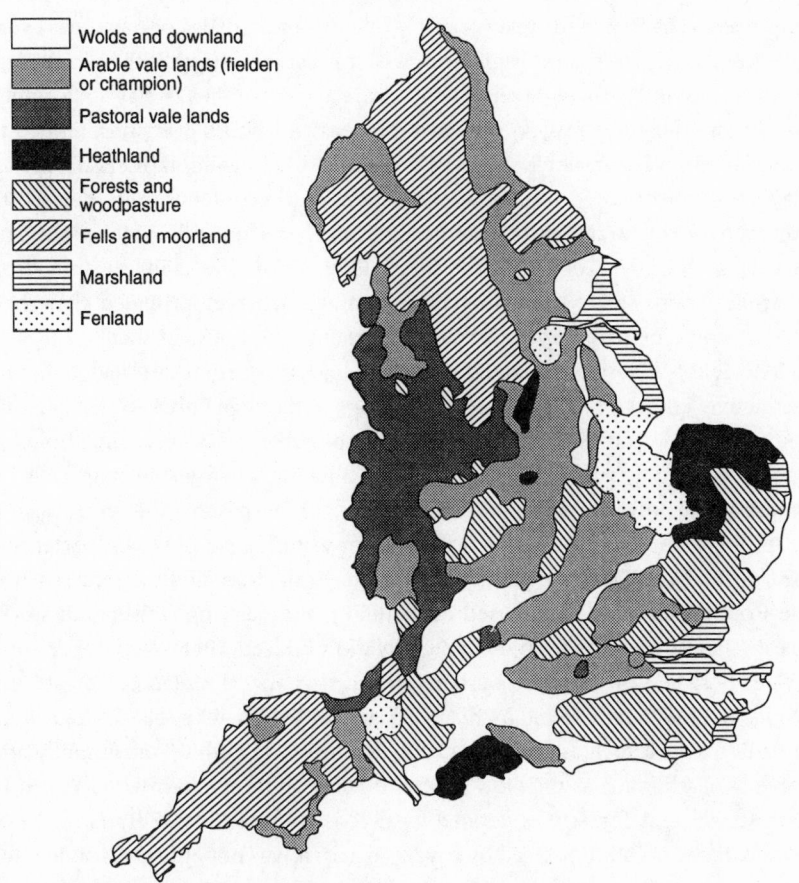

Wolds and downland
Arable vale lands (fielden or champion)
Pastoral vale lands
Heathland
Forests and woodpasture
Fells and moorland
Marshland
Fenland

FIG. 2.1. Farming regions of England, *c*.1700

Source: J. Thirsk, *England's Agricultural Regions and Agrarian History, 1500–1750* (1987), 39.

The vales of the lowlands were more suitable for growing crops, or for pastoral agriculture based on fattening and dairying. The degree of specialization varied between districts, producing a broad distinction between two lowland farming systems. One was the predominantly arable 'fielden' or 'champion' system which dominated in the east Midlands, Hertfordshire, Buckinghamshire, Berkshire, and the vale of York. Cattle and sheep were kept, but they were subordinate to arable cultivation in order to maintain soil fertility. The other lowland system, which dominated in the west Midlands, was pastoralism based on dairying and fattening with the cultivation of some grain as a subsidiary element. The boundaries between these two systems were by no means fixed, for farmers could adjust, particularly in the Midlands, which lay on the division between the predominantly pastoral and fielden zones. This was in part a response to changes in the relative prices of grain and cereals, for there was every incentive to shift to pastoralism at times of low cereals prices, such as in the late seventeenth and early eighteenth centuries. Farmers on heavy clay soils, which were more difficult to work, such as in the east and south Midlands, tended to leave them under grass when prices were low. Meanwhile, farmers on lighter clay soils concentrated on arable cultivation, and techniques were devised to cultivate the free-draining soils on the chalk and limestone hills of the wolds and downs, such as the Cotswolds and South Downs, and the sandy heathlands of Norfolk. These soils were easily ploughed and worked, provided that their fertility could be maintained by manuring them with flocks of sheep.

The fens of eastern England and the 'levels' of Somerset had a highly distinctive agrarian system. These low-lying, waterlogged areas of fertile, peat soil permitted a family to support itself with arable crops on a smallholding, complemented by grazing animals, fishing, trapping wildfowl, cutting reeds for thatch and willows for baskets. The marshlands on the eastern and south-eastern coast were superficially similar, with their waterlogged soils and extensive grazing land, but there were striking contrasts. Agriculture in these areas, such as the Romney marshes, was based on fattening and dairying rather than stock-rearing, and there was more arable cultivation. Indeed, there were more similarities between the agrarian systems in the fens and woodlands. Forests and woods were generally found on marginal land, either on heavy clays which were difficult to work such as the Forest of Arden in Warwickshire, or on sandy and gravelly heaths such as the New Forest in Hampshire or Charnwood Forest in Leicestershire. A forest was defined legally, as an area for the preservation of game which was administered by royal officials: it was not entirely wooded, for there were arable open fields or 'ridings' on which deer and cattle could graze, and 'lawns' where hay was grown for fodder. Other wooded areas, such as the beechwoods of the Chilterns or the Weald of Kent and Sussex, were not forests in the legal sense, although they shared many of the same ecological features. Much as in the fens, families could supplement small plots of arable with the resources of the woods. Pigs foraged for acorns and beechmast; horses, sheep, and cattle were bred and sent elsewhere for fattening; dairying and fattening developed where there were extensive clearings; nuts and berries were gathered for food; rabbits, birds, and deer were trapped and hunted; timber was available for wood-working, charcoal-burning, and tanning, which encouraged the development of furniture-making in the Chilterns, iron-smelting in the Weald and Forest of Dean, and leather in Northamptonshire. These industries grew by utilizing the resources of the woods, but industrialization could emerge for other reasons. In some cases, woods and forests attracted landless squatters from neighbouring parishes, placing pressure on resources and encouraging diversification into industries such as framework knitting in the Charnwood Forest in order to supplement the meagre living from common rights.

These different regional systems of agriculture provide the matrix for the analysis of many features of British economic and social history between the late seventeenth and mid-nineteenth centuries. The economies of scale differed between agrarian systems, which helps to account for variations in the survival of small farms; the distinctive labour needs of stock-rearing and arable farming shaped the pattern of employment; the availability of resources in the fens or woods could create a class of small, independent squatters. Such differences affected the social structure of areas, shaped demographic behaviour, and influenced the location of rural industry. Of course, it is necessary to avoid the trap of reducing everything to the underlying geography of soil types and climate, for apparently similar regions differed as a result of legal and institutional factors. Forest regulations broke down in some areas, but were enforced in others; farmers in some areas were able to gain the backing of the courts for customary tenure, which gave them more rights than their counterparts who were reduced to holding their land on short lets at the will of the landlord; and Scotland had its own highly distinctive patterns of landholding, of which the clan was simply the most obvious. Farming systems were shaped by an interplay between topography and climate on the one hand, and laws and institutions on the other, which in turn influenced the response to market forces.

Clearly, it is extremely difficult to measure the changing level and composition of agricultural output in these agrarian regions. Historians have, necessarily, concentrated on the production of cereals which provided the basis of the agricultural economy. Bread and beer formed the staple diet, and it was only when there was a reasonable quantity of grain to supply bakers and brewers that resources could be released for meat. Pressure on the supply of grain would create problems in the provision of wood and charcoal for industry, or would reduce the supply of fodder for horses, which provided the motive power for industry and transport. Cereals were far from the whole of British agriculture, but trends in their output and productivity are the foundation for an understanding of the agrarian economy. Accordingly, it is crucial to calculate the output of grain, which can be done in two ways, both of which have their problems. The first is from the 'bottom up', estimating total output by calculating movements in yield per acre and in the area under cultivation. The second is from the 'top down', dealing with national aggregates and using a simple demand and supply equation to move from statistics of population and prices to the missing variable of agricultural output.

The initial step of the bottom-up approach is the compilation of data on yields, which are normally expressed as bushels per acre. Unfortunately, comprehensive data on yields are only available for the harvests of 1794, 1795, 1800, and 1801, when the government was alarmed about food supplies during the wars with France. Overall, the yield for wheat was about 20 bushels per acre, but there were marked short-term fluctuations as a result of the weather, ranging from 15.6 bushels per acre in 1795 to 22.6 in 1801. These variations between harvests make it difficult to be certain about longer-term trends in the course of the eighteenth century, especially in view of the scarcity and poor quality of information in earlier periods. During his tours of the 1760s, Arthur Young recorded the wheat yields claimed by the farmers he met, which came to about 23 bushels per acre. Of course, the farmers he visited could be atypical, their claims exaggerated, and the harvests unusual. Earlier estimates are even more problematical, relying upon ingenious statistical procedures and heroic assumptions to extrapolate from limited sources. One measure relies upon the use of wage data: workers were paid either by the amount of work or by the day, and it seems plausible that if the piece-rate for cutting an acre of wheat was 4s. and the day-rate 2s., then it took two days to perform the task. Higher yields entailed an increase in the density of the crop in the field, which affected the effort of cutting and the number of sheaves to be bound and stacked, so that an increase in the number of man-days required to reap an acre of wheat provides a rough proxy for yields. The wage data suggest that yields improved substantially in the seventeenth century, for the man-days required to cut an acre of wheat rose from 1.86 in 1561–1649 to 2.47 in 1650–74, and again in the eighteenth century from 2.59 in 1768–71 to 2.90 in 1794–1810; there was little or no increase in the late eighteenth and early nineteenth centuries, with 2.92 man-days per acre in 1850.[1]

The chronology produced by the wage data is confirmed by somewhat tenuous calculations based upon probate inventories made on the death of a farmer. The content of the inventories depended upon whether the farmer died before the harvest, when acreage under crops was listed; or after the harvest, when the volume of grain in the farmer's barns was returned. It is possible to calculate yields by applying the volumes of grain in the second group of inventories to the acreages in the first, on the assumption that both sets of inventories reflect the overall distribution of farms, and were reasonably accurate in estimating both the acreage in the fields and the volume of grain in the barns. These are very large assumptions and the statistical techniques are open to dispute and modification, but most studies have produced results which are consistent with the wage data. Only Hampshire has so far suggested that productivity gains were greater in the *later* eighteenth century. In East Anglia and Hertfordshire, most of the improvement in productivity came in the first half of the eighteenth century, and an even more striking result has emerged in Oxfordshire, where wheat yields by the end of the seventeenth century were apparently already as high as in the early nineteenth century. The sample of farms in Oxfordshire is too small to give much confidence of massive gains in the seventeenth century followed by stasis in the eighteenth century, but it does appear from most analyses of probate inventories that there was a major increase in wheat yields in the seventeenth century and first half of the eighteenth century, which in many cases exceeded the gains of the later eighteenth century (Table 2.1).

The calculation of *output* from the 'bottom up' requires an estimate of the acreage under crops as well as yields per acre. This was influenced by two processes, neither of which can be measured with any accuracy. One was the enclosure of waste land, particularly on the moors and hills; the second was expansion of the cultivated acreage by changes in farming practices which reduced the amount of fallow. A two-course rotation meant that half the land was fallow each year, and a change to a three- or four-course rotation reduced the proportion to a third or a quarter. More sophisticated rotations could completely remove the need for fallow: root crops such as turnips were grown which helped to clean the soil, and leguminous crops such as clover and sainfoin which fixed nitrogen; animals were fed on these crops, manuring the soil and improving yields for the next cereal crop. The decrease in fallow is impossible to measure, for it depended upon the decisions of hundreds of individual farmers. It was, in any case, offset by an opposite trend, for in some regions land was taken out of arable cultivation and converted to permanent pasture. Not surprisingly, there is no accurate estimate of the cultivated acreage over the eighteenth and early nineteenth centuries.

Measurement of total agricultural output must turn to a different, top-down, approach which relies upon a simple demand and supply equation to move from the known level of prices and demand to the unknown level of agricultural output. The initial step is to calculate the demand for food, which gives the shape

TABLE 2.1. *Wheat yields, 1600–c.1800*

	Source	Bushels per acre
Norfolk and Suffolk		
1660–99	Probate inventories	15.3
1700–39	Probate inventories	18.5
1760s	Young's tours	26.5
1800	Government return	22.4
Hertfordshire		
1610–39	Probate inventories	12.1
1675–99	Probate inventories	19.0
c.1800	Government return	24.0
Oxfordshire		
1550	Probate inventories	9.0
1650	Probate inventories	16.5
1700	Probate inventories	20.6
c.1800	Government return on enclosed, light soils	19.7
Hampshire		
1619–28	Probate inventories	14.5
1683–9	Probate inventories	16.9
1690–9	Probate inventories	13.8
c.1800	Government return	21.0

Sources: Oxfordshire: R. C. Allen, *Enclosure and the Yeoman: The Agricultural Development of the South Midlands, 1450–1850* (Oxford, 1992), 136, 208; Hampshire and Hertfordshire (using Allen's method): P. Glennie, 'Measuring Crop Yields in Early Modern England', in B. M. S. Campbell and M. Overton (eds.), *Land, Labour and Livestock: Historical Studies in European Agricultural Productivity* (Manchester, 1991), 273, 278; Norfolk and Suffolk: M. Overton, 'The Determinants of Crop Yield in Early Modern England', in Campbell and Overton (eds.), *Land, Labour and Livestock*, 302.

of the demand curve DD (see Fig. 2.2). The next stage is to determine the movement in agricultural prices, and the level of agricultural output may then be deduced from a simple demand and supply equation. If the demand curve in 1700 was $D_1 D_1$ and the price was A, then output must have been B; if the demand curve in 1800 was $D_2 D_2$ and the price stood at C, then output must have been D. Of course, everything depends upon the accuracy of price statistics, and the calculation of the demand curve.

Price statistics are based upon institutional purchasers in towns in the south, and it is a moot point whether price trends were the same for individual purchasers in other areas of the country. The general trend is, however, clear: grain prices fell by about 12 per cent between 1640 and 1750, with a particularly marked short-term fluctuation in the 1730s and 1740s, when they fell 15 to 20 per cent below the level of the 1720s (see Fig. 2.3). More problematical is the calculation of demand. Consumption was only in part determined by population trends; the difficulty is knowing how far consumption of food per capita was influenced by changes in incomes and prices. It is usually assumed that consumption of food did not vary in proportion to changes in income or prices: the elasticity of demand was less than unity so that a rise in income or fall in prices of 1 produced a rise in demand for food of less than 1. The crucial question is how much less, for the answer will affect estimates of aggregate demand. Crafts has placed the income elasticity of demand for food at 0.7,[2] suggesting that consumption was close to unity and more responsive to changes in income than has usually been assumed. Unfortunately, the figure rests upon the slight basis of two surveys of a small number of poor agricultural workers in the south in the 1790s, and a group of factory workers in Lancashire in 1836, which are of doubtful validity as a measure of the responsiveness of food consumption for the entire country. Nevertheless, it is likely that the elasticity of demand for agricultural products was close to unity in the eighteenth century. Many urban workers even in the late nineteenth century were eating less than they needed to maintain physical efficiency, and the initial response to a reduction in food prices or an increase in incomes would be a better diet. Further, grain was not only used to make bread, for it was brewed into beer and distilled into gin, whose consumption was much more responsive to changes in price and income. Falling food prices and rising real incomes did, it is true, release consumption for industrial goods, but this in turn increased demand for agricultural products. Transport and industry relied upon horses for motive power, which increased demand for hay and oats; major industries such as shoemaking and linen relied upon agriculture

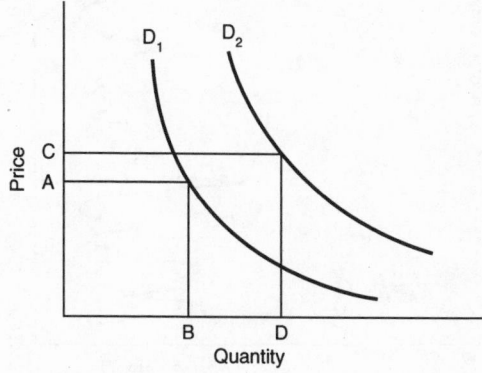

FIG. 2.2. Demand for agricultural products

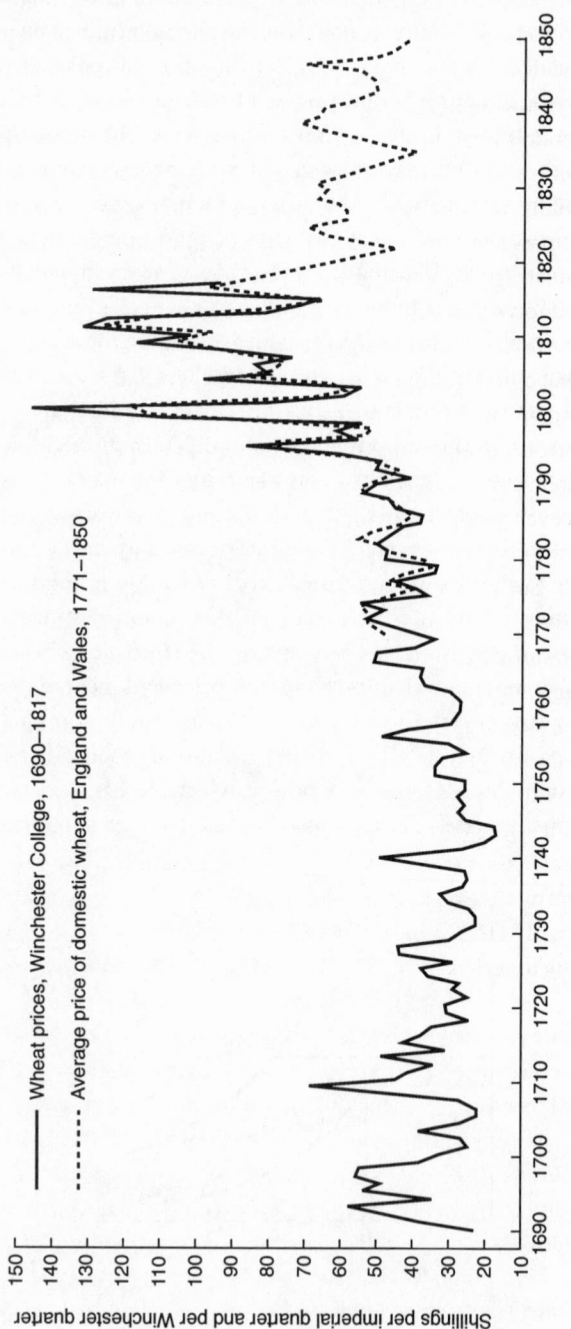

FIG. 2.3. Wheat prices, Winchester College, 1690–1817, and average price of domestic wheat, England and Wales, 1771–1850

Source: B. R. Mitchell, *British Historical Statistics* (Cambridge, 1988), 754–6.

for supplies of leather and flax. Consequently, it is reasonable to assume that the price and income elasticity of demand for agricultural products was well above zero, and possibly close to unity. It then becomes possible to calculate the total level of demand for food in response to changes in the level of prices and incomes—always assuming that movements in income levels can be measured.

Although scepticism is sensible, any reasonable set of assumptions confirms the fears of Malthus and Ricardo that agriculture at the end of the eighteenth century was failing to meet the demands of an increasing population. The eighteenth century may be divided into two, with a line drawn in the 1740s. Growth of population was low until 1740, but there was a higher demand for agricultural products as a result of rising real wages and falling prices. After 1740, population growth accelerated, real wages stagnated or fell, and prices rose. The implication is that agricultural output was rising faster than population until the 1740s, permitting an increase in per capita consumption at falling prices. After 1740, agricultural output lagged behind population growth, forcing up prices, and reducing per capita consumption. The contention that agricultural output decelerated survives even the least favourable assumptions, which minimize the rise in incomes and the fall in prices up to 1740, and exaggerate the rise of incomes and prices after 1740. Such an approach will depress the growth rate in the earlier period and boost it in the second, so that there can be considerable confidence that any deceleration of growth after 1740 was more than a statistical illusion. On these assumptions, agricultural output in England grew by *at least* 4.3 per cent per decade between 1660 and 1740, and *at most* by 2.7 per cent per decade between 1740 and 1790. Despite doubts on individual figures, the broad trend is clear: 'agricultural growth slowed just as population growth began to accelerate'.[3] One sign of the change in the market is the transformation of Britain from a net exporter of wheat in the first half of the eighteenth century to a net importer, on a modest scale from the 1760s and a large scale from the 1790s. The gloomy prognostications of Malthus and Ricardo, that the diminishing returns of agriculture were leading to serious problems for growth and forcing down wages, had a basis in reality.

These elaborate calculations answer one question, only to raise another. Why was there an increase in production at a time of relatively stable population in the later seventeenth century? Perhaps the important point was less the size of the population than its concentration in London, which placed pressure on sources of supply, encouraging regional specialization as the area of supply expanded. Another possibility is that gentry families were turning to their estates in order to make good the losses of the civil war, and were pioneering new methods. The fact that prices were falling could itself produce an incentive for agricultural improvement, for landlords' profits were squeezed, making it difficult to purchase land from rent income and capital appreciation, and encouraging the adoption of new techniques which could yield a decent return. By contrast, the increase in prices in the late eighteenth century removed the incentive to invest in new techniques and instead encouraged land purchases, especially because the rate of return on agricultural improvements was likely to fall as the agrarian economy reached a new equilibrium of yields, and could make further gains of productivity only with great difficulty and expense. Such an explanation assumes that the landlords were the dynamic force in the improvement of agriculture, and the traditional explanation for the agricultural revolution of the eighteenth century has simply been extrapolated back into the seventeenth century: the role of the modernizing landowner consisted of sweeping aside the restraints of tradition embedded in open-field agriculture and the conservatism of small farmers. The emphasis in such an interpretation is placed on a 'landlords' agricultural revolution' which created efficiency by parliamentary enclosures, the creation of large tenant farms, and the consolidation of great estates. But could the shift in the periodization of rising yields also entail a shift in the dynamic of change? Perhaps the agent for agricultural improvement in the seventeenth and early eighteenth centuries was the small yeoman farmer rather than the modernizing landowner. The rise in yields preceded the emergence of larger farms and the consolidation of estates in the eighteenth century, so that it could be small-scale yeomen farmers 'who accomplished the biological revolution in grain growing'.[4] The landlord could be displaced as the agent of change, and reinterpreted less favourably, merely facilitating a modest gain in productivity in the later eighteenth century which was just enough to escape the worst prognostications of dearth and demographic disaster, at the expense of a considerable increase in prices and rents, and a redistribution of income towards a small landed élite.

Raising Yields: Two Routes?

The new emphasis upon the improvement of yields in the seventeenth century has shifted attention away from the landlords' agricultural revolution of the later eighteenth century, bringing into question the importance of parliamentary enclosures and the significance of 'improvers', such as the sophisticated rotations of the second earl of Leicester at Holkham, or the development of new breeds of sheep by Robert Bakewell. On closer inspection, their significance disappears. The Holkham estate had invested a higher proportion of rental in improvements before the second earl inherited in 1776; and leases specified rotations of turnips and temporary grass from the early eighteenth century. The second earl was more of a publicist than an innovator, and much the same applies to Bakewell, whose long line of less fêted precursors stretched back to the seventeenth century and men such as Sir Thomas Gresley, who had a uniform herd of Longhorn cattle in Derbyshire by 1720.

The discovery of early eighteenth-century 'improvers' simply alters the chronology without affecting the mechanism of change. Perhaps a more radical reinterpretation is needed, which transfers responsibility for increased yields in the late seventeenth and early eighteenth centuries to a 'yeoman's agricultural revolution'. Rather than the heroic, pioneering example of a few publicists battling against the ignorance of farmers to disseminate new techniques, could it be that yields were raised by the tedious, back-breaking seasonal labours of countless anonymous farmers and their workers? The small yeomen farmers become the agents of improvement rather than the custodians of inertia.

There is much to be said for such an interpretation. The probate inventories of Hertfordshire in the late seventeenth century suggest a connection between areas with a high valuation per acre of growing crops and a valuation for ground prepared for crops. Valuers, it seems, were recognizing that farmers spent more time and effort in the labour-intensive tasks of systematically preparing the field bed for sowing, by ploughing and weeding the fallow. A greater use of spring-sown crops meant that more time was available for preparation in the autumn and winter months, which had the additional advantage of spreading the risks of crop failure. They could apply lime and marl to the soil in order to regulate acidity, which was a significant factor in the breakdown of farm manure and the ability of crops to take nutrients from the soil. More trouble was taken in selecting seed, and in regulating the rotation of crops to prevent the spread of disease. There was certainly scope for improvement in yields through the simple expedients of more careful husbandry, using techniques which were well known in medieval agriculture and more widely diffused by gardening. Changes in cropping patterns entailed the diffusion of crops such as peas and pulses which were available in the Middle Ages rather than the adoption of new crops of clover and turnips. Inventories for east Worcestershire, for example, show that pulses accounted for 28 per cent of the crop acreage in 1670–99, as part of a rotation of barley–pulses–wheat–fallow which was similar to the pattern on high-output estates in the Middle Ages. These leguminous crops fixed nitrogen, an essential element for growth: experiments at the research farm at Rothamsted between 1881 and 1917 found that the yield from land with a course of legumes was 26.4 per cent higher than that from land left fallow between crops.[5]

The high yields of the late seventeenth century were less a decisive break with medieval agricultural techniques than the result of changes in the social and institutional structure of agriculture which permitted more farmers to adopt labour-intensive techniques of careful ground preparation. Farm size was probably not the crucial consideration, for there is little sign that large farms had higher yields, and neither was enclosure a necessary precondition, for yields in Oxfordshire also rose in the open fields. One explanation for the wider adoption of high-yield agricultural practices is that yeomen farmers in the sixteenth and seventeenth centuries had greater security of tenure, which encouraged them to invest more time and effort in improving the soil, in the expectation that they would obtain the benefits. They had less incentive if their efforts simply raised rents and benefited the landlord, which was increasingly the case in the course of the eighteenth century as the tenurial system shifted towards short leases or tenancy-at-will, which allowed landlords to adjust rents and capture most of the gains of improved yields. In the sixteenth and seventeenth centuries, farmers were more likely to hold their land on long leases or copyhold and customary tenures which gave them a beneficial interest in the land. Rather than landlords playing a positive, modernizing role, it would appear that their relative weakness provided the context for a yeoman's agricultural revolution. 'It was only the yeomen of early modern England', argues R. C. Allen, 'who had a long-term interest in the soil and who thereby benefited from the rise in land value caused by a rise in productivity.'[6]

The adoption of best-practice agricultural techniques, and an increase of yields within an apparently 'traditional' agricultural system, was also encouraged by a growth of specialization within an integrated economy. Farmers were able to concentrate on what they, and their land, did best by abandoning regional self-sufficiency in cereals. This decision involved risks as well as opportunities, for the margin between food supply and consumption was precarious, with a constant danger that population would outstrip resources, and that imports of grain would disappear in years of dearth. Regional self-sufficiency in grains continued as an insurance, even in areas which were not best suited to cereal cultivation, until there was a wider margin between supply and demand, and an efficient marketing system could move grain from areas of production to consumption. When self-sufficiency could safely be abandoned, some regions could concentrate on pastoral agriculture and rural industry, while others devoted themselves to arable cultivation. It is impossible to measure the change directly in the absence of regional output statistics, but an indirect indication is available from the timing of marriages.[7] In arable parishes, most weddings took place in the autumn after the harvest; in pastoral parishes, most weddings were held in the spring and summer after lambing and calving; and in non-agricultural parishes, there was no marked seasonal peak. The seasonal incidence of weddings therefore provides a rough indication of regional specialization. In the second half of the sixteenth century, arable-type autumn marriages were found in all parts of the country, and no region was free of grain production. Pastoral marriages were relatively scarce, but there was a cluster of non-seasonal industrial marriage in the Weald of Kent and Sussex, and in the north-west of England. Marriage patterns were very different by 1701–40: arable-type autumn weddings were now predominantly in the east; pastoral marriages clustered in the north and west; and the location of non-seasonal industrial marriages shifted, with a decline in the south-east and a rise in the south-west, north Midlands, and the West Riding of Yorkshire. The new geography of marriage suggests that cereal cultivation for autonomous regional markets had disappeared by the end of the seventeenth century, allowing regions to devote their land to its best use.

The dating of change to the second half of the seventeenth century is consistent with trends in population growth and agricultural yields and output. In the sixteenth and early seventeenth centuries, growth of population placed pressure on food supplies, and prices rose; more land was devoted to growing grain in marginal areas, and reliance on external supplies was risky. When population pressure eased in the later seventeenth century, the need to grow grain for self-sufficiency was reduced; prices and profits fell, and areas which were less suited to grains had every incentive to shift to pastoral agriculture, benefiting from the buoyant demand for meat and dairy products without fearing dearth. Reduction in the pressure of population on food supplies permitted specialization, which in turn raised yields and output as farmers concentrated on commodities which offered them the greatest comparative advantage. The chronology is also consistent with the decay of rural industry in some areas and its emergence in others. A shift from labour-intensive cereal cultivation to pastoralism resulted in surplus labour which provided a work-force for industry: many parishes which emerged as centres of industry in the later seventeenth century were formerly arable and newly pastoral, such as in the West Country. On the other hand, parishes which specialized in labour-intensive arable crops were likely to deindustrialize, contributing to the decline of the cloth industry in Kent, Sussex, and East Anglia.

Although individual statistics have their weaknesses, the interpretation has the great virtue of internal consistency, making sense of movements in prices, population, regional specialization, shifts in tenure, and the development of food markets. The myth of the improving landowner, enlightening ignorant small farmers, has been dispelled; there is little doubt that many features of the landlords' agricultural revolution were means to raise rents by renegotiating leases rather than improving yields. But does this mean that the importance of new crops, rotations, and agricultural techniques should be completely rejected? Revision should not lead to over-reaction. The claims for the 'yeoman's agricultural revolution' at the expense of a 'landlords' agricultural revolution' have, after all, been most strongly urged on the basis of data from Oxfordshire, the only county where probate inventories suggest that yields failed to rise over the eighteenth century. The 'ground preparation' route was labour intensive, with little evidence of economies of scale or an increase in the number of animals per acre. By contrast, 'alternate' and 'convertible' husbandry were more capital intensive, entailing economies of scale, an increase in the number of animals, and the consequent application of greater amounts of manure to the soil.

Alternate husbandry, as the name suggests, switched between arable and pastoral farming, with a fixed rotation based upon the introduction of new leguminous fodder crops such as sainfoin, clover, and turnips which allowed a reduction in the amount of fallow and an increase in the number of livestock. The most famous was the so-called Norfolk four-course rotation of wheat, roots, barley, and clover, which was sometimes extended to cover five or six years. The principle was that clover and sainfoin provided fodder for sheep or cattle, who manured the soil; the nitrogen left by the legumes was taken up by roots, which provided winter feed; the livestock manured the soil for a crop of cereals. The rotation meant that land was more constantly cropped, so that productivity was higher even if yields per acre remained stable; there was, however, a good chance that yields would rise as a result of better care of the soil from ploughing and hoeing, and from the input of manure. Animals could be substituted for human effort, permitting the release of labour from farming which was one of the most striking changes in the late seventeenth and eighteenth centuries. Convertible husbandry or ley farming also switched between arable and pastoral farming, but did not have regular rotations. Instead, land was put under temporary grass (leys) for several years and used to raise livestock or for dairying, followed by several cereal crops. Turnips were grown by some farmers, but by no means all, and they were more concerned to maintain the fertility of the ley by treating it with manure, lime, marl, potash, bones, blood, or 'night soil' from towns. Convertible husbandry offered a considerable degree of operational freedom, for farmers could decide on the precise point of conversion from grass to cereals according to the relative movement of prices of grain and livestock, and their assessment of the most profitable use of their land. Livestock was not subsidiary to arable cultivation as in alternate husbandry, where it was primarily a means of maintaining the fertility of the soil; it was an important concern in its own right.

The more extreme supporters of the yeomen farmers' agricultural revolution deny the significance of 'alternate' husbandry with its 'great herds of prize animals fertilising corn lands and raising yields'.[8] Certainly, the 'yeoman's agricultural revolution' offered higher yields, but revisionist zeal should not lead to a dismissal of the possibilities of raising yields by 'alternate' husbandry. Much depended upon soil types. It was expensive to grow turnips on heavy soils which were difficult and expensive to work, and where the crop was liable to rot. Clay soils created problems in feeding sheep on the turnip field, for they compacted the ground and wet, muddy conditions made them liable to foot rot. Accordingly, it was necessary to lift roots from the ground at an additional cost. Alternate husbandry was therefore more significant on light, free-draining soils which were cheap to work and dry enough for animals to feed off fodder crops in winter. These light, sandy soils of East Anglia or the chalk downs of Hampshire had previously been too infertile for permanent cultivation, but the spread of alternate husbandry made them specialist cereal growers from the later seventeenth century. Instead of grazing sheep on rough pasture, larger numbers of animals were kept as a source of manure for cropped land, and agricultural output rose during the period of low population growth and prices in the late seventeenth and early eighteenth centuries, as a result of both higher yields and a larger cultivated acreage.

These changes in farming practices led to adjustment in agrarian regions. Light soils areas adopted alternate husbandry and became major cereal growers, which led to a decay of rural industry in areas such as East Anglia where more labour was required for farming. Arable farmers on heavy soils were less able to compete with light soil alternate husbandry, and faced depression with the fall in cereal prices, especially in the 1730s and 1740s. On the heavy Midland clays, rents were static and arrears high, and landlords' investment a smaller proportion of gross rentals. The duke of Kingston in the east Midlands, for example, ploughed back only about 4 per cent of his gross rental on repairs and buildings before 1750, falling to 1.4 per cent in the 1750s and 0.6 per cent in the 1760s and 1770s; by contrast, landlords' investment in East Anglia was 8.3 per cent in 1746–50 and 10.4 per cent in 1751–5.[9] Yet the extent of agricultural depression should not be exaggerated, for farmers and landlords could respond by cutting costs or by switching to dairying and livestock where the market was more buoyant as consumers spent more on better-quality food at a time of low cereal prices. Indeed, cattle prices *rose* by 13 per cent between 1640 and 1750, and arable farmers were encouraged to turn to convertible husbandry, as in the south-west of England, or to move from convertible husbandry to permanent pasture, as on the heavy soils of the Midlands. Adjustment was not always easy, for farmers in the Midlands who wished to switch to livestock and dairying did not have access to large areas of waste for grazing, such as existed on Dartmoor and the Pennines, which led to pressure on the common grazing of the open arable fields after harvest. Changes in land use were hindered by the communal regulations of farming, unless members of the village could negotiate agreements which allowed grass to be grown on the open fields. Enclosure removed these communal controls and permitted the conversion of the open arable fields to pasture, so that the chronology of enclosure affected the extent of depression on heavy soils and permitted some estates to escape its worst impact. On the Leveson-Gower estate, early enclosure allowed a switch to pasture after 1700 which meant that rents were stable and arrears an insignificant 0.8 per cent in the 1740s, in contrast to the Kingston estates where rents fell and arrears mounted. Of course, pastoralism is less labour intensive than arable farming, which released labour for rural industry such as hosiery in Leicestershire and Nottinghamshire. The pastoral stock-rearing districts of the upland zone, which supplied young animals for fattening in the lowlands, were not seriously affected by changes in agricultural techniques and benefited from the demand from lowland fatteners. Many farmers and landlords escaped lightly during the period of low cereal prices in the early eighteenth century, which is more accurately described as a time of restructuring and regional adaptation than agricultural depression.

The extent of agricultural change must be kept in perspective. Farming was not released from the restraints of an organic economy, and the limits were being reached by the late eighteenth century. Yields were raised both by taking greater pains in preparing the soil, and by increasing the number of animals it could sustain; indeed, one of the most striking characteristics of British agriculture in the eighteenth century was that it supported a larger number of animals per acre than in Europe. The process of raising crop yields and increasing livestock rested upon a virtuous circle of organic progress, and the increase of nitrogen in the soil and manure on the fields took several decades to reach a new equilibrium, at which point agriculture hit a ceiling of output. The restraints of the organic economy had been weakened rather than broken, which made the gloom of Ricardo and Malthus understandable. Whichever route to higher yields was followed, the crucial consideration remained the resources of nitrogen and manure available *within* the farm; further gains would rely upon larger inputs of fertilizers from external sources, which was to be a characteristic of 'high farming' in the mid-nineteenth century.

Labour Productivity and the Release of Labour

Agricultural improvements involved raising the productivity not only of *land* but also of *labour*. The 'yeoman's agricultural revolution' relied on labour-intensive farming practices at a time of rising real wages, and soon faced a constraint of mounting costs unless there were also significant gains in labour productivity. Similarly, an increase in yields through the development of new fodder crops required the use of more labour, for fields had to be ploughed more frequently, turnips had to be hoed, and increased output meant that there was more work in reaping and threshing the crop. An increase in the productivity of land would, it is true, raise output per worker for those tasks where labour requirements depended upon the acreage of land under cultivation rather than its output. The labour involved in ploughing and harrowing was the same, regardless of the size of the crop; and ditches had to be cleared and buildings maintained. Nevertheless, the amount of labour needed for cereal production was affected by output. This was obviously true of threshing grain, but at first sight it would appear that the labour for reaping depended upon the area cultivated, so that an increase in yields per acre would not affect labour inputs. In fact, higher yields meant that there were more plants per acre, which increased the effort of cutting the crop, and produced more sheaves to be bound and stacked. The demands for harvest labour in a few weeks of the year potentially created a bottle-neck which was much more serious than the demands of threshing, where labour could be utilized over the slack winter months. Higher output was the result of applying more labour to the soil, and in turn created a need for more labour: the process of agricultural improvement and the release of labour from the land would soon grind to a halt unless there were significant gains in labour productivity.

Britain achieved a higher level of labour productivity than the rest of Europe by the early nineteenth century. A comparison of day and piece wage rates for agricultural labourers can again be used in order to produce a rough estimate of the number of bushels of grain a worker could reap or thresh in a day. The threshing and reaping rate in medieval England was similar to that in early nineteenth-century Europe, by which time England had made substantial gains (see Table 2.2). Confirmation is provided by estimates based on the proportion of

TABLE 2.2. *Agricultural labour productivity, estimated from day and piece wage rates (bushels per worker-day)*

	Threshing	Reaping
Medieval England	2.8	2.8
Britain *c.*1850		
north	5.3	10.1
south	3.8	8.1
Hungary 1850	n/a	3.4
Germany		
Berlin 1812	n/a	4.0
Prussia 1812	2.0	n/a
Bohemia	2.2	n/a

Source: G. Clark, 'Productivity Growth without Technical Change: European Agriculture before 1850', *Journal of Economic History*, 47 (1987), 427, 429.

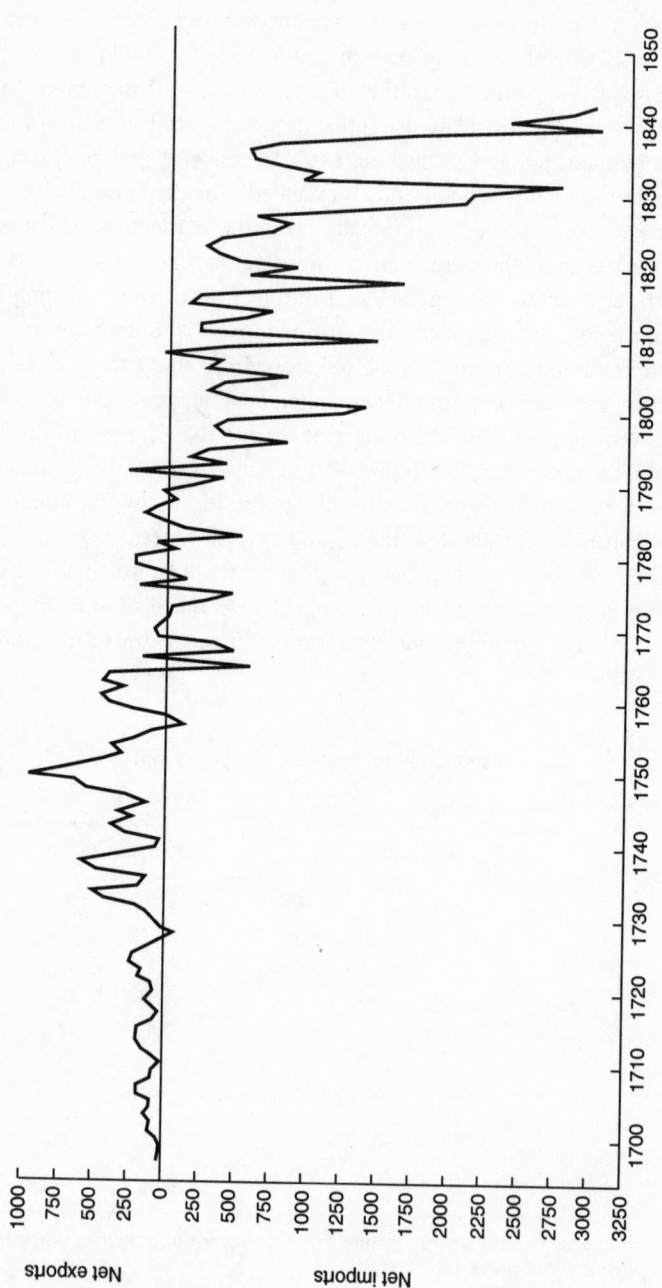

FIG. 2.4. Net import and export of wheat and wheaten flour, Great Britain, 1697–1842

Source: Mitchell, British Historical Statistics, 221.

TABLE 2.3. *Structure of English population, by major sector, 1600–1801*

	Urban		Rural agriculture		Rural non-agriculture		Total	
	%	no. (m.)	%	no. (m.)	%	no. (m.)	%	no. (m.)
1600	8.0	0.34	70.0	2.87	22.0	0.90	100.0	4.11
1700	17.0	0.85	55.0	2.78	28.0	1.43	100.0	5.06
1750	21.0	1.22	46.0	2.64	33.0	1.91	100.0	5.77
1801	27.5	2.38	36.25	3.14	36.25	3.14	100.0	8.66

Source: E. A. Wrigley, *People, Cities and Wealth* (Oxford, 1987), 170.

the population engaged in agriculture. The marked increase in the proportion of the population living in towns or employed outside agriculture in the country must entail an increase in the productivity of agricultural labour, unless food was supplied by imports. In fact, England was an exporter in the early eighteenth century, and only started to import at the end of the eighteenth century (see Fig. 2.4), so that any gains in labour productivity will be understated in the seventeenth and early eighteenth centuries, and overstated at the end of the period. The exact distribution of occupations is not easily measured: the urban population is reasonably precise, but it is difficult to calculate the number employed in rural industries and services, or to be certain how many were engaged in agriculture. However, the general picture (Tables 2.3 and 2.4) could only be overturned if the level of non-agricultural employment were reduced to an unrealistically low figure. Each agricultural worker in England supported considerably more people in the course of the eighteenth century, in contrast with France where a much lower proportion of the population was engaged in

TABLE 2.4. *Total population per 100 rural agricultural population and gains in agricultural labour productivity, 1600–1800*

	England		France	
	Total pop. per 100 in agriculture	Productivity gain (%)	Total pop. per 100 in agriculture	Productivity gain (%)
1600	143	—	145	—
1700	182	27.3	158	9.0
1750	219	20.3	163	3.2
1800	276	26.0	170	4.3

Source: Wrigley, *People, Cities and Wealth*, 187.

non-agricultural pursuits, far fewer people were released into towns, and labour productivity grew much more slowly. Accurate estimates of agricultural output per worker are available for the end of the period, amounting to £53.0 per worker in Britain in 1845–54, compared with £29.7 in France,[10] and it is likely that the gap had started to open in the seventeenth century.

Growth in labour productivity could be achieved by simple improvements in the technology of hand tools. A harvest-worker could cut about three times the acreage of wheat with a long-handled scythe as with a short-handled sickle; after making allowance for additional ancillary work of gathering and binding, the use of a scythe saved about 40 per cent of the labour in harvesting an acre. The scythe had long been used for cutting grass, but had a major shortcoming in the harvesting of cereals: a considerable wastage of grain, which had to be set against savings in labour. Although the price of grain fell relative to wages in the early eighteenth century, the scythe was only adopted for grain harvesting in the early and mid-nineteenth century with the disappearance of a large and elastic supply of labour for the few crucial weeks of the harvest. The release of labour into urban industry reduced the elasticity of the labour supply, forcing farmers to recruit temporary or casual workers from Ireland, Wales, and Scotland, or from towns, at wages in excess of the normal weekly rate. The bottle-neck in the supply of labour encouraged farmers to use scythes, long after significant increases in labour productivity had already been achieved.

A more significant factor in raising labour productivity was the presence of considerably more animals than elsewhere in Europe. Of course, a greater number of animals helped to raise yields, so contributing indirectly to an improvement in labour productivity. Animals also had a direct impact, for animal products were more valuable than arable crops, which increased the value of output per worker above the level in France; and they supplied considerable amounts of energy for carrying hay and corn from the fields to the barns and ricks, returning manure from the farmyard, and pulling ploughs and harrows across the fields. An increase in the number of draught animals for these tasks would raise output per capita, and allow labour to be released from agriculture or reallocated to other tasks on the farm. Labour productivity was affected by the type as well as the number of draught animals, for one horse was roughly equivalent to five men and one ox to about three men. A striking feature of English agriculture was that horses formed about 60 per cent of the draught stock as early as 1600, and were virtually universal by the end of the eighteenth century. Gregory King estimated that there were 502,000 cart and plough horses in England around 1695, amounting to 2.75 manpower per adult male in agriculture; in 1881 there were about 700,000, amounting to 3.50 manpower per adult male in agriculture, or an increase of 27.3 per cent. The contrast with France is marked, for there was only one draught animal for 2.6 agricultural workers in 1892, when oxen still slightly outnumbered horses; in Britain, there was one draught animal for 1.6 agricultural workers, and horses had completely replaced oxen.[11]

The adoption of horses was influenced by soil types, for they were less able to cope with heavy, slow-moving conditions such as on the clay soils of the Midlands, or where high rainfall required more energy to pull the plough through wet soils. Horses were more suited to light, easily worked soils such as in Norfolk, and stony soils which damaged the hooves of oxen: these were precisely the areas of expanding grain cultivation in the later seventeenth and eighteenth centuries. Horses were also more expensive to feed than oxen, for they needed grain, and farmers had to balance their higher costs against their greater speed and stamina which allowed a faster pace of work for an extra one or two hours a day. Many farmers in Britain felt that the gains were worth the additional costs of upkeep, particularly small yeomen farmers who favoured horses because they provided multi-purpose energy. Oxen were more suitable for ploughing than for harrowing and hauling; horses could be used for all three functions, as well as riding to market and carrying packs. Small farmers, who could not keep specialist plough teams, were more likely to invest in a versatile, multi-purpose horse which allowed considerable gains in efficiency. Of course, the decision to invest in an expensive horse only made sense when farmers were incorporated into a commercialized, market economy and wished to maximize earnings rather than to gain a subsistence living with enough cash simply to cover rent, taxes, and specialized purchases. Horses allowed an increase in labour productivity which farmers could exploit either to reduce the number of family members and workers employed, or to apply more effort to improving the soil by ploughing the fallow, more frequent harrowing, weeding, digging in lime or marl, breaking down clods, carting and spreading manure, or burning the turf to kill weeds. The adoption of horses resulted, at least initially, in improved soil preparation and higher yields in the later seventeenth century, before releasing labour into industry and services.

Animal power alone cannot explain increased labour productivity, for there was a considerable improvement in threshing and reaping, which used only human power. One very important influence was improved diet, which allowed workers to expend more energy. Changes in the organization and control of labour also intensified the pace of work and the effective utilization of labour, largely through the emergence of larger farms during the eighteenth century (see Table 2.5), particularly in arable districts of the southern Midlands, East Anglia, and southern England; small farms survived in the pastoral districts of the north-west, north Midlands, Lincolnshire fens, Wales, and the south-west. Economies of scale were most apparent in the arable farms of the fielden regions, where large farmers employed more landless labourers. Alternate husbandry on the light soils of East Anglia and the downs similarly offered economies of scale in the management of large flocks and sophisticated rotations, and social differentiation in these areas widened as large farmers gained at the expense of their smaller neighbours. In lowland pastoralism, there was a difference between areas where fattening was linked to arable farming, which produced large farms and graziers with considerable amounts of capital; and areas where fattening was associated with dairying, which required less labour and could allow the development of industrial by-employment. Stock-rearing was usually undertaken by small farms, and most upland areas therefore had a relatively egalitarian social structure, without a large number of landless labourers; an exception was Scotland, where landowners 'cleared' large numbers of people from the land and created great sheep runs. In the forests and fens, the availability of grazing and other resources created a relatively egalitarian social structure of small and middling peasants which was threatened by attempts by the crown to capture more of the assets of the forests, and by capital-intensive drainage schemes which created highly productive arable farming. Small owner-occupiers were gradually bought up by great landowners, and tenant farms were reorganized by landed estates. On the Leveson-Gower estates in Staffordshire, Shropshire, and Yorkshire, for example, the proportion of land farmed by large tenants of 200 acres and above increased threefold between 1714–20 and 1829–33, from 18.8 per cent to

TABLE 2.5. *Farm sizes in the south Midlands, c.1700–c.1800*

	Percentage of farms		Percentage of acres	
	*c.*1700	*c.*1800	*c.*1700	*c.*1800
Open fields				
Family farms (under 60 acres)	59.2	29.6	24.7	7.6
Intermediate (60 to 100 acres)	18.3	15.2	21.7	7.6
'Capitalist' farms (100+ acres)	22.4	55.1	53.6	84.7
Average size (acres)	65.0	145.0		
Enclosed fields				
Family farms (under 60 acres)	42.8	34.8	12.6	8.1
Intermediate (60 to 100 acres)	19.0	11.9	15.1	6.4
'Capitalist' (100+ acres)	38.2	53.3	72.2	85.5
Average size (acres)	100.0	147.0		

Source: R. C. Allen, *Enclosure and the Yeoman* (Oxford, 1992), 73–4.

59.3 per cent; farms with 20 to 200 acres became much less significant, falling from 74.9 per cent to 31.1 per cent of acreage.[12] Rural society on the Leveson-Gower estate became increasingly polarized, dominated by a group of large tenant farms (see Fig. 2.5 for the process on the Vernon estate in Worcestershire). Although large farms did not have noticeably higher *yields*, they did offer economies of scale in the use of *labour*. Arthur Young's data from his tours in the late 1760s show clear savings in labour costs and employment on large farms (Table 2.6), which accounted for a major part of gains in labour productivity in the eighteenth century.

Even small family farms were more likely to release members than in continental Europe, for the right to relief from the poor law provided protection against insecurity and permitted movement away from kin. The family farm in England was less a means of supporting kin during crises of the life-cycle, or of supporting the maximum number of family members, than an efficient unit of production which merely retained the number of hands which was economically rational. However, the main outcome of the 'yeoman's agricultural revolution' was to raise the productivity of *land* by labour-intensive farming which had some secondary benefit for labour productivity; the 'landlords' revolution' of consolidation of estates and the creation of large tenanted farms employing waged workers allowed gains in labour productivity and a release of population. Tenant farmers paying a rack-rent and employing wage labour were more concerned

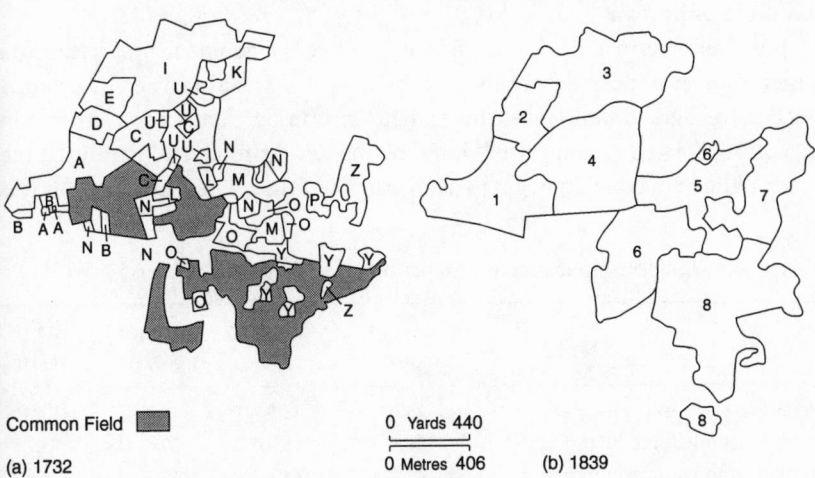

Common Field ▓

0 Yards 440

0 Metres 406

(a) 1732　　　　(b) 1839

FIG. 2.5. Reorganization of farms on the Vernon estates, Hanbury, Worcestershire

Note: Letters and numbers indicate individual farms

Source: J. A. Yelling, *Common Field and Enclosure in England 1450–1850* (1977), 128.

TABLE 2.6. *Labour cost and employment, arable farms, c.1770*

Farm size (acres)	Labour cost per acre (£)	Employment per acre		
		Men	Women	Boys
0–50	1.50	0.036	0.033	0.039
200–50	0.62	0.020	0.010	0.010
600–50	0.49	0.019	0.003	0.008

Source: Allen, *Enclosure and the Yeoman*, 213, 215; estimated from Arthur Young.

about producing an adequate return on their working capital, and had no reason to retain a worker unless his output was sufficient to support himself and his family. Tenants were more likely to release labour, and there were economies of scale on large farms. On a small farm, there was not likely to be much hired labour, and workers were often members of the family who were generalists rather than specialists. On a larger farm, specialization was possible, which was more efficient than the use of generalists, and less skilled workers could be hired to undertake simpler tasks, so freeing skilled men to concentrate on those tasks they were best able to perform. Farmers and landowners increased their control over the work-force, reducing the autonomy of the rural community by eroding custom and 'contingent' property rights, and creating a 'proletarianized' work-force which was more dependent and more disciplined because it had fewer resources of its own.

Improvements in agricultural efficiency created the potentiality of releasing a larger number of people from the land by 1700, which was realized by changes outside the agricultural sector. Investment in transport and improvements in marketing created an integrated domestic market for food, and permitted the redeployment of population in towns and rural industry. The structural shift was

TABLE 2.7. *European economies at $550 per capita income (1970 prices)*

	Britain 1840	Belgium 1850	France 1870	Italy 1910
% labour force in primary sector	25.0	48.9	49.3	55.4
% male labour force in agriculture	28.6	51.4	50.6	54.2
% male labour force in industry	47.3	34.4	28.7	26.5
% of income in primary sector	24.9	27.0	33.5	38.2
% of income in industry	31.5	24.0	36.0	23.4

Source: N. F. R. Crafts, *British Economic Growth during the Industrial Revolution* (Oxford, 1985), table 3.4.

striking, with a more precipitous fall in the proportion of the population employed in agriculture than in other European countries at the same level of income (see Table 2.7). These figures also indicate another striking feature of British economic development: the absence of any large productivity gap between industry and agriculture. The percentage of the labour force engaged in the primary sector was almost identical to its share of income, unlike in France where workers in the primary sector produced a lower share of income. The share of income produced by British industry was less than its share of the labour force, which implies that labour was released from agriculture into low-productivity industry. Britain experienced an industrial revolution in one sense, of rapid structural change in the deployment of labour. But the figures in Table 2.7 also suggest that Britain had not experienced an industrial revolution in another sense, of rapid growth of productivity in manufacturing industry. 'The "triumph" of the British economy in the late eighteenth and early nineteenth centuries', argues Crafts, 'lay in employing a lot of people in industry and relatively few in agriculture rather than achieving outstanding productivity levels or growth rates in industry taken as a whole.'[13] Britain, he argues, had a greater comparative advantage in agriculture than in industry, and the success of agriculture in raising labour productivity created an industrial sector based upon a low level of skill and training which made low value-added goods. The release of labour from the land could therefore be a matter of regret rather than celebration, and it has been argued by some critics of British economic development that the French pattern of retaining labour on the land was in many ways preferable for the welfare of the bulk of the population. In Britain, most of the gains from rising yields and labour productivity went to landowners and capitalist farmers; perhaps the French peasantry was better off in staying on the land until the environmental conditions in towns had improved. The rapid structural change in Britain also shaped the market for industrial goods, and led to a particular pattern of growth based on low value added production. The domestic market in Britain was more likely to be dominated by urban working-class demand than in France, where demand was more traditional and differentiated. There was also a divergence in the significance of export markets. British industry was heavily dependent on export markets, to which it supplied cheaper goods and semi-finished yarn or iron for processing by local industry to meet local tastes. By contrast, French industry was less reliant on overseas markets, and its exports were largely high-quality consumer goods. There were two divergent paths of industrialization, shaped by the process of agricultural development and release of labour from the land: the French pattern of small owner-occupying farms and labour retention arguably had some virtues, for French industry followed a path of development based upon high value added goods; by releasing people from the land, British industry followed a path of development based upon low value added goods and low levels of training in sectors such as cheap cotton goods. Perhaps Britain would have been more prosperous if it had retained small yeomen farmers rather than shifting to great estates and large tenant farms.

Landlords and Rent: Parasites or Stimulus?

The yeomen farmers of seventeenth- and early eighteenth-century England were clearly capable of raising yields, and were not so benighted as claimed by the proponents of large-scale capitalist agriculture. Their position was eroded by the emergence of large farms on consolidated estates in the eighteenth century, and many tenants lost the quasi-ownership of life-leases and customary tenure. Parliamentary enclosure was a means of capturing the property rights of tenants and transferring rents to landowners, who took a large part of the increase in agrarian incomes in the late eighteenth and early nineteenth centuries. The social structure of the countryside was changed as landownership became much more concentrated, and radicals from William Cobbett to Henry George were quick to point out that a pattern of landownership which was created by the use of political power could legitimately be destroyed by state power, and 'unearned' economic rents appropriated by the community. Some recent historians concur, arguing that landowners were shifting risks to tenants by fixing rents regardless of harvest fluctuations, so that farmers' incomes were more variable than landlords' incomes. 'The landed estate was not a device for sharing risk,' claims Avner Offer. 'The English tenure system was an arrangement for converting agriculture, an inherently risky enterprise, into landownership, a secure and stable one.'[14]

A more sanguine interpretation of British history is that the landed élite assisted economic growth, by their willingness to invest in commercial agriculture, mines, and transport. Defenders of the landed aristocracy and gentry claim that their responsibility for estate improvement allowed tenant farmers to devote their resources to investment in animals and implements, which was preferable to peasant owner-occupiers who were more likely to devote surpluses to the purchase of land. The rental of land to tenant farmers should be seen, in this benign account, as a device by which landowners could share risks by allowing arrears and remissions in periods of depression. On such a view, the system was preferable to the pattern of French agriculture, where competition for land forced up land prices and rents, leaving less surplus to reinvest in animals. Small peasant proprietorship, on this view, held down yields by checking investment in livestock and retaining underemployed labour, and the British pattern of large landowners renting to capitalist tenant farmers was more efficient.

Critics of landowners certainly have a strong case at the end of the eighteenth and early nineteenth centuries when rents rose sharply, and landlords were largely successful in retaining their increased share of agricultural income. In the second half of the eighteenth century, agriculture started to lag behind the growth of population, so that the slack in the agricultural system disappeared by the 1780s and plenty gave way to shortages. During the initial rise in prices between 1745 and 1780, the rate of growth of agricultural output decelerated, and it was only the rapid increase in prices at the end of the century which at length produced a recovery. Agriculture ran into high cost barriers to further expansion, and 'a heavy price had to be paid to landowners and farmers in order to obtain a fairly mediocre response to the demands of the new urban economy'.[15] One response was to place greater emphasis upon the corn side of alternate and convertible husbandry, and to extend those systems to areas of permanent pasture. The area of sheep walks and rough pasture was reduced, which did not necessarily entail a reduction in livestock production relative to cereals, for the spread of convertible husbandry allowed more animals to be kept and more crops to be grown, and permitted a speedy response to changes in the relative prices of cereals and animals. There was also an extension of cultivation into the uplands and fenland, precisely the type of marginal land on which Ricardo based his analysis.

Optimists such as Arthur Young took high rents as proof that productivity was increasing and that farmers could pay more without sacrificing their profits. A more realistic explanation is that the landlord had more power over his tenants, and that rent increases entailed a transfer of income from tenants to landowners rather than simply an increase in profitability. The general phenomenon is clear from the Leveson-Gower estates at Trentham and Lilleshall in Staffordshire, a predominantly pastoral estate which escaped the worst consequences of low cereal prices in the early eighteenth century. Rents rose modestly to about 1750, with rapid increases between the mid-1790s and about 1810 when tenant farmers faced a more efficient management and a harsher attitude (see Fig. 2.6). There was a shift from long leases, so that tenants were more vulnerable to rent increases, and the declining importance of political influence in shaping estate policy made the landlord less sensitive to opinion. The change in attitude is apparent from the contrast between the views of two agents on the Leveson-Gower estate. George Plaxton was reluctant to 'bring a great clamour on a good landlord'; by contrast, James Loch, when he was faced with opposition to high rents in 1817, commented that 'this, like other rebellions, must be put down by the strong hand of power'.[16]

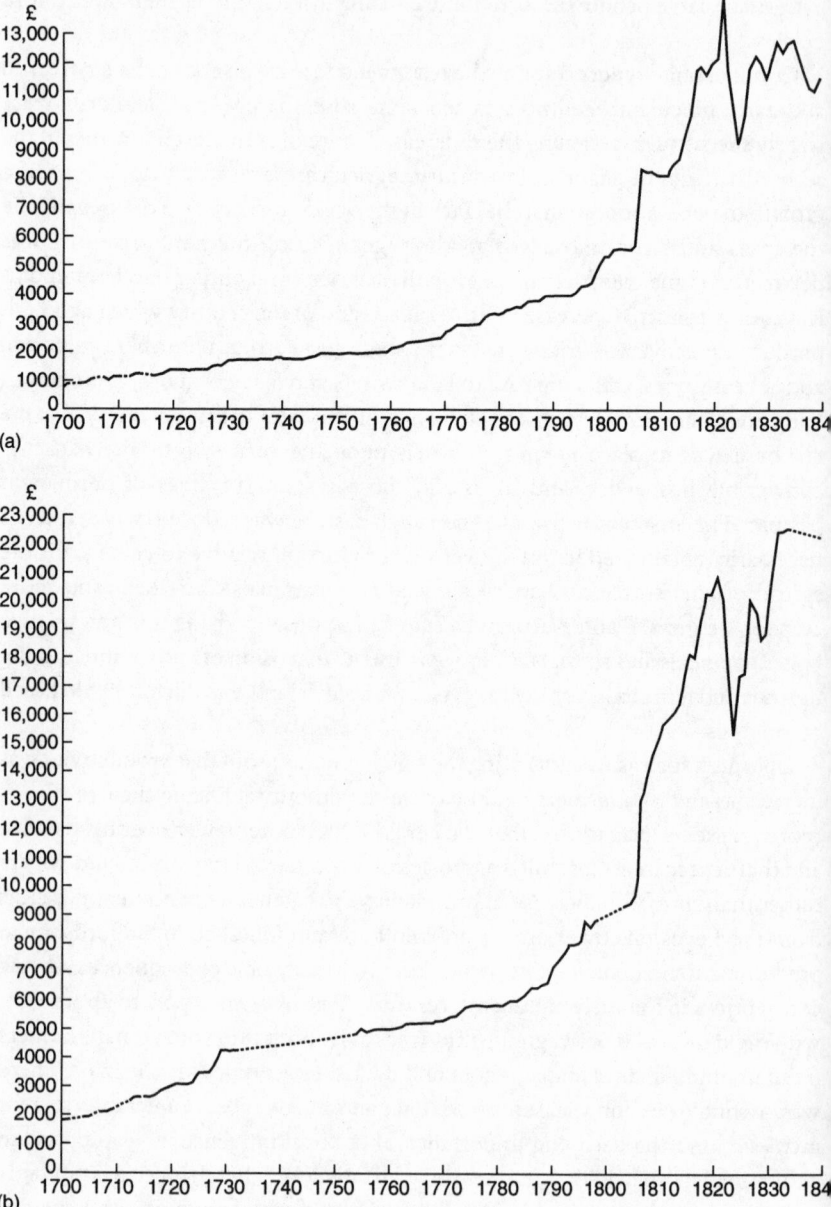

FIG. 2.6. Rent due at (a) Trentham and (b) Lilleshall, Leveson-Gower estate 1700–1839

Source: J. R. Wordie, 'Rent Movements and the English Tenant Farmer, 1700–1839', Research in Economic History, 6 (1981), app. 1.

Rents outstripped prices between 1790 and 1815, and did not fall in line with prices after the war. Landlords, who had adjusted to a higher standard of living, were reluctant to reduce their income, and tenant farmers in the early nineteenth century were probably worse off than their counterparts at the beginning of the revolutionary wars. The result, as Ricardo argued in his complex prose and radicals such as William Cobbett asserted with venom, was a golden age for landlords, who not only increased their rent rolls to unprecedented levels, but also benefited from the fees and perquisites of public office. Certainly, land-owners had little compunction about using state power to their own advantage in order to maintain their gains at the end of the war. The burden of taxation was shifted on to other classes, for the income tax was abolished in 1816; and protective duties were erected in 1815 in order to sustain high grain prices. Ricardo's *Principles* appeared in 1817, a product of the concern over the shape of the British economy and society. The radicals argued that the distribution of income was skewed, and that landlords deployed their high incomes in ways which were less conducive to growth. Cobbett wished to return to the rural community of the mid-eighteenth century, before the increase in rents and large farms destroyed stability; and urban radicals such as John Gast, the leader of the London artisans, feared the consequences for industry of an unequal income distribution. Higher food prices and raw material costs reduced the rate of return on industrial capital, and the lack of buoyancy in the domestic market forced a switch to more unstable foreign markets, which placed pressure upon profits and wages, with the result that less money was available for reinvestment and risks were increased. Great landowners were more likely to spend their income upon luxury imports than other groups; their investment in buildings competed with industry; they employed retinues of servants and boosted the provision of luxury services. The critics of the aristocracy could point to the lavish rebuilding of town houses in London, the blatant parading of wealth at the court of the Prince Regent, and the luxury trades of London, which had its clearest expression in 1820–1 with the grandiose coronation of the Prince Regent as George IV. The tenurial system of British agriculture was not necessarily the best in the best of all possible worlds, and a high price was paid in order to persuade farmers and landowners to respond to the increasing demand from towns and industry. In the late twentieth century, the great aristocratic country houses are portrayed as proud symbols of 'heritage'; to the radicals of the early nineteenth century they were symptoms of class robbery and misappropriation through state power, symbols of the distortion of the economy. Political reform, they argued, was necessary in order to redress the balance, for the power of the state was crucial to the wealth of landowners, which rested upon the tax system, the corn laws, and the profits of office.

The radicals had a point, but the alternative was not necessarily without its problems. The last serious famine in Britain was in Scotland in 1697–9; in France, there were sixteen nation-wide famines between 1700 and 1789, and a serious subsistence crisis as late as 1819. In nineteenth-century France, the survival of small farms was at the expense of rigid controls on fertility in order to prevent pressure on resources, so that there was virtually no population growth; and food prices were maintained by tariffs. Ricardo was right to suggest that rent formed a rising share of income, and Cobbett was correct in his belief that many small farmers and labourers were better off in the mid-eighteenth century. But could the agrarian system of the early eighteenth century feed a rapidly growing population, and avoid a subsistence crisis such as Malthus feared, without a sizeable increase in rents and a consolidation of farms? Britain achieved high labour productivity in agriculture, allowing it to release labour and feed the rising population, without a disastrous increase in food prices which would lead to a collapse of wages and a 'positive' check on population. Of course, gains in output in the late eighteenth century were hard won, as agriculture hit the ceiling of yields and farming moved to marginal land. But was any other response possible in the face of accelerating population growth at the end of the eighteenth century which threatened prosperity and economic growth? Far from being necessary to provide a work-force for farming and industry, population growth was a potential threat which placed pressure on resources, leading to increased prices and rents; agriculture was able to release labour to meet the needs of industry. Population growth threatened the onset of a 'stationary state', and agriculture in the late eighteenth and early nineteenth centuries was only able to supply food by dint of great efforts. Its success was that it *was* able to feed the population without a subsistence crisis or a serious erosion of real wages.

Conclusion

Changes in agrarian society had wide implications. The comparative advantages of light and clay soils affected the location of rural industry, which in turn had demographic consequences, for the emergence of industry in the countryside weakened constraints on the formation of families which were imposed by the need to acquire a holding. In districts where agriculture continued to dominate, the reduction of the population to dependent wage labour could remove any incentive to delay marriage in order to serve an apprenticeship or to acquire a few animals, and so ease constraints on population growth. Agricultural change could weaken restraints upon population growth, which in turn placed pressure on the supply of food. The increased demand for food, to which agriculture was able to respond only sluggishly, meant higher food prices and a check to the growth of the market for industrial goods. Rents rose, and landowners took an increasing share of the national income—a process which was intensified because they paid lower taxes than other groups in society, and benefited from the high proceeds of office during the Napoleonic wars. The nature of landed society could have been a hindrance to industrialization, rather than a help by providing investment in mines, transport, and commercial agriculture. It is conceivable that the rise of food prices and the fall in per capita consumption could, as Ricardo claimed, have led to a deterioration in the standard of living and a squeeze on industrial profits. The growth of markets for industrial goods was less the result of a release of demand by agricultural change than the result of developments within the industrial sector which allowed an extension of markets at lower prices within the urban-industrial economy and abroad, where there was a greater risk of fluctuations and disruption. The major changes in agricultural productivity occurred in the late seventeenth and early eighteenth centuries, within a framework of relatively small-scale yeoman farming, through their greater care of the soil and intensification of the work-rate on the farm. The emergence of the great estates and the process of parliamentary enclosure were not so much means of increasing the productivity of land, as part of the shift in income from the farmer to the great landowners. This discussion clearly leads to a major question: why precisely did British agriculture follow its distinctive route towards consolidation and the demise of the yeoman farmer? The emergence of great estates and the destruction of coincidental use-rights led to a much more polarized rural society, which had immense consequences for the nature of social relations in the countryside. Increasingly, landless labourers faced large landowners and tenant farmers across a gulf produced by the disappearance of small proprietors.

NOTES

1. G. Clark, 'Yields per Acre in English Agriculture, 1250–1850: Evidence from Labour Inputs', *Economic History Review*, 2nd ser. 44 (1991), 449.
2. N. F. R. Crafts, 'Income Elasticities of Demand and the Release of Labour by Agriculture during the British Industrial Revolution', *Journal of European Economic History*, 9 (1980).
3. R. V. Jackson, 'Growth and Deceleration in English Agriculture, 1660–1790', *Economic History Review*, 2nd ser. 38 (1985), 349.
4. R. C. Allen, *Enclosure and the Yeoman* (Oxford, 1992), 18.
5. G. P. H. Chorley, 'The Agricultural Revolution in Northern Europe, 1750–1800: Nitrogen, Legumes and Crop Productivity', *Economic History Review*, 2nd ser. 34 (1981), 77; J. A. Yelling, 'Changes in Crop Production in East Worcestershire, 1540–1867', *Agricultural History Review*, 21 (1973), 20.
6. Allen, *Enclosure and the Yeoman*, 208.

7. A. Kussmaul, *General View of the Rural Economy of England, 1538–1840* (Cambridge, 1990).

8. Allen, *Enclosure and the Yeoman*, 125.

9. B. A. Holderness, 'Landlord's Capital Formation in East Anglia, 1750–1870', *Economic History Review*, 2nd ser. 25 (1972), 439; G. E. Mingay, 'The Agricultural Depression, 1730–50', *Economic History Review*, 2nd ser. 25 (1972), 330.

10. P. K. O'Brien and C. Keyder, *Economic Growth in Britain and France, 1780–1914: Two Paths to the Twentieth Century* (1978).

11. J. Langdon, *Horses, Oxen and Technological Innovation: The Use of Draught Animals in English Farming from 1066 to 1500* (Cambridge, 1986); O'Brien and Keyder, *Economic Growth*, 117; E. A. Wrigley, *Continuity, Chance and Change: The Character of the Industrial Revolution in England* (Cambridge, 1988), 41.

12. J. R. Wordie, 'Social Change on the Leveson-Gower Estates, 1714–1832', *Economic History Review*, 2nd ser. 27 (1974), 596.

13. N. F. R. Crafts, *British Economic Growth during the Industrial Revolution* (Oxford, 1985), 256.

14. A. Offer, 'Farm Tenure and Land Values in England, c.1850–1950', *Economic History Review*, 2nd ser. 44 (1991), 9.

15. P. K. O'Brien, 'Agriculture and the Industrial Revolution', *Economic History Review*, 2nd ser. 30 (1977), 175.

16. J. R. Wordie, 'Rent Movements and the English Tenant Farmer, 1700–1839', *Research in Economic History*, 6 (1981), 221, 222.

FURTHER READING

Allen, R. C., 'Inferring Yields from Probate Inventories', *Journal of Economic History*, 48 (1988).

—— 'The Efficiency and Distributional Consequences of Eighteenth-Century Enclosures', *Economic Journal*, 92 (1982).

—— *Enclosure and the Yeoman: The Agricultural Development of the South Midlands, 1450–1850* (Oxford, 1992).

Beckett, J. V., 'Regional Variations and the Agricultural Depression, 1730–50', *Economic History Review*, 2nd ser. 35 (1982).

Broad, J., 'Alternate Husbandry and Permanent Pasture in the Midlands, 1650–1800', *Agricultural History Review*, 28 (1980).

Campbell, B. M. S., and Overton, M. (eds.), *Land, Labour and Livestock: Historical Studies in European Agricultural Productivity* (Manchester, 1991).

Chambers, J. D., and Mingay, G. E., *The Agricultural Revolution, 1750–1880* (1966).

Chorley, G. P. H., 'The Agricultural Revolution in Northern Europe, 1750–1800: Nitrogen, Legumes, and Crop Productivity', *Economic History Review*, 2nd ser. 34 (1981).

Clark, G., 'Productivity Growth without Technical Change: European Agriculture before 1850', *Journal of Economic History*, 47 (1987).

—— 'Yields per Acre in English Agriculture, 1250–1850: Evidence from Labour Inputs', *Economic History Review*, 2nd ser. 44 (1991).

Collins, E. J. T., 'Harvest Technology and Labour Supply in Britain, 1790–1870', *Economic History Review*, 2nd ser. 22 (1969).

Crafts, N. R. F., 'Income Elasticities of Demand and the Release of Labour by Agriculture during the British Industrial Revolution', *Journal of European Economic History*, 9 (1980).

——*British Economic Growth during the Industrial Revolution* (Oxford, 1985).

Flinn, M. W., 'Agricultural Productivity and Economic Growth in England, 1700–60: A Comment', *Journal of Economic History*, 26 (1966).

Glennie, P., 'Continuity and Change in Hertfordshire Agriculture, 1550–1700: ii, Trends in Crop Yields and their Determinants', *Agricultural History Review*, 36 (1988).

——'Measuring Crop Yields in Early Modern England', in B. M. S. Campbell and M. Overton (eds.), *Land, Labour and Livestock* (Manchester, 1991).

Gould, J. D., 'Agricultural Fluctuations and the English Economy in the Eighteenth Century', *Journal of Economic History*, 22 (1962).

Holderness, B. A., 'Landlord's Capital Formation in East Anglia, 1750–1870', *Economic History Review*, 2nd ser. 25 (1972).

Hueckel, G., 'Relative Prices and Supply Response in English Agriculture during the Napoleonic Wars', *Economic History Review*, 2nd ser. 29 (1976).

Ippolito, R. A., 'The Effects of the "Agricultural Depression" on Industrial Demand in England, 1730–50', *Economica*, 42 (1975).

Jackson, R. V., 'Growth and Deceleration in English Agriculture, 1660–1790', *Economic History Review*, 2nd ser. 38 (1985).

John, A. H., 'Farming in Wartime, 1793–1814', in E. L. Jones and G. E. Mingay (eds.), *Land, Labour and Population in the Industrial Revolution: Essays Presented to J. D. Chambers* (1967).

Jones, E. L., 'Agriculture and Economic Growth in England, 1660–1750: Agricultural Change', *Journal of Economic History*, 25 (1965).

——*Agriculture and the Industrial Revolution* (Oxford, 1974).

——(ed.), *Agriculture and Economic Growth in England, 1650–1815* (1967).

Kussmaul, A., *A General View of the Rural Economy of England, 1538–1840* (Cambridge, 1990).

Langdon, J., *Horses, Oxen and Technological Innovation: The Use of Draught Animals in English Farming from 1066 to 1500* (Cambridge, 1986).

MacDonald, S., 'Agricultural Response to a Changing Market during the Napoleonic Wars', *Economic History Review*, 2nd ser. 33 (1980).

——'The Diffusion of Knowledge among Northumberland Farmers, 1780–1815', *Agricultural History Review*, 27 (1979).

Mingay, G. E., 'The Agricultural Depression, 1730–50', *Economic History Review*, 2nd ser. 8 (1955–6).

——'The Size of Farms in the Eighteenth Century', *Economic History Review*, 2nd ser. 14 (1961–2).

O'Brien, P. K., 'Agriculture and the Industrial Revolution', *Economic History Review*, 2nd ser. 30 (1977).

——'Agriculture and the Home Market for English Industry, 1660–1820', *English Historical Review*, 100 (1985).

O'Brien, P. K., and Keyder, C., *Economic Growth in Britain and France, 1780–1914: Two Paths to the Twentieth Century* (1978).

Offer, A., 'Farm Tenure and Land Values in England, c.1750–1950', *Economic History Review*, 2nd ser. 44 (1991).

Overton, M., 'Agricultural Productivity in Eighteenth-Century England: Some Further Speculations', *Economic History Review*, 2nd ser. 37 (1984).

—— 'Estimating Crop Yields from Probate Inventories: An Example from East Anglia, 1585–1735', *Journal of Economic History*, 39 1979).

—— 'The Determinants of Crop Yields in Early Modern England', in B. M. S. Campbell and M. Overton (eds.), *Land, Labour and Livestock* (Manchester, 1991).

—— 'The Diffusion of Agricultural Innovations in Early Modern England: Turnips and Clover in Norfolk and Suffolk', *Transactions of the Institute of British Geographers*, 10 (1985).

Parker, R. A. C., 'Coke of Norfolk and the Agrarian Revolution', *Economic History Review*, 2nd ser. 8 (1955–6).

Roberts, M., 'Sickles and Scythes: Women's Work and Men's Work at Harvest Time', *History Workshop Journal*, 7 (1979).

Rowe, D. J., 'The Culleys, Northumberland Farmers, 1767–1813', *Agricultural History Review*, 19 (1971).

Thirsk, J. (ed.), *The Agrarian History of England and Wales*, v: *1640–1750*, 1: *Regional Farming Systems*; 2: *Agrarian Change* (Cambridge, 1984, 1985).

Timmer, C. P., 'The Turnip, the New Husbandry, and the English Agricultural Revolution', *Quarterly Journal of Economics*, 83 (1969).

Turner, M. E., 'Agricultural Productivity in Eighteenth-Century England: Evidence from Crop Yields', *Economic History Review*, 2nd ser. 35 (1982).

—— *English Parliamentary Enclosure: Its Historical Geography and Economic History* (Folkestone, 1980).

—— 'Agricultural Productivity in Eighteenth-Century England: Further Strains of Speculation', *Economic History Review*, 2nd ser. 37 (1984).

Wilkes, A. R., 'Adjustments in Arable Farming after the Napoleonic Wars', *Agricultural History Review*, 28 (1980).

Wordie, J. R., 'Social Change on the Leveson-Gower Estates, 1714–1832', *Economic History Review*, 2nd ser. 27 (1974).

—— 'Rent Movement and the English Tenant Farmer, 1700–1839', *Research in Economic History*, 6 (1981).

—— *Estate Management in Eighteenth-Century England: The Building of the Leveson-Gower Fortune* (1982).

Wrigley, E. A., *People, Cities and Wealth: The Transformation of Traditional Society* (Oxford, 1987).

—— *Continuity, Chance and Change: The Character of the Industrial Revolution in England* (Cambridge, 1988).

Yelling, J. A., 'Changes in Crop Production in East Worcestershire, 1540–1867', *Agricultural History Review*, 21 (1973).

....

CHAPTER 3

The Rise of the Great Estates
and the Decline of the Yeoman

'The distribution of landed property', remarked James Caird in 1878, 'is, by the growing wealth of the country, constantly tending to a reduction in the number of small estates.'[1] The increasing concentration of landownership fuelled political controversy in the nineteenth century, and one outcome was the compilation of figures on English landownership in 1873 which defenders of landed society hoped would refute the claim that the countryside was in the grip of a few great magnates. They were disappointed, for the 'new domesday' showed a concentrated pattern of ownership (Table 3.1). At the top were great magnates with 10,000 acres and above, such as the dukes of Bedford or Devonshire with their country seats at Woburn and Chatsworth, and their great London mansions. They shaded into the greater gentry and squires, who were more likely to have local influence than a national role. An estate of about 1,000 acres marked the boundary of a gentry life-style, with three or four tenants and a manor house, although some owners of 300–1,000 acres aspired to gentry society, particularly those who had non-agricultural income and had bought a small estate as an investment or a guarantee of social status. The proportion of land held by genuine 'yeomen' or owner-occupying farmers was probably about 10 per cent in England in 1873.

The survey of 1873 provides an accurate picture of the outcome of two centuries of consolidation, but earlier figures are much less reliable. The estimates for 1790 do suggest that small owners of less than 1,000 acres and owner-occupying farmers or yeomen were more significant, and large estates less dominant. Earlier estimates rest upon Gregory King's figures for 1688, which suggest that landownership was dominated by country gentlemen with 45–50 per cent of land and small owner-occupiers with 25–33 per cent. Over the two centuries, there was a rise in great estates and a decline in peasant proprietors and

TABLE 3.1. *Structure of landownership, 1790 and 1873*

	Percentage of land held by owners of various sizes
1790 (England and Wales)	
Great owners (5,000 acres and above)	20–5
Greater squirearchy (1,000–6,000/7,000 acres)	25–33
Smaller owners (under 1,000 acres)	42–55
of whom small owner-occupiers	15–20
1873 (England)	
Great owners (10,000 acres and above)	24
Greater gentry (3,000–10,000 acres)	17
Squirearchy (1,000–3,000 acres)	12.4
Smaller owners (under 1,000 acres)	38.5
Greater yeomen (300–1,000 acres)	14
Lesser yeomen (100–300 acres)	12.5
Under 100 acres	12
of whom small owner-occupiers	10

Source: 1790: G. E. Mingay, *English Landed Society in the Eighteenth Century* (1963), 19–20, 22, 24, 26; 1873: F. M. L. Thompson, *English Landed Society in the Nineteenth Century* (1963), 32, 114, 115, 117.

yeomen who farmed their own smallholdings, with middling owners more or less holding their share. The decline of smallholders was, indeed, more stark than the statistics suggest, for many tenants in 1688 were copyholders or 'beneficial' lessees with some stake in the property; by 1790, tenants were more likely to hold farms on short leases which eroded their interest. The rise of large owners went further in some counties than others. In 1873, after two centuries of consoli-

TABLE 3.2. *Percentage of land occupied by estates of various sizes, 1873 (acres)*

	10,000+	3,000–10,000	1,000–3,000	300–1,000	100–300	Under 100
Nottingham	38	17	7	10	9	12
Lincoln	28	13	10	15	12	14
Cumberland	19	10	12	16	22	16
Essex	9	19	15	20	17	10
Surrey	10	16	18	22	13	12
England	24	17	12.4	14	12.5	12

Source: Thompson, *English Landed Society*, 32, 114–15, 117.

dation, the share of great estates of 10,000 acres ranged from 38 per cent in Nottinghamshire to only 9 per cent in Essex; small owners of less than 300 acres still owned 38 per cent of the land in Cumberland but only 21 per cent in Nottingham (see Table 3.2). These regional variations are of great assistance in explaining the rise of great estates and the decline of the yeoman, for comparison between regions can help to establish which variables were most important, whether tenure, soil type, composition of output, or simply the presence of successful aristocratic families who could play the land market.

Settlements, Inheritance, and the Marriage Market

The great magnates, so their critics complained, were able to grow because they shaped the law to favour accumulation and constrain fragmentation. 'A land system', claimed George Brodrick, 'founded on the Law of Primogeniture and guarded by strict family settlement has a direct tendency to prevent the dispersion of land.'[2] The wrath of the radicals was particularly directed against the 'curious and exquisite' device[3] of strict settlement, which they believed allowed estates to be handed down intact from generation to generation, permitting continuity of landed families, a low level of new entrants, and an inactive land market. Their explanation of the rise of the great estates stressed the artificial constraints of the legal system rather than any economic rationale, and they were confident that an unfettered market and free trade in land would restore small owners. Such an analysis was an integral part of the ideology of nineteenth-century liberalism with its faith in the benefits of competition; but was it really the case that the rise of great estates was the outcome of the legal system frustrating the operation of the free market?

The legal device of settlement developed in the mid-seventeenth century as a means of providing for widows. Common law gave a widow the right to 'dower', a third share for life in her husband's estate, which caused difficulties because her claim on the income of the entire estate made the sale of land and management of the estate more complicated. The solution was a 'jointure', by which the groom assigned a specific part of his estate to support his widow during her life, so that the rest of the estate could be managed without restriction. Jointures were usually less generous than the dower, and the statute of uses of 1536 restricted the widow's right to renounce the jointure and elect to receive dower. In future, she could make a choice only when a settlement was made *after* marriage, with the obvious result that settlements were usually negotiated prior to marriage. Their emergence, therefore, was primarily as a means of setting the bride's jointure rather than preventing the dispersal of land.

Of course, negotiation of the marriage settlement provided an opportunity to consider the future of the estate and to arrange the orderly transmission of property by restricting the freedom of succeeding generations to sell or bequeath land. The usual procedure in the early seventeenth century was the 'life estate and entail': the head of a family (A) made a settlement prior to the marriage of his eldest son (B), providing the groom with a life interest in the estate on the death of A, with an entail to C, the eldest surviving son of B, and a jointure to B's wife. A shortcoming was that there was nothing to prevent B from selling land during his life tenancy, so that C's inheritance could be dissipated by a dissolute or incompetent father. This was removed by the 'strict settlement' which emerged in the mid-seventeenth century in order to prevent life tenants disposing of the estate. The competing needs of freedom in managing the estate and protection of the family's interest were balanced by the legal device of a 'trust to preserve contingent remainders': the life tenant in possession could no longer sell the estate, for the rights of the 'contingent remainder' (C) were protected by trustees and the family head (A) could be confident when he made a settlement on the marriage of his son (B) that any grandson (C) would inherit the estate intact. The arrangement was repeated in successive generations. When B had possession of the estate and C wished to marry, C gave up his entail in return for a life estate to commence on the death of B and an income in the mean time, with an entail to his prospective son D.

Although the strict settlement was more rigid than its immediate predecessor, it did not completely prevent sales, which would obviously threaten the family's ability to manage its estates. Henry Brougham, the future Lord Chancellor, was sanguine in 1828: 'I consider the English law as hitting very happily the just medium between too great strictness and too great latitude, in the disposition of landed property.'[4] The concerns were immediate—to fix jointures and the orderly transmission of property—rather than a complete bar on land sales, and there was more freedom of manœuvre than the critics of strict settlement claimed. Some land was usually kept outside the settlement to permit freedom of action, and land was in any case tied up only for a single generation so that decisions could be made to sell land at each resettlement, and there was a constant stream of private Acts to circumvent the provisions of settlements. In any case, demographic realities could countermand the neat legal model, which assumed that successive family heads were alive on the marriage of their eldest son. Where the father died before the marriage of his eldest son, the heir had a virtually free hand; or there might simply be no direct male heir to inherit the estate, which consequently passed to distant kin or through the female line. The rise of great estates could, contrary to the ideology of nineteenth-century liberals, have very little to do with the law, for the strict settlement could be subverted by demography.

The survival of eighteenth-century landed families was threatened by a shortage of direct male heirs, for there was a 'biological failure' on the part of the landed class in the first half of the eighteenth century. British peers born between 1600 and 1624 produced 1.1 sons; their successors born between 1650 and 1674 could manage an average of only 0.95 sons, and the generation born between 1700 and 1724 a mere 0.79, and by no means all survived to adulthood. The aristocracy was committing collective suicide in the first half of the eighteenth century, and much the same applied to gentry families. In Glamorgan, for example, 21.9 per cent of gentry born between 1721 and 1740 left no surviving children and 43.8 per cent no adult male heir. Clearly, there was a high chance that successive resettlement of estates would be disrupted by the absence of a male heir. Even in families which were able to produce sufficient sons, there was a further threat to successive resettlement: death of the father before the marriage of his eldest son. Demographic data on the British peerage indicate that, on average, a father born in 1675 would marry in 1701, and his eldest son would be born in 1705; the father had a life expectancy of a further 26.2 years and the son's median age of marriage was 28.4 years. Consequently, the average son married two years after the death of his father and successive resettlements were the exception rather than the rule. Only 28.0 per cent of aristocrats born between 1675 and 1699 could expect both to produce a son and to survive to his marriage, a startling demographic pattern which affected the market in land. Where the father died before his son's marriage, the restraints of settlement were removed; where there was no direct male heir, land passed to female heiresses or indirect, collateral heirs who were more likely to dispose of property. Demography was unfavourable to the use of the strict settlement as a device to preserve and expand estates in the late seventeenth and early eighteenth centuries. The demographic pattern started to change in the later eighteenth century, for the urge to reproduce was rediscovered by the generation of peers born between 1725 and 1749, who had 1.1 sons; the next generation, born between 1750 and 1799, had an average of 1.4 sons. More sons were born and there was a better chance that fathers survived to their marriage when the land could be resettled. Aristocrats born between 1725 and 1749 had a life expectancy of a further 29.25 years at the birth of their eldest son, whose median age of marriage was 27.8 years; they could expect, on average, to live for eighteen months after their son's marriage, and strict settlement could be used with a greater degree of success in the late eighteenth and early nineteenth centuries.[5] The process of consolidation had already gone far by this stage, and there were more significant factors at work: reform of the law was not likely to have a startling effect in restoring small-scale ownership, for large estates were more likely to have arisen from the operation of a relatively unfettered land market than the constraints of strict settlement.

An alternative, and more sophisticated, account argues that marriage settlements were an important part of a complicated pattern of estate consolidation, providing the occasion for bargains to be struck between the families of the bride and the groom. The wife's family brought a 'portion' to the marriage, and she received a jointure from her husband's family for support in widowhood. A fall in the value of the jointure relative to the portion made the wife more dependent on her husband and implied a shift towards a more patriarchal marriage; a fall in the portion relative to the jointure implied that the balance was moving towards the wife and a more egalitarian marriage. The marriage settlement also struck a balance between the eldest son of the marriage and his younger brothers and sisters. The eldest son received the estate, but its income was encumbered with a jointure for his widowed mother, annuities for younger brothers, and portions for his sisters which could be spread in an egalitarian or patriarchal manner. A rise in the proportion of income received by younger sons and daughters suggests a trend towards an egalitarian and affectionate family; a fall implies that aristocratic families were becoming more patriarchal and weighted towards primogeniture.

Aristocratic families in the eighteenth century were, Habakkuk has argued, concentrating wealth in favour of the male heir at the expense of younger sons and daughters, so that the marriage settlement was moving in the direction of patriarchy and primogeniture.[6] 'These contracts would never be made', complained Sir William Temple in 1750, 'but by men's avarice, and greediness of portions with the people they marry . . .; so that our marriages are made, just like other common bargains and sales, by the mere consideration of interest or gain, without any love or esteem.'[7] Marriage, Habakkuk claims, was the most important factor in the rise of great estates: portions increased at the expense of both jointures to support widows and annuities for younger sons, so that eldest sons secured more for their brides; and there was a more systematic search for brides who were wealthy heiresses or had large portions for the purchase of land. The outcome was not simply a redistribution of assets from the father of the bride to the groom which merely shuffled assets amongst great magnates, for Habakkuk argues that large owners were able to gain by a sort of ratchet effect. The groom's family used the portion to buy land, and the bride's father raised the funds by mortgaging his own estate rather than selling land. Of course, the increased burden of mortgage debt might in time lead to financial strain and forced sales, but Habbakuk believes that the danger was avoided by increased rent income in the later eighteenth century. The marriage market, if Habakkuk is to be believed, increased the scale of large estates; marriages were dynastic rather than affectionate, and the needs of the eldest son and the estate were given primacy over the widow and younger sons.

There is little doubt that portions did rise: the average value in a sample of peers was £5,050 in 1625–49 and £9,350 in 1675–1729.[8] More questionable is whether the surge in portions provides evidence of a calculating attitude to marriage, and a sacrifice of widows and younger sons on the altar of dynastic ambition. Rather, the eighteenth century was marked by the rise of an affectionate family structure which protected the rights of widows, daughters, and younger sons in a way which threatened the disintegration rather than the consolidation of estates. This might seem unlikely, for titles passed through the male line, and inheritance of the landed estate followed in order to maintain dignity and status: Mrs Bennet in *Pride and Prejudice* must have had many real counterparts when she complained 'bitterly against the cruelty of settling an estate away from a family of five daughters, in favour of a man whom nobody cared anything about'.[9] The appearance of dynastic continuity was preserved in such cases by the use of 'fictive kin', who were required to change their names to suggest the uninterrupted possession of the estate through the generations. The Pusey estate in Oxfordshire, for example, was inherited by John Allen and Philip Bouverie, both of whom were obliged to adopt the name of Pusey. Yet this was not to say that the interests of widows, daughters, and younger sons were neglected and that the strict settlement was a patriarchal device to protect the eldest son or male heir. Although the marriage settlement attempted to keep the estate intact in the hands of the eldest son or inheritor of the title, it was treated as a capital asset to raise income to be shared between members of the family in a more egalitarian way, which increased the rights of both daughters and younger sons. Until the end of the seventeenth century, settlements left the provision for daughters and younger sons to the discretion of the heir; by the early eighteenth century, they were freed from the tender mercies of their eldest brother or more distant kin, and were given a definite right to specified amounts. The result could be the fragmentation of the estate and an active land market, rather than the subordination of the family to a drive for consolidation.

Once charges became mandatory, they had to be met regardless of circumstances. The tenant for life was, complained Lord Winchilsea, made into 'the slave of the family'[10] under pressure to meet the claims of portions and annuities created by his father, and with the prospect of creating more for his own children. Estates were frequently mortgaged to raise the money, which created financial difficulties, for the interest paid on mortgages was higher than the yield on the land. Landowners were not rescued from the mounting burden of debt created by portions so easily as Habakkuk assumes, and his argument could be reversed. Marriage settlements were not made on dynastic considerations to the exclusion of all else; rather than the eldest son benefiting at the expense of his widowed mother and younger brothers and sisters, the relatively generous provision for other members of the family created heavy costs of debt service which might lead to a crisis in landed families and a disintegration of estates. The strain was greatest in cases of indirect inheritance, which were increasingly common in the late seventeenth and early eighteenth centuries, for there was a temptation to pile up charges on the estate when it was inherited by a collateral heir 'whom nobody cared anything about'. In 1705, for example, Lord Petre provided a portion of £15,000 for his daughter if his son inherited the estate, but £30,000 if his son died and the estate passed to anyone else. The windfall of inheritance could lead to an active land market in an attempt to reduce the burden of debt, such as happened after the death of Sir Samuel Grimston in 1700. He left his estate, with a gross income of £4,400 a year, to his great-nephew William Luckyn, who had to finance a portion of £30,000 to Grimston's granddaughter and £17,000 to his daughter; he was not free of the debts for thirty years, despite selling a fifth of the estate.[11] Even when the collateral heir was not stretched by debt, he might well place his acquisition in a different category from his paternal property. The land might be distant from his main holdings, and there was every incentive to sell in order to reduce debt on the 'core' estate or to create a more coherent holding. In some cases the beneficiary might not be interested in landownership, and would be tempted to sell the land and invest in stocks or trade and industry. Even when a man was fortunate enough to marry a rich heiress, her estate was not necessarily absorbed into the family estate, for it could return to her lineage on his death or pass to a younger son in order to retain a separate identity. The third earl of Bute, for example, married Mary Wortley Montagu, who inherited her father's vast estates in 1761. The earl received the rents until his death in 1792, when the estate passed to his younger son rather than to the extensive holdings of his eldest son. Whether or not a family gained from the marriage market was less a long-term strategy than a lottery in which the odds were set by the chances of demography. There were some winners, such as the Stuarts of Bute, who were minor Scottish landowners at the beginning of the eighteenth century and rose to become one of the very wealthiest families of nineteenth-century Britain through a series of fortunate inheritances and marriages. The first marquess married, 'upon prudential considerations only' according to one cynic, the coheiress of Lord Windsor, who brought him large mineral-bearing estates in south Wales; on her death, he married the daughter of Thomas Coutts, who brought a portion of £100,000.[12] Few were so lucky or calculating, and the marriage market was not a major reason for the rise of great estates.

The increase in portions was not the outcome of a deliberate strategy to consolidate estates so much as the product of an imbalance in the marriage market caused by the fall in the supply of eligible potential husbands as a result of the low birth rate of aristocratic and gentry families. Women generally outnumber men, and the surplus was exacerbated by the loss of men to war and the colonies, and accentuated by considerations of status transmission. A woman's status was given by her husband, so she could not marry into a lower social rank: a landowner's daughter could not marry a merchant's son. A man's status could be preserved despite a marriage to a woman of a somewhat lower rank, so that a landowner's son could, if necessary, marry a merchant's daughter. Higher-status men were able to marry down the social scale, whereas women needed to find husbands of the same or higher social status. The result was to force up the price of portions to secure a suitable match, particularly because of competition with the daughters of wealthy merchants and financiers such as Henry Hoare and Thomas Coutts, who were offering generous portions for the marriage of their daughters to landed sons. The rise in portions was less a calculated bid to 'buy' land which led to a systematic increase in great estates than a response to an unbalanced marriage market which led fathers to protect the status of their daughters. The behaviour of landed families in the late seventeenth and eighteenth centuries reflects a social and cultural shift to a more affectionate and less patriarchal family structure which made children more costly and valued. One consequence was a fall in the birth rate, which created indirect inheritance and fuelled the land market; another was the encumbrance of estates by portions and annuities, which led to sales. Certainly, neither the adoption of strict settlements nor the marriage market can explain the rise of great estates.

Tenure: Custom Versus Contract

The consolidation of land ownership arose largely from the gradual, piecemeal acquisition of land from farmer-occupiers, who ranged from peasant smallholders to substantial yeomen. The explanation should be sought less in the internal dynamics of aristocratic society, with the smallholders and yeomen as passive victims, than in the changing balance of power between aristocrats and yeomen. Between 1700 and 1850, tenure was redefined to create a starker division between owning and renting property, which allowed larger owners to acquire property from smaller owners or to reduce occupiers with some interest in property to simple tenancy. In 1700, the distinction between a tenant who farmed the land of another man, and a freeholder who owned his own farm, was still very hazy. In contemporary usage, a peasant or yeoman did not necessarily own the freehold: his right to land could rest upon manorial custom or a relatively secure form of leasehold, and there was a variety of claims or 'use-rights' which overlapped or coincided, such as foraging for timber or the right to cut peat. Landowners became increasingly hostile to constraints upon their exclusive use of property; they wished to reduce ownership to a single, pre-eminent right to the use of property which would allow them to exploit 'their' land without restraint. The replacement of customary tenure or long leases by contracts and short leases might well threaten peasants and yeomen, who could counter by claiming a use-right in property by appealing to a custom which existed 'time out of mind', continued without interruption, and applied to a specific area and group of people. In the north-east and north-west of England, for example, customary tenure derived from 'border service', which required the tenants of a manor to provide a horse and undertake military service against the Scots.

Customary tenants were liable to two types of payment to the lord of the manor: a small annual rent which was below the full market or rack-rent of the land; and the occasional payment of a lump sum or 'fine'. 'Dropping' fines were paid on the death of the tenant in order to admit his heir, and 'general' fines on the death of the lord of the manor; they could be 'fixed' as a multiple of the annual rent or 'arbitrary', that is, open to negotiation according to the current value of the holding. The tenants were virtually freeholders, for they had an 'estate of inheritance' which they could sell or bequeath. Another form of customary tenure was 'copyhold', based on a contract in the manorial court which was entered in the manorial roll and copied for the tenant. The annual 'quit' or 'reserved' rent was below the market or rack-rent, with a fine for 'admission' when the holding passed into new hands. Copyhold tenancies offered a greater or lesser degree of security. Fixed fines were obviously beneficial to the copyholders at times of inflation; arbitrary fines could be increased to reflect market values, although the courts did rule that they should be 'reasonable' in order to prevent lords setting them so high that the copyholder was forced to surrender the land. Some copyholds were based upon a number of 'lives', such as the tenant and two children; the lord of the manor could renew the term as each life 'dropped', but there was no legal compulsion and he could decide to allow the copyhold to expire. By contrast, in the east and Midlands, copyhold often gave tenants the security of an inheritable interest.

The erosion of customary tenure and the manorial court by written contracts and the power of the landlord was shaped by the ability of tenants to secure legal backing, and by the matrix of copyholds for lives and inheritance with fixed or arbitrary fines. Tenants in the north-west of England, for example, secured the backing of the courts for their customary tenure in 1625; in other areas, it was not always possible to prove continuity without interruption in a defined area or group. Similarly, variation between types of copyhold could permit a more or less rapid replacement by leases. In the south-east of England and east Midlands, for example, copyhold had largely disappeared by 1750, whereas in the south-west and west Midlands it still had a tenacious survival. Leases themselves gave a greater or lesser degree of security to the tenant. In western England, life-leaseholds were close to copyholds for life, creating a tenancy for, say, the life of the tenant, his wife, and his eldest son in return for a small annual 'reserved' or 'chief' rent, and a fine for admission to the tenancy. In practice, the tenancies became hereditary, for landlords usually permitted the automatic renewal of the lease on the payment of a 'dropping' fine as each life ended. By contrast, leases in the eastern half of England charged a full market or rack-rent, without fines or any right of inheritance, for short periods of one to twenty-one years. The final step, which was becoming the norm by the nineteenth century, was a tenancy-at-will without any written agreement, which could be terminated or adjusted at any time to reflect market or rack-rents. Tenants increasingly lost all property rights in the land, and held on short-term contracts.

What determined the location and timing of change from, at one end of the spectrum, customary or copyhold tenure and life-leaseholds to, at the other end, short annual leases and tenancies-at-will? Certainly, there was a wide-ranging attack upon manorial custom in the seventeenth and eighteenth centuries, as lords of the manor inspected custom and attempted to increase their power by pushing up fines, substituting short leases, and converting themselves into landlords. Explanation of the process is controversial. The 'Brenner hypothesis' suggests that the English peasantry failed to establish secure property rights in the sixteenth century, in contrast with French peasants who retained political and economic rights. The structure of agrarian society was linked, he argues, with the formation of the state. Peasant proprietorship and an absolute state were interdependent in France, for the crown relied on taxes paid by the peasantry and consequently had an interest in defending them against landlords' demands for rent. By contrast, the finances of the English crown were dependent on the landlords, so that they allied and secured the destruction of peasant property.[13]

Brenner's hypothesis has a seductive simplicity, but can easily be challenged. Where customary or copyhold tenants could not make a case, the courts allowed the lords of the manor to acquire the freehold and reduce the occupiers to tenants on short leases or at will, without a right to inheritance. But where a case could be made, English courts protected copyholds of inheritance, and supported customary tenure such as in the ruling on 'border service' in 1625. The law was not, as some historians have suggested, simply a capitalist agency for the destruction of 'moral economy' and the substitution of the market relations of 'political economy'; it was concerned to define what property had a legal right to protection, which could work to the advantage of copyholders and customary tenants. Indeed, the Brenner hypothesis could be reversed, by suggesting that the shift to leases was an unintended consequence of the legal strength of customary tenure and copyhold of inheritance. In the first half of the sixteenth century, the replacement of copyhold by leases was uncontentious. Lords viewed the change as a simple expedient to anticipate income by securing a fine at the time of conversion; their tenants did not feel threatened, for conversion was an opportunity to avoid further fines during the term of the lease. At this stage, neither side saw the substitution of leases as a means of evicting the tenant or his heirs, or of increasing rents. Expectations changed at the end of the sixteenth century and first half of the seventeenth century. Prices were rising and lords had an incentive to increase rents; equally, tenants had the motive to defend their custom in the courts, and in many cases they were successful. The lords, in a weak legal position and economically straitened, could take two courses of action. One was to sell confirmation of the custom as a way of raising capital: Sir John Lowther, for example, sold a confirmation to the tenants of the manor of Thirkeld in Cumberland for £1,200 in 1633, which entrenched custom and made it difficult to substitute leases at a later date in the eighteenth century. An alternative response was to sell the freehold to the copyholders, like the lord of the manor at Aynho in Northamptonshire in 1611. Ironically, the ability of the tenants to assert their rights and secure the freehold created a future opening for landlords to purchase their land and let it to tenants at rack-rents: at Aynho, the last freehold yeoman sold to the lord of the manor in 1787, and much the same process was repeated in the north-west of England in the early nineteenth century. Landlords made a renewed attempt to undermine customary tenure in the late eighteenth century by raising fines to a level which the tenants could not afford; the tenants won support from the courts which ruled that their fines were fixed, and about two-thirds of the manors in Cumbria and Westmorland consequently still had customary tenure in the late eighteenth century. This successful defence of property rights backfired, for lords of the manor opted to grant the freehold to the customary tenants, so increasing the marketability of holdings and leading to sales in times of hardship such as the 1830s when prices fell and the textile industry, which supplied supplementary income, collapsed. Similarly, in the Forest of Dean the 'free miners' were able to defend their right to sink shafts in the royal forest, which was embodied in an Act of Parliament in 1838. But the Act was double-edged, for it permitted free miners to sell or lease their rights to coal, so dislodging the title coal from the community of free miners and making it a marketable commodity which could be sold to outsiders. The custom was confirmed, but embedded in a different intellectual framework which turned rights into discrete, saleable commodities. The demise of smallholders and yeomen farmers was, therefore, not a simple outcome of an attack by the courts on the rights of customary tenants. On the contrary, the courts were willing to defend rights where a case could be made, which led either to the confirmation of custom or to the substitution of freehold, which could result in sales and consolidation.

The process of transforming tenures was slow, and there was a haze of ambiguity throughout the eighteenth century, for by no means all copyhold and customary tenures had been clarified, whether by conversion into freehold, confirmation as customary tenure, or decline into short leases and tenancies at will. The lord of the manor had to decide whether the cost and effort of testing the legality of customary rights were justified, or whether he should allow copyholds and long leases to expire as lives 'dropped'. His decision was affected by the economic context. Short leases and rack-rents offered the landlord a more regular and certain income than annual reserved rents supplemented by irregular fines. However, conversion to short leases entailed a short-term loss, for he had to forgo 'dropping' fines which added a further life interest; the landlord would be obliged to rely upon the modest reserved rents until the existing lives died and rack-rents could be introduced. The switch would be delayed where the proportion of income derived from fines was high, for landlords would experience a long period of hardship before securing any gain from rack-rents. This applied to the Welsh border, and south-west and north-west England. Where reserved rents were a higher proportion of income, such as in the east Midlands, south-east, and east England, it was easier to forgo fines and convert to rack-rents.

The timing of the shift to short leases was influenced by price trends. When prices were falling, long leases and copyhold were more attractive, for reserved rents were rising in real terms, and tenants had a strong incentive to pay the periodic fines which secured the entry of the next 'life'. Life-leaseholders and copyholders paid taxes and were responsible for repairs, which was particularly appealing to landlords at a time of low prices. By contrast, rack-rents were more likely to fall into arrears and to increase the problems of management. When prices were rising, the assessment of gains and losses was reversed. Tenants benefited from falling real rents and captured most of the gains of rising prices and profits; landlords stood to lose from the low level of reserved rents which no longer reflected economic reality, and had a strong incentive to convert to short leases and rack-rents. Life-leases and copyholds were therefore challenged during the period of rising prices and rents in the late eighteenth century. Rising land values made it worthwhile for lords of the manor to bear the expense and trouble of returning to the courts to test the claim of customary tenants and copyholders to various use-rights which they had previously condoned, such as the rights of customary tenants to timber, minerals, stone, and peat. How should this process be interpreted?

Social conflict in the eighteenth and early nineteenth centuries is often placed within a framework of a clash between the 'moral economy' of a customary, non-market culture based on 'just' prices and 'fair' wages which was defended by rural communities against the imposition of a 'political economy' based on a market culture of competitive individualism, which came from outside through the actions of land stewards and landlords. This dichotomy is overdrawn, for cottage- and smallholders who defended their contingent property rights or customary tenure were not necessarily rejecting market relations, which were reflected in their culture and ideology; they were attempting to ensure that their property rights were recognized as market relations were redefined. What was at stake was an attempt by both sides to turn the terms of the market to their own advantage: conflict was over the definition rather than the abrogation of market forces. The process of change was not simply through the incursion of market relations from outside the farming community, through the 'seigneurial' route to the emergence of large estates by converting the lord of the manor's rights into outright ownership as a landlord at the expense of small peasant and yeomen farmers. This was by no means a foregone conclusion, for customary tenants were able to protect their position or gain the freehold. Change could also take place within the village community, through the operation of an active land market, as smallholders sold to their larger neighbours, allowing some yeomen to climb into the lesser gentry and moving the distribution of land up a notch. This was the 'kulak' route to consolidation through internal differentiation within the yeomanry without the involvement of manorial lords.

Consolidation of small freeholders, copyholders, and customary tenants was greater in arable districts than in pastoral areas. In early eighteenth-century Cambridgeshire, for example, rural society was more differentiated in the arable parish of Chippenham than in the pastoral fenland parish of Willingham. In Chippenham, a class of substantial yeomen emerged during the sixteenth and seventeenth centuries as the result of small owners selling their land, either when harvests failed or in response to a long downward trend in prices. Although a poor harvest resulted in high prices, this was little consolation to a small producer with little or no surplus for sale; larger farms benefited because they had a surplus for sale. Similarly, a long downward trend in prices allowed large arable farms to gain at the expense of small units, for there were economies of scale in arable agriculture. Larger holdings emerged from within the peasant land market, through the efforts of prosperous yeomen or 'kulaks' such as Thomas Dillamore whose holding in the 1630s had been in the possession of fifteen men in 1544. By 1712, 63 per cent of tenants in the parish held no land of their own, and 14 per cent owned more than 90 acres. Willingham was more egalitarian; only 31 per cent of tenants in the 1720s had no land of their own, and no one had more than

90 acres. Small farmers and owners held their own in pastoral areas, for they benefited from low grain prices which allowed consumers to purchase meat, and the more constant labour demands of pastoral farming allowed small farmers to engage in domestic industry or, as at Willingham, to supplement a fragment of land with grazing rights on common fenland.[14]

There were certainly cases in which the process of differentiation and creation of middling sized holdings took place *within* the peasantry, without the active involvement of lords of the manor or landlords. The contrast between France and England was less the imposition of landlord power in England, and its failure in France; rather, the exploitation of French peasants by crown, Church, and seigneurs hindered the development of a prosperous yeoman class which raised yields as in England. There was a period in the seventeenth century when yeomen farmers had greater security, which contributed to their willingness to raise yields by improving land in the 'yeoman's agricultural revolution'. However, many prosperous yeomen families did not survive the eighteenth century, and their holdings were acquired by larger landowners rather than a gradual move of yeomen upwards into the gentry. The 'kulak' route of rich peasants buying up their neighbours stopped, and consolidation of land owner-ship became much more a top-down process of purchases by great owners. The holdings of the prosperous yeomen were often transitory, soon acquired by large landowners who consolidated their estates by gradual accretion of small free-holds. The Colchester family at Westbury in Gloucestershire, for example, spent £10,530 between 1693 and 1744 on thirty-one purchases from twenty-eight ven-dors, and the process of change was cumulative.[15] Once land was aggregated from small units, it was returned to the market in consolidated blocks which were purchased by larger owners. The nature of the land market changed, checking the ability of yeomen to rise into the gentry by reducing the pool of smallholdings within their means. The 'seigneurial' route to consolidation was not simply the result of a destruction of copyhold or customary tenure and its conversion into ownership by landlords; it also arose from purchases of small freehold or copyhold interests.

The ability of great owners to shift from fines to rack-rents, and to purchase the freehold or copyhold interests of yeomen, may be explained by the de-velopment of mortgages rather than by the 'Brenner thesis' of an alliance of crown and landlords. Mortgages were an important element in the rise of great estates, less through their role in the marriage market than in allowing land-owners to replace fines and reserved rents by short leases and rack rentals, and to raise large sums to enter the land market. Essentially, 'fines' raised a capital sum from the land, in return for allowing the yeoman to farm the land and retain a share of the profits above the reserved rent. The lord was, in effect, paying the

tenant a generous rate of interest, as much as 9 per cent on church estates in the
1720s. There was less incentive to use long leases or copyhold to raise capital
sums when mortgages were readily available, without the risk that lenders
would retain the land. Mortgages also eased the hardship of conversion to rack
rentals by providing money to compensate for the immediate strain to estate
finances in forgoing fines. Further, mortgages gave great landowners a competitive edge in the land market, for they could borrow capital more readily and on
better terms than yeomen. A rise in the value of land from about 1710 and a fall in
interest rates gave an edge to large owners who could borrow larger sums on the
security of appreciating assets and could service the debt more easily. Large
owners could build up their holdings, releasing capital gains through mortgages
when required for marriage settlements, rebuilding of a country seat, or estate
improvement. Smaller owners, who were less able to borrow on favourable
terms, could react in a different way. The rise in land values could provide an
inducement for men with a modest amount of land to sell in order to obtain
capital, or to concentrate on more profitable ventures in trade and industry. This
was most likely where individuals who were not established farmers inherited
land indirectly, but even small owners who wished to remain in agriculture could
realize their capital in order to increase their scale of activity or level of stock on a
rented farm.

The rise of great estates was largely the result of a piecemeal process of
accretion on the perimeter of the holding, as the odd field or occasional farm was
purchased, rather than large sales, which were usually designed to reorganize the
estate by selling windfall inheritances to reduce the burden of debt or to acquire a
holding nearer the 'core'. The rise of great estates was not the outcome of strict
settlements and the marriage market, or the simple destruction of property rights
through an alliance of crown and aristocrats at the expense of the peasantry. It
was the product of a complex legal tussle over customary tenure, which could
protect the tenants and confirm their rights; a careful economic assessment of the
economies of rack-rents versus fines and reserved rents, which varied according
to price movements; the availability of mortgage finance, which gave a competitive edge to large owners and allowed them to abandon fines and reserved rents;
and the outcome was mediated by variations in farming systems.

Economic Rationality, the Land Market and New Men of Wealth

Nineteenth-century critics of the land law and settlements assumed that they
prevented an unfettered, competitive market which would preserve the maintenance of small estates. In reality, the land market was buoyant and active:
demography, generous portions, and a desire by small owners to release capital

TABLE 3.3. *Median price for freehold land in years' purchase, 1670–1679 to 1805–1814 (multiples of annual rent)*

	Price in years' purchase
1670–9	18
1700–9	21
1735–44	26
1765–74	29.75
1780–9	25
1805–14	28

Source: C. G. A. Clay, 'The Price of Freehold Land in the Later Seventeenth and Eighteenth Centuries', *Economic History Review*, 2nd ser. 27 (1974), 174.

brought a steady flow of land on to the market. Movements in land prices (see Table 3.3) were the outcome of variations in demand rather than constraints on supply, which raises the question whether purchases were based on financially rational calculation of the rate of return, or were more concerned with social position and status, at the expense of a lower rate of return than could be achieved from alternative investments.

Variations in land prices were sensitive to competing attractions, for a low yield on Funds released a flood of money on to the land market and drove up prices in the 1760s and 1770s, when some owners took advantage of the buoyant market to sell in order to pay off encumbrances. Conversely, a high yield on Funds drew money away from the land market and prices fell, such as during the American War of Independence. Although the land market was sensitive to economic variables, purchasers who borrowed to buy land were apparently forgoing income: the net return was about 3.02 per cent in the 1720s at a time when the mortgage interest rate was 4.5 per cent. The explanation favoured by some historians is that there were non-economic reasons for purchase, the lower rate of return serving as the fee for 'admission into the charmed circle of English landed society'.[16] Status was obviously a consideration, but the purchase of land was usually financially rational. A prosperous merchant who bought land was often seeking a secure investment away from the risks of business, and providing security for his family as well as status. Landownership also offered the attraction of an appreciation in capital values, which could be realized by selling or by mortgaging the property to secure money without disposing of the underlying asset. The introduction of short leases and enclosures allowed landowners to increase rack rentals and appropriate a greater part of the proceeds of agriculture, especially when pressure on food supplies from the mid-eighteenth century led to an increase of rent. Land was not over-priced and purchases were rational, largely because of the redefinition of power within the market: the lower risks of landownership and the ability to raise rents rested upon the replacement of customary tenure and long leases by rack-rents, which took a larger part of the farmers' income without sharing in their risks. The reasonable economic return was essentially a matter of *power* between landowner and tenant. The tenant was weak, for he could not easily withdraw his assets from the farm and sell the crop at short notice; the landowner was strong, for he had power to seize goods for non-payment of rent, and could usually find another tenant. The landowners' bargaining advantages were translated into higher rents and lower risks. The apparent choice between the returns of social status and power on the one hand and economic returns on the other was somewhat unreal, for the admission fee charged for entry into the social and political élite assisted in obtaining power to restructure market relations and permit landowners to increase their level of appropriation.

The outcome of the active land market varied across the country. There was virtue in accumulating a coherent block of land which was easier to manage, and great owners gradually extended their hold in areas such as the 'Dukeries' of Nottinghamshire where they were strongest, ploughing profits into land and seizing any opportunities created by the vicissitudes of their neighbours. In other areas, great magnates sold in order to realize capital for investment in their central holding, such as in Lincolnshire where the market was left open to existing gentry families, and to men who had made fortunes in commerce, finance, or industry. Modest estates were acquired by men from the expanding industrial towns of the north and Midlands, such as Joseph Banks, an attorney and money-lender from Sheffield, and by local families who formed a prosperous middle stratum of food-processors, traders, and professionals in the market towns of the county, such as the Dealtrys who were oil-millers in Gainsborough. The influence of commercial and financial wealth was particularly marked around London, where Middlesex, Essex, and Surrey had the lowest proportion of great estates in 1873. The wealth of the metropolis and empire could also flow into the provinces, as with Edward Stephenson, who invested profits gained from service with the East India Co. in an estate in Cumberland which produced an annual income of £1,245 in 1750.

The conventional wisdom is that English landed society was 'open' to self-made men from the law, public office, trade, and finance, which diffused social conflict and allowed policy to respond to the needs of industry and commerce. But can this view be reconciled with the rise of great estates and the consolidation of landownership which might imply an increasingly oligarchic, closed social and political system? The Stones have argued that there is in fact a contradiction, and they propose that the notion of an open landed élite should be rejected and the concept of a closed caste substituted. Their analysis of the ownership of 362 large country houses in Hertfordshire, Northamptonshire, and Northumberland between 1540 and 1880 led them to the conclusion that new-comers were rare: country seats were kept from the market, even in the absence of a direct male heir, by indirect inheritance and surrogate heirs, and by the sale of parts of the estates to avoid the indignity of the loss of the ancestral home. In Northamptonshire, for example, only 9 per cent of all changes of ownership of country houses between 1540 and 1879 arose from sales, which were often made by the purchasers themselves or their heirs, which suggests that new entrants were transient in comparison with older families who rarely sold. There was, the Stones argue, 'a very large, very stable core of well-established families who continued to retain their hereditary seats from generation to generation',[17] so that the landed élite was closed and new entrants from the world of business rare. However, the data compiled by the Stones are not conclusive. The case is biased against openness by considering the market for country houses rather than land, for many entrants were content with a relatively modest manor house, and few merchants could aspire to build on the scale of the great magnates. It was the *gentry* which was in a state of flux and entry was more easily gained at this less exalted level, which provided a safety-valve and helped maintain social stability. Despite the bias of the Stones' data against openness, their figures can be read to show that 'the rate of upward mobility ... is little short of astonishing'.[18] There were 2,246 owners in their sample between 1540 and 1879, of whom 480 or 21.4 per cent were newcomers, with 157 coming from business. Stability or closure may also be exaggerated by interpreting indirect inheritance and surrogate kin as a means of maintaining continuity. In fact, indirect inheritance could lead to an active land market and bring in 'new men'. In 1716, Aldenham Place in Hertford-shire passed from Henry Coghill, a bachelor, to his sister Sarah, and hence to her husband Robert Hucks, a London brewer; his son died unmarried in 1814, when the estate passed to his unmarried nieces; and on the death of the surviving niece in 1842, the estate passed to a distant relative, George Gibbs, a London merchant. The Stones interpret the indirect inheritance of Aldenham Place by a London brewer and merchant as a sign of continuity; it could equally be a measure of discontinuity and fluidity. There is no contradiction between the continued entry of new men and the consolidation of great estates by larger owners, for the mechanism was the same: an active land market. The high incidence of indirect inheritance and the erosion of the position of smallholders brought land on to the market, which could be purchased either by prosperous newcomers to enter the lower ranks of the landed élite, or by large owners to build up their core estates.

Lairds and Crofters: the Case of Scotland

The structure of landed society was very different in Scotland, where there was scarcely any class of yeomen to experience decline. Rural society was more polarized, with a starker divide between landowners and tenants, and without the complications of customary or copyhold tenure and life-leaseholds. At the top was a small group of about a hundred nobles and Highland chiefs who held their land direct from the crown, such as the great house of Argyll. Below them were the 'lairds' who held their land as vassals or subvassals of the crown or a 'superior'. This feudal tenure took two forms. In the case of wardholding, the land reverted to the superior on the death of the wardholder, and the heir paid 'relief' which was equivalent to about a year's income of the estate. Where the heir was a minor, the estate went into 'wardship' and was administered by the superior until his majority; and in the absence of an heir, the land was 'escheated' or returned to the superior. By 1700, wardholding was confined to the Highlands, where it was linked to the survival of the clan system. It was completely abolished after the rebellion of 1745, which left a second form of tenure: the 'feu-ferme'. The vassal paid his superior a large lump sum to obtain land, followed by an annual feu-duty in perpetuity and a payment to renew the charter when the land passed to an heir. When feu-fermes were initially created, the crown and Church wished to secure money income, so that the lump sums were large and the feu-duties fixed at economic rents. Consequently, the purchasers came from existing landed families who augmented their estates, or office holders and lawyers who entered the ranks of landowners. It was unusual for the tenants who farmed the land to acquire land, with the exception of some areas in the south-west of Scotland where abbeys such as Melrose were feued in small parcels to the so-called 'bonnet lairds' who were the closest equivalent to the yeomanry of England.

The tenants of the nobles and lairds could not follow the pattern of copyhold-ers, customary tenants, and life-leaseholders in England and obtain a right to hereditary occupation. Unlike English common law, the Scottish legal system did not recognize unwritten tradition and therefore offered no protection to custom-ary tenure, and gave considerable power to the landlord. Neither was there anything equivalent to long life-leaseholds. Most tenants in the seventeenth century held their land on verbal agreements as tenants-at-will, which gave very little security, and they could be removed when the landlord wished. By 1700, there was a trend towards written leases, particularly on Lowland estates, for periods of up to nineteen years. Although written leases offered greater legal security to tenants during the term of the lease, and provided an incentive to make improvements, they also marked a shift in attitudes which could disrupt the farming community. Verbal leases reflected the existence of a traditional, patriarchal community based on personal ties, and there was likely to be a high level of security for tenants who were part of the proprietor's following. The trend towards written leases reflected a more commercial attitude to the estate, an attempt to increase the money income which challenged an older social system.

The settlement pattern was dispersed, with the exception of nucleated villages in the south-east, and was based on 'fermetouns' consisting of the houses of the farm's tenants and subtenants. By 1700, about 10 per cent of farms were held by two or more joint tenants on a single lease who farmed the land communally, providing their family labour, sharing the crop, and paying the rent in a lump sum. Much more common were multiple-tenant farms, which were worked by two or more tenants, with the lease specifying a share of the rent for each tenant: on Whelmes farm on the Buccleuch estate in 1708, for example, shares ranged from James Grieve with one half to John Riddell with a twelfth; each managed his own share of the farm and paid rent separately. In some areas, multiple tenancies gave way to single-tenant farms where the farm and holding were conterminous. Single tenancies were most common in arable areas, accounting for 70 per cent of farms on the fertile Lowlands of Aberdeenshire by 1696, and also on the southern uplands of the borders where subsistence farming by multiple tenants was replaced by large commercial sheep farms by 1700. Generally, the number of multiple tenants was reduced in the course of the eighteenth century, such as at Eckford on the Buccleuch estate where there were nine tenants in 1710, three in 1766, and one in 1792. The multiple- and single-tenant farms usually had subtenants who were granted land by larger tenants in return for seasonal labour.

The process of change in Scottish agriculture accelerated after about 1780 with a consolidation of multiple tenancies, a reduction in the ranks of the tenantry, and the destruction of subtenants. The higher price of grain and cattle in the later eighteenth century meant that land was more valuable for the production of marketable goods than for providing subsistence for an underemployed workforce of subtenants, and farmers preferred more regular, disciplined labour to operate large holdings. Subtenants' plots were absorbed into larger farms, and people were, as William Cobbett remarked on his visit to the Lothians, 'studiously swept from the land'.[19] The work-force for these large farms was not supplied by day wage labour as in the arable counties of England, where seasonal underemployment was supported by the poor law. One solution in the north-eastern Lowlands of Banff and Aberdeenshire was the creation of smallholders and crofters at the end of the eighteenth century in order to absorb waste land and provide labour for larger farms. Unmarried 'servants' were housed in 'bothies' or outhouses, forming a distinct part of the life-cycle on the lines of

English servants in husbandry. An alternative system emerged elsewhere in the Lowlands, which in England was adopted only in the border county of Northumberland: married servants were hired for the year and paid largely in kind, which usually consisted of accommodation, keep for a cow, and ground for potatoes.

Lowland society underwent major change, particularly from the 1780s to the 1820s, with the emergence of three clear-cut categories: a small group of landlords, a few substantial tenant farmers, and a large number of landless labourers. There was, however, nothing equivalent to the rural unrest found in the south of England. The use of married farm servants certainly eased the transfer from subtenancy, for the disruption was less violent than a shift to day wage labour, and at least an element of subsistence agriculture survived. Long hires provided a greater degree of security than the daily or weekly hiring of the south of England, and payment in kind insulated the workers from the impact of inflation. Scottish Lowland agriculture required a more constant use of labour over the year than the cereal-growing areas of southern England with their marked harvest peak. Mixed farming was the norm, with a reliance on turnips and artificial grass to feed livestock, which required regular ploughing and encouraged the employment of married farm servants as ploughmen on large farms, rather than the use of short hires such as were found in many parts of England. Additional labour was supplied by drawing on the wives and daughters of married servants, and day labourers were much less significant than in southern England. The absence of underemployed day labourers was in part a response to the farming system, and much the same pattern emerged in similar circumstances in Northumberland. But it was also the result of a conscious policy of removing excess population from the land to the growing towns of Scotland or overseas to North America, in order to retain a relatively small, productive work-force. Farmers and landowners had the power to dispossess subtenants, and the poor law was less generous than its English counterpart in providing relief to the able-bodied poor. Clearance of the *Lowlands* did not lead to overt social tension, for the population which remained had a reasonable degree of security and was insulated from inflation.

Clearance of the *Highlands* was more overtly violent, imposing a greater strain upon social stability, which led to collective resistance, a sense of betrayal, and a harsh, unbending religion. Change was more traumatic, in part because Highland society was less commercialized than the Lowlands, where the market had a greater influence and leases were formal, written documents based upon economic considerations. By contrast, land-holding in the Highlands in 1700 was still associated with clan loyalty. A clan, remarked Duncan Forbes in his survey of

Scotland in 1746, was 'a set of men all bearing the same surname and believing themselves to be related the one to the other and descended from the same common stock ... all agree in owing allegiance to the Supreme Chief of the clan or kindred and look upon it to be their duty to support him at all adventures.'[20] An important word is 'believing', for clans were not simply kinship networks: they were means of extending loyalty by bonds based, as an Act of 1587 put it, on 'a pretence of blude' which made people act *as if* they were kin. The chief of a clan granted land to 'tacksmen' in return for military service; they were a sort of subordinate gentry who left farming to subtenants, receiving a middleman's income from the difference between the rent they paid to the chief and received from the subtenants. The subtenants in turn sublet to cottars. The system was not intended to raise agricultural production so much as to maintain a customary standard of living, and provide men for military expeditions. Although cash was becoming more common in the early eighteenth century, the payment of rent contained at least an element of food which was essential to the maintenance of the clan system. The chief's store offered protection against crop failure in an area prone to food deficits, provided hospitality to gain status, and supported fighting men to sustain feuds.

Whether or not the clan system survived depended upon the chief, who had absolute control over the allocation of land. By the late seventeenth century, the ideology of the clan chiefs was a hybrid based upon an uneasy meeting of the Gaelic world of the Highlands and metropolitan society of Edinburgh and London, an attempt to maintain some of the values of the clan while adopting the behaviour of Lowland landlords. Feuding, cattle raids, and feasting ceased to be the means by which social order was maintained and came to be seen as threats to stability. Chiefs gradually shifted to the marketing of produce in order to raise cash income to improve their standing within a wider society, rather than to maximize internal consumption and social credit within the clan. Their desire to increase money rents came into conflict with their wish to retain the support of tacksmen who felt that they had a hereditary right to their land. In fact, the tacksmen's customary tenure had no legal protection and the chiefs would dispense with them as soon as they felt that agricultural efficiency and money income were more important than maintaining a large following. Clan chiefs started to act as landlords, utilizing the clan lands as their own personal property, and letting land direct to commercial farmers without the mediation of tacksmen. The policy was initiated by the second duke of Argyll, the chief of Clan Campbell, who started to reorganize the clan lands at Kintyre around 1710, in order to increase money rents, treating his estate as a source of revenue rather than a reward for allegiance and a means to support armed followers. He leased farms at open auction to the highest bidder, encouraging subtenants to bid in defiance of their tacksmen. Yet the new policy had its dangers. The second duke had already moved from the culture of the Highlands to incorporation into metropolitan society; the allegiance of 5,000 armed men was less relevant than an income of £5,000 to maintain his status in London society. The problem was that the pursuit of landlordism undermined political stability at a time of Jacobite unrest, removing the tacksman's role as a source of order and loyalty, and placing greater burdens on the tenants by increasing money rents. The response was not to restore tacksmen and to reverse the transformation of tenure, but to reduce rents and make sound politics a precondition for a lease. Change was well under way before the defeat of the rebellion of 1745, which merely permitted the process to be completed by abolishing the judicial powers of chiefs, enforcing restrictions on bearing arms, and imposing a ban on the wearing of Highland dress. Whether legislation was the crucial point is doubtful; more significant was the solvent of commercialism, money rents, and contracts which meant that the policies pioneered by Argyll were more widely adopted. More chiefs treated the land as their own, the position of the tacksmen was eroded, and traditional tenancies replaced. The demise of Jacobitism as a serious political threat simply removed the remaining restraint on commercial imperatives, allowing the completion of transformation from clan chief to landlord.

Transformation of the clan system and the rise of landlordism did not mean that rural society in the Highlands simply converged with the Lowlands. A bastard clan system emerged, as a result of landlords raising regiments for the British army by offering tenancies. Although the motivation was a commercial desire to earn money from military entrepreneurship, this neo-feudalism preserved a feeling that land was granted for service rather than rent, and a sense of lordship and loyalty survived into the nineteenth century. Rural society was even more starkly differentiated than in the Lowlands. Prosperous tenants were less apparent, and the profits of the cattle trade did not filter far down the social scale. A tenant normally supplied a cow to his landlord at an agreed price, which was deducted from the rent, and it was sold to a drover: tenants' involvement in the market was slight, and there was less opportunity for commercially minded farmers to emerge from the ranks of rural society. When change did come, its impact was much more sudden and disruptive than in the Lowlands. There, the ranks of the tenantry had been thinned by a gradual reduction of the number of tenants on a farm, usually when leases came to an end. In the Highlands, the process was much more disruptive, involving the removal of whole communities at a stroke by the policy of clearances. Large sheep farms were created in the Highlands from the 1760s, which led to the dispossession of existing tenants and subtenants and consolidation into single tenancies. The result, it was claimed, would be the replacement of an inefficient, subsistence agriculture by a more economical, commercialized system. The population was relocated on crofts, where kelping, fishing, and spinning of linen yarn were supplemented by small holdings of land. The crofters were not survivors of a traditional small peasantry, but a new phenomenon of the late eighteenth and early nineteenth centuries. The smallholdings could not feed a family and provide sufficient cash for the rent, so that tenants were forced into a precarious reliance upon supplementary income and provided a cheap, dependent labour supply. The process was often brutal and harsh, such as the forced eviction and resettlement of 430 families on the Sutherland estate at Strathnaver; the agent, Patrick Sellar, occupied the land as a sheep-farmer. Not surprisingly, the overturning of joint tenancies and forced resettlement on the coast led to bitter resentment.

The labour-intensive crofting economy was threatened at the end of the Napoleonic wars when fishing and kelp were hit by depression. The small plots of land were inadequate to support the crofters, who were in a desperate plight. The population was now considered to be 'redundant', and landlords sought to remove the crofters whom they had recently created as a central prop of estate management. This sudden turn around in policy created intense social strain in contrast to the more constant process of clearances in the Lowlands. Their removal was not total, for crofters hung on in some places, making a bare living and harbouring bitter resentment. Certainly, it was naïve for men such as Sellar to believe that poor tenants could be wrested from a traditional agrarian system and dumped on the sea-shore, where they would be transformed into models of enterprise; it was a recipe for dislocation and immiseration which benefited only men such as Sellar and the Leveson-Gowers who owned the Sutherland estate.

The pattern of landownership in Scotland was even more concentrated than in England. Unfortunately, there is no Scottish equivalent to the 'new domesday' of 1873 to provide a reasonably accurate measure of the level of concentration at the end of the period, but valuation rolls for the land tax do provide an approximate measure of landownership in 1770 (see Table 3.4). The role of great landlords was least, and of the bonnet lairds greatest, in the west and centre where the impact of small-scale feuing of church and crown lands was still apparent. The great landlords were dominant in the borders and most of the Highlands, especially in Sutherland. Ross and Cromarty was somewhat less skewed towards the great landlords, and had more in common with the Lowlands, where the great landlords and the lairds were of more or less equal importance. Overall, the structure of ownership in 1770 was certainly more concentrated than in England, and there are signs of further consolidation by the time of Sir John Sinclair's survey of landownership in 1814.

The rise of great estates in England was associated with an active land market; rather than strict settlements holding land off the market, the nature of marriage

TABLE 3.4. *Pattern of landholding, Scotland, 1770 (percentages)*

	Great landlords (£2,000 p.a. and above)	Lairds (£100–£2,000)	Bonnet lairds (less than £100)	Institutions
West and central				
Ayr	34.1	54.9	10.2	0.8
Lanark	27.8	54.0	13.5	4.7
Borders				
Roxburgh	73.6	22.0	5.4	1.0
East Lothian	69.7	26.7	1.4	2.2
Lowlands				
Midlothian	40.8	53.9	3.7	1.6
Fife	44.4	48.7	3.7	3.2
Highlands				
Sutherland	67.7	31.6	0.7	0.0
Ross and Cromarty	40.0	50.1	0.9	9.0

Source: L. Timperley, 'The Pattern of Landholding in Eighteenth-Century Scotland', in M. L. Parry and T. R. Slater (eds.), *The Making of the Scottish Countryside* (1980), 144–6.

settlements and the demographic behaviour of landed society brought land on to the market. In Scotland, settlements were 'stricter', for 'unbarrable' entails without duration were permitted in 1685, which tied up land in the long term without the need for the English device of resettlement in each generation. Agreements on inheritance and marriage were part of the same process in England, but in Scotland marriage settlements were separate contracts between the families of the bride and groom which did not involve the rearrangement of inheritance within the groom's family. These legal differences reflected a more patriarchal family structure in Scotland, which gave more power to the head of the family to preserve the patrimony. But the cumulative extension of permanently entailed land did not close off all opportunities for sales, for most families placed only part of their property under strict entail, and the demography of Scottish landowners was likely to generate sales. Glasgow merchants, Edinburgh lawyers, and nabobs from the East Indies entered the land market, creating a turnover amongst the lairds and preventing Scottish landed society from becoming 'an oligarchy of birth'.[21] Certainly, the Scottish landed class underwent greater social and cultural change in the eighteenth century than the English, as the old order of clan chieftains in the Highlands gave way to landlordism, and as the proprietors in the Lowlands adopted a more commercialized attitude. There was a revolution of manners, a turning away from fortified castles and large retinues, which were still common in the late seventeenth century, to elegant country houses such as Mellerstain and Hopetoun, designed by rising architects such as William Adam and his sons, with their delicate plasterwork, fine furniture, and works of art. Land was valued as a source of rent rather than to sustain a retinue, paying for a town house in the New Town of Edinburgh or London and maintaining a grand house in the country. The Scottish nobles and lairds were Anglicized, becoming part of a wider British upper class.

NOTES

1. Quoted in J. V. Beckett, 'The Pattern of Landownership in England and Wales, 1660–1880', *Economic History Review*, 2nd ser. 37 (1984), 2.
2. G. C. Brodrick, *English Land and English Landlords* (1881), 152.
3. F. Pollock, *The Land Laws* (3rd edn., 1896), 118.
4. *Hansard Parliamentary Debates*, NS 18, col. 181, 7 Feb. 1828.
5. J. P. Jenkins, 'The Demographic Decline of the Landed Gentry in the Eighteenth Century: A South Wales Study', *Welsh History Review*, 11 (1982–3), 37; T. H. Hollingsworth, 'The Demography of the British Peerage', supplement to *Population Studies*, 18 (1964); L. Bonfield, 'Marriage Settlements and the Rise of the Great Estates: The Demographic Evidence', *Economic History Review*, 32 (1979), 490, 492.
6. Habakkuk's position has developed over his career in a series of articles: see Further Reading.
7. H. J. Habbakuk, 'Marriage Settlements in the Eighteenth Century', *Transactions of the Royal Historical Society*, 4th ser. 32 (1950), 25.
8. J. P. Cooper, 'Patterns of Inheritance and Settlement by Great Landowners from the Fifteenth to the Eighteenth Centuries', in J. Goody *et al.* (eds.), *Family and Inheritance: Rural Society in Western Europe, 1200–1800* (Cambridge, 1976), 307.
9. J. Austen, *Pride and Prejudice* (1813), ed. D. J. Gray (New York, 1966), 42.
10. R. Trumbach, *The Rise of the Egalitarian Family: Aristocratic Kinship and Domestic Relations in Eighteenth-Century England* (New York, 1978), 77.
11. C. G. A. Clay, 'Marriage, Inheritance and the Rise of Large Estates in England, 1660–1815', *Economic History Review*, 2nd ser. 21 (1968), 511.
12. J. Davies, *Cardiff and the Marquesses of Bute* (Cardiff, 1981), I, 4–10.
13. R. Brenner, 'Agrarian Class Structure and Economic Development in Pre-Industrial Europe', *Past and Present*, 70 (1976).
14. M. Spufford, *Contrasting Communities: English Villagers in the Sixteenth and Seventeenth Centuries* (Cambridge, 1974), 73, 149.
15. C. G. A. Clay, 'Landlords and Estate Management in England', in J. Thirsk (ed.), *The Agrarian History of England and Wales, v: 1640–1750, ii: Agrarian Change* (Cambridge, 1985), 182.

16. H. J. Habakkuk, 'The English Land Market in the Eighteenth Century', in J. S. Bromley and E. H. Kossman (eds.), *Britain and the Netherlands* (1960), 171.

17. L. and J. F. Stone, *An Open Elite? England, 1540–1880* (Oxford, 1984), 179.

18. H. Perkin, 'An Open Elite', *Journal of British Studies*, 24 (1985), 498.

19. Quoted in T. M. Devine, 'Social Responses to Agrarian "Improvement": The Highland and Lowland Clearances in Scotland', in R. A. Houston and I. D. Whyte (eds.), *Scottish Society, 1500–1800* (Cambridge, 1989), 154.

20. *Culloden Papers . . . from the Originals in the Possession of D. G. Forbes* (1815), 298.

21. T. C. Smout, *A History of the Scottish People, 1560–1830* (1969), 284.

FURTHER READING

Allen, R. C., 'The Price of Freehold Land and the Interest Rate in the Seventeenth and Eighteenth Centuries', *Economic History Review*, 2nd ser. 41 (1988).

Beckett, J. V., 'The Pattern of Landownership in England and Wales, 1660–1880', *Economic History Review*, 2nd ser. 37 (1984).

—— 'The Decline of the Small Landowner in Eighteenth and Nineteenth-Century England: Some Regional Considerations', *Agricultural History Review*, 30 (1982).

—— 'The Peasant in England: A Case of Terminological Confusion?', *Agricultural History Review*, 32 (1984).

—— 'English Landownership in the Later Seventeenth and Eighteenth Centuries: The Debate and the Problems', *Economic History Review*, 2nd ser. 30 (1977).

Bonfield, L., *Marriage Settlements, 1601–1740: The Adoption of Strict Settlement* (Cambridge, 1983).

—— 'Marriage Settlements and the "Rise of Great Estates": The Demographic Aspect', *Economic History Review*, 2nd ser. 32 (1979).

—— '"Affective Families", "Open Elites" and Family Settlements in Early Modern England', *Economic History Review*, 2nd ser. 39 (1986).

—— 'Marriage Settlements, 1660–1740: The Adoption of the Strict Settlement in Kent and Northamptonshire', in R. B. Outhwaite (ed.), *Marriage and Society: Studies in the Social History of Marriage* (1981).

Brenner, R., 'Agrarian Class Structure and Economic Development in Pre-industrial Europe', *Past and Present*, 70 (1976).

Carter, I., 'Social Differentiation in the Aberdeenshire Peasantry, 1696–1870', *Journal of Peasant Studies*, 5 (1977).

Chibnall, A. C., *Sherington: Fiefs and Fields of a Buckinghamshire Village* (Cambridge, 1965).

Clay, C. G. A., 'Lifeleasehold in the Western Counties of England, 1650–1750', *Agricultural History Review*, 29 (1981).

—— 'Marriage, Inheritance and the Rise of Large Estates in England, 1660–1815', *Economic History Review*, 2nd ser. 21 (1968).

—— 'Landlords and Estate Management in England', in J. Thirsk (ed.), *The Agrarian History of England and Wales, 1640–1750*, 2: *Agrarian Change* (Cambridge, 1985).

—— 'Property Settlements, Financial Provision for the Family and the Sale of Land by the Greater Landowners, 1660–1790', *Journal of British Studies*, 21 (1981–2).

—— 'The Price of Freehold Land in the Later Seventeenth and Eighteenth Centuries', *Economic History Review*, 2nd ser. 27 (1974).

—— ' "The Greed of the Whig Bishops?": Church Landlords and their Leases, 1660–1760', *Past and Present*, 70 (1976).

Cooper, J. P., 'The Social Distribution of Land and Men in England, 1663–1700', *Economic History Review*, 2nd ser. 20 (1967).

—— 'Patterns of Inheritance and Settlement by Great Landowners from the Fifteenth to the Eighteenth Centuries', in J. Goody *et al.* (eds.), *Family and Inheritance: Rural Society in Western Europe 1200–1800* (Cambridge, 1976).

Creegan, E. R., 'The Tacksmen and their Successors: A Study of Tenurial Reorganisation in Mull, Morven and Tiree in the Early Eighteenth Century', *Scottish Studies*, 13 (1969).

Croot, P., and Parker, D., 'Agrarian Class Structure and Economic Development', *Past and Present*, 78 (1978).

Devine, T. M., 'Social Responses to Agrarian "Improvement": The Highland and Lowland Clearances in Scotland', in R. A. Houston and I. D. Whyte (eds.), *Scottish Society, 1500–1800* (Cambridge, 1989).

Dodgshon, R. A., 'West Highland Chiefdoms, 1500–1745: A Study in Redistributive Exchange', in R. Mitchison and P. Roebuck (eds.), *Economy and Society in Scotland and Ireland* (Edinburgh, 1988).

—— ' "Pretense of Blude" and "Place of thair Duelling": The Nature of Highland Clans, 1600–1745', in R. A. Houston and I. D. Whyte (eds.), *Scottish Society, 1500–1800* (Cambridge, 1989).

—— 'The Economics of Sheep Farming in the Southern Uplands during the Age of Improvement, 1750–1833', *Economic History Review*, 2nd ser. 29 (1976).

—— 'Agricultural Change and its Social Consequences in the Southern Uplands of Scotland, 1600–1780', in T. M. Devine and D. Dickson (eds.), *Ireland and Scotland 1600–1850* (Edinburgh, 1983).

Erickson, A. L., 'Common Law versus Common Practice: The Case of Marriage Settlements in Early Modern England', *Economic History Review*, 2nd ser. 43 (1990).

Fisher, C., *Custom, Work and Market Capitalism: The Forest of Dean Colliers, 1788–1888* (1981).

Gray, M., *The Highland Economy, 1750–1850* (Edinburgh, 1957).

Gregson, N., 'Tawney Revisited: Custom and the Emergence of Capitalist Class Relations in North-East Cumbria, 1600–1830', *Economic History Review*, 2nd ser. 42 (1989).

Habakkuk, H. J., 'Marriage Settlements in the Eighteenth Century', *TRHS* 4th ser. 32 (1950).

—— 'English Landownership 1680–1740', *Economic History Review*, 10 (1939–40).

—— 'La Disparition du paysan anglais', *Annales*, 20 (1965).

—— 'The English Land Market in the Eighteenth Century', in J. S. Bromley and E. H. Kossman (eds.), *Britain and the Netherlands* (1960).

Holderness, B. A., 'The English Land Market in the Eighteenth Century: The Case of Lincolnshire', *Economic History Review*, 2nd ser. 27 (1974).

Hollingsworth, T. H., 'The Demography of the British Peerage', *Population Studies*, supplement to 18 (1966).

Hoyle, R. W., 'Tenure and the Land Market in Early Modern England: Or a Late Contribution to the Brenner Debate', *Economic History Review*, 2nd ser. 43 (1990).

Hunter, J., *The Making of the Crofting Community* (Edinburgh, 1976).

Jenkins, J. P., 'The Demographic Decline of the Landed Gentry in the Eighteenth Century: A South Wales Study', *Welsh History Review*, 11 (1982).

——*The Making of a Ruling Class: The Glamorgan Gentry, 1640–1790* (Cambridge, 1983).

Martin, J., 'Private Enterprise versus Manorial Rights: Manorial Property Disputes in Mid-Eighteenth Century Glamorgan', *Welsh History Review*, 9 (1978).

Mingay, G. E., *English Landed Society in the Eighteenth Century* (1963).

Offer, A., 'Farm Tenure and Land Values in England, c.1750–1950', *Economic History Review*, 2nd ser. 44 (1991).

Outhwaite, R. B., 'Marriage as Business: Opinions on the Rise in Aristocratic Bridal Portions in Early Modern England', in N. McKendrick and R. B. Outhwaite (eds.), *Business Life and Public Policy* (Cambridge, 1986).

Parker, R. A. C., *Coke of Norfolk: A Financial and Agricultural Study, 1707–1842* (Oxford, 1975).

Perkin, H., 'An Open Elite', *Journal of British Studies*, 24 (1985).

Richards, E., *A History of the Highland Clearances*, i: *Agrarian Transformation and the Evictions* (1982); ii: *Emigration Protest, Reasons* (1985).

Searle, C. E., 'The Cumbrian Customary Economy in the Eighteenth Century', *Past and Present*, 110 (1986).

Simpson, A. W. B., 'Entails and Perpetuities', in *Legal Theory and Legal History: Essays on Common Law* (1987).

Skipp, V., *Crisis and Development: An Ecological Case Study of the Forest of Arden, 1540–1674* (Cambridge, 1978).

Smout, T. C., *A History of the Scottish People, 1560–1830* (1969).

Spring, D. and E., 'Social Mobility and the English Landed Elite', *Canadian Journal of History*, 21 (1986).

——'The English Landed Elite 1540–1880: A Review', *Albion*, 17 (1985).

Spring, E., 'The Family, Strict Settlement, and Historians', *Canadian Journal of History*, 18 (1983).

——'The Strict Settlement: Its Role in Family History', *Economic History Review*, 2nd ser. 41 (1988).

Spufford, M., *Contrasting Communities: English Villagers in the Sixteenth and Seventeenth Centuries* (Cambridge, 1974).

Stone, L. and J. F., *An Open Elite? England, 1540–1880* (Oxford, 1984).

Thirsk, J. (ed.), *The Agrarian History of England and Wales*, v: *1640–1750*, 1: *Regional Farming Systems* (Cambridge, 1984).

Thompson, F. M. L., 'The Social Distribution of Landed Property in England since the Sixteenth Century', *Economic History Review*, 2nd ser. 19 (1966).

—— *English Landed Society in the Nineteenth Century* (1963).

—— 'The End of a Great Estate', *Economic History Review*, 2nd ser. 8 (1955–6).

Timperley, L., 'The Pattern of Landholding in Eighteenth-Century Scotland', in M. L. Parry and T. R. Slater (eds.), *The Making of the Scottish Countryside* (1980).

Trumbach, R., *The Rise of the Egalitarian Family: Aristocratic Kinship and Domestic Relations in Eighteenth-Century England* (New York, 1978).

Whyte, I., *Agriculture and Society in Seventeenth-Century Scotland* (Edinburgh, 1979).

—— 'Written Leases and their Impact on Scottish Agriculture in the Seventeenth Century', *Agricultural History Review*, 27 (1979).

Wordie, J. R., 'Social Change on the Leveson-Gower Estates, 1714–1832', *Economic History Review*, 2nd ser. 27 (1974).

Youngson, A. J., *After the Forty-Five: The Economic Impact on the Scottish Highlands* (Edinburgh, 1973).

CHAPTER 4

Open Fields and Enclosure: The Demise of Commonality

> Enclosure came, and trampled on the grave
> Of labour's rights and left the poor a slave.
>
> (John Clare, *c.*1821–4)

The sentiments of John Clare, the Northamptonshire poet, were put more prosaically by a lace-dealer of that county. 'I lament that this field is now agoing to be enclosed', wrote David Hennell of Wollaston. 'Some that have large quantities of land are set upon it, and pay no regard to the many little ones that may be injured, and I fear many ruined.'[1] All change is likely to inspire laments, exaggerating destruction and ignoring benefits: were Clare and Hennell correct in seeing enclosure as socially disruptive, an attack upon the poor?

Much depended upon the way in which enclosure arose. Clare and Hennell saw it as a force coming from outside the village community, imposed by men of property and influence who dispossessed the poor of their rights. But was this how enclosure was experienced in all parts of the country? Perhaps in some areas enclosure emerged by agreement within the village community. The nature of open-field agriculture was highly diverse, with a variety of agrarian systems and social organization which had an important influence on how the process of enclosure was implemented, and the degree of social conflict it generated.

Even if enclosure was, to use E. P. Thompson's words, 'a plain enough case of class robbery',[2] there still remains the possibility that it contributed to an increase in agricultural output which allowed an escape from subsistence crises and falling real wages. Clare and Hennell were sceptical of such a comforting interpretation, preferring to believe that enclosure had only a limited impact on agricultural productivity, and that its major role was in permitting landowners to raise rents and renegotiate leases. Rather than providing an escape route from the dire consequences which alarmed Malthus, dispossession could have stimulated population growth by weakening the 'prudential restraint' on marriage. A cottager had the incentive to save in order to acquire the stock for a smallholding; a landless waged labourer did not. Enclosure, suggests its critics, did not allow Britain to escape from the Malthusian trap; it entailed a shift in the distribution of agricultural income towards landowners which threatened the onset of Ricardo's 'stationary state'.

The impact of enclosure on output and the distribution of agricultural income might depend on how it was implemented, for enclosure could possibly contribute to raising yields when it was undertaken by the farming community by agreement, and redistribute income when it was imposed by landowners. Timing was also likely to have an influence, with enclosure in the seventeenth and early eighteenth centuries affecting rural society in a different way from enclosure in the later eighteenth century when output was lagging behind population growth. A central feature of Ricardo's analysis was the shift of cultivation to marginal land, which raises a further consideration: how far did enclosure entail a reorganization of cultivated land, and how far an extension on to the waste?

Open Field and Runrig

An open-field parish is usually imagined as a nucleated village of houses and barns clustered around the village church and green. The village was in the midst of two or three large, unfenced open fields which grew different crops or lay fallow according to a rotation. The fields were divided into strips, with the holdings of individual peasants or tenants scattered rather than consolidated into blocks. The cultivation of the fields was agreed communally, for it was necessary to decide what crops were grown, when to leave the field fallow, and when to sow, plough, and reap. The heart of the system was the grazing of animals on the stubble after the harvest and on the fallow, with communal controls on their numbers to prevent over-grazing, and on their date of entry after the harvest and removal before ploughing. Beyond the open fields, there was an area of common waste where stock could graze (see Fig. 4.1). Families without land had rights to glean on the open fields after the harvest, to turn a few animals on to the common waste, and to forage for wood. Such a system of open-field agriculture was highly organized and communal, regulated by a manorial court or an assembly of the villagers which determined the farming schedule and controlled access to the 'contingent property rights' of gleaning, grazing, and foraging. There was, argues Edward Thompson, a 'delicate agrarian equilibrium' based on a hierarchy of use-rights and 'the inherited grid of customs and controls within which the right was exercised':

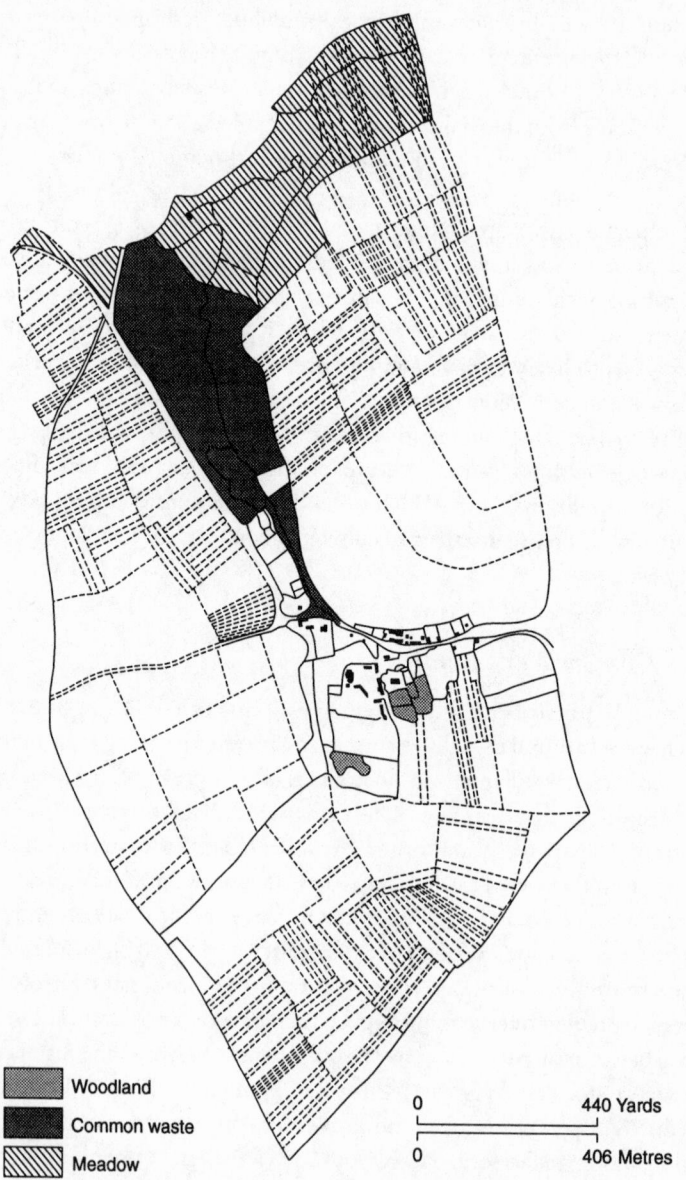

FIG. 4.1. Three-field common field-system of Cuxham, Oxfordshire, 1767

Note: Note the reorganization of strips in some areas of the common fields.

Source: J. L. G. Mowat, *Sixteen Old Maps of Properties in Oxfordshire* (1888), from D. Roden, 'Field Systems of the Chiltern Hills and their Environs', in A. R. H. Baker and R. A. Butlin (eds.), *Studies of Field Systems in the British Isles* (Cambridge, 1973), 346.

The farmer confronted with a dozen scattered strips in different hands, and with prescribed stints in the commons, did not (one supposes) feel fiercely that he *owned* the land, that it was *his*. What he inherited was a place within the hierarchy of use-rights; the right to send his beasts, with a follower, down the lane-sides, to tether his horse in the sykes or on the baulks, the right to unloose his stock for lammas grazing, or for the cottager the right to glean and to get away with some timber-foraging and casual grazing. ... Indeed one could say that the beneficiary inherited both his right *and* the grid within which it was effectual: hence he must inherit a certain kind of social or communal psychology of ownership: the property not of his family but of his family-within-the-commune.[3]

This ideal (and possibly romanticized) open-field agriculture was not universal in medieval England and Wales; it was characteristic of the centre of the country, in an area stretching from part of Yorkshire through the Midlands. What is being described is more accurately *common*-field agriculture, for a field could be open—that is, subdivided into strips—without being subject to common rights and communal management. The fully developed common-field system made most sense in areas with a large population, which compelled the intensive cultivation of land. The expansion of arable cultivation at the expense of rough pasture led to a shortage of land for grazing, so that the arable fields had to serve for this purpose after the harvest. Such pressure did not exist in all areas of the country, and the full-fledged common-field system with strict controls of common grazing on the arable was less apparent on the Pennines, wolds and downs, fens and woodland with their abundant grazing.

The number of open fields varied, because of the nature of the soil. Land was more heavily cropped in the three-field system, which left a third of the land fallow each year; a field would grow four crops in six years and be grazed and manured in two years. In the two-field system, half the land was fallow each year; a field grew three crops in six years, and the land was manured for three years. Consequently, the two-field system in the Middle Ages concentrated on less-fertile soil than the three-field system. The field system could, however, be much more complex than two or three large fields. In Kent, for example, the arable land was divided into rectangular areas called 'tenementa' or 'iuga'; the absence of a large, compact fallow field reduced the need for control of communal grazing, and permitted a gradual consolidation and enclosure of scattered plots from the late Middle Ages. In East Anglia, there were large open fields but the fallow was not common pasture for the entire body of landholders; instead, portions of the fallow or 'fold courses' were assigned to particular landholders (see Fig. 4.2). Such regional variations had major consequences for the ease with which land could be enclosed. The absence of a fully developed common-field system meant that there were fewer interests to be offended, and enclosure could be relatively

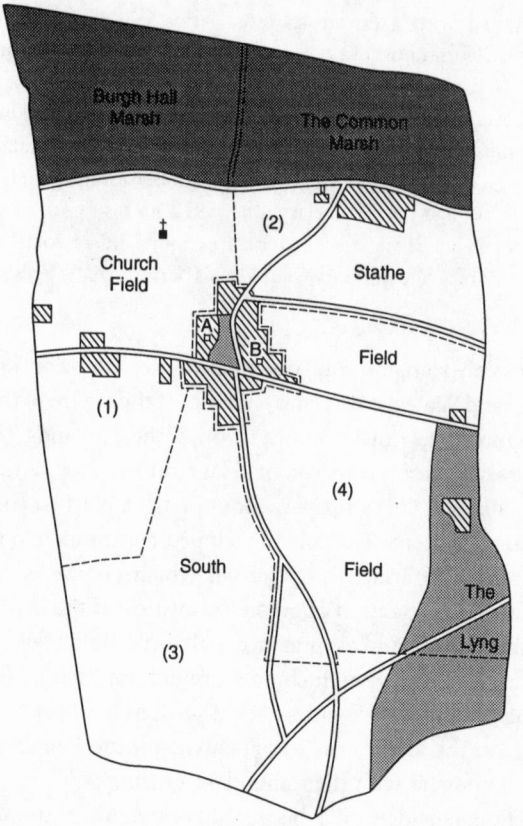

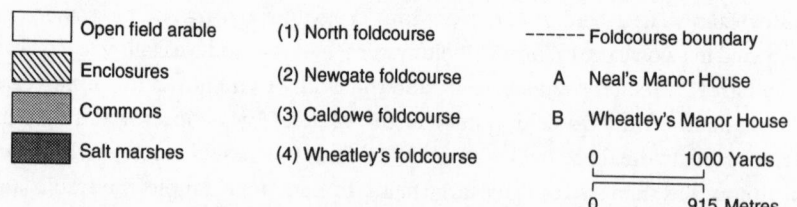

FIG. 4.2. Open fields of Holkham, Norfolk, 1590

Source: Holkham MS, map 1, from M. R. Postgate, 'Field Systems of East Anglia', in Baker and Butlin (eds.), *Studies*, 316.

peaceful; by contrast, enclosure in the Midlands was delayed by communal controls of the common fields and the hierarchy of contingent property rights.

The operation of the open fields did not remain unchanged until their demise in enclosure, for greater flexibility could be negotiated within the constraints of communal regulations, even in the heartland of the common-field system. The organization of common-field agriculture was usually decided by the farming community in the manorial court or vestry meeting, and by-laws were agreed to ensure that the existing system operated smoothly. Although this could result in rigidity and conservatism, husbandry agreements could introduce substantial changes in farming practices and field layout. In many cases, the two-field system was converted to four fields by the early eighteenth century, and more complicated rotations were developed for 'furlongs' within the fields, such as at Shenington in 1732, where the arable was divided into twelve sections; and management could be ceded to groups of individuals for part of a field.[4] Common-field agriculture was adapted to allow the replacement of fallow by temporary grass, which supported more livestock, so producing more manure and raising or at least maintaining fertility despite the greater intensity of cropping. In Oxfordshire, for example, agreements were made to sow strips in part of the field with clover or sainfoin, or to place 5 acres under grass for every yardland in the cornfield. The common-field system had a degree of flexibility and responsiveness to changing market conditions, and it was even claimed by Thomas Davies in 1811 that common fields raised the general standard of farming by allowing progressive farmers to impose their views upon others. Perhaps he was exaggerating; but it is clear that the open fields of England were neither uniform nor static.

Holdings were usually scattered across the open fields in strips rather than consolidated into a block. Scattering, it is suggested by some recent economic historians, was a rational response, spreading the farmer's risk by giving him a share of different soils and aspects, in the same way that an investor holds a diversified portfolio to spread risks. An alternative explanation is based on an analysis of property rights.[5] Open fields combined private ownership of the arable with communal grazing, which could only operate if each farmer was willing to abide by rules governing access of animals to his land; and the lack of hedges meant that animals had to be managed in large herds to prevent their straying on to the crops. Scattering of strips, it is argued, prevented an individual farmer withdrawing from the communal grazing system which required the herd and open field to be treated as a unit. These explanations of scattering rely upon theoretical and *post hoc* deductions, assuming that the consequences of scattering are also the causes. Scattering could, in fact, have arisen with scant regard for economic rationality. It could have been produced by colonization or 'assarting' of waste under the influence of population pressure, with those who took part sharing the new land out among themselves so that holdings were divided between land taken into cultivation at successive stages. Equally, blocks of land were broken up by partible inheritance, or as a result of an active land market produced by population pressure. Of course, when scattering had emerged it might well be sustained because the benefits of spreading risks were realized, or because the pattern of property rights prevented rationalization.

Scotland had a distinctive system of open-field agriculture. The bulk of permanent pasture was held in 'commonty', communally regulated grazing land which was not subdivided between owners and could not be enclosed or converted to arable. Winter fodder for the animals was provided by meadows which supplied hay, and grain was grown on arable land which was divided into an open infield and outfield. The infield was the best land, closest to the farm, which received manure from the stableyard; it was mainly used to grow oats and barley, with wheat and flax in some areas. The outfield was manured by folding livestock on it for part of the summer; it was sown with oats for several years until yields fell, at which point it was left fallow (see Fig. 4.3). Whether holdings were scattered and cultivation was regulated depended upon the tenancy of the farm. There was no need to scatter holdings in joint-tenant farms, for the land was worked communally as a single unit, with the rent and crop shared between the tenants. In multiple tenancies, each tenant managed his own share of the farm. It was consequently necessary to define the holding of each tenant by 'runrig', which converted the share of the farm specified in the lease (say, John Riddell's twelfth of Whelmes farm in 1708) into specific strips scattered in the fields. Although multiple tenants had more freedom than joint tenants, they still had to co-operate in deciding when to sow, reap, and plough; in regulating the grazing of animals on the stubble; and sharing equipment and labour. Regulation was a matter of farming custom overseen by the Baron Court which covered the estate of the laird. The lord or his agent presided, often assisted by a panel of 'birlaymen' who advised on agricultural matters, such as the number of animals to be kept and their herding. They tended to maintain traditional practices, and in the eighteenth century were replaced by factors directly employed by the laird, who gave directions to the tenants on farming practices, and acted as a solvent to tradition. Of course, single-tenant farms had no need for runrig or communal regulation of the farming year, and consolidation of holdings and the removal of runrig were easily achieved by replacing multiple tenancy of a farm by a single tenancy. It was not necessary to reallocate the land of each tenant in order to produce consolidated holdings as in English common fields; rather, the number of tenants was reduced and the size of each holding increased by a simple decision of the landlord at the renewal of the lease. More problems would arise where land belonging to different *owners* was intermingled, which was more likely on feuar settlements on church lands, where holdings were smaller. The removal of 'proprietary runrig' posed greater difficulties than a simple reduction in the number of tenants, for the strips of all owners in a parish had to be

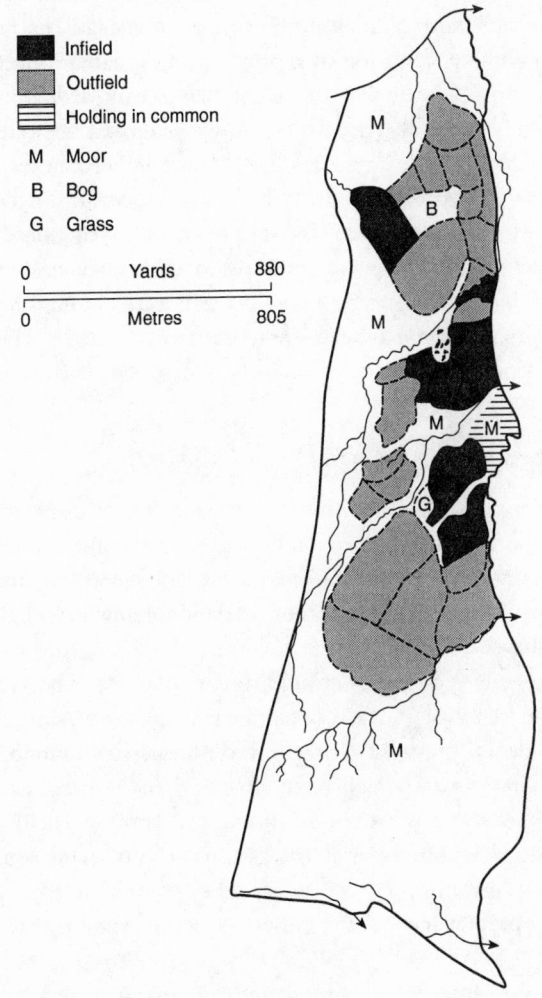

FIG. 4.3. Infield–outfield at Westertown, 1753

Source: Survey in Scottish Record Office, RHP 3485, reproduced in G. Whittington, 'Field Systems of Scotland', in Baker and Butlin (eds.), *Studies*, 555.

reallocated into consolidated holdings, and it might be difficult to obtain general agreement.

Open-field agriculture was neither uniform nor static, and its varieties shaped the process of enclosure. The task of transforming open fields to consolidated, enclosed holdings was more difficult in the common fields of central England, where reliance on arable fields for common grazing created a need for tight communal regulations; Clare and Hennell's complaints came from this heartland of the common-field system. By contrast, in looser systems of open-field farming with grazing on adjacent hills or moors, there were fewer constraints on the gradual emergence of consolidated holdings and enclosure by agreement amongst farmers. In Scotland, the removal of tenant runrig was a relatively simple matter of converting farms from multiple to single tenancies; only in cases of proprietary runrig would there be a need to reallocate holdings into consolidated blocks. This matrix shaped the extent to which enclosure had transformed the landscape by 1700.

The Chronology and Geography of Enclosure

Enclosure in England and Scotland involved three distinct actions, which could be undertaken at the same time or separately. One was to consolidate properties, bringing together scattered strips in the open fields. The second was the abolition of coincidental use-rights and the substitution of landholding 'in severalty', that is individual or unshared tenure. The third element was enclosure in a physical sense, by creating hedges or fences around the holding and subdividing it into individual fields. In many ways, the most significant change was the second, the removal of coincidental use-rights and common husbandry practices of open-field agriculture; Clare and Hennell were attacking this element of enclosure. Tensions were likely to be most severe in areas of common-field cultivation where access to grazing on the arable was crucial, but there could also be problems in enclosing common wastes where they were an integral part of the farming system, or used by families for gathering fuel and running a few sheep or cattle.

Enclosure was implemented in three ways in England, which had different social implications. One was piecemeal enclosure: proprietors gradually withdrew from open or common-field husbandry with the two systems coexisting for a considerable period, such as at Tibberton in Worcestershire where 56 per cent of the land was in common fields and 44 per cent enclosed in 1776, and enclosure was not completed until 1813 (see Fig. 4.4 for an example in Leicestershire).[6] Piecemeal enclosure was most difficult in nucleated villages with a fully developed common-field system. It was most likely where irregular field systems

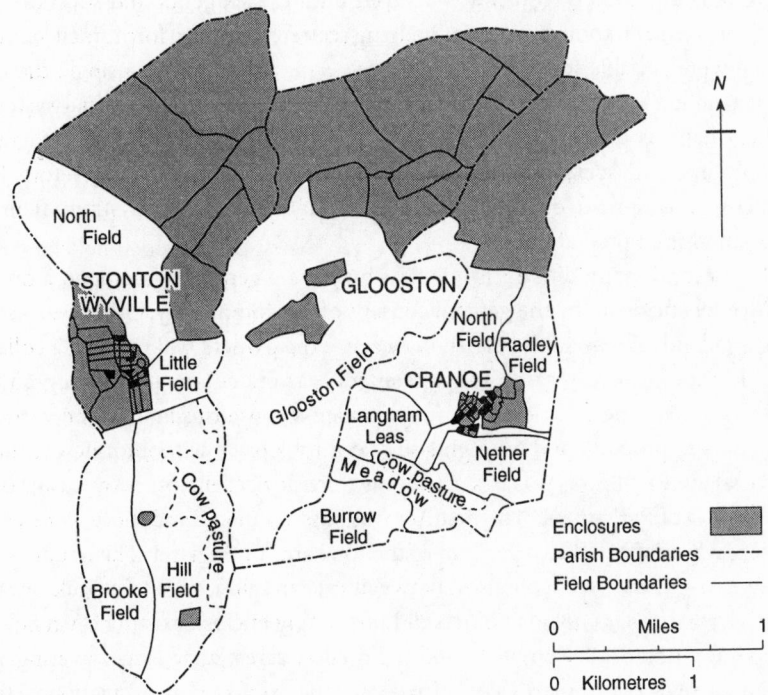

FIG. 4.4. Partial enclosure at Stonton Wyville, Glooston, and Cranoe, Leicestershire, *c*.1635

Source: J. A. Yelling, *Common Field and Enclosure in England, 1450–1850* (1977), 48.

and dispersed settlement removed the necessity for agreement by the entire farming community, particularly in pastoral districts which required fewer communal controls than arable farming with its complex rotation systems and scattered strips. In Devon, for example, abundant moorland reduced pressure on pasture, the field system was flexible, and communal controls of agriculture did not develop; cultivated land was almost fully enclosed by 1700. The process took somewhat different forms in the south and the east of the county. In the south, piecemeal enclosure resulted in compact fields and larger holdings. The population was declining, there was little industry, and the land was not suitable for pastoralism. Consequently, the demand for land was weak and the dwindling community of arable farmers consolidated and enclosed holdings, a process which was virtually complete by the mid-fifteenth century. In the east of the county, holdings were fragmented and fields smaller. Textile production and conversion from mixed farming to pastoralism created a buoyant demand for land and led to population growth. Consequently, consolidation of holdings was more difficult, and enclosure was delayed until the sixteenth and seventeenth centuries, when it took the form of hedging scattered strips to form small 'closes' which were suitable for pastoralism. These were variations on a single theme: piecemeal enclosure permitted slow change within the existing social system, rather than disruption. Piecemeal enclosure could take place without great disruption to the social structure and without destroying small proprietors, for the cost was spread over a longer period and imposed less strain than a once-and-for-all procedure.

The second method of enclosure was by private general agreement, a once-and-for-all enclosure by the general consent of the community, either because a single individual owned the parish or because the owners had reached a collective decision. In many cases, the agreement was the culmination of a gradual process of piecemeal enclosure, and it entailed a consensus among the various claimants to property and use-rights so that it took place without much dispute or social upheaval. This was less true of the third device: enclosure by means of a private Act of Parliament. The first Act was passed in 1604, and there were 5,265 by 1914 which affected 20.9 per cent of the total area of England. The majority of these Acts—3,828—were obtained between 1750 and 1819, with two peaks in the 1760s–1770s and 1793–1815. The Acts did not simply enclose existing open fields, which accounted for 3,093 Acts and 4.5 million acres; 2,172 Acts covering 2.3 million acres were primarily concerned with the extension of cultivation to the waste.[7] These private Acts could simply validate enclosure by agreement, and did not necessarily mark a fundamental shift in agrarian society. Until the early eighteenth century, most Acts were found in parishes where one or a few landlords had acquired most of the property, so that enclosure was a response to the emergence of concentrated ownership rather than the cause of the demise of the yeomanry. However, private Acts could also be used to force dissentients into line, by imposing the wishes of the owners of the majority of the land. Again, a private Act did not necessarily entail a major disruption in rural society for the initiative up to the 1780s and 1790s often came from yeomen freeholders who wished to improve their farms, marking the next stage in the process of adapting farming practices within the common fields. The improvers used compulsion against the laggards, but this did not necessarily entail a major disruption of the local social structure, and usually common land was set aside for members of the community who lost use-rights. Serious social conflict and disruption was more likely in the late eighteenth and early nineteenth centuries, when parliamentary enclosure was associated with rising rents and a shift of power to large land-owners. Private Acts were concentrated in densely populated villages where there was opposition from a large body of small owners and cottagers who felt, with good reason, that they would lose out. Enclosure in the late eighteenth and early nineteenth centuries was concentrated in parishes where it was not possible to secure consensus to abandon communal controls: areas with a nuclear pattern of settlement, scattered holdings, dominance by arable agriculture, highly organized communal rotation, and control of grazing on the open fields, predominantly in the east and south Midlands. The impact of enclosure by private Act consequently varied widely, affecting a mere 0.8 per cent of the total acreage of Kent and only 2.5 per cent of Devon, compared with 54.3 per cent of Oxfordshire and 53.0 per cent of Northamptonshire (see Fig. 4.5).[8]

Parliamentary enclosure, it has been suggested by Edward Thompson, marked the culmination of the imposition of 'the universal currency of capitalist definitions of ownership. Property must be made palpable, loosed for the market from its uses and from its social situation, made capable of being hedged and fenced, of being owned quite independently of any grid of custom or of mutuality.'[9] The nature of property was redefined, he argues, with the displacement of custom and communal rights by contract and individual ownership. The hierarchy or 'grid' of property rights was overturned: rights which did not amount to 'ownership' were not compensated and were captured by landowners who increased their cash income. The claim must be kept in

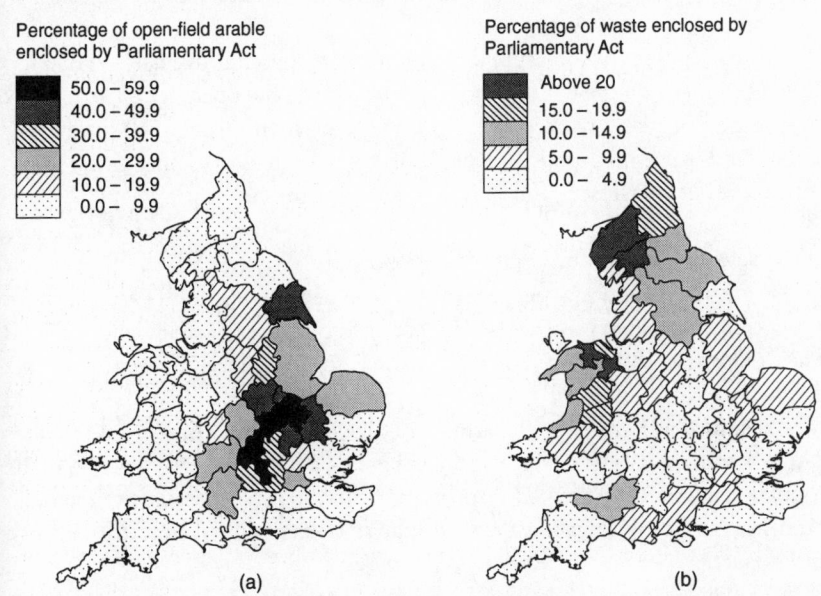

FIG. 4.5. Parliamentary enclosure, England and Wales, *c.*1730–*c.*1850. (*a*) Open-field arable; (*b*) waste

Sources: M. Overton, 'Agriculture', in J. Langton and R. J. Morris (eds.), *Atlas of Industrialising Britain, 1780–1914* (1986), 45, using English data of M. E. Turner, *English Parliamentary Enclosure*, Folkestone (1980); Welsh data supplied by Dr. J. Chapman.

perspective, for the complaints of men such as Clare and Hennell refer to the common fields of the Midlands in the final phase of parliamentary enclosure, rather than to the process in its entirety. The contrast between the older 'moral economy' of the common fields and the new 'political economy' of enclosure is overdrawn, for farmers had a sense of individual property within the village community. The open fields of England and runrig in Scotland were not survivals of communal *ownership* of land by the parish which was destroyed at enclosure. Land was held by separate title and, as Maitland commented, the open fields were 'not incompatible with a very perfect individualism, a very complete denial that the village has any proprietary rights whatever'.[10] The trend in land law and parliamentary enclosure was not a dramatic shift from communal to individual ownership so much as the emergence of a more precise definition of what constituted an individual's property. Individual property rights and market relations were firmly entrenched; what was at stake was a tussle over which claims would be recognized and how the market should be structured. Parliamentary enclosure excluded contingent use-rights from the equation, unlike enclosure by agreement, which often set aside common land for cottagers as compensation for their loss of grazing rights. It was not a defeat of custom by the market, and of moral economy by political economy, so much as a redefinition of the market and property rights.

Only parliamentary enclosure left reasonably comprehensive data, so that it is difficult to measure the entire process of enclosure. The open fields had already disappeared in many parts of England by 1600, when virtually all productive arable land in Kent, Cornwall, Devon, Essex, Cheshire, Monmouthshire, and Lancashire was enclosed, and about 75 per cent in Shropshire, 59 per cent in Herefordshire, and 48 per cent in Sussex. There was a further spate of enclosure in the seventeenth century, with the proportion of enclosed land in Leicestershire rising from about 17.5 per cent in 1600 to 51 per cent in 1700.[11] Overall, about 47 per cent of England was enclosed in 1600 and about 71 per cent in 1700. England was predominantly enclosed in 1700, at least so far as existing areas of arable cultivation were concerned; large areas of open moorland in the enclosed counties, such as Exmoor and Dartmoor in Devon, were incorporated at a later date. Parliamentary enclosure was the tail end of a long process of change in the countryside, and has received disproportionate attention because it generated extensive records which allow detailed analysis of its timing, scale, location, cost, and impact.

In Scotland, the consolidation of tenants' holdings into blocks was a relatively simple matter of replacing multiple tenancies by single tenancies at the discretion of the landowner. The removal of 'proprietary runrig' was more difficult, and the Scottish parliament in 1695 gave sweeping powers to reformers: the Act 'anent lands lying runrig' allowed one or more owners to enforce change by requesting the local court to divide the land. The creation of single tenancies and consolidated holdings did not imply an end to the use of an open infield and outfield, with grazing on the 'commonty'. This led to problems, for the major constraint on Scottish agriculture was the supply of winter fodder for animals. This bottle-neck could only be eased by converting the best commonty to arable, which entailed overturning communal regulations of grazing, ending the ban on conversion, and subdividing the land. Change had always been possible where all owners were in agreement, and an Act of 1647 allowed conversion in the Lothians, Lanarkshire, and Ayrshire where the *majority* of owners agreed. In 1695, a commonty Act for the entire country permitted a single owner to force change by requesting the courts to appoint an officer who would divide the commonty and add it to existing farms or create new farms. The commonty and runrig Acts of 1695 created a national framework which was simpler and less open to challenge than in England, where a separate private Act was necessary for each division. In Scotland, an 'improving' landowner had general powers to enforce change without the cost of obtaining an Act or facing counter-petitions, and with less scope for opposition. The problem for the historian is that Scotland's general permissive legislation makes it difficult to measure the pace of implementation.

The Acts of 1695 did not require the physical enclosure of land when holdings were consolidated or taken from the commonty. The government had attempted to encourage enclosure in 1661 and again in 1685 when owners of land worth £1,000 or more a year were obliged to enclose at least 4 acres a year for ten years and to plant it with a border of trees, in return for tax exemptions. Most enclosure in the seventeenth century was around country houses, with the remodelling of the 'policy' or park and 'mains' or home farm on the lines of English country houses. The motivation was in part cultural, a change from fortified mansions and armed retainers to refinement and 'politeness'; and in part functional, for belts of trees provided shelter and timber, and enclosed grassland was used to fatten animals paid in rent. The next stage of enclosing the farms of tenants did not develop until later in the eighteenth century, starting in the Lothians from about 1760. In England, the physical enclosure of land took place over a long period; in Scotland, it was concentrated in a later and shorter period. Enclosure simply did not matter greatly in the Scottish system of farming, for farms were large and dispersed, and the need to control livestock was less of a problem. Scottish landowners could create large, single-tenant farms with economies of scale, and abolish tenant runrig, without the necessity of a complicated redivision of land and the need to enclose separate holdings. In England, enclosure was an essential part of reallocation and consolidation; in Scotland, it was not. Parliamentary enclosure could, in any case, be a device by which

English landowners broke existing leases and increased their share of agricultural income, rather than a means of improving productivity. In Scotland, landowners were not fettered by copyhold and customary tenure or long leases and were able to set market rents. But this is to jump ahead: was parliamentary enclosure a device to increase landlords' appropriation rather than efficiency?

Parliamentary Enclosure and English Rural Society

The literature on enclosure has concentrated on parliamentary enclosure of open fields, especially in the late eighteenth and early nineteenth centuries, rather than piecemeal enclosure, enclosure by agreement, or parliamentary enclosure of the waste. The emphasis has therefore been upon the type and period of enclosure which was most likely to cause social tension. Parliamentary enclosure was less sensitive to 'labour rights', and Lord Chancellor Thurlow complained in 1781 of the 'mode in which private bills were permitted to make their way through both Houses . . . in matters in which property was concerned, to the great injury of many, if not to the total ruin of some private families'.[12] Some historians have nevertheless denied that parliamentary enclosure was 'class robbery', pointing out that it was remarkably free from overt strife, contending that it was a sign of progress and efficiency, and that the procedure was fair and reasonable. An alternative—and more plausible—interpretation is that parliamentary enclosure was so biased that opposition through the formal channels was usually pointless.

The first stage was to draft a bill, which was signed by the owners of land who supported the measure. The informal rule, which was often ignored, was that around 75 to 80 per cent of the *land* had to consent. 'Suffrages were not counted but weighed',[13] and small owners, who formed a large part of the *population*, could be overruled. In many parishes, opponents accounted for a majority of owners and a small proportion of land, and the easy passage of the Act masked deep division within the village. The enclosure bill for Wigston Magna in Leicestershire, for example, sped from its first reading to royal assent in two months in 1764, despite the opposition of three-quarters of owners who held 16 per cent of the land.[14] Where small owners held about a quarter of the land, they had some chance of forcing the withdrawal of bills, such as in Northamptonshire where 22 per cent were withdrawn between 1750 and 1815 as a result of opposition from owners of more than a third of the acreage in the parish, mainly smallholders of up to 20 acres who were frequently small traders and domestic industrial workers alarmed at the cost of enclosure and the loss of contingent rights. Where the opponents held a smaller proportion of land, their only legal means of opposition was to present a counter-petition to the Commons, an expensive course which was unlikely to succeed: in Northamptonshire, for example, counter-petitions were presented against only 11 per cent of enclosure bills between 1750 and 1815, and only five succeeded.[15]

The procedures for obtaining an enclosure bill were usually followed with scrupulous care, and some historians believe that they have disproved the case of the critics by showing that there was little sign of collusion between landowners and friendly MPs. But the issue is a deeper one than the observance of administrative and legal niceties. Parliament is not the place to find opposition, and silence should not be taken to mean consent. What was at stake was less the 'fairness' of parliamentary procedures than the fact that the bills embodied a different conception of property from the contingent use-rights which were at the heart of the case of the opponents. The relative weakness of opposition through parliamentary procedure does not necessarily mean that dissenters were supine, for opposition was expressed through different channels: the collection of information met delay, obstruction, and non-compliance; the landed gentry were petitioned (or threatened); and in some cases there was direct action such as at West Haddon in Northamptonshire in 1765, where a football match spilled over into a two-day riot and the destruction of fencing worth £1,500. The opponents were not inarticulate peasants trapped in the small world of the village who were incapable of expressing their grievances. Many small owners and cottagers were traders and artisans in rural industry, firmly embedded in a capitalist world, who saw little point in appealing to parliamentary procedures which failed to recognize their claims. Small landowners were at least consulted about enclosure, and their claims were recognized by the award of land. The claims of many other members of the village within the grid of use-rights were not recognized by the process of parliamentary enclosure, and they had no voice within official procedures which dealt only with the *ownership* of land. Enclosure could spell disaster for landless families who supplemented their income by gathering fuel, grazing a few sheep or a cow, or feeding pigs or geese. Such supplementary income allowed many families to take part in trade and crafts serving the local community, such as carriers, shopkeepers, blacksmiths, and wheelwrights. Enclosure marked the demise of these small rural traders and craftsmen, leaving a more polarized society of landless labourers and farmers. Defenders of the process of parliamentary enclosure claim that a 'perfectly proper distinction'[16] was drawn between owners (who were compensated) and tenants (who were not) without appreciating that the distinction was 'perfectly proper' within capitalist property relations, and 'improper' according to a definition of property as coincidental use-rights. The fact that rules of the game were 'fair' misses the point that the game had been changed at half-time.

Although small owners received an allocation of land at enclosure, expenses might force them to sell. Enclosure entailed public costs: the legal and parliamentary expenses of obtaining the Act, which were highest where opposition was most persistent; the fees and expenses of commissioners who implemented the enclosure; and the construction of new roads, bridges, culverts, and drains which were needed because of the changed layout of land. Generally, the later was the enclosure, the greater were the difficulties. Public costs were high and rising, in Warwickshire growing from 11s. per acre in 1753–9 to 34.1s. in 1790–9 and 61.9s. in 1801–65.[17] Small owners were often charged at a higher rate per acre, and they were likely to experience more strain in meeting the public costs than larger owners, who were able to meet the demand out of current income, particularly when they could channel funds from other parts of their estate. The private costs of physically enclosing the land with hedges or fences were often as much again as the public costs. A boundary fence or hedge was usually required within two months, with the provision of internal fences or hedges around individual fields left to the discretion of the owner. These costs were heavier for small holdings, which required proportionately more external fences than large holdings, where owners could spread internal fencing costs over a longer period. Small owners clearly had good reason to be wary of parliamentary enclosure, and it was little consolation to them that commissioners were generally careful that there was 'no overt injustice to anyone who could establish a legal claim'.[18]

Whether parliamentary enclosure produced a more concentrated pattern of landownership and a decline of small freeholders depended upon the nature of the community and the period of enclosure. In many parishes, consolidation *preceded* and facilitated enclosure. Some optimistic historians have argued that the number of small owner-occupiers actually rose and that enclosure did not destroy small farmers.[19] Such an interpretation rests on a statistical illusion. A cottager with a claim to common rights might well not appear in lists of owners in land tax records before enclosure, and might enter the list after being granted a small allotment at enclosure. The result was not a genuine increase in the number of small occupiers so much as a transfer of coincidental use-rights into a smallholding which was often of less practical value, and imposed considerable costs which were a prelude to sale and decline into the mass of landless labourers. In any case, counting numbers of small owners provides only part of the story, for there was a considerable turnover of membership, such as in Buckinghamshire where 38.7 per cent of the original owners disappeared in parishes enclosed between 1780 and 1820.[20] The costs of enclosure clearly had serious disruptive effects upon even those members of the rural community whose rights were recognized, let alone the larger number who received no acknowledgement. The result was the destruction of the peasants of common-field villages who had access to land or to common right, which had provided the framework for their way of life. 'Land and common right came first. They were considered the most desirable, most satisfactory basis for a living. Agricultural labour or rural trade and manufacture enhanced or even enabled this economy to continue, but land itself came first.'[21] The importance of the land question in British politics, from the Chartists through radical Liberalism to Lloyd George, is not surprising.

The loss of common rights affected the relative contribution of men and women to the family budget. There was a broad distinction between male waged labour and the exploitation of use-rights by women and children who augmented the family income by caring for livestock, gathering wood for fuel, and gleaning after the harvest. These rights were valuable, for the net profit of a cow kept on the commons in the Midlands in 1797 was about £4. 6s. 8d., or half an adult man's wages; and a woman could probably glean 3 or 4 bushels, at a time when a bushel of wheat was equivalent to two weeks' wages for a labourer.[22] When enclosure was implemented by agreement, an area of common land was usually set aside for the cottagers, but in parliamentary enclosure they were less likely to be compensated. The relationship between male and female contributions to the household budget was destroyed by the loss of common rights, and the family became more dependent on the male wage. Capitalist cereal farmers wished to remove working-class independence, which threatened the supply of labour at critical stages of the farming calendar. The supply of harvest labour could be ensured by making families more dependent on the male wage-earner, so that he was more committed and more susceptible to discipline. Not only did women lose access to various use-rights, but gender roles were also redefined in the labour market. Women were less likely to work for wages in the fields, for increased dependence of families on male wage-earners made men fear that competition from women would reduce wage rates.

It was not a change to which villagers easily agreed, and they continued to defend the surviving vestiges of use-rights. Women persisted in entering the enclosed fields after harvest to glean grain, which was challenged by a ruling of the Court of Common Pleas in 1788 that there was no right to gleaning in common law, and that anyone who entered a field without permission was guilty of trespass. Although the High Court adopted an absolute conception of property based upon the principle of exclusive enjoyment, farmers had to rely upon local courts to implement the ruling. Unless there was a breach of the peace, trespass was a matter for civil courts and many magistrates and jurors were sympathetic to gleaners who acted collectively to defend rights. Indeed, two-thirds of gleaning cases in south-east Essex between 1785 and 1808 arose from *gleaners* bringing cases of assault against farmers. The legal system was not entirely on the side of the farmers, for the ruling of 1788 had simply stated there was no right in common law. Villages could still appeal to local customary law, claiming that gleaning existed 'time out of mind'. Usually, the best that farmer could expect was the enforcement of the medieval practice that gleaning coul start only when the crop was cleared from the fields. The law and the courts wer not mere agents of a capitalist transformation of property rights, redefinin, customary rights as trespass and theft, for tension between the different prin ciples of the common law, custom, and equity meant that the courts were resource for the village community rather than a simple device to impos capitalist property relations. The transformation of property rights was lon, drawn out and contentious.

Parliamentary enclosure, it was suggested by some commentators, provide labour for industry, by dispossessing families of rights and forcing them int waged labour. 'The hardy yeomanry', remarked J. Wedge in 1794, 'have bee driven for employment into Birmingham, Coventry, and other manufacturin, towns.'[23] Such a view was challenged in the 1950s by J. D. Chambers, who argue that the number of owner-occupiers increased between 1790 and 1830, and tha agricultural improvements after enclosure entailed a larger and more continuou demand for labour in cultivating fodder crops, maintaining stock, hedging, anc ditching. The emergence of a wage-dependent work-force, in Chambers's opinion, arose from the natural increase of the population rather than from institutional change or compulsion.[24] Chambers's interpretation is problem atical, for the increase in owner-occupiers is an illusion, and he confused a simple measure of numbers employed and the extent to which enclosure saved labour by reducing the amount used in relation to output. If a smaller proportion of a larger population was needed to provide food, the result was to release men and women into towns and industry. Since Chambers believed that enclosure led to gains in labour productivity, his own analysis implies there *was* a release of labour. It is, in any case, questionable where enclosure did create a more continuous demand for a larger work-force, for the payment of poor relief shifted from a relatively even seasonal distribution before enclosure to a greater degree of fluctuation after enclosure. The most plausible explanation is that the erosion of use-rights led to a shift from a quasi-independent family economy in which the poor could gather fuel or keep livestock, to a greater reliance on wage labour which followed the seasonal cycle of harvest labour. The result was a glut of underemployed labour in the country, which was supported by the payment of poor relief. Whether enclosure created a larger demand for labour is also doubtful. Enclosure in the Midlands often meant a switch of land from arable to pasture, which *reduced* the demand for labour, and it is not clear that employ ment rose even in arable farming. Much has been made of the additional labour of hedging and turnip cultivation, but a contemporary remarked in 1808 that hedges were cut only every twelve years; and cultivation of turnips entailed less abour than grain, for roots were often eaten by sheep in the field without the effort of harvesting, carting and threshing cereals. Detailed calculations of the cost of various farming practices from Board of Agriculture surveys in the south Midlands around 1810 suggest that the amount of labour in enclosed villages on light arable soils was 7.2 per cent less than in open villages, and only 1.1 per cent higher on heavy soils. After allowance is made for conversion to pasture, enclosure possibly reduced farm employment in the south Midlands by 12 per cent.[25]

Although the population of enclosed villages did rise, it was not because enclosure used more labour. Rather, modification of the family economy removed restraints on the natural increase of the rural population. The decline in opportunities for semi-independence reduced 'prudential constraints' against early marriages, for there was little incentive to serve an apprenticeship in a trade, or to save in order to acquire stock or build a cottage. The point was made by Arthur Young in 1801, who reported the sentiments expressed in alehouses in enclosed counties:

For whom are they to be sober? For whom are they to save? (Such are their questions.) For the parish? If I am diligent, shall I have leave to build a cottage? If I am sober, shall I have land for a cow? If I am frugal, shall I have half an acre of potatoes? You offer no motives; you have nothing but a parish officer and a workhouse!—Bring me another pot.[26]

Defenders of enclosure, who stress that population increase was the crucial factor in supplying labour for industry, neglect the possibility that population growth itself was the product of changes in social organization fostered by enclosure. In any case, the surplus labour created by population growth did not necessarily move to towns and industry, for rural and urban industry were located in different parts of the country from high-output agriculture, which led to stagnant pools of underemployed labour in the south of England until the end of the nineteenth century. It is, indeed, unlikely that population growth was necessary for industrialization: agriculture was able to release sufficient labour and the acceleration in population growth placed strains on resources which could threaten the process of growth.

Enclosure of the Wastes

Parliamentary enclosure was not confined to open-field villages, for there was a considerable extension of the margin of cultivation at the end of the eighteenth and in the early nineteenth centuries which entailed the enclosure of common waste. 'We have begun another campaign against the foreign enemies of the country,' remarked Sir John Sinclair, the President of the Board of Agriculture in

1803, '... Why should we not attempt a campaign also against our great domestic foe, I mean the hitherto unconquered sterility of so large a proportion of the surface of the kingdom? ... Let us not be satisfied with the liberation of Egypt or the subjugation of Malta, but let us subdue Finchley Common.'[27] A precise measure of enclosure of waste is difficult, for the enclosure Acts do not include land which was taken into cultivation by private agreement or encroachment; on the other hand, they include large areas which were only gradually taken into enclosed fields. What is clear is that high prices in the late eighteenth and early nineteenth centuries led to a considerable reduction in the area of common waste on the uplands of the north, the moors of the West Country, the fens of eastern England, the sand or gravel soils of East Anglia, Surrey, and Hampshire, the chalk downs of Wiltshire, and the wooded clays of Warwickshire.

Whether the war on the common waste led to social tension depended on how far it was an integral part of the agrarian system. In Devon, enclosure of Dartmoor and Exmoor was usually uncontentious, and did not require Acts. Farms around Dartmoor and Exmoor were separated from each other by moorland waste, and there was no pressure on grazing which made it necessary to 'stint' livestock; any farmer could take in a piece of the waste without harming his neighbours, adding a few fields to existing farms. In areas of cloth production around the moors, poor households took in small areas from the waste, and some landlords carved new farms from the moors. The outcome is clear from the estate of the Dean and Chapter of Exeter at Thorverton, which rose from 932 acres held by leasehold or copyhold tenure in 1661 to 1,257 acres in 1800, and 1,353 in 1813–14.[28] Even in areas where enclosure of the waste was undertaken by an Act of Parliament, there might be few financial strains upon the existing farming community. Rather than levying a rate as in open-field parishes, commissioners could sell a proportion of land at auction to cover public costs, and there was a greater degree of flexibility and discretion than in settled lowland areas where existing fields had to be converted at a stroke. In some cases, commissioners established a fixed timetable for the enclosure of land over a period of years; in other cases, they did not fix a precise area or timetable, and allowed the owner to graze stock on the unenclosed land until he built drystone walls around his own allotment.

Enclosure of the waste did cause tension when lowland farmers lost essential grazing land. In Wiltshire, for example, the downs provided crucial summer grazing for farms in the valleys, and the agrarian system was disrupted by enclosure. Enclosure could also impose financial costs which in some cases exceeded those of enclosure of the open fields. On the 'levels' of Somerset, enclosure was a preliminary to large-scale drainage schemes of waterlogged, peaty soils to prevent flooding; in 1798, public costs were about 6s. per acre. On the Mendips, the conversion of land from common grazing to arable entailed a much larger expenditure than did the simple construction of drystone walls on the moors of Yorkshire for summer grazing: the public costs on the Mendips were about 51s., with very substantial private costs such as the creation of Wigmore Farm at Chilton Mendip in 1807, which cost £9.09 per acre.[29] The social impact of enclosure of the waste therefore depended upon the precise agrarian structure, and it would be wrong to draw a simple contrast between disruptive enclosure of existing open fields and unproblematic enclosure of waste land. Of course, expenditure of large sums of money might well create problems in the future, if rents and food prices were to fall: the defeat of Napoleon left the country with a national debt, and the subjugation of Finchley Common equally created problems for farmers and landowners who spent money in the expectation of high prices. Both issues were to obsess governments after 1815.

Enclosure and Agricultural Productivity

When Arthur Young submitted *The General Report on Enclosures* to the Board of Agriculture in 1808, he was convinced of the benefits of enclosure for agricultural production and productivity:

there can be no doubt of the superior profit to the farmer by cultivating enclosures, rather than open-field arable. In one case he is in chains—he can make no variations according to soil, or circumstances, or times. He is bound down to the production of corn only. . . . Whatever may be the advantages of varying the crops, it cannot operate to his benefit—a mere horse in a team, he must jog on with the rest.[30]

Strips were 'promiscuously dispersed' in the fields, which increased the costs of cultivation: ploughs and carts had to make pointless journeys and more horses were needed. The rotation of the crops was fettered by custom, so that corn was grown where clover and sainfoin would be better. Stock was kept on open fields, deriving inadequate feed from the stubble or fallow. The common pastures were over-stocked and unimproved, so that animals were prey to the spread of disease and lacked shelter. Improvement of stock was well nigh impossible. 'Such is the uniform picture', wrote Young in a state of despair, 'and a more wretched or melancholy one is hardly within the compass of imagination.' It was, complained Young, 'a system of barbarism':

What a gross absurdity, to bind down in the fetters of custom ten intelligent men willing to adopt the improvements adapted to enclosures, because one stupid fellow is obstinate for the practice of his grandfather! To give ignorance the power to limit knowledge, to render stupidity the measure of talents, to chain down industry to the non-exertions of indolence, and fix an insuperable bar, a perpetual exclusion, to all that energy of improvement which has carried husbandry to perfection by means of enclosure! Yet it is all done by the common-field system.[31]

Enclosure was, in Young's opinion, the answer for all the ills of British agriculture:

By giving an exclusive property to the soil, the proprietor has his industry unfettered; he is allowed to expend his capital; he is permitted to apply his lands to whatever use will pay him best; he neither burdens his neighbour, nor is shackled by him: no barbarous customs prohibit his exertions: his talents, his energy, and his capital, are free to be employed for his own benefit; he thrives, and national prosperity follows in his train.[32]

Although small farmers might lose, everyone else benefited: the poor gained employment from the cultivation of the wastes and common; landlords doubled their rents; farmers trebled their profit; consumers in towns and industry had sufficient food; and the nation as a whole had a higher output. 'That it must be highly beneficial to enable every land proprietor to apply the soil to the purpose for which it is best adapted, can scarcely be doubted.'[33]

Of course, piecemeal enclosure and enclosure by agreement achieved many of these potential benefits by the early eighteenth century, so that the spate of parliamentary enclosure in the late eighteenth and early nineteenth centuries did not necessarily lead to an acceleration in the rate of growth of yields and output. On the contrary, the evidence suggests that the improvement of yields, output, and labour productivity was *slower* in the later eighteenth century. Neither did the chains of common-field agriculture bind so tightly as Young argued, for it was possible to rearrange the fields and to introduce new crops. Nor was there such a stark contrast as Young claimed between open and enclosed parishes in the creation of consolidated holdings, and the consequent saving on costs in comparison with scattered strips. There was a gradual process of consolidation in the open fields as farmers exchanged strips, and piecemeal enclosure often resulted in small, irregular fields and scattered holdings. Certainly, parliamentary enclosure resulted in a radical redivision of holdings, better access on new roads, and led to reduced carting costs for manure and crops. What is not clear is whether the costly investment in new roads led to either private profit or social savings. Young was certainly exaggerating the benefits of enclosure: the problem is deciding by how much, and establishing whether enclosure was a marginal or a major contributor to agricultural improvement.

It is one thing to argue that open fields allowed some flexibility; it is another to suggest that they were just as able to introduce new techniques as enclosed parishes. Young had a point, for the rate of adoption of new methods was somewhat faster in enclosed parishes. Crop returns made as a result of the Tithe Commutation Act of 1836 show a clear contrast in the light arable districts of the south Midlands between enclosed villages (where 3.4 per cent of arable land was fallow and 22.9 per cent under clover) and open villages (where even in the more progressive parishes which grew turnips, 11.2 per cent of arable land was fallow and only 14.3 per cent under clover).[34] Young's case that open fields delayed innovation has some validity. But whether these differences were crucial for the improvement of yields is a different matter. Young was confident that enclosure led to a considerable improvement in yields, and supported his argument by comparing adjoining parishes on identical soil in Cambridgeshire: in the open parish of Hardwicke, the yield of wheat was 16 bushels per acre; in the enclosed parish of Childersley, the yield was 24 bushels or 50 per cent higher. However, a more sophisticated statistical analysis of Young's own data reaches a different conclusion. In his tours around England in the late 1760s, Young collected data on 231 farms, of which 159 were enclosed, 27 open, and 45 partly open, drawn predominantly from mixed and arable farms in the Midlands, East Anglia, and the north-east. Yields were higher in enclosed villages, but the differential was by no means as great at Young implied: the yield of wheat was 22.6 bushels per acre in open and 24.5 in enclosed parishes, or an increase of 8.4 per cent.[35] A comparison between 52 open and 62 enclosed parishes in government returns for the harvest of 1801 produces a larger differential of 26.4 per cent.[36] These comparisons of different parishes at a single point in time are problematical, for there could have been a similar differential in yields before enclosure, and it is not at all obvious that enclosure had made the difference. A better test is a comparison of yields before and after enclosure within the same parishes or within natural districts with the same soil. In the south Midlands, yields in open and enclosed villages on the same soil types around 1800 were not markedly different: in the light arable district, the wheat yield in open parishes was 20.0 bushels per acre, which was *higher* than the yield of 19.7 bushels in enclosed parishes; in the heavy arable district, the yields were respectively 19.7 and 20.2 bushels, or an increase of 2.5 per cent.[37] The gains of enclosure were less than Young imagined, and even on the most generous estimate enclosure could only account for a small part of the doubling of yields between the Middle Ages and the nineteenth century.

What parliamentary enclosure did allow was an increase in rents. Young, in his *General Report* of 1808, argued that higher rents 'should alone be accepted as a sufficient proof of increased productivity, 'for what can be the inducement to the farmer to give double or treble his former rent unless with a view to the profit of his business? And how is he to increase his profit without increasing the value of his produce?'[38] Young, of course, was convinced that enclosures were efficient, and that rents reflected the benefits of changed layout and improved practices. There is, however, another possibility, that 'enclosure caused a massive redistribution of income from farmers to landowners',[39] and produced a decent rate of return for landlords who were able to renegotiate leases and increase

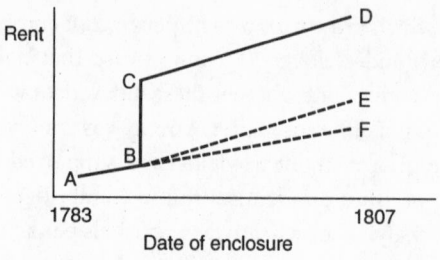

FIG. 4.6. Enclosure and rent levels

rents. Enclosure meant a sharp rise in rents (B to C), and the landlord's rate of return on the public costs may be calculated by taking the difference between rents after enclosure and the level of rents which would hypothetically have been charged in the absence of enclosure (see Fig. 4.6). This figure can be calculated on two different assumptions. The first assumption is that the level of rent would have risen at the same rate as in the past (B to F), which produces a higher return for enclosure; the second, more contentious, assumption is that the rate of increase would have been the same as for enclosed land (B to E) which produces a lower return. Data for Nottinghamshire suggest that landlords secured a good return even on the second, lower, estimate. The enclosure of Weston in 1796 produced an annual return of 26.1 per cent on the lower and 31.6 per cent on the higher estimate; the enclosure of Cotgrove in 1790 produced a return of 9.9 or 12.3 per cent.[40] Landlords did well, but the higher rents could be paid either from an increase in farmers' profits as a result of greater efficiency, or from a redistribution of income from the farmers to the landlords.

Young's data of the late 1760s can be used to test the competing hypotheses of efficiency or redistribution. The surplus of both open and enclosed farms may be calculated by taking the revenue of the farm, and deducting the costs of seed, implements, and labour, with an allowance for the time, board, and lodgings of the farmer and his family. The 'farmer's surplus' is obtained by making further deductions for rent, tithes, and taxes. If the 'farmer's surplus' was roughly the same before and after enclosure, rents were raised by increasing efficiency; on the other hand, a fall in the farmer's surplus after enclosure suggests that income was redistributed to the landlord. Young's data indicate that the farmer's surplus in open farms was £1.22 per acre, and that half the surplus went to the landlord as rent, the Church as tithes, and the state as taxes. Enclosure broke existing leases, allowed rents to be renegotiated, and introduced free competition into the market for leases; rents were doubled, and the landlord appropriated a larger part of the farmer's surplus, which fell to £0.24 per acre. Young's own data support the conclusion that 'the major economic consequence of the enclosure of open field arable in the eighteenth century was to redistribute the existing agricultural income, not to create additional income by raising efficiency'.[41] Ricardo would not have been surprised, and even Young, the arch-advocate of enclosure, hinted at the possibility of redistribution. 'If profit be measured by a percentage on the capital employed, the old system might, at the old rents, exceed the profits of the new; and this is certainly the farmers' view of the comparison.'[42] He nevertheless went on to argue that higher rents reflected efficiency; there was a discrepancy between his data and his ideology. He took high rents as a sign of progress, and emphasized the introduction of new crops such as clover and turnips as a result of the initiative of landlords, who merited their higher rents as the agents of modernization. In fact, parliamentary enclosure was a final step in a long process of change which produced a further small increment of improvement rather than a sudden, revolutionary change in farming and spectacular gains in output. Its most important outcome was to increase the share of income taken by the landed élite; it was part of the creation of a more hierarchical rural society of large landed estates and tenant farmers facing a mass of landless labourers. The rise of the great estates, enclosure, and clearances produced a major change in rural society, but were not crucial to the improvement of yields and output. Perhaps Ricardo and the late nineteenth-century critics of landowners were right: they obtained an unearned increment which could be appropriated through taxation. In the early nineteenth century, the outcome was very different, for landowners instead shifted the burden of taxation to other groups in society, and maintained their higher rents by protection. The redistribution of income, and its maintenance by state policy, had serious political and economic repercussions, leading to radical attacks and demands for parliamentary reform to make policy more accountable, and encouraging a shift from domestic markets to exports.

NOTES

1. J. M. Neeson, 'The Opponents of Enclosure in Eighteenth-Century Northamptonshire', *Past and Present*, 105 (1984), 139.

2. E. P. Thompson, *The Making of the English Working Class* (1963), 218.

3. E. P. Thompson, 'The Grid of Inheritance', in J. Goody *et al.* (eds.), *Family and Inheritance* (Cambridge, 1976), 337.

4. M. A. Havinden, 'Agricultural Progress in Open-Field Oxfordshire', *Agricultural History Review*, 9 (1961), 79.

5. D. N. McCloskey, 'English Open-Fields as Behaviour towards Risk', *Research in Economic History*, 1 (1976); C. J. Dahlman, *The Open Fields and Beyond: A Property Rights Analysis of an Economic Institution* (Cambridge, 1980).

6. J. A. Yelling, *Common Field and Enclosure in England, 1450–1850* (1977), 71.

7. M. E. Turner, *English Parliamentary Enclosure: Its Historical Geography and Economic History* (Folkestone, 1980), 62.

8. Ibid. 180–1.

9. Thompson, 'Grid', 341.

10. Quoted in R. A. Dodghson, 'Runrig and the Communal Origins of Property in Land', *Juridical Review* (1975), 191.

11. J. R. Wordie, 'The Chronology of English Enclosures, 1500–1914', *Economic History Review*, 2nd ser. 36 (1983), 490–1, 497, 502.

12. Quoted in J. L. and B. Hammond, *The Village Labourer, 1760–1832: A Study in the Government of England before the Reform Bill* (1911), 54.

13. Ibid. 49.

14. W. G. Hoskins, *The Midland Peasant: The Economic and Social History of a Leicestershire Village* (1957), 247–9.

15. Neeson, 'Opponents', 124, 126, 127, 131–2.

16. J. D. Chambers and G. E. Mingay, *The Agricultural Revolution 1750–1880* (1966), 97.

17. J. M. Martin, 'The Cost of Parliamentary Enclosure in Warwickshire', in E. L. Jones (ed.), *Agriculture and Economic Growth in England, 1650–1815* (1967), 132.

18. Hoskins, *Midland Peasant*, 249.

19. J. D. Chambers, 'Enclosure and the Small Landowner', *Economic History Review*, 10 (1940), 123, 127.

20. M. E. Turner, 'Parliamentary Enclosure and Landownership Change in Buckinghamshire', *Economic History Review*, 28 (1975), 568.

21. J. M. Neeson, *Commoners: Common Right, Enclosure and Social Change in England, 1700–1820* (Cambridge, 1993), 329.

22. J. Humphries, 'Enclosure, Common Rights and Women: The Proletarianization of Families in the Late Eighteenth and Early Nineteenth Centuries', *Journal of Economic History*, 50 (1990), 26, 35.

23. Quoted in Yelling, *Common Field*, 222.

24. J. D. Chambers, 'Enclosure and the Labour Supply in the Industrial Revolution', *Economic History Review*, 2nd ser. 5 (1952–3), 332–3.

25. R. C. Allen, *Enclosure and the Yeoman, The Agricultural Development of the South Midlands, 1450–1850* (Oxford, 1992), 156–7.

26. K. D. M. Snell, *Annals of the Labouring Poor: Social Change and Agrarian England 1660–1900* (Cambridge, 1985), 213–14.

27. M. Williams, 'The Enclosure and Reclamation of Waste Land in England and Wales in the Eighteenth and Nineteenth Centuries', *Transactions of the Institute of British Geographers*, 51 (1970), 57.

28. W. G. Hoskins, 'The Reclamation of Waste in Devon, 1550–1800', *Economic History Review*, 13 (1943), 86.

29. M. Williams, 'The Enclosure of Wasteland in Somerset', *Transactions of the Institute of British Geographers*, 57 (1972), 107; 'The Enclosure and Reclamation of the Mendip Hills, 1770–1870', *Agricultural History Review*, 19 (1971), 80–1.

30. A. Young, *General Report on Enclosures* (1808), 32.

31. Ibid. 219.

32. Ibid. 220.

33. Ibid. 37.

34. Allen, *Enclosure and the Yeoman*, 114.

35. R. C. Allen and C. ÓGráda, 'On the Road Again with Arthur Young: English, Irish and French Agriculture during the Industrial Revolution', *Journal of Economic History*, 48 (1988), 98; J. J. Purdum, 'Profitability and Timing of Parliamentary Land Enclosures', *Exploration in Economic History*, 15 (1978), 322.

36. M. E. Turner, 'Agricultural Productivity in England in the Eighteenth Century: Evidence from Crop Yields', *Economic History Review*, 35 (1982), 500.

37. Allen, *Enclosure and the Yeoman*, 136.

38. Young, *General Report*, 37–8.

39. R. C. Allen, 'The Efficiency and Distributional Consequences of Eighteenth-Century Enclosures', *Economic Journal*, 92 (1982), 937.

40. Purdum, 'Profitability', 318.

41. Allen, *Enclosure and the Yeoman*, 181.

42. Young, *General Report*, 31–2.

FURTHER READING

Allen, R. C., *Enclosure and the Yeoman: The Agricultural Development of the South Midlands, 1450–1850* (Oxford, 1992).

—— 'The Efficiency and Distributional Consequences of Eighteenth-Century Enclosures', *Economic Journal*, 92 (1982).

—— and O'Grada, C., 'On the Road Again with Arthur Young: English, Irish and French Agriculture during the Industrial Revolution', *Journal of Economic History*, 38 (1988).

Baker, A. R. H., 'Some Terminological Problems in the Studies of British Field Systems', *Agricultural History Review*, 17 (1969).

Buchanan, B. J., 'The Financing of Parliamentary Waste Land Enclosure: Some Evidence from North Somerset, 1770–1830', *Agricultural History Review*, 30 (1982).

Butlin, R. A., 'The Enclosure of Open Fields and Extinction of Common Rights in England, c.1600–1750: A Review', in H. S. A. Fox and R. A. Butlin (eds.), *Change in the Countryside: Essays on Rural England, 1500–1900* (1979).

Chambers, J. D., 'Enclosure and Labour Supply in the Industrial Revolution', *Economic History Review*, 2nd ser. 5 (1952–3).

—— 'Enclosure and the Small Landowner', *Economic History Review*, 10 (1940).

—— and Mingay, G. E., *The Agricultural Revolution, 1750–1880* (1966).

Chapman, J., 'The Chronology of English Enclosure', *Economic History Review*, 2nd ser. 37 (1984).

—— 'Parliamentary Enclosure in the Uplands: The Case of the North York Moors', *Agricultural History Review*, 24 (1976).

Crafts, N. R. F., 'Enclosure and Labour Supply Revisited', *Explorations in Economic History*, 15 (1978).

Dahlman, C. J., *The Open Field System and Beyond: A Property Rights Analysis of an Economic Institution* (Cambridge, 1980).

Dodgshon, R. A., 'Towards an Understanding and Definitions of Runrig: The Evidence for Roxburghshire and Berwickshire', *Transactions of the Institute of British Geographers*, 64 (1975).

—— 'Runrig and the Communal Origins of Property in Land', *Juridical Review* (1975).

—— 'The Removal of Runrig in Roxburghshire and Berwickshire, 1680–1766', *Scottish Studies*, 16 (1972).

Fox, H. S. A., 'The Chronology of Enclosures and Economic Development in Medieval Devon', *Economic History Review*, 2nd ser. 28 (1975).

—— 'The Alleged Transformation from Two-Field to Three-Field Systems in Medieval England', *Economic History Review*, 2nd ser. 39 (1986).

Gray, H. L., *English Field Systems* (Cambridge, Mass., 1915).

Gray, M., 'The Abolition of Runrig in the Highlands of Scotland', *Economic History Review*, 2nd ser. 5 (1952–3).

Hammond, J. L. and B., *The Village Labourer 1760–1832: A Study in the Government of England before the Reform Bill* (1911).

Havinden, M. A., 'Agricultural Progress in Open-Field Oxfordshire', *Agricultural History Review*, 9 (1961).

Hoskins, W. G., *The Midland Peasant: The Economic and Social History of a Leicestershire Village* (1957).

—— 'The Reclamation of the Waste in Devon, 1550–1800', *Economic History Review*, 13 (1943).

Humphries, J., 'Enclosure, Common Rights and Women: The Proletarianization of Families in the Late Eighteenth and Early Nineteenth Centuries', *Journal of Economic History*, 50 (1990).

Hunt, H. G., 'The Chronology of Parliamentary Enclosure in Leicestershire', *Economic History Review*, 2nd ser. 10 (1957–8).

—— 'Landownership and Enclosure, 1750–1830', *Economic History Review*, 2nd ser. 11 (1958–9).

King, P., 'Gleaners, Farmers, and the Failure of Legal Sanctions in England, 1750–1850', *Past and Present*, 125 (1989).

McCloskey, D. N., 'English Open Fields as Behaviour towards Risk', *Research in Economic History*, 1 (1976).

Martin, J. M., 'The Cost of Parliamentary Enclosure in Warwickshire', *University of Birmingham Historical Journal*, 9 (1964).

—— 'Village Traders and the Emergence of a Proletariat in South Warwickshire, 1750–1851', *Agricultural History Review*, 32 (1984).

—— 'The Parliamentary Enclosure Movement and Rural Society in Warwickshire', *Agricultural History Review*, 32 (1984).

—— 'The Small Landowner and Parliamentary Enclosure in Warwickshire', *Agricultural History Review*, 15 (1967).

—— 'Members of Parliament and Enclosure: A Reconsideration', *Agricultural History Review*, 27 (1979).

Mingay, G. E., *Enclosure and the Small Farmer in the Age of the Industrial Revolution* (1968).

Neeson, J. M., 'The Opponents of Enclosure in Eighteenth-Century Northamptonshire', *Past and Present*, 105 (1984).

—— *Commons: Common Right, Enclosure and Social Change in England, 1700–1820* (Cambridge, 1993).

Purdum, J. J., 'Profitability and Timing of Parliamentary Land Enclosures', *Explorations in Economic History*, 15 (1978).

Smout, T. C., *A History of the Scottish People, 1560–1830* (1969).

Snell, K. D. M., *Annals of the Labouring Poor: Social Change and Agrarian England, 1660–1900* (Cambridge, 1985).

Thirsk, J., 'The Common Fields', *Past and Present*, 29 (1964).

Thompson, E. P., *The Making of the English Working Class* (1963).

—— 'The Grid of Inheritance', in J. Goody *et al.* (eds.), *Family and Inheritance: Rural Society in Western Europe, 1200–1800* (Cambridge, 1976).

Turner, M. E., 'Enclosure Commissioners and Buckinghamshire Parliamentary Enclosure', *Agricultural History Review*, 25 (1977).

—— 'The Cost of Parliamentary Enclosure in Buckinghamshire', *Agricultural History Review*, 25 (1977).

—— 'Agricultural Productivity in England in the Eighteenth Century: Evidence from Crop Yields', *Economic History Review*, 2nd ser. 35 (1982).

—— *English Parliamentary Enclosure: Its Historical Geography and Economic History* (Folkestone, 1980).

—— *Enclosures in Britain, 1750–1830* (1984).

—— 'Cost, Finance, and Parliamentary Enclosure', *Economic History Review*, 2nd ser. 34 (1981).

—— 'Parliamentary Enclosure and Landownership Change', in A. R. H. Baker and R. A. Butlin (eds.), *Studies of Field Systems in the British Isles* (Cambridge, 1973).

—— 'Parliamentary Enclosure and Landownership Change in Buckinghamshire', *Economic History Review*, 2nd ser. 28 (1975).

Whyte, I., *Agriculture and Society in Seventeenth-Century Scotland* (Edinburgh, 1979).

—— 'The Emergence of the New Estate Structure', in M. L. Perry and T. R. Slater (eds.), *The Making of the Scottish Countryside* (1980).

Williams, M., 'The Enclosure and Reclamation of the Mendip Hills, 1770–1870', *Agricultural History Review*, 19 (1971).

—— 'The Enclosure of Wasteland in Somerset', *Transactions of the Institute of British Geographers*, 57 (1972).

—— 'The Enclosure and Reclamation of Waste Land in England and Wales in the Eighteenth and Nineteenth Centuries', *Transactions of the Institute of British Geographers*, 51 (1970).

Wordie, J. R., 'The Chronology of English Enclosures', *Economic History Review*, 2nd ser. 36 (1983).

Yelling, J., 'Common Land and Enclosure in East Worcestershire, 1540–1870', *Transactions of the Institute of British Geographers*, 45 (1968).

—— *Common Field and Enclosure in England, 1450–1850* (1977).

PART II

Industry and Urban Society

CHAPTER 5

Diversities of Industrialization

British society underwent a fundamental transformation in the eighteenth century, as a large proportion of the population was released from the land and absorbed into industry and the towns. This amounted to an industrial revolution in terms of the structure of the economy, but did it also entail an industrial revolution in terms of economic growth? In the 1950s and 1960s, many historians believed that there was a spurt in the rate of growth, the level of capital formation rose, and the economy was able to achieve a take-off into self-sustained growth. The classical economists of the late eighteenth and early nineteenth centuries were more sceptical, and presented a picture of an economy which was resolutely tied to the ground, unable to escape from the restraints of gravity. Could it be that workers were released from agriculture, where a high level of productivity had been reached, and employed in industry and services where productivity was little higher? Was it even possible that population growth and the redeployment of workers from the land led to underemployed pools of cheap labour which removed the incentive of industrialists to invest in capital-intensive production in factories using powered machinery?[1] Despite the existence of an industrial *revolution* in terms of the *structure* of the economy, could it be that there was industrial *evolution* in terms of rates of *growth*?

The issue can only be resolved by measuring industrial output and productivity, a task which is by no means easy. The underlying data are extremely weak, and much rests upon the methods which are adopted in moving from a few glimpses of some sectors to the overall growth of industry. A number of historians have been sufficiently bold or foolhardy to make the attempt, and Lord Brougham's words of warning are particularly apt: 'I have found how insecure all details of mere figures are upon which to build an argument. . . . It is easy to add a little here, and subtract a little there; gently to slip in a figure . . .; slyly to make what seems to be a reasonable postulate in your premises, but which turns out in the result to be a begging of the question.'[2] Not surprisingly, there are wide

TABLE 5.1. *Growth of industrial production, 1700–1831 (% p.a.)*

	Hoffman	Deane/Cole	Harley	Crafts	CLM
1700–60	0.8	1.0		0.71	0.8
1760–80	1.4	0.5		1.51	0.9
1780–1801	3.9	3.4		2.11	1.9
1801–31	2.8	4.4		3.00	2.7
1700–70	1.0	1.0		0.78	0.9
1770–1815	2.5		1.6/1.7	2.15	1.4
1801–31	3.6		3.1/3.2	3.6	
Per capita					
1700–60	0.5	0.7		0.4	0.5
1760–80	0.7	−0.2		0.8	0.3
1780–1801	2.8	2.4		1.1	0.9
1801–31	1.3	3.0		1.5	1.3
1700–70	0.6	0.6		0.4	0.6
1770–1815	1.4		0.5/0.6	1.0	0.3
1815–41	2.2		1.7/1.8	2.2	

Source: R. V. Jackson, 'Rates of Industrial Growth during the Industrial Revolution', *Economic History Review*, 2nd ser. 45 (1992), tables 1 and 2.

variations in the various indices of industrial production, reflecting different premises and adjustments made in their compilation (see Table 5.1).

Measuring Industrial Growth

The most influential recent attempts to measure industrial growth have suggested that it remained slow in the late eighteenth century, and that the onset of more rapid growth was delayed until after 1815. These estimates stand in marked contrast with earlier figures produced by Hoffman and Deane and Cole, which indicated the onset of rapid growth after 1780, in both aggregate and per capita output.[3] Indeed, the index of Crafts, Leybourne, and Mills (CLM) suggests a *deceleration* in per capita industrial output between 1770 and 1815.[4] The period which earlier historians had so confidently branded as the industrial revolution and the period of take-off into self-sustained growth assumes a very different pattern of slower growth of both agricultural and industrial output. The emphasis is placed upon the success of agriculture in releasing labour from the land to a greater extent than in other European countries, which led to major structural change in the economy. It did not mean, according to Crafts's interpretation, faster growth: labour moved from high-productivity agriculture to an industrial economy dominated by small-scale organization and a low level of capital investment. The 'revolutionized' or 'modern' sectors of industry formed, according to Crafts, islands of modernity in a sea of tradition.[5]

Revisionary zeal has led some historians into extreme and untenable positions. 'Far from being revolutionized by industry', Lee has remarked, 'the low rate of growth of the British economy before 1914 and the modest and faltering contribution of manufacturing to that growth is witness to the weakness and fragility of industrialization in the first industrial nation.'[6] This is a curious interpretation of Britain's unprecedented dominance of world trade in manufactures, and the uniquely high level of employment in industry and residence in towns. The industrial revolution was, according to J. C. D. Clark, 'a fictitious entity',[7] and he proceeds to present a picture of English society as an *ancien régime* characterized by slow growth and the survival of small units of production, in which social relations remained patriarchal and hierarchical and class conflict largely absent. Unfortunately, Clark has misunderstood the implications of revisionist quantification which shows a major transformation in the structure of the economy. Rather than denying the existence of an industrial revolution, Crafts and other quantifiers have tried to explain Britain's extreme and atypical industrialization. British industrialization, they contend, was different from that of other countries: it combined rapid structural change and slow growth, characterized by an early release of labour from agriculture into industry in the absence of a wide differential in productivity, and with a high reliance upon exports. There was the expansion of what Blackstone called 'a polite and commercial people', who were no longer willing to accept 'old feudal actions' which were ill-suited to 'commercial modes of property'.[8] Although a large part of the industrial population continued to work in small units, these were often far removed from the nostalgic picture of apprentices, journeymen, and masters in a cohesive family unit: the expansion of production in the domestic system of manufacture could strain social relationships, and the status of artisans could be challenged by the use of unskilled workers who had not served apprenticeships. Social tension did not depend upon the appearance of the factory and steam engine, and could emerge within domestic production and the workshop.

The act of quantification has not added the industrial revolution to the list of spurious revolutions; it has redefined the industrial revolution and made it more puzzling and interesting than older accounts of heroic inventors transforming Britain with their steam engines and spinning-jennies. But can the statistics of slow growth be believed? What is the evidence upon which these estimates of industrial output are based, how trustworthy are the figures for the sectors which are covered, and how far do the statistics provide an adequate cover of British industry throughout the period?

The government's need to raise money provides a number of sources for measuring industrial output: excise duties were levied on a number of industries such as glass, brewing, distilling, soap, and candles; and customs duties applied to imports of industrial inputs such as raw cotton. Historians have to place their faith in the efficiency of eighteenth-century tax collectors; contemporaries had a more jaundiced view. In 1783, the Commons was sufficiently concerned to appoint a select committee to make inquiries into the 'illicit practices used in defrauding the revenue', which concluded that the excise officers collected about 75 per cent of the revenue which was due.[9] Of course, the 'black economy' is a problem in statistics for all periods, and the important point is whether the level of under-recording changed, as it did in the paper industry, where the apparent increase in output in the 1780s was the result of new administrative procedures. Care must be taken to understand the basis of the excise figures and the extent to which they provide a realistic measure of output in any sector. For example, Crafts relies on the excise data on strong beer which exaggerate the growth of the brewing industry, for there was a decline both in 'small' beer and in home brewing which fell outside the excise. Imports of raw materials can be of some help, such as in the silk and cotton industries where raw materials came from overseas, but care is again needed in understanding the structure of the industry and the composition of output. Imports of raw silk are not, as Crafts assumes, an accurate guide to the growth of the silk industry. In the mid-eighteenth century, British weavers imported about half their yarn and produced the remainder from imported raw silk; by 1820, about 90 per cent of yarn was processed in Britain so that figures based on imports of raw silk exaggerate the growth of the industry. Volumes of imported raw material are, in any case, only a partial guide to the growth of any industry. Imported silk was turned into cheap ribbons in Coventry or exquisite dress fabric in Spitalfields, and cotton could be used for spinning coarse yarns for export or converted into high-value printed cloth. The changes in the composition of output need to be considered as well as the volume of inputs.

Industries liable to excise or import duties formed only a part of industrial activity, and it is remarkably difficult to calculate trends in the output of textiles or ironwares, which were spread across the country in the hands of thousands of domestic workers. Only a few industries are included in the statistics of output, and it is difficult to share Crafts's confidence that 'the omitted sectors must be of only very minor importance'.[10] How realistic is a view of the economy which excludes glass and pottery; lead, brass, and chemicals; the plethora of metal manufacturers from clocks and guns to 'toys' and nails; the processors of sugar, salt, bread, and spirits; the producers of furniture and upholstery; the domestic producers of baskets, straw plait, and lace; the coopers and coach-makers. Only one 'modern' industry—cotton—is included and many expanding industrial sectors are excluded, such as the Potteries, the chemical industries of Merseyside and south Lancashire, and the metal trades of the Black Country. He concentrates on intermediate products rather than the final goods sold to the consumer. The growth of the iron industry, for example, is based upon the output of pig iron, which exaggerates the growth of the industry, for pig iron output grew more rapidly than other sectors as a result of the substitution for Swedish and Russian imports. In any case, pig iron could be used for a wide variety of purposes ranging from cheap castings to conversion into bar iron for the manufacture of low-value nails or valuable clocks and guns. Perhaps two-thirds of Crafts's data on industrial output are based upon the input of raw materials or the production of intermediate goods, which fail to capture vital parts of the manufacturing process. It is difficult to tell how far the growth rate is biased and in which direction: on the one hand, some expanding industries are excluded; but handicraft and domestic industries are under-represented, and these were likely to have a *lower* level of productivity.

It is difficult to compile output data on a single industry, and it is even more difficult to combine them into an aggregate index of industrial production. The first stage is to convert the highly disparate products of industries into a common measure so that the number of candles and yards of cloth can be brought into an aggregate figure. One procedure is to convert volumes of output into money terms by the use of 'price weights'. Unfortunately, information on the relative price of commodities is sketchy, and there is a methodological problem of whether relative prices are taken at the beginning or end of the period. Suppose the price of a candle in 1700 was 6d. and the price of a brass candlestick 2s. 6d.; one candlestick has the 'weight' of five candles. Development of new techniques in the metal trades meant that the price of candlesticks fell relative to candles during the eighteenth century: assuming a candlestick in 1800 cost 2s. and a candle 8d., the 'weight' of one candlestick was now three candles. Calculation of the rate of growth of output is consequently influenced by the choice of prices from the beginning of the period (a Laspeyeres index) or the end (a Paasche index). An alternative and preferable procedure would be to measure value added in each industry, taking the difference between the costs of inputs and the price received for the finished product. This could vary widely, for an ingot of brass could be used to manufacture a cheap, utilitarian candlestick for the working-class market, or an elegant and sophisticated item for fashionable houses in London or Bath. The quantity of brass and the price of the input might be the same; the price received differed by a wide margin. Unfortunately, estimates of value added are extremely fragile. Prices might be available for inputs, but there is little information on the composition of output, or on price trends for various styles and designs. Once the output of an industry has been expressed in cash terms, a further serious problem arises in moving from data on individual industries to the sector as a whole. Data are available for only a few industries, and any estimate of overall trends depends on the assumptions made about their share of total output and how it changed over time. 'Weights' are crucial to the shape of the index of industrial production, for the impact of a rapidly growing sector can be minimized by assuming that it comprised a small part of total activity, or exaggerated by assuming that it accounted for a large and growing share of output. Above all, the weight assigned to the rapidly growing cotton industry is important for calculating growth at the end of the eighteenth and early nineteenth centuries. In the Hoffmann index, the cotton industry is assumed to account for 6.7 per cent of all value added in industry in 1783 and 12.2 per cent in 1812, which is effectively increased by assuming that the rate of growth of industries for which he had data was the same as those for which he had no information. By contrast, Crafts assumed that the share of cotton was 2.6 per cent in 1770 and 17.0 per cent in 1801, compared with Harley's extremely low estimate of at most one per cent. These assumptions shape the pattern of industrial growth, and the margins of error are extremely wide.[11]

The case for slow industrial growth until the end of the Napoleonic wars has not been proved by the act of quantification, and a reworking of Crafts's index to remove some of its more glaring weaknesses can produce a different outcome.

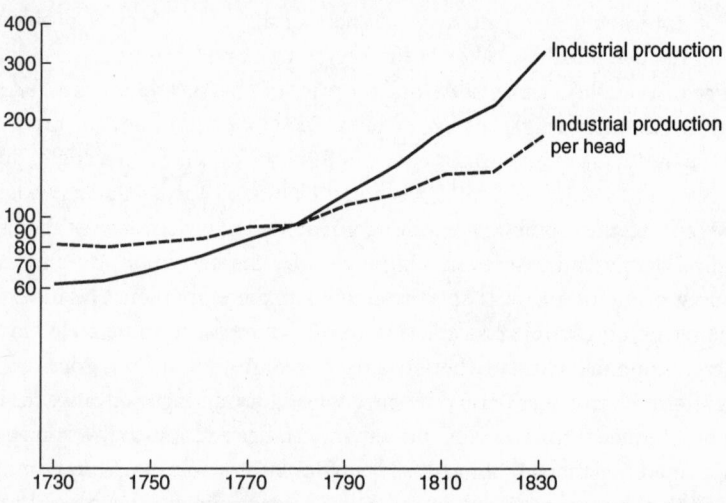

FIG. 5.1. Industrial production: index of revised estimates (R. V. Jackson)

Source: R. V. Jackson, 'Rates of Industrial Growth during the Industrial Revolution', *Economic History Review*, 2nd ser. 45 (1992), 19.

TABLE 5.2. *Growth of industrial output: revised estimates, 1730–1830 (% p.a.)*

	Industrial output	Per capita
1730–70	0.9	0.4
1740–80	1.1	0.5
1750–90	1.4	0.7
1760–1800	1.7	0.8
1770–1810	2.1	1.0
1780–1820	2.2	1.0
1790–1830	2.7	1.3

Source: Jackson, 'Rates of Growth', table 10, p. 19.

'Industrial activity', suggests Jackson, 'grew faster and accelerated more sharply after 1780' (see Table 5.2 and Fig. 5.1).[12] Of course, these revised figures are themselves open to challenge, for the margins of error are huge. Brougham's point remains valid, that it is easy to insinuate assumptions into calculations to gain a point, 'until it is found that your adversary, having access to the same stores of arithmetic, just proves his case and refutes yours with the same facility'.[13] Confident statements about the rate of industrial growth are mis- placed, and a contrast should not be drawn between the apparent precision and objectivity of statistics and the subjectivity of qualitative material. In reality, the compilation of statistics of industrial output rests upon a number of assumptions about the nature of eighteenth-century Britain which can only be tested through the use of a wide range of non-quantitative material. What exactly are these underlying assumptions, and how realistic are they?

'Modern' Versus 'Traditional' Industries: a False Dichotomy?

The Crafts–Harley approach to the industrial revolution assumes that rapid structural change and an unusually high level of industrialization were associated with a slow rate of growth. The paradox is explained by the release of labour from high-productivity agriculture into an industrial sector which was still largely 'traditional', with a relatively small 'revolutionized' or 'modern' sector. Their interpretation rests upon the unevenness of productivity advance between a few progressive sectors such as cotton, where factories and powered machinery raised productivity, and a laggard mass of industries based upon hand labour in which productivity was low and static. The Birmingham metal trades, for example, rested upon extreme division of labour so that a button could pass through fifty hands; and simple hand tools were used, such as stamps and presses for shaping the blanks for buttons, treadle-operated lathes to trim the buttons after they had been stamped, and draw-benches to make wire. Industrialization is interpreted as a gradual movement from production on the Birmingham model as modernized industries increased their share of output and employment, and the traditional sectors of hand labour fell away. A similar dichotomy is central to Wrigley's contrast between two different patterns of growth. The first followed Adam Smith's route of growth through *specialization*, based on a *flow* of organic energy from the annual growth of crops and wood, and the vagaries of wind and water power, which would soon reach a ceiling of growth. These limits were broken by the application of large *stocks* of mineral fuel, for a coal-mine could supply a large input of energy without any immediate danger of exhaustion. An organic economy and asymptotic growth gave way to a mineral-based energy economy and exponential growth. The statistical calculation of rates of growth is in many ways less important than these assumptions: if they are accepted, it is clear that growth must have been slow until the 'revolutionized' industries were able to counterbalance the dead weight of the 'traditional' sectors, and growth by the use of mineral fuel could escape from the constraints of growth by special-ization. Should the dichotomies be accepted? Have the possibilities of pro-ductivity gains in so-called 'traditional' industries been neglected, and the rate of growth by specialization underestimated?

Although 'traditional' and 'modern' industries are defined as successive and separate stages of development, in reality the two categories of industries and the two types of growth were interdependent. The distinction between intermediate and final products indicates some of the shortcomings of the 'stage' approach to industrialization. The output of pig iron from new blast furnaces, and of cotton cloth from textile mills, provided inputs for a wide range of final commodities produced in apparently 'traditional' ways, such as the diverse metal trades of Birmingham and the Black Country, and tailors, dressmakers, and upholsterers. Centralized production did not operate independently of the rest of manufactur-ing, and the relationship between the two sectors was complex. In some cases, 'traditional' sectors competed directly with centralized factory production and they eventually disappeared, such as the hand-loom weavers in the cotton industry. But even in these cases, there was often an extended period of coexistence and complementarity. It did not make sense to undertake large-scale investment in factories when demand for cloth was highly cyclical; the hand-loom weavers could meet periods of high demand and then be laid off in slack periods without placing a burden on the employer. Complementarity between small-scale workshops and centralized factories could remain an integral feature of an industry, so that parts produced in a centralized plant were finished by hand-workers in workshops or their homes. Indeed, a 'traditional' industry could integrate vertically in order to secure materials and take an active role in the 'modern' sector, such as the Birmingham metal trades which moved into the brass and copper industries. The path of development was not linear, away from 'traditional' workshops towards 'revolutionized' industries adopting centralized mass production.

A linear model of industrialization based on a simple movement from one stage to another should be rejected, but it could still be argued that productivity growth was overwhelmingly concentrated in processes based on factories and mineral energy. Could it be that productivity gains in the production of a shirt were located in textile factories with centralized, powered machinery rather than in the workshops of tailors and seamstresses in London; and that productivity gains in the manufacture of a brass candlestick arose from the coal-fired furnaces of smelters rather than from workshops in Birmingham? These claims have been challenged by a number of historians who argue that 'traditional' industries offered an alternative route of growth based on flexible craft production which could make gains in productivity apart from the inputs of semi-finished materials from textile mills and metal-refiners.[14] Perhaps, they suggest, the introduction of factories in the place of workshops had less to do with any exhaustion of productivity growth in 'traditional' sectors and more to do with issues of *control* over the process of production. 'Traditional' production processes could certainly be well adapted to the market and capable of flexibility and innovation. Industries producing consumer goods could continue to be based on small workshops using labour-intensive methods of production, concentrating their innovations on the organization of production and marketing rather than the adoption of new technology, and devising a wider range of goods to exploit new markets and cultivate fashion. They could economize on the use of materials by substituting cheap alloys for more expensive metals, or developing new types of cloth which did not need fulling and complex dyeing. Relatively simple hand tools could be used, such as the metal stamps and presses of the Birmingham trades, and women and children could be substituted for men in order to secure lower wages and manual dexterity. 'There is a cunning crept into the trades', remarked one late seventeenth-century commentator, 'artificers, by tools and lathes fitted for different purposes, make such things as would puzzle a stander by to set a price on, according to the worth of men's labour.'[15] This could lead to 'flexible specialization' as an alternative to centralized mass production.

The choice between flexible specialization or mass production depended in part upon the nature of the market. Mass production made most sense where a large market existed for standardized goods, which depended upon the distribution of incomes and cultural expectations. In the United States, for example, farmers provided a widespread demand for basic consumer goods and tools, in contrast to France where peasants tended to direct surplus income into land purchases. The slow pace of urbanization and the continuation of artisan production meant that there was a smaller working-class market for standardized goods in France, and demand for manufactures largely came from well-to-do urban and rural élites, with highly varied tastes and an expectation that goods would be differentiated. The production of high-quality, short-run goods using flexible technologies made sense. Britain came somewhere between France and the USA. On the one hand, there was a mass market for cheap consumer goods at home and in foreign markets, which encouraged the development of mass production in some sectors. On the other hand, there was considerable demand from well-to-do urban professionals and merchants, as well as members of landed society, which created flexible production to supply them with high-quality furnishings, sporting guns, or riding boots. The structure of demand in any society therefore helped to determine the mix between mass production and flexible production.

The traditional sectors were certainly not static, and had a continued viability. Small producers were responsive to markets, and manufacturers of Birmingham 'toys' could turn out 50 or 500 different types of buckle, and could substitute cheap children or women for skilled men. But could 'flexible specialization' and innovations in products and processes offer a significant break in productivity? Adam Smith made a large claim for growth through the division of labour, suggesting that it permitted each worker in the pin industry to increase output by *at least* 240-fold. The claim is implausible: he assumed that ten men could make 48,000 pins a day, which entailed 864,000 separate operations a day; in a ten-hour day, each worker would need to complete 2.4 tasks a second without cease. Although specialization would allow some gains in productivity, they were likely to disappear when the market passed a certain size. Once the production of a pin had been divided into its separate tasks, it was only possible to replicate teams of workers, and there is no reason why a workshop employing 100 workers should have a higher productivity than a workshop employing ten or fifty. The economies of scale were low, and growth by specialization was likely to meet a ceiling of productivity.

The prospects for growth were also limited by the existence of many trades which were unable to improve productivity through either the application of power or division of labour. This was especially true of trades serving local markets, which employed large numbers of carpenters, masons, tailors, bakers, shoemakers, and so on. In 1831, when the census for the first time provided data on employment, only 10 per cent of the adult male work-force in England was engaged in manufacturing, a category including factory workers and outworkers making goods for distant markets. Workers in these trades were able to increase their productivity by specialization or the application of power. Workers making

;oods for purely local markets were assigned to retail trade and handicraft: they accounted for 516,979 men or 32.0 per cent of the adult male work-force in 1831, including 110,122 shoemakers, 83,810 carpenters, and 60,166 tailors. In these trades and handicrafts, per capita output was relatively stable and there was a large dead weight to shift before the potential of higher productivity in manufacturing could affect the overall growth of the economy. In the early nineteenth century, slow growth continued to have a basis in structural reality, until sectors with high output per worker had developed sufficiently to dominate the movement of the economy as a whole. Between 1831 and 1841, employment in manufacturing rose by 4.1 per cent per annum in comparison with 2.4 per cent for handicrafts and trade, and constraints on growth were slowly removed as the balance of the economy shifted.[16]

The prospects of growth remained limited so long as the economy relied upon organic flows of energy and specialization, and it was only in the nineteenth century that these constraints were removed. This is far from arguing that eighteenth-century Britain was characterized by stagnation and conservatism. On the contrary, Britain's achievement in the eighteenth century was to develop the organic economy and specialization to a point which surpassed other countries in Europe. An emphasis upon the slow pace of growth, and the difficulty of breaking the limits on productivity, must not overlook the emergence of Britain as the most industrialized and urbanized country in Europe with the exception of the Netherlands, and of London as the largest city in western Europe. The rate of population growth was also unusually rapid: the population of France, Spain, Germany, Italy, and the Netherlands grew by 50 to 80 per cent between 1550 and 1820; in England, the population grew by 280 per cent.[17] Such a striking rate of population growth might have been expected to place pressure upon the available resources and lead to an erosion of the standard of living; in fact, real incomes per head rose in the eighteenth century and overtook the Netherlands. The conjunction of a faster rate of population growth with an increase in the standard of living relative to other countries leads to an obvious conclusion: the rate of growth of Britain's gross national product was greater than elsewhere in western Europe in the eighteenth century. Britain's growth in the eighteenth century was rapid in relative terms, as it caught up with and overhauled its European neighbours.

Britain was making relative gains during the seventeenth and eighteenth centuries, in part by raising the organic economy to the limits of its possibilities by the development of a more integrated market which allowed a greater degree of specialization. Improvement in transport, marketing, finance, and credit allowed agricultural and industrial areas to specialize in the crops and trades in which they had the greatest comparative advantage. Britain's success in increasing market integration and reducing transaction costs allowed it to catch up with other countries. Yet part of the success of the British economy in the seventeenth and eighteenth centuries already rested upon the emergence of mineral-based energy growth, which lessened some of the competing demands on the land, and mitigated the restraints of an organic economy. Coal was used for domestic heat, and was gradually extended to boil liquids in pans for the production of salt, sugar, and beer and in dye-works; to heat ovens to bake bricks and bread; and to fuel furnaces for the production of glass and metals. British coal output in 1700 was between 2.5 and 3 million tons, and each ton was roughly equivalent to the output of wood from an acre of land. Coal output expanded during the eighteenth century to about 15 million tons in 1800, so reducing pressure upon the land for fuel and freeing it to grow food. The British economy was much more successful in escaping from the constraints of an organic economy than the Dutch, who were heavily dependent upon peat. Heat-intensive industries such as the manufacture of bricks and tiles, salt-refining, bleaching and dyeing textiles developed in Holland, but constraints soon appeared as reserves of peat were exhausted and costs rose. By contrast, British coal production could sustain high levels of output for longer periods of time provided that the problems of winning coal at greater depths could be overcome. The application of mineral energy permitted the land to support more people before running into constraints.

Urbanization and Craft Regions

Clearly, one reason for the success of the British economy relative to other European economies was the increase in agricultural productivity, which made it possible to sustain more workers in industry and towns. In Europe, urban growth between 1500 and 1750 was concentrated on large cities, and particularly state capitals; cities with a population of less than 40,000 only grew in line with the general rise in population, and the number of small towns of 5,000 to 10,000 actually declined between 1600 and 1750. Industry in Europe was shifting to the countryside from the towns, and a number of cities lost political autonomy with the rise of nation-states and the emergence of capital cities. In England, the pattern was different. The number of small towns doubled between 1600 and 1750, and industrial growth in the countryside was not at the expense of urban expansion.[18] In England, the proportion of the total population living in towns with 10,000 or more inhabitants rose fourfold between 1600 and 1800, whereas the level in the rest of Europe was stable. There was also a major change in the urban hierarchy of England, unlike in Europe where the largest cities of 1600 were still dominant in 1800. Smith's emphasis upon the interconnection between

TABLE 5.3. *Largest six towns in England, 1600, 1700, and 1801. (Population shown in 000s)*

1600		1700		1801	
London	200	London	575	London	959
Norwich	15	Norwich	30	Manchester/Salford	89
York	12	Bristol	21	Liverpool	83
Bristol	12	Newcastle	16	Birmingham	74
Newcastle	10	Exeter	14	Bristol	60
Exeter	9	York	12	Leeds	53

Source: E. A. Wrigley, *People, Cities and Wealth* (Oxford, 1987), 160.

agriculture and urbanization was understandable, for the agricultural surplus allowed a rapid rate of growth in towns such as Leeds and Birmingham. Indeed, England accounted for well over half the total increase in Europe's urban population in the eighteenth century (see Tables 5.3 and 5.4).

The growth of large towns was constrained by the need for large volumes of domestic fuel for cooking and heat, even more than by limits on the supply of food. London had a great advantage over Paris and other Continental cities, for it could draw supplies of coal from the north-east of England, using cheap water transport along the river Tyne, the east coast, and the Thames. London was free

TABLE 5.4. *Urbanization in England and Europe, 1600–1800*

	Percentage of total population in towns of 10,000 and above		
	1600	1700	1800
England	6.1	13.4	24.0
North and west Europe (excl. England)	9.2	12.8	10.0
Europe (excl. England)	8.1	9.4	9.5
English percentage of net gain in European urban population:			
1700–50	57		
1750–1800	70		

Source: Wrigley, *People, Cities and Wealth*, 177, 179.

to grow to become the largest city in Europe, with a high proportion of the total national population: in 1750, 11 per cent of the population of England lived in London, in comparison with about 2.5 per cent of the population of France in Paris. The result was to encourage developments in the rest of the economy. London's demands for food helped to encourage the commercialization of agriculture, the development of mines in the north-east, investment in a fleet of ships to carry the coal down the east coast, improvement in the transport network, and the creation of marketing and credit facilities. The City of London was at the centre of the 'fiscal-military state', providing loans to the British government to fight a succession of wars with the French between 1689 and 1815. Success in these wars contributed to the growth of merchants and the development of London as a major entrepôt which gradually took over the role of Amsterdam in the supply of colonial products, and as a centre of shipping and marine insurance. The auctions of tea at East India House, the import of sugar from the West Indies and of tobacco from Virginia, attracted merchants from Europe, and generated a host of specialist brokers and processors in London. Sugar, for example, was 'boiled' in the City, and the dangers of fire led to the emergence of the Phoenix fire insurance company which was subsequently to move into the insurance of cotton-mills in the north. Indeed, the City was not simply involved in government finance and international trade, for it co-ordinated the supply of credit and marketing services to the specialist regions of the country. Its involvement in the import of cotton cloth from India, for example, led to the development of specialist printers and dyers who were involved in the production of domestic cloth, providing advice on markets and fashions. The bankers of Lombard Street drew surplus funds from agricultural districts such as East Anglia, and redirected them to areas of credit deficit such as Lancashire. The notion that London was the product of older patterns of development, and that it was absent from the process of industrialization, is a travesty of its central role.

London was the single most important industrial centre in the country. It was the centre for the luxury trades for landed society, supplying carriages and fine bindings, picture frames and ball gowns, chandeliers and cabinets. The lawyers, doctors, bankers, and merchants who serviced the City and the state emulated their social superiors, so increasing the social depth of demand. Not only did they buy goods to adorn their persons and homes: doctors bought specialist surgical instruments; ships' captains needed chronometers and telescopes; lawyers, merchants, and government had an insatiable appetite for stationery and printing; London newspapers and publishers catered to a literate public in search of information and entertainment. London was more than a playground of the rich, for such demands generated a highly specialist engineering industry, able to produce printing presses and scientific instruments, turning out high-value machinery. The huge size of London meant that it was also the largest single market for basic consumer goods, which stimulated the production of shoes, clothing, furniture, beer, and the other necessities of life. Cattle driven to market at Smithfield were slaughtered for meat, and provided hides for the tanners at Bermondsey who produced leather to be used in shoes, saddles, coaches, and book bindings, and bones which were boiled to make glue and varnish for the furniture trades. The port generated a host of industries. The building of standard cargo ships migrated to the north-east, but London still produced highly specialized and sophisticated naval vessels at the royal dockyards at Deptford and Chatham, and East Indiamen at Blackwall. Vessels were repaired and refitted in London, and there was a demand for myriad pieces of iron, copper, cables, pumps, rope, sail, anchors. Imported goods were processed: sugar from the West Indies was refined, tallow from Russia turned into soap and candles. Coopers toiled to produce barrels to hold these and many other commodities. The construction of London was another source of demand for industrial goods, with iron foundries producing railings, kitchen ranges, and specialized items such as gas meters. London was the centre for the transport network on land as well as sea. The fast mail coaches which left for the provinces every evening were built and serviced at extensive works on Millbank. Coal brought down the coast kept vats and boilers steaming along the banks of the Thames, producing commodities from printers' ink to coal gas tar. The scale of some industrial concerns in London rivalled anything in the northern towns, where factories and mills were simply more visible. 'The densely packed masses of building forming the eastern districts of the metropolis, on both sides of the river,' commented George Dodd in the 1840s, 'include individual establishments which, although they would appear like little towns if isolated, scarcely meet the eye of a passenger through the crowded streets.'[19] London's highly diverse industrial structure and skilled work-force meant that it was a dynamic generator of new products and processes. It was a nursery of trades, which could subsequently relocate in the provinces in order to expand by using cheaper labour. The hosiery industry moved to the east Midlands by the eighteenth century, and the shoe industry followed suit. The weaving of cheaper grades of silk shifted to the north from Spitalfields. One result of competition from cheaper provincial labour was to intensify the division of labour in these trades in London, subdividing the tasks of skilled men who had served apprenticeships in order to employ unskilled workers—and often women—at lower wages. Whether the outcome was a faltering in the industrial economy of London and a stagnation of real wages by the end of the eighteenth century, as some historians have argued, is doubtful. The huge breweries of Truman and Whitbread, gin distilleries, and flour mills were highly capitalized enterprises, with a small work-force of regularly employed labourers under the control of skilled foremen. There was little reason for retaining capital goods such as heavy engineering in London, with its high costs, and these migrated to the coalfields. But London retained a large number of specialized engineering firms, making high-value products such as scientific instruments with a high value added. In the specialized engineering workshops, skilled men were *more* likely to be regularly employed than their counterparts in the Midlands and north, which were more prone to the trade cycle. By contrast, many luxury and consumer trades were dependent on Society and seasonal demand, and had a high degree of insecurity. What does seem unlikely is that London experienced any deindustrialization, which certainly did affect many parts of southern England.

The emergence of London as the largest city in Europe is much more dramatic than the second striking feature of seventeenth- and eighteenth-century Britain: the widespread growth of small towns, which formed a well-developed network of markets and services throughout the country. The country towns were flourishing centres for crafts, services, and professions catering for local land-owners and farmers and for their own residents: lawyers, doctors, surveyors, architects, teachers, publishers, bankers, insurance offices, shop- and innkeepers. Many developed as cultural centres for the gentry from the surrounding area, with the provision of promenades, assembly rooms, and literary and musical societies, which amounted to an 'urban renaissance' in the eighteenth century.[20] Although the position of small yeomen farmers was deteriorating in the eighteenth century, their urban counterparts were flourishing. Urban craftsmen formed an expanding sector of the work-force, and were often the largest single occupational category in country towns. Growth of the local market allowed some specialization, as an all-purpose carpenter evolved into a specialist furniture-maker, or a wheelwright into a coach-builder. The prosperity of the local gentry or merchants created new luxury trades, for high-quality furniture and tableware, for stucco and fine carving to decorate their houses, for fashionable clothes to impress local society. The scope for the division of labour was limited, for each craftsman was catering for the locality and had little incentive to subdivide his workshop into a large number of separate tasks; rather, he would take on an apprentice to learn the skill, without creating too much competition which would undermine his prosperity. Craftsmen might well try to limit the right of 'settlement' by outsiders who might threaten the balance of the local economy.

All towns had their blacksmith, carpenter, shoemaker, cabinet-maker, stone-mason, saddle-maker, wheelwright, coach-maker, and tailor to service the needs of the locality, and these urban craftsmen formed a high proportion of all industrial workers in the eighteenth and early nineteenth centuries. But a striking

:ature of the late seventeenth and early eighteenth centuries was the de-
elopment of highly specialized industries serving a national or international
narket. Crafts which had once been widely diffused became more concentrated
nto a defined area so that 'a distinct *craft-region* emerges, with its own character,
ts own traditions, its own sense of identity, and its own distinctive culture',
usually centred upon an 'entrepreneurial' town.[21] Birmingham was the hub of
he small metal trades of the west Midlands, Sheffield for the cutlery trades of
'orkshire, Leicester and Nottingham for hosiery, Northampton for shoes, Leeds
or the woollen industry, Manchester for cotton, Newcastle upon Tyne for coal
nd heavy engineering, and so on. In the course of the eighteenth century, the
roduction of staple goods became increasingly concentrated in these regions,
vhich became more differentiated from each other and more internally special-
zed as towns and villages concentrated on a particular stage of production or
ype of commodity. In the west Midlands, for example, one town in the Black
Country made chains, another pieces of horses' harnesses, another nails; in
Lancashire, some areas concentrated on spinning and others on weaving.
Specialization between and within regions rested upon the provision of market-
ng and financial services, and the co-ordination of different stages of production
rom the regional 'entrepreneurial town'. These towns were frequently themselves centres of production, but their distinctive role was to process raw
naterials or to finish goods for sale; they provided the marketing and distribution
system, and acted as the hub of credit networks. Leon Faucher captured the
character of one industrial region in 1844:

Manchester, like a diligent spider, is placed in the centre of the web, and sends forth roads
and railways towards its auxiliaries, formerly villages but now towns, which serve as
outposts to the grand centre of industry.... An order sent from Liverpool in the morning
is discussed by the merchants in the Manchester Exchange at noon, and in the evening is
distributed amongst the manufacturers in the environs. In less than eight days cotton
spun at Manchester, Bolton, Oldham or Ashton, is woven in the sheds of Burnley,
Stalybridge or Stockport, dyed and printed at Blackburn, Chorley or Preston and finally
measured and packed at Manchester.[22]

Leeds and Birmingham were similar spiders at the centres of webs woven from
turnpikes, canals, and railways, and from networks of credit and finance. Regions
were internally integrated, creating highly distinctive patterns of growth around
major regional capitals which brought together manufacturers from the surrounding towns with merchants and financiers.

The industrial and urban geography of Britain underwent a major change
between 1700 and 1850. In the late seventeenth century, industry and towns were
concentrated along the line from Norwich to London and Bristol, the three

largest towns in the country. The major centres of textile production were in East Anglia, the West Country, and the southern counties, with significant production of iron in the Weald of Kent and Sussex. By 1800, the regional geography had changed. London remained the largest city and industrial centre in Britain, and the massive naval dockyards at Portsmouth and Deptford were amongst the largest industrial enterprises in Britain, but generally southern Britain deindustrialized during the eighteenth century. The centre of gravity of towns and industry shifted to the west Midlands, the West Riding of Yorkshire, Lancashire, south Wales, the north-east of England, and the Clyde. Clearly, it is necessary not only to account for growth but also to explain decline and deindustrialization which aborted the process of industrial development in the south.

The location of industry was in part shaped by the changing geography of agrarian regions, with the demise of self-sufficiency in grain. Regions which specialized in high-productivity, labour-intensive arable crops were likely to deindustrialize, and the production of wool textiles virtually disappeared during the eighteenth century in Essex and Suffolk, and in a wide swathe of the south across Kent, Surrey, Berkshire, and Hampshire; it was in relative decline in Norfolk. These areas became more agricultural and less industrial, and the trades which survived were on a relatively small scale, utilizing cheap female labour in occupations such as straw-plaiting and lace. Deindustrialization and increased dependence on seasonal wage labour in the fields meant that the south ceased to be an area of high wages, and was blighted by underemployment and poverty throughout the nineteenth century. In other areas, the abandonment of labour-intensive cereal crops resulted in surplus labour, and industrial growth tended to concentrate in areas which were formerly arable and newly pastoral such as in the West Country, and areas of marginal soils such as the Pennines.

The changing matrix of agrarian regions affected the location of rural industry, but did not determine success or failure, which also reflected the internal dynamic of the industrial economy. Existing industrial regions had more or less ability to adapt to changing circumstances. The cloth industry, for example, was in absolute decline around Exeter and in relative decline in the Cotswolds by the end of the eighteenth century, whereas the West Riding of Yorkshire was increasingly dominant. The explanation is largely that the organization of industry could produce inflexibilities, by creating barriers to the introduction of machinery or making production less sensitive to changing markets. Consider-able attention will need to be paid not only to the location of industry in response to changes in the agrarian economy, but also to the organization of rural industry and its ability to change and adapt in the face of economic change.

The shifting location of industry also reflected the availability of wood for fuel, minerals, and, increasingly, supplies of coal. The iron industry of the Weald of Kent and Sussex virtually disappeared in the early eighteenth century, as a result of pressure on supplies of charcoal and iron ore. It was overtaken by the development of a major industrial district strung along the Severn and its tributaries, from the Forest of Dean to Shropshire: iron forges, furnaces, slitting mills, and smithies clustered in centres such as Coalbrookdale. By the early nineteenth century, the Severn was in turn becoming an industrial backwater as the major centre of the iron industry moved to south Wales and Scotland, with their abundant supplies of cheap coal. Another major centre of industry in 1700 was Cornwall, where deep mines for tin and copper were the first to use steam power. By the late eighteenth century, it was being challenged by copper ore from Anglesey and, when this threat disappeared, by imports from South America, Australia, and Spain. In the seventeenth and eighteenth centuries, lead and copper were mined and smelted in the Peak District of Derbyshire and Staffordshire, and Richard Arkwright and his imitators were attracted to the area in the 1770s by the availability of water power for large spinning mills. But the main centre of the cotton industry soon shifted to Lancashire when steam power freed the industry from reliance on water, and the lead and copper industry encountered problems of exhaustion and drainage by the early nineteenth century. Increasingly, the mineral workings of Cornwall and the Pennines could compete only at times of high prices, and the workers combined industrial and rural labour or emigrated. Deindustrialization was a significant feature of large parts of Britain in the eighteenth and early nineteenth centuries, whose visible signs are barely perceptible workings on the hills of the Peak District or Yorkshire Dales and the attractive villages of the miners; and the lavish churches and houses built in the heyday of prosperity by clothiers in the Cotswolds and East Anglia. Now, these areas present an idyllic myth of the English countryside; in the eighteenth and early nineteenth centuries, they were experiencing decay and depression.

Expanding industrial regions emerged, in some cases, from pre-existing rural outwork, as in the cotton industry of Lancashire or wool textiles in the West Riding. Domestic production or 'protoindustrialization', it has been argued by some historians, passed through stages. Independent artisans who produced goods for their own profit were reduced to wage labourers dependent on 'putting out' merchants who supplied raw materials. Putting out in turn encountered difficulties by the later eighteenth century, they argue, for expansion entailed a spread of production over an ever-widening area, which ran into problems of controlling labour and maintaining quality. The solution, so it is argued, was to switch to centralized factory production for which 'protoindustrialization' had created a dependent work-force and accumulated capital.

Can this interpretation be accepted, or were artisan production and putting ou
alternatives which produced different routes to factory production, rather than
successive stages? How far was the construction of factories a response to
technological change rather than a means of resolving the tensions of rura
outwork and imposing labour discipline? To what extent did factories draw upor
the work-force and capital created by outwork, or turn to alternative sources?

Of course, many industrial areas were based upon the availability of cheap
mineral fuel rather than the existence of rural outwork. Initially, the use of coa
was limited to areas with easy access to water, and above all the north-east o
England where coal was mined along the river Tyne and shipped down the coas
to London. The Tyne, and subsequently the Wear and Tees, emerged as major
centres of fuel-intensive industries such as salt, glass, and chemicals; and the coa
trade stimulated wooden shipbuilding and the construction of steam engine
which formed the basis of heavy engineering and the construction of iror
steamships in the nineteenth century. In the course of the eighteenth century
coal-based industrialization spread to the Mersey with the production of glass
and chemicals in St Helens and Warrington; to the area around Swansea, where
copper and tin could be brought by sea from Cornwall and Devon for smelting
with large quantities of coal; and in Scotland, where salt, chemicals, and iror
were produced, and shipbuilding and engineering developed on the Clyde
Coal-based industrialization usually required more fixed capital than industries
based on outwork, which could impose greater problems of accumulation. Ir
some cases, fuel-based industries were able to tap internal sources of capital as ir
the north-east of England, or to draw funds from local merchants in Liverpool or
Edinburgh and Glasgow. In other cases, however, there was no prior experience
of industry, and enterprise and capital were brought from outside. In south
Wales, the growth of the iron industry on the northern outcrop of the coalfield
relied largely upon capital from London and Bristol, and much of the profit was
removed rather than reinvested. The economy was unable to move from the
production of semi-finished goods such as bar iron and tin-plate to shipbuilding
and heavy engineering as in the north-east of England and the Clyde, and when
the iron industry encountered competition around 1850, south Wales turned
increasingly to the export of coal rather than to manufacturing.

The complexities of industrialization are obscured by an over-reliance
on national aggregates rather than regional economies. The experience of
eighteenth- and early nineteenth-century Britain included a wide range
of patterns: deindustrialization and immiseration in southern England, where
domestic outwork faltered and declined; the halting development of factories in
the West Country, which created tension and conflict; a swifter and more
successful emergence of factory production in Lancashire and the West Riding of

Yorkshire; the erosion of artisan production and a slide into sweat-shops in some London trades; and the emergence of coal-based industries in the north-east, south Wales, the Mersey, and the Clyde. This matrix of industrialization affected the labour market and the gender division of work; influenced patterns of income distribution; shaped demographic behaviour; created a greater or lesser susceptibility to cyclical or seasonal depression; and determined the relations between merchants, financiers, and producers according to the needs for fixed capital or credit.

NOTES

1. N. F. R. Crafts, *British Economic Growth during the Industrial Revolution* (Oxford, 1985); J. G. Williamson, 'Debating the British Industrial Revolution', *Explorations in Economic History*, 24 (1987).

2. Quoted in J. Hoppit, 'Counting the Industrial Revolution', *Economic History Review*, 2nd ser. 43 (1990), 173.

3. W.-G. Hoffman, *British Industry, 1700–1950* (1955); P. Deane and W. A. Cole, *British Economic Growth, 1688–1959* (Cambridge, 1969); Crafts, *British Economic Growth* and 'British Economic Growth, 1700–1831: A Review of the Evidence', *Economic History Review*, 36 (1983); C. K. Harley, 'British Industrialisation before 1841: Evidence of Slower Growth during the Industrial Revolution', *Journal of Economic History*, 42 (1982).

4. N. F. R. Crafts, S. J. Leybourne, and T. C. Mills, 'Trends and Cycles in British Industrial Production', *Journal of the Royal Statistical Society*, ser. A 152 (1989).

5. Crafts, *British Economic Growth*, 8, 69, 87.

6. C. H. Lee, *The British Economy since 1700* (Cambridge, 1986), 106.

7. J. C. D. Clark, *English Society, 1688–1832* (Cambridge, 1985), 4.

8. Quoted in D. Lieberman, *The Province of Legislation Determined: Legal Theory in Eighteenth-Century Britain* (Cambridge, 1989), 47, 48.

9. Hoppit, 'Counting', 179.

10. Crafts, 'British Economic Growth', 181; and *Economic Growth*, 20.

11. R. V. Jackson, 'Rates of Industrial Growth during the Industrial Revolution', *Economic History Review*, 2nd ser. 45 (1992), 9, 12.

12. Ibid. 21.

13. Quoted in Hoppit, 'Counting', 173.

14. For critiques, see C. Sabel and J. Zeitlin, 'Historical Alternatives in Mass Production', *Past and Present*, 108 (1985); M. Berg and P. Hudson, 'Rehabilitating the Industrial Revolution', *Economic History Review*, 2nd ser. 45 (1992).

15. Quoted in M. Berg, *The Age of Manufactures* (Oxford, 1985), 51–2.

16. E. A. Wrigley, *Continuity, Chance and Change* (Cambridge, 1988), 84–6.

17. Ibid. 13.

18. E. A. Wrigley, *People, Cities and Wealth* (Oxford, 1987), 177–8.

19. G. Dodd, *Days at the Factories; on the Manufacturing Industry of Great Britain Described* (1843), 158.

20. P. Borsay, *The English Urban Renaissance: Culture and Society in the Provincial Town, 1660–1770* (Oxford, 1989).

21. A. Everitt, 'Country, County and Town: Patterns of Regional Evolution in England', *Transactions of the Royal Historical Society*, 5th ser. 29 (1979), 94.

22. Quoted in J. Langton, 'The Industrial Revolution and the Regional Geography of England', *Transactions of the Institute of British Geographers*, NS 9 (1984), 156–7.

FURTHER READING

Ashton, T. S., *The Industrial Revolution, 1760–1830* (1948).

Behagg, C., *Politics and Production in the Early Nineteenth Century* (1990).

Berg, M., *The Age of Manufactures: Industry, Innovation and Work in Britain, 1700–1820* (Oxford, 1985).

—— 'Women's Work, Mechanisation and the Early Phases of Industrialisation in England', in P. Joyce (ed.), *The Historical Meanings of Work* (Cambridge, 1987).

—— 'Revisions and Revolutions: Technology and Productivity Change in Manufacture in Eighteenth-Century England', in J. A. Davis and P. Mathias (eds.), *Innovation and Technology in Europe from the Eighteenth Century to the Present Day* (Oxford, 1991).

—— 'Commerce and Creativity in Eighteenth-Century Birmingham', in M. Berg (ed.), *Markets and Manufacture in Early Industrial Europe* (1991).

—— and Hudson, P., 'Rehabilitating the Industrial Revolution', *Economic History Review*, 2nd ser. 45 (1992).

Borsay, P., *The English Urban Renaissance: Culture and Society in the Provincial Town, 1660–1770* (Oxford, 1989).

Clark, J. C. D., *English Society, 1688–1832: Ideology, Social Structure and Political Practice during the Ancien Regime* (Cambridge, 1985).

Cole, W. A., 'The Measurement of Industrial Growth', *Economic History Review*, 2nd ser. 11 (1958–9).

Corfield, P. J., *The Impact of English Towns, 1700–1800* (Oxford, 1982).

Crafts, N. R. F., *British Economic Growth during the Industrial Revolution* (Oxford, 1985).

—— 'British Economic Growth 1700–1831: A Review of the Evidence', *Economic History Review*, 2nd ser. 36 (1983).

—— and Harley, C. K., 'Output Growth and the British Industrial Revolution: A Restatement of the Crafts–Harley View', *Economic History Review*, 2nd ser. 45 (1992).

—— Leybourne, S. J., and Mills, T. C., 'Trends and Cycles in British Industrial Production', *Journal of the Royal Statistical Society*, ser. A 152 (1989).

Deane, P., and Cole, W. A., *British Economic Growth, 1688–1959* (Cambridge, 1962).

De Vries, J., *European Urbanization, 1500–1800* (Cambridge, Mass., 1984).

Everitt, A., 'Country, County and Town: Patterns of Regional Evolution in England', *Transactions of the Royal Historical Society*, 5th ser. 29 (1979).

Harley, C. K., 'British Industrialisation before 1841: Evidence of Slower Growth during the Industrial Revolution', *Journal of Economic History*, 42 (1982).

Hoffmann, W.-G., *British Industry, 1700–1950* (Oxford, 1955).

Hoppit, J., 'Counting the Industrial Revolution', *Economic History Review*, 2nd ser. 43 (1990).

Hudson, P., *The Industrial Revolution* (1992).

——(ed.), *Regions and Industries: A Perspective on the Industrial Revolution in Britain* (Cambridge, 1989).

Jackson, R. V., 'Rates of Industrial Growth during the Industrial Revolution', *Economic History Review*, 2nd ser. 45 (1992).

Langton, J., 'The Industrial Revolution and the Regional Geography of England', *Transactions of the Institute of British Geographers*, NS 9 (1984).

Lee, C. H., *The British Economy since 1700: A Macroeconomic Perspective* (Cambridge, 1986).

Lieberman, D., *The Province of Legislation Determined: Legal Theory in Eighteenth-Century Britain* (Cambridge, 1989).

Mokyr, J., 'Has the Industrial Revolution been Crowded out? Some Reflections on Crafts and Williamson', *Explorations in Economic History*, 24 (1987).

Rostow, W. W., *The Stages of Economic Growth: A Non-Communist Manifesto* (Cambridge, 1960).

Sabel, C., and Zeitlin, J., 'Historical Alternatives to Mass Production: Politics, Markets and Technology in Nineteenth-Century Industrialisation', *Past and Present*, 108 (1985).

Williamson, J. G., 'Debating the British Industrial Revolution', *Explorations in Economic History*, 24 (1987).

Wrigley, E. A., *Continuity, Chance and Change: The Character of the Industrial Revolution in England* (Cambridge, 1988).

——*People, Cities and Wealth: The Transformation of Traditional Society* (Oxford, 1987).

···

CHAPTER 6

The Domestic System of Manufactures

Daniel Defoe, in *A Tour through the Whole Island of Great Britain* (1724–6), described his journey across the Pennines to Halifax. He was surprised to find that the hills, despite their steepness, were 'spread with houses, and that very thick; for the land being divided into small enclosures, that is to say, from two acres to six or seven acres each, seldom more; every three or four pieces of land had a house belonging to it.' The explanation was not far to seek: outside most houses was a tenter on which was stretched a piece of cloth. The land alone, Defoe estimated, could support only a fifth of the population. When he visited a master manufacturer, Defoe found 'a house full of lusty fellows, some at the dye-vat, some dressing the cloths, some in the loom, some one thing, some another, all hard at work'. Scattered amongst the houses of the master manufacturers, Defoe found 'an infinite number of cottages or small dwellings, in which dwell the workmen which are employed, the women and children of whom are always busy carding, spinning, etc so that no hands being unemployed, all can gain their bread, even from the youngest to the ancient; hardly any thing above four years old, but its hands are sufficient to itself.'

In this landscape of industrious domestic producers, agriculture was very much an ancillary activity:

as every clothier must keep a horse, perhaps two, to fetch and carry for the use of his manufacture, (viz) to fetch home his wool and his provisions from the market, to carry his yarn to the spinners, his manufacture to the fulling mill, and, when finished, to the markets to be sold, and the like; so every manufacturer generally keeps a cow or two, or more, for his family, and this employs the two, or three, or four pieces of enclosed land about his house, for they scarce sow corn enough for their cocks and hens.

The area could not feed itself, so that 'they must then necessarily have their provisions from other parts of the country'. Grain came from Lincoln, Nottingham, and the East Riding; cattle and horses from the North Riding; butter from the East and North Riding; cheese from Cheshire and Warwickshire; and sheep and mutton from the adjacent counties on every side. 'Thus this one trading, manufacturing part of the country', commented Defoe, 'supports all the countries round it.'[1] There was a symbiosis between the areas which specialized in domestic industry and in commercial agriculture.

The industrial goods produced by the cottage industry of the Pennines were not simply for the use of the immediate area, for they had a wide national and international market. Defoe visited Leeds and witnessed the sale of cloth at the twice weekly market. Tables were set up in the street, and the clothiers displayed their goods to merchants and factors who bought cloth to the value of £20,000 in the space of about an hour. 'By this quick return the clothiers are constantly supplied with money, their workmen are duly paid, and a prodigious sum circulates through the county every week.'[2] Merchant capital therefore linked the areas producing commodities to wider markets. The buyers in Leeds fell into three categories. First, there were the travelling merchants who bought cloth to take to fairs and market towns around the country, supplying shops and providing large amounts of credit. Secondly, there were the buyers who sent cloth to London in order to meet the demands of the metropolis and to supply export markets. These buyers either received a commission from London merchants to meet their orders or themselves paid a commission to warehousemen in London to sell the cloth. The third group of buyers 'are truly merchants, that is to say, such as receive commissions from abroad to buy cloth for the merchants chiefly in Hamburg, and in Holland, and from several other parts: and these are not only many in number, but some of them are very considerable in their dealings, and correspond as far as Nuremberg, Frankfurt, Leipzig, and even to Vienna and Augsburg, in the farthest provinces of Germany.'[3]

Defoe provided a graphic account of the 'domestic system of manufactures' or—to use a more recent and contentious term—'protoindustrialization', which has been defined as 'the development of rural regions in which a large part of the population lived entirely or to a considerable extent from industrial mass production and inter-regional and international markets'.[4] The domestic system of manufactures is a simple descriptive phrase; 'protoindustrialization' implies a particular model of development which, despite its flaws, does at least locate some important areas of debate. Both terms apply to a number of important trades which could be carried on within a domestic setting. The spinning of yarn and the weaving of cloth on hand-powered spinning-wheels and looms was found in many parts of the country, using wool, flax, and cotton. The production of hosiery was concentrated in the east Midlands, using knitting frames. The forging of small metal goods by nailors, cutlers, and implement-makers was a major trade in the Black Country and around Sheffield. Defoe's account raises a number of the central questions about this domestic production or protoindustrialization.

One issue is the apparently simple matter of location: why did some areas become dominated by rural industry and others by commercialized agriculture? The protoindustrial model suggests that urban merchants were fleeing from the monopolies of towns and their guild restrictions, which created inelasticities of production. They sought rural areas with surplus, cheap population which, unlike the towns, included women and children. Rural industry became feasible where feudal ties were weakened, so that lords did not appropriate the surplus product of the peasants. But why did some areas of abundant, cheap labour develop as industrial centres, while others failed to attract industry or even *de*industrialized? According to the protoindustrialization model, industry was most likely to settle in areas with low agricultural productivity, smallholdings, dispersed settlement, and partible inheritance, particularly in the mountains. In lowland, arable areas, the argument runs, economic and social structures were more inflexible: nuclear villages and regulated common fields meant that lords and the village community had more power in restricting settlement and population growth, so that cheap labour was not available. The agrarian basis of protoindustrialization, on this view, was a small, subsistence farm, with food supplied by adjacent areas of commercialized agriculture which generated demand for labour and prevented the growth of rural industry. Clearly, this model must be tested.

A second question relates to the organization of domestic production. Defoe distinguished between the master manufacturers and the cottages 'in which dwell the workmen who are employed', which implies that many of the inhabitants of the hills around Halifax were not independent artisans producing goods on their own account so much as dependent wage labourers who were working, with the assistance of their families, for larger clothiers. Such a system may be described as 'putting out': a merchant or a master manufacturer supplied raw materials for spinning and weaving; the yarn or cloth was returned to the 'putter out' for sale; and the worker received payment according to the amount produced. At no point did the worker own the materials, or engage in the commodity market: he was simply selling his labour and that of his family. The protoindustrialization model claims that domestic industry passed from an initial stage of independent artisan production to 'putting out', as a result of internal tensions. In artisan production, the pace of work and level of output was determined by family needs of the petty producer, who might—so the proto-industrial model argues—slow down as real income per unit of output increased, in order 'to satisfy the traditional socio-culturally determined needs of familial subsistence'.[5] The work effort fell precisely at the point where production should increase to meet demand. More control was possible, so it is argued, by shifting to putting out, which was also encouraged by the slide of artisans into debt as a result of subdivision of holdings and population growth. A merchant supplied raw materials and equipment, and the petty producers declined into piece-workers who could only work when commissioned. He could control the pace of work and output by adjusting the piece-rate and the flow of raw materials, and by supplying materials to a greater or lesser number of producers: in a period of normal trade, he could keep a large number of workers slightly underemployed, who could then be drawn upon in a boom. Putting out offered the advantage of increasing the merchant's profit margin, for he could take more of the surplus of the producer, who was now dependent; and it was possible to divide tasks between different specialists rather than to rely upon the family unit as in artisan production. Such is the theory, which assumes there were two successive stages; is this correct, or were the two types of organization alternative responses to local circumstances which could exist alongside each other?

Thirdly, there is the complex issue of the relationship between domestic production and the rise of the factory, for Halifax and Leeds became factory towns in the nineteenth century. How far did the domestic system of industrial production provide the basis for this later development of centralized production? The protoindustrialization model claims that the domestic system of manufacture was the precursor of full-fledged factory production, which formed a third stage of development after artisan production and putting out. Output in putting out was increased by spatial expansion over wider and wider areas which led, so the model assumes, to increasing difficulties of control over production. Materials were liable to be pilfered; it became difficult to control quality; the cost of transport rose; and the turnover of capital declined as a result of a larger interval between handing out materials and receiving goods from the scattered producers. These problems were solved, it is claimed, by centralization in factories. Putting out allowed, it is argued, a higher profit rate which led to accumulation of capital in the hands of large merchant-manufacturers, which was needed for the construction of factories. It also created a dependent, waged work-force by stimulating population growth and training skilled handcraft workers. How far can this model explain the coming of the factory?

The Location of Domestic Industry

Defoe's description of the cloth industry around Halifax highlighted a number of factors which could explain the location of industry in the area. Halifax was in the Pennine uplands, where agricultural productivity was low and the land was not capable of supporting a large population. Nevertheless, the presence of extensive

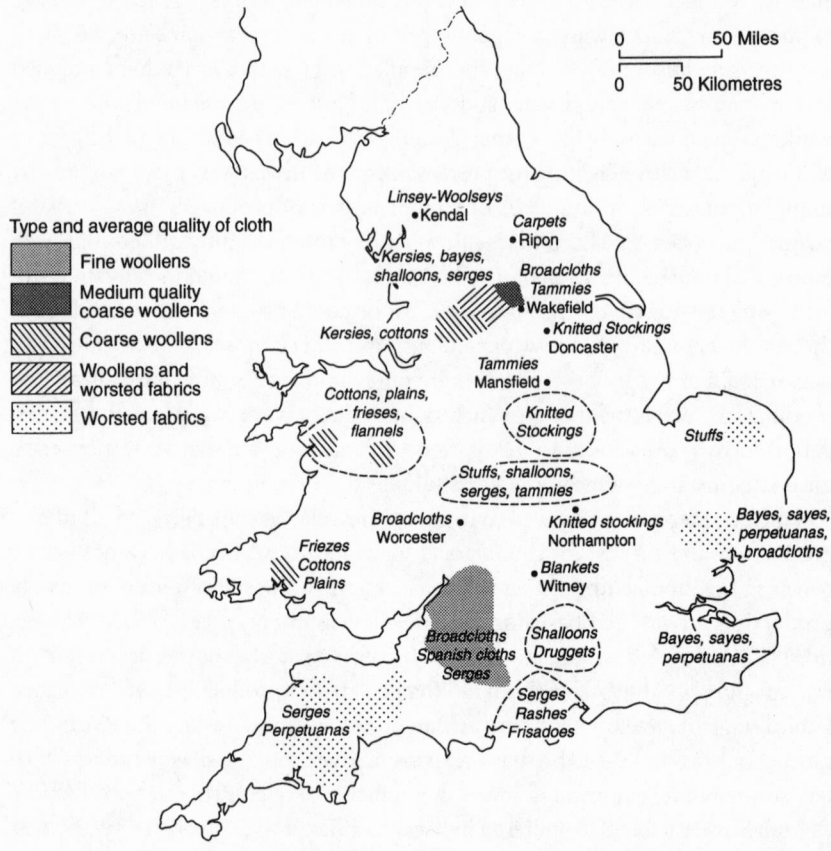

FIG. 6.1. Distribution of textile specializations, England and Wales, c.1700

Source: P. D. Glennie, 'Industry and Towns, 1500–1730', in R. A. Dodghson and R. A. Butlin (eds.), *An Historical Geography of England and Wales* (2nd edn. 1990), 206.

grazing lands on the hills and the absence of community controls meant that there were few limits on settlement. The result was serious pressure on the land, which obliged families to find some supplementary income. How far does Defoe's explanation fit the location of domestic industry in other parts of Britain? Upland areas were certainly important locations of domestic industry, such as wool and cotton on the Pennines of Yorkshire and Lancashire, or wool in the Lake District around Kendal (see Fig. 6.1). However, a simple topographical explanation does not work in all cases, and the exceptions are just as striking. The framework knitting industry of Nottinghamshire and Leicestershire, the metal trades of the Black Country, the wool textile industries of East Anglia and southern England, and the Scottish linen industry were all located in *lowland* districts.

Perhaps more important than topography was the type of agriculture. The area around Halifax had poor soil and was devoted to pastoral farming, which meant that the demand for labour was less intense and more constant than in arable agriculture, allowing farmers to devote part of their time to alternative employment. Such an explanation could account for the fact that the textile industry in Wiltshire and Gloucestershire was located in the stock-rearing and dairying districts rather than in the area devoted to sheep and corn. Similarly, the metalworkers in the Sheffield region were located on less fertile soils on the edge of the Pennines, rather than on better soils further east. Nevertheless, farming systems still do not provide a completely satisfactory answer, for some pastoral and dairying districts failed to develop domestic industry. More than half the Wiltshire dairying region, for example, lacked industry. There were also cases where industry was found in areas of arable agriculture, such as around Leeds, where farms were larger than near Halifax and devoted part of their land to growing crops. Arguments which rely upon geographical determinism, whether of topography or farming systems, are not entirely satisfactory.

The social structure and pattern of power in rural communities could modify the impact of topography and the ecological system, for rural industry was more likely to develop where landlord or communal control over the population was relatively weak. Defoe commented that land in the hills around Halifax was enclosed and freehold, with a dispersed pattern of settlement and abundant common grazing on the hills, which provided a resource for small freeholders and allowed squatters to settle in the area. There was therefore an absence of community controls over farming and settlement, which were more likely to be found in areas of arable farming based on common fields and nucleated villages. Neither was there a dominant landholder who attempted to maintain a hold over the population through manorial controls. The small freeholders of the Pennines adopted a system of partible inheritance, and subdivision of farms meant that the population outran the ability of agriculture to support a family. Similarly, the framework knitting village of Shepshed in Leicestershire was an unregulated freehold village on the edge of Charnwood Forest, which provided resources for smallholders and encouraged the settlement of cottagers; the census of 1831 found 553 workers in manufacturing.[6] Much the same factors explain the existence of textiles in the Weald of Kent: its infertile clay soils and small farms were largely devoted to pastoralism; early enclosure removed the need for communal supervision; manorial control was difficult, for manors were usually divided and spread over several parishes so that an individual lord could not impose his will upon the parish; and freehold tenure meant that there were no manorial controls over the division of holdings. Such factors could lead to marked divergence between areas with apparently similar ecological systems. Although the Chilterns and New Forest both had poor soils and abundant timber, only the Chilterns developed diverse trades of wood-turning, paper-making, lace-making, and plaiting. The most likely explanation is that the crown was able to impose restrictions on settlement in the New Forest, preventing the growth of cottagers; in the same way, large landowners in Sherwood Forest were able to prevent the area following the route of Charnwood Forest. Similarly, the distinctive legal system and social structure of Scotland explains why the linen industry was predominantly located in the arable Lowlands rather than pastoral uplands. It was much more difficult for smallholdings to be taken from the 'commonty' in the Scottish uplands than from the waste in England, in areas such as Halifax. In the Scottish Lowlands, tenants devoted their time to agriculture and many of the cottars who sublet smallholdings could spend part of their time spinning and weaving in the slack season of the farming year. The production of textiles in the arable Lowlands was threatened from the late eighteenth century when cottars were replaced by waged landless labourers and migrant workers, forcing the cottar-weavers either to become agricultural labourers or to migrate to the towns. The influences of ecology and topography were always mediated by tenure and the social system.

The stress on the internal structure of farming regions begs a crucial question: was the development of domestic industry in any region the result of internal initiatives or of external forces? The protoindustrial model assumes that the process was controlled by *external* merchant capital: urban merchants were fleeing from towns where production was being stifled by guild regulations which made the supply of goods unresponsive to demand, in order to tap pools of cheap rural labour. The distribution of rural industry, on such a view, reflected the locational choices of urban merchants within the matrix of agrarian society. Although there were cases where industry was controlled by urban merchants, the location of protoindustry often arose from *internal* initiatives. Capital could come from smallholders who were looking for new ways of making money, such as Jenings Berrington of Hathern in Leicestershire, who died in 1740: he had a yardland in the open fields, four cow pastures, and a stocking frame, and he was able to raise capital by mortgaging his land. The arrival of protoindustry did not depend merely upon the existence of a mass of impoverished labour and the arrival of urban merchants, so much as on a modicum of wealth and a group of enterprising individuals. Towns were, in any case, less inimical to industry than the protoindustrial model suggests. The role of towns, on such an account, was predominantly financial and commercial, providing merchant capital to organize the rural system and to sell the goods, with any industrial role limited to trades associated with marketing, such as finishing and dyeing cloth. The reality was different from this model of rural protoindustrialization, for domestic industry was urban as well as rural, and the growth of industry in the countryside during the eighteenth century was not necessarily at the expense of the towns.

The right to produce a commodity or to provide a service was, at least in theory, restricted to members of the guild who had served an apprenticeship with a master and obtained their 'freedom'. The guilds were responsible for regulating standards, practices, and prices in order to prevent fraud and to maintain the reputation of the town's goods; the Weavers' Company of Norwich, for example, had the power to inspect and seal all worsted cloth from the city and its hinterland. The guilds usually provided feasts and ceremonies which were an important part of civic life; they ran almshouses and schools; and they were closely connected with corporations which governed the town. The result, it was claimed at York in 1736, was conservatism and decay:

Our magistrates have been too tenacious of their privileges, and have for many years last past, by virtue of their charters, as it were locked themselves up from the world, and wholly prevented any foreigner [i.e. outsider] from settling any manufacture amongst them; unless under such restrictions as they are unlikely to accept of. The paying a large sum of money for their freedoms, with the troublesome and chargeable offices they must often undertake, would deter any person of an enterprising genius in regard of manufacture, for coming to reside at York.[7]

Supporters of a liberal, free market economy argued that the increase in industrial production during the eighteenth century was concentrated in the countryside or in towns such as Birmingham, Halifax, or Oldham which did not have charters and guild controls. 'A town without a charter is a town without a shackle', commented an early historian of Birmingham,[8] for there were no guilds to hinder development by apprenticeship regulations, and Dissenters were not barred from the town.

The correlation was not as clear as they asserted, for many expanding towns had charters and guilds, such as Liverpoool, Newcastle upon Tyne, Leeds, Hull, and Preston. The causation could be reversed: the pattern of growth affected the nature of regulations, rather than the existence of regulations limiting the prospects of growth. Industry was not fleeing from the stranglehold of guilds but was shifting its location for other reasons, from the south to new industrial districts in the Midlands and north, as a result of changes in the regional division of labour and in response to the location of coal. There were simply fewer guilds and chartered towns in the north than the south because of the distribution of population in the Middle Ages. The explanation of the decay of trade and industry at York was the shift in the location of the cloth industry to the West

Riding, and the emergence of Leeds and Hull as major trading centres. Stagnation was not caused by the survival of guilds in York, and merchants and
manufacturers were indeed offered complete freedom from controls in 1713 and
again in the 1740s. They were not tempted, and economic stagnation permitted
the persistence of guilds as craftsmen and tradesmen clung to their old forms of
organization in a desperate attempt to preserve their position. They had little
success, and a committee which was appointed to punish defaulters admitted
defeat in 1775: 'as it always has been, so it will ever continue impossible to find
out, or if found to compel, every individual who may be liable, to purchase his or
her freedom, from the various causes of poverty, contrivance, secretion, conniv-
ance and deceit.'[9] Leeds and Hull themselves had charters and guilds, which
were swamped by expansion: restrictions were easily circumvented where the
town and its trade were buoyant. In Norwich, for example, the sealing of cloth
was evaded by merchants in the later seventeenth century, and the Weavers'
Company lost control in 1705.

In London, the expansion of production in the suburbs beyond the limits of
the City undermined guild regulations by the early eighteenth century; the best
the guilds could achieve was a compromise in 1750 which preserved the principle
of regulation in return for a controlled licensing of non-freemen. Although the
guilds or livery companies of the City of London attempted to maintain their
monopoly over trades, and the whole system theoretically survived until 1856,
their powers had in practice long ceased to be effective. The authority of the
guilds was weakened by the sixteenth century as London expanded beyond the
City limits, most significantly into suburbs to the east such as Spitalfields, Bethnal
Green, and Whitechapel. The companies had two responses. They could try to
prevent the development of suburban industry, which proved ineffective; the
suburbs to the east of the City were amongst the major industrial areas of the
country, producing a wide range of consumer goods such as silk, clothing, and
furniture, as well as processing imports, servicing the port, and building ships.
The alternative was to relax the terms of freedom, sacrificing the realities of
control for the illusion of influence. In the first half of the eighteenth century,
both the City Corporation and the companies retreated from the enforcement of
controls, and in 1750 a system of licensing non-freemen was substituted. Guilds
took on a new guise as social clubs or property-owning trusts. The magnificent
hall of, say, the Drapers' Company in the City of London was the venue for lavish
dinners for members drawn from the ranks of City merchants and businessmen,
and their properties were managed to support schools and other charities.

The emphasis upon the rural origins of industry leaves London out of the
picture, the largest single industrial district in Britain. The metropolis was a
major protoindustrial town: it had textile trades as in the Pennines, framework

TABLE 6.1. *English provincial towns with a population in excess of 20,000, 1750 and 1801*

Specialism	1750			1801		
	Number of Towns	Population	%	Number of Towns	Population	%
Manufacturing	2	60,000	37.3	7	348,462	49.6
Dockyard	—	—	—	2	76,360	10.9
Port	3	101,000	62.7	5	242,661	34.5
Spa/resort	—	—	—	1	34,990	5.0
Total	5	161,000	100.0	15	702,473	100.0

Source: P. J. Corfield, *The Impact of English Towns, 1700–1800* (Oxford, 1982), 25.

knitting and shoemaking as in the east Midlands, and metal trades as in Birmingham and the Black Country. Framework knitting, silk-weaving and shoemaking were, it is true, in relative decline as production shifted to the provinces, and London merchant capital did play a role in their relocation. But other sectors survived and flourished, such as the production of watches in Clerkenwell and the adjoining parish of St Luke's, which employed about 8,000 at the end of the eighteenth century. Parts were produced by a process of minute subdivision under the control of a maker who assembled the watch. The trade combined elements of putting out and artisan production, with some workmen employed by watchmakers, and others making parts on their own account which they offered for sale. London also continued to produce high-value scientific instruments, specialized machinery, a wide range of furnishings and furniture, coaches and clothing.

London was not alone as a centre for urban domestic industry. Norwich, the second largest city in England in 1700, had a large industrial sector which produced worsted cloth of high quality for the national market. Weavers were concentrated in the city and neighbouring villages; they were supplied with yarn by spinners who were more widely spread in the surrounding countryside, drawn from the wives and daughters of agricultural labourers. Rural and urban industry were as often complementary as opposed. In the east Midlands knitting industry, for example, 19.4 per cent of 'frames' in 1727 were located in Nottingham and Leicester. Similarly, in the cutlery and edge-tool trades of south Yorkshire and north Derbyshire, 37.6 per cent of smithies in 1672 were based in Sheffield, and this proportion increased in the eighteenth century, with urban producers concentrating on high-class cutlery and rural producers on cheap knives or specialized items such as scythes.[10] Much the same pattern applied in the Black Country, where the manufacture of specialized goods such as metal parts for saddles was concentrated in Walsall, and lower-value goods such as nails in the countryside. Above all, Birmingham was the major producer of a wide range of metal goods and an integral part of the protoindustrialization of the west Midlands. Not only did it provide markets and commercial expertise for rural crafts, but it was also a major centre of production in its own right, specializing in the manufacture of jewellery, guns, and swords, and the so-called 'toy' trades of buckles, buttons, watch-chains, tapestry hooks, and the like. The organization of many urban trades was similar to the rural domestic system, and the protoindustrial model exaggerates the rural origins of industry in opposition to the towns.

Indeed, manufacturing towns were growing rapidly in eighteenth-century Britain, and they came to rival ports as the largest provincial towns in the eighteenth century (see Table 6.1). Whether new or old, towns had a number of advantages which gave them a continuing vitality and allowed them to compete with cheap rural labour. Access to markets, knowledge of changes in fashion, availability of mercantile and legal services, a wide range of skilled craftsmen, could all give an edge to urban production. Much depended upon the type of commodity, for urban production made most sense where rapid changes in style were important, where a high level of skill was demanded, or where accessibility to the consumer was vital. The production of nails could take place at scattered forges in the Black Country, for they were a crude product with a low value added which required relatively little skill, and were devoid of any changes in fashion. The manufacture of guns made more sense in Birmingham, for they were more sophisticated, with a high value added, requiring a considerable degree of skill and supervision, and were much more closely attuned to the requirements of a differentiated market. The weaving of woollen cloth was feasible in the Pennines around Halifax; the tailoring of a coat was undertaken in London. Pressure to disperse production into the countryside was countered by forces for concentration, for at some point high costs of transport and supervision over a wide area made urban production attractive, even before the rise of the factory. Protoindustrialization was an urban as well as rural phenomenon.

The release of a large number of workers from direct employment on the land could induce a switch into domestic industry, especially in areas of poor soil, pastoralism, and weak community or landlord controls. Equally, the surplus population could migrate, both from pastoral areas which failed to develop industrial by-employment and, to a greater extent, from arable parishes with strict controls over settlement. These migrants moved both to other rural areas where it was possible for them to settle and for industry to develop, and to towns which were experiencing industrial growth. In both cases, the labour released from agriculture was absorbed into production, which led to economic growth. There was, however, a third possible outcome: rural underemployment by maintaining unproductive labour in the countryside which was neither absorbed into protoindustry within the area nor transferred to expanding industrial districts elsewhere. Surplus labour did not necessarily lead to the growth of manufacturing, and there were cases, such as spinning in the country around Norwich, or the cloth industry of Essex, Suffolk, and southern England, where existing rural industry shrank in the eighteenth century. Indeed, the areas which were most likely to shed labour from agriculture were precisely those whose social structure was least suited to industrialization. The release of labour was facilitated by the consolidation of estates and the rise of large farms; great landowners did not welcome the development of industry in their parishes; and large tenant farmers who engaged in commercial, capitalist farming wanted a work-force which was available to meet the demands of production. The erosion of contingent property rights such as the right to graze a few animals after the harvest, and a strict control over industrial by-employment, permitted the development of a more dependent, servile work-force which was paid low wages. A 'reserve' was maintained in the slack season by the poor law, so that workers were available for the harvest peak. The result was proto-*deindustrialization*, as areas such as East Anglia turned to commercialized farming and abandoned industry. Rural industry was not likely to emerge from a highly differentiated social structure of landless labourers and large tenant farmers and landowners; it was more likely to emerge where there was a 'middling' group of small traders and yeoman farmers, who had more assets and were able to draw upon communal resources. The 'proletarianization' of agrarian society by the landlords' agricultural revolution eroded the position of such groups in many parts of the country, so that the release of labour from agriculture could create a supply of cheap labour and impose restraints upon its absorption, leading to underemployment, low wages, and low productivity. The simple availability of cheap agricultural labour did not lead to its complete absorption into rural protoindustry, for it could also mean underemployed, surplus labour: agrarian reorganization could lead to immiseration rather than industrialization.

The argument of the protoindustrialization model is that the mounting demands of protoindustrial districts for food encouraged other areas to abandon industry in order to concentrate upon commercial agriculture. This could mean that the consequent demand for agricultural labour removed the elastic labour supply which was essential for domestic industry, and the result was a process of deindustrialization. Such an argument can be applied to the Black Country, where the demands of the metalworkers of the south Staffordshire plateau for food encouraged the lighter soils on the periphery to shift from a pastoral–industrial economy in the sixteenth century to mixed farming, with a higher proportion of arable crops. It would, however, be wrong to assume that specialized commercial agriculture created a 'tight' labour market which removed the cheap and flexible work-force needed by industry; on the contrary, the result could be a glut of underemployed workers. The most striking example of such a process was East Anglia. Changes in agricultural techniques between 1650 and 1750 favoured areas of light soil, and there was a shift to consolidated estates and larger farms, and a need for a more dependent, proletarianized work-force which was available during the harvest. The labour market was not 'tight' for much of the year, for a pool of underemployed labour was supported by the poor law, and held in reserve to meet the needs of large, capitalist farmers during the harvest and other crucial points of the farming year. Specialization led to deindustrialization, not so much by removing labour surpluses as by creating a pool of dependent wage labour to meet the seasonal needs of farmers. New rural industries did, it is true, sometimes emerge on the ruins of the old, such as straw-plaiting, glove-making, and lace. But these were not direct replacements for the old cloth industry, for they were smaller and relied upon cheap female labour which had been eased out of work in agriculture and had lost the ability to exploit contingent use-rights. These trades were, unlike their predecessors, complementary to the development of a highly commercialized arable agriculture. By contrast, areas such as Yorkshire, Lancashire, and the east Midlands with their poor or heavy soils were less able to switch to the new agricultural techniques, which gave them an incentive to concentrate on rural industry. There was a two-way process: protoindustry stimulated commercial agriculture, and the emergence of a more efficient agricultural system in one area forced other districts to develop industrial by-employment.

Patterns of change were not simply internal to rural domestic industry as is assumed by the protoindustrialization model. Equally important was the process of change within the agrarian economy, and the ability of any region to respond to new market conditions and exploit new techniques, which depended upon its soil, topography, and social structure. The success and failure of protoindustrial regions is, in other words, often a matter of comparative advantage between industry and agriculture: Essex and Norfolk shifted to commercialized agriculture and abandoned rural industry. The correlation is, however, by no means perfect, for the cloth industry also disappeared in the Weald of Kent, an area of poor soils where the comparative advantage clearly lay with industry, and the Cotswolds were not amongst the most productive agricultural districts. Industry also survived in areas of commercial, arable agriculture where comparative advantage might have been expected to lead to decline, such as in

Scotland where the linen industry was found in the arable Lowlands rather than the pastoral districts of the Highlands and southern uplands, which were superficially similar to the Pennines in Yorkshire and Lancashire. Comparative advantage alone is not an adequate explanation; it is also necessary to consider organizational and social structures which could frustrate the development of industry in areas where it might be expected to flourish.

The Organization of Domestic Industry: Artisans, Putters Out, and the Factory

The protoindustrialization model assumes that the internal dynamic of independent artisan production reduced workers to destitution and dependency, and resulted in the emergence of 'putting out'. It argues that domestic industry sought rural areas with an abundant supply of labour, and then produced a rapid increase in the population by removing traditional 'prudential' restraints against early marriages. There was no need to delay marriage until a holding was available, for it was possible to form a productive unit in which the husband and wife shared tasks, and the maximum output of a domestic worker was likely to come in early adulthood. There was also an incentive to have a large number of children in order to maximize the family's output. The population rose, outstripping the supply of land and reducing many families to entire dependence upon industrial employment. The result, so it is claimed, was that domestic workers were pauperized, without small plots of land which could act as a buffer against periods of depression. The producer lost autonomy, working only when commissioned by a putting out merchant-manufacturer who owned the raw materials and, possibly, the tools: there had been a decline from independent artisan to dependent wage labourer. The 'putter out', according to this model of protoindustrialization, appropriated an ever-larger part of the profits of production as the domestic producer lost bargaining power and the division of labour in the industry was extended from specialization within a single family to the entire work-force. The outcome, according to this interpretation, was social polarization. Small producers fell into debt, but merchants and some larger producers made fortunes, accumulating capital to cover the greater costs of raw materials and equipment which were required by the putting out system. Eventually, their assets and expertise allowed them to shift to factory production, for which the dependent domestic workers provided a ready-made work-force. Artisan production and putting out were, on this view, successive stages, and the first gave way to the second as a result of internal tensions. How far does this model of protoindustrialization stand up to scrutiny?

Certainly, some industries did experience a succession of stages, with immiseration and decline from artisan production into dependence on putting out. From the middle of the eighteenth century, the framework knitting industry of the east Midlands shifted from independent artisans such as Jenings Berrington towards putting out under the control of large hosiers with warehouses in Leicester, Nottingham, and other towns. In the 1840s, Ward and Co. of Belper had about 4,000 frames in Nottinghamshire, Derbyshire, and Leicestershire, as well as 2,000 seamers, 800 winders, 100 dyers and bleachers, 300 embroiderers, 200 menders and trimmers, and 100 framesmiths and needle-makers.[11] Control of a large and dispersed work-force created problems, and the merchant-manufacturers relied upon middlemen or 'bag hosiers' in the villages, themselves small producers, who collected the work of framework knitters on Friday night or Saturday morning, and handed out material on Monday afternoon. The 'bag hosiers' made it easier for the hosiers to control dispersed production, but they also introduced tension. They charged the knitter a 'frame-rent' as a commission for the supply of work, and they could increase their income by spreading work around a large, underemployed work-force, which had the further advantage of creating slack capacity to call upon in a boom. Charges were made for the collection of goods, and payment was often in goods or 'truck' which further reduced the knitter's income, who was far removed from an independent artisan producing and selling on his own account. There were, however, other industries in which artisanal production and putting out coexisted, emerging from particular agrarian structures rather than from an internal dynamic of protoindustrialization.

When Defoe visited the West Riding of Yorkshire, the woollen textile industry was undergoing a process of differentiation, and he was describing parts of two systems of production. Around Halifax, artisan production of woollen cloth was giving way to the production of worsted cloth by putting out; around Leeds, artisan production of woollen cloth continued to dominate. The Halifax worsted trade relied upon dependent domestic workers with little or no land, with raw material 'put out' by merchant capitalists or the larger cloth manufacturers. Society was polarized, as the subdivision of plots reduced some to landless labourers and allowed others to buy up small parcels of land. Worsted was largely sold to fluctuating foreign markets, which encouraged putting out, for small concerns found it difficult to ride out slumps. In the area around Leeds, industry remained more closely associated with agriculture. Society was less polarized, for enclosure came later, and the continuation of manorial controls and copyhold tenure checked the emergence of small cottagers or landless families. The possession of farms gave clothiers a degree of independence, which could survive because woollen cloth was less reliant on export markets and had a more stable demand. Artisans in the woollen cloth industry were accordingly less prone to debt, and independent artisan production survived into the nineteenth century.[12]

There was, then, not a simple succession of stages from artisans to putting out as a result of internal tensions in artisan production. Similarly, it is doubtful whether the argument of the protoindustrialization model that tensions within putting out led to the factory can be sustained. When the demand for industrial goods was high, so it is argued, the putter out ran into problems in his attempt to mobilize all available resources. Workers are assumed to have conventional standards of consumption, so that they did not aim to maximize monetary income so much as to satisfy the traditional needs of family subsistence. An outworker who was paid a higher piece-rate for producing a length of cloth would consequently slow down production and still reach the conventional level of consumption. The consequences were alarming for the putter out, for the supply of labour fell at precisely the point where he wanted to increase production. A further difficulty arose because the domestic system tended to increase production by geographical expansion, and the merchant's control was stretched to breaking point. Raw materials were pilfered, the quality of production was not easily monitored, transport costs rose, and turnover of capital slowed down because of longer intervals between handing out materials and receiving back manufactured goods. These problems, so the protoindustrial model contends, threatened profitability, and the factory emerged to resolve the internal tensions of putting out. Merchants shifted to centralized production, by adding workshops to their warehouses, especially where raw materials were valuable, in order to secure more control over work effort and pilfering. This did not entail technological change or a great increase in productivity, but it prepared the way for the next stage of mechanization. Further, putting out created the necessary preconditions for a shift to factory production, for merchant-manufacturers accumulated capital to invest in the new technology, and had a skilled workforce ready to hand. How far does this model describe the realities of eighteenth- and early nineteenth-century Britain?

The model is somewhat contradictory and confused on the relationship between protoindustry, labour supply, and the emergence of the factory. It suggests that expansion of production was constrained by labour shortages at periods of prosperity, and by weak labour discipline which led to the introduction of factories in order to escape from the problems of absenteeism and embezzlement. This is a social rather than a technological explanation of the emergence of the factory; centralization emerged to impose labour discipline, which then led to mechanization as a consequence. This is disputable, for mechanization could just as well be a *cause* of centralization which made it worth facing the serious problems of discipline which were created rather than solved by factories. Neither are proponents of the protoindustrial model agreed on how rapid growth of population affected the development of the factory. Did it stimulate factory production by producing a supply of labour at low wages, which permitted putters out to accumulate capital and to secure a work-force for the new factories? Or did low wages and abundant labour check the development of factories, by removing the need for capital-intensive techniques? The result could be 'industrial involution'[13] rather than industrial revolution, a vicious circle of glutted labour and low wages which could be broken in two ways. One was a sudden spurt in demand to which protoindustry could not respond, so that centralized factory production was needed to release the bottle-neck. The other was competition from a low-cost region, possibly overseas, which forced a change in the organization of production in order to survive.

It does seem unlikely that protoindustrialization was necessary to create an abundant, low-wage labour supply for factory production. It is not obvious that population growth *was* more rapid in protoindustrial districts, for prudential restraints were weakened in predominantly agrarian districts as a result of 'proletarianization' of the work-force, which removed the incentive to accumulate savings for a smallholding. In any case, agriculture was releasing a large amount of labour, so that population growth was not necessary to create the labour supply for industry; if anything, it posed a danger by placing strain on food supplies. Neither were factory workers recruited directly from the ranks of outworkers. In the cotton industry, for example, hand-loom weavers were predominantly male, with large numbers in north-east Lancashire; power looms were initially located in southern Lancashire and Cheshire, and employed women and children. The location of the large, water-powered spinning factories of Richard Arkwright and his imitators was determined by the presence of power rather than labour, which created problems of securing workers in remote, sparsely inhabited districts. Rather than recruiting from an abundant pool of labour created by protoindustry, these mills turned to children apprentices. The poor law authorities were willing to pay employers a premium of between £3 and £5 to take children, who were usually orphaned or illegitimate girls. There was by no means a neat connection between the work-force employed in domestic production and factories, which tended to rely largely upon young women.

There was no reason why capital engaged in protoindustry should be directed into the construction of factories, for the vital point about protoindustrial capital was its fluidity, whether into commercial agriculture, brewing, innkeeping, retailing, or into land and stocks. A characteristic feature of the early eighteenth-century textile industry was that most assets were held as working capital and credit, or invested in fixed capital which was not specific to a particular trade and could easily be transferred. Clothiers in the west of England rarely owned a fulling mill, preferring to rely on specialist mill-owners working on commission; their workshops and warehouses were frequently converted buildings with general rather than specific uses, such as the property insured in 1729 by Philip Hoste, a clothier at Sturminster Newton, as 'a new workhouse or malthouse'. Inns were often owned by clothiers or merchants, operated as businesses in their own right as well as places to store cloth and transact trade. A common practice was to run a number of distinct businesses, which avoided commitment to one sector. John Anstie of Devizes, for example, took out an insurance policy in 1751 as a 'shop-keeper, snuff-maker and clothier', and his property valuation included the drink trade and malting. Many clothiers in the West Country and East Anglia combined industry with farming, investing in land in order to enter the gentry and engaging in agrarian-based trades such as maltsters or grain-dealers. A retreat from industry into agriculture could be a gradual process as they shifted their assets in response to the comparative profitability of industry and agriculture. The whole investment strategy was based upon 'the need to limit their commitment to, and insulate themselves against, the erratic course of industrial change that had been characteristic of the economy as far back as anyone remembered or cared to record'.[14]

The protoindustrialization model's emphasis upon a linear development from artisan production to putting out to the factory is misleading for factories emerged from both forms of domestic production, by different routes. In the West Riding of Yorkshire, the transition to the factory differed between the artisan-based woollen districts around Leeds and the putting out worsted industry around Halifax. In the first case, the emergence of the factory was long drawn-out. Centralized production initially involved preparing wool for domestic spinners by 'carding' and 'scribbling', and finishing the cloth after it was woven on hand looms by fulling, dyeing, and shearing. These preparatory and finishing processes were carried out in 'mills', centralized plant with powered machinery, to which materials were brought for processing in the same way that a farmer had his grain ground into flour. Producers of woollens had for centuries taken their cloth to be fulled in water-powered mills, where it was beaten in a mixture of water and fuller's earth; there were about 200 fulling mills in the West Riding of Yorkshire in 1800. Many were 'public' mills owned by landowners or lords of the manor to serve the producers in the area, but as the industry expanded 'private' mills were erected by local businessmen. By the mid-1770s, carding and scribbling of raw wool had also moved into mills, and from the early nineteenth century cloth was sent for mechanical shearing. These power-driven and centralized stages of production complemented rather than disrupted domestic spinning and weaving, and were often undertaken in 'company mills' which were jointly owned by groups of clothiers, without upsetting the existing organization of artisan production. When centralized factories subsequently developed for spinning yarn and weaving woollen cloth, they were small in scale: they emerged from the ranks of artisan producers who had fewer assets than putters out in the worsted sector; and they employed workers from the artisan trades. By contrast, the transition to the factory was much quicker in the worsted district. There was no prior stage of powered, centralized mills complementing domestic production, for worsted cloth was not fulled and the raw wool was not scribbled. Factory production of yarn and cloth was technically easier, for the long-fibre wool used in producing worsteds was amenable to mechanical spinning and weaving. Dispersed wage labour created more problems of pilfering in putting out than in artisan production; and the swifter growth of demand for worsteds placed strains on the domestic system. The greater scale and capital resources of putting out manufacturers in the worsted trade meant that factories in Halifax and Bradford were larger than in the woollen trade of Leeds and Huddersfield; and they were less likely to recruit their workers from the ranks of domestic workers.

Although the transition to the factory was swifter in the worsted industry of the West Riding, which was organized on the basis of putting out, there was by no means an invariable rule that putting out encouraged the process. The organizational structure of industry could be more rigid and less flexible in one area than in another. In the West Country woollen cloth trade, the structure of putting out created barriers to change rather than an impetus to transition. The ability of domestic systems to transform to centralized production was affected by two points of organization. One was the precise relationship between the various stages of production. In the woollen industry, scribbling and fulling mills could either disrupt or complement domestic producers in spinning and weaving, creating tensions or opportunities. The West Country experienced greater disruption and tensions than the West Riding. Josiah Tucker saw the difference in the structure of the industry as one reason for the contrast. In the West Riding, he argued, the journeymen could set up as small masters, which was an incentive to frugality and industry; in the West Country, they had no incentive, for 'they shall always be chained to the same oar (the clothier), and never be but journeymen'. The clothier, Tucker remarked, had a 'great stock and large credit', buying the wool and controlling and paying for spinning, weaving, dyeing, shearing, and dressing; 'he is the clothier whom all the rest are to look upon as their paymaster. But will they not also look upon him as their tyrant.'[15] Tucker was exaggerating the contrast in social mobility, but there was clearly a variation in the organization of the woollen cloth industry in the two areas. In the West

Country, there were large-scale merchant-manufacturers, and the dominance of a small, cohesive group with strong links to gentry society could make the emergence of new methods more difficult. Perhaps more significant than the cultural milieu was the divergence in the organization of the industry, which created barriers to the adoption of new technology. Gentlemen clothiers co-ordinated groups of dependent waged workers who specialized in one task, so that a new machine threatened the affected workers with redundancy, and technological change was consequently resisted. The new machinery benefited a small group of wealthy clothiers and reinforced a hierarchical structure which limited opportunities for new enterprise and created social tension. In the West Riding, small independent artisan clothiers were more likely to view new machinery as complementary, offering opportunities. A new machine reduced the time an artisan spent on one process, freeing him to concentrate on another stage of production (see Fig. 6.2). 'The same machine', remarks Adrian Randall, 'might liberate labour from drudgery and open up more profitable and even

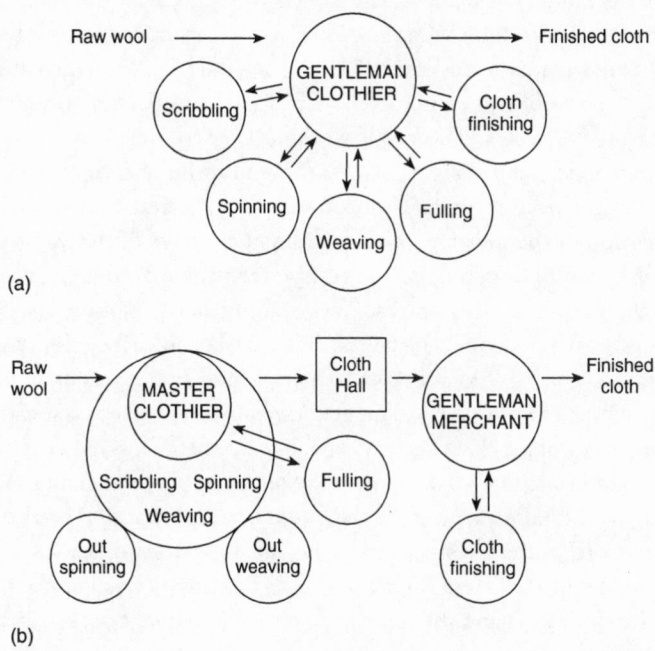

FIG. 6.2. Organizational structure of the woollen industry. (a) West of England; (b) West Riding of Yorkshire

Source: A. J. Randall, 'Work, Culture and Resistance to Machinery in the West of England Woollen Industry', in P. Hudson (ed.), Regions and Industries: A Perspective on the Industrial Revolution in Britain (Cambridge, 1989), 180–1.

socially mobile prospects in one area and break down customary work relations, throw labour onto the scrap heap and widen the gap between capital and labour in another.'[16] The putting out system of the West Country woollen industry led to resistance, delaying the growth of centralized production compared with the artisan system of the West Riding. This contrast was reinforced by a second organizational difference: the relationship between production and marketing.

The gentlemen merchants of the West Riding woollen industry were based in local towns, and particularly Leeds, where they formed an oligarchy which was closely associated with the landed society of the district, from which many had been recruited. They purchased cloth from artisan clothiers, which they finished by sending to a specialist dresser. It was very unusual for them to become engaged in the production of cloth; they saw themselves as more akin to country gentlemen, leading a cultured life and aiming to create a landed dynasty. Close attention to production and employment of large numbers of workers was alien to their culture. Accordingly, the capital and enterprise for factories came from artisan master clothiers who gradually shifted into centralized production, rather than from merchants, who were more likely to divert their profits into land or finance. In the worsted sector of the West Riding, the tasks of manufacturing and marketing were often combined. The merchant-manufacturers directly employed large numbers of domestic workers; they co-ordinated their activities from a warehouse; and often provided the enterprise and capital for factory production. But putting out did not always aid the retention of capital for transformation of the industry. The gentlemen clothiers of the West Country were wealthy putters out, but their direct involvement in production was largely confined to the preparatory stages. They had financial resources to purchase large quantities of raw wool, which was sorted, dyed, and scribbled very carefully under their close supervision in order to maintain quality; it was then put out to domestic spinners and weavers. The gentlemen clothiers were associated with the landed gentry of the West Country and, like the merchants of Leeds, they had little ambition to become involved with the direct employment and supervision of a factory work-force. Neither did they take a direct interest in marketing, for the sale of cloth in the West Country was left to factors at Blackwell Hall in London, unlike in the West Riding where marketing was undertaken locally through the cloth halls and the merchants of Leeds. There was, as a result, less flexibility in response to market change.

In the woollen industry of the West Riding, the gentlemen merchants' lack of interest in production gave an opportunity to artisan master clothiers; in the woollen industry of the West Country, the gentlemen clothiers' lack of interest meant that there were few substitutes. Specialist workers had less experience of the whole process of production than the artisans of the West Riding, and mechanization was likely to generate intense hostility because of the disruption of the existing social system. The extreme craft specialization of the putting out system in the woollen industry of the West Country created a social system which gave rise to friction and conflict, to a greater extent than either the artisan system in the woollen industry or the putting out system in the worsted trade of Yorkshire. There was, therefore, no necessary connection between the accumulation of capital in putting out and a transition to mechanization and factory production. Putting out could impose barriers, and artisan production could accommodate change: generalized models are less useful than careful analysis of the dynamics of each case.

Conclusion

Protoindustrialization excludes too much to provide the key to developments in eighteenth-century industry. Not only does it ignore domestic industry in the towns; it also ignores rural and urban industry based upon non-domestic organization. In the country, there was a wide variety of mines, mills, forges, and furnaces, and historians have made little effort to explain how these fitted into the agrarian economy, or to analyse their impact upon demographic behaviour. Domestic and plant-based industry coexisted in some areas, such as the Weald of Kent with its blast furnaces, paper-mills, and gunpowder plants as well as domestic textile production. In other areas, the two types of industry were distinct. On Tyneside, there was little in the way of domestic industry, and the industrial economy was dominated by coal-mining, salt-pans, glassworks, sulphuric acid production, and soap. Much the same was true of the Mersey, the Clyde, and south Wales. Many plant-based industries were located in the country, but they were also found within towns. Textiles were dyed and finished; there were food-processing industries such as the production of sugar; the drink trades such as beer, porter, and gin; the construction of ships and ancillary trades such as the manufacture of sails and ropes; and naval dockyards were amongst the largest industrial concerns in the eighteenth century. There were, indeed, probably more workers in plant-based industries than in protoindustrial activities. Although the debate over protoindustrialization has focused attention upon some major issues, it has also distorted the analysis of change in the eighteenth-century British economy. Perhaps the word 'protoindustrialization' with its associated explanatory model should be avoided; the older descriptive term of the 'domestic system of production' is more realistic and less prescriptive.

The rise and fall of domestic industry was influenced by the structure of farming regions and patterns of land tenure, by the ability of some areas to retain freehold or customary tenures which created the preconditions for domestic industry, by variations in the pace of enclosure or the dominance of large estates and by changes in farming practices. Domestic production was both a conse quence and a cause of changes in demography and family structure. The remova of restraints on marriage created the potentiality for rapid population growth and the organization of production in family units affected the relationship between husband and wife, and parents and children. Relationships within families engaged in domestic production were not necessarily symmetrical, fo domestic industry allowed young adults to marry and start a new production unit, which might clash with the desire of parents to retain children in thei productive unit for as long as possible. The precise relationship between dom estic production and merchanting could affect the responsiveness to changes in the market, and influence the sources of capital for factory development Further, the organization of various stages of domestic production affected the impact of mechanization and the ability of the work-force to resist changes. And were domestic workers trapped in a world of conventional consumption defending a 'moral' economy against the incursion of the market and a cash nexus? These issues are pursued in later chapters.

NOTES

1. D. Defoe, *A Tour through the Whole Island of Great Britain* (1724–6) (Everyman edn. repr. 1974), ii, 193–202.
2. Ibid. 206.
3. Ibid. 207.
4. P. Kriedte, H. Medick, and J. Schlumbohm, *Industrialisation before Industrialisation* (Cambridge, 1981), 6.
5. Ibid. 41.
6. D. Levine, *Family Formation in the Age of Nascent Capitalism* (New York, 1977), 17.
7. Quoted in K. J. Allison and P. M. Tillott, 'York in the Eighteenth Century', in P. M Tillott (ed.), *Victoria County History, City of York* (1961), 215.
8. W. Hutton, quoted in E. Hopkins, *Birmingham: The First Manufacturing Town in the World, 1760–1840* (1989), 5.
9. Allison and Tillott, 'York in the Eighteenth Century', 215–16.
10. D. Hey, *The Rural Metalworkers of the Sheffield Region: A Study of Rural Industry before the Industrial Revolution* (Leicester, 1972), 11; J. D. Chambers, *Nottinghamshire in the Eighteenth Century: A Study of Life and Labour under the Squirearchy* (1932), 95.
11. Chambers, *Nottinghamshire*, 125.
12. P. Hudson, *The Genesis of Industrial Capital: A Study of the West Riding Wool Textile Industry, c.1750–1850* (Cambridge, 1986), for the outstanding account.
13. Levine, *Family Formation*, 33–4.
14. S. D. Chapman, 'Industrial Capital before the Industrial Revolution: An Analysis of

the Assets of a Thousand Textile Entrepreneurs, c.1730–50', in N. B. Harte and K. G. Ponting (eds.), *Textile History and Economic History* (Manchester, 1973), 130, 137.

. Quoted in M. Berg, *The Age of Manufactures* (1985), 119, 53–4.

. A. J. Randall, 'Work, Culture and Resistance to Machinery in the West of England Woollen Industry', in P. Hudson (ed.), *Regions and Industries: A Perspective on the Industrial Revolution in Britain* (Cambridge, 1989), 185.

URTHER READING

llen, R. C., *Enclosure and the Yeoman: The Agricultural Development of the South Midlands, 1450–1850* (Oxford, 1992).

llison, K. J., and Tillott, P. M., 'York in the Eighteenth Century', in P. M. Tillott (ed.), *Victoria County History: City of York* (1961).

erg, M., *The Age of Manufactures: Industry, Innovation and Work in Britain, 1700–1820* (Oxford, 1985).

——Hudson, P., and Sonenscher, M., 'Manufacture in Town and Country before the Factory', in M. Berg *et al.*, *Manufacture in Town and Country before the Factory* (Cambridge, 1983).

ythell, D., *The Handloom Weavers: A Study in the English Cotton Industry during the Industrial Revolution* (Cambridge, 1969).

hambers, J. D., *Nottinghamshire in the Eighteenth Century: A Study of Life and Labour under the Squirearchy* (1932).

hapman, S. D., 'Industrial Capital before the Industrial Revolution: An Analysis of the Assets of a Thousand Textile Entrepreneurs, c.1730–50', in N. B. Harte and K. G. Ponting (eds.), *Textile History and Economic History* (Manchester, 1973).

larkson, L., *Proto-industrialisation: The First Phase of Industrialisation?* (1985).

oleman, D. C., 'Proto-industrialisation: A Concept too Many', *Economic History Review*, 2nd ser. 36 (1983).

orfield, P. J., *The Impact of English Towns, 1700–1800*, (Oxford, 1982).

——'A Provincial Capital in the Late Seventeenth Century: The Case of Norwich', in P. Clark and P. Slack (eds.), *Crisis and Order in English Towns 1500–1700: Essays in Urban History* (1972).

ourt, W. H. B., *The Rise of the Midland Industries, 1600–1838* (1938).

rost, P., 'Yeomen and Metalsmiths: Livestock in the Land Economy in South Staffordshire, 1560–1720', *Agricultural History Review*, 29 (1981).

George, M. D., *London Life in the Eighteenth Century* (1925).

Hey, D., *The Rural Metalworkers of the Sheffield Region: A Study of Rural Industry before the Industrial Revolution* (Leicester, 1972).

Hopkins, E., *Birmingham: The First Manufacturing Town in the World, 1760–1840* (1989).

Houston, R., and Snell, K. D. M., 'Proto-industrialization? Cottage Industry, Social Change and Industrial Revolution', *Historical Journal*, 27 (1984).

Hudson, P., 'Proto-industrialisation: The Case of the West Riding Wool Textile Industry in the Eighteenth and Early Nineteenth Centuries', *History Workshop Journal*, 12 (1981).

—— *The Industrial Revolution* (1992).

Hudson, P., *The Genesis of Industrial Capital: A Study of the West Riding Wool Text* Industry, *c.1750–1850* (Cambridge, 1986).

—— (ed.), *Regions and Industries: A Perspective on the Industrial Revolution in Brita* (Cambridge, 1989).

Jenkins, D. T., *The West Riding Wool Textile Industry, 1770–1835: A Study of Fixed Capit* Formation (Edington, 1975).

—— 'Early Factory Development in the West Riding of Yorkshire, 1770–1800', in N.) Harte and K. G. Ponting (eds.), *Textile History and Economic History* (Manchester, 1973)

Jones, E. L., 'Agricultural Origins of Industry', *Past and Present*, 40 (1968).

Kellett, J. R., 'The Breakdown of Gild and Corporation Control over the Handicraft an Retail Trade in London', *Economic History Review*, 2nd ser. 10 (1957–8).

Kriedte, P., Medick, H., and Schlumbohm, J., *Industrialization before Industrializatio* (Cambridge, 1981).

Lane, J., Apprenticeship in Warwickshire Cotton Mills, 1790–1830', *Textile History*, 10 (1979)

Large, P., 'Urban Growth and Agricultural Change in the West Midlands during th Seventeenth and Eighteenth Centuries', in P. Clark (ed.), *The Transformation of Englis* Provincial Towns (1984).

Levine, D., *Family Formation in an Age of Nascent Capitalism* (New York, 1977).

Mills, D. R., 'Rural Industries and Social Structure: Framework Knitters in Leicestershire 1670–1851', *Textile History*, 13 (1982).

Randall, A., 'Work, Culture and Resistance to Machinery in the West of England Woolle Industry', in P. Hudson (ed.), *Regions and Industries: A Perspective on the Industria Revolution in Britain* (Cambridge, 1989).

Rogers, A., 'Rural Industries and Social Structure: The Framework Knitting Industry o South Nottinghamshire 1670–1840', *Textile History*, 12 (1981).

Rowlands, M. B., *Masters and Men in the West Midlands Metalware Trades before th Industrial Revolution* (Manchester, 1975).

Short, B. M., 'The Deindustrialisation Process: A Case Study of the Weald, 1600–1850', ir P. Hudson (ed.), *Regions and Industries: A Perspective on the Industrial Revolution in Britain* (Cambridge, 1989).

Thirsk, J., 'Industries in the Countryside', in F. J. Fisher (ed.), *Essays in the Economic and Social History of Tudor and Stuart England* (Cambridge, 1961).

—— (ed.), *The Agrarian History of England and Wales*, v: 1640–1750, I: *Regional Farming Systems* (Cambridge, 1984).

Wilson, R. G., 'The Supremacy of the Yorkshire Cloth Industry in the Eighteenth Century', in N. B. Harte, and K. G. Ponting (eds.), *Textile History and Economic History* (Manchester, 1973).

....

CHAPTER 7

The Coming of the Factory

Edward Baines in 1835 expressed a cataclysmic view of the impact of the factory system and powered machinery in reshaping work and industry:

It is by iron fingers, teeth, and wheels, moving with exhaustless energy and devouring speed, that the cotton is opened, cleaned, spread, carded, drawn, roved, spun, wound, warped, dressed, and woven. . . . All are moving at once—the operations chasing each other; and all derive their motion from the mighty engine, which, firmly seated in the lower part of the building, and constantly fed with water and fuel, toils through the day with the strength of perhaps a hundred horses. Men, in the meanwhile, have merely to attend on this wonderful series of mechanisms, to supply it with work, and to check its slight and infrequent irregularities—each workman performing, or rather superintending, as much work as could have been done by *two or three hundred men* sixty years ago. . . . When it is remembered that all these inventions have been made within the last seventy years it must be acknowledged that the cotton mill presents the most striking example of the dominion obtained by human science over the powers of nature, of which modern times can boast.[1]

This captures a common view of the industrial revolution as a nightmare vision of smoking chimneys, large factories, a dense urban setting, and workers as the slaves of power-driven machinery. Yet the transition to centralized urban factory production was slow and piecemeal: large parts of British industry in 1835 were still based upon hand labour and outwork, and many early factories were located in the country in search of water power. Recent historical revisionism has played down the impact of the factory until a relatively late stage of industrialization; it has also questioned the explanation of the emergence of factory production (see Fig. 7.1).

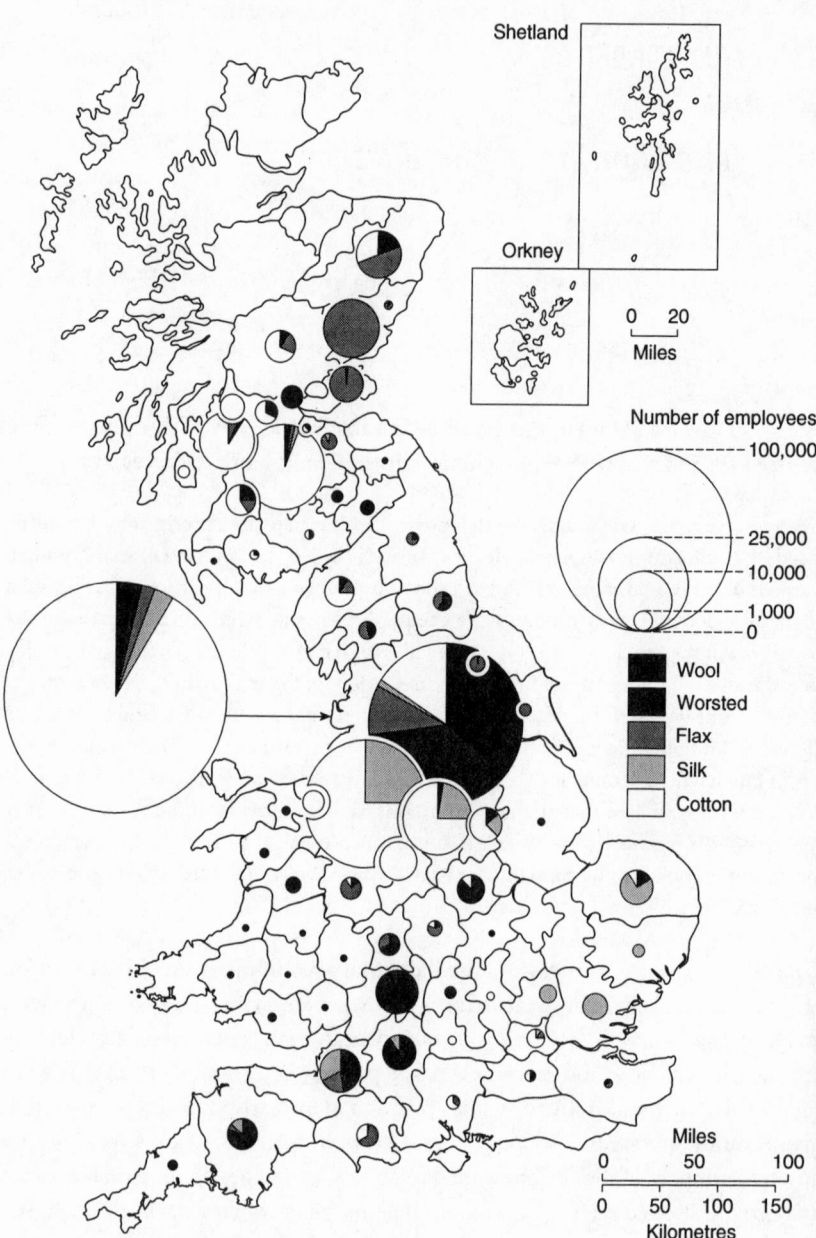

FIG. 7.1. Employment in textile factories, 1838

Source: P. Laxton, 'Textiles', in J. Langton and R. J. Morris (eds.), *Atlas of Industrialising Britain, 1780–1914* (1986), 110, using data from PP 1839, xliii.

Centralization of Production: Labour Control and Transaction Costs

The simplest, common-sense, view of the coming of the factory is that it had a technological motivation: the centralized power source of a 'mighty engine' permitted the synchronization of specialized machines and the processing of materials through a sequence of operations in order to produce a standardized good at a low unit cost. Of course, such an argument begs the question of what determined technological change. Could it be argued that the development of new machinery was a *consequence* of the emergence of the factory for other reasons? Centralized production which brought labour together under one roof could, after all, exist before powered machinery was used to produce standardized goods. In some cases, it allowed control over expensive materials, such as valuable metals or Spanish wool in the broadcloth trade of Leeds; in others, scattered production was uneconomic because of the cost of transporting bulky, low-value raw materials, such as in the production of pottery. The production of sophisticated or luxury commodities, such as steam engines and high-quality furniture, might require careful control to ensure uniform quality, or close co-ordination of the stages of manufacture. Centralization could arise from the need to supervise and organize workers who were minutely specialized, such as in the pin factory of Adam Smith's famous analysis, which continued to rely upon hand labour until the slow adoption of powered machinery in the 1830s (see Fig. 7.2).

The 'non-technological' interpretations of the coming of the factory fall into two categories. One is social, arguing that factories developed in order to solve the problem of labour discipline, reducing 'embezzlement', imposing stricter work discipline, transforming the attitude of workers towards time and leisure, and making it possible to employ children and apprentices. The second is economic, arguing that factories permitted savings on 'transaction costs' by reducing the expense of transport of raw materials to scattered domestic producers, lowering the level of inventories, and imposing stricter controls over the quality of production. Both explanations interpret technological development as a consequence rather than a cause of change. Adherents of the social explanation of the coming of the factory argue that the prior existence of a hierarchically organized firm made it possible to adopt expensive patents, so that the social relations of production gave a bias to technical innovation. Adherents of the transaction cost approach claim that closer monitoring of production led to rationalization, making it easier to locate the points for technical improvements. Such approaches have challenged the primacy of technical change in explaining the rise of the factory. 'The emphasis in much of the literature in the industrial

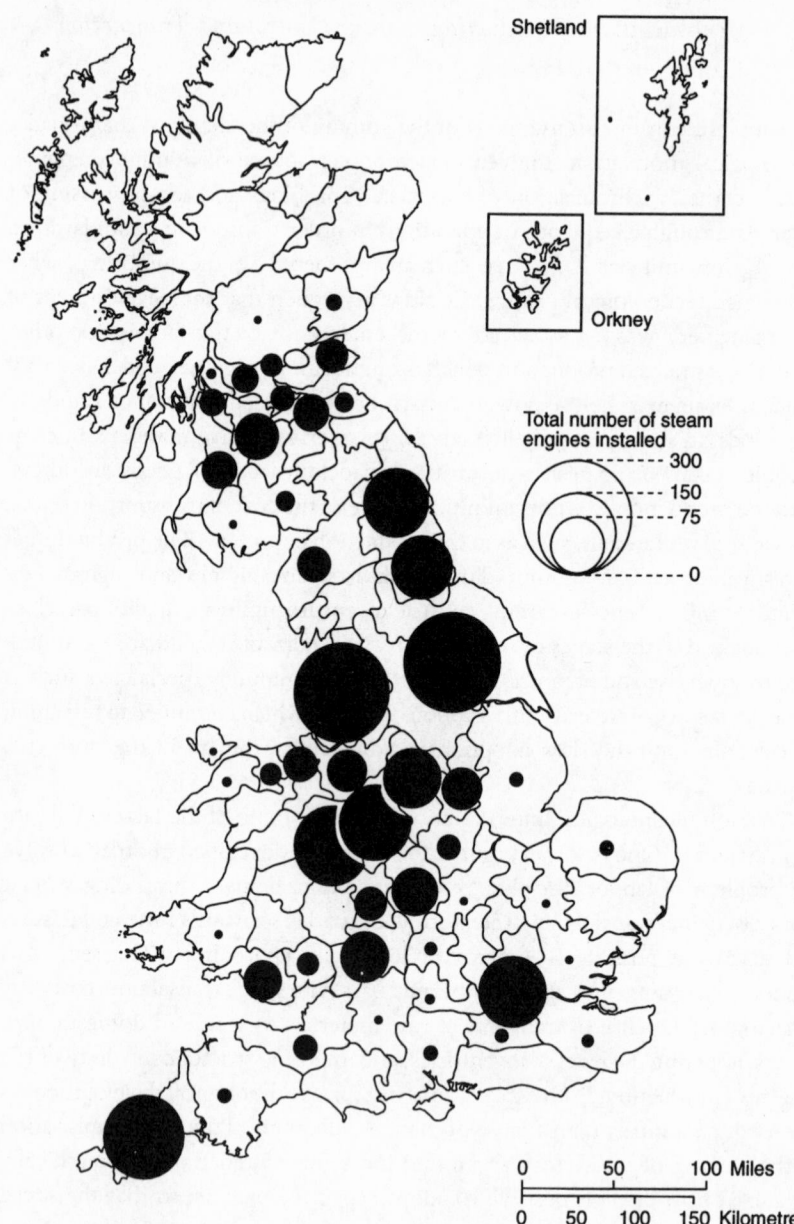

FIG. 7.2. Steam engines built by 1800

Source: G. N. von Tunzelmann, 'Coal and Steam Power', in Langton and Morris (eds.), *Atlas*, 77, from J. W. Kanefsky and J. Robey, 'Steam Engines in Eighteenth-Century Britain: A Quantitative Assessment', *Technology and Culture*, 21 (1980).

evolution goes the wrong way', D. C. North has remarked, 'from technological change to the factory system; rather than from central workplace, to supervision, to greater specialization, to better management of input contributions, to technical change.'[2] Clearly, the coming of the factory raises major issues about the social organization of work, the nature of 'transaction costs', and the determinants of technical change.

A common complaint of eighteenth-century commentators was that workers had a high leisure preference, responding to higher wage rates by reducing their supply of labour rather than continuing to work to secure a higher income. 'There's nothing more frequent', commented Defoe in 1704, 'than for an Englishman to work until he has got his pocket full of money, and then to go and be idle, or *perhaps drunk*, till 't is all gone.'[3] Low wages, it appeared, were necessary for a hard-working, reliable labour force. 'Everyone but an idiot knows', commented Arthur Young in 1771, 'that the lower classes must be kept poor or they will never be industrious.'[4] Workers would actually benefit from low wages, argued David Hume, for in 'years of scarcity, if it be not extreme, the poor labour more and really live better than in years of great plenty when they indulge themselves in idleness and riot'.[5] The assumption was that a higher wage rate did not produce a commensurate increase in earnings, for much of the benefit was taken in shorter hours of paid work which allowed more leisure or unpaid activities such as tending a small plot of land.

These concerns were part of the debate over 'luxury' in the late seventeenth and early eighteenth centuries, with its fear that higher real wages would raise the price of exports and endanger the nation. The question is whether the participants were articulating a political concern or describing social behaviour. If they were correct in arguing that leisure preference was high and labour discipline weak, it would be difficult to expand production within the constraints of domestic industry, for any increase in wage rates would reduce work effort and constrain output at a time of prosperity. The answer, on such an interpretation, was centralized production as a means of imposing strict discipline and wresting control from the work-force. But leisure preference would not only provide a motivation for the construction of factories; it would also increase the scale of the task facing factory owners, who had to reform the social behaviour of the workers. Indeed, the argument could even be reversed: the task of weaning a recalcitrant work-force from high leisure preference and conventional consumption could create disincentives to would-be factory owners who feared that capital investment in machinery and buildings would be jeopardized. Andrew Ure in 1835 commented that the main difficulty of the pioneer factory master, Richard Arkwright, was not in developing a powered spinning-machine; it was 'above all, in training human beings to renounce their desultory habits of work, and to identify themselves with the unvarying regularity of the complex automaton. To devise and administer a successful code of factory discipline, suited to the necessities of factory diligence, was the Herculean enterprise, the noble achievement of Arkwright.'[6] Ure was not suggesting that Arkwright built factories in order to reshape the social organization of work; on the contrary, the existence of factories for technical reasons required new standards of diligence, without which investment in new machinery and production processes would not be profitable. Ure implied that a less determined man than Arkwright would be loath to introduce factories because of the magnitude of the task of reshaping social attitudes. The 'Herculean task' of creating factory discipline would, on this reading, only be undertaken when the development of new machinery made it imperative.

Both interpretations assume that workers had a high leisure preference and conventional patterns of consumption. But is this correct? Defoe and other commentators on leisure preference were probably confusing a short-term lag before consumption caught up with opportunities with a permanent structural feature. Indeed, Defoe was making two contradictory complaints, that high wages meant absenteeism and at the same time led to emulation and 'flourishing pride' in London, which 'has dictated new methods of living to the people; and while the poorest citizens live like the rich, the rich like the gentry, the gentry like the nobility, and the nobility striving to outshine one another'.[7] It was impossible to take higher wage rates both in leisure and in consumption, and the choice depended upon a number of factors. One was the nature of the increase in wage rates. A short, seasonal upturn in rates (as at the harvest or during a short, cyclical boom in the industrial sector) gave little incentive to workers to adjust consumption patterns. There was no expectation of a long-term gain in the standard of living and it made more sense, in a life of privation, to 'blow' the windfall in a spree of drinking and leisure. Savings were unlikely to be adequate to meet the hardships of life, and membership of friendly societies depended upon regular earnings to pay subscriptions. These attitudes continued to apply throughout the nineteenth century to groups such as casual dockers. In expanding sectors of the economy, the prospects of longer-term gains made it feasible and rational to adjust patterns of consumption. In the later eighteenth century, the debate over luxury and wages shifted to an acceptance that higher wages stimulated demand and efficiency. 'That a little more plenty than ordinary may render some workmen idle, cannot well be doubted', remarked Adam Smith, 'but that it should have this effect upon the greater part, or that men in general should work better when they are ill-fed than when they are well fed ... seems not very probable.'[8] Did this amount to a change in the behaviour of the British population during the eighteenth century, or a shift in the perceptions of economists and moralists? Certainly, the emergence of factories would be easier where the work-force had already changed its attitudes and viewed increases in wage rates as a way to move beyond conventional expectations of consumption, so reducing the 'Herculean task' to manageable proportions. It does, indeed, seem more plausible that the work-force had developed new attitudes to work and consumption than that the factory emerged as a device to discipline a recalcitrant work-force prior to technical advance. The imposition of stricter labour discipline was unlikely to be a sufficient explanation for centralization of production. There were many forces leading to new attitudes to consumption and work without the need to sink capital in factories, and there was little sense in imposing labour discipline through the construction of expensive factories unless continuous, large-volume production was justified by the market and powered machinery offered reductions in costs. When these economic incentives were present, the task of the factory owner in imposing discipline was made easier by changes which had already taken place in workers' attitudes.

The gradual emergence of new attitudes to work and consumption was shaped by the extent to which workers were incorporated into a monetized, market economy, and by their ability to raise their standard of living through a non-waged economy, by exploiting customary rights such as collecting wood, gleaning, or keeping a few animals. Time devoted to such activities might well yield a higher marginal return than time devoted to, say, weaving more cloth, so that workers were not simply pursuing a traditional 'moral economy' which was opposed to the market: they had a clear sense of their best economic interests. Employers had a different perception, for they needed to keep their circulating capital moving as quickly as possible in order to maintain profitability, and it was easy for them to denounce workers as feckless. The ability of workers to allocate time to non-industrial or non-waged work was weakened by the erosion of customary perquisites and coincidental use-rights, which was clearly one method of creating a more 'disciplined' work-force by reducing the autonomy of cottagers and transforming them into dependent wage labourers. External pressure was one means of bringing the perceptions of employer and worker into line, but it was also the result of integrating workers into a money economy which gave them the ability and incentive to maximize the receipt of cash to purchase a wider range of commodities.

The spread of market-oriented consumption patterns depended upon the substitution of cash wages, which was by no means synonymous with factory employment. The endemic shortage of small coin and problems of liquidity meant that factory owners were often faced with difficulties in paying cash wages, so that their workers were consequently paid in goods or 'truck'. The response of workers to higher cash incomes also depended upon their ability to buy goods in shops, which did not follow the same pattern as centralized production. Obviously, there were more shops in large towns, so that urban residents were likely to have a much less conventional attitude to consumption and to be less prone to 'leisure preference'. Workers in the small metal trades of Birmingham, or furniture-makers and tailors of London, accepted the imperatives of rising consumption earlier than workers in scattered rural industries with a similar domestic organization. By contrast, workers in Arkwright's early cotton-mills were in isolated country districts, where there were few shops for workers to spend their earnings; his 'Herculean task' was exacerbated because workers had little incentive to maximize their earnings in the absence of the temptations of urban life. Further, the consumption of goods has as much to do with social position as with use. A wooden platter or brown pottery is just as functional as Wedgwood porcelain, which acted as a 'positional good' and indicated aspirations to refinement. A choice was made between leisure and 'positional goods', which varied between occupations and communities. Expenditure on 'positional goods' was more likely in areas with a diversified social structure which provided models to emulate; it was less likely in the south Wales iron and coal industries, where labour was dangerous and unpleasant, and communities were dominated by a single class and occupation. Leisure preference continued in south Wales, where miners were more likely to stop work when they had reached their conventional expectations. By contrast, there were many complaints that workers in London were aping their social superiors and subverting the social order. There was, in other words, a variation in the extent to which there was a 'commodification' of consumption, a pursuit of goods rather than leisure which both created a more disciplined work-force and raised the level of demand for goods, so producing a more favourable climate for investment of fixed capital in factories.[9]

New attitudes towards time and consumption outside the factory cleared the way for the investment of large sums of fixed capital in centralized production. The domestic outworker was not necessarily feckless and undisciplined, insensitive to changes in wage rates, with a conventional pattern of expectations. Nevertheless, factory production threw up new issues of labour control, which were only worth facing where mechanization and the application of a central power supply offered the incentive of higher productivity. A broad distinction may be drawn between a task orientation to work, which applied to agriculture and domestic industry, and a time orientation, which became necessary in factories. A worker who was mowing a field, reaping grain, weaving a piece of cloth, or making a pair of shoes could decide to take a break at midday and work into the evening, or devote time to other tasks. Cornelius Ashworth, a weaver from Wheatley in Yorkshire, recorded in his diary on 24 December 1782 that he 'wove 2 yards before 11 o'clock. I was laying up the coal heap, sweeping the roof and walls of the muck midden till 10 o' clock at night'; on 21 January 1783 he 'wove 2¾ yards the Cow having calve she required much attendance'.[10] In the Potteries, for example, male potters employed children who assisted them, and paid for power and light as if they were independent contractors; they could work at their own pace. 'There were always the mornings and nights of the last days of the week', commented An Old Potter in his memoirs, 'and these were always trusted to make up the loss of the week's early neglect.'[11] A task orientation to work did not necessarily imply a high leisure preference, a conventional pattern of consumption, and adherence to 'moral economy': Ashworth and the Old Potter could work long hours and be part of a sophisticated market economy with high levels of consumption. The shift to a time orientation to work in factories with powered machinery nevertheless entailed major adjustments in social behaviour; the entire work-force had to be present at fixed hours when the plant was being operated. 'If a steam-engine had started every Monday morning at six o'clock', remarked the Old Potter, 'the workers would have been disciplined to the habit of regular and continuous industry.'[12] He contrasted the Potteries, where precise hours and days of work were of little consequence, with Lancashire, where the use of machinery meant that minutes mattered. It was not that workers developed a new attitude to consumption and worked for longer hours; the crucial issue was a loss of control over *which* hours were worked.

In the cotton-mills, early factory masters had to teach time thrift. Richard Arkwright, it was remarked, 'had to train his work people to a precision and industry altogether unknown before, against which their listless and restless habits rose in continued rebellion'.[13] What was denounced as desultory and restless could be seen in another way, as resentment at a loss of autonomy and subjugation to the machine. The factory bell marked the start of the day, and workers who were late lost a considerable part of their day's pay as a punishment. Once in the factory, strict attention to work was enforced by dismissal or fines. In one mill in 1830, for example, 'Any person found from the necessary place of work, except for necessary purposes, or talking with anyone out of their own Ally [sic], will be fined 2d for each offence.'[14] Factory employers sometimes attempted to take charge of the whole life of the worker and his family, especially in 'Arkwright' mills in remote areas which involved the provision of a factory village. Henry and Edward Ashworth, for example, informed a government inquiry in 1833 that

Most of the workpeople in our employ reside in houses belonging to us. We exercise a control or superintendence over them, for their moral and social improvement ... at frequent and irregular periods visits are paid to the dwelling of every workman. ... The state and cleanliness of their rooms, their bedding and furniture are very minutely examined, and the condition of their children, their income and habits of life, are carefully enquired into, and remarks thereon are entered in books which are kept for the purpose.[15]

Few factory masters persisted once production moved into the towns, and increasingly they relied less on fines and direct control, and more on the use of wages. Factory owners increasingly assumed that the prospect of higher earnings was an incentive to hard work rather than a deterrent. Payment by output was increasingly adopted to provide an incentive, with 47.1 per cent of workers in 225 cotton-mills in 1833 paid on piece-work.[16] There was also a decline in long hirings which were seen as counter-productive, making the work-force resentful and hampering the use of wages to control work habits. There was, generally, a move from long to short agreements, and a more frequent payment of wages.

Factory masters could sidestep the issue of control to some extent by relying on 'internal subcontracting', which passed the task of imposing discipline on to overseers, 'butties', and minders who controlled and paid subordinate labour. The new technology did not fully reshape production institutions in the first phase of factory development, and the new spinning mills did not simply rely upon a capitalist factory master facing a homogeneous proletariat; labour discipline over a large part of the work-force was imposed by one grade of workers over the other. This is not to argue that the early cotton-mills simply continued the pattern of labour control of the domestic system, by hiring families who worked as a unit. The family was often not a self-contained unit of production even in the domestic system, for a male weaver required several spinners to keep his loom at work. Spinning mills rarely relied upon family labour. The early mills were often located in the country to obtain water power, and they usually employed single adults with a high level of turnover, often supplemented by pauper apprentices who were usually orphaned or illegitimate adolescent girls. Families were only part of the work-force of the mills, and they did not necessarily work as a unit based upon a domestic pattern of employment. The gender division of labour changed, for domestic spinning was female and factory-based spinning machinery was usually operated by men. The machines were only partially powered, and they required some strength to operate, which was one reason why men displaced women. Perhaps more significantly, men excluded women from trades which offered an opportunity of securing high rates of pay. Mule spinning-machines initially required continuous adjustments to maintain tension on the yarn and to produce a given 'count' or fineness of thread, and male operatives seized on the strong bargaining position. The mules were operated by an adult spinner or 'minder', who was paid a piece-rate according to output; he controlled a 'big' and 'little piecer' in an 'internal subcontract', paying them a day-rate. The minder had an incentive to increase output, which led to an increase in his payment, without a need to pass it on to his assistants. The task of keeping them at work fell on him rather than the factory owner. Although this had clear parallels with the pattern of control in the domestic system, it did not necessarily entail a family-based unit of employment. At Horrocks and Jackson's mill in Preston in 1816, for example, 57.9 per cent of children were employed by the workers, but only 14.0 per cent were employed by a parent or sibling.[17] The social structure of work had clearly changed between the domestic system and factories, with a shift in the gender division of labour and in the role of the family as a work unit. There *was* continuity in the use of the internal subcontract system, which eased the problems of labour discipline at the expense of entrenching the power of the male 'minders'. This was to cause concern to the factory owners, particularly when the minders exploited their strong bargaining position in the strikes of the late 1820s.

The mill-owners attempted to regain the initiative by approaching an engineer, Richard Roberts, to design a fully mechanized or 'self-acting' mule to break the power of the minders. He took out his first patent in 1825 and completed the task by 1830. Here was a clear example of socially determined technical change, which arose from a desire to replace expensive and militant men by cheap and docile women. The self-acting mules could perfectly well be operated by women, as they were in Scotland. But in Lancashire, the factory owners failed to readjust the gender division of labour. This was in part the result of a breakdown in the transmission of skills in the female work-force as a result of the use of large, semi-powered mules in Lancashire. More importantly, it was an outcome of the economics of the industry. Employers had to judge whether the long-term gains of substituting cheaper women and a direct hierarchical system of control outweighed the short-term losses in production and productivity. The Scottish cotton-masters decided that the costs were worth bearing. They were under pressure from their rivals in Lancashire, and their profits were squeezed by a large wage increase and a fall in yarn prices in 1836. Consequently, they were willing to accept the costs of a strike which would break the unions and introduce self-acting mules operated by women. The result was a more direct, hierarchical system of labour control which employed unskilled women piecers under the supervision of a male overseer who controlled several sets of mules. In Lancashire, the mill-owners came to a different conclusion and the internal subcontract of minders and piecers survived. The industry was highly competitive and the risks of altering the system of labour control were too great, for rivals would take advantage of any disruption to increase their market share. Cotton-masters were reluctant to overturn the existing system of internal subcontracting which had eased their problems of recruitment and control in the 1790s, and to substitute a new system of direct, hierarchical labour control at the expense of an initial loss of output. The survival of internal subcontracting was, therefore, not simply a capitalist strategy to intensify the pace of work by 'co-exploitation' of subordinate workers by industrialists and higher grades of workers: the minders were not, as some historians have argued, part of a conscious strategy by which capitalists divided the proletariat by creating allies in a new 'labour aristocracy'.[18] The minders were the legatees of an older system of labour management, which survived as a result of their own powers of organization against the wishes of capitalists who were constrained by the highly competitive structure of the industry in Lancashire. It follows from this comparison between Scotland and Lancashire that the precise structure of labour control in factories was contingent rather than technically determined, shaped by the struggle for control of the shop-floor rather than the demands of a particular machine. Production *technology* should be distinguished from production *institutions*, for the social organization of work was incorporated into a set of institutional arrangements to negotiate wages and work conditions, so creating inflexibilities which limited future technical change in the late nineteenth century.

The emergence of time and work discipline was not synonymous with the introduction of machinery and its need for a greater degree of synchronization of labour; it was a much more general phenomenon, taking different forms: the erosion of customary rights and the reduction of cottagers to agricultural labourers; the spread of notions of punctuality and discipline by schools; and the preaching by Nonconformists that idleness produced sin and immorality. Older styles of leisure were challenged, and gentlemen started to draw apart from plebeian culture, which was particularly marked with the emergence of the movement for the 'reformation of manners' in the late eighteenth century. There were a variety of motives apart from a simple desire to reshape workers for the discipline of factories. The evangelical movement emphasized social and self-discipline, and a suspicion of 'the world' and its pleasures which were opposed to service to God and holiness. There was concern over the loss of the American colonies, and a fear of corruption and decline as in imperial Rome. The end of transportation of criminals to the American colonies meant that the population of gaols and the number of executions rose, and attention turned to the social processes which led to criminality. There was also concern that social change was challenging public order in growing towns. Sunday schools and prison reform were equally designed to produce moral reform, the one by inculcating moral precepts and the other by solitary confinement to induce reflection. Even when 'St Monday' or wakes did survive, they were internally transformed by the spread of 'rational recreation'. The wakes weeks in

Lancashire became an annual factory holiday, when families took a seaside holiday at Blackpool or went on railway excursions. At Birmingham 'St Monday' was observed into the middle of the nineteenth century, but it became the day for cheap railway excursions, concerts sponsored by the Street Commissioners, and the opening of the Botanical Gardens to workers on preferential terms. In 1853, a regular Saturday half-day holiday was substituted, and leisure in Birmingham shifted from irregular disruptions which affected a whole day, to a regularized half-day with the emergence of professionalized, controlled sporting events. 'A mighty revolution', remarked William Howitt in 1840, 'has taken place in the sports and pastimes of the common people.'[19] The change to a stricter time discipline was resented by cottagers who had less freedom to attend a cricket match, as it was by factory workers who complained of their loss of independence. But complaints about excessively long hours in poor conditions did not mean that workers were rejecting work discipline; in many ways, they had internalized the notions of time thrift. The Old Potter felt that the habit of calculation amongst workers in Lancashire affected their whole life, and helped them to develop their own organization. 'Their great co-operative societies would never have arisen to such economic and fruitful development but for the calculating induced by the use of machinery,'[20] and the point applied equally to friendly societies. Workers stopped fighting *against* the changed attitude to time and fought *about* time, through demands for the ten-hour day and strikes for overtime and time-and-a-half. 'They had accepted the categories of their employers and learned to fight back with them.'[21]

Clearly, the creation of new attitudes to consumption and time was a much wider phenomenon than the construction of factories. It was scarcely economically rational to invest in centralized production simply as a means of imposing discipline, for there were other, less costly, methods of securing control over labour. Outwork, after all, had attractions for employers. Most of the burdens of adjustment to fluctuations in demand were borne by workers who could be laid off, whereas a factory incurred capital charges in slack periods. The fixed costs of factories only made economic sense when demand passed a threshold which offered some certainty of continuous working, and the opportunity of securing economies from the application of a centralized source of power. The recasting of work discipline was in most cases a *consequence* of the construction of factories rather than a cause, and there was always the possibility that labour control would be ceded to subcontractors, which could entrench the power of workers within the factories. The social structure of the factories was not the result of a simple imposition of discipline by the factory masters; it involved a process of negotiation and conflict, which often meant factory employers did not have total control over the labour process. After 1875, the erosion of profits in many industries, as other areas of the world industrialized and prices fell, gave an incentive to impose tighter discipline and more direct control, but the production institutions created during the early nineteenth century proved remarkably resilient.

Technology and the Factory

The social and transaction cost approaches to the coming of the factory, with their assumption that technology was a dependent variable, cannot explain the long gap in the emergence of the factory in two branches of the same trade, even within a single firm. The silk industry is a case in point. The first trade to enter a factory in the full sense of a continuous process using a centralized power source was silk 'throwing', when Thomas Lombe built a mill at Derby between 1718 and 1721. His motivation was neither a need to impose discipline on workers nor a desire to save transaction costs, but the disruption of imports of silk yarn during the wars with France. Factory workers remained difficult to control, and a ready supply of cheap outworkers continued to be used in weaving, which only started to move into factories from 1815. In 1835 there were still only about 1,750 power looms in a total of 40,000 looms in Britain, largely in cheaper lines of the ribbon trade.[22] Power weaving was not feasible for the delicate and intricate patterns of broad silks produced in Spitalfields, where hand weaving continued at least to the 1850s, with lower grades being sent to the East End or the provinces where labour costs were cheaper. Although there was concern for quality and transaction costs, the response was to integrate throwing and weaving within a single firm rather than to replace the domestic system by hierarchically controlled factories. Outwork was not a static system rendered ineffective by problems of discipline and transaction costs. The ribbon manufacturers of Coventry, for example, changed the organization of outwork rather than building factories. They removed the middlemen or 'undertakers' and dealt directly with workers, so capturing the profits of the undertakers and placing the burden of supplying looms and working space upon the work-force. Alternatively, they made an agreement with the undertakers and workmen to employ adolescent 'apprentices' who received half the pay of a journeyman, and could be laid off at will because they did not have a formal apprenticeship secured by an indenture. Power looms had little attraction, for they imposed interest charges and increased the wastage of silk, when there was abundant underemployed labour to continue with hand weaving. Even when power weaving did arrive in Coventry, it was often used in 'cottage factories' which allowed journeymen to work from their home by providing a power supply at the end of a row of cottages. The long survival of domestic weaving and alternative means of economizing on labour and transaction costs suggest that there was a technological motivation for the introduction of factories in silk-throwing which required a central power source to operate the machinery.

There were similar divergences in the chronology of mechanization and centralization in cotton and wool, where mechanization and centralization were determined less by concerns for supervision and transaction costs than by the technical nature of different types of fibre. Preparatory processes and spinning were more easily mechanized than weaving, and more readily in cotton, which could better withstand rough handling than wool. Mechanized spinning was a difficult task, which involved pulling out fibres at an even tension, and then twisting them together at constant speed. Even when powered machinery was used, constant attention was needed to ensure a smooth, steady operation. The first significant development was James Hargreaves's 'spinning-jenny', which was initially hand-powered before moving into factories with a central power supply. When Richard Arkwright's water-frame was patented in 1769, it did not at once destroy domestic spinning, for it was only suitable for coarse yarns and was more expensive than the jenny, which did not need power and was better suited to spinning fine yarn. Machine-spun yarn was only able to compete with the finest hand-spun yarn with Samuel Crompton's 'mule' of 1780, which was not fully mechanized or 'self-acting' until 1830. In wool textiles, it was technically easier to introduce machinery in the preparatory 'scribbling' of short-staple wool for woollen cloth than in combing long-staple wool for worsted cloth. By contrast, worsted wool was strong and could better withstand machine spinning, so that domestic spinning declined earlier than in the woollen branch of the industry.

The mechanization of weaving was even more halting than spinning. Relatively sophisticated hand machines had existed for some time: William Lee's knitting frame of 1589 formed the basis of the hosiery trade of the east Midlands; Jedediah Strutt's stocking frame of the 1750s made ribbed stockings; and hand weaving was improved by Kay's flying shuttle of 1733. These improvements in hand looms and the mounting needs of weavers placed pressure on the supply of yarn, for a hand-loom weaver needed several spinners to keep him supplied with yarn, which stimulated the mechanization of spinning. Centralized, powered production of yarn arose from the appetite of hand weavers, and it might be expected that the removal of constraints on yarn supplies would create an incentive to improve weaving techniques. It was, however, some time before a successful power loom was developed and adopted. Although the first practicable power loom was patented by William Horrocks in 1803, there were only about 2,400 power looms in the British cotton industry in 1813 and still only 14,150 by 1820. Hand-loom weavers were able to keep pace with the flow of machine-spun yarn, for productivity was high and efforts were devoted to further improvement in the hand loom as much as to the development of a power loom. There was no bottle-neck in the supply of hand-loom weavers, whose numbers increased until the 1820s, when there was a peak of between 200,000 and 250,000 in Britain. Indeed, fluctuations in demand for cloth meant there were periodic gluts of labour. A manufacturer who invested in powered machinery would face problems of high overheads in periods of slack trade, whereas a manufacturer who employed hand-loom weavers could simply lay them off without the problem of making valuable capital idle. Widespread adoption of power weaving came in the 1820s, when the number of looms increased rapidly to 55,500 by 1829 and 100,000 by 1833.[23]

The rapid spread of power weaving in the cotton industry created one of the most notorious social problems of industrialization: the decline of the hand-loom weavers. The problem was largely one of location, a mismatch between the centres of power- and hand-loom weaving. Mechanized weaving was initially undertaken by factory spinners with experience of powered machinery; it was therefore concentrated in 'integrated' spinning and weaving factories in south Lancashire and Cheshire, where most of the spinning mills were located. In these areas, hand-loom weavers were absorbed more easily than in the country district of north-east Lancashire, where the rise of weaving-only firms came later. Until the 1820s, many weavers kept at their hand-looms, forming a 'reserve army' of labour which was drawn upon when factories were operating at full capacity; in slumps, costly power looms were kept in production and domestic workers laid off. The turning-point came in 1826, when the piece-rate for hand-loom weaving ceased to recover in periods of buoyant trade, forcing hand-loom weavers to work longer hours for lower rates as they faced the spectre of technological unemployment.

The spread of power weaving came later in the case of wool than cotton, and later in woollen than worsted cloth. There were only 2,768 power looms in the worsted industry of the West Riding in 1836, which had increased to 29,539 in 1850. In woollens, there were only 9,417 power looms in Britain in 1850, and the shift to power weaving only started in the late 1850s with a rapid increase to 46,984 power looms by 1867.[24] The explanation was largely technical. Woollen yarn was more susceptible to breakages, which meant that power looms were confined to low-grade cloth and had to work slowly until the 1850s and 1860s, when they could weave at higher speeds and in better-quality cloth without damaging the yarn. Clearly, there was an important technical dimension to the pace of mechanization and centralization in the textile industries at a time when powered machines were crude and unreliable. This is not to deny that the pace of mechanization was shaped by legal, institutional, and social factors. In the West

Riding, the protoindustrial organization of worsteds reinforced technical reasons for the earlier development of mechanization than in woollens. Embezzlement and control caused greater problems for putters out in the worsted districts than for independent artisans in the woollen industry, which gave a greater incentive to shift into factory production. Further, large-scale putters out in the worsted district developed larger factories in Halifax and Bradford than did small artisan clothiers in the woollen trade of Leeds and Huddersfield. It was, however, also possible for putting out to *delay* the development of centralized factory production and for artisan production to ease the transition. In the West Country, the technical problems of mechanizing woollen cloth were exacerbated by the organization of putting out, for the introduction of machinery into one specialized sector created technological unemployment, and led to resistance. In the artisan structure of the West Riding woollen industry, mechanization of one stage of production released members of the artisan workshop to undertake other tasks, and so caused less hostility. Technical and social explanations of mechanization and centralization interacted.

The pattern of technical change was also affected by the extent of legal protection of new techniques by patents. Inventions were often the result of a conscious and costly process of development, rather than the product of trial and error from existing practices. Industrial towns developed an interest in science, most notably the Lunar Society in Birmingham, whose members included James Watt and Matthew Boulton. The costs of developing a patent could be high, and Richard Roberts claimed to have spent £29,944 on his patent of 1825, which took nine years to make a profit.[25] Financing a new patent required considerable capital, and very few inventors were able to follow the example of Henry Bessemer in financing his work from the proceeds of past patents. More usual was a partnership between the patentee and user of a new technique. The patent established a property right in the invention, and protected it against exploitation by firms which had not shared in the costs. A careful balance had to be struck between the encouragement of investment in developing new techniques, and the diffusion of best-practice production methods. A high level of protection of property rights would allow patentees to take high profits, encouraging them to develop new techniques at the expense of slowing down the diffusion of best-practice technology; a low level of protection would allow the more rapid diffusion of best-practice technology, but slow down the flow of inventions. The patent system of 1536 gave an inventor the right to exclude others from using a patent for fourteen years, which could be extended by private Act of Parliament such as the unprecedented extension of James Watt's patent for twenty-five years in 1775. But the system was not noticeably skewed towards the patentees. In 1778 Lord Mansfield ruled that a patent was a social contract between the patentee and society which required a precise specification of how a technique could be utilized, and this principle was used in 1785 to overturn Arkwright's patent of 1769 on the water-frame. The balance between the conflicting aims of protecting inventors and encouraging diffusion of new technology was somewhat in favour of users until the 1830s, when the courts started to take a more favourable view of property rights and shifted the balance to the protection of patentees.

A further technical dimension to the spread of centralized, power-driven factories was the cost of providing a power source relative to the wages for hand labour. It took a considerable time before cheap sources of power were available, and it was only in the 1830s and 1840s that a decisive fall in the cost of steam power permitted a shift to factory production in cotton and wool. Until then, domestic and factory production were complementary, with only part of the spinning and weaving of cotton and wool moving into centralized, powered factories. When Baines referred to the 'mighty engine' in the cotton-mills of 1835, he was still describing a striking novelty rather than the norm.

Sources of Power

Factories applied a central source of power, so allowing a considerable increase in the amount of work performed by each worker. Machines were initially very similar to hand-operated devices used in the domestic system, such as the spinning-jenny; a central source of power allowed an increase in their scale, pace, and length of operation, and permitted a worker to supervise several machines rather than to operate a single machine. In Adam Smith's example of the pin factory, workers increased their productivity by division of labour and the possibilities of further productivity growth disappeared as the market was integrated by improvements in transport and distribution, and specialization of function went as far as was practicable. Despite improvements to hand tools and the development of specialized skills, there were strict limits to productivity. By applying power and energy to production, a new level of productivity became possible which far exceeded the potential offered in Adam Smith's model of growth.

When *The Wealth of Nations* was published in 1776, Smith was scarcely aware of the possibilities of applying power to production, and even in the census of 1831 the number of workers in energy-intensive factories was still small. The impact on overall productivity was slight, and the onset of the 'stationary state' still a real danger. Baines was certainly exaggerating the extent to which steam power had transformed industry by 1835, when the typical industrial worker had more in common with the pin-maker. Renewable 'soft' energy from the animate power of men and horses, or from wind and water, continued to be more important than steam at least to 1850, and perhaps to 1870. There were serious constraints on these sources of energy, and all were susceptible to declining marginal returns. Both human and animal power depended on the annual flow of crops from the soil, and an increase in the use of horses would reduce the human food supply. Wind could not be stored or controlled, and was often available in unsuitable locations. Water power could be harnessed by building dams, which offered a more flexible and responsive source of energy, but the search for water took industrialists to remote locations or obliged them to construct more costly dams and mill-races. Coal was a different matter, permitting an escape from the constraints of short-term *flows* of energy and allowing the input of a large *stock* of mineral energy into the economy. Once coal could be harnessed to the steam engine to supply mechanical energy, growth by specialization on the model of the pin-makers could give way to growth by application of energy, which loosened the constraints on productivity.

For much of the eighteenth century, coal was limited to providing *heat* energy in a few industrial processes, and it was a slow process to harness the steam engine to provide *mechanical* energy. Animal and human energy, wind and water, remained important. Horses were used in small factories to drive carding machines; in coal-mines, they were used initially for winding and pumping, and subsequently for underground transport; they were employed to operate grinding wheels in potteries or to mix clay in brickyards. Wind power reached a peak at the end of the eighteenth century, and possibly exceeded the total of steam power in 1800. Windmills were expensive to build and very cheap to run; their main problem was irregular operation, so that they could only be used where *time* was cheap. They made most sense in milling corn or crushing seeds, which could be spaced over the year as the produce of the harvest was processed by a miller and a few assistants. There was little urgency, for speedy completion of milling or crushing would simply leave the plant idle for the rest of the year. An industrial sector with a large work-force and a constant flow of materials was a different proposition and here water power offered greater regularity for driving textile machinery, grinding flint and mixing clay in the Potteries, turning cutlers' wheels in Sheffield, powering slitting mills in the iron industry, or pounding rags to produce paper.

Water power greatly exceeded steam in 1800, and continued to expand and improve its efficiency. The initial extension of water power to the preparatory processes of carding and scribbling wool did not require any great increase in power requirements, and it was possible to adapt corn-mills and fulling mills or to apply their techniques. However, Arkwright cotton-mills applied power in new ways, and specialist engineers such as John Smeaton, Thomas Brindley, John Rennie, and William Fairbairn introduced more efficient wheels, iron axles, and gears. The mounting demands for water power in Manchester, Leeds, or Nottingham forced textile producers to search for new sources in remoter country districts. Arkwright, for example, moved to Cromford, where he was obliged to build not only a mill but also housing and social facilities for the work-force. The capital costs of sophisticated water-wheels, with their dams and mill-races, often exceeded the fixed cost of a steam engine. They were, of course, cheaper to run, for the main variable cost was the payment for water rights, and they needed no coal and considerably less labour than steam engines. Continued improvements in the efficiency of water power over the eighteenth and early nineteenth centuries meant that its overall cost remained very close to steam power as late as 1830.

It took some time to realize the greater potentiality of the cheap, energy-intensive mechanical power which was offered by steam power. The first steam engine was developed by Savery in 1695, and was improved by Thomas Newcomen in 1712 (see Fig. 7.3). Application of these engines was limited, for they could not provide a continuous source of power for machines which required an even, constant rotary motion. They were used for pumping, initially in Cornish tin-mines and subsequently in coal-pits, and could be used to supplement water power by pumping water back into the mill-pond after it had passed over the wheel, so freeing industry from some of the limitations imposed by the flow of water. The direct application of steam power to machinery required further technical changes in order to produce constant, rotary power, which was achieved in the 1780s. Whether it made economic sense was another matter, depending on the cost of steam engines in relation to other sources of mechanical energy.

A Savery engine consumed about 30 lb. of coal to produce one horsepower for one hour. The Newcomen engine was slightly more efficient in the early eighteenth century, when it consumed between 20 and 30 lb. of coal; later improvements in the accuracy of cylinders and valves reduced consumption to 17 to 18 lb. by the late eighteenth century. Watt improved the efficiency of steam engines in a patent of 1769, which brought fuel consumption down to 12.5 lb. per horsepower per hour by the 1790s. A significant part of the gain was, however, taken by the high premium he charged for the use of the patent. The major savings in fuel consumption came with the development of high-pressure compounding engines, which were first used in Cornish mines, where as little as 2.5 to 3 lb. of coal were needed per horsepower per hour. The choice of engine depended upon the importance of fuel economy versus capital costs. The Savery engine had a high coal consumption, but cost about a quarter of a Newcomen engine for small sizes; they made sense when small amounts of power were needed. At the end of the eighteenth century, the capital cost of a Newcomen engine was about three-quarters that of a Watt's engine, but fuel costs were higher. Much depended on the price of coal, and Newcomen engines persisted for much longer on the coalfields than in London. High-pressure compound engines offered fuel economy, but cost more to build; they were initially developed in Cornwall, where coal was expensive. These engines only spread to the Lancashire cotton industry on any scale from 1845, when the McNaught patent offered a compromise between lower fuel consumption of between 4.5 and 5 lb. per horsepower per hour, and capital costs. The costs of steam power in Manchester were stable between the 1790s and 1830s, and it was only in the 1840s that there was a marked fall in total costs which allowed a decisive shift to factory production in cotton and wool textiles. Manufacturing industry started to experience the growth potential of energy-intensive production.

There was not a sudden shift in the relative cost of power with the coming of steam, and it made economic sense in many cases to continue to use water power, particularly in view of the different structure of costs. The total cost of water power in 1830 was £18. 3s. 4d. per horsepower, of which the variable cost was only £2. 4s. 8d. or 12 per cent; steam power had a slightly lower total cost of £17. 11s. 6d. per horsepower, with variable costs amounting to £13. 7s. 4d. or 76 per cent.[26] In cotton, the choice between water and steam power depended on the type of spinning machinery. Water-frames produced cheap, coarse yarns and used large amounts of power, about one horsepower per hundred spindles; mule-spinning needed only about 0.2 horsepower per hundred spindles for coarse yarns and less for fine yarns of much greater value. The larger power requirements of frame-spinning and the lower value of output encouraged the continued use of water power, for the marginal cost of additional power was low after the high fixed costs of building the dam and mill-race had been incurred. In mule-spinning, power costs were a small proportion of value added, and the use of steam was encouraged because mills had to be heated to spin fine yarn. The fine spinners were the leaders in the use of steam power, until it spread to other sectors of the cotton industry with the fall in the price of steam power from the 1840s. Adoption of steam was also encouraged by a reduction in the working day to ten hours and a fall in profit margins in the depression of the late 1830s and early 1840s which gave an incentive to increase the speed of machinery and labour effort. Baines's graphic description was starting to describe the typical rather than the exceptional.

At the beginning of the nineteenth century steam engines were not found predominantly in towns or in manufacturing industry, and Cornwall had about three times the amount of steam power of London, and six times the level of Manchester. By 1850, steam was used more widely in towns and manufacturing, and above all in textile factories: steam accounted for 86 per cent of power in

(b) Watt's Double Acting Rotative Engine, 1784

(a) Newcomen's Atmospheric Engine, 1712

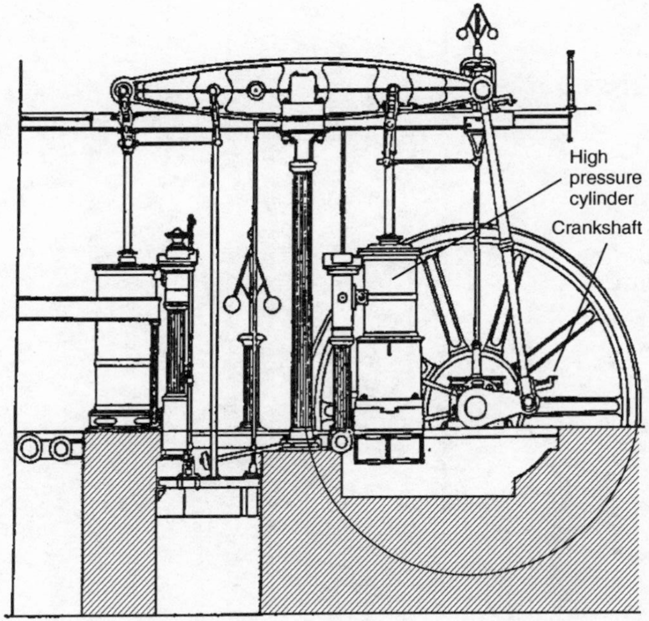

FIG. 7.3. Development of the steam engine

Source: H. V. Dickson, *A Short History of the Steam Engine* (Cambridge 1938), 30; C. Singer *et al*. (eds.), *A History of Technology, iv: The Industrial Revolution c.1750–c.1850* (Oxford, 1958), 187, 194.

(*a*) Newcomen's Atmospheric Engine, 1712 [The top of the cylinder was open, and the piston descended under the weight of the atmosphere when the steam in the cylinder was condensed by the injection of water. The piston was returned to the top of the stroke by the weight of the beam, while steam was admitted to the cylinder. Power was transmitted by the beam only on the down stroke, by pulling on a chain connected to the pump rod.]   (*b*) Watt's Double Acting Rotative Engine, 1784 [The top of the cylinder was closed, and a separate condenser added in the patent of 1769. When the piston was at the top of the cylinder, steam was admitted above it, and the piston was forced down. When the piston reached the bottom of the cylinder, it was pulled up by the weight of the beam. The engine could now transmit power on both strokes, if some means other than a chain could be found for connecting the piston to the beam as it described an arc: a chain could pull and not push. In order to produce rotary motion, the up-and-down movement of the beam had to be converted into circular motion. The simplest way of creating circular motion was by a rigid connecting rod and crankshaft, which was patented by a rival in 1780; Watt's solution in 1781 was the 'sun and planet' gear. The remaining problem was solved in 1784, by the parallel motion bars.]   (*c*) McNaught's Compound Beam Engine, 1848 [McNaught added a high-pressure cylinder midway along the beam.]

High pressure cylinder

Crankshaft

(c) McNaught's Compound Beam Engine, 1848

cotton factories and water for 14 per cent; in other textile factories, steam supplied 71.8 per cent and water 28.2 per cent. The only manufacturing industry which came close to rivalling cotton was iron, where steam power was used for smelting, founding, forging, and engineering. Steam was little used in London, where it was mainly located in waterworks, breweries, distilleries, dyehouses, corn-mills, and some foundries and machine-makers. In Birmingham, steam power was largely confined to the primary processes of rolling copper and brass, and iron-founding; it was not adopted to any extent in the manufacture of screws, buttons, guns, and other small metal goods which formed the basis of the economy of the town. Steam was also used in grinding of clays and chemicals, and the polishing of glass. But the spread of steam into British industry must not be exaggerated. As late as 1870, only two sectors of manufacturing industry were affected on any scale: cotton and the primary processes of iron production, which accounted for 30.8 per cent and 22.7 per cent respectively of steam power in factories and workshops. Most steam was still used to pump water in mines and waterworks; to supply forced ventilation for blast furnaces or mines; to turn rollers and drive hammers in metal forges and foundries; and to grind and mill. The production of most manufactured goods continued to rely upon the extensive use of hand labour and simple tools, and even in the forges and foundries, hard physical labour was used to charge the furnaces with raw materials, and to drag heavy ingots and bars to the hammers and rollers. The coming of the factory, the emergence of powered machinery, and the overturning of work-practices still had far to go by 1850.[27]

Who were the Factory Owners?

Industry before the industrial revolution, François Crouzet has suggested, was 'an industry without industrialists':[28] putting out merchant manufacturers were more concerned with selling than production processes, they had little fixed capital and plant, and their business was centred on a warehouse. The factory owner was a new breed of businessman, an industrialist who placed production at the centre of his concerns and sought a fortune by producing rather than selling goods. The first half of the nineteenth century was therefore the period of the 'making of the northern employing class'.[29] The number of cotton-mills increased from between 15 and 20 in 1780 to 1,932 in 1850, so that on the cautious assumption of an average of two partners a mill, there were about 4,000 cotton-masters in 1850. Crouzet's 'extremely wild guess' is that there were about 10,000 industrialists in all sectors.[30] How were they recruited?

It is often assumed that there was a break in industrial leadership, as a new group of factory masters emerged to replace artisan producers and putters out whose management style and business ethos were inappropriate to the new order. Many contemporaries argued that there was a considerable degree of openness, and John Kennedy, the Manchester cotton-spinner, assured a French visitor that he had 'never seen a firm established with a large capital which has ever succeeded. The only men who have made fortunes have been those who started with nothing.'[31] Samuel Smiles in *Self Help* (1859) propagated an ideology of the self-made man, stressing the possibility of rising from a lowly social origin to industrial eminence on the basis of thrift, hard work, and character. These views have some plausibility, for early factories required little fixed capital and much industrial capital came from the reinvestment of profits, which could allow small firms to grow in gradual stages. Yet the assertion that mobility was open to anyone with ability could be a useful means of condoning inequality, forming an important myth to justify industrial capitalism rather than a description of reality. It was, remarked Charles Dickens, 'among the fictions of Coketown. Any capitalist there, who had made sixty thousand pounds out of six pence, always professed to wonder why the sixty thousand nearest Hands didn't each make sixty thousand pounds out of sixpence.'[32] Contrary to the myth of the self-made man, the limited importance of fixed capital did not encourage the emergence of new men, for success depended upon access to circulating capital and credit, which was precisely the expertise gained by merchant-manufacturers in the domestic system. Could it be argued that putting out provided the expertise and capital for the coming of the factory, so that there was no marked shift in industrial leadership and few opportunities for men to rise from rags to riches? On such an interpretation, established businessmen maintained their leadership by a slow transfer of resources and expertise into centralized production.

Surveys of the social origins of industrialists have shown that few were drawn from landowners (see Table 7.1), who played a greater role in investing in docks and mining rather than manufacturing, where their involvement was usually as *rentiers* in leasing furnaces or mills. Neither did many industrialists come from the professional middle class. Benjamin Gott was the son of a surveyor, a profession which was involved with industry; John Roebuck was a doctor in Birmingham before moving into the refining of precious metals and subsequently chemicals and iron production; and Thomas Williams became involved in the copper industry as a result of his involvement in a lawsuit over mining rights. Such men were exceptional, and it was also rare for industrialists to be recruited from the other end of the social scale. Only 7.1 per cent of industrialists had fathers who were wage-earning manual workers. The most striking instances of social mobility were in sectors where technical skill provided the basis for entry, such as William and Peter Fairbairn. Their father had been an agricultural labourer and farm manager, and they were apprenticed as engineers

TABLE 7.1. *Social origins of founders of large industrial undertakings in Britain 1750–1850* (%)

	Father's occupation of 226 founders	Last occupation of 316 founders
Upper class (peer, gentry, officer)	8.8	2.5
Professions	7.1	2.5
Merchants and traders	23.0	19.6
Industry	29.2	41.8
Land (yeoman/farmer, yeoman and manufacturer, coal-master)	21.7	4.1
Working class	7.1	9.8
Various	3.1	3.8
Set up directly	—	15.8

Source: F. Crouzet, *The First Industrialists: The Problem of Origins* (Cambridge, 1985), table 2, p. 147, and table 4, p. 149.

and millwrights. After working as journeymen, they started firms in Manchester and Leeds which produced driving shafts for spinning mills and flax-spinning machinery. But the chances of gradual progression from small concerns to large were limited; failure was more likely than gradual growth. In the Manchester cotton industry, 85 per cent of small firms (those employing between 1 and 150 workers) failed between 1815 and 1833, compared with a failure rate of 36 per cent for firms employing between 151 and 500 workers. Small firms declined from 80 per cent of all concerns in 1815 to 43 per cent in 1833, and the increased dominance of medium and large firms was not the result of small firms moving up the scale. Rather, new firms entered at a 'mature' size, leap-frogging the first stage.[33] The prospects for social mobility were few. Although there were many small firms in British industry—in Birmingham metal trades, Sheffield cutlery, or the east Midlands hosiery and lace trades—they were usually subordinated to larger firms, forming dead ends rather than stairways to success. A small producer in Birmingham was unlikely to rise to be a large producer, for he was more likely to be a subcontractor in the grip of a larger firm, with a somewhat spurious independence. The ideology of mobility, the assertion that men could rise from the shop-floor to ownership, was less an expression of social reality than a means of justifying the changes which were taking place in the social structure. In the craft trades of Birmingham or London in the eighteenth century, journeymen could expect to become masters, and the workshop was based upon a common identity of interest as producers, protecting the workman's property in his skill, paying a decent wage, and selling goods at a fair price. But increased competition overturned the sense of identity between workers and masters, and the development of specialization and minute subdivision eroded the property of skill, removing workers' general knowledge of the production process, and reducing the prospects of becoming an independent producer. The attempt to preserve the older form of artisan production was a key element in early nineteenth-century artisan radicalism, which was challenged by an emerging liberal ideology of free competition and self-help.

Although the initial investment of fixed capital was often modest, it was necessary to obtain circulating capital, which depended upon being known. Kinship and reputation within a middle-class community were essential to success. John Heathcoat, one of the major producers of lace, appears as a self-made man in *Self Help*. In fact, he was the son of a small farmer who was apprenticed to a framesmith and hosier, and the key to his success was access to funds through contacts in the middle-class business community of the Midlands. It is, after all, scarcely surprising that the great majority of early industrialists were drawn from the business middle class. Inland traders, drapers, and shop-keepers could shift into industry, such as John Marshall, the Leeds flax-spinner, who was the son of a draper; Henry Blocklow, who was a grain and commission merchant before establishing the iron industry in Middlesbrough; or Miles Mason, who was a china-dealer in London before establishing a pottery. The motivation was often backward and forward integration, as suppliers of raw materials moved forward into production, or retailers and wholesalers moved backwards to acquire their own sources of supply. Nevertheless, the role of purely mercantile capital should not be exaggerated; more significant was recruitment from within the industrial sector. Many industrialists came from the ranks of merchant-manufacturers who were already involved in production in the domestic system and had the incentive of backward integration to acquire sources of materials for outworkers. John Foster, for example, employed 700 hand-loom weavers in the worsted industry at the time he commenced the construction of Black Dyke Mills in 1835. In the metal trades, there were similar examples of backward integration into forges and furnaces from the seventeenth century; a striking case in the later eighteenth century was the shift of John Roebuck and Samuel Garbett from the metal trades of Birmingham into the production of sulphuric acid in Scotland and the establishment of the Carron ironworks. Similarly, it was possible to move from centralized finishing trades such as bleaching, printing, or dyeing into cotton-spinning, such as Robert 'Parsley' Peel, who was one of the largest calico-printers. By comparison, forward integration was rare: one of the few examples was the movement of Cornish copper-miners into smelting at Swansea.

Rather than a change in industrial leadership, there was 'a kind of endogenesis:

industry bred a large number of the leaders who "revolutionised" it.'[34] There may have been few instances of rags to riches, but there were many cases in which men rose from relatively modest beginnings. John Kennedy and his partner James McConnel, for example, were the sons of Scottish farmers who were apprenticed to McConnel's uncle as engineers. They started to make textile machinery, initially in partnership with a firm of warehousemen, before moving into fine cotton-spinning. They were self-made men on a less strict definition, drawing on social groups below the landowners and rich merchants. The striking feature of British society was the highly diverse and flexible business community, and the large number of men of a 'middling sort' who were actively engaged in a variety of trading and commercial activities. How should they be viewed? One view is that the industrialists were a marginalized group, 'heartily despised by the traditional ruling class for their low birth and bad manners, and for decades they remained beyond the pale of "gentle" society'.[35] They were, in this interpretation, a group of outsiders who were able to concentrate on their business ventures, and industrialization took place almost despite the state. The faltering of British economic performance, it is often suggested, came when they succumbed to the embrace of the traditional ruling class, seeking acceptance on the terms of the landed élite so that the offspring of dynamic entrepreneurs such as Arkwright and Peel were transformed into landed gentlemen. This interpretation has a superficial attraction, for British society and politics in the eighteenth century appeared to be increasingly dominated by the landed élite, with the consolidation of great estates, a shift of income towards rents, and an unreformed parliament. But it *is* a superficial interpretation, for the men of a 'middling sort' had influence upon civil society. They were faced with the task not only of managing their individual firms, but also of running the factory towns of the industrial revolution. Labour relations and urban politics were as important as machines and steam engines in the creation of a new urban industrial society. This entailed a widening of the boundaries of civil society by creating a plethora of voluntary organizations such as hospitals and schools, and pressure groups such as trade associations and societies for moral reform. Towns which lacked formal parliamentary representation could secure 'virtual representation' through petitions and pressure on members of parliament drawn from the landed class. The apparent oligarchic stability of national politics should not obscure the vigour of political life at the local level, and the susceptibility of landed representatives to influence. The state was, in reality, sensitive to the needs of industry and commerce, providing encouragement and support for the development of new trades by adjusting commercial law and providing protection against foreign competition. Further, the rise of the great estates encouraged an unprecedented release of labour from the land, leading to the emergence of a

arge industrial, urban, and commercial sector. It is a travesty of the economic
nd social history of eighteenth-century Britain to reduce it to the entrenchment
of an *ancien régime* or 'old corruption' in which the great landowners controlled
parliament and the levers of state power, in association with the established
Anglican Church. The British political and social system was more fluid and
flexible, providing opportunities for the 'middling sort' and encouraging commercial and industrial development.

NOTES

1. E. Baines, *History of the Cotton Manufacture in Great Britain* (1835), 243–4.

2. D. C. North, *Structure and Change in Economic History* (New York, 1981), 168–9.

3. E. S. Furniss, *The Position of the Laborer in a System of Nationalism: A Study in the Labor Theories of the Later English Mercantilists* (Boston, 1920), 10.

4. Ibid. 118.

5. Ibid. 122.

6. A. Ure, *The Philosophy of Manufactures; or, An Exposition of the Scientific, Moral and Commercial Economy of the Factory System of Great Britain* (1835), 15.

7. Quoted in H. J. Perkin, *The Origins of Modern English Society 1780–1880* (1969), 92.

8. A. Smith, *An Inquiry into the Nature and Causes of the Wealth of Nations* (repr. 1937), 82–3 (book i, ch. viii).

9. M. Douglas and B. Isherwood, *The World of Goods: Towards an Anthropology of Consumption* (1979).

10. E. P. Thompson, 'Time, Work Discipline and Industrial Capitalism', *Past and Present*, 38 (1967), 71–2.

11. Ibid. 75.

12. Ibid.

13. Quoted in S. Pollard, *The Genesis of Modern Management: A Study of the Industrial Revolution in Britain* (1965), 183–4.

14. Ibid. 184.

15. Quoted in M. J. Daunton, *House and Home in the Victorian City: Working Class Housing, 1850–1914* (1983), 189.

16. S. Pollard, 'Factory Discipline in the Industrial Revolution', *Economic History Review*, 16 (1963–4), 264.

17. M. M. Edwards and R. Lloyd-Jones, 'N. J. Smelser and the Cotton Factory Family: A Reassessment', in N. B. Harte and K. G. Ponting (eds.), *Textile History and Economic History* (Manchester, 1973), 312–13.

18. See J. Foster, *Class Struggle and the Industrial Revolution: Early Industrial Capitalism in Three English Towns* (1974), ch. 7.

19. R. V. Malcomson, *Popular Recreation in English Society, 1700–1850* (Oxford, 1973), 170.

20. Thompson, 'Time', 75.

21. Ibid. 86.

22. S. R. H. Jones, 'Technology, Transaction Costs, and the Transition to Factory

Production in the British Silk Industry, 1700–1870', *Journal of Economic History*, 4 (1987), 82.

23. D. Bythell, *The Handloom Weavers: A Study in the English Cotton Industry during th Industrial Revolution* (Cambridge, 1969), 88.

24. D. Jenkins and K. G. Ponting, *The British Wool Textile Industry, 1770–1914* (Aldershot 1982), 111, 112.

25. H. I. Dutton, *The Patent System and Inventive Activity during the Industrial Revolutio 1750–1852* (Manchester, 1984), 157, 159.

26. G. N. von Tunzelmann, *Steam Power and British Industrialisation to 1860* (Oxford, 1978) 160.

27. J. W. Kanefsky, 'Motive Power in British Industry and the Accuracy of the 187 Factory Returns', *Economic History Review*, 2nd ser. 37 (1979); and A. E. Musson 'Industrial Motive Power in the United Kingdom, 1800–70', *Economic History Review* 2nd ser. 29 (1976).

28. F. Crouzet, *The First Industrialists: The Problem of Origins* (Cambridge, 1985), 4.

29. P. Joyce, *Work, Society and Politics: The Culture of the Factory in Later Victorian Englan* (1980), 3.

30. Crouzet, *First Industrialists*, 36.

31. Ibid. 38.

32. C. Dickens, *Hard Times* (1854; Oxford edn., 1955), 117.

33. R. Lloyd-Jones and A. A. Le Roux, 'Marshall and the Birth and Death of Firms: The Growth and Size Distribution of Firms in the Early Nineteenth-Century Cotton Industry', *Business History*, 24 (1982), 144, 146.

34. Crouzet, *First Industrialists*, 116.

35. Ibid. 142.

FURTHER READING

Berg, M., Hudson, P., and Sonenscher, M., 'Manufacture in Town and Country before the Factory', in M. Berg *et al.*, *Manufacture in Town and Country before the Factory* (Cambridge, 1983).

Bythell, D., *The Handloom Weavers: A Study in the English Cotton Industry during the Industrial Revolution* (Cambridge, 1969).

Catling, H., 'The Development of the Spinning Mule', *Textile History*, 9 (1978).

Chapman, S. D., 'Industrial Capital before the Industrial Revolution: An Analysis of the Assets of a Thousand Textile Entrepreneurs, c.1730–50', in N. B. Harte and K. G. Ponting (eds.), *Textile History and Economic History* (Manchester, 1973).

—— 'Financial Constraints on the Growth of Firms in the Cotton Industry, 1790–1850', *Economic History Review*, 2nd ser. 32 (1979).

—— 'The Textile Factory before Arkwright: A Typology of Factory Development', *Business History Review*, 48 (1974).

—— 'The Cost of Power in the Industrial Revolution in Britain: The Case of the Textile Industry', *Midland History*, 1 (1971–2).

Chapman, S. D., 'The Peels in the Early English Cotton Industry', *Business History*, 11 (1969).

—— *The Early Factory Masters: The Transition to the Factory System in the Midlands Textile Industry* (Newton Abbot, 1967).

Chapman, S. J., and Marquis, F. J., 'The Recruiting of the Employing Classes from the Ranks of the Wage Earners in the Cotton Industry', *Journal of the Royal Statistical Society*, 75 (1911–12).

Crouzet, F., *The First Industrialists: The Problem of Origins* (Cambridge, 1985).

Douglas, M., and Isherwood, B., *The World of Goods: Towards an Anthropology of Consumption* (1979).

Dutton, H. I., *The Patent System and Inventive Activity during the Industrial Revolution, 1750–1852* (Manchester, 1984).

—— and Jones, S. R. H., 'Invention and Innovation in the British Pin Industry, 1790–1850', *Business History Review*, 57 (1983).

Edwards, M. M., and Lloyd-Jones, R., 'N. J. Smelser and the Cotton Factory Family: A Reassessment', in N. B. Harte and K. G. Ponting (eds.), *Textile History and Economic History* (Manchester, 1973).

Foster, J., *Class Struggle and the Industrial Revolution: Early Industrial Capitalism in Three English Towns* (1974).

Freifeld, M., 'Technological Change and the "Self-Acting Mule": A Study of Skill and the Sexual Division of Labour', *Social History*, 11 (1986).

Furniss, E. S., *The Position of the Laborer in a System of Nationalism: A Study in the Labor Theories of the Later English Mercantilists* (Boston, 1920).

Gatrell, V. A. C., 'Labour, Power, and the Size of Firms in Lancashire Cotton in the Second Quarter of the Nineteenth Century', *Economic History Review*, 2nd ser. 30 (1977).

Greenberg, D., 'Reassessing the Power Patterns of the Industrial Revolution: An Anglo-American Comparison', *American Historical Review*, 87 (1982).

Habakkuk, H. J., *American and British Technology in the Nineteenth Century: The Search for Labour-Saving Inventions* (Cambridge, 1962).

Harris, J. R., 'The Employment of Steam Power in the Eighteenth Century', *History*, 52 (1967).

Hills, R. L., 'Hargreaves, Arkwright and Crompton: Why Three Inventors?', *Textile History*, 10 (1979).

—— *Power in the Industrial Revolution* (Manchester, 1970).

Honeyman, K., *Origins of Enterprise: Business Leadership in the Industrial Revolution* (Manchester, 1982).

Howe, A. D., *The Cotton Masters, 1830–60* (Oxford, 1984).

Hudson, P., 'From Manor to Mill: The West Riding in Transition', in M. Berg, P. Hudson, and M. Sonenscher (eds.), *Manufacture in Town and Country before the Factory* (Cambridge, 1983).

—— *The Genesis of Industrial Capital: A Study of the West Riding Wool Textile Industry, c.1750–1850* (Cambridge, 1986).

Jenkins, D. T., 'Early Factory Development in the West Riding of Yorkshire, 1770–1800', in N. B. Harte and K. G. Ponting (eds.), *Textile History and Economic History* (Manchester, 1973).

—— *The West Riding Wool Textile Industry, 1770–1835: A Study of Fixed Capital Formation* (Edington, 1975).

—— and Ponting, K. G., *The British Wool Textile Industry, 1770–1914* (Aldershot, 1982).

Jones, S. R. H., 'The Organization of Work', *Journal of Economic Behaviour and Organization*, 3 (1982).

—— 'Technology, Transaction Costs, and the Transition to Factory Production in the British Silk Industry, 1700–1870', *Journal of Economic History*, 47 (1987).

Joyce, P., *Work, Society and Politics: The Culture of the Factory in Later Victorian England* (1980).

Kanefsky, J. W., 'Motive Power in British Industry and the Accuracy of the 1870 Factory Return', *Economic History Review*, 2nd ser. 32 (1979).

Lane, J., 'Apprenticeship in Warwickshire Cotton Mills, 1790–1830', *Textile History*, 10 (1979).

Lazonick, W. H., 'Production Relations, Labor Productivity, and Choice of Technique: British and US Cotton Spinning', *Journal of Economic History*, 41 (1981).

—— 'Industrial Relations and Technical Change: The Case of the Self-Acting Mule', *Cambridge Journal of Economics*, 3 (1979).

Lee, C. H., *A Cotton Enterprise, 1795–1840: A History of M'Connel and Kennedy, Fine Cotton Spinners* (Manchester, 1972).

Lloyd-Jones, R., and Le Roux, A. A., 'Factory Utilization and the Firm: The Manchester Cotton Industry, c.1825–40', *Textile History*, 15 (1984).

—— 'Marshall and the Birth and Death of Firms: The Growth and Size Distribution of Firms in the Early Nineteenth Century Cotton Industry', *Business History*, 24 (1982).

—— 'The Size of Firms in the Cotton Industry: Manchester, 1815–41', *Economic History Review*, 2nd ser. 33 (1980).

Lloyd-Jones, R., and Lewis, M. J., *Manchester and the Age of the Factory: The Business Structure of Cottonopolis in the Industrial Revolution* (1988).

Lyons, J. S., 'Vertical Integration in the British Cotton Industry, 1825–50: A Revision', *Journal of Economic History*, 45 (1985).

Malcomson, R. V., *Popular Recreations in English Society, 1700–1850* (Cambridge, 1973).

Marglin, S. A., 'What Do Bosses Do? The Origins and Function of Hierarchy in Capitalist Production', *Review of Radical Political Economics*, 6 (1974).

Mathias, P., 'Leisure and Wages in Theory and Practice', in *The Transformation of England* (1979).

Musson, A. E., 'Industrial Motive Power in the United Kingdom, 1800–70', *Economic History Review*, 2nd ser. 29 (1976).

—— and Robinson, E., 'Science and Industry in the Late Eighteenth Century', *Economic History Review*, 2nd ser. 13 (1960–1).

North, D. C., *Structure and Change in Economic History* (New York, 1981).

Perkin, H. J., *The Origins of Modern English Society, 1780–1880* (1969).

ollard, S., 'Fixed Capital in the Industrial Revolution in Britain', repr. in F. Crouzet (ed.), *Capital Formation in the Industrial Revolution* (1972).

—— 'Factory Discipline in the Industrial Revolution', *Economic History Review*, 2nd ser. 16 (1963–4).

—— *The Genesis of Modern Management: A Study of the Industrial Revolution in Britain* (1965).

eid, D. A., 'The Decline of Saint Monday, 1766–1876', *Past and Present*, 71 (1976).

arn, J., 'The Textile Millwright in the Early Industrial Revolution', *Textile History*, 5 (1974).

hompson, E. P., 'Time, Work Discipline and Industrial Capitalism', *Past and Present*, 38 (1967).

on Tunzelmann, G. N., *Steam Power and British Industrialisation to 1860* (Oxford, 1978).

adsworth, A. P., and Mann, J. de L., *The Cotton Trade and Industrial Lancashire, 1600–1780* (Manchester, 1931).

illiamson, O. E., 'The Organization of Work', *Journal of Economic Behaviour and Organization*, 1 (1980).

ilson, R. G., 'The Supremacy of the Yorkshire Cloth Industry in the Eighteenth Century', in N. B. Harte and K. G. Ponting (eds.), *Textile History and Economic History* (Manchester, 1973).

....

CHAPTER 8

Furnaces, Forges, and Mines

The debate on rural industrialization and its metamorphosis into factory production ignores trades, in both town and country, which were based upon fixed, centralized plant. These included some of the most important industries of the eighteenth and early nineteenth centuries: the mining of coal and minerals such as iron, lead, tin, and copper; the smelting of ores in furnaces and their refining in forges; the processing of domestic and imported agricultural commodities by sugar-refiners, leather-tanners, seed-crushers, flour-millers, maltsters, brewers, and distillers; and the production of salt, paper, and glass. Although the dynamic of growth in plant-based trades was very different from protoindustrial industries, they were often mutually dependent. The nail-makers of the west Midlands, cutlers of Sheffield, and the producers of buckles, buttons, and small metal goods of Birmingham could only grow by specialization because their supplies of iron, steel, copper, and brass were freed from restraints through the use of coal as a source of heat in furnaces and forges. The impact of the 'modernized' sector was much greater than is suggested by the low proportion of the work-force directly employed, for a change in the supply of materials to domestic workers disrupted the existing social relations of production in the 'traditional' sectors.

The growth of plant-based industries rested on the application of greater amounts of both mechanical and heat energy. Mechanical energy was used for operating millstones, rollers, and hammers in order to grind grains, crush seeds, pound clay, cut bar iron, roll sheets of metal, pump water, and raise coal and minerals from mines. Horse, wind, and water power had long been used, and there were fewer technical difficulties in substituting steam than in textile factories, which needed a regular, constant source of power. Whether it made economic sense depended on whether a bottle-neck existed. In some cases, there was no point in speeding up the processing of materials, for a water-powered 'pug mill' could process enough clay to keep the potters at work; in other cases, ıch as coal-mines, the installation of steam engines was crucial to mining at reater depths. The availability of heat energy was a greater restraint on some ıdustries, for the amount of energy needed to fire kilns in potteries, or to smelt nd refine iron or copper, was greater than the energy needed to pound clay or to perate the rolling and slitting mills. Growth of these heat-intensive industries ˌas limited so long as they were restricted to using wood or charcoal produced ˎy covering mounds of wood with turf and burning it slowly to produce pure ˌarbon. The availability of energy was limited to the sustainable output of wood, ɔr a serious shortage of fuel would soon appear if more timber was cut than the ınnual growth; there was also direct competition with the use of land for ˌrowing food for men and animals. The management of coppices and the ˌroduction of charcoal were slow and labour intensive. By contrast, coal did not ompete with land for crops, and a miner was able to produce about 200 tons of oal a year, which was far more energy than any other worker. It became ˌossible to inject large *stocks* of mineral energy into the economy.

The winning of coal led to formidable technical challenges, as the exploitation ˌf easily worked outcrops of coal on the surface gave way to deeper pits, with the ːonsequent difficulties of pumping water, ventilation, raising coal from the ˌvorkings, and transporting the bulky commodity to the consumer. Larger ˌuantities of coal had to be produced without running into barriers of falling ˌroductivity and mounting costs. It was also necessary to devise ways of applying ːoal to a wider range of industries, a gradual process which started well before ˌ700 and was only reaching completion in 1800. The use of coal for domestic ˌeating and cooking posed no technical problems; the major difficulty was ˌransport, which limited coal largely to towns with easy access to coalfields by ˌvater (see Fig. 8.1). Above all, coal from the north-east of England was carried in ˌeels along the river Tyne to ships which sailed down the east coast and up the Γhames to the heart of London, which consumed about 15 per cent of total ɔutput in 1700, and a third of the production of the north-east throughout the ˌeighteenth century. The use of coal in domestic hearths reduced pressure on the ˌupply of wood for industry, and coal was also used from the sixteenth century in ˌndustrial processes which simply heated or boiled materials in pans where there ˌvas no direct contact with materials and no danger of contamination. Sea water ˌvas boiled to produce salt; molasses to refine sugar; animal fats and bones to ˌroduce tallow and glue; water and malt to brew beer; dyestuffs and bleaches to ˌinish cloth. Whether these industries were located in the coalfields depended on ːhe ratio of the cost and quantity of coal to materials, and the value of the final ˌroduct. A large volume of sea water was boiled with considerable amounts of ˌoal in order to produce a small amount of salt: a location close to coal made ˌsense and the production of sea-salt was concentrated along the Tyne. By

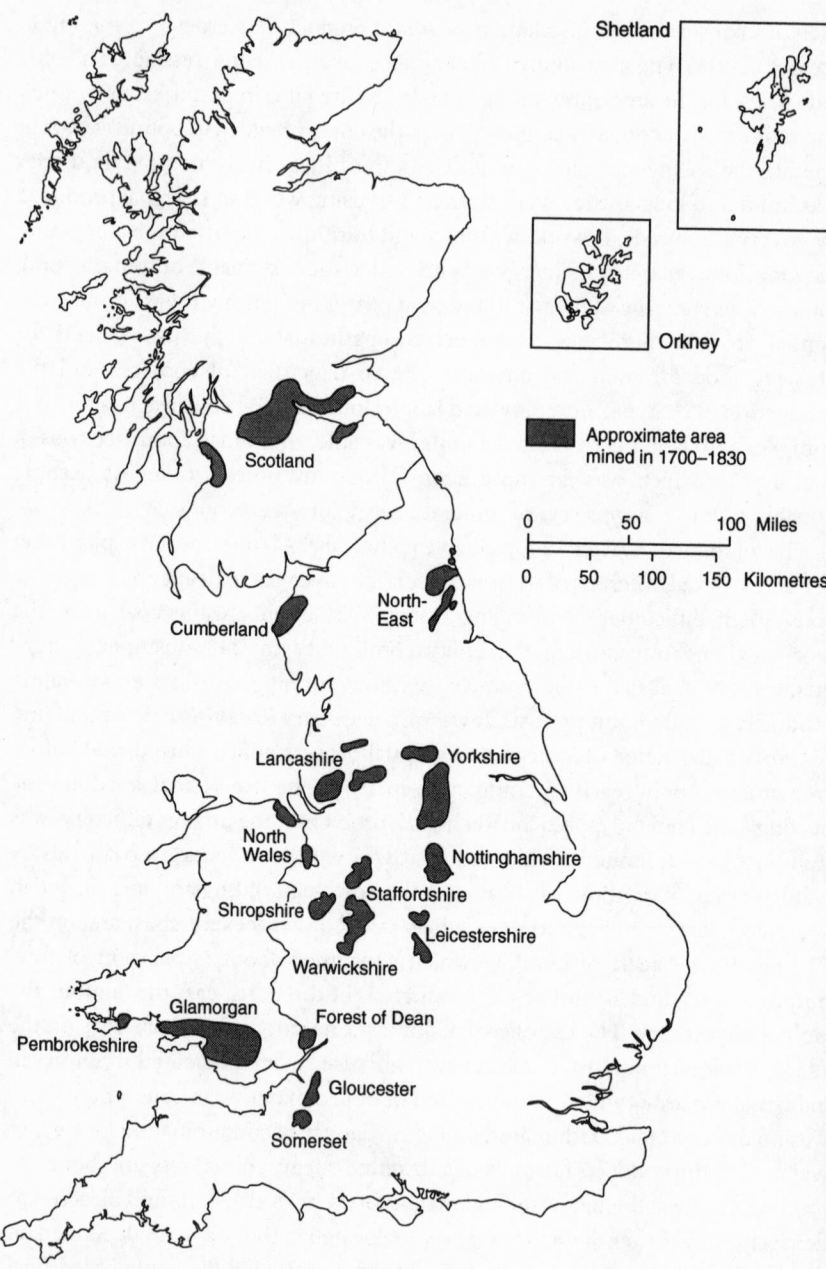

FIG. 8.1. Coalfields in Britain

Source: M. W. Flinn, *History of the British Coal Industry*, ii: *1700–1830: The Industrial Revolution* (Oxford, 1984).

contrast, the amount of coal was small in relation to the volume of costly molasses, so that sugar-refining was located in London. Glue and tallow production were located close to major meat markets, such as the noxious trades on the south bank of the Thames which obtained fat and bones from Smithfield. Similarly, coal was a relatively low proportion of the total cost of production of beer and spirits, which was located close to the final market. Technical innovation in these trades was a matter of economizing in the use of coal and labour, especially where coal was expensive and the size of the plant allowed economies of scale. In the 1790s, dyers and bleachers started to replace separate fires under each vat with a central source of steam heat, which allowed savings in the use of fuel and labour at the cost of greater capital investment. Coal could also be used without too much difficulty in ovens and kilns to bake bread and bricks, or in heating metal sufficiently to be passed through rolling mills and worked in smithies by nailers or locksmiths, for the metal was not molten and was consequently not affected by impurities in the coal. Serious difficulties arose when much higher temperatures were required in furnaces and forges; impurities in the coal interacted with molten raw materials and affected the chemical composition of metals. It was crucial to remove these technical constraints on the application of coal to industry in order to complete the escape from the limited flow of energy of the organic economy.

The Reverberatory Furnace

The use of coal at high temperatures was made possible by the reverberatory furnace: a tall, cone-shaped funnel produced a fierce draught when a coal fire was lit at the base; a curved dome deflected heat back on to raw materials contained in covered pots for protection from smuts and soot; and raw materials and coal were not in direct contact, so that impurities did not affect the final product. The process was first used in 1612 to heat sand and alkali to produce glass. Initially, 'glasshouses' were located in London and Bristol, for coal was a less significant element in total costs than the skilled, labour-intensive working of molten glass. In 1696 there were still twenty-four glasshouses in London catering for the large local market, and producing high-quality, fragile items such as wineglasses and chandeliers. During the eighteenth century, as output expanded and the value of glass fell, production concentrated on the coalfields, initially in the north-east, but increasingly in south-west Lancashire around St Helens and Warrington.

In the 1680s, the reverberatory furnace was applied to the smelting of lead and copper at Bristol. Copper and brass—an alloy made by adding zinc—became increasingly important during the eighteenth century for tools, scientific instruments, guns, clocks, steam engines, and a wide range of Birmingham trades from bedsteads to shoe buckles. They were used in the furniture industry for fixtures and fittings, turned into cooking utensils for the home, and vats and vessels for the food-processing industry. Copper was used to sheathe the bottom of ships in order to protect timbers from damage by wood-boring insects in the tropics. Smelting shifted from Bristol to Swansea, which had the great advantage of cheap fuel and easy access across the Bristol Channel to the Cornish ores, which accounted for 80 to 85 per cent of output for most of the eighteenth century: ships carried coal to Cornwall to operate steam engines at the mines and to smelt tin; they returned with cargoes of copper ore. Location on the coalfield made economic sense, for the fuel-intensive 'Welsh method' used 28 to 35 tons of coal to produce a ton of copper in the early eighteenth century and between 15 and 20 tons in the early nineteenth century, which accounted for about 45 per cent of total costs.[1] The Swansea smelters were highly concentrated, for costs of entry were high: they built specialist furnaces, held large stocks of a variety of ores, and often owned coal-mines. By contrast, the bargaining position of Cornish mine-owners was weak, for they were less concentrated, had widely varying costs and profit margins, and were loath to stop production because their mines needed constant pumping. This unequal relationship between Cornwall and Swansea was disrupted when copper ore was discovered in Anglesey in the 1770s and a local attorney, Thomas Williams, secured control of the largest mines. In 1779 he established his own smelting plant in south-west Lancashire to capture the high profits made by the Swansea cartel, and he expanded to form a large integrated concern which extended from Swansea to north Wales and the Thames valley, with warehouses in London, Birmingham, and Liverpool as well as a bank in north Wales and a chemical works in Liverpool. The price of copper fell, and the Swansea smelters paid less for Cornish ore, which provoked the mine-owners to counter-attack by establishing the Cornish Metal Company in 1785 to smelt their own ores, which entered an alliance with Williams not to undercut each other. Although Williams's dominance soon declined with the exhaustion of the Anglesey ores, and the Cornish cartel was weakened by wide variation in costs, the industry did not simply revert to its earlier pattern of dominance by the Swansea smelters. In the early nineteenth century Cornish mine-owners moved into the Swansea smelting industry, and in the 1820s a new challenge appeared with the discovery of copper ore in Latin America and Australia. Initially, ore was imported and smelted at Swansea, but by the 1840s the preliminary process of refining was undertaken in simple furnaces at the mines. The dominance of Swansea was further threatened by the production of copper from Spanish pyrites, which were also used in making sulphuric acid. Consequently, copper production shifted from Swansea to the major centres of the chemical industry on the Tyne, Clyde, and Mersey. The erosion of Swansea's position was completed in the 1860s and 1870s, when improvements in smelting technology reduced the amount of fuel needed to smelt and made it more rational to smelt close to the source of the ore.

Growth in 'traditional' sectors based on specialized hand production was intimately connected to growth through the application of mineral energy: steam engines were initially developed to pump water from deep mines in Cornwall; and copper and brass were produced by the application of massive quantities of cheap coal for use in a wide range of trades. The development of labour-intensive hand trades in Birmingham and the Black Country, using hand-operated presses, punches, and lathes, and relying on minute subdivision into specialized trades, rested upon the availability of cheap copper and brass from the reverberatory furnaces. Indeed, the so-called 'traditional' sectors might well, in the longer term, have greater potential for growth and development. Matthew Boulton specialized in the production of brass fittings for furniture and houses, supplying fashionable markets and adding considerable value to the input of brass and copper. He collaborated with James Watt in the production of steam engines, and in the later nineteenth century his successors were pioneers in the development of bicycles, motor cycles, and motor cars. Meanwhile, the smelters were in decline. The attraction of Britain for the production of copper and other metals in the eighteenth century was the availability of cheap coal and a work-force with the 'knack' of using it in furnaces. Dominance was short term, for Britain did not have abundant sources of ores and soon ran into declining marginal returns in the production of tin, copper, lead, and iron ores. Increasingly, the small lead-mines of the Pennines, and the deep copper- and tin-mines of Cornwall, were only profitable when prices were high. It was unattractive to refine and smelt imported ores as soon as producing countries could tap their own sources of coal, master the techniques of coal-fired furnaces, and obtain capital to construct works.

The Iron Industry

The reverberatory furnace allowed the application of coal to glass and non-ferrous metals, but it could not reach the high temperatures needed for smelting iron in 'blast' furnaces, where fuel was in direct contact with ore and limestone, and a forced draught was provided by water-driven bellows. Until some means could be found of preventing impurities in the coal from contaminating the iron, ironmasters were obliged to use charcoal, which limited the size of the blast furnace because the fragile fuel would be reduced to dust by the weight of ore and limestone. The furnace was kept in blast for as long as possible, until repairs were needed or the supply of water to the bellows failed: in the early eighteenth century a furnace might be in production for about thirty weeks, producing from 150 tons in a small furnace in the Weald to 1,000 tons in a new, large furnace. Location was dependent upon the availability of charcoal, for its fragility and high transport cost limited the area from which supplies could be drawn; it was also necessary to have iron ore in the vicinity and a supply of water for the bellows. Furnaces were consequently dispersed rather than concentrated, and the search for charcoal, water, and iron ore forced ironmasters to move from the Weald of Kent and Sussex to more distant, isolated areas in the Forest of Dean, south Wales, Lancashire, and Scotland. The Backbarrow Company, for example, built a furnace at Furness in Lancashire in 1711, and the partners erected another furnace at Invergarry in the Highlands of Scotland in 1727. Furnaces sprang up on the desolate uplands of northern Monmouthshire and Glamorgan, which were transformed in the course of the eighteenth century from an area of marginal grazing into the world's greatest centre of the iron industry. The dynamics of protoindustrialization had little relevance, and the search for timber supplies often forced ironmasters to locate in areas with sparse population and limited capital (see Fig. 8.2).

The output of iron grew at a modest rate from about 25,000 tons a year in the 1710s to 28,000 tons in 1750, but British furnaces' share of domestic consumption fell from about 54 per cent in 1716–20 to 43 per cent in 1750.[2] The shortfall was made up by imports from Sweden and Russia. The relative decline in British iron production was not caused by an absolute shortage of charcoal, for the increased use of coal for domestic and industrial uses meant that its price stabilized between the 1690s and 1750, and ironmasters could still obtain charcoal from coppices or by moving to areas of virgin wood. Rather, their problem was that charcoal production was labour intensive, which made it difficult for British furnaces to compete with low-wage economies in Sweden and Russia, particularly because poor-quality iron ore required a larger input of fuel. Indeed, British iron production only remained profitable and avoided absolute decline because it was protected by import duties and Swedish export duties which together amounted to between a quarter and third of the price of Swedish bar iron in Britain.

Blast furnaces produced pig iron, a brittle material with a high carbon content. In the early eighteenth century, about 5 per cent was cast into pots, cannon, stoves, railings, and fire-backs; the bulk of pig iron was refined in forges, removing carbon to produce more malleable and less brittle bar or wrought iron which was suitable for manufacture into nails, locks, and small arms. The forges were heated with charcoal rather than coal, and water power was used to produce a draught and to operate a hammer which beat the iron into a bar. The location of forges was somewhat less constrained than furnaces, for they did not

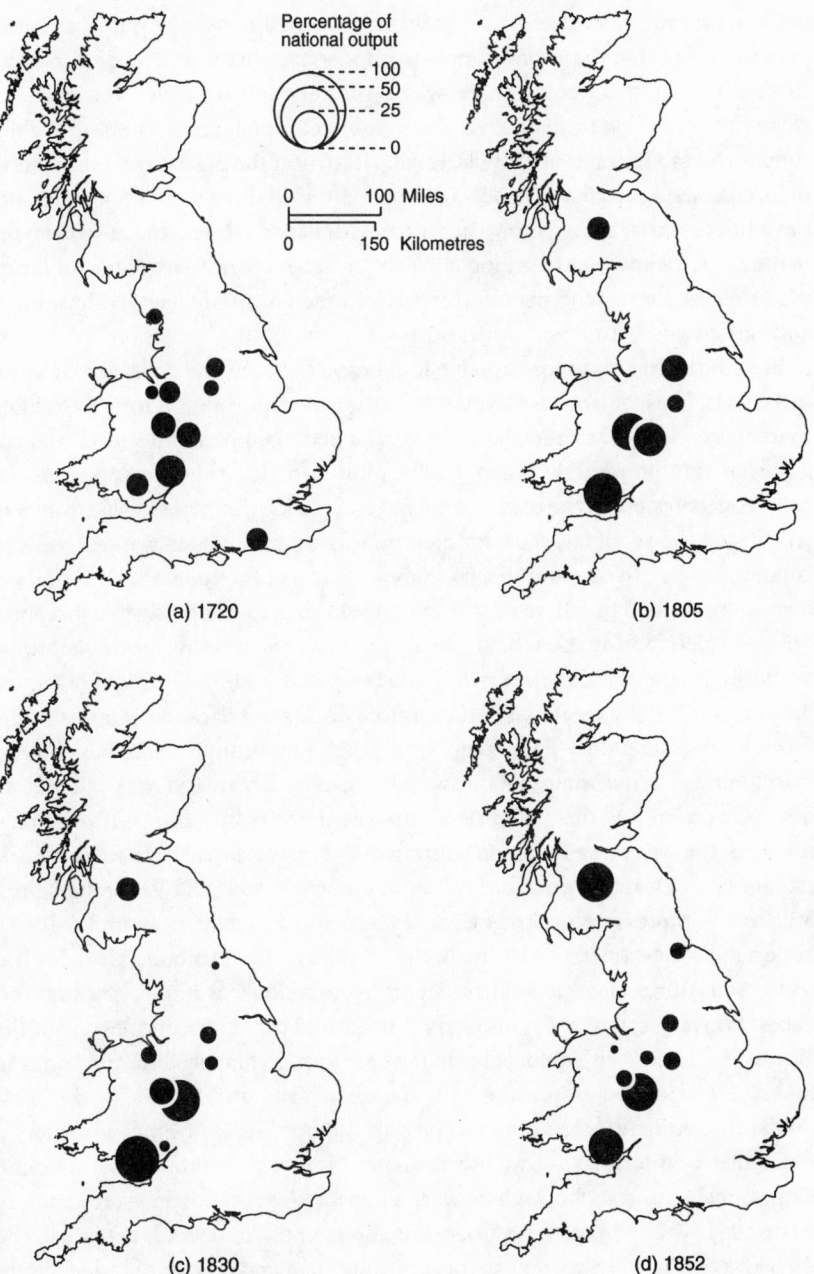

FIG. 8.2. Pig iron production by region

Source: P. Riden, 'Iron and Steel', in J. Langton and R. J. Morris (eds.), *Atlas of Industrialising Britain, 1789–1914* (1986), 129.

use iron ore, and needed less fuel and water power. Although the high wastage of pig iron meant that there was some attraction in locating near a furnace in order to save on transport costs, there was a greater pull towards the users. The character of pig iron from different districts varied, and forge-masters drew their supplies from a number of districts, mixing it to meet the precise requirements of their customers. A cluster of forges supplied the tool-makers of Sheffield and, most importantly, a large group in the west Midlands catered for the iron trades of the Black Country and Birmingham. The river Severn, a 'free' river, connected the furnaces, forges, and manufacturers from the Forest of Dean to Shropshire, and carried goods to Bristol for export.

British bar iron was most suitable for cheap hardware and nails, and Swedish or Russian bar iron was used where quality was important. Before it could be used by iron manufacturers, bar iron was heated, flattened into sheets, and cut into rods at rolling and slitting mills. The mills were driven by water power, and were concentrated on the banks of the Severn and its tributaries; unlike furnaces and forges, they could use coal for the iron was not molten and was less liable to contamination. Rolling and slitting mills were sometimes operated by independent owners, who purchased bar iron and sold rods to ironmongers who put it out to nailers and marketed the final product. There were, however, some vertically integrated concerns which co-ordinated widely separated stages of production, usually created by an ironmonger moving backwards into slitting, forging, and smelting. The Foley enterprise, for example, was based on a warehouse at Stourbridge in the west Midlands, where rod was put out to domestic nailers and the final product marketed; the family also controlled nine furnaces, thirteen forges, and four slitting mills in 1704, spread over south Wales, the Forest of Dean, Staffordshire, Cheshire, north Wales, and Worcestershire.[3] Still more impressive was the Crowley enterprise, which was probably the largest industrial concern in the early eighteenth century. Ambrose Crowley II, a nailer and ironmonger at Stourbridge, moved backwards into forges and furnaces; his son, Ambrose III (1658–1713), supervised the entire business from the City in association with his brother-in-law, the Birmingham ironmaster Sampson Lloyd. He operated a 'putting out' business from warehouses in the west Midlands, and he extended the business to the north-east of England, where a series of workshops used Swedish iron and local coal to produce nails, locks, hinges, chains, and anchors which were shipped down the east coast to London, where large warehouses held stocks for the country trade and, above all, the Royal Navy. Crowley was able to meet the huge demands of the royal dockyards, both because he held large stocks and because he had sufficient resources to wait for the Admiralty to pay. Indeed, his fixed capital was modest, amounting only to £12,000 in 1728; more significant were stocks of £92,856 and trade debts of £71,737.

The enterprise was, Michael Flinn remarked, a giant in an age of pygmies,[4] with an exceptional degree of economic integration and centralized control, employing about a thousand men in the early eighteenth century and moving commodities between the west Midlands, north-east, London, and the royal dockyards. Geographical dispersion made control difficult, and the typical organizational structure in iron firms was a series of flexible, interlocking partnerships and alliances which were dissolved and reformed as family circumstances and business needs changed; each forge or furnace was treated as a separate profit centre, with relatively loose co-ordination.

The dominant figure in the early eighteenth-century iron industry was the *manufacturer* or ironmonger who produced nails, locks, and hinges, rather than the iron*master* who produced pig and bar iron. The British industry was a high-cost producer of pig and bar iron, with a falling share of the market which was only sustained by import and export duties; the competitive advantage of the British iron industry in the early eighteenth century was in the production of rods and their manufacture into a wide range of commodities, which rested on a high degree of specialization and the use of cheap coal. British furnaces and forges only became competitive with Sweden and Russia when the high costs of charcoal and labour were offset by the application of coal to smelting and refining. The crucial breakthrough is often credited to Abraham Darby, who used coke to smelt iron at Coalbrookdale in Shropshire in 1709. In reality, it was only after 1750 that coke was widely used: in 1750, only 5 per cent of pig iron was produced with coke, which increased to 55 per cent by 1775, and 90 per cent by 1791.[5] The explanation for the failure to adopt coke smelting was cost, for pig iron produced with coke had a high silicon content which made it more costly to convert into bar iron. Darby was not concerned, for he had patented a new method of making thin castings for cast-iron pots in 1707; coke pig iron was suitable because it was more fluid as a result of its high silicon content. Coke pig iron was only economically viable for a few specialized uses until the 1750s, when charcoal prices rose, and coke pig prices fell sharply as a result of a fall in coal prices and greater efficiency. It became economically rational to close existing charcoal furnaces and build coke furnaces, for the total capital and running or variable costs of producing coke pig iron fell below the running cost of charcoal furnaces. At the Plymouth works at Merthyr Tydfil in 1766, for example, the variable cost of producing pig iron in a coke furnace was £2.85 a ton and the capital cost £0.50, or a total of £3.35; the variable cost at an efficient charcoal furnace at Staveley was £5.4 a ton.[6] Efficient charcoal furnaces were able to survive for a time, for the buoyant demand for iron kept the selling price of pig iron above their variable costs, and the construction of coke furnaces was delayed by the need to recruit labour and accumulate capital. The shift was, however, largely complete by 1790, when the efficiency of coke blast furnaces was further increased by the replacement of water power by steam, which allowed furnaces to be used for longer periods, increased in scale, and grouped together at a site.

The fall in the price of pig iron meant that cast iron could be substituted for wood, copper, lead, brass, and stone in a wide variety of engineering and construction, which was strikingly symbolized by the iron bridge built at Coalbrookdale between 1777 and 1780. Cotton-mills relied on cast iron for pillars, beams, and machinery; and it was used for rails for tramways, lock gates on canals, steam engines, gas and water pipes. Castings accounted for 25 per cent of pig iron by about 1800, a considerable increase since the early eighteenth century. The bulk of pig iron was still converted into bar iron by forge-masters, who faced a serious fall in their profits in the mid-eighteenth century. The price of charcoal rose from £1.28 a 'dozen' in the 1740s to £1.86 in the 1770s, and a ton of pig iron from £5.79 to £6.70, but foreign competition held down the price of bar iron. The forge-masters clearly had an incentive to use coal for refining pig iron. By the 1760s, coal was used to heat refined iron for working under the hammer, but it was more difficult to apply coal to the refining process, for contamination with sulphur made the iron brittle, particularly when combined with silicon in coke pig iron. The answer was 'potting and stamping', which was devised in the 1760s. Pig iron was heated with raw coal in order to remove silicon, and the sulphur was subsequently removed by 'stamping' the iron into small pieces which were mixed with limestone and heated in covered pots in a coal-fired reverberatory furnace, so that carbon was oxidized and sulphur absorbed by the limestone. Costs were about £2 to £3 a ton lower, and the process was used in the production of about half the output of bar iron by the 1780s; it contributed to the growth of coke smelting, which had been checked by the fact that it cost more to refine than charcoal pig iron. In many cases, potting was the crucial breakthrough, allowing the British iron industry to increase its market share from 43 per cent of consumption in 1750 to 60 per cent in 1788. The more famous process of puddling, which was patented by Henry Cort in 1783–4, marked a further advance rather than a fundamental break. Pig iron was placed in a coal-fired reverberatory furnace, and carbon was burned off by stirring a puddle of molten iron on the furnace floor; lumps of wrought iron and slag were reheated and 'shingled' into slabs under a hammer; and finally the slabs were heated and passed through a roller to produce bars. The process only worked where pig iron had a low silicon content, for the preliminary stage of removing silicon was abandoned, and much depended on the skill of workmen in judging when the carbon was burned off. The initial cost savings were slight, and puddling only became a viable proposition after further development by Richard Crawshay at Cyfarthfa, where the variable costs of 'puddled' bar iron fell from £12.30 in 1790–1 to £10.71 in 1793–4.[7]

The application of coal to smelting and refining transformed Britain from a high cost, uncompetitive producer of pig and bar iron, into the largest iron smelter and refiner in Europe. Swedish and Russian iron was priced out of the home market by the start of the nineteenth century, as British costs fell and tariffs increased from £2.08 per ton of bar in 1781 to £6.49 by 1813. Retained imports fell from 41,000 tons a year in the 1790s to 7,000 tons in 1815–19, and British output meanwhile increased from about 90,000 tons of pig and 32,000 tons of bar iron in 1788–90 to 395,000 tons and 150,000 tons in 1815.[8] In the mid-nineteenth century, British exports were almost as much as the total output of the rest of Europe, and its output of pig iron in 1873 was as much as Europe and the USA combined. British ironmasters overtook iron manufacturers in scale and competitive efficiency. Growth of output in the later eighteenth and early nineteenth centuries was concentrated in south Wales and Staffordshire, and the industry was dominated by a few large firms. In 1805, the largest fifteen producers accounted for 53 per cent of coke pig iron output, and 75 per cent of bar iron.[9] The fixed capital required for a furnace increased from about £4,000 in the early eighteenth century to £20,000 in the early nineteenth century, with the replacement of charcoal by coal; and the replacement of water power for bellows and forge hammers by steam allowed mills to cluster together, and made it possible to integrate smelting and refining on the same site. Economies of scale above all came from the efficient utilization of expensive rolling mills, and firms had an incentive to build five or six blast furnaces to keep them fully employed. Bar iron producers were mammoth enterprises, operating mines for coal and iron, quarries for limestone, as well as blast furnaces, puddling furnaces, and rolling mills; the capital valuation of the Dowlais Company, one of the largest firms, rose from about £61,000 in 1798 to £503,200 in the 1850s.[10] The dominance of south Wales and Staffordshire was challenged from about 1820 by the rise of the north-east of England and Scotland. In 1828, John Nielson patented a method of heating air before it entered the furnace; the 'hot blast' reduced fuel consumption and reduced costs, particularly in Scotland, which replaced south Wales as the lowest cost producer. The reduction in regional dominance meant an increase in competition in the mid-nineteenth century, with a marked decline in prices and a lower level of concentration. By 1871, the largest fifteen firms accounted for only a quarter of both pig iron and bar iron output (see Table 8.1).

The protoindustrialization model of a transfer of enterprise, capital, and workers from 'putting out' has little relevance to the iron industry. Initially, the *manufacture* of iron had the competitive edge, and Britain lagged behind European producers of pig and bar iron; by the early nineteenth century, British

TABLE 8.1. *Regional distribution of pig iron output, 1788–1790, 1815, and 1871* (%)

	1788–90	1815	1871
S. Wales	16.2	35.4	16.4
S. Staffs.	9.8	31.6	10.9
North-east		0.0	27.5
Scotland		6.3	17.5

Source: C. K. Hyde, *Technological Change and the British Iron Industry, 1700–1870* (Princeton, NJ, 1977), 114, 181.

smelters and refiners were highly competitive and were major exporters. In cotton and woollen textiles, 'putters out' or artisan producers could shift into centralized production, but this was scarcely feasible in the iron industry, where the scale of smelting and refining increased so much relative to iron manufactures. On the contrary, the rapid growth of the iron industry ended the earlier pattern of major manufacturers such as the Foleys integrating backwards into the ownership of forges and furnaces. This was less feasible as the industry became more dependent upon coal, particularly in south Wales and Scotland without a significant iron manufacturing industry. An important source of entrepreneurship and capital in south Wales was the merchant community of Bristol and London, rather than putting out ironmongers. The Cyfarthfa ironworks, for example, were established around 1776 by Anthony Bacon, a London merchant involved in shipping iron ore from Cumberland and supplying the Board of Ordnance with cannon. On his death, the works were leased by Richard Crawshay, who was a partner in Bacon's merchant house in London; his son William I, a prosperous West Indian merchant in the City, eventually became the sole owner. Another source of capital came from landowners who were eager to develop their estates, such as Lord Mansel in south Wales, the duke of Devonshire at Barrow-in-Furness, and the earl of Balcarres at Wigan. But the most significant source of recruits was the ironmasters themselves, who moved around the country in search of sites for their furnaces. Those who were fortunate to settle in areas close to coal supplies were able to transfer to the new mineral fuel, and grow on the basis of a high level of retained profits.

The coal industry allowed Britain to escape the constraints of organic energy to a much greater extent than any other economy in the eighteenth century, permitting the injection of large stocks of mineral fuel without encountering declining marginal returns. The process was gradual, extending over at least two centuries as coal was applied to a wider range of purposes and transported to a larger geographical area. New techniques were needed to overcome problems of contamination, and a large investment in transport was necessary to make coal available to consumers at a reasonable price. Neither could the expansion of coal output be taken for granted, for there was a danger that mining would encounter rising marginal costs as pits went deeper, underground workings became more extensive, and problems of pumping, ventilation, and underground transport became more pressing. Coal could only offer an escape from the constraints of an organic economy and declining marginal returns if it was able to overcome its own geological and technical problems, and increase its output without significant price rises or a collapse in productivity.

Coal

Increased demand for coal threatened to force up prices unless two constraints on supply could be removed. The first was transport, for the movement of a bulky commodity over land was expensive, and production was limited to areas adjacent to the coast or navigable rivers. Investment in river improvements, canals, and tramways was needed to escape from the tight geographical limits upon the application of coal. The second constraint arose from the technical problems of mining coal at greater depths as easily worked seams were exhausted. Workings had to be supplied with fresh air to allow men to work, and to prevent accumulations of gas; safe lighting was essential to guard against explosions; extraction had to be planned to prevent collapse of the roof or an upward 'creep' of the floor; water had to be pumped from the mine; and coal hauled from the face to the shaft and raised to the surface. Technical ingenuity and capital were needed as pits became larger and more costly, and managerial expertise was essential to handle the increased scale of the mines and their work-force. The ability of the coal industry to increase output without a collapse of productivity and increase in prices could not be taken for granted.

The output of the British coal industry increased about tenfold between 1700 and 1830, from 3.0 million tons to 30.4 million tons (see Table 8.2). Domestic heating and cooking were by far the largest user of coal in 1700, and increased faster than the population, in large part because more people lived in towns. Industry only became the major consumer in the last quarter of the eighteenth century. The demand for coal in non-ferrous metals such as copper grew only slowly, and probably declined as a proportion of demand in the eighteenth century; other uses, such as bricks, glass, soap, and the food and drink trades, probably increased faster than population growth as income levels rose and bricks were used in place of wood and stone, without accounting for a large part of coal output. The most striking growth in consumption came from the iron industry, which accounted for about a quarter of the increase between 1775 and

TABLE 8.2. *Distribution of British coal consumption, 1700–1830*

	1700		1775		1830	
	000 tons	%	000 tons	%	000 tons	%
Domestic	1,420	47.6	3,760	42.5	11,500	37.9
Iron	—	—	200	2.3	5,635	18.6
Copper	30	1.0	80	0.9	240	0.8
Salt	250	8.4	310	3.5	350	1.2
Gas	—	—	—	—	500	1.6
Other	890	29.8	3,160	35.7	7,250	23.9
All industry	1,170	39.2	3,750	42.4	13,975	46.0
Collieries/waste	255	7.5	920	10.4	3,650	11.9
Export	140	4.7	420	4.7	1,250	4.1
Total	2,985	100.0	8,850	100.0	30,375	100.0

Source: M. W. Flinn, *History of the British Coal Industry*, ii: *1770–1830: The Industrial Revolution* (Oxford, 1984) 252.

1830, and shifted the regional structure of the coal industry away from the north-east of England towards the inland coalfields.

The dominance of the north-east of England over the London coal trade led to attempts to regulate output and force up prices (see Table 8.3 and Fig. 8.3). Monopoly profits could be secured most easily when mining was limited to the area close to the river Tyne, for three leading coal-owners controlled 60 per cent of output. In 1726, they formed the 'Grand Alliance' to prevent newcomers from opening pits by purchasing land and limiting access to the Tyne, but their power declined as production moved further afield, particularly to the Wear. A period of 'open' trade followed from the 1750s and capacity outstripped demand. In 1771,

TABLE 8.3. *Regional coal output, 1700, 1775, and 1830*

	1700		1775		1830	
	000 tons	%	000 tons	%	000 tons	%
North-east	1,290	43.2	2,990	33.8	6,915	22.8
West Midlands	510	17.1	1,400	15.9	5,600	18.4
Scotland	450	15.1	1,000	11.3	3,000	9.9
Yorkshire	300	10.1	850	9.6	2,800	9.2
Lancashire	80	2.7	900	10.2	4,000	13.2
South Wales	80	2.7	650	7.3	4,400	14.5

Source: Flinn, *Coal Industry*, ii, 26.

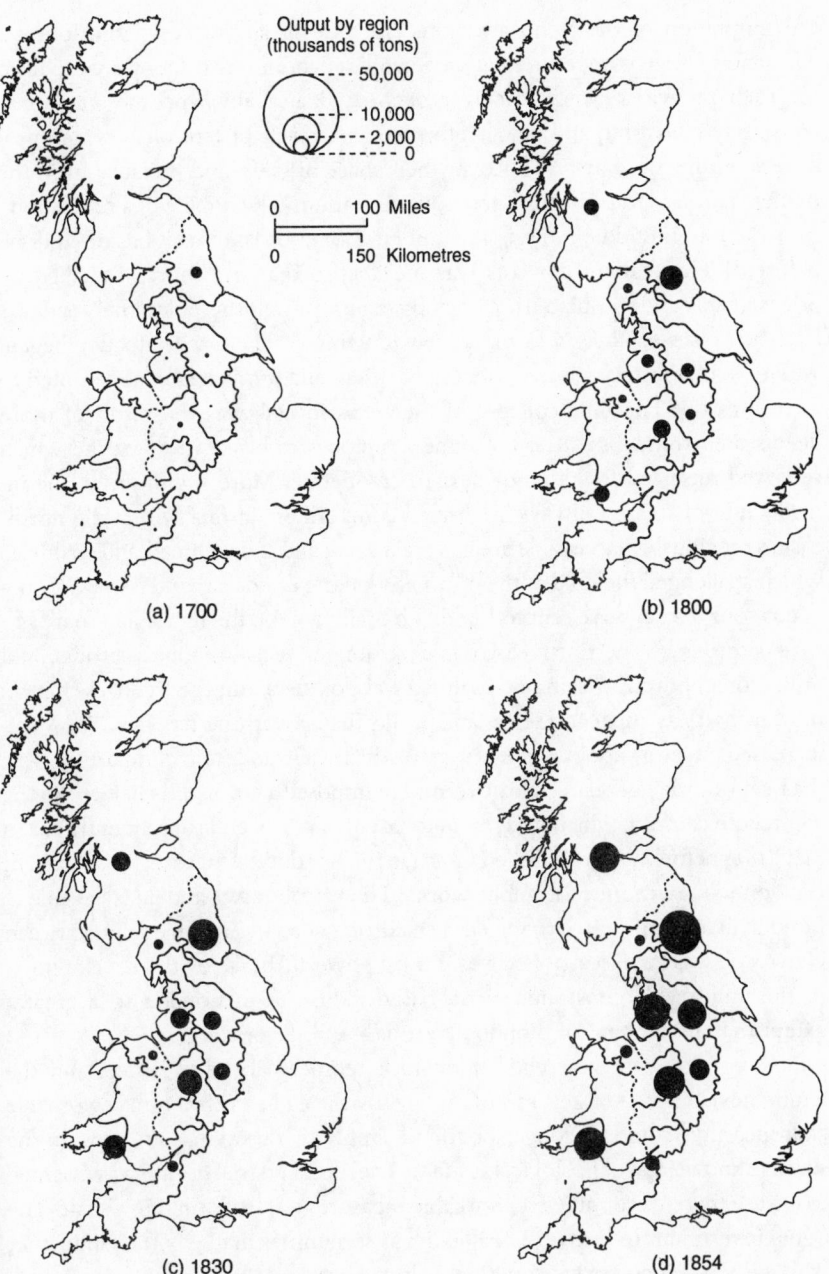

FIG. 8.3. Coal output by region

Source: G. N. von Tunzelmann, 'Coal and Steam Power', in Langton and Morris (eds.), *Atlas*, 73, from Flinn, *Coal Industry*.

the Limitation of the Vend attempted to raise profits by restricting output, eliminating price competition, and controlling labour costs. Quotas were fixed for each pit which were usually renegotiated annually, and the Vend was constantly collapsing and being reformed as a result of tension between producers on the Tyne and Wear over their share of sales, and pressure from the owners of new, large pits for a generous allocation. 'The bubble of a regulation', remarked John Buddle in 1823, 'must burst sooner or later, as it has often done before.'[11] The demand for coal was inelastic so that any shortfall pushed up prices steeply and stimulated the opening of new pits. At this point, the Vend was likely to collapse. There was a relatively long interval before production began, when the market was glutted, prices collapsed, and producers were tempted to form a cartel. The final collapse of the Vend in 1845 was the result of more deep-seated trends. In 1844, the miners' union was broken by a strike which removed the need for mine-owners to co-operate. More significantly, the introduction of steam railways intensified competition, at first within the north-east as previously inaccessible areas were mined, and soon from inland coalfields which challenged the hold of the north-east on the London market. In 1850, only 55,000 tons of coal were sent to London by rail; by 1855, the figure had soared to 1,138,000 tons.[12] The north-east could no longer seek monopoly profits, and limitation of output within one coalfield was pointless. But the Vend, even in its heyday, had less impact on prices and profits than government policy. The Vend increased prices by about 6 to 8 per cent, which was modest in comparison with the heavy burden of taxes. The government imposed a tax of 5s. a chaldron in the eighteenth century, which was raised to 12s. 6d. in 1809, and subsequently cut to 6s. in 1824 before it was abolished in 1831; a further duty of 3s. to 4s. was levied in London to raise money for public works. The various taxes and dues payable at London in 1824 amounted to 10s. 6d. a chaldron, when the average selling price at Newcastle was 13s. Fiscal policy was 'a most powerful brake on the development of the industry',[13] constraining coal-based industries in London to a greater extent than the pursuit of monopoly profit by producers.

Finding new reserves relied upon luck tempered by experience, and the willingness to invest large sums of money. By the eighteenth century, workable coal measures could no longer be found simply by observing outcrops on the surface: knowledge of geological strata was needed, and trial boring was essential to ensure there were sufficient workable measures to justify sinking a shaft. The initial investment to 'prove' a coalfield was sometimes made by the landowner who wished to increase his mineral royalties, such as the Bute estate, which sank a shaft to the deep steam coal seams of the Rhondda valley in 1851. In the north-east, some of the largest pits were operated by landowners: in 1828 they ran at least sixteen of forty-one Tyneside 'sea-sale' collieries; and others leased collieries to operators, such as the duke of Northumberland, who owned six pits. However, direct involvement of landowners became increasingly unusual, and their role was rather to lease minerals for a royalty and ensure that the estate as a whole was worked profitably. A balance had to be struck between the mine-owners, who preferred long leases which offered protection for their investment, and landowners, who preferred short leases which could be renegotiated; the level of royalty had to be fixed so that it did not hold down production nor give too large a share of profit to the operator of the pit. John Buddle, the most experienced 'viewer' and agent in the north-east, felt that a fair royalty would give the landowner a third of the profit.

The 'viewers' formed the basis of a new profession of mining engineers, who solved the formidable technical problems of working deep mines, planning large pits with their complex systems of ventilation, drainage, and roadways. The deepest mines in the north-east were around 300 or 400 feet in the early eighteenth century, increasing to around 800 feet in the 1790s and more than 1,000 feet in the 1820s, which involved a large expense before production could start and often entailed considerable technical difficulties of driving through unstable or water-bearing strata. Water was an endemic problem, which entailed the construction of a network of drains to a sump. In some cases, water could be removed from the sump by driving a channel into a nearby valley, but in most cases it was necessary to pump the water to the surface. At the beginning of the eighteenth century horses were used, but this was not practicable in larger deeper pits. The development of steam pumps in the mineral mines of Cornwall and subsequently coal-pits was crucial in preventing the onset of declining marginal returns. The technical problems had only just started, for coal had to be removed without the roof closing on the workings. The 'pillar and stall' system was used in the north-east, removing coal from passages or stalls and leaving a pillar to hold up the roof. The drawback was that large pillars were needed to withstand pressure in deep pits, so that as much as half the coal was abandoned. In 'longwall' mining, coal was completely removed at the cost of considerable additional labour in ancillary tasks. The roof at the coal-face was supported by timber props and was allowed to collapse as the face advanced, and roadways were maintained from the shaft to the face by packing waste in the cleared area. Longwall mining became more attractive as the cost of sinking and maintaining a pit increased, but was not always practicable for geological reasons. The alternative, which was adopted in parts of the north-east, was a second phase of extraction which removed about 75 per cent of the coal by 'robbing' the pillars. The technique was dangerous and inefficient, and in the early nineteenth century 'panel' working was developed. The pit was worked in large blocks separated from adjacent areas by thick barriers of coal, which permitted the coal to be entirely removed without adjacent areas being disturbed as the roof settled. The adoption of panel working required a sophisticated ventilation system to take air into the workings, and safety lamps to avoid the dangers of explosion from accumulated gas. Indeed, ventilation and gas posed the greatest difficulties in deep mines. Two shafts were usually required to draw in fresh air and to expel gases. An updraught was created by lighting a fire in the upcast shaft, which posed a constant threat of explosion until steam-driven fans were adopted in the 1820s. The layout of the pit had to be carefully planned so that air could be directed through the workings, which usually involved boys opening and closing doors across the roadways. The depth and size of pits increased faster than the ability of engineers to provide adequate ventilation, which led to a constant risk of accumulating gas being ignited by the miners' candles. Fatalities in the north-east rose from 1.2 per 1,000 employed in 1795–1809 to 4.4 in 1815–19,[14] and mine-owners encouraged inventors to devise a safety lamp. The adoption of safety lamps from 1816 made it possible to work deeper areas which had previously been considered too dangerous.

Large, deep pits faced a further constraint: the transport of coal from the face to the shaft and surface. Underground haulage was a major cost, and gradually evolved from dragging containers along the roadway, to the use of wooden sledges or wheeled waggons on planking, to the construction of underground tramways with iron rails. The containers or wagons were usually pulled by women and children. Horses were used in larger pits by the early nineteenth century when capacity increased sufficiently to justify investment in larger roadways, and made it feasible to pay the high costs of feeding horses and employing male drivers rather than the low wages of boys and women. When coal reached the shaft, it was wound to the surface. Until the late eighteenth century horse gins were used, which imposed a major constraint on the scale of mines, for one horse gin on a single shaft could only raise about 100 tons a day. The application of steam engines to winding from about 1790 removed a significant constraint on the scale and output of pits.

Technological change had little effect on the cutting of coal with hand tools. Although coal transformed the amount of energy available to workers in other industries, and one miner produced more energy than was possible by any other means, it was wrested from the ground by unremitting physical labour. There was no prospect of a major gain in productivity at the face, so that the expansion of output required more miners, and labour recruitment was a possible constraint on the industry. Mine-owners generally accepted that men had to be 'bred' to the pit, acquiring experience over many years from the age of 8 to 10 to survive in the dangerous environment. When parliament threatened to ban the employment of boys underground in 1842, Buddle protested vehemently that 'our peculiar race of pitmen . . . can only be kept up by *breeding*—it never could be recruited from an *adult population*.'[15] The high premium on experience meant that mine-owners were tempted to 'poach' labour from their neighbours, which resulted in long contracts to tie workers to their employer.

The most extreme form of long contract was in Scotland, where miners were 'serfs' tied to the pits for life. In 1606, employment at a Scottish coal-mine was forbidden without a certificate from the last employer; anyone who absconded was considered to be a thief who was 'stealing' his labour and was to be returned within twenty-four hours on penalty of a fine of £100, provided the request was made within a year and a day. The intention of the Act was to stop employers poaching labour, but in the seventeenth century it became an increasingly strict system of binding labour. The collier was bound to a pit by signing a formal agreement or, more usually, simply by working for a year and a day, and owners claimed that miners' children were automatically bound to the pit. Although colliery serfdom was repressive and a threat to liberty, it did not entail low wages, for Scottish miners were probably better paid than their counterparts in England. In fact, serfdom did not so much solve the problems of recruitment as discourage entry and force up wages. 'The slavery of the slave', commented the *Edinburgh Review*, 'had become his strength in the battle for wages. It gave him the advantage of a monopolist. It frightened competition away.'[16] The solution, some owners argued, was to end serfdom and encourage an influx of free labour. Others were less convinced, fearing increased competition, and in 1775 a compromise was reached. Serfdom was abolished for new workers, and existing workers were to be freed between 1778 and 1782. In fact, the influx of free labour did not materialize, and mine-owners replaced serfdom by long engagements, paying 'binding money' to men who agreed to work for several years, and encouraging miners into debt as a means of restricting their mobility. These devices secured a stable work-force, but also allowed miners to organize and force up wages. Their power would, it was hoped, be broken by legislation in 1799 which aimed to introduce a 'free' labour market by stopping actions for recovery of debts, and encouraging the introduction of annual bindings.

In the north-east of England a similar pattern of annual bindings developed in the second half of the eighteenth century and became increasingly formalized by the early nineteenth century. The attempt to secure a stable work-force had the same outcome as in Scotland, of increasing the bargaining power of the workers. Bonds were signed on one day of the year, which provided an opportunity for the two sides to test each other. A lump sum or 'binding money' was paid when the bond was signed, reaching as much as £21 or half the annual wage in boom years such as 1804. On the whole, miners supported the bond, for it gave them an opportunity to bargain over wages and reinforced the assumption that hewers were a 'pit-bred' caste with property in their skill and cohesion against outsiders. They had considerable power, for the supply of skilled mining labour lagged behind demand, and they were able to form trade unions such as the United Association of Colliers in 1825 which developed a strategy of 'restriction' controlling effort and output as a means of maintaining wages, and opposing attempts of the owners to increase the intensity of work. For their part, viewers became more concerned to impose control over the miners as pits became larger and more complex, and a tussle ensued for control over the work-place and market relations. Owners were willing to regulate the commodity market in the Vend, claiming that the maintenance of profits was in the best interests of consumers by ensuring a secure supply of coal. In the same way, miners argued that a regulated labour market was the best means of securing a supply of 'pit-bred' miners. They were not rejecting the market and 'political economy', and demanding the maintenance of an older 'moral economy' which determined a 'fair' wage by non-market criteria; rather, they accepted that wages were determined by the market, and sought to establish market relations which they considered fair and equitable.

In 1831, the owners laid pits idle to secure higher prices for coal, which meant that miners suffered a loss of earnings. They formed a union, and demanded a revision of the bond to provide a guarantee of work. After an initial victory, the union was defeated in 1832, and the bond was changed on the owners' terms: a monthly bond replaced the single annual 'binding', which allowed owners to impose tighter discipline. Market relations were redefined, and 'pit-bred' hewers or 'independent colliers' gave way to free wage labour with one month's notice. The colliers had not seen themselves as wage labourers so much as independent contractors, and their strategy was to maintain their status by limiting output and hours of work. The policy was based upon a sense of the interests of the trade, for it would keep up coal prices as well as miners' income. The owners tolerated such a strategy when pits were small and the market local, but it did not make sense for large pits which needed regular production throughout the year. The culture of the independent collier, who believed that wages could be controlled by organizing the pit-bred skill of the miner through an exclusion of 'foreigners' and controls of output, gave way to a new strategy based upon organizing newcomers into an inclusive union.

How far did these technical and organizational changes allow coal to escape the onset of decreasing marginal returns and mounting costs (see Table 8.4 and Fig. 8.4)? Coal became cheaper in real terms in the eighteenth century, falling more than other prices in the first half of the eighteenth century, and rising less until the early nineteenth century. The trend was reversed in the early nineteenth century, when coal prices fell less than other prices. The overall result was

TABLE 8.4. *Coal and general price movements, 1700–1830*

	General prices	Coal prices
1700/4–1750/4	−4.8	−8.7
1746/50–1788/92	+32.7	+23.4
1788/92–1809/15	+74.1	+54.6
1809/15–1826/30	−37.1	−21.2

Source: Flinn, *Coal Industry*, ii, 311.

that coal prices were stable or fell slightly between 1700 and 1830, which was a significant achievement. It was, furthermore, profitable for landowners with coal on their estates and for industrialists who were willing to risk large sums in sinking a pit; there was compensation for high risks and an adequate return to allow continued investment of retained profits in new technology. The coal industry increased its output tenfold between 1700 and 1830, and per capita consumption rose from about half a ton to almost 2 tons without an increase in the real costs of production. Britain escaped from the constraints of an organic economy, with its inelastic supplies of energy. The industry also stimulated technical changes of the greatest importance. Pumping water from deep mines led to the development of the steam engine, at first in tin- and copper-mines in Cornwall and soon in coal. The 'punctiform' movement of large quantities of minerals placed pressure on the transport system, which was crucial for the development of canals and railways. Technical developments in the mines secured greater output at stable prices; and the creation of an improved system of transport made coal available to a greater number of consumers, breaking down the constraints on winning of coal in inland coalfields. London escaped from limits to growth, which in turn stimulated the development of agriculture to feed the metropolis. The increase in the use of coal for heat and energy lessened pressure on the land, which could be used to feed the population. The success of the coal industry in providing a massive injection of energy at a stable real price formed a crucial breakthrough in the British economy.

The Labour Process

Mines and plant-based industries relying upon mineral fuel clearly differed from protoindustrial outwork and artisan production: workers were brought together in a centralized plant rather than scattered in small units. The pattern of work and labour discipline also differed from the emerging cotton or woollen textile mills, for work to a considerable extent remained *task* rather than *time* oriented. In the glass industry, for example, the pattern of work was determined by the

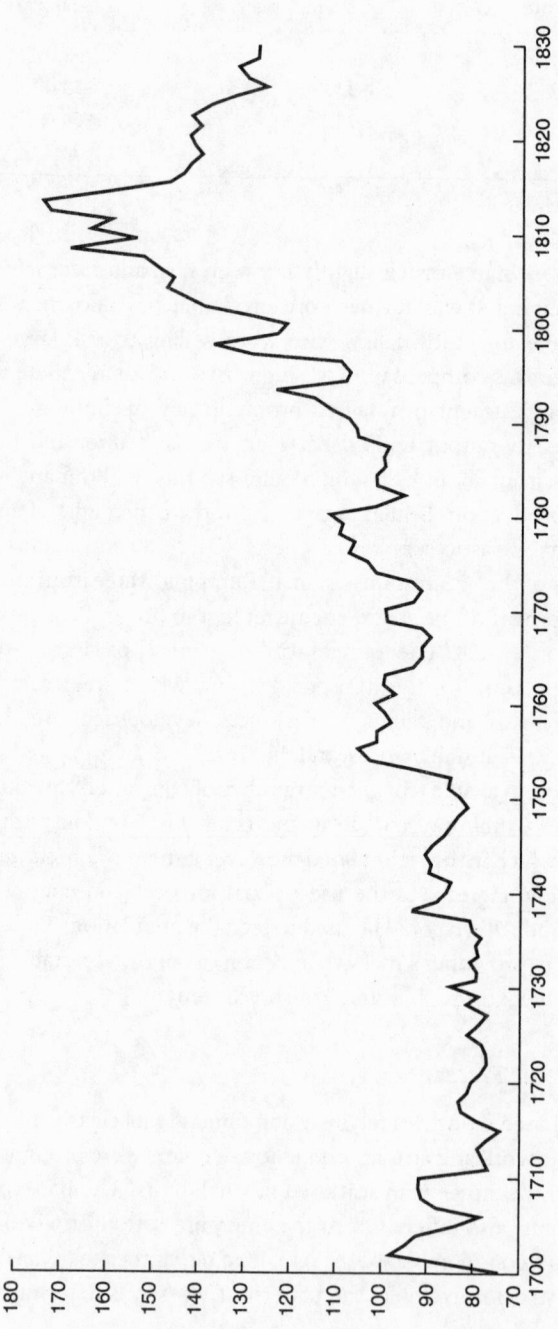

FIG. 8.4. Index of coal prices, England (1770–1900)

Source: Flinn, Coal Industry, ii, table 9.4, 303–4.

flow of molten glass from the furnace. Each 'charge' took about twenty-four hours to produce molten glass, which was processed by glass-blowers in a shift of ten hours followed by a break of twenty-four hours while the furnace was reheated. The skilled glass-blowers served a seven-year apprenticeship and attempted, with some success, to limit entry to their sons. The employers, for their part, were anxious to secure a work-force and they offered long contracts of six or seven years with a 'binding fee' and the guarantee of a minimum wage when the furnace was not in operation. Despite the application of coal to the production of molten glass, the industry did not use machinery on any scale until the 1840s, when grinding and polishing machinery was installed to produce sheet glass. Until then, production of glass was energy and labour intensive, with considerable bargaining power in the hands of the skilled workers who were crucial to the process.

Much the same point applied to furnaces and forges in the metal trades. A blast furnace had a life of its own, demanding fuel and ore until the molten metal was discharged. In the early eighteenth century, a furnace usually employed a team of seven workers, consisting of two 'keepers' who controlled the charge and blast, two 'servers' who filled baskets with raw materials, and two or three 'fillers' who carried them to the furnace. They were helped by labourers, often women and children, who undertook the preparation of the ore and limestone and the other ancillary tasks around the furnace. Similarly, forges in the early eighteenth century were under the supervision of a master hammerman, who was assisted by two 'finers' and a boy. The work groups had a degree of autonomy from the owner of the plant, and the keepers and master hammermen were often subcontractors who employed the rest of the team, rather than waged labourers. When the industry shifted to the coalfields and large, integrated concerns such as Dowlais and Cyfarthfa, production continued to be in the hands of skilled men such as the puddlers with the experience of controlling furnaces and forges, judging how much ore to add and when the iron should be drawn from the furnace. The plants were, in fact, a collection of teams under the control of workmen, rather than a monolithic enterprise under the immediate direction of the owners. Beyond the furnaces and forges, scattered across the uplands of the northern rim of the south Wales coalfield, workmen dug, mined, and quarried coal, iron ore, and limestone to supply the works at Merthyr Tydfil. The iron masters relied upon subcontractors who struck a contract with the companies for the supply of materials, rather than directly employing waged labour and managing the mines and quarries. Any attempt by the companies to remove independence and reduce workers to wage labour was bitterly resented and resisted. Skilled men such as puddlers were in short supply, and their 'knack'

could only be learned by experience; and it was easier to devolve the management of scattered mineral workings than to impose central control.

Miners were often employed on a 'bargain' or 'tribute' system, selling the
produce of their labour rather than the labour itself. In the tin- and copper-mines
of Cornwall, 'pitches' in the mine were auctioned to gangs of miners every one
or two months, and the owner accepted the lowest bid, which was a 'tribute' or
share of the sum for which the ore was sold. The miners decided what rate to bid
according to the expected ore content of the 'pitch': where the ore content was
low, they might bid 12s. in the pound and where it was high they might take 2s. in
the pound. A team which struck a rich vein would make a good profit, and there
was a danger that other gangs would compete at the next auction and force down
the 'tribute'. However, there was a convention by the end of the eighteenth
century that the gang in possession had priority, and the miners did not indulge
in cut-throat competition against each other. In the lead-mines of the Pennines
the bargain did not take direct account of the price received for the ore: teams of
four to eight miners struck a bargain with the mine-owner, usually for three
months, to produce ore at an agreed rate per ton (a 'bingtale') or to dig ground at
an agreed rate by distance (a 'fathomtale'), according to their assessment of the
hardness of the vein, the quality of the ore, the depth of the workings, and the
conditions of ventilation and drainage. The agreements were, legally, leases and
the miners had a sense of independence as contractors working for their own
profit rather than waged labour. In reality, the bargain system was skewed
towards the mine-owners; it was a means of passing some of the risks of irregular
seams on to the miners, and there was a surplus of miners seeking bargains
except at times of high demand. The independence of miners became increasingly illusory in the early nineteenth century. In the eighteenth century, the
ore was washed by the miners' wives and children, but mine-owners increasingly
operated washing floors with water-powered machinery, and charged the
miners for the service. The owners also switched to 'fathomtale' bargains for
extraction rather than, as in the eighteenth century, driving levels through barren
ground. Consequently, the ore remained the property of the mine-owner, and
the miner lost any ability to share in profits as his status was gradually reduced
from independent subcontractor to a waged labourer on piece-work.

In the coal industry, there was pressure to impose stricter control over the
miners as pits become deeper and more complex, with a need for regular
production and careful control of layout. The mine-owner did not, however,
always take entire responsibility for operating the pit. In the 'big butty' system of
the west Midlands and Yorkshire, mine-owners supplied the fixed capital of shaft,
drainage, winding gear, and ventilation plant, and their agents handled sales and
accounts; the operation of the pit was subcontracted to a 'charter master' or

'butty' who supplied workers, horses, tools, and timber. In the 'little butty' system, owners made an agreement with a face-worker who supplied and paid a team of miners, in much the same way as a minder in the cotton industry controlled and paid his piecers. Miners in the north-east had long been waged labourers, but they clung to at least a vestige of autonomy. They were paid by output, which varied according to geological conditions; in order to ensure equity, the colliers operated a system of 'cavilling' by which lots were period-ically drawn for a place at the face. In the south Wales coalfield, by contrast, owners allocated workers to their places in the seams, which could lead to considerable resentment on the part of those who had difficult places.

The social organization of work on the coalfields was by no means uniform. In the north-east, boys progressed from opening and closing ventilation doors, to driving ponies on the roadways, 'putting' the coal from the face, and finally employment as a hewer. The division between haulage and face-work was by age, forming part of a process of acclimatization to the pit; and adolescent haulage workers operated one long shift to cover two short shifts of hewers, who shared a single place at the face and pooled their earnings. In south Wales, haulage and face-workers were separate grades of workers, and boys joined one or the other when they first entered the pit. There was less chance of progression, and a wide wage differential between adult wages. The social pattern of employ-ment varied between coalfields, affecting income distribution, earnings over the life-cycle, patterns of labour control, and class formation.

Historians have devoted considerable attention to the social and demographic structures of protoindustrial parishes, and to the emergence of factories in the textile trades. By contrast, little attention has been paid to the processes of growth in plant-based industries, and how they fitted into the social structure of localities. The lead-miners of Derbyshire and the Pennines, the copper- and tin-miners of Cornwall, the copper-smelters of Swansea, the shipbuilders at Sunderland, or the workers in paper-mills in Kent, have not been adequately considered in discussions of marriage patterns, or relationships with the agrarian structure. The law on mineral rights varied, in the same way as the tenure of land. In the Forest of Dean, only 'free' miners had the right to work coal and iron ore, which excluded capitalists; and in 'free' mining areas, such as Derbyshire, the rights to lead were vested in the crown, and anyone could claim to work the veins of ore, provided they paid a duty and obeyed regulations. In other areas, and for other minerals, the rights belonged to private owners who charged a royalty. In the Pennines and Derbyshire, lead-miners often had small plots of land, where they grew some food and kept a horse and cow; this allowed them to sustain themselves at times of low prices of ore, or when the vein disappeared. How did this affect the age of marriage and birth rate; what was their relationship with other families in the locality who concentrated on pastoral agriculture What opportunities existed for women to work? In the heavy industrial town such as Merthyr Tydfil, women were often employed in sorting materials for the furnace: how did their experience change, and what were the family structures Questions abound; answers are few.

Clearly, coal-based industrialization varied as much as did regions of proto industry. Iron poured from the forges and furnaces of south Wales, but was exported as semi-finished bars and rails to manufacturers in the west Midlands or the railways of Britain and the world. The industrialization of south Wales relied upon abundant cheap fuel and did not develop a wide industrial base as in other coalfields. There were no naileries and hardware manufactories as in the Mid lands, and no significant shipbuilding or engineering industry as in the north-east of England or Clydeside; at most, iron was rolled into thin sheets and coated with tin in the tin-plate works around Swansea and Llanelli. When the iron industry faltered in the middle of the nineteenth century, the prosperity of the area was to rest upon the export of 'steam' coal for use in steamships and railway engines. The presence of coal and iron ore in south Wales, and the availability of copper and tin across the Bristol Channel in Cornwall, overcame the absence of skilled labour or an established industrial base, and attracted enterprise and capital from other regions. The pattern of industrialization on other coalfields was very different. On the Tyne and the Mersey, coal was used in the eighteenth century to produce salt, glass, and chemicals, and there was a more diverse industrial structure which drew upon local finance and enterprise. In the early nineteenth century, iron was increasingly used in the production of capital goods such as steam engines, textile machinery, ships, and machine tools. Shipbuilding and heavy engineering concentrated on the rivers of the Clyde, Tyne, Wear, and Tees, where iron and coal were available close to water. Textile machinery and machine tools were found close to the textiles centres, in towns such as Oldham and Leeds, and in Birmingham where the wide range of small metal manufac-turers could supply parts for specialist machine- and engine-builders. Each region generated its own peculiarities of industrial structure, relations with merchants and financiers, and patterns of employment.

Conclusion

Britain in 1800 produced five times as much coal as the rest of Europe, and British workers gradually built up expertise in the use of the fuel as it spread from trade to trade. The diffusion of new coal-based technologies to other countries was, it is true, hampered because workers lacked knowledge, but too much can be made of Britain's advantage in the exploitation of coal. Whatever the difficulties of earning the 'knacks' of the trade, they were more easily transferable than earlier patterns of growth by specialization where the whole institutional, legal, and political context was crucial. The structure of landownership and tenure helped to determine the location of industry and the release of labour from agriculture; the legal system encouraged risk-taking and credit; and the demographic system helped to preserve a balance between resources and reproduction. These features were deeply embedded in English society and were not easily transferable to other societies. The result was a long period, from the seventeenth to the early nineteenth centuries, in which 'the English economy steadily strengthened in comparison to its continental rivals'.[17] Growth by the application of mineral energy was less affected by the institutional context of politics, law, landholding, and marriage, and became more 'footloose and exportable in contrast to the position when the organic economy prevailed. Previously the institutional framework of growth had been more important than its material technology and therefore far less easy to transfer.'[18] One result was to shift the location of industry within Britain to areas which had not previously been at the forefront of industrial development, such as south Wales and the Clyde. Another was to create the possibility that areas outside Britain would adopt the technology of mineral-based growth and erode Britain's lead. It was still a distant prospect in the first half of the nineteenth century, for Britain had an unusual degree of comparative advantage both in its highly developed organic economy, and in its lead in the application of mineral fuel. The Great Exhibition of 1851 marked the peak of British economic dominance, but also the beginning of its erosion as other countries started to apply even cheaper supplies of energy to their economies, which often had more abundant raw materials.

NOTES

1. E. Newell, 'Copperopolis: The Rise and Fall of the Copper Industry in the Swansea District, 1826–1921', *Business History*, 32 (1990), 75; A. H. John, *The Industrial Developments of South Wales, 1750–1850* (Cardiff, 1950), 150.
2. C. K. Hyde, *Technological Change and the British Iron Industry, 1700–1870* (Princeton, NJ, 1977), 43.
3. B. L. C. Johnson, 'The Foley Partnership: The Iron Industry at the End of the Charcoal Era', *Economic History Review*, 2nd ser. 4 (1952).
4. M. W. Flinn, *Men of Iron: The Crowleys in the Early Iron Industry* (Edinburgh, 1962), 174–5, 252.
5. Hyde, *Technological Change*, 67.
6. Ibid. 59, 60.
7. Ibid. 79, 93, 102.
8. Ibid. 105, 106, 113.
9. Ibid. 124
10. Ibid. 178.

11. C. E. Hiskey, 'The Third Marquess of Londonderry and the Regulation of the Coa Trade: The Case Reopened', *Durham University Journal*, NS 44 (1982–3), 5.

12. B. R. Mitchell, *British Historical Statistics* (Cambridge, 1988), 245.

13. M. W. Flinn, *History of the British Coal Industry*, ii: *1700–1830: The Industrial Revolutio* (Oxford, 1984), 283.

14. Ibid. 137.

15. C. Hiskey, 'John Buddle 1773–1843: Agent and Entrepreneur in the North-East Coa Trade' (unpublished M.Litt. thesis, University of Durham, 1978).

16. Quoted in B. Duckham, *A History of the Scottish Coal Industry*, i: *1700–1815: A Social an Industrial History* (Newton Abbot, 1970), 262.

17. E. A. Wrigley, *Continuity, Chance and Change* (Cambridge, 1988), 117.

18. Ibid. 117–18.

FURTHER READING

Addis, J. P., *The Crawshay Dynasty: A Study in Industrial Organisation and Development 1765–1867* (Cardiff, 1957).

Ashton, T. S., *Iron and Steel in the Industrial Revolution* (Manchester, 1924).

Barker, T. C., *The Glassmakers: Pilkington: The Rise of an International Company, 1826–197* (1977).

Birch, A., *The Economic History of the British Iron and Steel Industry, 1784–1879* (1967).

Campbell, R. H., *The Carron Company* (Edinburgh, 1961).

Coleman, D. C., *The British Paper Industry, 1495–1960: A Study in Industrial Growth* (Oxford 1958).

Colls, R., *The Pitmen of the Northern Coalfield: Work, Culture and Protest, 1790–1850* (Manches ter, 1987).

Duckham, B. F., *A History of the Scottish Coal Industry*, i: *1700–1815: A Social and Industria History* (Newton Abbot, 1970).

—— 'Serfdom in Eighteenth-Century Scotland', *History*, 54 *(1969)*.

Evans, C., *The Labyrinth of Flames: Work and Social Conflict in Early Industrial Merthyr Tydfi* (Cardiff, 1993).

Evans, J. D., 'The Uncrowned Iron King: The First William Crawshay', *National Library o Wales Journal* (1951).

Flinn, M. W., 'The Growth of the English Iron Industry, 1660–1760', *Economic History Review*, 2nd ser. 11 (1958–9).

—— *Men of Iron: The Crowleys in the Early Iron Industry* (Edinburgh, 1962).

—— *The History of the British Coal Industry*, ii: *1700–1830: The Industrial Revolution* (Oxford, 1984).

Hammersley, G., 'The Charcoal Industry and its Fuel, 1540–1750', *Economic History Review*, 2nd ser. 26 (1973).

Harris, J. R., *The British Iron Industry, 1790–1850* (1988).

—— *The Copper King: A Biography of Thomas Williams of Llanidan* (Liverpool, 1964).

—— 'Skills, Coal and British Industry in the Eighteenth Century', *History*, 61 (1976).

arrison, R. (ed.), *Independent Collier: The Coal Miner as Archetypal Proleterian Reconsidered* (Hassocks, 1978).

ausman, W. J., 'Cheap Coals or Limitation of the Vend: The London Coal Trade, 1770–1845', *Journal of Economic History*, 44 (1984).

liskey, C. E., 'The Third Marquess of Londonderry and the Regulation of the Coal Trade: The Case Reopened', *Durham University Journal*, NS 44 (1982–3).

unt, C. J., *The Lead Miners of the Northern Pennines in the Eighteenth and Nineteenth Centuries* (Manchester, 1970).

lyde, C. K., *Technological Change and the British Iron Industry, 1700–1870* (Princeton, NJ, 1977).

iffe, J. A., *The Struggle for Market Power: Industrial Relations in the British Coal Industry, 1800–40* (Cambridge, 1991).

ohn, A. H., *The Industrial Development of South Wales 1750–1850: An Essay* (Cardiff, 1950).

ohnson, B. L. C., 'The Foley Partnership: The Iron Industry at the End of the Charcoal Era', *Economic History Review*, 2nd ser. 4 (1951–2).

—— 'The Midland Iron Industry in the Early Eighteenth Century', *Business History*, 2 (1960).

Aathias, P., *The Brewing Industry in England, 1700–1830* (Cambridge, 1959).

Minchinton, W. E., *The British Tinplate Industry* (Oxford, 1957).

Jamier, L. B., 'Anthony Bacon, MP: An Eighteenth-Century Merchant', *Journal of Economic and Business History*, 2 (1929).

Jewell, E., 'Copperopolis: The Rise and Fall of the Copper Industry in the Swansea District, 1826–1921', *Business History*, 32 (1990).

laistrick, A., *Dynasty of Ironfounders: The Darbys and Coalbrookdale* (1953).

liden, P., 'Output of the British Iron Industry before 1870', *Economic History Review*, 2nd ser. 30 (1977).

lule, J., *The Experience of Labour in Eighteenth-Century Industry* (1981).

weezy, P. M., *Monopoly and Competition in the English Coal Trade, 1550–1850* (Cambridge, Mass., 1938).

Fann, J., 'Fuel Saving in the Process Industries during the Industrial Revolution: A Study in Technological Diffusion', *Business History*, 15 (1973).

Faylor, A. J., 'Combination in the Mid-nineteenth Century Coal Industry', *Transactions of the Royal Historical Society*, 5th ser. 3 (1953).

Wrigley, E. A., 'The Supply of Raw Materials in the Industrial Revolution', *Economic History Review*, 2nd ser. 15 (1962–3).

—— 'Metropolitan Cities and their Hinterlands: Stimulus and Constraints to Growth', in E. Aaerts and P. Clark (eds.), *Metropolitan Cities and their Hinterlands in Early Modern Europe* (Leuven, 1990).

—— *Continuity, Chance and Change: The Character of the Industrial Revolution in England* (Cambridge, 1988).

CHAPTER 9

Capital and Credit:
Financing Industrialization

In 1935, M. M. Postan asked a fundamental question: was the supply o investible funds adequate for industrialization, or did shortages impose limits His surmises were largely confirmed by detailed research, and a consensus wa firmly established. Britain, he argued, was wealthy beyond the relatively modes requirements of early industrialization. Eighteenth-century Britain was able t find funds for major undertakings. Naval vessels and dockyards were hug enterprises, overshadowing most industrial concerns; great country houses such as Chatsworth or Holkham exceeded the investment in the largest factory; an the pleasure resort of Bath absorbed more money than the entire cotto industry. A country which could afford these expensive investments could mee the needs of industry, for Postan claimed that these were 'modest': machiner was relatively simple and often hand-driven; production was labour intensive buildings could be converted or extended piecemeal. Capital shortages, whe they did occur, were localized rather than general. The earl of Leicester wa willing to invest in the construction of his Palladian house at Holkham in nortl Norfolk; his wealth was of little use to a cotton-master in Lancashire. Areas witl commercial and industrial wealth might be in relative decline, such as the west o England or Kent; industrialization could be located in areas such as south Wale which lacked prosperous commercial and industrial families. The problem wa not absolute shortages of capital so much as the provision of effective channel for savings to flow into productive enterprise. In Postan's words, 'the in sufficiency of capital was local rather than general, and social rather tha material'.[1]

The interpretation rests upon the modesty of fixed capital and the significance of circulating capital and credit. Fixed capital consisted of a factory or workshop its power source, machinery, and tools. Circulating capital had two elements

he first was materials in the course of production and stocks of goods; together
ith the fixed capital, this comprised the inventory capital. The second was
edit for the purchase of raw materials and the sale of goods; this and the
ventory capital comprised total capital. Finally, credit received by the firm is
educted to arrive at the net capital employed, which consists of fixed capital and
ocks (inventory capital) plus the difference between the credit extended and
ceived (see Table 9.1 for an example). The consensus is that the amount of fixed
apital was strictly limited, and much of it simple, cheap, or adapted over time.
ven such striking examples as the Soho works of Boulton and Watt, and
Vedgwood's pottery works at Etruria, achieved their pre-eminence—so it is
rgued—by organization and marketing rather than using expensive machinery.
his is not to say that raising short-term capital for credit was necessarily easier
1an finding long-term capital: the problems were simply different. The propor-
on of fixed to circulating capital varied, and so did the 'credit matrix' of credit
eceived and extended. A firm might be a net debtor, receiving more credit from
s suppliers than it gave to its customers, or it might 'buy' markets by offering
enerous credit. It was highly dependent on an assessment of risks, which could
e mitigated by intermediaries or intensified by commercial panics and bank-
uptcies. The 'credit matrix' could be crucial to success or failure.

The consensus after Postan's article was that the investment requirements of
ndustrialization were low, and that accumulation of capital was driven by the
nvestment demands of the private sector rather than facing limits caused by lack
f savings. Consequently, 'the aggregate volume of investment was a relatively
mall proportion of national income'[2] and the level of capital accumulation did
ot rise significantly until the railway age. Of course, consensus usually inspires a
hallenge, and revisionists have argued that investment in industry was limited
y a savings constraint which restricted the supply of capital, forcing industry to
ompete with other users and 'crowding out' investment.[3] Assessment of the
evisionist challenge depends upon establishing how much capital was needed by
lifferent sectors, and how this varied over time. And even if capital needs were
nodest, the precise methods by which capital was raised are of great importance.
The accumulation of considerable wealth in the hands of rich landowners or
nerchants was of little use if they ignored the needs of industry and diverted
onsumption and investment into less productive channels. Did the impressive
growth of mercantile wealth in eighteenth-century Britain assist in the process of
ndustrialization, or did it constrain development? Marx felt that mercantile
wealth was a barrier, arguing that 'it cannot by itself contribute to the overthrow
f the old mode of production, but tends rather to preserve and retain it as its
orecondition';[4] he believed that the 'really revolutionary path' entailed the
oroducer moving into merchanting. But it does not follow that a lack of direct

involvement in industry meant that the wealth of landed and mercantile famili
was unavailable. Much depended upon how capital markets were organized an
funds obtained. Could local markets in funds, based upon mortgages and trust
direct money from those with surpluses to those who wished to invest?

Industry was not the only market for savings, and it could be squeezed b
competing demands on the limited sums available. War was endemic in th
eighteenth and early nineteenth centuries, and taxes and public loans coul
possibly 'crowd out' industry, driving up interest rates and choking off ir
vestment. Should the scale of warships and naval dockyards be taken as evidenc
of the absorption of available funds rather than an abundance of capital? An
emphasis upon the modest capital needs of production within the individual firr
could neglect the large sums required for social overhead capital such as housing
sanitation, and water supplies which were provided outside the individual firr
Could it be that the capital needs of industrialization were less modest than i
usually assumed, and shortages of capital led to problems of investment in socia
overhead capital?

The Legal Context: Partnerships, Trusts, and Companies

Certainly the greater needs of large undertakings for fixed capital require
change in the legal and institutional structure, and it would be easy to conclud
that the slow pace of reform created rigidities which held down capital forma
tion. The formation of joint-stock companies with limited liability was restricte
by the Bubble Act of 1720, and corporate status could only be obtained by mean
of a royal charter or a private Act of Parliament which was often associated witl
exclusive trading privileges, such as the Bank of England, the East India Com
pany, or the Royal Exchange Assurance. The overwhelming majority of indus
trial concerns remained partnerships under the law of contract, with each partne
fully liable and shares only transferable with the consent of the other partners
The law of partnership in England and Scotland, unlike many European coun
tries, did not permit a form of limited liability known as *commandite*, which reste
upon a distinction between active partners with unlimited liability, and 'sleeping
partners with limited liability who provided capital and took no part in manage
ment. The debate over the merits and drawbacks of *commandite* provided the
context for liberalization of company law. *Commandite*, according to its propo
nents, allowed retired businessmen to keep their money in business withou
endangering the family fortune and so made capital available to capable mer
who did not have funds of their own. The opponents of *commandite* contended
that capital was more abundant than in Europe, so that reform was unnecessary
France needed to encourage enterprise; the problem in Britain was, they felt, tc

revent *over*-trading and speculation. Indeed, pressure for the introduction of *commandite* partnerships did not come from business so much as from middle-class philanthropists and Christian Socialists who wished to encourage co-operative enterprises, an ambition partly achieved by the Industrial and Provident Societies Act of 1852. The extension of unlimited liability to partnerships was slower. In 1865, it became possible to lend money to a partnership at a rate of interest which varied with the profit of the firm without, as previously, becoming liable for debts; and in 1867 a distinction was drawn between directors with unlimited liability and shareholders with limited liability. Eventually, the Limited Partnership Act of 1907 extended limited liability to partnerships.

In the mid-1850s, pressure for reform shifted from *commandite* partnerships to the introduction of joint-stock companies with limited liability, which were permitted by Acts of 1855–6 and 1862. Pressure for change came less from industrialists concerned by constraints in investment or from *rentiers* seeking safe outlets for their savings, than from 'free traders' in parliament who wished to sweep away the last vestiges of control over trade; regulations over the formation of corporations were seen as barriers to enterprise, smacking of monopolies and privilege. Industrialists did not rush to adopt joint-stock organization, and did not appear to be aware that the law of partnerships imposed any serious constraints. They could usually obtain additional capital by recruiting a new partner from their kin or co-religionists, and adjust the structure of the firm as others retired and withdrew their assets. Although unlimited liability posed an ever-present threat, the risks of failure were lessened by changes in the law of bankruptcy and by ensuring that part of the family fortune was held in marriage settlements which were legally separate. Partnerships were flexible and responsive, and suited manufacturing industry when most concerns required only modest amounts of fixed capital, and when credit was more readily available to individuals who were known and trusted.

A more serious problem emerged in ventures requiring considerable amounts of fixed capital, such as transport undertakings and public utilities, which needed to draw upon a wide circle of investors who would not be actively involved in management. The constraints of partnership could be circumvented by obtaining a private Act of Parliament to create a corporation with limited liability; this course was usually adopted by canal and railway companies. The alternative was the legal device of an unincorporated company under the law of trusts, which was based on a legal decision of 1673 that property and assets held on trust could not be claimed by the trustee's creditors. This was unlike European law, where the only legal relationship recognized was a contract which required corporations to have a separate legal identity so that they could sue and be sued. In England, the development of trusts allowed the creation of unincorporated societies without a separate legal personality. Trustees held the property of society, club, charity, marriage settlement, or estate for the benefit of membe: or beneficiaries, and they could dissolve and divide the property at any time. Th society or estate had no legal identity, and could not sue or be sued in its ow right; any legal action was in the name of the trustees. The legal device had number of virtues. It allowed the emergence of political clubs and chariti without the need for official sanction and registration, and there was an e: plosion of such bodies in the eighteenth century. It was a device used by bodi such as the Stock Exchange, which became a trust in 1808, removing the need t apply to parliament for incorporation with its corollary of public scrutiny. Trust overcame the limits of the Bubble Act on joint-stock organization, for the asset of individual members could not be claimed, so allowing investment in publi works and utilities which would otherwise have been difficult; they provide urban services such as paving and street lighting; and they were the legal devic used by turnpikes. They also offered a means of extending industrial part nerships, for the Court of Chancery permitted unincorporated business assoc ations to vest their assets in trustees through a deed of settlement, so tha individual shareholders were liable only in proportion to their share in th company rather than to the full extent of their wealth. The procedure wa regularized by an Act of 1844, which required the registration of unincorporate societies which had twenty-five or more partners and transferable shares. Th significance of the legal device is clear from the number of registrations betwee 1844 and 1856: 910 companies registered, of which 219 were in insurance, 211 in ga and water, 106 in manufacturing, 85 in markets or halls, and 46 in shipping.[5] Th development of the law of trusts by the Court of Chancery meant that there wer no serious legal and institutional constraints upon investment, and the Englis legal system was arguably more flexible and responsive than in other Europea countries.

Fixed Capital

Any attempt to establish the modesty of industry's needs for fixed capital face serious problems of evidence and its interpretation. One source used in th cotton and woollen textile industries is insurance policies taken out by factory masters on their premises and stocks, but most firms insured only part of thei assets, and many took out policies with more than one company, whose records often do not survive. Where comparison can be made between policies and a firm's own accounts, the results do not inspire confidence: in the case of McConnel and Kennedy, a large firm of Manchester fine cotton-spinners, in- surance policies varied from 41.4 per cent to 137.6 per cent of their own valuation of fixed capital between 1797 and 1806. Care is also needed in interpreting the firms' own accounts, for fixed capital might be inflated by non-productive assets such as workers' housing or under-recorded by showing only capital owned rather than controlled through leases, with a wide variation in allowances made for depreciation. There is also a danger of drawing definite conclusions from an occasional surviving balance sheet, for the ratio of fixed to total capital varied at different stages of growth. The demand for fixed capital might well be high during the construction phase, such as in McConnel and Kennedy, where fixed capital stood at 64 per cent of total capital in 1800; as output rose, the ratio fell to 40 per cent in 1821 (see Table 9.1).[6]

Care is certainly needed in interpreting evidence, but the consensus remains that circulating capital and the 'credit matrix' were more important than fixed capital in the textile industries. Most of the fixed investment in the first generation was undertaken by established firms in fustians, cotton, and hosiery which had 'little difficulty in making the marginal shifts from working to fixed capital necessary for building'.[7] McConnel and Kennedy stand at one end of the spectrum, for they had not previously been a major concern in the domestic system, and they became one of the largest firms in factory-based mule-spinning. The burden of fixed capital was usually less even in the construction phase, for the cotton industry grew in a piecemeal fashion. Early mills were often a collection of buildings adjacent to the fustian manufacturer's house, often converted from other uses and involving a modest capital which was built up slowly over time. Arkwright-style mills, it is true, required a large mill and power source which often involved expensive engineering works on dams and water-wheels, but the firms often emerged from the domestic system so that the ratio of fixed capital in the concern as a whole was still modest. McConnel and Kennedy's fixed capital of £13,129 in 1800 was modest in comparison with the sums involved

TABLE 9.1. *Capital of McConnel and Kennedy, 1800 and 1821* (£)

	1800	1821
Fixed capital	13,129	81,177
Stocks	853	44,390
Inventory capital	13,982	125,567
Credits	6,678	76,802
Total capital	20,660	202,369
Debts	4,873	636
Net capital	15,787	201,733

Source: P. Richardson, 'The Structure of Capital during the Industrial Revolution Revisited: Two Case Studies from the Cotton Textile Industry', *Economic History Review*, 2nd ser. 42 (1989), 493.

in a large putting out merchant-manufacturer moving into factory production John Foster and Sons, putters out and merchants in the West Riding worsted trade, constructed the sizeable Black Dyke Mills from 1835, yet fixed capital was only 32 per cent of total capital between 1834 and 1847, falling to 25 per cent between 1848 and 1852.[8] Even in the case of McConnel and Kennedy, the importance of trade credit *granted* by the firm in 1821 is striking: it far exceeded the credit received by the business, and was roughly equal to the amount of fixed capital. Ability to manipulate credit could be crucial to success.

Potentially more serious is the criticism that historians have concentrated on fixed capital formation in manufacturing industry, and have neglected sectors in which fixed capital was of greater importance. One was extractive industries such as copper, tin, and coal. The amount of fixed capital increased as pits became deeper, bigger, and more complex in the eighteenth century. When John Lambton developed a new pit near Houghton in Co. Durham between 1823 and 1828, for example, he spent £38,276 solely on the mine, without allowing for expenditure on a wagonway.[9] Circulating capital was of limited importance, for the only significant inputs were pit-props and feed for horses, and there were no raw materials in the course of production. Mine-owners usually did not offer much credit, and fixed capital in coal-mining consequently amounted to the unusually high figure of about 90 per cent of inventory capital. Similarly, transport undertakings and social overhead capital required major investments. Canals, railways, and public utilities such as piped water, sanitation, and gas depended upon 'lumpy' investment of considerable sums in tunnels, cuttings, bridges, reservoirs, pumping stations, retorts, and miles of underground pipes and sewers. This could not be financed piecemeal from prior accumulation or retained profits, for the work had to be largely completed before there was any prospect of a flow of income. The growth of urban factory production necessitated investment in social overhead capital and housing, so that the fixed capital requirements of industrialization are less modest than appears from a narrow concern with investment in workshops and factories. Arguably, fixed capital formation was low not only because of the modest needs of manufacturing industry, but also because investment in social overhead capital was held down by the difficulties of raising funds.

The provision of long-term capital for industry was influenced by the nature of landholding. Fixed capital investment was in some cases directly provided by the owners of estates. Milling of corn and fulling of cloth were frequently manorial monopolies, and some landowners continued to provide facilities on a modest scale as the cloth industry expanded. Landed capital had a greater role on the coalfields and in mineral extraction, where large landowners often provided capital for mines and the infrastructure of docks, canals, and railways. They could draw upon their estates, which provided security for raising larger sums of money through mortgages than were available to the business community. In south Wales, for example, the second marquess of Bute wished to stimulate coal exports in order to increase mineral royalties and ground rents from his land at Cardiff: he invested at least £338,000 in the first dock which opened at Cardiff in 1839, and a further £401,000 in a second dock which was completed in 1859.[10]

The involvement of landowners in the provision of capital for mining is not surprising, for they owned the minerals under their estates and common land, and they had the necessary resources to develop the asset. It was part of their long-standing interest in exploiting their estates, whether by improved agriculture, urban development, or the winning of minerals. The Devonshire estate, for example, worked copper- and lead-mines at Ecton in the Peak District on its own account from 1760 to 1825, and subsequently invested heavily in the iron and steel industry at Barrow-in-Furness. But, as time passed, landowners adopted a more passive role, simply drawing a royalty from the mine-owner. Royalties were often interpreted as a drain upon productive enterprise by parasitical landowners; more realistically, leases reduced capital requirements and allowed mine-owners to devote their funds to developing the mine rather than buying mineral-bearing land. Most coal-mines were operated by partnerships which drew together merchants, bankers, lawyers, landowners, industrialists, ship-owners, and 'viewers'. In some areas, coal-mining was an adjunct of another industry, such as in south Wales where pits were initially operated by iron companies such as Dowlais and Cyfarthfa, until the development of the sale coal trade in the mid-nineteenth century brought in capital from other sources such as shipowners and merchants from the ports, local tradesmen from the coalfield, or 'viewers' drawn from elsewhere in the country. By the 1820s, mining companies were emerging in the north-east of England, where ventures such as the Hetton Coal Co. marked the beginning of a major change in the ownership and finance of industry: a shift to a wide diffusion of ownership which was separate from management.

Although direct investment by landowners was rare outside mining and transport, 'the complex relationship between landholding and the evolution of rural industry had important financial consequences'.[11] Mortgages, by allowing loans to be raised on the security of land, permitted an expansion of private credit during the eighteenth century. Mortgages were not only used by large land-owners as a means of releasing capital from their estates in order to finance portions, build country houses, buy more land, or improve the estate; they were also used by small owners to secure funds for trade and industry. Many industrialists inherited or purchased small quantities of land which they could use as security for a loan, particularly where industry emerged in rural districts with a wide diffusion of land ownership. In the West Riding of Yorkshire, many clothiers were able to mortgage their freehold or copyhold land in order to secure capital, and a Register of Deeds was established in 1703 in order to provide proof of title to lenders. By contrast, there were fewer small owners and a dearth of available funds in south Wales, allied to a pattern of industrialization based on mines and metal production which required large investments. Although the destruction of property rights in copyhold land and the erosion of small free-holders reduced the possibility of raising mortgage finance on the security of land, mortgages could also be raised on urban and industrial property such as housing, ships, inns, warehouses, and factories.

The mortgage was a central feature in the emergence of a sophisticated capital market, which channelled funds to those who wished to invest. The legal system made it easier to borrow on the security of real property, which allowed mortgages to be used in a wider range of circumstances. Initially, the mortgagor (borrower) conveyed the land outright to the mortgagee (lender), with a covenant returning the land to the borrower provided the loan was repaid in time. This procedure could only be used where the mortgagor held the land freehold, and in the late seventeenth century the device of 'lease and release' was adopted to allow the mortgage of leasehold land: the mortgagor granted a long lease to the mortgagee, who gave back possession when the loan was repaid. There was always a risk that the mortgagee would opt to retain the land rather than accept repayment and this threat was removed by the concept of 'equity of redemption': the Court of Chancery drew a distinction between the debt and the underlying security. Although there was a risk that property would be over-mortgaged with a danger of defaults, there was no shortage of people willing to lend money on mortgage and the flow of funds was encouraged by the growth of trusts in managing family investments. The English concept of a trust gave executors a greater degree of discretion than in continental Europe. When making a will, a testator appointed an executor to act as his trustee after his death, holding the family property in the interests of his beneficiaries, and particularly widows, daughters, and minors. A trust was also a means by which women in the middle and upper classes could keep property which was settled on them at marriage apart from their husbands' property. Husbands were not able to use the money, which was protected against extravagance or bankruptcy, and it was invested by trustees in the wife's interests. Executors and trustees of marriage settlements accordingly had wide discretion in the use of large amounts of personal wealth, which was protected against creditors. The device of the trust was 'indicative of a legal framework closely aligned to private accumulation':[12] it was important not only in creating flexible organizations in a wide range of

ctivities, but also in making assets available for investment in a variety of
utlets.

Mortgages and trusts gave considerable power to attorneys who were in close
ouch both with landowners and with traders and merchants. They collected
ents and handled legacies, marriage settlements, and conveyances, which gave
hem considerable knowledge of finance and large sums of money to invest.
Capital markets were essentially local and personal rather than national and
nstitutional up to the early nineteenth century, and attorneys were key figures in
matching the funds of trustees to the needs of mortgagors, acting as intermediaries between borrowers and lenders. Investors sought local outlets, and the
national debt—the most obvious alternative—was part of the local capital
market of London and the south-east. Eighteenth-century attorneys concen-
rated on mortgage loans secured on local property; on new outlets in turnpikes,
canals, and utilities which were local and personal; and they sometimes made
direct loans to industrialists. In the early nineteenth century, the role of attorneys
was curtailed, as a result of competition from banks and stricter legal controls
over trust funds which directed *rentier* savings away from industry and trade
towards house property and the public debt.

The 'primary accumulation' of capital in centralized production came from
assets transferred from putting out and internal trade, and funds borrowed
through mortgages on real property. Once a firm was established, a major source
of funds for expansion came from 'ploughing back' profits. The significance of
self-finance varied between sectors and over the growth cycle of a firm, for there
was always the possibility of a discrepancy between a gradual flow of profits and
an irregular and discontinuous demand for fixed capital. A new factory building
or pit shaft could over-stretch the provision of funds from retained profits,
forcing a firm to find external finance for larger projects, which was influenced by
the extent to which fixed capital investment was 'lumpy'. In some trades, such as
the small metal trades of Birmingham, or cutlery in Sheffield, investment was
piecemeal and small scale, and ploughing back profits was usually adequate.
Where a large mill or plant was needed for a new blast furnace, for example,
external funds would be required. Most manufacturing industries fitted the first
category, for even trades such as shipbuilding and heavy engineering used fairly
traditional methods of production in a collection of workshops rather than in a
single, continuous process plant.

Whether profits were available to be ploughed back depended upon a number
of considerations, which were social as much as economic. Usually, partners in a
firm were credited with interest on their capital, plus an allowance for profits. If
they drew out less than was credited to them in the accounts, the balance
increased the capital of the firm: £108,286 was available to the partners of John

Foster and Sons in 1856, but withdrawals were only £7,105. Much depended upon the level of profits, which varied with fluctuations in exports, raw material prices and labour costs. More complicated is the issue of whether businessmen wished to retain profits in the business, for alternatives might be more appealing in terms of status, family security, or a higher rate of return. Business ventures were inextricably entangled with the families of the partners, and the motivation was to provide security to the family as much as to foster the growth of the firm. These considerations could be intermingled. Land purchase offered status to successful textile magnates such as John Foster, who bought an estate for £205,000 in 1860, but it was not simply a device to secure recognition from the landed élite for it could also be a means of withdrawing assets from the perils of industry, spreading risks, and providing a safe outlet for surplus capital to provide family security. Land was not the only outlet for industrial profits, for families could make a careful decision between the relative return on real property and government stocks, and successful firms could develop a diverse portfolio of investments, such as John Foster and Sons, which accumulated £696,176 in British and foreign government stocks and railways between 1853 and 1867.[13] The extent to which profits were ploughed back into the firm also depended upon a 'property' cycle, as the business moved from an initial stage of paying off debts, to the accumulation of assets, and the subsequent withdrawal of resources in order to establish sons in business, provide marriage settlements for daughters, or put aside income for retirement and dependants.

Industry in Britain was essentially 'family capitalism' in which the aim was to maximize the welfare of the family rather than industrial growth and profitability. Did the reliance upon ploughing back profits in family concerns act as a barrier to industrial investment, holding back the rate of growth? On the whole, it probably did not and it does not seem likely that the growth of industry was constrained by a lack of funds. When government borrowing was at its peak, during the French revolutionary and Napoleonic wars, industrial firms were insulated, and were able to reinvest their own profits; they were less sensitive to the interest rate on government securities than to a desire to establish the firm as the basis for their family fortune. There is no sign that firms were neglecting opportunities for reinvestment in the business; their problem was how to find an outlet for surplus funds, for continued investment in the firm might expose them to the dangers of over-commitment and diseconomies of scale, to a glut of capacity and a collapse of profits. The creation of a diverse portfolio made sound economic sense, and contributed to the creation of an active capital market.

The 'Credit Matrix'

Although fixed capital was relatively less important than circulating capital, historians have concentrated on sources of fixed capital and have neglected the vital role of circulating capital and credit which were at the heart of the economy between 1700 and 1850. A firm could obtain working capital by inserting itself into the local web of credit, and pay for fuel, raw materials, and even machinery after the production of the finished article and after it had gained some return, possibly by obtaining cash from a merchant before the goods were sold to the consumer. By obtaining credit, it was possible for an industrialist to devote his own limited assets to fixed capital. Such a firm would be a net debtor within the web of credit, and it follows that other firms were net creditors, purchasing markets for their goods by offering generous credit terms. The whole edifice of business rested upon the shifting sands of credit, and any disruption threatened large-scale collapse. An understanding of credit is central to the industrial economy of the eighteenth and early nineteenth centuries, but the 'credit matrix' of firms is complex and less visible than steam engines, spinning-jennies, and factory buildings, which embodied fixed capital.

The first type of credit was internal or 'open', consisting of book debts and credits covering the purchase of raw materials and the sale of goods which allowed transactions to be financed with a smaller stock of money, deferring payment and allowing the purchase of goods without the use of currency. The mutual indebtedness of traders and producers created a pyramid of credit which could prop up smaller men, such as in the drink trade where shopkeepers were in debt to innkeepers, who were in turn in debt to maltsters, brewers, and wine-merchants. The position of manufacturers within this pyramid deteriorated in the late eighteenth and early nineteenth centuries. In the eighteenth century, they usually obtained raw materials on long credits of between six and eighteen months, but the terms shortened from about 1815 and were normally two to four months by the 1830s and 1840s. Consequently, labour became the most flexible item in costs and industrialists were, in effect, obtaining credit from their workers through 'truck', by delays in payment of wages, and by the use of tokens rather than coin. The ability of manufacturers to *obtain* credit was reduced, and at the end of the eighteenth century they were obliged to *grant* credit to customers. Producers of woollen cloth in the eighteenth century were net creditors: they obtained credit from the staplers who supplied wool; and sold their output at cloth halls in return for cash or at most short periods of credit. Their position changed with a switch to direct selling to customers or commission arrangements with merchants, and the need to gain a competitive edge in volatile, long-distance trades forced them to offer more extended credit from the late 1790s. A similar pattern applied to cotton, where the need to offer credit is clear from the accounts of McConnel and Kennedy (Table 9.1). The pattern altered again from the 1820s, when a change in the market environment reduced the need to offer long credit to secure sales. Of course, long credit was expensive, and firms preferred to concentrate on reducing their costs: mechanization increased the turnover of capital in production; improved communications meant that goods could be realized more quickly; and the development of banking provided an alternative source of credit. Although some industrialists continued to 'buy' custom in slumps, such as shipbuilders who offered generous credit to shipowners, the underlying trend is clear: a contraction of internal credit by the 1830s and 1840s, and an increased reliance upon a second form of *external* credit (see Fig. 9.1).

External credit drew upon sources of funds outside the circle of producers and merchants directly involved in production and marketing. A merchant or manufacturer who was selling goods worth, say, £100 would send a bill of exchange to the purchaser requesting payment in, say, three months. The purchaser signed and 'accepted' the bill and returned it to the issuer, who could either retain it until it fell due or release his funds into more productive use. He could pass it in payment of a claim to a creditor, who could repeat the process so that the bill became a type of paper currency; or he could obtain cash by 'discounting' it at a bank. The creditor or bank offered somewhat less than face value for the bill, paying, say, £98 for a three-month bill for £100; the purchaser earned £2 over three months or an annual interest of 8.2 per cent. Bills consequently offered a very attractive short-term holding for banks, who could usually realize the asset at short notice, and the significance of external credit from the banks increased as open credit declined in the 1830s and 1840s. The legal framework in England was favourable to the emergence of a commercialized credit-based economy, for bills of exchange could not be used in this way in other countries. In France, a bill was defined as a contract of exchange which required that value had been given; it was simply a means of transferring a trade debt from one area to another. In England, it was not necessary for value to be given, and bills could be drawn and paid in the same place; in 1765, they could be payable to the bearer, who could be completely separate from the original transaction which had led to their creation. Bills could, as a consequence, be used as a common currency rather than for the payment of inter-regional debts.

The bill of exchange, and the development of the law of mortgages and trusts, fostered an economy based on credit which had vices as well as virtues. Credit, it seemed to some, eroded the social fabric, leading to gambling, avarice, irresponsibility, and ambition; to others, it was essential to business and a mark of confidence in a man's moral standing. Certainly, credit removed some constraints. Bills were a close substitute for money, which moderated the demand for cash at a time of slow growth of the supply of currency. They were means of transferring assets between areas of capital surplus and deficit, helping to overcome the social and local insufficiencies of capital. Bills drawn on Lancashire were transferred to bankers in London, who sold them to country bankers in areas such as East Anglia which had surplus funds, so that the wealth of one locality and social class was fed to another locality and class through the provision of external credit rather than direct investment in fixed capital. But extensive use of credit also threatened instability. Bills of exchange relied upon confidence that the issuer would meet payment, but personal knowledge of credit-worthiness declined and risks increased as bills passed from hand to hand. Although external credit could stimulate the economy, it could also lead to over-extension, fluctuations, and trade crises. Reliance upon credit made business failure an ever-present possibility, and parliament and the courts had to decide how to view bankrupts: were they men of overreaching ambition and avarice who were dishonestly evading their creditors and deserving of punishment; or were they enterprising men who deserved sympathy?

Initially, the law of bankruptcy was concerned with fraudulent defaulters who sought to evade their creditors, but from 1706 protection was offered to honest bankrupts. Traders and persons with debts of at least £100 were covered by the law; the bankrupt surrendered his estate, which was divided amongst his creditors; he was discharged from his debts when four-fifths of the creditors by number and value agreed; and if he paid 8s. in the pound, he received 5 per cent of the realized estate to start life anew. The motivation of the law was clear: the trading and financial limits were intended to liberalize the law for wholesalers and manufacturers but not for retailers and artisans who must, as Sir William Blackstone said, 'take the consequences of their own indiscretion ... for the law holds it to be an unjustifiable practice, for any person but a trader to encumber himself with debts of any considerable value'.[14] Bankruptcy—like mortgages, bills of exchange, and trusts—was tailored to meet the needs of businessmen who were crucially dependent upon credit, and it was intended to encourage a culture of enterprise. 'In a Trading Country', remarked a pamphleteer in 1734, 'those who have become Insolvent, by pursuing Projects, or by any other Losses incident to Trade, ought to be gently dealt with; so even this of venturing another Man's Money upon a *reasonable* Project, or Scheme of Trade, ought not to be looked on as a very gross Fault.'[15]

The industrial revolution was a period of growth *and* of business failures, creating the unfortunate bankrupt as well as the spectacular successes of Arkwright or Wedgwood. Increased opportunities meant that more men were willing to take risks, and more intense competition meant that there was a

(a)

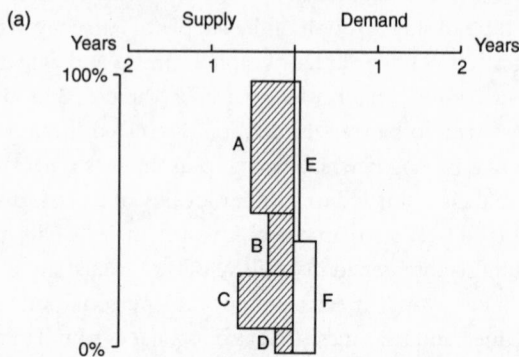

A Purchase of wool from staplers at average of 6 months' credit
B Labour payment (largely weaving and spinning) at 3–4 months' credit
C Fulling, scribbling, and carding at 6–8 months' credit
D Other inputs, tools, and rents at 2–3 months' credit
E Sales at cloth halls at under 14 days' credit
F Direct sales to merchants or middlemen for short bills at 3 months

(b)

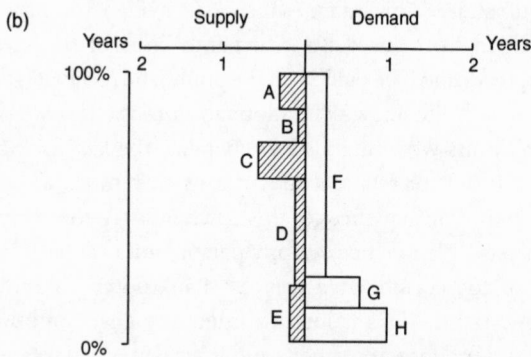

A Purchase of wool from growers and dealers at 3–4 months' credit
B Purchase of wool from growers and fairs at 14 days' credit or less
C Purchase of wool from staplers at 6–8 months' credit
D Labour payment at average of 1–2 months' credit
E Tools, carriage, oil, soap, etc., at 2–3 months' credit
F Cloths sold to Leeds merchants at 3 months' credit
G Cloths sold direct to Europe at average of 8 months' credit
H Cloths sold direct to American market and to the home trade at average of 12 months' credit

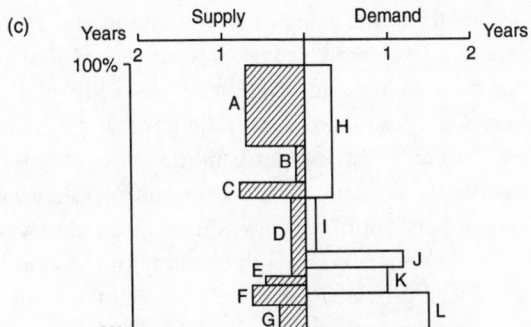

(c)

A Purchase of wool from staplers at 6–10 months' credit
B Direct purchase of wool from growers and middlemen at an average of 1 month's credit
C Purchase of wool from importers at 6–11 months' credit
D Labour, part centralized, part domestic, at an average of 2 months' credit
E Rental of premises at 6 months' credit
F Dyeing and dressing services at 6–12 months' credit
G Other inputs: oil soap, tools, carriage at an average of 4 months' credit
H Sales to local merchants at 4 months' credit
I Sales to shippers for advances at 6 weeks' credit
J Direct sales to Europe at credit averaging 14 months
K Sales to the home trade at credit averaging 12 months
L Sales to North and South America at 18 months' credit

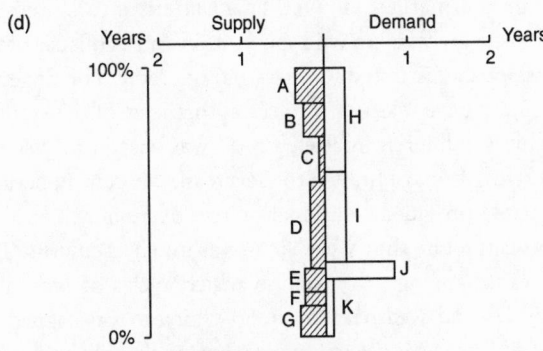

(d)

A Purchase of recycled wool at 4 months' credit
B Purchase of wool from staplers at 3 months' credit
C Purchase of wool at auction at 2 weeks' credit
D Labour at credit averaging 2 months
E Dyeing and carriage at 3 months' credit
F Rental of premises/fixed capital charges at an average of 3 months' credit
G Machinery, tools, utensils, residual inputs at 4 months' credit
H Direct sales or through intermediaries to the home trade at 3 months' credit
I Direct sales abroad at 3 months' credit
J Direct sales abroad on long credits
K Direct sales to foreign houses in England for immediately discountable bills: 1
    month's credit

FIG. 9.1. Credit matrix in the West Riding wool textile industry. (*a*) Domestic artisan woollen manufacturer before 1815; (*b*) Worsted putting out manufacturer, *c*.1780–1810; (*c*) Large-scale manufacturer, woollen branch, *c*.1800–1820s; (*d*) Factory woollen manufacturer, 1820s–1840s

Source: P. Hudson, *The Genesis of Industrial Capital: A Study of the West Riding Wool Textile Industry, c.1750–1850* (Cambridge, 1986), 191–3, 195.

greater chance of failure. Credit offered the allure of success and an opportunity for wealth in periods and sectors of growth: it also posed a danger of failure and bankruptcy by making firms more vulnerable when there was a loss of confidence. The number of bankruptcies rose sharply from the 1770s, and it is likely that the rate also increased. Certainly the level of bankruptcy was higher in expanding sectors such as overseas trade, Lancashire cotton, and Yorkshire wool textiles than in declining areas such as Norfolk textiles. Above all, London was at the heart of business failure until the later eighteenth century, for it was at the centre of high-risk overseas trade; it provided a vast web of credit for domestic trade and production; and it was the home of fashion with its uncertainties. Generally, risk was increased by novelty and the emergence of new firms such as in Lancashire cotton and West Riding wool; and uncertainty was intensified by regional specialization and reliance on external markets with the difficulties of obtaining accurate information. The gradual replacement of regional economies by an integrated national economy in the later eighteenth century, with the development of coastal shipping, turnpikes, canals, newspapers, and marketing networks, led to the onset of business cycles and cyclical depressions. Further, increased reliance upon bills of exchange after about 1770, and the creation by country banks of an integrated market, allowed financial crises to sweep the country. Prudence could easily give way to wild speculation and a collapse of the network of bills, which seriously disrupted the pyramid of credit. The finger of blame was pointed at the country banks which were at the heart of the system. Whether they were at fault is a different matter. Credit was based on trust and confidence, which could swing from optimism to gloom and despair. In periods of optimism the country banks provided additional sources of credit and encouraged growth; when pessimism set in, they were victims as much as culprits. The nature of the economy was changing, from one in which cycles of economic activity rested on the harvest and weather, to one in which it was shaped by business and financial cycles. The response of governments in the first half of the nineteenth century was to draw a distinction between 'real' bills, based on trade, and speculative paper which subverted the social order. Collapse was therefore seen as a useful corrective, purifying the economy and society. Although the distinction was in fact difficult to sustain, and led to problems for businesses based on genuine trade as well as for speculators, the Bank Charter Act of 1844 installed these assumptions at the heart of economic policy.

'Crowding Out' and Social Overhead Capital

The delay in capital-intensive growth has been explained by two competing interpretations. The first account argues that fixed capital investment in industry was low because existing techniques were adequate for the expected growth of the market. This is to argue that the *demand* for investment was the key. The alternative is to suggest that industrialists were prevented from adopting capital-intensive technology, and might even have developed capital *saving* methods, because funds were not available. This argument has two variants: it could be that savings were low, or that competing demands for government loans 'crowded out' investment until the second quarter of the nineteenth century. 'Britain', argues Williamson, 'tried to do two things at once—industrialize *and* fight expensive wars, and she simply did not have the resources to do both.'[16] The limitation of private investment, he argues, meant that there was a low level of accumulation with little capital deepening; productivity was kept within strict limits, and living standards did not improve until a reduction in government borrowing from the 1820s ended crowding out and allowed resources to be channelled into production.

The 'crowding out' hypothesis rests on a number of questionable assumptions. It implies full employment, for government borrowing would otherwise 'crowd in' underemployed resources and stimulate the economy by injecting demand and raising the rate of growth. It also assumes that private business and government drew upon a single pool of resources. Both assumptions rest on shaky foundations. Indeed, the initial impact of war in 1793 was probably beneficial, with deficit finance injecting demand into the economy which compensated for a slower rate of growth of trade with America and the end of the canal mania. By 1797, the budget deficit was reduced by higher taxes and a large part of expenditure went abroad or in interest to holders of the national debt who had a low propensity to consume. Even so, 'crowding in' remained a possibility for bank loans augmented the means of payments. Neither should resources of labour and capital be treated as a single pool. Government employment of adult male soldiers did not necessarily harm industry, for their replacement by children and women might well encourage the use of factories and powered machinery. Similarly, it is doubtful that resources were allocated to competing uses by a single capital market. The demands of the state led to a higher yield on consols but not necessarily to a rise in real interest rates, for the capital market was segmented. Government debt attracted investors from the south of England, drawn from particular social groupings; capital for industry was raised from family and friends, through local networks and retained profits. The mobility of capital between different uses was limited and social groups reacted to changes in interest rates in a variety of ways, rather than simply selecting the highest rate of return in the market. An industrialist who was building up a family firm would not switch his funds between competing uses according to the rate of interest, for he was more concerned with pursuing a family strategy to provide security and employment. His decision to invest would also be influenced by expectations of market expansion. By contrast, a *rentier* or landed aristocrat could choose between purchasing government stock and luxury consumption rather than between investment in industry and the national debt.

The 'crowding out' hypothesis does not seem plausible, and it also seems unlikely that investment in capital-intensive production was hampered by a low level of savings. There was probably an increase in the savings ratio in the later eighteenth and early nineteenth centuries, partly as a result of high and regressive taxation. The cost of government fell disproportionately upon poorer members of society, which held down the demand for goods; interest payments on the national debt benefited the better off, shifting the distribution of income towards groups with a higher propensity to save. Trends in agriculture had a similar outcome, for output lagged behind population growth and the terms of trade shifted towards agriculture. Higher food prices depressed the demand for industrial goods, and income shifted to large landowners with a greater propensity to save. How these factors affected investment is uncertain: was it beneficial by encouraging savings, or harmful by depressing domestic demand and reducing the incentive to invest? A neo-classical economist would take the first position, arguing that the supply of savings was the crucial variable: a dog called savings wagged a tail of investment. A Keynesian economist would take the second position, arguing that the expected rate of expansion of the market determined investment demand for savings: a dog called investment wagged a tail of savings. The Keynesian model does seem more plausible in the eighteenth and early nineteenth centuries, for industry generated a large part of its own funds for investment from the prior process of domestic production and through ploughed-back profits as it responded to the growth of the market. In this case, constraints on the market created by a regressive system of taxation and a shift of income towards rent held back growth, reducing the ability of industrialists to generate funds and limiting their demand for investment.

The neo-classical emphasis upon a savings constraint could possibly be more applicable to investment in the growing cities, which required housing, paving, sewers, water supply, street lighting, and the erection of public buildings such as market halls, hospitals, schools, prisons, and churches. The modesty of investment in industrialization could appear in a different guise, as 'an attempt to achieve an industrial revolution on the cheap'[17] by failing to commit resources to the urban infrastructure. Edwin Chadwick certainly protested against urban squalor in his *Report on the Sanitary Conditions of the Labouring Population of Great Britain* of 1842, and contended that increased investment would pay by reducing poor law expenditure and allowing workers to be more productive. 'Low investment requirements', Williamson suggests, 'reflect a growth strategy which starved housing, public works and other social overhead investment', leading to an 'enormous deficit' in social overhead capital by 1830. Britain adopted, he argues, an 'ugly-city and industrialisation-on-the-cheap development strategy'.[18]

Concentration on individual industrial concerns has led to a neglect of the large investment needs of the urban infrastructure, but was there *under-investment*? The contention relies upon a comparison between Britain and the modern Third World, where cities are more capital intensive and there is lower mortality in urban areas than there is in the countryside; and a belief that investment in social overhead capital would have paid, as Chadwick contended, by reducing the costs of ill-health both directly in terms of poor law expenditure and indirectly in terms of lost production and earnings. But are these points convincing proof that investment opportunities were neglected? More realistic than spurious comparisons with the modern Third World would be comparison with cities in France, Holland, or Germany in the eighteenth and early nine-teenth centuries in order to establish whether British cities had a lower level of investment in the urban infrastructure. Continental cities spent more on grand schemes of boulevards and palaces, so that they were more aesthetically impress-ive than their British counterparts. Despite the ambitions of the Prince Regent and John Nash, London was not rebuilt as the capital of a great empire; it was constructed by aristocratic landowners such as the duke of Bedford and a mass of small builders catering for a market of prosperous professionals, merchants, and gentlemen. London, unlike other eighteenth-century capitals, was 'raised by private, not by public wealth. ... The land speculator and the adventuring builder have contributed more to the character of the Georgian city than the minister with a flair for artistic propaganda, or the monarch with a mission for dynastic assertion.'[19] London became the largest city in Europe, and also one of the best housed and healthiest, with a death rate lower than the birth rate by about 1800, at a time when most European cities were 'devourers of men'.

It is difficult to accept that social overhead investment in Britain was lower than it should have been either because of a primitive state of public health technology or because of constraints on investment. Many facilities were neither necessary nor available until the second quarter of the nineteenth century. In London, for example, it was still possible to draw water with relative safety from the Thames, wells, and rain-water cisterns until the appearance of cholera in the 1830s. Although the provision of piped water supplies had started with the New River Company in the sixteenth century, investment was limited both by the restriction of demand to better-off members of the middle class and by problems of distribution through expensive, leaking wooden pipes. The construction of piped water and gas depended upon a fall in the price of cast-iron pipes with the new technology of iron-smelting, and it is by no means obvious that the supply of capital was a crucial constraint. Trusts allowed local funds to be raised for 'lumpy' investments such as turnpikes, bridges, market halls, or hospitals, and much sanitary reform was less a matter of massive investment in drains and sewers than in piecemeal improvements. Although London lacked a unified system of government and many expanding industrial towns relied on the governmental machinery of a medieval village, action was possible and a spate of public measures continued from about 1750 until the reforms of the 1830s. In most towns, street, paving, or lighting commissions were established by act of parliament, with the right to levy rates and to take over responsibilities which had previously been placed on individual householders. Rather than these powers accruing to existing corporations, the scope of civil society was widened by the creation of new bodies of trustees which were often given the right to raise a rate and to borrow money, which created a market for local authority debt. The first improvement commission was created in 1725, for the prestigious St James's Square, with power to raise a rate and borrow £6,000; more impressive in scale were the Westminster paving commissioners who were appointed by an Act of 1762 and spent £400,000 by the early 1770s.[20] Similarly, in Manchester the medieval institutions of the manorial court and parish vestry were joined by the Police Commission in 1792, a body consisting of everyone with property of £30: it provided public order, street scavenging and lighting, and started the gas works in 1824.

Although these efforts did allow some improvement in the urban environment, rapid growth of industrial towns exposed the inadequacy of the solution. Improvement commissions were more likely to be found in cities where merchants and gentry had their town houses and warehouses, which were oriented to trade rather than production; in 1801, expanding towns such as Warrington, Wigan, Oldham, and Blackburn had no improvement commission. Large, 'lumpy' investment in sanitation became necessary by the 1830s, with the threat of cholera epidemics and a deterioration in the urban death rate. The social return on urban overhead capital rose, and constraints on investment were largely political. Public investment was limited by the structure of local government finance, for the majority of borough corporations were closed Tory cliques, which could use their assets for the benefit of members rather than the inhabitants of the town. Although the Municipal Corporations Act of 1835 created elected councils, problems remained, for the reformed corporations did not necessarily extend their functions, and new corporations were not immediately created for towns such as Manchester and Merthyr Tydfil. Above all, taxes consisted of a property rate which fell on housing, and owners of house property were often able to mount a successful campaign for 'economy' against those who advocated investment in the urban environment and supported Chadwick's argument that it was rational in terms of social savings. Opposition was not simply obscurantist, for higher rates might well force up the cost of working-class accommodation, and many had reason to be suspicious of the centralizing tendencies of the Public Health Act of 1848, which continued the challenge of the new poor law of 1834 to local self-government.

The largest single investment in towns was housing. Many towns were rebuilt in brick and tile by 1750 as a result of a fall in price relative to wood. Towns were, as a result, less prone to fire, and brick houses were less liable to disease and dirt. But did investment in housing keep pace with the increase in the urban population? House building was a matter for small concerns with modest capital, heavily dependent on credit and susceptible to wide fluctuations as over-expansion gave way to bankruptcies and collapse. In some towns, small builders were aided by large landowners, who planned the general layout, invested in roads, drains, and garden squares, and then offered sites to individual builders on 99-year leases which had the virtue of reducing the amount of capital they needed. Landowners who sold the freehold either prepared the roads and supplied credit themselves, or sold to intermediary developers, often syndicates of merchants, attorneys, and surveyors who were more likely to have access to capital and credit than individual builders. The landowners and developers were investing in building land ahead of construction, fuelling speculation by builders. These small-scale concerns took on a handful of sites, often erecting only the brick carcass and roof and leaving completion of the interior to a team of artisans who shared the profits from the sale. Materials were often obtained on credit, and construction took place in a flurry of speculation with builders and artisans eager to share in the profits of running up a few houses. Of course, heavy dependence on a fragile network of loans and confidence meant that building was prone to collapse. A tightening of credit as a result of competing demands might cause problems, such as at the outbreak of war in 1793, but on the whole the building cycle had an internal dynamic. Builders could not easily stop, for their survival depended on a continued flow of income from sales. They tended to over-build, glutting the market as in the London boom of 1788–91, so that the credit restriction of 1793 acted as a trigger rather than the cause of the slump. The over-supply of housing led to a period of low prices and rents until the shortage was removed, and an increase in rents eventually triggered renewed activity. The response of builders to market indicators was slow, rather than the highly sensitive reaction to slight changes in interest rates assumed by the 'crowding out' hypothesis.

Builders were usually erecting houses at their own risk rather than to order, and their success depended upon finding a purchaser who would buy the house and let it to tenants. The purchasers of houses were mostly of modest means, drawn from the ranks of shopkeepers or traders, widows and retired people, who wished to withdraw funds from the risks of trade or industry and invest small sums in order to obtain a secure income with low risk, for their retirement or to support dependants; often they borrowed money with a mortgage from a local solicitor. Houses were a sort of pension fund which had the virtue, in the eyes of the purchasers, of being visible and easily realizable when capital was needed. The construction of London's suburbs and provincial towns came about by a piecemeal reinvestment of funds generated within the locality, tending to attract a particular segment of the capital market which was not easily tempted by alternative outlets. Any shortage of funds was likely to be localized rather than general, the result of industrial development in isolated areas, where the factory owner might himself be forced to build, as with the Greg family at Styal. In general, there is little sign of a savings constraint, with hundreds of people investing directly in housing and many more providing loans and credit.

Rather than a constraint on savings or 'crowding out' by alternative claims on funds, the problem was that landowners, builders, and investors were more attracted by the market for middle-class property in Bloomsbury than working-class property in Bethnal Green. The provision of healthy housing for the working class at market rents was more difficult in the late eighteenth and early nineteenth centuries, for costs of construction rose with wartime inflation of building materials, and the price of urban land increased by perhaps 50 per cent between the 1780s and 1810s. Builders and house owners were caught in a trap of increased outgoings encountering sticky rents and house prices, so that 'the choice lay between squeezing profit margins or skimping on the use of materials, or both'.[21] The quality of housing probably fell, with lower standards of construction, smaller houses, and a denser use of land through in-filling the existing built-up area and subdividing housing. Housing quality was therefore under pressure at the end of the eighteenth and early nineteenth centuries, but quantity kept pace with the rise in the urban population. The average number of inhabitants per house in England and Wales remained fairly stable, at 5.67 in 1801, 5.68 in 1811, and 5.76 in 1821,[22] which was an important consideration in view of the expectation that newly married couples would establish a new household. Quality started to rise after the building boom of 1825, when the price of building land fell and working-class incomes started to improve.

Conclusion

The demand for fixed capital in industrialization has been under-estimated by concentrating on the individual firm, particularly in manufacturing, and neglecting investment in the urban infrastructure and social overhead capital. The balance should be redressed, both for a better understanding of capital markets, and because a major source of productivity growth was external economies and a reduction in transaction costs. Nevertheless, Postan's basic point remains valid: there was no general shortage of funds, and growth was neither limited by a savings constraint nor 'crowded out' by government borrowing. Restrictions on joint-stock organization and the shortcomings of local government finance were overcome by alternative means of raising funds through the use of trusts and mortgages, and there is little sign that the organization of capital markets or a shortage of funds imposed significant constraints on growth. Rather, growth was constrained by the structure of demand at the end of the eighteenth and early nineteenth centuries: there was, as Malthus and Ricardo argued, a shift of income to landowners and a rise in food prices relative to industrial goods which were respectively intensified by the incidence of taxation and agricultural protection. Growth was constrained by the nature of an organic economy, until it became possible to apply larger amounts of mineral fuel and steam power.

Calculation of the level of fixed capital accumulation is fraught with difficulties, and the margin of error is extremely wide. Nevertheless, the most recent estimates do cast doubt on Rostow's contention that investment was a relatively small proportion of national income in the mid-eighteenth century, and that the net investment rate doubled from about 5 to over 10 per cent of the net national product over the late eighteenth and early nineteenth centuries. The level of fixed capital investment was probably higher in the mid-eighteenth century as a result of investment in social overheads and extractive industries, and Feinstein has suggested that gross domestic fixed capital was stable at about 10 per cent of GDP from the 1780s until after 1860, rather than experiencing a sudden spurt or 'take-off' into self-sustained growth.

Nevertheless, the importance of fixed capital increased, more as a result of savings in circulating capital than through a surge in fixed capital formation. The ratio of fixed to circulating capital in British industry and commerce shifted, Feinstein calculates, from 1:1 to 3.3:1 between the mid-eighteenth and mid-nineteenth centuries, which seems plausible. Improvements in organization, communications, and technological change allowed a swifter turnover of capital, and the amount of circulating capital fell relative to fixed capital. The gradual adjustment in the ratio between circulating and fixed capital was intensified in the second quarter of the eighteenth century by the spread of steam power and the emergence of capital goods industries such as heavy engineering and machine building. The fixed capital stock of Britain, on Feinstein's estimates, grew by 1.6 per cent per annum between 1761 and 1860, with the most rapid growth of 2.3 per cent between 1831 and 1860.[23] Although the precise figures are open to serious doubt, the general trend is plausible in terms of the development

TABLE 9.2. *Distribution of gross domestic fixed capital formation, excluding residential dwellings, 1761–1770 to 1841–1850*

	Agriculture	Mineral-based industries	Other industries, services
1761–70	39.0	12.9	48.0
1801–10	34.4	18.1	47.4
1841–50	15.8	58.6	25.5

Source: E. A. Wrigley, *Continuity, Chance and Change* (Cambridge, 1988), 107, from C. H. Feinstein, 'National Statistics, 1760–1920', in C. H. Feinstein and S. Pollard (eds.), *Studies in Capital Formation in the United Kingdom, 1750–1920* (Oxford, 1988).

of British industry, with the relatively slow emergence of factory production and centralized sources of power until the second quarter of the nineteenth century. But the argument for continuity and the absence of an 'industrial revolution' should not be pressed too far, for aggregate figures can disguise changes in the composition of investment and its impact on society. A rough categorization of investment (Table 9.2) suggests that a major change took place in the early nineteenth century, with a fall in the share of investment in agriculture and a rise in mineral-based sectors such as coal, gas, iron, and railways. The relative stability in the *aggregate* level of capital investment is only part of the picture, for change is more evident than continuity in the *composition* of investment.

NOTES

1. M. M. Postan, 'Recent Trends in the Accumulation of Capital', *Economic History Review*, 6 (1935), repr. in F. Crouzet (ed.), *Capital Formation in the Industrial Revolution* (1972), 71.
2. D. Landes, *Unbound Prometheus: Technological Change and Industrial Development in Western Europe from 1750 to the Present* (Cambridge, 1969), 79.
3. Above all, J. G. Williamson, 'Why was British Growth so Slow during the Industrial Revolution?', *Journal of Economic History*, 44 (1984).
4. K. Marx, *Capital*, iii (1959 edition), 393.
5. H. A. Shannon, 'The First Five Thousand Limited Companies and their Creation', *Economic History*, 2 (1930–3), cited in P. Cottrell, *Industrial Finance, 1830–1914: The Finance and Organisation of English Manufacturing Industry* (1980), 44–5.
6. P. Richardson, 'The Structure of Capital during the Industrial Revolution Revisited: Two Case Studies from the Cotton Textile Industry', *Economic History Review*, 2nd ser. 42 (1989), 493.
7. S. D. Chapman, 'Fixed Capital Formation in the British Cotton Industry, 1770–1815', *Economic History Review*, 2nd ser. 23 (1970), 253.

8. P. Hudson, *Genesis of Industrial Capital: A Study of the West Riding Wool Textile Industry, c.1750–1850* (Cambridge, 1986), 51.

9. M. W. Flinn, *History of the British Coal Industry*, ii: *1700–1830: The Industrial Revolution* (Oxford, 1984), 194.

10. M. J. Daunton, *Coal Metropolis: Cardiff, 1870–1914* (Leicester, 1977), 28.

11. Hudson, *Genesis of Industrial Capital*, 104.

12. B. L. Anderson, 'Law, Finance and Economic Growth in England: Some Long-Term Influences', in B. M. Ratcliffe (ed.), *Great Britain and her World, 1750–1914* (Manchester, 1975), 103.

13. E. M. Sigworth, *Black Dyke Mills: A History* (Liverpool, 1958), 224.

14. J. Hoppit, *Risk and Failure in English Business, 1700–1800* (Cambridge, 1987), 25.

15. Ibid. 23.

16. J. G. Williamson, 'Why was British Growth so Slow during the Industrial Revolution?' *Journal of Economic History*, 44 (1984), 689.

17. J. G. Williamson, *Coping with City Growth during the Industrial Revolution* (Cambridge, 1990), 270.

18. Ibid. 273, 280.

19. J. Summerson, *Georgian London* (1945), 9–10.

20. E. L. Jones and M. E. Falkus, 'Urban Improvement and the English Economy in the Seventeenth and Eighteenth Centuries', *Research in Economic History*, 4 (1979), 212, 214; M. D. George, *London Life in the Eighteenth Century* (1925).

21. C. W. Chalklin, *The Provincial Towns of Georgian England: A Study of the Building Process, 1740–1820* (1974), 225.

22. Ibid. 305.

23. C. H. Feinstein, 'Capital Formation in Great Britain', in P. Mathias and M. M. Postan (eds.), *Cambridge Economic History of Europe*, vii, part 1 (Cambridge, 1978), 83, 90–1.

FURTHER READING

Anderson, B. L., 'Provincial Aspects of the Financial Revolution of the Eighteenth Century', *Business History*, 11 (1969).

—— 'Money and the Structure of Credit in the Eighteenth Century', *Business History*, 12 (1970).

—— 'Law, Finance and Economic Growth in England: Some Long-Term Influences', in B. M. Ratcliffe (ed.), *Great Britain and her World 1750–1914: Essays in Honour of W. O. Henderson* (Manchester, 1975).

Ashton, T. S., 'The Bill of Exchange and Private Banks in Lancashire, 1790–1830', *Economic History Review*, 15 (1945).

—— *Economic Fluctuations in England, 1700–1800* (Oxford, 1959).

Beresford, M. W., *East End, West End: The Face of Leeds during Urbanisation, 1684–1842* (Leeds, 1988).

—— 'The Back-to-Back House in Leeds, 1787–1937', in S. D. Chapman (ed.), *The History of Working-Class Housing* (Newton Abbot, 1971).

Black, R. A., and Gilmore, C. G., 'Crowding out during Britain's Industrial Revolution', *Journal of Economic History*, 50 (1990).

Borsay, P., The English Urban Renaissance: Culture and Society in the Provincial Town 1660–1770 (Oxford, 1989).

Chalklin, C. W., The Provincial Towns of Georgian England: A Study of the Building Process 1740–1820 (1974).

Chapman, S. D., 'Working-Class Housing in Nottingham during the Industrial Revolution', Transactions of the Thoroton Society, 67 (1963).

——'Fixed Capital Formation in the British Cotton Industry, 1770–1815', Economic History Review, 2nd ser. 23 (1970).

Cottrell, P., Industrial Finance, 1830–1914: The Finance and Organisation of English Manufacturing Industry (1980).

Daunton, M. J., Coal Metropolis: Cardiff, 1870–1914 (Leicester, 1977).

Errazurez, A., 'Some Types of Housing in Liverpool, 1785–1890', Town Planning Review, 19 (1943–7).

Feinstein, C. H., 'Capital Formation in Great Britain', in P. Mathias and M. M. Postan (eds.), Cambridge Economic History of Europe, vii, part 1 (Cambridge, 1978).

——and Pollard, S. (eds.), Studies in Capital Formation in the United Kingdom, 1750–1920 (Oxford, 1988).

Flinn, M. W., The History of the British Coal Industry, ii: 1700–1830: The Industrial Revolution (Oxford, 1984).

George, M. D., London Life in the Eighteenth Century (1925).

Heim, C. E., and Mirowski, P., 'Interest Rates and Crowding out during Britain's Industrial Revolution', Journal of Economic History, 57 (1987).

Hennock, E. P., Fit and Proper Persons: Ideal and Reality in Nineteenth-Century Urban Government (1973).

Holderness, B. A., 'Credit in a Rural Community, 1660–1800: Some Neglected Aspects of Probate Inventories', Midland History, 3 (1975–6).

Hoppit, J., 'Attitudes to Credit in Britain, 1680–1790', Historical Journal, 33 (1990).

——Risk and Failure in English Business, 1700–1800 (Cambridge, 1987).

Hudson, P., The Genesis of Industrial Capital: A Study of the West Riding Wool Textile Industry, c.1750–1850 (Cambridge, 1986).

——'From Manor to Mill: The West Riding in Transition', in M. Berg, P. Hudson, and M. Sonenscher (eds.), Manufacture in Town and Country before the Factory (Cambridge, 1983).

Jenkins, D. J., The West Riding Wool Textile Industry, 1770–1835: A Study of Fixed Capital Formation (Edington, 1975).

Jones, E. L., and Falkus, M. E., 'Urban Improvement and the English Economy in the Seventeenth and Eighteenth Centuries', Research in Economic History, 4 (1979).

Landes, D., Unbound Prometheus: Technological Change and Industrial Development in Western Europe from 1750 to the Present (Cambridge, 1969).

Miles, M., 'The Money Market in the Early Industrial Revolution: The Evidence from West Riding Attorneys, c.1750–1800', Business History, 23 (1981).

Morris, R. J., 'The Middle Class and the Property Cycle during the Industrial Revolution', in T. C. Smout (ed.), *The Search for Wealth and Stability: Essays in Economic and Social History Presented to M. W. Flinn* (1979).

Olsen, D. J., *Town Planning in London: The Eighteenth and Nineteenth Centuries* (New Haven, Conn., 1964).

—— *The City as a Work of Art: London, Paris, Vienna* (New Haven, Conn., 1986).

Pollard, S., 'Fixed Capital in the Industrial Revolution in Britain', *Journal of Economic History*, 24 (1964).

Postan, M. M., 'Recent Trends in the Accumulation of Capital', *Economic History Review*, 6 (1935); repr. in F. Crouzet (ed.), *Capital Formation in the Industrial Revolution* (1972).

Richardson, P., 'The Structure of Capital during the Industrial Revolution Revisited: Two Case Studies from the Cotton Textile Industry', *Economic History Review*, 2nd ser. 42 (1989).

Rimmer, W. G., 'Working-Men's Cottages in Leeds, 1770–1840', *Publications of the Thoresby Society*, 46 (1960).

Rose, M. B., 'Diversification of Investment by the Greg Family, 1800–1914', *Business History*, 21 (1979).

Rostow, W. W., *The Stages of Economic Growth* (Cambridge, 1960).

Saville, J., 'Sleeping Partnership and Limited Liability, 1850–56', *Economic History Review*, 2nd ser. 8 (1955–6).

Shannon, H. A., 'The First Five Thousand Limited Companies and their Creation', *Economic History*, 2 (1930–3).

Sigsworth, E. M., *Black Dyke Mills: A History* (Liverpool, 1958).

Summerson, J., *Georgian London* (1945).

Taylor, I. C., 'The Court and Cellar Dwelling: The Eighteenth-Century Origins of the Liverpool Slum', *Transactions of the Historic Society of Lancashire and Cheshire*, 112 (1970).

Vigier, F., *Change and Apathy: Liverpool and Manchester during the Industrial Revolution* (Cambridge, Mass., 1970).

Weatherill, L., 'Capital and Credit in the Pottery Industry before 1770', *Business History*, 24 (1982).

Williamson, J. G., *Coping with City Growth during the British Revolution* (Cambridge, 1990).

—— 'Why was British Growth so Slow during the Industrial Revolution?', *Journal of Economic History*, 44 (1984).

Wrigley, E. A., *Continuity, Chance and Change: The Character of the Industrial Revolution in England* (Cambridge, 1988).

PART III

Integrating the Economy

....

Integration and Specialization

Prosperity, argued Adam Smith in *The Wealth of Nations*, depended on he pursuit of 'comparative advantage'. No family would make at home any rticle which it could buy more cheaply: a tailor would not make his own shoes, or a shoemaker his own clothes, for they would produce more, and be more prosperous, by specializing on the tasks at which they were most adept. 'All of hem', argued Smith, 'find it for their interest to employ their whole industry in a way in which they have some advantage over their neighbours.'[1] What was true of the conduct of families applied equally to national policy: each country should specialize in the goods to which it was most suited, removing barriers to free exchange of goods and allowing comparative advantage to flourish.

The same arguments applied to regional specialization within a country, for agricultural yields would increase if land were devoted to the cultivation of the most appropriate crops, and industrial productivity rise if craftsmen were able to devote themselves to making specialized goods. Of course, regions could never be entirely self-sufficient, for commodities such as salt or copper or iron were only available in certain localities, and there had long been an international trade in woollen textiles. However, traded commodities could form a relatively small proportion of total output, and a family (and region) could try to live 'within itself' as far as possible, growing its own cereals, keeping a few animals, making household goods, and selling any surplus to obtain cash. This was a very different matter from maximizing cash income by concentrating on a few goods and purchasing other commodities from outside. Specialization depended upon integrating the economy and removing barriers to exchange, so that a region had a larger market for its output and was confident that other goods could be secured from outside.

The emergence of an integrated and specialized economy was a slow, piece-meal process which was under way in 1700 and was scarcely complete by 1850. The initial stage of abandonment of regional self-sufficiency in cereals had been reached by 1700 (see Chapter 2), and increased reliance on inter-regional trade i apparent in the movement of wheat prices. An integrated market does no necessarily mean that prices are the same in all regions, for price levels reflec differences in transport costs and the level of demand; rather, prices respond a the same speed to a shortage or glut. By 1700, wheat prices were moving to th same rhythm, so that the marketing system was providing clear price signals an ensuring supplies to areas of deficit. These statistics are reflected in the change i the organization of grain marketing and public policy in the later seventeentl century, from a stress in Tudor and early Stuart legislation upon preserving loca food supplies, to encouragement of an active trade in grain. Grain marketin; moved from local, face-to-face contacts to a more complex system of intermedi aries, and imperfections in the market were reduced.

Transaction Costs and Imperfect Competition

Abandonment of regional self-sufficiency in grains was important, but it wa. only the first step towards an integrated national market, with labour and capita devoted to producing the goods in which they had the greatest comparativ advantage. Completion of the process was one of the major themes in th economic, social, and political history of Britain during the next 150 years Specialization would only be feasible when the anticipated gains exceeded th 'transaction costs' of transport and storage, provision for wastage and spoilage credit to hold stocks, and the expenses and profits of merchants and retailers. I only made sense for one region to purchase goods from another when th difference in costs of production exceeded transaction costs; until this happened a region would continue to make goods for its own use, even if it was a high-cos producer. In the eighteenth and early nineteenth centuries, there was often more scope for reducing transaction costs, which formed a high proportion of tota costs, than for cutting production costs. Indeed, a reduction in transaction costs could provide the incentive for changes in the organization of production and the adoption of new technology, by allowing regional concentration on a particula commodity, and providing access to a larger market.

The cost of moving goods was a major constraint on specialization. Goods with relatively low value and high volume, such as coal, were less able to bear transport over long distances than a commodity such as cotton cloth with a relatively high value and low volume. Transport of bulky commodities was cheaper by water than by land, so that the production of coal was confined to areas with access to rivers or the coast, even when it was more easily mined elsewhere. By contrast, producers of cotton goods could more readily shift to areas with the lowest production costs, for raw cotton, yarn, and cloth could bear ie costs of transport. A reduction in transport costs obviously led to a direct aving on freights, and increased speed and reliability allowed savings in stocks nd trade credit. More significantly, it allowed specialization in a wider range of oods, and permitted production to move to low-cost sites, particularly in the ase of mining and fuel-intensive industries such as iron. The results were often iore significant than changes in industrial technology and organization, which iight well become possible as a result of improved transport.

Clearly, the dating of significant improvements in the transport system has onsiderable implications for the chronology of economic growth. The most bvious and striking innovations were the construction of canals in the later ighteenth century and steam-powered railways in the second quarter of the ineteenth century. But did they have the greatest economic impact? There was more gradual improvement of water transport from the late seventeenth entury: the construction of breakwaters, quays, and enclosed docks protected hipping from storms and allowed more rapid loading; straightening and deepen- ng rivers and the construction of locks allowed ships and barges to reach a wider rea. Changes in ship design reduced the size of crews, and allowed ships to perate in less favourable winds which, combined with the improvement of iarbour facilities, reduced the amount of idle time and increased productivity. iimilarly, road transport could be improved by the construction of bridges which emoved expensive detours, and by better maintenance which reduced dis- uption in times of bad weather. Improved carrier and coach services involved onsiderable investment in inns, stables, teams of horses, and fleets of vehicles. ndividual improvements were relatively insignificant; could their combined veight reduce transport costs before the construction of canals and steam- owered railways?

Transaction costs also involved merchants and traders, who linked producers ind consumers within Britain and abroad, and created a constant market with mproved flows of information. Marketing and transport costs were, indeed, nterrelated. First, changes in marketing allowed goods to be supplied directly from producer to consumer. When grain was carried to the market for sale, there vere often expensive transshipments and detours: the farmer loaded his cart and carried grain to the market-place; and the merchant who bought the grain irranged transport to his granary for distribution to millers or for export. By purchasing from farmers on the basis of a sample after the harvest, merchants could transport grain direct from the farm to the customer. The same point applied to the sale of cloth by small producers riding to the piece hall, and merchants selling to drapers at annual fairs: there would be considerable savings in transport costs and inventories by relying on commercial travellers or sending out circulars. Secondly, intermediaries created an active market for transport services which allowed them to be more efficiently utilized. A merchant who wished to export a valuable consignment of textiles and metal goods from London to North America was eager to secure the lowest freight at a convenient time so that goods were not kept in store; and the owner of an expensive ship wished to reduce the time spent in port waiting for a cargo to be assembled. The emergence of specialist brokers and exchanges reduced imperfections in the market, allowing freight rates to be established and the needs of merchants and shipowners to be balanced.

The development of specialist brokers and exchanges from the coffee houses clustered around the Royal Exchange in the City of London was an important part of the gradual reduction in market imperfections not only for shipping but also for stocks issued by the government, improvement commissioners, and trusts. Investors would not purchase long-term stocks unless a permanent market existed where they could be sold and converted into cash: an active market increased 'liquidity' and made it possible to utilize previously idle balances. The general improvement in market information, and the emergence of specialist brokers and exchanges, led to a reduction in the cost, both in time and money, of discovering the cheapest goods and services from the most efficient suppliers. 'Imperfections' in competition were reduced, and manufacturers were able to keep their assets more fully employed, which contributed to improvements in productivity.

Brokers and exchanges were complemented by developments in retailing which created a constant market drawing goods from a wide range of suppliers. In the late seventeenth century, a narrow range of goods was carried to the weekly village market or annual fair, or touted around the countryside by hawkers and pedlars. Their turnover was modest, and they spent considerable time travelling rather than selling goods; they could not hold large stocks and did not provide a constant market, so that customers had a limited knowledge of goods and prices. Many items were still purchased from small craftsmen retailers in the village or market town, ranging from cobblers and blacksmiths who made shoes and agricultural tools for the local market, to skilled silversmiths or clockmakers in Norwich or Exeter who supplied the gentry and middling class. The emergence of permanent shops, drawing their goods from a wider area and range of suppliers, provided a constant market with a better flow of information about prices and qualities, and permitted a greater degree of specialization.

Regional specialization rested upon an ability to raise capital and credit: a region could not concentrate on the production of, say, cotton goods unless it had sufficient financial resources to cover purchases of raw cotton, to hold materials in the course of production, and to provide credit to purchasers. The emergence of a more reliable transport system and a constant, active market meant that credit was used more efficiently, by reducing the level of stocks in transit or held to insure against disruptions to supplies. However, a greater commitment to the market entailed a considerable increase in the amount of credit, and a change in its character. In local or regional trade, it was possible to assess credit-worthiness from personal knowledge and information gleaned from a network of kin and co-religionists. In long-distance trade, specialist intermediaries were needed, and it was necessary to draw on sources of credit outside the region. Different specialisms created different needs for finance. In East Anglia, for example, there was a surplus of money after the grain harvest, which could be held within the region, or made available to the cotton manufacturers of Lancashire with their need for trade credit. Regional specialization created the need for a banking system to channel short-term credit from areas of surplus to deficit, and to maintain liquidity. But an integrated market for credit had costs as well as benefits, for the banking system might be liable to failures which disrupted credit and spread depression between regions.

The level of specialization and the benefits of comparative advantage were determined by the timing and scale of the reduction in transaction costs produced by changes in transport, marketing, and the provision of trade credit. Change was piecemeal and gradual, depending on the relationship between production costs and transaction costs, and affecting different commodities at different times. The timing of the fall in transaction costs clearly has major consequences for the chronology of economic growth. Were there major gains before the construction of canals and railways, as a result of improved waterways, harbours, shipping, and roads? When did permanent retail shops spread from large towns and affluent consumers to reach the bulk of the population?

Public Policy and Integration

A national economy is also a political space, and the emergence of an integrated and specialized economy could be aided or hindered by public policy. Adam Smith attacked the existence of protective duties, subsidies, and regulations by which the government tried to shape international trade. The visible hand of public policy, he argued, should be withdrawn so that the invisible hand of the market could allow each country to devote its resources to their most efficient uses. Where England differed from the rest of Europe was in the lack of significant *internal* tariff barriers, which made it the largest and most prosperous free trade area. Much of Europe in the eighteenth century was divided into small city-states or principalities, and even nation-states had internal trade barriers such as the *octroi* levied on goods entering towns in France. In England, customs duties were paid at the point of entry, and goods within the country paid a

uniform excise duty regardless of where they were sold. The only tax whic
resembled the *octroi* was the duty levied by the Corporation of London on coa
entering the Thames, which was used to finance public works in the City. Ther
was, however, still one internal border in 1700, between the kingdoms o
Scotland and England.

The crowns of Scotland and England were united in 1603, but the Scottisl
parliament retained autonomy until 1707, when the Scots gained free entry t
English and colonial markets without the payment of customs duties. The Unio
of 1707, Defoe assured the Scots, would soon make them prosperous: they woul
have markets for their linen and cattle in England, money and capital would flow
into Scotland, its balance of payments deficit would disappear, and funds woul
be available to exploit the natural resources of the country. Of course, apologist
such as Defoe did not mention any disadvantages, preferring to stress that th
Scottish economy was rescued from imminent collapse by the blessings o
Union. They argued, with some justice, that the Scottish economy was i
disarray at the turn of the seventeenth and eighteenth centuries. There had bee
serious harvest failures in the 1690s; an ill-conceived scheme to establish a colony
in Central America had collapsed; trade with Europe was declining as a result o
wars and tariff barriers; and there was a deficit on the balance of payments.
Nevertheless, the vulnerability of the Scottish economy around 1700 should no
be exaggerated. The famine of the 1690s was serious, but the agrarian economy
was already changing in the later seventeenth century with the erosion of clans
the growth of single tenancies, and the emergence of commercial farming. Trade
patterns were altering, with a growth of exports of linen, coal, cattle, and salt tc
England. In the towns, guild regulations and the trading privileges of roya
burghs were dissolving in the later seventeenth century. Indeed, Union with
England could be interpreted less as a desperate attempt to fend off economic
collapse than as a means of capitalizing on changes which were in progress.

The critics of Union saw dangers rather than opportunities in creating a free
market between a larger, more prosperous country and a smaller, poore
neighbour. A flow of goods across the border might, they feared, abort the
development of Scottish industry, and merchants in London and Bristol would
not welcome competitors from Glasgow. Integration could mean a loss of
economic independence, so that the Scottish economy was reduced to the
provision of basic food, raw materials, and labour for a more developed and
dynamic English economy. Union did not simply give membership of the
colonial system and the protection of the navy; it transferred the power of
taxation from Edinburgh to Westminster, with the danger that Scotland would
pay for expensive wars which benefited English interests. And aristocratic
landowners who were incorporated into the British political élite could concentrate on raising money rents, rejecting the old tradition of the clan, and with-

drawing income to spend in their London town houses. 'This country now and for some years past', complained James Erskine in 1733, 'has lookt on it self as deserted, not only by its courtiers, but by the principall part of its nobility and gentry.'[2]

The immediate experience of Union gave some support to the sceptics, for there was no sudden spurt of growth. But neither was there a collapse of Scottish industries and trade as a result of English competition and excessive taxes. Although the power of legislating for Scotland had moved to Westminster, existing statutes were not affected and new legislation was shaped by the distinctive Scottish legal code. It could be argued that Scotland was able to derive benefit from Union, without losing all of the advantages of independence. Scotland retained its own banking system, which was able to mobilize funds for economic development; at the same time, it was able to rely upon the Bank of England to maintain stability. The Scottish poor law was more limited and cheaper than in England; its education system produced a higher level of literacy; and the land law gave greater powers to landowners to reshape tenure. It could even be argued that absentee landlords encouraged economic development: the appetite of landowners such as the duke of Atholl for money rents to sustain a lavish life-style stimulated the commercialization of Scottish agriculture. Whether this amounted to 'improvement' or expropriation is another matter; what is clear is that the immediate impact of Union was modest, neither rescuing the Scottish economy from imminent collapse nor reducing it to dependency.

In the longer term, incorporation into the imperial system of protection encouraged the development of two sectors of the economy: the linen industry was stimulated from about 1740 by export subsidies and protection; and Glasgow emerged as a major entrepôt in the middle of the eighteenth century, specializing in the import of North American tobacco for re-export to France. These developments would not have been possible outside the system of 'mercantilism', but Union alone was not enough to guarantee prosperity. The crucial point in the case of the linen industry was the agrarian and social structure. In Ireland, the linen industry was associated with fragmentation of holdings which prepared the way for famine and immiseration. In Scotland, agriculture was under the control of landowners who consolidated tenancies and moved population off the land. Consequently, linen production in Scotland was not linked with subsistence agriculture but was located in towns and villages with a permanent industrial work-force, providing the basis for future economic development. Neither was incorporation into the system of protection crucial to the continued development of Scottish commerce. Scottish merchants were in the forefront of exploiting new areas of trade outside the colonial system, which were linked to the retention of a degree of independence, with distinct systems of banking, insurance, and finance based in Glasgow and Edinburgh. The development of Scotland after 1707 was not simply the result of incorporation into a wider British and imperial economy; it was equally a result of internal factors such as the banking system, the ability of landowners to impose change on the countryside a high level of literacy created by universal primary education, and universitie and medical schools which were in the forefront of European thought.

Although Britain was a free trade area from 1707, the visible hand of public policy could nevertheless shape the development of an integrated nationa economy and restrain the mobility of resources. Econometric historians' in terpretations of the British economy in the eighteenth and early nineteenth centuries take it for granted that prices and wages were determined by demand and supply, with liberty to buy and sell in a free market. But these assumption were part of an ideological battle which was fought out during the period. The classical economists and 'Manchester school' argued that regulation was un natural and that the free play of the market was natural and beneficial, rejecting the view of medieval and early modern governments and commentators that regulation was necessary to the functioning of society, and competition a disruptive force which had to be controlled. The crown granted charters to lords of the manor or municipalities to operate markets with a local monopoly of trade, for which they could charge tolls. These charters were valuable assets and it was worth fighting to preserve them against merchants who circumvented the regulations, with the result that new forms of distribution might be limited. The success of the chartered markets in preserving their rights depended not only on their tenacity, but also on the wider context of government policy: chartered markets could be seen either as an essential part of a system of regulation or as a barrier to efficient distribution. In Tudor England, farmers were required to carry goods to the market-place and 'pitch' them for inspection, in order to ensure that exchange relationships were transparent. The margin between food supply and consumption was narrow, and it was feared that supplies of grain would be bought direct from farmers by 'forestallers' or cornered by 'engrossers' aiming to manipulate prices for private gain. Food supplies were crucial for the maintenance of social stability and the avoidance of dearth, and policy rested upon regulation of the market and control of prices. Public policy started to change in the later seventeenth century, towards encouraging free trade in grain in order to secure an increase in production and a rapid movement of foodstuffs into areas of deficit. The change was contentious, and consumers could still appeal to the earlier codes of regulations into the early nineteenth century. But in general, the British marketing system diverged from the pattern in France, where Paris placed greater pressure on the available food supply and the authorities relied upon forced levies of grain in times of dearth.

The production of manufactures in medieval and early modern towns was similarly regulated by guilds, which were granted monopoly rights and privileges by municipal by-laws or royal charter. By the eighteenth century, their importance was considerably reduced. Guilds had never existed in many expanding industrial towns in the north and Midlands; where guilds did exist, they were usually undermined by urban growth and survived mainly in towns which were stagnating for other reasons (see Chapter 6). There was, indeed, a striking contrast between Britain and other European countries, where guilds survived longer. Artisans who worked for the court were usually granted exemption from guild control, but this was simply another form of regulation; and in some areas of Paris, *ouvriers libres* could work outside the guilds. These exemptions are confirmation that guild regulations remained powerful in European cities during the eighteenth century, and corporate assumptions persisted into the nineteenth century. When the guilds were swept away in France in 1791, trades were still defined by *patentes*, a licence which was a means of raising revenue: they created a group identity and provided the basis for social and political mobilization.[3]

Although guild regulation of production and entry of apprentices into the 'mystery' of their craft had largely disappeared by the early eighteenth century, there was another possible constraint upon a free market economy: public control over the movement of labour in the statute of artificers of 1563 and the Elizabethan poor law of 1598–1601. Social stability, it was feared, was threatened by unemployed men wandering the country in search of work, and the statute of artificers aimed to limit mobility by requiring that workers in a wide range of occupations should be hired for at least a year, and permitting the authorities to compel labourers to work on the land. It also established a national system of apprenticeship regulated by legal indentures as an alternative to guild control, and gave power to justices to make an annual assessment of wages, taking account of the price level and the state of the economy. The regulation of the labour market was completed by the poor law, which required parishes to provide work for the able-bodied poor and to relieve the 'impotent'. It was, like the statute of artificers, concerned to control 'rogues, vagabonds and sturdy beggars' who could be seized, whipped, and returned to their place of work. It could, however, potentially create more general restrictions on mobility, for parishes would obviously be concerned at the cost of relieving migrants. How far did these laws restrain a free labour market?

The apprenticeship clauses of the statute of artificers were abandoned in practice in most trades long before their repeal in 1814. Indeed, apprenticeship was abolished in the rural woollen industry as early as 1694 on the grounds that it was 'very inconvenient and a great prejudice to the clothing trade'. It was unusual in rural outwork industries, where children picked up a trade by helping adults, and in mining, where children undertook ancillary tasks such as opening ventilation doors rather than learning specific skills from a master. Apprenticeship survived as a means by which parishes placed orphans and pauper children with employers, who supplied board, lodging, and a small wage in return for a premium. Although some fortunate parish apprentices might learn a trade, in many cases they were a source of cheap domestic labour or a means of recruiting workers for cotton-mills in isolated country districts. Apprenticeship continued in some professional and commercial occupations, and well-to-do families paid sizeable premiums for their sons to learn the business of a merchant, lawyer, doctor, or civil engineer. In established crafts such as silversmiths or tailors, apprenticeship was the first stage on a career progression from apprentice to waged journeyman and master of a small workshop. But in many skilled manual trades such as masons, shipwrights, or cabinet-makers, and in new trades such as boiler-makers, the nature of apprenticeship changed. Boys served 'time' with an adult under the protection of trade societies rather than the statute of artificers. Organizations such as the Friendly Society of Shipwrights, which was formed in 1794, confined membership to men who had served a full seven-year apprenticeship in an attempt to limit the labour supply, maintain wages, and preserve the 'property' of skill. The employers, of course, had an incentive to take on more apprentices in order to reduce skilled wages, or to subdivide jobs and employ cheaper, semi-skilled labour. The struggle over apprenticeship was central to trade disputes in the 1800s and 1810s, above all in London where the United Artisans Committee made a concerted effort to reactivate the statute of artificers. At a time of hostility to 'combinations', workers could appeal to the old code of regulations, which legitimized their demands and made employers into the destroyers of the traditional rights of 'freeborn Englishmen'. The immediate result was the repeal of the apprenticeship clauses in 1814. The challenge was not simply to the legal code, for many small employers rejected the notion that the workshop was an artisan 'republic' in which apprentices, journeymen, and masters had a common identity in the protection of trade, prices, and wages through limitation of competition. In the early nineteenth century, the norms of artisan 'republicanism' were countered by an ideology of social mobility which stressed the opportunities for rising within a competitive, free market.

Although assessments of wages virtually disappeared in the course of the eighteenth century, they could still provide a bargaining weapon or legitimization for workers seeking higher wages. Workers appealed to parliament to regulate wages and conditions, and did secure measures such as the Spitalfields Act of 1773 which regulated wages in the London silk industry. In particular, the inflation of the Napoleonic wars led workers to petition justices for increased assessments. Tailors in London had some success in 1800, and they were

ollowed by carpenters in 1803 and shoemakers in 1804. More alarming to the
government and employers was the cotton-weavers' petition of 1812 for an
assessment of wages, which they justified on the grounds that the unlimited
movement of unapprenticed workers into industry led to 'a surplus of manufacturing poor, and an unnecessary competition, ruinous to the commercial capital
and industry of the nation'.[4] Their case rested upon the joint interest of workers
and capital in regulating mobility, limiting output, and controlling prices. It was a
view which was rejected by the Prime Minister, Lord Liverpool, who remarked
in 1813:

The wisest principle of proceeding, with respect to commerce and manufactures, was ...
laissez faire—This principle was particularly necessary to be kept in view with respect to
the machinery and mechanical inventions of this country, which more than any other
case, had raised this kingdom to its high rank among the commercial nations of the
world.[5]

Consequently, the wage-fixing clauses of the statute of artificers were repealed in
1813, removing a bargaining weapon from the hands of the workers. The law was
the forum in which market relationships were defined: workers appealed to
sixteenth- and seventeenth-century codes as a way of defending their property in
skill in the same way as the law defended real property; an increasing number of
employers and politicians sought to reshape the law in accord with the norms of
free markets and competition. Clearly, economic historians who assume that the
market was a neutral device for the allocation of labour and capital according to
their relative prices in order to optimize efficiency are ignoring the fact that
market relations were determined within a contested institutional and legal
framework.

The repeal of the apprenticeship and wage assessment clauses of the statute of
artificers did not completely remove the hand of the government from the
labour market, for there still remained the Elizabethan poor law. The impact of
the poor law on labour mobility could run in two directions. On the one hand,
the poor law was criticized for frustrating the movement of labour: subsidies paid
to the wages of underemployed labourers in the south of England, it was argued,
reduced their incentive to leave areas of low productivity; and parishes concerned by the cost of providing poor relief restricted settlement. On the other
hand, it could be argued that the right to poor relief made people more willing to
leave their family of origin and take their chance in expanding towns or industrial
districts where they could not turn to kin for support. The poor law, on this view,
eased the release of labour from the land and led to gains in productivity.
The second interpretation is probably more realistic, for modifications to the law
of 'settlements' in the later seventeenth century encouraged economically

desirable migration; and subsidies in aid of wages at the end of the eighteenth and early nineteenth centuries did not so much create pools of underemployed labour as mitigate the worst features of rapid population growth.

The role of the state in creating an integrated economy and removing the barriers to the pursuit of comparative advantage entailed a slow, piecemeal process of standardizing the legal and institutional system. The distinctive land law of Scotland remained after the Union, and there were marked variations within England and Wales. The persistence of copyhold and customary tenure, and the divergence between areas of long and short leases, meant that landowners, farmers, and industrialists took their decisions within different contexts, which affected the speed of their response to price movements and the distribution of benefits. In an area where customary tenure or life-leases survived, for example, landowners were less able to increase rents or the size of farms than in areas where land was let on short leases. Variations in land law and tenure shaped market relations, and landlords and tenants fought out their differences over the validity of customary holdings or the terms of enclosure in the courts and parliament. The complexities of the tenurial system also increased the transaction costs of selling land. Registers of land giving clear title existed only in Middlesex and two ridings of Yorkshire; elsewhere, it was necessary to make expensive enquiries. The need for a free market in land was a rallying cry of radicals and liberals in the nineteenth century, who wished to simplify conveyancing and abolish strict settlements and primogeniture which, they complained, created large landed estates and high rents which stifled enterprise and competition.

There were marked differences in weights and measures, which created uncertainties and costs. A 'stone' was 8 lb. in Hertford but 16 lb. in Leeds; and in Sussex alone areas were measured in statutory acres of 160 rods, forest acres of 180 rods, and short acres of 100 or 120 rods. These variations in weights and measures were, complained reformers, so many internal barriers to free trade by creating uncertainty and imperfect competition, and the long process of standardization provides one measure of the emergence of an integrated national market. The government was concerned to create uniformity for purposes of tax collection, and the onset of rapid inflation in the 1790s encouraged stricter inspection of weights and measures, but it was not until 1824 that common standards were created for the whole country. There were also deficiencies in the supply of currency which could cause strains and impose costs. The relocation of the iron industry to the northern rim of the south Wales coalfield was a sign of an increasingly integrated economy with production at low-cost sites, but at the same time it created difficulties in supplying small coin to pay workers, who were forced to accept tokens or 'truck', which limited their market freedom. The

mergence of a competitive, integrated market could itself impose strains as
egions readjusted.

The market was shaped by political and social conflict, and by a complex
nterplay between the development of an integrated economy and the legal
ystem. The market was a power relationship, and the legal system was the main
rena in which the contest was played out. Workers and consumers could appeal
o the statute of artificers or to the law against engrossers and forestallers in order
o strengthen their position; the government could retreat and deny the rele-
ance of public regulation. The market was far from being the abstraction of
eo-classical economic theory, which can be taken for granted in writing the
conomic history of Britain between 1700 and 1850: the redefinition of market
elations was a crucial theme which shaped how the economy responded.

Regional Identity, National Identity

'The first effect of early industrialisation', Asa Briggs remarked, 'was to differ-
entiate English communities rather than to standardize them',[6] and much the
same could be said of developments in agriculture. Far from producing homo-
geneity, the emergence of an increasingly integrated economy led to a greater
degree of specialization between regions which were tied together by more
efficient transport, marketing, and financial systems. Price signals were transmitted from one area to another more quickly and clearly, but they were not simply
received and acted upon uniformly: they were filtered and interpreted by
differences in economic structure, land tenure, and social relations. Arable,
pastoral, and forest areas had different ecologies, which led to differences in
social structure, modified by variations in systems of tenure, access to common
rights, or patterns of employment, and the response to changes in prices or wages
was by no means uniform. Marriage patterns varied between districts with
'service in husbandry' or day labourers; the existence of customary tenure and
long leases or 'rack-rents' determined the distribution of benefits between
farmers and landlords; the geography of common fields shaped the pace and
nature of enclosure. Similarly, craft regions differed in their response to economic forces, depending on the existence of artisan production or 'putting out',
the relationship between producers and merchants, and the ease with which new
technology could be inserted into the social organization of production.

The regional geography of Britain underwent considerable change as the
economy became more integrated and specialized between 1700 and 1850. Some
districts deindustrialized, others emerged as centres of domestic industry which
subsequently transformed into factory production, and others grew on the basis
of coal with no prior experience of domestic production. The new industrial

regions were different from the older craft regions, and also different from each other. Textile towns tended to employ more women than heavy industrial districts, which affected the age of marriage and birth rates. Towns relying on the export of heavy engineering goods or shipbuilding were prone to extreme cyclical swings of boom and slump, whereas areas concentrating on domestic markets such as tailoring had sharp seasonal fluctuations. Differences might equally arise within a single sector such as coal-mining or cotton-spinning. Coal was won from the seam by hand, but in Scottish pits the workers were 'collier serfs', in the north-east of England they were employed on annual 'miners bonds', and in Staffordshire they were engaged by subcontractors or 'big butties'. The Lancashire and Scottish cotton industry used the same spinning-machines but the one employed men by a system of subcontracting, and the other, women under the control of male supervisors. Indeed, distinctive regional identities were in many ways reinforced rather than weakened in the process of industrialization. The development of transport systems in the eighteenth and early nineteenth centuries increased the *internal* integration of regions, such as in south Lancashire where the improvement to river navigation and the construction of canals permitted the exchange of raw materials and coal within the area, with most shipments over relatively short distances or to the port at Liverpool. The canal-based transport system, John Langton has suggested, consisted of 'dense patches', and the 'canal-based economies became more specialised, more differentiated from each other and more internally unified'.[7]

Of course, specialization of highly distinctive regional economies was only feasible because of the development of national and international markets, and London was the hub around which the regions revolved, with its specialist stock-brokers, money-dealers, discount houses, merchant bankers, and commodity brokers. But this did not mean that the regions were subordinated to London. Banks were locally owned, with close connections to industrialists and traders within the regions; the role of the City of London was to *co-ordinate* the balancing of credit between deficit areas such as Lancashire and surplus areas such as East Anglia, rather than to control the banks and dictate their lending policy. Most industrial concerns were still family businesses which raised their capital from ploughed-back profits or local contacts through a network of kin and co-religionists. Each industrial region had its 'capital' with its bankers, merchants, and brokers who supplied credit, raw materials, and specialist goods to the different towns within the district: there was not a simple divide between the industrial Midlands and north, and the provision of banking and commercial services in London. In Lancashire, for example, cotton brokers and warehousemen at Manchester provided raw cotton to the spinners, supplied yarn to weavers, and provided facilities for the sale of yarn and cloth to foreign markets;

and in Liverpool, merchants and shipowners imported raw cotton from the United States, provided credit for sales in foreign markets, and owned ships to handle imports and exports. There was, as Langton has remarked, a 'full regional containment of the whole social spectrum that was produced by manufacturing and commerce'.[8]

These regional economies developed their own distinctive institutions and interests. Manchester, most famously, was associated with the demand for free trade by the Anti-Corn Law League, and the members of the Chamber of Commerce presented the views of the cotton trade to the government when its interests were threatened. Birmingham in the early nineteenth century was associated with the anti-bullionist doctrines of Thomas Attwood and the campaigns of the Birmingham Political Union for reform of the franchise. Employers' associations and trade unions were usually locally based, often within a particular town, and attempts to move to a national coverage were short lived. The attempt to create a General Chamber of Manufacturers in 1785, for example, soon foundered on regional disagreements over the impact of the commercial treaty with France in 1786; it proved impossible to create a successful national organization from the regional body formed in the Midlands by Samuel Garbett and Matthew Boulton. The main concern of many employers was their own town and its immediate surroundings. Its efficiency depended on investment in adequate supplies of water or gas; social order and stability depended on the construction of schools, churches, and hospitals by local voluntary associations. The same point applies to organizations formed by workers. Unions with national ambitions such as the Miners' Association of Great Britain did not succeed for long before retreating to a single coalfield. The friendly societies which provided sick pay, for example, were strongest in the north-west of England, which was reflected in names such as the Manchester Unity of Oddfellows. Such bodies were less likely to arise in industrial regions with a highly cyclical pattern of employment, where workers were less able to maintain regular contributions and there was a greater need to provide unemployment pay. Instead, workers in districts such as Tyneside were more likely to insure against unemployment through trade unions.

The 'nationalization' of employers' and workers' organizations was a slow process which was only completed when the First World War stimulated the creation of national bodies to negotiate with the government over taxation or import controls, and the depressed industries in the 1920s and 1930s became increasingly involved with national schemes of 'rationalization'. Industrialists retreated from involvement in urban government and voluntary associations as problems of local taxation shifted the balance towards central government finance and control; national policy on the social services and taxation became more important than local initiatives. The decline of family firms and the rise of large corporations meant that power shifted from the regions to the centre. By 1850, these trends had made little progress, and the regional dimension of economic and associational life remained crucial. But regionalism was not an alternative to a national economy and politics. Specialization between regions was only possible because the economy had become more integrated as a result of improved systems of distribution, marketing, and banking which permitted regions to specialize and to exploit the benefits of comparative advantage.

Regional identity was counterpoised by a wider consciousness of British identity. The growth of a provincial press shaped regional identities, but also reported national news and the latest prices on the London markets. And Britain was at war more often than at peace up to 1815. Taxes and loans to finance the war, and the demands of the army and navy for materials and men, affected industries and trade in different ways; they might not agree on their response, but they were part of a national debate. Could it be argued that war also fostered a sense of being British, encouraging a patriotic national identity which contained radical attacks on society?

Certainly, the peerage was becoming more national, with the admission of more landowners from the Celtic fringe and a shift from provincial centres of sociability to the London Season. There was a concern to map and count the nation with the formation of the Ordnance Survey in 1791 and the first census in 1801. But, suggests Linda Colley, 'when we examine how far the British government promoted *popular* national consciousness, what is striking is not how much it attempted, but how much it left deliberately undone'.[9] The state resisted any involvement in education until it gave a modest grant to voluntary bodies in 1833, and there was no attempt to foster a cult of national heroes. Resources were effectively mobilized for war without sponsoring state nationalism, and there was, in any case, a tension between nationalism and the role of the Anglican Church. Membership of the established Church was necessary for full participation in civic and national life, and the government could not both support an exclusive Church of England and foster an inclusive nationalism. An appeal to patriotism was a double-edged sword: it might secure popular support, but it could also be seized upon by those who were excluded as a means of self-assertion. The Patriotic Fund of 1802, for example, was seen as a device by City traders to challenge the landed aristocracy; and an appeal to serve in the militia or armed forces could be used as a justification of the extension of the franchise. Patriotic and nationalist language was not simply a tool of control, for it could just as readily provide a weapon for the opponents of the government. An appeal to nationalism and patriotism was much safer in the late nineteenth century when it was a way of *sustaining* the rule of the landed ruling class after the franchise had been extended and education introduced.

The creation of a national economy and a sense of national identity were controversial, contested processes with a political dimension. They involved, amongst other processes, a reshaping of the land law, a dismantling of market regulations, an abandonment of apprenticeship and wage assessments, the formulation of laws on credit. These changes were subjects of dispute and contention, which raise the whole issue of the nature of the British state. And how important were the reductions in transport costs and market imperfections? The driving force of economic growth, in the opinion of some historians, was an increase in demand, whether from exports or at home. But could it be that changes on the side of *supply* were more important, by reducing costs, which allowed British manufacturers to capture foreign markets and expand domestic sales within the existing demand schedule?

NOTES

1. A. Smith, *An Inquiry into the Nature and Causes of the Wealth of Nations* (repr. 1937), 424 (book iv, ch. ii).
2. Quoted in T. M. Devine, 'The Union of 1707 and Scottish Development', *Scottish Economic and Social History*, 5 (1985), 29.
3. See G. J. Crossick, 'Shopkeepers and the State in Britain, 1870–1914', in G. J. Crossick and H.-G. Haupt (eds.), *Shopkeepers and Master Artisans in Nineteenth-Century Europe* (1984), 260–1.
4. Quoted in I. Prothero, *Artisans and Politics in Early Nineteenth-Century London: John Gast and his Times* (Folkestone, 1979), 56.
5. Ibid. 56.
6. A. Briggs, *Victorian Cities* (1964), 32.
7. J. Langton, 'The Industrial Revolution and the Regional Geography of England', *Transactions of the Institute of British Geographers*, NS 9 (1984), 162.
8. Ibid. 163.
9. L. Colley, 'Whose Nation? Class and National Consciousness in Britain, 1750–1830', *Past and Present*, 113 (1986), 105.

FURTHER READING

Black, I., 'Geography, Political Economy, and the Circulation of Finance Capital in Early Industrial England', *Journal of Historical Geography*, 15 (1989).

Braggs, A., *Victorian Cities* (1964).

Colley, L., *Britons: Forging the Nation, 1707–1837* (New Haven, Conn., 1992).

—— 'Whose Nation? Class and National Consciousness in Britain, 1750–1830', *Past and Present*, 113 (1986).

Crossick, G. J., 'Shopkeepers and the State in Britain, 1870–1914', in G. J. Crossick and H.-G. Haupt (eds.), *Shopkeepers and Master Artisans in Nineteenth-Century Europe* (1984).

Devine, T. M., 'The Union of 1707 and Scottish Development', *Scottish Economic and Social History*, 5 (1985).

—— *The Tobacco Lords: A Study of the Tobacco Merchants of Glasgow and their Trading Activities c.1740–90* (Edinburgh, 1975).

Granger, C. W. J., and Elliott, C. M., 'A Fresh Look at Wheat Prices and Markets in the Eighteenth Century', *Economic History Review*, 2nd ser. 20 (1967).

Gregory, D., 'The Fiction of Distance? Information Circulation and the Mails in Early Nineteenth-Century England', *Journal of Historical Geography*, 13 (1987).

—— 'The Production of Regions in England's Industrial Revolution', *Journal of Historical Geography*, 14 (1988).

Hoppit, J., 'Reforming Britain's Weights and Measures, 1660–1824', *English Historical Review*, 108 (1993).

Kussmaul, A., *Servants in Husbandry in Early Modern England* (Cambridge, 1981).

—— *A General View of the Rural Economy of England, 1538–1840* (Cambridge, 1990).

Langton, J., 'The Industrial Revolution and the Regional Geography of England', *Transactions of the Institute of British Geographers*, NS 9 (1984).

—— 'The Production of Regions in England's Industrial Revolution: A Response', *Journal of Historical Geography*, 14 (1988).

Minchinton, W. E. (ed.), *Wage Regulation in Pre-industrial England* (Newton Abbot, 1972).

Prothero, I., *Artisans and Politics in Early Nineteenth-Century London: John Gast and his Times* (Folkestone, 1979).

Smout, T. C., *Scottish Trade on the Eve of the Union, 1660–1707* (Edinburgh, 1963).

—— 'The Anglo-Scottish Union of 1707: The Economic Background', *Economic History Review*, 2nd ser. 16 (1963–4).

Sturmer, M., 'An Economy of Delight: Court Artisans of the Eighteenth Century', *Business History Review*, 53 (1979).

CHAPTER II

Transport

The growth potential of the economy could be released by a reduction in transaction rather than production costs, which allowed agricultural and industrial goods to be exchanged more cheaply, so reducing market imperfections and encouraging areas to specialize in those goods to which they were best suited. Such a process of specialization could have a greater impact on total costs than changes in production technology, which could well emerge from an ability to concentrate on one commodity and to devise new methods of production and organization. Above all, transport costs could impose severe limits on the creation of an integrated, competitive market, preventing low-cost producers from supplying a wide area and allowing high-cost producers to survive. The crucial point for understanding the chronology of British economic growth is: when did transport costs fall sufficiently to make a difference to specialization and competition? Can a case be made for a reduction in transport costs *before* the construction of canals in the late eighteenth and early nineteenth centuries, by placing an emphasis on investment in rivers, harbours, and roads, technical improvements in ships and wagons, or changes in business practices which allowed a better utilization of the transport system? Or was a significant drop in transport costs delayed until the age of canals and railways, which allowed an escape from constraints on growth at the end of the eighteenth century or even in the first half of the nineteenth century?

Transport developments in the late seventeenth and early eighteenth centuries were, at first sight, less spectacular and heroic than the construction of flights of locks, the engineering feats of impressive tunnels, embankments, and viaducts, and the incursion of railway lines into densely settled towns and cities. But there is a danger that the achievements of men such as Isambard Kingdom Brunel have obscured the less spectacular developments of his precursors, who devised better road surfaces, altered the design of coaches, modified the rigging or hull design of sailing ships, or improved access to harbours and rivers. These changes were gradual and easily overlooked in comparison with the striking construction of canals and railways in short, intense bursts. Much more important than the visibility and intensity of construction is the extent to which investment offered 'social savings', by freeing producers from constraints and allowing them to specialize. After all, the investment of large sums in impressive feats of engineering may well offer modest social savings compared with the investment of small sums in removing a crucial bottle-neck. Could it be argued that canals and railways produced more modest social savings?

The creation of an efficient transport system rested not only on the solution of technical and engineering difficulties, but also on overcoming organizational and financial problems. The demand for fixed capital in manufacturing industry was slight, and small-scale units owned by families and partnerships were typical. Although ships and coaches could be owned in relatively small units by family firms or partnerships, investment in the transport infrastructure was a different matter. Improvement of water navigation entailed large-scale investment in making rivers navigable, digging canals, and constructing harbours and docks, which required considerable sums of capital and usually necessitated some form of corporate enterprise. Similarly, the construction of improved roads involved replacing piecemeal maintenance by individual parishes with an organization based upon larger areas which could raise sizeable sums of money. Railways were simply a further stage in the process of innovation in business organization and capital markets, which was necessary to build and operate concerns requiring large-scale 'lumpy' investment beyond the reach of an individual or partnership. The belief that industrialization was somehow 'cheap' and unproblematic because of the low capital needs of manufacturing industry ignores investment in the urban and transport infrastructure, where innovation in organization and finance were more striking.

Investment in transport facilities involved raising considerable amounts of money in advance of any revenue from tolls levied on the users of a new bridge, harbour, waterway, canal, or railway. Unlike most industrial concerns, it was less feasible to grow by ploughing back profits, and there was less chance of relying on credit. The scale of investment was usually beyond the means of individual businessmen, and it was only owners of exceptionally large coal-mines with a constant, high-volume traffic who were likely to build their own facilities. A single putter out in the nail trade, or the owner of a forge, could not improve the navigation of the river Severn which formed the main artery connecting forges, furnaces, slitting mills, and warehouses, and the port at Bristol. Neither was it possible for an individual parish or farmer to provide a better road to the market town. What was needed was an institutional structure which transcended the individual small concern, and which could attract funds from businessmen with an immediate interest in better transport, from public bodies or landowners with a general interest in encouraging economic development, or from passive investors looking for a secure outlet for their savings. The form of organization varied, depending in part on whether there was a prospect of private profit to investors or whether most of the benefit was taken by a high social rate of return to the economy of a town or region. Investment in transport facilities often produced a low return from tolls, and the initiative could be taken by landowners or town councils who were willing to make a large investment in a new harbour or dock because they would obtain some of the wider social return through the increased value of their estates. But in most cases the solution was to create trusts or improvement commissions which brought together a range of interests and tapped various sources of money. These were non-profit-making bodies on the boundary between the private and public spheres, obtaining revenue from a combination of tolls and subventions from local taxation, and raising capital through the sale of interest-bearing bonds which attracted local investors in search of a secure income. The next stage was the creation of joint-stock companies seeking private profit which raised capital both from subscribers to ordinary shares, who incurred risk in return for participating in any profits of the concern, and from holders of loan stock, who received a fixed return. There was, of course, always the possibility that the rate of return could be low for both the individual investor and the economy as a whole, for canal or railway companies were often floated during speculative manias, when rational expectations were suspended, and a railway company which took over traffic from an existing canal or navigable waterway might produce modest social savings.

Moving Goods by Water

Water transport, Adam Smith was confident, was more efficient than road. The economic geography of Britain was shaped by access to water:

As by means of water-carriage a more extensive market is opened to every sort of industry than what land-carriage alone can afford, so it is upon the sea-coast, and along the banks of navigable rivers, that industry of every kind naturally begins to subdivide and improve itself, and it is frequently not till a long time after that those improvements extend themselves to the inland parts of the country. A broad-wheeled waggon, attended by two men, and drawn by eight horses, in about six weeks time carries and brings back between London and Edinburgh near four ton weight of goods. In about the same time a ship navigated by six or eight men, and sailing between the ports of London and Leith, frequently carries and brings back two hundred ton weight of goods. Six or eight men, therefore, by the help of water-carriage, can carry and bring back in the same time the same quantity of goods between London and Edinburgh, as fifty broad-wheeled waggons, attended by a hundred men, and drawn by four hundred horses.[1]

Water transport by coastal ship and river was considerably cheaper than carriage on land. A pack-horse could carry perhaps 2 or 3 cwt.; a wagon pulled by a team of horses was limited by statute in 1662 to a load of 30 cwt., which was raised to 6 tons by 1763. On a river, a single horse could pull a load of 30 tons, and on a canal as much as 50 tons. At the beginning of the eighteenth century, the average cost of transport on inland waterways was perhaps 2.5*d*. per ton-mile, and even less in coastal shipping; by comparison, road transport cost about 1*s*. per ton-mile.

Water was ideal for low-value, bulky goods which could not bear a high transport cost, and particularly raw materials such as coal with a 'punctiform' pattern of distribution from one point to another in large quantities along a single route. By contrast, high-value goods could bear a greater transport cost, and speed was often of greater importance. Many industries had an 'areal' pattern of production and delivery, which required a transport system based on a large number of routes carrying relatively modest volumes to collect goods from a wide area for delivery to small shops and fairs across the country. Road transport was more suitable for domestic manufacturers of hosiery or cloth in workshops scattered across the country, and investment in an expensive, high-volume transport infrastructure would be inappropriate. Commodities such as grain shared features of both patterns of transport, for wheat and barley were collected from a large number of farms, carried to granaries and malt-houses, and then shipped in bulk to millers and brewers in the towns. Roads were an important ancillary to water, and Smith was guilty of exaggerating the superiority of water by comparing their costs in the long-distance movement of bulk commodities where they were obviously non-competitive. Water transport was equally inappropriate for the movement of high-value commodities produced over a wide area for dispersed consumers.

Water transport entailed considerable fixed costs. The initial stage was to make rivers navigable by deepening, straightening, and constructing locks, which started on a large scale from 1694 when powers were obtained to make the Mersey navigable as far as Warrington. The river systems of the Mersey and Trent in particular were improved in the first quarter of the eighteenth century, usually on the initiative of urban merchants rather than landowners, who feared a loss of income from mills and damage to their land by the construction of embankments. By the 1750s, improvement of existing waterways was supplemented by the construction of canals, which made economic sense where a heavy tonnage was concentrated on a single route. 'A good canal', remarked the duke of Bridgewater, 'should have coal at the heels of it.'[2] The first canals were built in the area drained by the Mersey and its tributaries, which had already been improved to carry large quantities of low-value goods such as crude salt from Cheshire and coal from the Lancashire coalfield. In 1754, the corporation of

Liverpool, with the support of leading merchants who subscribed to shares, embarked on the Sankey navigation in order to increase competition in the supply of coal. The Sankey navigation was completed in 1757, and was soon imitated by the third duke of Bridgewater, who constructed a canal between 1759 and 1761 to transport coal from his estate at Worsley to Manchester and Liverpool.

Until the construction of canals, industries which relied on bulky raw materials and coal such as salt, glass, pottery, and the metal trades were clustered on natural waterways such as the Tyne, Mersey, Severn, and Thames. Canals initially had little impact on their location, for they improved communications within existing self-contained river systems. Interconnection between river systems started in 1772 when the Staffordshire and Worcester canal joined the Mersey to the Severn, but the process was not complete until about 1810. Even then, the real importance of canals remained their short-distance trade, which made it easier to bring bulky raw materials to inland sites, and to provide food and fuel to large urban settlements, which were previously confined to the coasts or rivers. This is by no means to minimize their significance, for carrying coal 10 miles by land doubled its cost, and was equivalent to about 200 miles of water transport. The construction of navigable waterways and canals allowed inland coalfields to compete with coastal coalfields, permitting pits with low production costs to challenge higher-cost producers who had previously had a competitive advantage because of their location near water. Canals lowered the supply price of coal in regions with economic potential, reversing 'the relationship between water transport and the economy: bulk water transport could be brought to favourable manufacturing sites instead of a forced movement in the opposite direction'.[3] The growth of the iron industry on the northern rim of the south Wales coalfield, for example, was hampered by the costs of transporting iron on pack-horse across the hills to the coast, until the Glamorganshire canal was completed between Merthyr Tydfil and Cardiff in 1794, and the Monmouthshire canal to Newport in 1799. The canals allowed south Wales, the cheapest producer of iron in the early nineteenth century, to expand at the expense of Shropshire, where the transport links of the Severn compensated for higher costs of production. Similarly, the construction of a canal network in south-west Lancashire led to the growth of existing trades, and to the emergence of a new industrial district around St Helens based on fuel-intensive trades of copper, glass, and iron which competed with the glass industry of Newcastle and the copper industry of Swansea. Canals permitted industrial growth to shift to inland coalfields where the pit-head price of coal was lowest, especially in the east and west Midlands and Lancashire, giving fuel-intensive industries access to low-cost producers and reducing costs of transport. The supply of coal became more

elastic, industrial regions became more competitive, and costs were reduced.
Canals, as a contemporary remarked in 1785, 'converted the internal parts of our
island into coasts'.[4]

Canals were built by joint-stock companies, with the single exception of the
aristocratic Bridgewater canal. Since the Bubble Act of 1720, it was necessary to
obtain a private Act of Parliament to establish a joint-stock company, which also
gave powers for the compulsory purchase of land along the route. The initial
capital for the construction of the canal was raised from subscribers to shares, and
it would be natural to assume that industrialists, who had the incentive of
obtaining cheap supplies of raw materials, would be major investors. The
Glamorganshire canal, it is true, was largely under the control of the Crawshays
of the Cyfarthfa ironworks, but many industrialists preferred not to put money
into the infrastructure. Josiah Wedgwood, for example, built his factory at
Etruria on the banks of the Trent and Mersey canal, but did not subscribe to a
single share. This was often a sensible strategy, for a diverse investing public was
willing to subscribe to shares, so freeing industrialists to invest in their own
enterprises. Most shareholders were drawn from the locality, with the exception
of speculation in canals in southern England between 1807 and 1811, which was a
short-lived phenomenon rather than a permanent widening of the capital
market. The purchasers of canal shares were largely concerned with their private
profit from dividends; more important for the economy as a whole were the
'social savings' from the reduction in transport costs, or savings as a result of the
need to hold smaller stocks of goods. Unfortunately, no estimate has been made
of the social savings of the canal system as a whole. Certainly, some canals
produced neither a profit to their owners nor a social saving to society, particularly in rural areas where canals were not economically justified in the absence of
a steady movement of bulky raw materials. Construction of the Herefordshire
and Gloucestershire canal, for example, cost £105,000 for the first stage, which
was completed in 1798, and a further £141,500 for the second stage between 1839
and 1845. By contrast, the Glamorganshire canal produced a high social saving on
its investment of £103,600 by reducing the costs of shipping iron to the coast.[5]
(See Fig. 11.1.)

Overall, the social savings were probably high, until the latter speculative
manias in southern England. Improvement of rivers and construction of canals
were often associated with investment in harbour facilities, which increased the
productivity of shipping by reducing the constraints of weather and tides, and
allowing vessels to turn round more quickly. Investment in docks was 'lumpy',
and social savings might well exceed the private return to investors. Construction could therefore draw upon public finance, such as at Liverpool where the
corporation took over responsibility for the docks as trustees in 1762, which

.llowed money to be borrowed on the security of the rates and its sizeable landed state. The corporation could hope to capture at least some of the social return on the docks, in addition to the direct income from dock dues, through an increase in the rateable value of the town and the value of its landed estate. The corporation was dominated by traders who stood to benefit from the provision of additional shipping facilities, but the trustees became more directly responsive to the needs of trade in 1825, when dock ratepayers were allowed to elect representatives. A burst of dock building followed under the direction of Jesse Hartley, who was responsible for building 140 acres of docks, about 10 miles of quays, and massive warehouses, at a cost of something over £5 million by the time of his death in 1860.[6] Public bodies were not always so responsive, such as at Bristol where the corporation was reluctant to invest and the port fell behind its competitors. Alternatively, the initiative could be taken by landowners such as the second marquess of Bute at Cardiff or the marquess of Londonderry at Seaham Harbour in Co. Durham, who stood to benefit from an increase in the value of their urban estate or in the development of coal-mines as a result of improved shipping facilities. Landowners were able to raise much larger sums than industrialists and merchants by mortgaging their estates.

In other cases, and above all in London, companies were formed to make the investment, sometimes against the opposition of public bodies. The port of London was facing crisis by 1800, for trade was limited in 1558 to the 'legal quays' which amounted to a mere 1,419 feet, supplemented by the so-called 'Sufferance Quays' below Tower Bridge. Goods were discharged from ships into lighters in mid-stream, and transferred to the quays, which led to confusion and congestion. High-value colonial goods had to thread their way through a mass of colliers and coasting vessels, with frequent delays and endemic pilfering; there was also a shortage of warehousing for seasonal imports such as sugar which needed to be stockpiled for the rest of the year. The problem was particularly marked during the revolutionary and Napoleonic wars, when ships sailed in convoy and arrived in harbour in a bunch. In 1795 the West Indian merchants started a campaign to construct an enclosed dock where ships could unload within the protection of walls and police, and the goods could be safely stored in warehouses owned by the dock company. The merchants were opposed by the City Corporation, which feared a loss of income from the legal quays, but the government offered generous compensation and the West India Dock Act was passed in 1799; the first stage of the new dock opened in 1802. Similar powers were granted for the construction of an East India Dock in 1803. In both cases, parliament accepted that the huge investments could only make a profit if the docks were granted a monopoly which required all ships from the West and East Indies to unload there. This strategy was rejected in 1823 when the St Katherine's Dock Co.

(a) 1770

(b) 1780

(c) 1790

(d) 1800

(e) 1810

——— Canals

·············· Rivers/river navigations

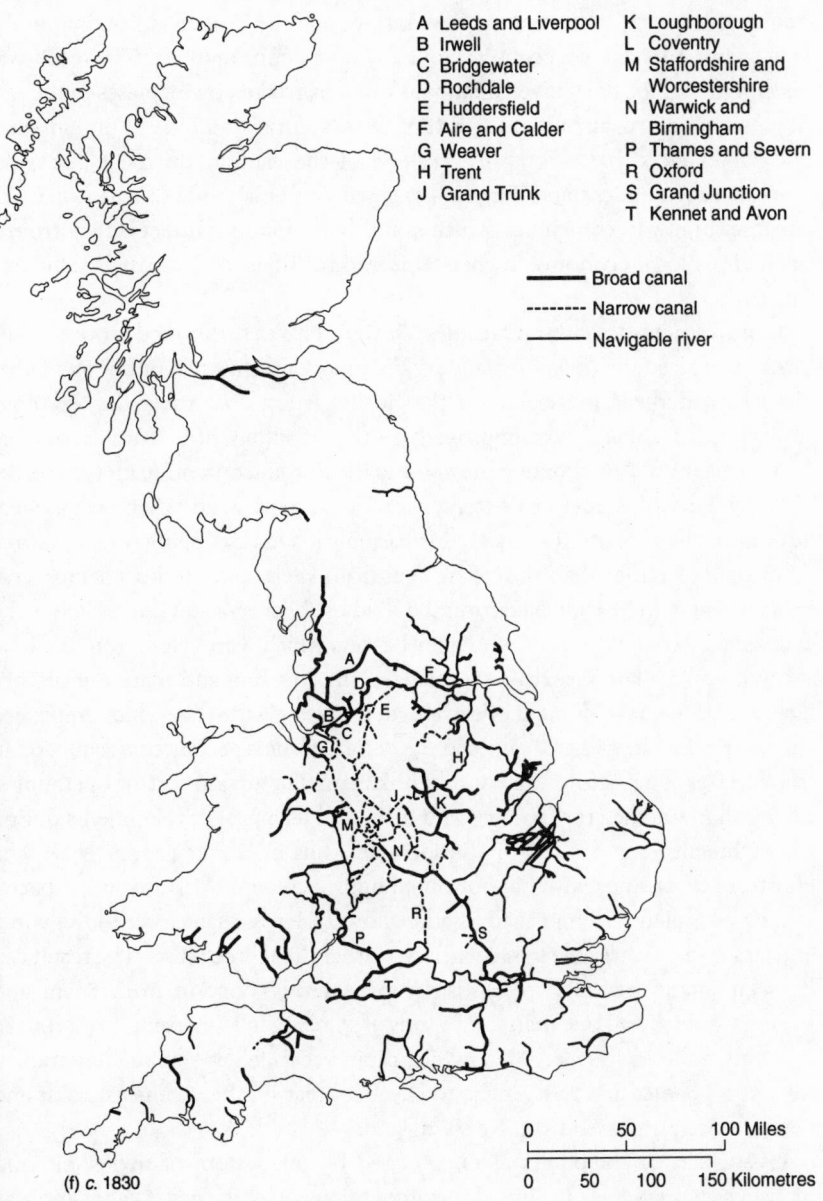

A Leeds and Liverpool
B Irwell
C Bridgewater
D Rochdale
E Huddersfield
F Aire and Calder
G Weaver
H Trent
J Grand Trunk

K Loughborough
L Coventry
M Staffordshire and
  Worcestershire
N Warwick and
  Birmingham
P Thames and Severn
R Oxford
S Grand Junction
T Kennet and Avon

—————— Broad canal

-------- Narrow canal

———— Navigable river

(f) c. 1830

0   50   100 Miles

0   50   100   150 Kilometres

Fɪɢ. ɪɪ.ɪ. (*a–e*) The growth of the English canal system, decadal increments, 1770–
1810, and (*f*) inland navigation, *c*.1830

Source: G. Turnbull, 'Canals, Coal and Regional Growth during the Industrial
Revolution', *Economic History Review*, 2nd ser. 40 (1987), 547; M. J. Freeman,
'Transport', in J. Langton and R. J. Morris (eds.), *Atlas of Industrialising Britain, 1780–
1914* (1986), 85.

obtained powers to construct a new dock beside the Tower of London, in the expectation of making a profit without any restrictions on trade. The result was disappointing, for dock investment was often overtaken by increases in the size of vessels before an adequate return was secured, and the London dock companies faced bankruptcy by the end of the century. In most cases, the construction of docks and harbours was left to public bodies, landowners, or canal and railway companies which could hope for an indirect return from a prosperous local economy, higher rents and royalties, or increased traffic (see Fig. 11.2).

Improvements to harbour facilities allowed ships to turn round more quickly which increased the utilization and productivity of the merchant marine. Other changes had the same effect. In the north-eastern coal trade, for example utilization of colliers was improved by the adoption of a 'turn' system at Newcastle in 1766 and London in 1799, and the introduction of steam tugs on the Tyne in 1818 allowed ships to enter and leave port even when winds were adverse. Colliers on the Tyne were increasingly loaded by tipping wagons of coal from staithes rather than shovelling coal from keels; and on the Thames, coal was less likely to be shovelled from the hold by 'heavers', and more likely to be unloaded by coal 'whippers' who filled baskets which were raised from the hold using a pulley. The growth of specialized ship brokers and marine insurance agents, and the development of exchanges for hiring and selling ships, improved the market for shipping. Changes in the design of ships permitted a reduction in freight rates long before the coming of steam. The major cost of operating a sailing ship was the crew's wages and food, and technical developments during the eighteenth century led to considerable gains in labour productivity. The construction of ships with flat-bottomed hulls increased their carrying capacity and saved on labour; improved rigging allowed ships to sail closer to the wind; and larger ships were able to sail with two rather than three masts. The result can be seen in the manning of British ships entering London from Spain and Portugal, which had one man for 7.9 tons of shipping in 1686, rising to 9.1 tons in 1726 and 12.6 tons in 1766.[7] Meanwhile, capital costs fell as shipbuilding moved from the Thames and East Anglia to cheaper areas on the north-east coast and vessels were purchased from New England.

Investment in shipping was encouraged by the system of ownership and management, which contributed to competition and efficiency. Ownership was usually divided into shares of eighths, sixteenths, thirty-seconds, and sixty-fourths, which in most cases were held by ten to twenty individuals. The pattern of ownership was diffuse, for most investors spread their shares among a number of vessels in order to minimize risks, and there was usually little sense of common identity among the owners of a ship, in contrast to most concerns of the

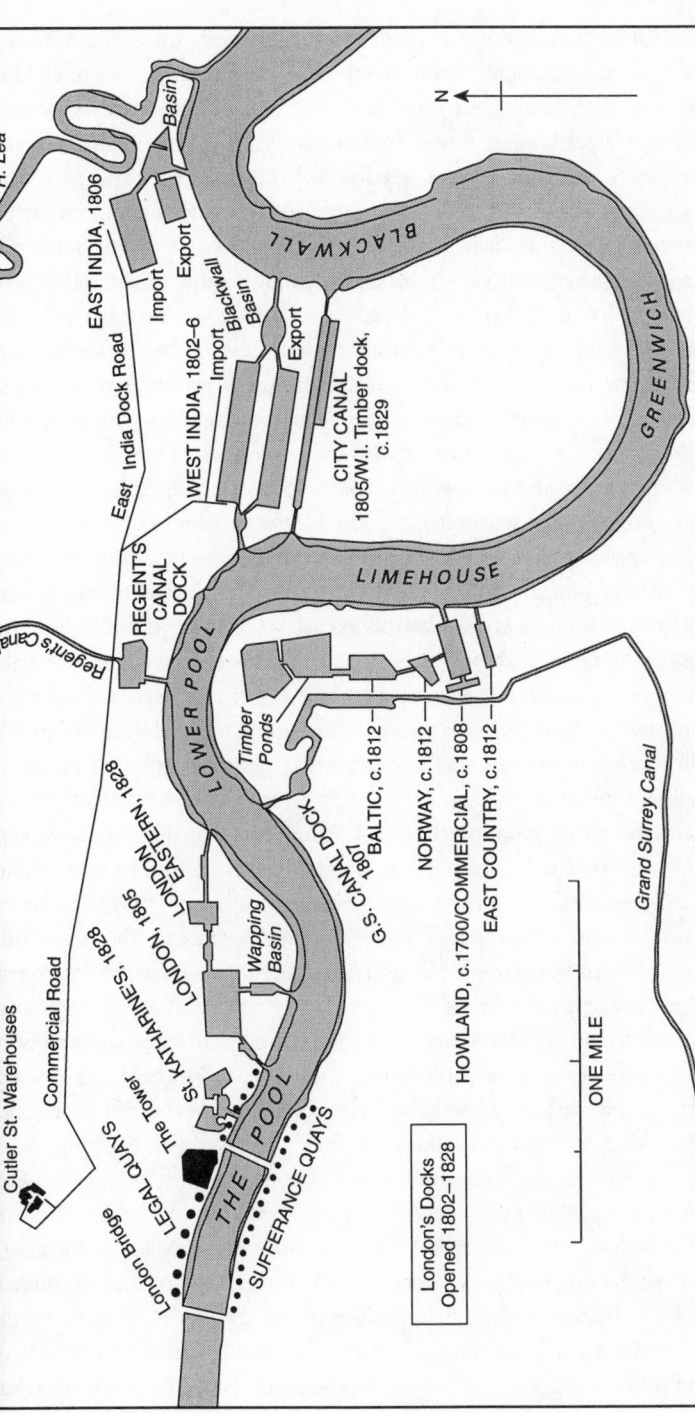

FIG. 11.2. London dock construction, 1802–1828

Source: G. Jackson, 'The Ports', in D. H. Aldcroft and M. J. Freeman (eds.), *Transport in the Industrial Revolution* (Manchester, 1983), 204.

eighteenth century which had fewer partners and a greater commitment to th
business and its management. There were few specialist shipowners. On
exception was the coal trade of the north-east, where the shipowners took ove
the merchanting of coal. A second was the slave-trade, where merchants move
into shipowning. A large capital was needed to buy goods for export to wes
Africa, and to cover the heavy costs of a long voyage with slaves across th
Atlantic. Merchants in the slave-trade had an incentive to own ships, fo
transport was a large proportion of total costs, and the value of the slaves wa
heavily dependent upon the speed and care with which the master made th
voyage. Although merchants in other trades often held shares in ships, the
viewed them as separate ventures and preferred to buy cargo space as and whe
required, at the lowest possible price. Other shareholders came from peopl
involved with shipping, such as masters who took an interest in their vessel an
tradesmen who supplied food and stores. Shipping was, however, attractive tc
people who wanted a passive investment which offered a higher return than
mortgage, combined with the possibility of a share in the profits without the risk
and involvement of a partnership in industry or trade. The dangers of unlimitec
liability were low, for debts were unlikely to exceed the value of the ship; and the
Court of Admiralty allowed shares to be sold and transferred relatively easily
without reference to other owners, so that there was a reasonable level of
liquidity. Most shareholders played no part in the management of the ship, which
was left to the master or, more usually, to a managing owner or ship's husband
who held some shares as well as receiving a commission. The pattern of
ownership started to change in the late eighteenth century, when the level of
concentration increased as a result of the development of marine insurance,
which reduced the need to spread risks, and high wartime freights, which
encouraged new entrants. By the end of the eighteenth century, about half the
ships were owned by one or two people, and full-time professional ownership led
to greater efficiency and economies of scale.

The result was a considerable reduction in freight rates and transaction costs
before the coming of steam, as a result of investment in harbours and docks, an
improvement to ship design, and the development of commercial practices.
Total factor productivity (that is, total output in comparison with total input) of
the shipping industry in the trade between London and North America, for
example, rose by 0.7 per cent per annum between 1676 and 1776, and by 3.5 per
cent per annum between 1814 and 1860.[8] The result of these gains in productivity
was to hold down the price of coal shipped from Newcastle to London, of timber
imports from the Baltic, or colonial produce from the West Indies, North
America, and Asia. Clearly, productivity increases in eighteenth- and early
nineteenth-century Britain were not simply the result of the factory and powered

machinery; they were also the outcome of the efforts of dock engineers, harbour commissioners, and the ship brokers and insurers in the coffee houses of London.

Roads and Carriers

Roads were an essential complement to water transport. Barley for the great London brewers, for example, was gathered by cart from the farms of Hertfordshire and processed in malt kilns in small towns such as Ware and Hitchin, before it was shipped to London in barges along the rivers Lea and Stort, which were improved on the initiative of brewers and maltsters. Similarly, in East Anglia and Kent, grain was carried in carts to ports such as Ipswich and Faversham for shipment to London, or from the farms of the Thames valley to Henley and Abingdon, where it was loaded into barges for carriage downstream. A fall in the cost of this complementary road transport allowed the 'reach' of ports to be extended to a wider hinterland. But roads did not simply 'feed' water-borne transport, for many parts of the country, such as the uplands of the Pennines, Wales, and Scotland, could not be reached by rivers or canals. These areas concentrated on pastoral farming, and cattle and sheep could walk long distances along drove routes, if necessary being fattened close to the final market. The transport of minerals and industrial goods posed greater problems, and metals, cloth, and raw wool were often carried on pack-horses. In 1766 it was claimed that 2,000 horses a week carried lead along the road from Nenthead to Penrith. Even in lowland areas road transport might be preferable to water, where high charges might be imposed to cover improvements. Smith also exaggerated the price differential by ignoring the costs of loading and unloading carts at both ends, which led to delays and damage. 'The lock Dues, upon the Rivers Aire and Calder, being very high', it was reported in the early 1740s, 'the Manufactures of the Western Parts, as also Wool, Corn &c from Lincolnshire, and other Places, can be conveyed by Land Carriage . . . when [the roads] are passable, at an easier Expense than they are now carried by Water.'[9]

Investment in roads might make more economic sense than improvements in rivers and the construction of canals. Much depended upon the nature of the goods which were being carried, and the organization of production. High-value commodities of low bulk could bear higher transport costs than low-value commodities of high bulk, so that road transport was feasible in industries such as cutlery where 'great Quantities of Goods are weekly sent away in carriages, and on Horseback, from Sheffield, to London and other places'.[10] Water transport could damage certain cargoes, as William Stout, a shopkeeper at the port of Lancaster, was well aware: coastal shipping was cheaper but he complained of 'damage by rats, who eat out the corks in liquor and oyl casks, to the loss [of] some whole casks of oyle and vinigar'.[11] Where production was spread over a wide area, road transport made sense, such as in the wool and cotton industries whose raw materials, yarn, and cloth had a relatively high value in relation to their bulk. Road transport continued to be important even when large cotton-spinning factories were built, for many hosiers or weavers who purchased yarn had a hand-to-mouth existence and their orders for small amounts could be met more readily and quickly by road carriage. The marketing of cloth or small metal goods depended upon 'travellers' who went around the country in search of orders from drapers and ironmongers, whose small, regular consignments were more easily supplied by a pack-horse or cart than by ship or barge. Investment in a navigable river or canal was only a paying proposition where production was concentrated at a point which generated a sufficiently large trade, and where transport was a high proportion of the total cost. In the eighteenth century, these preconditions were met above all by coal and other bulky raw materials such as salt and iron. However, much industrial production in the eighteenth century was in the countryside with an 'areal' distribution, and goods such as cloth, hosiery, and small metalwares produced both in towns and country had a high value in relation to their bulk. Road transport was, consequently, much more important then Smith suggested, and investment in roads and improvement in carriers' services could have a considerable impact on the economy and the level of transaction costs.

The maintenance of roads in England and Wales was the responsibility of parishes, which elected two unpaid Surveyors of Highways each year. These reluctant amateurs supervised 'statute labour' supplied by the parishioners: anyone with land worth £50 a year or who kept a draught of horses supplied two men, a cart, and horses or oxen for six days; everyone else supplied one man or attended in person; fines were levied on defaulters. It was a system which treated each parish as a self-contained unit, which caused few problems in small, homogeneous communities where it was in the self-interest of all residents to maintain the roads between their farms. Tensions appeared if some residents felt that they were providing labour from which they did not benefit: why should a smallholder spend his time repairing a road damaged by the heavy traffic of a coal-mine or iron forge; why should a parish straddling a through route maintain the road for the benefit of carriers and coach-owners? The parish system was also unresponsive to changes in the direction of trade, for it was concerned with the maintenance of existing roads and there was no mechanism to co-ordinate the construction of new roads.

Although the parish system survived until 1835, it was reformed by two complementary processes. One was to supervise the work of parishes and to

ncrease their financial resources. The Quarter Sessions were given power to
order parishes to make repairs; statute labour was gradually commuted into a
money payment; and justices were given powers from 1662 to raise a rate of up to
6d. in the pound. But this still left parishes to raise money within their own
resources, and it did not solve the problem of major routes such as the Great
North Road which passed through dozens of parishes with limited money and
interest. The second process was to hand responsibility for through routes to
turnpike trusts which had the right to impose tolls on users, so shifting the
financial burden from the parish and local users to through traffic. Although
parishes were still liable to supply labour or a cash payment, this accounted for
only 8.2 per cent of the total income of turnpike trusts in 1834, and tolls were set at
low levels for short-distance traffic with exemptions for wagons used in agriculture or for hauling building materials, coal, or lime.

The first turnpike appeared in 1663 on part of the Great North Road, but
growth really started from 1695. Parliament authorized the creation of 143 trusts
by 1750, rising to 519 by 1770, and 942 by the time the last trust was created in 1836.
Initially, many trusts controlled only a few miles: 42 per cent of trusts formed
before 1720 had 10 miles or less and only 8 per cent had 30 miles or more.
Long-distance turnpikes could not be expected to emerge at once, for most traffic
was relatively short distance, and finance and management were drawn from the
locality. The early turnpikes were created on the most heavily used roads around
London and the expanding provincial towns, and gradually expanded to cover
the main routes out of the capital. The road from London to Bath and Bristol, for
example, was 125.5 miles long, of which 112.5 miles had been turnpiked by 1730,
and the whole by 1750. The crucial change in the character of the network came
with the turnpike boom of 1751–72. New trusts were larger, with only 14 per cent
in the 1750s responsible for 10 miles or less, and 40 per cent for 30 miles or more.[12]
The location of new trusts also shifted: routes were turnpiked across the
Pennines, linking the West Riding and Lancashire with their expanding wool and
cotton industries; trusts spread in Derbyshire and the east Midlands to serve the
lead industry and the expanding rural industry of hosiery; and made strides in
Shropshire and Staffordshire for the iron, coal, and pottery trades. By 1770
turnpikes were no longer localized and limited to certain routes leading to
London, and a reasonably well co-ordinated and integrated network had
emerged with a much greater level of interconnection between the provinces
(see Fig. 11.3).

How successful were these trusts in producing additional income which
allowed the roads to be kept in a better state of repair? The trusts were not
without their critics, who argued that they were unaccountable bodies which
were often too small and fragmented, and more concerned with exploiting their

monopoly powers to charge high tolls than with improving the road. Inactiv
trustees and incompetent or corrupt salaried staff, the critics complained, squar
dered resources on management and legal costs rather than repairs, which wer
often wasteful and inappropriate. How justified are their criticisms? There i
some substance in the claim that the trusts became more unaccountable afte
1706–7 when trustees were less likely to be drawn from justices of the peace, an
more often selected from landowners. However, their ability to exploit mon
opoly powers was limited, for they were forbidden to make a personal profit
tolls were established by a schedule of charges in the original Act; and the trus
was created for a limited term, usually of twenty-one years, so that renewal coul
be challenged. It is difficult to see that trustees had anything to gain from
charging high tolls, from which they would not benefit. Perhaps a more seriou.
charge was the absence of overall control, for turnpikes formed a loose system
which only gradually took on a semblance of order. In the early nineteenth
century, reformers argued for consolidation, which had some success in 182(
when the Metropolis Road Act brought together fourteen trusts operating 11
miles of road in London, but they failed in their wider campaign in the 1830s to

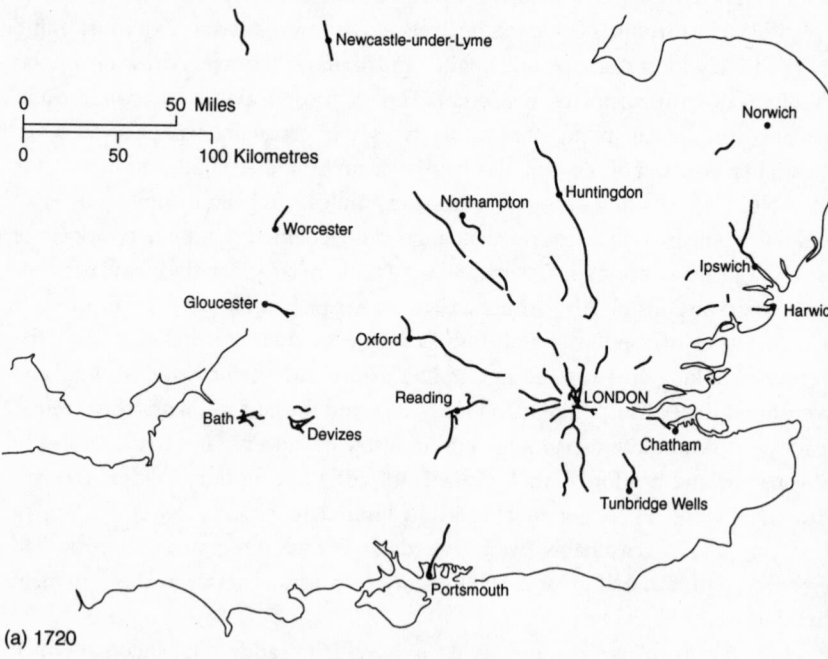

FIG. 11.3. Growth of the turnpike system, 1720–1770

Source: E. Pawson, *Transport and Economy: The Turnpike Roads of Eighteenth-Century Britain* (1977).

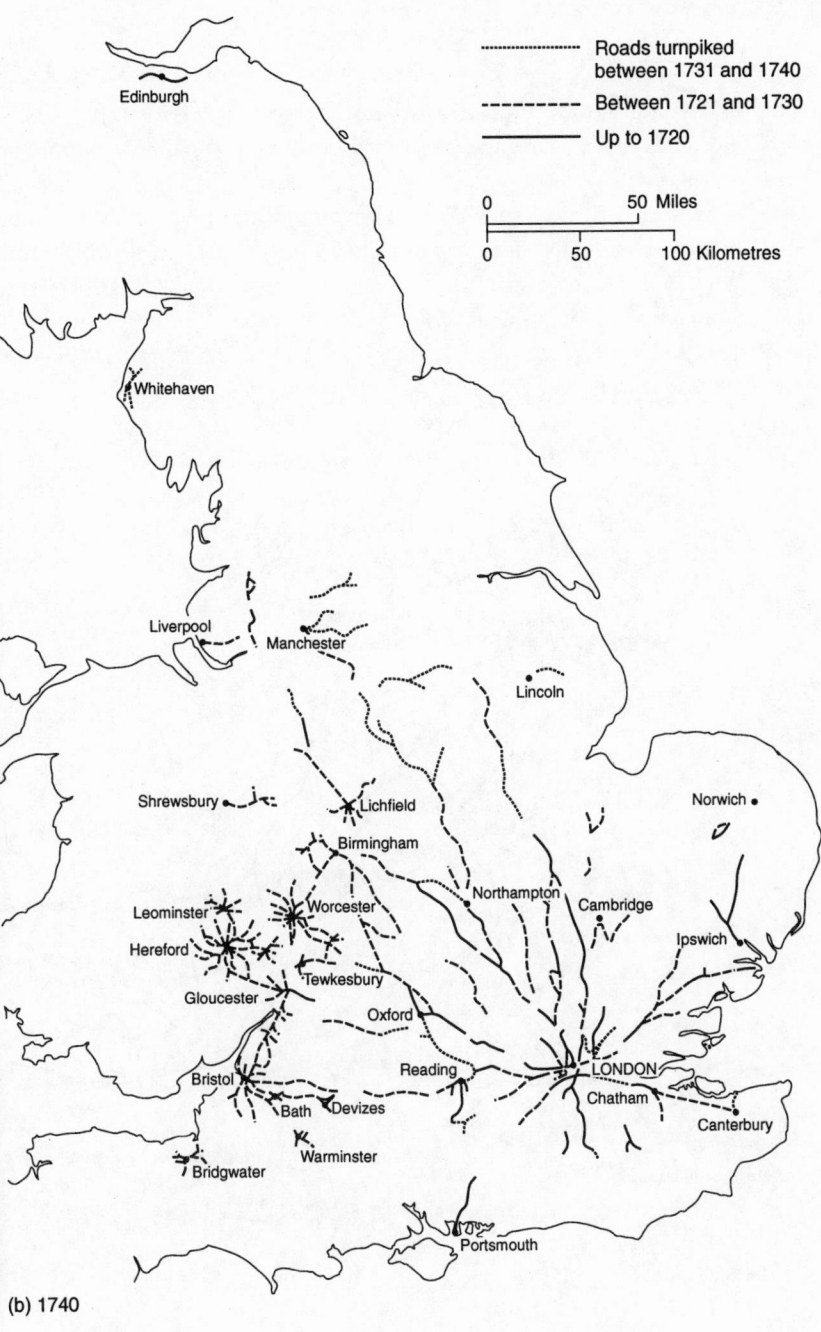

Roads turnpiked
between 1731 and 1740

Between 1721 and 1730

Up to 1720

0   50   Miles

0   50   100 Kilometres

Edinburgh

Whitehaven

Liverpool

Manchester

Lincoln

Shrewsbury

Lichfield

Birmingham

Norwich

Leominster

Worcester

Northampton

Cambridge

Hereford

Ipswich

Tewkesbury

Gloucester

Oxford

Reading

LONDON

Bristol

Chatham

Bath

Devizes

Canterbury

Warminster

Bridgwater

Portsmouth

(b) 1740

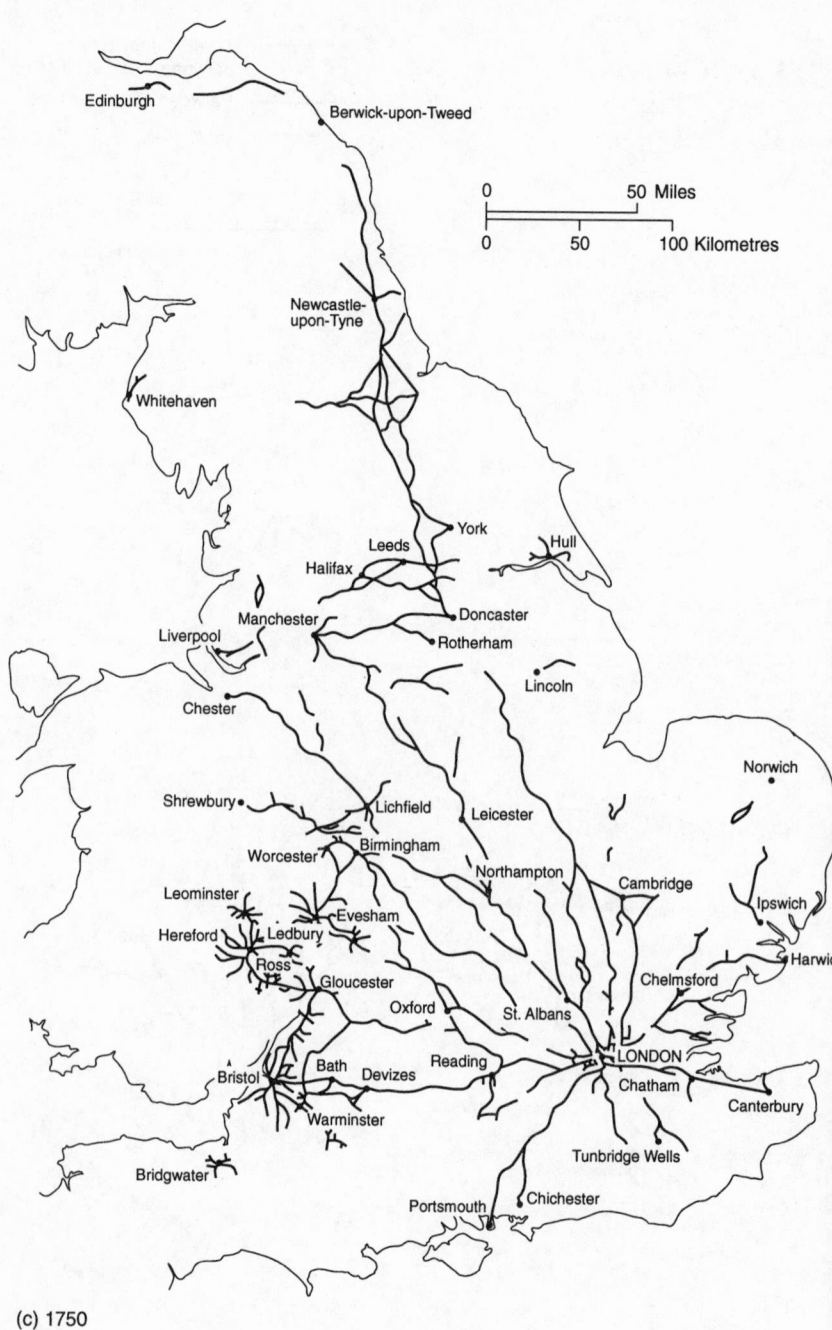

(c) 1750

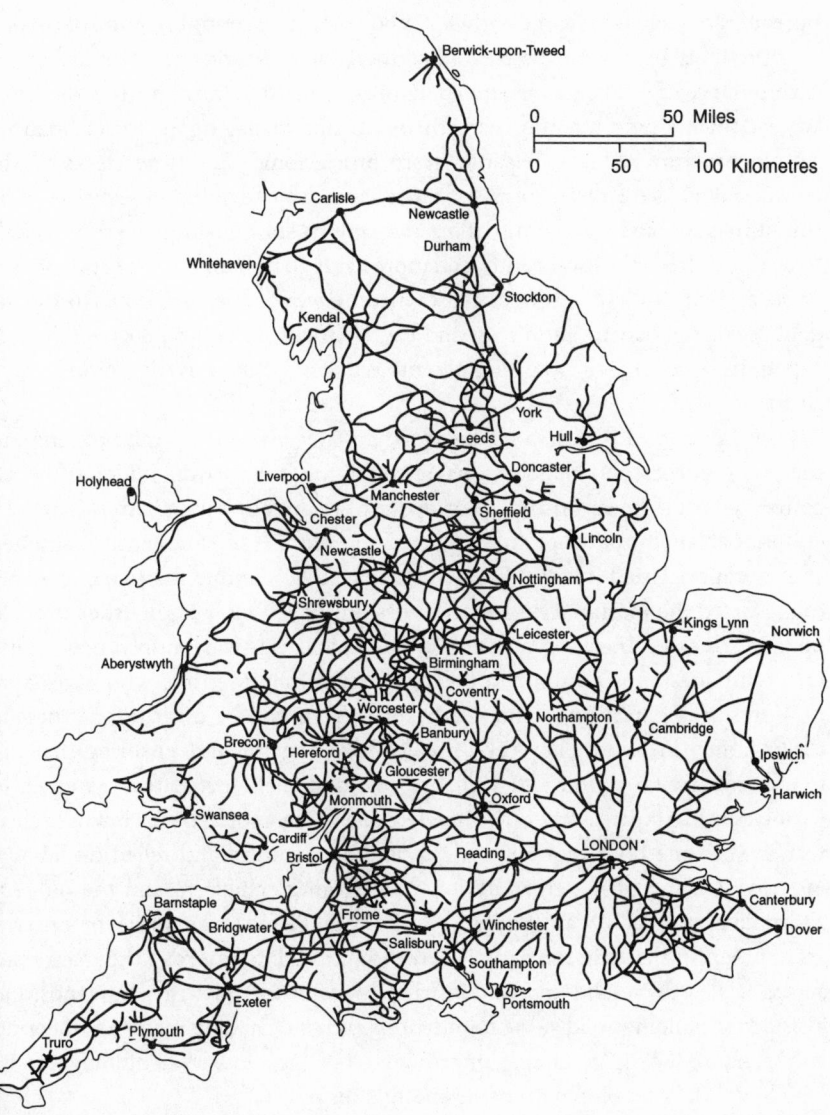

Berwick-upon-Tweed

0   50 Miles
0   50   100 Kilometres

Carlisle
Newcastle
Durham
Whitehaven
Stockton
Kendal
York
Leeds   Hull
Holyhead   Liverpool   Doncaster
Manchester
Chester   Sheffield
Newcastle   Lincoln
Shrewsbury   Nottingham
Aberystwyth   Leicester   Kings Lynn   Norwich
Birmingham
Coventry
Worcester   Northampton   Cambridge
Brecon   Banbury
Hereford   Ipswich
Gloucester   Harwich
Swansea   Monmouth   Oxford
Cardiff
Bristol   Reading   LONDON
Barnstaple   Canterbury
Bridgwater   Frome   Winchester   Dover
Salisbury
Exeter   Southampton
Truro   Plymouth   Portsmouth

(d) 1770

create a national system of consolidated trusts under a central board. The case was essentially political, part of a highly contentious campaign by centralizing bureaucrats such as Edwin Chadwick who wished to centralize control of local services; it is by no means clear that there were economies of scale in the maintenance of roads. Much depended, of course, upon how effective the trusts were in maintaining and improving the roads, and managing the trusts' finances. Administration gradually became more professional. Part-time clerks to the trustees who were often local solicitors gave way to full-time officials, who sometimes worked for a group of interlocking trusts; treasurers were less likely to be drawn from the local gentry and more likely to be bankers. The critics of the trusts argued that a high proportion of income went on legal costs, salaries, and debt servicing, leaving little to spend on the roads; in reality, 69.5 per cent of expenditure in 1834–8 was directly on repairs.[13] But was the money well spent?

John Loudon McAdam, a leading road engineer, was sceptical, pointing out that his predecessors included a baker, publican, and Lloyd's underwriter. Of course, it would be surprising if surveyors were initially much better than their counterparts in the parishes, for many had no expertise and frequently continued with traditional methods. But McAdam was a publicist rather than a pioneer, and exaggerated the inertia of his predecessors out of self-interest, in order to build up an extensive business advising trusts. McAdam was simply developing the techniques of professional surveyors such as John Metcalfe who was active in Yorkshire, Lancashire, and Derbyshire from the 1750s to 1790s, or the Collis family in Kent. They took greater care over repairs, ensuring that the foundations were sound and well drained, and then sorted the materials in various sizes to create a smooth, impenetrable convex surface which would shed water. Such methods required little capital expenditure and relied on labour-intensive sorting of materials by low-paid women, children, and the old. An alternative approach was adopted by Thomas Telford, the surveyor on two government projects in the early nineteenth century to improve the main road across Wales to Ireland and to construct roads in the Scottish Highlands. He insisted on building solid stone foundations and undertaking major engineering works on reducing gradients, improving drainage, and straightening roads, which was only feasible with government subsidy.

Although the techniques of road construction adopted by the trusts held down capital costs, they nevertheless needed to raise large sums of money by long-term borrowing secured by a mortgage on the tolls. Initially, loans were raised from a few individuals, who were often landowners attracted by a secure investment which would also assist in the development of their estate, rather than industrialists who preferred to invest in production. Josiah Wedgwood, for example, lent only £150 to the Burslem–Lawton–Newcastle under Lyme trust he helped to promote in 1764. From the middle of the eighteenth century, the trusts increasingly turned to modest loans from a wider social range, selling fixed-interest 'deed polls' by public auction or by advertisements in the local press, which attracted small urban savers from the ranks of gentlemen, clergymen, professionals, shopkeepers, and craftsmen and their widows and daughters who sought a decent, secure return from an asset which had the virtue of being visible and local. Investment in the turnpikes tapped local funds, which were distinct from the London capital market and interest rates, so that the crucial factor in the formation of turnpike trusts was the prosperity of the local economy which generated the need for road improvements and produced the toll income to pay for loans and repairs. This might well suggest that the social rate return on turnpikes was as high as that achieved by canals and railways, both of which were marked by speculative manias and investment in areas with insufficient traffic to secure a reasonable return. By contrast, turnpikes emerged from the needs of the local economy, and were less liable to speculative mania than canals and railways organized as public companies. Investment in better roads raised the productivity of horses, permitting the replacement of pack-horses by carts, and an increase in the size and speed of wagons and coaches. The greater efficiency and reliability of transport meant that firms could reduce their stocks of raw materials or goods for sale, increasing the turnover of their capital and saving on credit.

Certainly, the extent of road transport in the eighteenth century was far greater than was once assumed, for both passengers and freight. Stage-coaches provided an improved service which reached more destinations in a shorter time. In 1680, stage-coach services ran from London to 88 towns, increasing to 180 by 1705 and 216 by 1715.[14] The stage-coaches were usually run by owners of inns and stables, who co-operated in providing facilities and horses along the route in return for a share of the profits, and paid tolls for the use of turnpikes. At the end of the eighteenth century, they were challenged by mail coaches, which were first introduced between London and Bristol in 1784 on the suggestion of the theatre-owner John Palmer, as a joint initiative between three parties. The Post Office specified the type of coach, fixed the timetable, and provided an armed guard; the system was controlled by Palmer, who combined private enterprise and public service: he was appointed Surveyor and Comptroller of the Mails in 1786, receiving a salary and a commission based on the increase in the net revenue of the Post Office. The coaches were built, owned, and maintained by John Besant and John Vidler, who had extensive works in London, in return for a mileage rate from the Post Office and the contractors. The contractor charged passengers a high fare for a fast service, received a mileage rate from the Post Office, and was exempted from tolls. Mail coaches were expensive to operate, for each coach required six horses which were changed every 10 miles and had a working life of only three years, and investment in a large coaching inn was also necessary. The concerns were large, dominated by William Chaplin who operated 14 mail coaches a night in 1835, as well as 106 stage-coach services: he owned five inns in central London, employing 2,000 people and 1,800 horses. The mail coaches did not replace stage-coaches, which provided a slower, cheaper service on the mail routes, as well as covering a wider network. Indeed, by 1810 they started to compete directly with the mail coaches for their service was improving with better roads and coaches, and their times were not fixed by the needs of the mails. Mail coaches tried to compete by offering faster speeds, but the Post Office did not increase payments and their profitability started to fall.[15]

Better roads and coach services resulted in a considerable reduction in journey times, and helped to integrate markets. In 1750 a fast coach covered the 114 miles from London to Bristol in 40 hours; by 1811 the journey could be completed in 1 hours 45 minutes (see Fig. 11.4).[16] Mail coaches carried news more quickly from London to the provinces, for the stamp duty on newspapers gave them free conveyance: *The Times* was as cheap in Newcastle as in London. There were however, still constraints on communication, for letters continued to be charged by distance and rates were increased during the revolutionary and Napoleonic wars in order to produce revenue. Means were found to evade the high Post Office charges, by exploiting the right of members of parliament to free use of the mails or by sending letters in breach of the Post Office's monopoly by private carriers and stage-coaches. Finally, the Post Office introduced a uniform Penny Post in 1840 for the entire country, so that distance ceased to determine the cost of the transfer of information.

Fares for passengers remained more or less stable, in return for faster journeys. By contrast, freight charges fell in real terms during the eighteenth century, for better roads allowed fewer horses to haul more goods. Local freight services were provided by 'private' carriers, often farmers with horses and carts for working their land who supplemented their income by providing a service to other farmers or industrial producers. These private carriers could decide how much to charge and whether to take on a job, unlike 'common carriers' who provided a more regular, long-distance service, and were obliged to accept the custom of everyone wishing to use their services, at a reasonable charge which could be set by the justices of the peace. The common carriers ranged from small concerns with a single wagon to large ventures such as John Hick of Leeds, whose business in 1793 consisted of 102 horses, seven chaises, a coach, four carts, two farm wagons, harnesses, hay, straw, eight acres of oats, two farms of 127 and

2 acres, furniture and drink, and a lease on the Old Kings Arms. A dense, interconnected network of carriers' services emerged in the eighteenth century: there were services between London and most provincial towns, interconnected through inns where goods were collected and exchanged between carriers from different towns. The number of carriers' services from London listed in trade directories grew from 348 a week in 1690, to 565 in 1798, and 1,093 in 1838, but the pattern of growth in *capacity* was different. In the eighteenth century, long-distance routes were developed by better-organized firms with larger wagons and the capacity of carriers' services from London grew by about 260 per cent between the 1690s and 1798. In the early nineteenth century, new services were predominantly short distance, using small, light vans; capacity grew by about 34 per cent between 1798 and 1838.[17] Such a pattern of growth is plausible, for canals allowed the transfer of bulky goods to water in the late eighteenth and early nineteenth centuries, leaving roads to concentrate on high-value goods or short hauls. What these figures do confirm is the existence of considerable improvements in the transport system and market integration *before* the era of canals and railways.

The Coming of the Railway

'As I drew nearer and nearer to Newcastle', commented Celia Fiennes in the 1690s, 'I met with and saw abundance of little carriages with a yoke of oxen and a pair of horses together, which is to convey the coals from the pits to the barges on the river.'[18] The Jesmond pit to the north of Newcastle, for example, used more than 700 wagons in 1726 to carry coal to the nearest staithe on the river, which involved considerable costs of buying and feeding horses, and paying wages to drivers. Clearly, concentration of a high volume of traffic on a single route from pit to waterway made it economically rational to make a fixed capital investment in tracks which allowed a horse to pull a larger load. This started from the end of the seventeenth century in the north-east of England, spreading to south Wales, Derbyshire, and Shropshire. Canals and rivers were the arteries of the coalfields and mineral districts; the tram- and wagonways were the veins.[19]

Many wagon- and tramways were built by individual collieries or ironmasters to link their pits and furnaces to the nearest water, with firms sometimes agreeing to share a line. In other cases, the wagonway was provided by a company for use by anyone who cared to pay, such as the Sirhowy Tramroad Co. in Monmouthshire. Although wagon- and tramways often fed canals, they could also duplicate an existing canal, either to stimulate competition and reduce rates, such as the Penydarren tramway, which was opened in 1802 by ironmasters from Merthyr Tydfil in order to challenge the monopoly of the Glamorganshire canal,

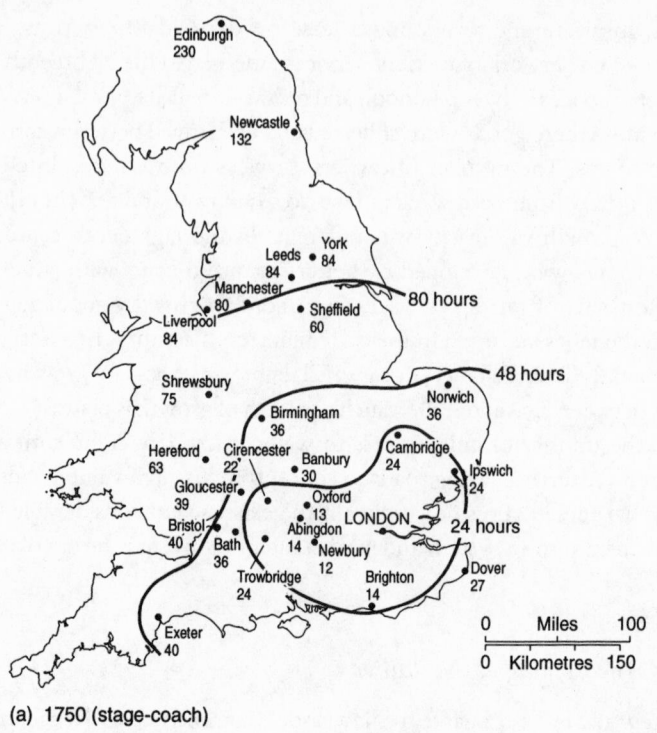

(a) 1750 (stage-coach)

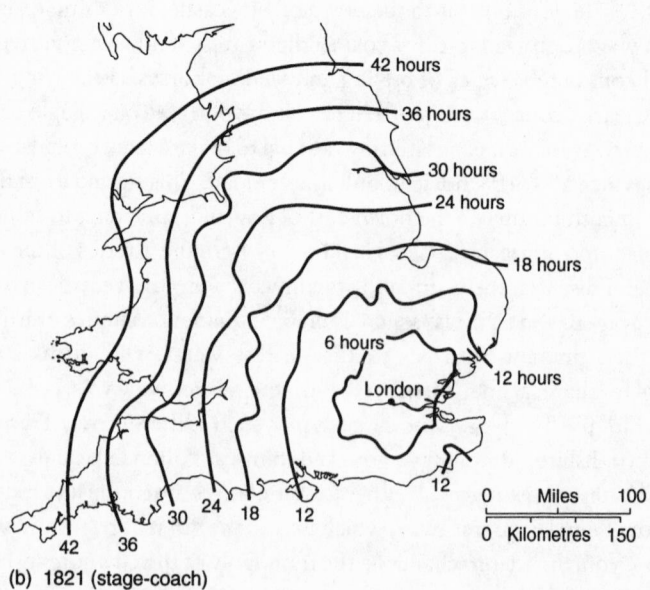

(b) 1821 (stage-coach)

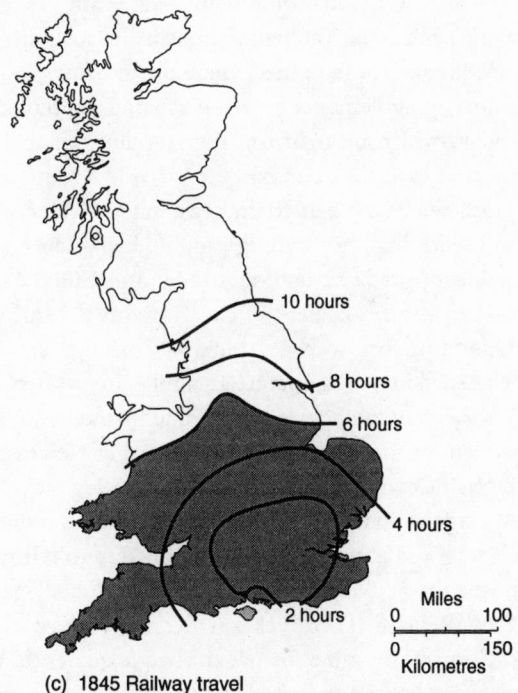

(c) 1845 Railway travel

FIG. 11.4. Travel time from London by fastest stage-coach and railway, 1750, 1821, and 1845

Source: Pawson, *Transport*, fig. 41a, and Freeman, 'Transport', 82, from M. J. Freeman and J. Longbotham, 'The Fordham Collection at the Royal Geographical Society: An Introduction', *Geographical Journal*, 146 (1980), and *Bradshaw's Railway Companion for August 1845*.

or by the canal company itself to reduce pressure, such as the Monmouthshire Canal Co. Most wagon- and tramways were short, with an average length of five miles on the Tyne in 1738, but some were longer and involved considerable engineering work, such as the Tanfield wagonway in Co. Durham, which tapped new areas of production south of the Tyne. Longer routes could be created in a piecemeal fashion by agreements between separate undertakings, such as the Sirhowy tramway, which brought together the lines of the public company, canal company, and various ironmasters to provide a route from the northern fringe of the south Wales coalfield to the coast in 1805. The capital costs of tram- and wagonways were high, for cuttings and embankments were necessary to produce gentle, steady gradients in order to economize on the use of horses. The wagonway built at Murton colliery in Co. Durham in 1810, for example, cost £1,203 a mile. Operating costs were also high. At Coxlodge and Fawdon collieries, 81 horses were needed in 1813 to operate a 5.5-mile line with 81 wagonmen and 8 horse-keepers: upkeep of the horses, wages, and maintenance of the track came to about 16 per cent of the selling price of the coal at Newcastle.

There were obviously incentives to reduce operating costs. Stationary steam engines hauled wagons on the steepest slopes in order to reduce the number of horses, and full wagons descending a slope were used to return empty wagons. The next step was the application of steam power to haulage, which was first demonstrated by Richard Trevithick on the Penydarren tramway in 1804. Trevithick, a Cornish tin-mine manager, had experience of high-pressure engines, which were lighter and needed less coal; even so, the cast-iron rails broke under the strain. Success depended upon strengthening the rail, which became possible with the use of wrought iron from 1808, and increasing the power of the engine in relation to its weight. Steam locomotives started to replace horses on colliery tram- and wagonways from around 1810, and the economic attractions are clear at Charles Brandling's colliery at Middleton near Leeds. A locomotive was installed in 1812 to haul coal to the Aire: the annual cost of horse haulage was £2,900 and of steam £830. The capital cost of three locomotives was about the same as the horses which were replaced, and the fuel for the locomotive cost about the same as feed for the horses. The major saving was in labour: one horse and wagonman could pull a single wagon of 2 to 4 tons, whereas a locomotive with a crew of one or two men could haul up to 20 wagons.

The steam locomotive gradually emerged as a substitute for horses on existing wagonways and tramways which carried coal and metals to rivers, canals, and the coast; it was some time before steam locomotives replaced water for the transport of bulk commodities *between* regions. The first purpose-built railway from Stockton to Darlington opened in 1825, and is often taken as the start of the

ailway age. In fact there were striking continuities with the existing colliery
ramways: it was a public line linking the collieries of southern Co. Durham to
he river Tees in order to ship coal to London; the surveyors of the line had
worked on the Penydarren and Sirhowy tramways; and the line used a mixture of
ocomotives, stationary engines, and horses. A more obvious departure was the
railway between Manchester and Liverpool, which was promoted as a replacement of the canals and rivers, on the grounds that they were expensive, slow, and
overwhelmed with traffic. There were still serious shortcomings with the pulling
power of locomotives, and the company offered a prize to any engineer who
could build a locomotive of less than 6 tons which could pull three times its
weight at a speed of 10 miles per hour, which was won in 1820 by George
Stephenson, an engineer from Tyneside. When the line opened in 1830, it was the
first to be operated entirely by steam, marking the beginning of the age of the
steam railway as a rival rather than an auxiliary to water.

The success of the Manchester–Liverpool line soon led to imitators, which
exploded in the railway manias of 1836–7 and 1844–7. In 1836, 29 companies were
sanctioned in Britain to construct 955 miles of line with an authorized capital of
£22.9 million; activity fell away in the late 1830s and early 1840s, with no company
sanctioned in 1840 and only one in 1841. The next mania reached a peak in 1846,
when 272 companies were sanctioned to build 4,540 miles of line with an
authorized capital of £132.6 million, before a dramatic drop to three companies in
1850 which were sanctioned to build a mere 6.75 miles. The construction of the
network was rapid, increasing from about 500 miles in 1838 to 2,000 miles in 1844
and 7,500 miles in 1852, when the main routes were completed between all
regions of the country (see Fig. 11.5).[20]

Clearly, large amounts of capital had to be raised and two mechanisms tapped
different sources: shares and loans. Subscribers to the ordinary shares in the
company paid an initial sum, with further 'calls' as the line was built. In the case
of the Manchester–Liverpool railway, most subscribers were drawn from the
locality, with 46.4 per cent of the initial share capital coming from Lancashire,
and 42.4 per cent from Liverpool alone. Generally, non-local capital was important in the manias of the 1830s and 1840s, particularly from Manchester, Liverpool,
and London. The north-west provided a considerable part of the share capital in
railways where it had no direct economic interest; for example 70.5 per cent of
the shares in the London and Birmingham railway in 1837 were held in Lancashire and Cheshire, in comparison with only 7.6 per cent in London and 2.9 per
cent in Birmingham.[21] The north-west was never heavily involved in the
national debt, and the railways mobilized savings from sources which had not
previously participated in the national capital market in quoted securities.
Lancashire was not only investing in the expanding cotton industry and the

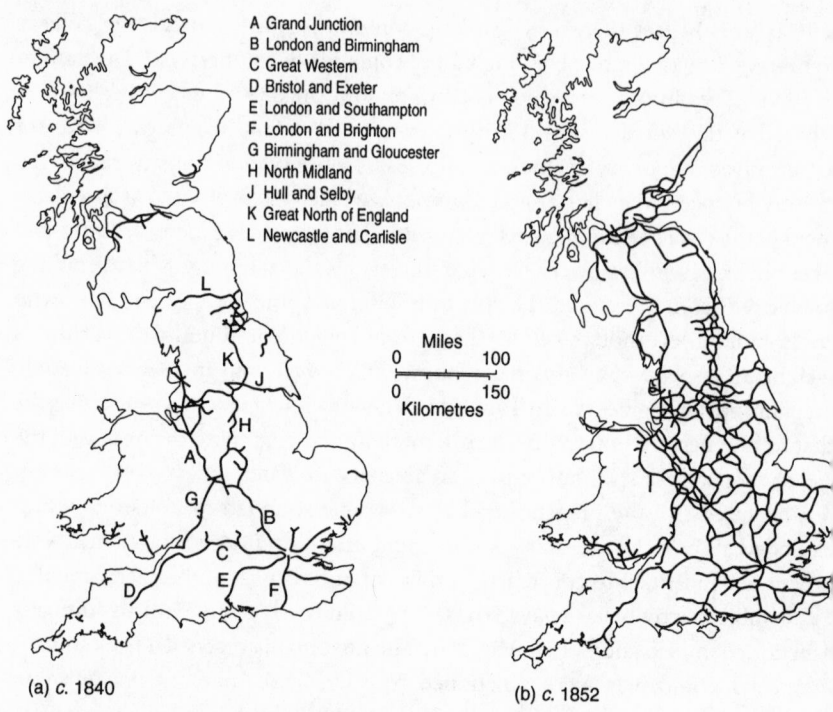

Key:

A Grand Junction
B London and Birmingham
C Great Western
D Bristol and Exeter
E London and Southampton
F London and Brighton
G Birmingham and Gloucester
H North Midland
J Hull and Selby
K Great North of England
L Newcastle and Carlisle

(a) *c.* 1840 (b) *c.* 1852

FIG. 11.5. Railway network, *c.*1840 and *c.*1852

Source: Freeman, 'Transport', 89, adapted from H. Pollins, *Britain's Railways: An Industrial History* (1971), 32, 42.

towns and shipping which it created; it was exporting capital to other regions of the country and helping to overcome imperfections in the capital market.

Railway shares experienced wide fluctuations in price, and shareholders were reluctant to pay 'calls' which might well be wiped out by falls in the market price, and share capital was inadequate during the phase of construction. Loans were the obvious answer, which amounted to 36.8 per cent of capital in England and Wales in 1844, and the early railway Acts gave permission for large sums to be raised: the London and Birmingham railway, for example, could borrow £2,250,000 when half of its authorized capital of £2.5 million was paid up. An attempt was made in 1836 to forbid borrowing until half the share capital was paid up, when loans were restricted to one-third of the authorized capital. In practice, the companies circumvented these limits, either by the legally dubious device of fixed-interest promissory loan notes, which were prohibited from 1844, or by overdrafts from the company's bankers, which were specifically allowed by railway Acts in Scotland and secured surreptitiously by some English companies.

The reduction in the volume and yield of the national debt made railway loans attractive both to institutional investors such as banks and insurance companies, and to private investors who were usually drawn from the locality, and were more quiescent and cautious than the shareholders. They tended to come from the same groups as the purchasers of deed polls in turnpikes, seeking a better yield than was offered by other similar investments and with greater security than shares. The 'intention of loans on debentures', the banker George Carr Glyn explained in 1846, 'was to introduce into the railway system a different class of money dealers'.[22]

Of course, the investment of large sums in railways does not necessarily mean that it had a major impact on the economy as a whole: this depends on the social rate of return from reduced freight rates, the lower level of inventories, speedier and more comfortable journeys, and linkages with industries which supplied materials for construction. The saving in transporting freight and passengers in England and Wales has been estimated for 1865 by taking the next best alternative to railways, whether coastal ships, canal barges, or stage-coaches and carts; the difference between the 'counterfactual' and real economy in 1865 places the social savings on freight and passenger travel at somewhere between 7 and 11 per cent of national income. A further social return arose from linkages with industries supplying materials. These were greatest in the iron industry, but even here technical development did not depend upon railway demand, which was largely confined to south Wales. Neither did railways have a major role in relocating industry and increasing external economies. Overall, the contribution of railways probably amounted to 10 per cent of the national income of England and Wales in 1865, which was equivalent to about five years' growth. The social savings of the railways were 15 to 20 per cent per annum on the investment between 1830 and 1870, exceeding the yield on consols which stood at between 3 and 4 per cent, and outstripping the private rate of return on the railways.[23] These calculations put the railways in perspective, suggesting that no single technical innovation could transform the economy and create a major spurt of growth. The figures also suggest that investment in railways was socially advantageous rather than a waste of money in speculation or the pursuit of private profit. Indeed, the surprise is that shareholders were willing to accept a private rate of return which was *lower* than the social return of their investment. This was understandable in dock construction, where investors were willing to accept a low private rate of return because they could capture part of the social return themselves. It was less rational in railways where the bulk of risk capital came from outside the area, and the private and social return went to different people. The obvious explanation is that investors simply miscalculated the private return, subscribing to shares before the lines were built and the real cost

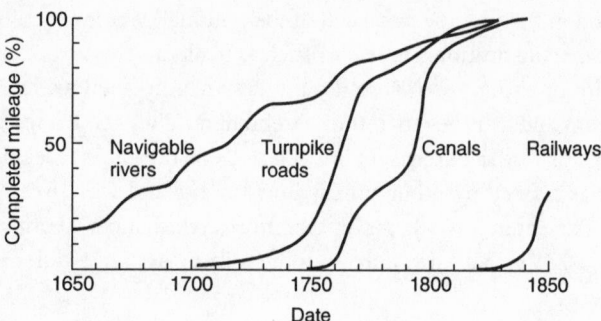

FIG. 11.6. Transport developments in Britain, 1650–1850

Source: Pawson, Transport, 13.

of construction was apparent. 'Private capital was forthcoming for railway investment on the scale on which it was undertaken in Britain in the later 1830s and early 1840s only because the eventual lowness of the private rate of return on some projects was not anticipated.'[24] The speculative manias, with their unrealistic expectations of profits, did not lead to the misallocation of capital, so much as encourage investment which offered a high social rate of return.

Conclusion

The railways offered a respectable social rate of return, but they were not the major factor in the transformation of the economy (see Fig. 11.6 for successive waves of investment). Canals, turnpikes, and coastal shipping were important, and they might well have offered social savings which rivalled or even exceeded the railways. There were significant changes in the organization and efficiency of transport throughout the eighteenth and early nineteenth centuries, which the railways continued rather than initiated. Canals and turnpikes laid the basis for the mobilization of savings to fund the railways, which were beneficiaries as much as creators of an active capital market. Above all, investment in transport reduced transaction costs in the economy, and this was in many ways more striking than improvements in industrial or agricultural productivity over the eighteenth century.

NOTES

1. A. Smith, *An Inquiry into the Nature and Causes of the Wealth of Nations* (repr. 1937), 18 (book i, ch. iii).

2. Quoted in M. W. Flinn, *History of the British Coal Industry*, ii: *1700–1830: The Industrial Revolution* (Oxford, 1984), 181.

3. G. Turnbull, 'Canals, Coal and Regional Growth during the Industrial Revolution', *Economic History Review*, 2nd ser. 40 (1987), 539–40.

4. J. Phillips, quoted ibid. 558.

5. J. R. Ward, *The Finance of Canal Building in Eighteenth-Century England* (Oxford, 1974), 53–4, 72.

6. G. Jackson, *Ports* (Tadworth, 1983), 77–88.

7. R. Davis, *The Rise of the English Shipping Industry in the Seventeenth and Eighteenth Centuries* (1962), 71.

8. J. F. Shepherd and G. M. Walton, *Shipping, Maritime Trade and the Economic Development of Colonial North America* (Cambridge, 1972), 69; D. C. North, 'Sources of Productivity Change in Ocean Shipping, 1600–1850', *Journal of Political Economy*, 76 (1968), 964.

9. E. Pawson, *Transport and Economy: The Turnpike Roads of Eighteenth-Century Britain* (1977), 25–6.

10. Quoted ibid. 29.

11. J. D. Marshall (ed.), *The Autobiography of William Stout of Lancaster, 1665–1752* (Manchester, 1967), 11.

12. Pawson, *Transport and Economy*, 96, 125; W. Albert, *The Turnpike Road System in England, 1663–1840* (Cambridge, 1972), 42.

13. Albert, *Turnpike Road System*, 88.

14. Pawson, *Transport and Economy*, 32–3.

15. B. Austen, 'The Impact of the Mail Coach on Public Coach Services in England and Wales, 1784–1840', *Journal of Transport History*, 3rd ser. 2 (1981); P. Bagwell, *The Transport Revolution from 1700* (1974), 50.

16. Pawson, *Transport and Economy*, 290–1.

17. D. Gerhold, 'The growth of the London Carrying Trade, 1681–1838', *Economic History Review*, 2nd ser. 41 (1988), 400, 403.

18. *The Journeys of Celia Fiennes*, ed. Christopher Morris (1947), 209.

19. Flinn, *British Coal Industry*, ii, ch. 5.

20. Bagwell, *Transport Revolution*, 93–5.

21. M. C. Reed, *Investment in Railways in Britain 1820–44: A Study in the Development of the Capital Market* (Oxford, 1975), 120, 135.

22. Ibid. 35, 225, 260.

23. G. R. Hawke, *Railways and Economic Growth in England and Wales, 1840–70* (Oxford, 1970), 400, 405.

24. Reed, *Investment in Railways*, 270.

FURTHER READING

Albert, W., *The Turnpike Road System in England, 1663–1840* (Cambridge, 1972).

Austen, B., 'The Impact of the Mail Coach on Public Coach Services in England and Wales, 1784–1840', *Journal of Transport History*, 3rd ser. 2 (1981).

Bagwell, P. S., *The Transport Revolution from 1770* (1974).

Barker, T. C., 'Lancashire Coal, Cheshire Salt and the Rise of Liverpool', *Transactions of the Historic Society of Lancashire and Cheshire*, 103 (1952).

—— 'The Sankey Navigation', *Transactions of the Historic Society of Lancashire and Cheshire*, 100 (1948).

—— and Harris, J. R., *A Merseyside Town in the Industrial Revolution: St Helens, 1750–1900* (Liverpool, 1954).

Broadbridge, S., *Studies in Railway Expansion and the Capital Markets in England, 1825–73* (1970).

Broeze, F. J. A., 'The Cost of Distance: Shipping and the Early Australian Economy, 1788–1850', *Economic History Review*, 2nd ser. 28 (1975).

Buchanan, B. J., 'The Evolution of the English Turnpike Trusts: Lessons from a Case Study', *Economic History Review*, 2nd ser. 39 (1986).

Chartres, J., 'Road Carrying in England in the Seventeenth Century: Myth and Reality', *Economic History Review*, 2nd ser. 30 (1977).

Davis, R., *The Rise of the English Shipping Industry in the Seventeenth and Eighteenth Centuries* (1962).

Duckham, B. F., 'Canals and River Navigations', in D. H. Aldcroft and M. J. Freeman (eds.), *Transport in the Industrial Revolution* (Manchester, 1983).

Flinn, M. W., *The History of the British Coal Industry*, ii: *1700–1830: The Industrial Revolution* (Oxford, 1984).

Freeman, M. J., 'Transporting Methods in the British Cotton Industry during the Industrial Revolution', *Journal of Transport History*, 3rd ser. 1 (1980).

—— 'Road Transport in the English Industrial Revolution: An Interim Reassessment', *Journal of Historical Geography*, 6 (1980).

Gerhold, D., 'The Growth of the London Carrying Trade, 1681–1838', *Economic History Review*, 2nd ser. 41 (1988).

Gregory, D., 'The Friction of Distance? Information Circulation and the Mails in Early Nineteenth-Century England', *Journal of Historical Geography*, 13 (1987).

Hadfield, C., *The Canals of South Wales and the Border* (Newton Abbot, 1960).

Hausman, W. J., 'The English Coastal Coal Trade, 1691–1910: How Rapid was Productivity Growth?', *Economic History Review*, 2nd ser. 40 (1987).

Hawke, G. R., *Railways and Economic Growth in England and Wales, 1840–70* (Oxford, 1970).

Hyde, F. E., *Liverpool and the Mersey: An Economic History of a Port, 1700–1970* (Newton Abbot, 1971).

Jackson, G., *Ports* (Tadworth, 1983).

Kenwood, A. G., 'Railway Investment in Britain, 1825–75', *Economica* (1965).

Langton, J., *Geographical Change and Industrial Revolution: Coal-Mining in South-West Lancashire, 1590–1799* (Cambridge, 1979).

—— 'The Industrial Revolution and the Regional Geography of England', *Transactions of the Institute of British Geographers*, NS 9 (1984).

Mitchell, B. R., 'The Coming of the Railway and UK Economic Growth', *Journal of Economic History*, 24 (1964).

North, D. C., 'Ocean Freight Rates and Economic Development, 1750–1913', *Journal of Economic History*, 18 (1958).

—— 'Sources of Productivity Change in Ocean Shipping, 1600–1850', *Journal of Political Economy*, 76 (1968).

Pawson, E., *Transport and Economy: The Turnpike Roads of Eighteenth Century Britain* (1977).

Reed, M. C., *Investment in Railways in Britain, 1820–44: A Study in the Development of the Capital Market* (Oxford, 1975).

Robinson, H., *The British Post Office: A History* (Princeton, NJ, 1948).

Shepherd, J. F., and Walton, G. M., *Shipping, Maritime Trade and the Economic Development of Colonial North America* (Cambridge, 1972).

Turnbull, G., 'Canals, Coal and Regional Growth during the Industrial Revolution', *Economic History Review*, 2nd ser. 40 (1987).

—— 'Provincial Road Carrying in England in the Eighteenth Century', *Journal of Transport History*, NS 4 (1977).

—— *Traffic and Transport: An Economic History of Pickfords* (1979).

Ville, S. P., *English Shipowning during the Industrial Revolution: Michael Henley and Son, London Shipowners, 1770–1830* (Manchester, 1987).

—— 'Total Factor Productivity in the English Shipping Industry: The North-East Coal Trade, 1700–1850', *Economic History Review*, 2nd ser. 39 (1986).

—— 'Defending Productivity Growth in the English Coal Trade during the Eighteenth and Nineteenth Centuries', *Economic History Review*, 2nd ser. 40 (1987).

Walton, G. M., 'Sources of Productivity Change in American Colonial Shipping, 1675–1775', *Economic History Review*, 2nd ser. 20 (1967).

Ward, J. R., *The Finance of Canal Building in Eighteenth-Century England* (Oxford, 1974).

Willan, T. S., *River Navigation in England, 1600–1750* (1936).

—— *The Navigation of the River Weaver in the Eighteenth Century* (Manchester, 1951).

....

CHAPTER 12

Merchants and Marketing

Britain's distinctive regional economies, with their particular social structures and patterns of production, were not self-sufficient: specialism only makes sense where markets permit the exchange of commodities, and connect the regions into a nationally integrated economy. The question is: how efficient were markets in providing these links? The operation of a market depends upon the quality and quantity of information which is available to participants, for a consumer or shopkeeper in, say, Devon might well have no knowledge of the price or design of clocks or cutlery manufactured in Birmingham or Sheffield, and might consequently continue to purchase from local craftsmen in Exeter whose costs were higher. Competition was 'imperfect', and the slow development of a more 'perfect' market depended upon improved flows of information through the distribution network, allowing areas to concentrate on the production of goods in which they had a competitive edge, and offering consumers access to the lowest-cost suppliers. Of course, the provision of trade networks to link production and consumption itself imposed 'transaction costs', and improvements in the efficiency of intermediaries could have a significant impact on the final price to the consumer. Economic historians have concentrated on changes in the production of goods, but changes in marketing which reduced transaction costs could have as great an impact on the final price to the consumer. The technical marvels of steam engines and spinning-machines are more striking than the mundane activities of merchants and shopkeepers who left fewer visible remains and records, but they are not necessarily of greater economic significance. After all, the greatest fortune in the textile trades was not made by Richard Arkwright in the production of yarn; it was accumulated by James Morrison, the 'Napoleon of shopkeepers', whose textile warehouse in the City of London supplied the inland trade with its handkerchiefs, ribbons, braids, and fabrics.[1]

The efficiency of markets and merchants affected the level of transaction costs, and the particular institutional structure shaped the pattern of economic development. Markets were far from the neutral abstractions of macroeconomic theory, for they were relationships which gave more or less power to the participants, and were renegotiated as circumstances changed. The producer was in some cases subordinate to the merchant, who captured a large part of the profit; in other cases, the producer took over merchanting in order to remove profits from the middleman. The relationship between the producer and merchant influenced the process of accumulation of capital, and helped to shape the pattern of economic development. The gentlemen merchants of Leeds, for example, withdraw their money from the cloth industry rather than investing it in factory production; by contrast, putting out merchants in the worsted trade of Halifax or in the metal trades of the Midlands moved into centralized production. The marketing structure could affect the responsiveness of a region: in Yorkshire, the reliance upon local merchants made producers more sensitive to market changes than in the West Country, where dependence upon Blackwell Hall factors in London created a barrier between producers and the final market. The marketing structure should not be viewed as something apart from production, for they reacted upon each other, with the balance of power between merchant and manufacturer shifting over time and varying between regions.

The market was also defined by changing social expectations and assumptions, which were adjusted through a process of conflict and political action. Economic historians who apply macroeconomic analyses to the British economy assume that prices were set by the unfettered operation of supply and demand, without considering whether the assumption was accepted or challenged. The *Book of Orders* of 1630 encapsulated a different view of the market, in which the 'visible hand' of charity and morality tempered the 'invisible hand' of supply and demand:

That all good means and persuasions be used by the Justices in their several divisions, and by admonitions and exhortations in sermons in the churches ... that the poor may be served of corn at convenient and charitable prices. And to the furtherance thereof, that the richer sort be earnestly moved by Christian charity, to cause their grain to be sold under the common prices of the market to the poorer sort.[2]

The stress upon 'charitable and convenient' prices was linked with public regulation of markets, limits to the power of merchants over farmers and consumers, and controls over prices by the Assize of Bread. The system of public regulation of prices and exchange was challenged by economists such as Adam Smith, who felt that 'charitable' prices were *inconvenient*, removing the incentive to produce and so making the problem worse. 'Unlimited, unrestrained freedom of the corn trade'[3] was, argued Smith, the best way of dealing with shortages. Of course, *The Wealth of Nations* is as much an ideological construct as the *Book of Orders* and its assumptions were by no means universally accepted. There was a long drawn out conflict between the two approaches, which was fought in books and pamphlets, and in tussles in market-places where aggrieved consumers demanded the restoration of regulation. The conflict has been portrayed by Edward Thompson as a displacement of 'moral economy', with its assumption that prices should be 'just', by political economy with its assumption that prices should be left to the invisible hand of supply and demand. Although his particular formulation is contentious, there is no doubt that the 'market' was an arena of contest in the eighteenth century, rather than the neutral process of price determination of macroeconomic theory.

Fairs and Markets

The hub of international trade in the Middle Ages was the annual fair, to which merchants travelled to exchange the specialities of different regions. The role of fairs was in many ways supplanted in the sixteenth and seventeenth centuries by entrepôts such as Amsterdam and Antwerp, where the grain and timber of northern and eastern Europe were exchanged for wines, spices, tea, and sugar from the Mediterranean and the colonies of Asia and America. Of course, London emerged as the great rival to the Continental entrepôts in the eighteenth century, with foreigners attracted by sales of tea and other colonial commodities in the auction rooms of the East India Co., and imports of sugar and tobacco by the West Indian and Virginian merchants. But fairs did not disappear completely, for the great fairs at Leipzig and Frankfurt continued to fulfil an important function into the early nineteenth century, attracting British textiles and other manufactures for sale to merchants from central and eastern Europe; and there were no fewer than 1,691 fairs in England and Wales in 1792.[4] What was their economic role?

At one extreme, major national fairs brought together a wide range of traders from around the country to exchange commodities and place orders. The largest was Sturbridge Fair, held near Cambridge in September.[5] Retail goldsmiths, turners, milliners, hatters, mercers, drapers, pewterers, and haberdashers from London erected their stalls; wholesale dealers in woollen cloth sold cloth on the spot and, more importantly, took orders to be supplied at a later date and settled accounts with itinerant hawkers and pedlars who travelled around the country. Wholesale grocers, iron-merchants, and brasiers took orders to be supplied from their warehouses in London. Clothiers from Halifax, Leeds, Wakefield, and Huddersfield in Yorkshire jostled with their competitors from the west of England and Norwich, and with the cotton and fustian cloths from Rochdale,

Bury, and Manchester in Lancashire. There was iron and brass from Birmingham, tools and knives from Sheffield, stockings from Nottingham and Leicester, and the last day of the fair was given over to horses. Amongst all this activity, Sturbridge specialized in two commodities: wool from Lincolnshire was sold to manufacturers from East Anglia; and hops from Kent and Surrey were sold to northern brewers. Sturbridge was exceptional in its scale and coverage, but most districts had a general purpose annual fair, usually held in the autumn, when the farmers and their workers had cash after the harvest to make purchases of consumer goods. They could act as a labour market which brought together farmers and workers in districts where annual contracts were the norm, as well as providing an outlet for the speciality of the area, and allowing retailers to order stocks of a wide range of goods for the coming year.

In the course of the eighteenth century, these fairs became less significant as retail and wholesale trade moved into new channels, and annual labour contracts declined. It was, of course, costly to transport goods to Sturbridge Fair from London, and already by the early eighteenth century much business was done by taking orders which were filled direct from London. It was an easy step to use travelling salesmen or 'riders' who toured the country, taking orders from shopkeepers and market traders, which could be supplied by the improved carrier system. The commercial traveller became a common sight from the early eighteenth century, removing the need for retailers to visit fairs to order stock. Iron-merchants or Manchester warehousemen sent out representatives to compete for the custom of shopkeepers, and to collect payment for goods. Small producers sometimes spent part of the year touting their wares around the neighbourhood, and as specialization increased they concentrated on manufacturing and relied upon specialist factors such as Tobias Bellaers of Birmingham, who travelled from farm to farm in the Midlands taking orders for nails, locks, and brassware, delivering the goods, and collecting payment. Others were larger operations, such as ironmongers from centres like Stourbridge who collected goods at their warehouse and left stock with agents on their 'circuit'. The largest producers such as Matthew Boulton and Josiah Wedgwood developed their own distribution system, and from the 1770s many smaller Birmingham and Sheffield manufacturers cut out middlemen by sending patterns and price lists direct to shopkeepers who could order items for customers. By the end of the eighteenth century, the commercial importance of fairs was largely confined to trade in livestock, horses, and pastoral products, with one cluster in the spring at which breeders from the upland areas sold young animals for fattening in the lowlands, and another in the autumn when animals were sold for slaughter. Cattle, sheep, and horses were only available at certain times of the year, and had to be inspected to judge their value. Otherwise, fairs were increasingly 'for diversion, more than for trade'.[6] Crowds with cash in their pockets had always attracted acrobats, jugglers, showmen, and races; what had once been peripheral became the prime purpose of many fairs.

In addition to annual fairs, the country was covered by a network of weekly markets with royal charters giving the lord of the manor or borough a local monopoly of trade and the right to charge for the use of the market square or hall. In 1693 there were around 680 active markets in England and Wales and 728 in 1792, ranging from wholesale markets which linked the region to the national or international economy down to small-scale local retailing.[7] At one extreme, specialist wholesale markets dealt in a single commodity and attracted merchants serving a national or even international market. Clothiers carried cloth to the 'piece halls' of Halifax and Bradford, renting a small room or stall to display their goods for sale to merchants from Leeds or drapers who served the country trade; corn factors, distillers, brewers, maltsters, and millers went to grain markets in the arable districts to buy their supplies; drovers bought livestock from farmers at cattle markets such as that on Castle Hill in Norwich and resold to wholesale butchers at Smithfield market in London. At the other extreme to these inter-regional wholesale markets there were local, retail village markets where farmers' wives sold their dairy produce, or a few itinerant traders displayed their haberdashery. But most markets fell somewhere between these two extremes, combining wholesale and retail services and trading in a variety of commodities. A farmer or producer of industrial goods who came to town to sell his output to a middleman would also sell direct to local consumers, and buy consumer goods from traders who set up stalls in the market-place to retail the products of other regions. At Norwich, for example, the long-distance trade of Castle Hill operated alongside the local 'ped' market, at which farmers supplied local consumers with commodities they carried to town in panniers or peds on their horses. In the eighteenth and nineteenth centuries markets became less important as hubs of the wholesale trade, except for the sale of livestock, where regular markets survived at which farmers sold cattle or sheep for fattening, breeding, or slaughter. Producers of industrial goods were less likely to transport their goods to the market for sale to merchants or the final consumer; and the sale of grain increasingly bypassed the market-place.

The supply of grain was crucial to public order and welfare in pre-industrial societies, where a Malthusian crisis was always a possibility. There was concern that rapacious speculators might corner the market and force up prices, so that public policy stressed the need to maintain supplies and prevent merchants from exploiting consumers. The grain market was to be open and transactions visible: grain was to be physically transported to the market where it was 'pitched' for inspection by the purchasers; sales were regulated by the market authorities and he justices; and the law prohibited sale of grain at the farm or by sample, which was undertaken in private and could therefore not be supervised. The *Book of Orders* gave the authorities the power to survey stores held in the barns and warehouses of farmers and dealers, and to order them to send grain to the market for sale at a reasonable price. The internal trade was regulated, exports were forbidden when prices rose above a certain level, and imports were seldom restricted. Such was the theory enshrined in statutes, common law, the *Book of Orders*, and market charters.

In reality, chartered markets were increasingly circumvented by millers and merchant factors who bought grain from farmers on the basis of a sample inspected at private markets held in inns, or purchased the crop while it was still in the ground, which had the attraction of easing the liquidity of farmers and assuring the purchaser of supplies. The use of 'pitched' markets became less important, particularly as supply lines became more extended. It was one thing to bring a cart of grain from a farm in the neighbourhood of a small town for sale to local bakers and brewers; it was quite another thing to supply grain deficit areas such as the pastoral West Country and industrial Lancashire from East Anglia or Yorkshire. Above all, London drew its grain for bread, brewing, and distilling from a large part of the country, by ship around the coast of Kent, southern England, and East Anglia, and by barge along the Thames, Lea, and Wey. Not surprisingly, the organization of London's grain trade diverged from the theory contained in legislation and the common law. In the seventeenth century, the organization of the trade still had something in common with 'pitched' markets, for the grain was sold when the cargo arrived at the quay. By the early eighteenth century, sales were usually made by sample before arriving in London, and the shift from visibility and public regulation culminated with the opening of a private corn exchange in 1750 which was owned and managed by the corn factors and dealers. The trade came to rely upon a complex pattern of specialists and middlemen, who linked farms with the final market in London. Grain was purchased from farmers by factors or merchants, who traded on their own account or worked on commission for sellers and buyers. The factors were often substantial businessmen, needing large resources to purchase grain and to store it in granaries; in some cases, such as in Kent, they also owned ships to transport the grain to market. The factors sold the grain to sizeable corn merchants such as Samuel Fitch who held stocks to supply the home market and, at least until the 1760s, for export to Europe, and to processors—millers and maltsters—who were often running large businesses which required considerable amounts of working capital and an investment in fixed plant. Indeed, food-processing was one of the most significant industries of the period.

Many millers operated on a small scale, grinding corn for local farmers and gleaners, in return for a proportion of the flour or a fee. Increasingly, they were displaced by large, capital-intensive mills which purchased grain in order to supply long-distance markets; water-powered mills on the Thames were some of the largest industrial concerns of the eighteenth century, and steam-powered mills were erected in London. The flour was in turn sold to mealmen, who supplied bakers and the retail trade. As the scale of firms increased, they integrated backward and forward. Large millers purchased their own supplies and cut out the factors, or they moved forward into the trade in flour and cut out the mealmen. The mealmen, in turn, integrated backwards and acquired mills. The whole pattern of supplying bread-stuffs, the basic necessity of life, had become a very different matter from a farmer pitching his wagon in the market-place: it had extended lines of distribution, involving capital-intensive plant and considerable amounts of working capital, with some of the largest concerns in the economy.

Factors also sold barley for conversion into malt, the crucial ingredient for beer. Maltsters required considerable amounts of working capital to purchase and hold stocks, and fixed capital in large, brick malt-houses where barley was germinated and roasted in kilns. Barley was an important specialist crop in East Anglia, Hertfordshire, south Nottinghamshire, and Lincolnshire, with major centres of malting in Burton-on-Trent, the ports of East Anglia, and the small towns of Hertfordshire such as Hitchin and Hoddesdon which supplied the London brewers. In some cases, malting and brewing were integrated such as at Ipswich, where the Cobbolds were involved in brewing, malting, and corn-merchanting, but it was only in the later eighteenth century that some of the largest London brewers purchased their own malt-houses; usually, they relied on independent maltsters and specialist brokers.

At the beginning of the eighteenth century, most beer was produced by small 'common brewers' or by publicans for sale on their premises. In the course of the eighteenth century, the scale of brewing increased, and in most towns it was amongst the largest and most prosperous businesses. Peter Greenall, a brewer at St Helens, for example, diversified into banking at Warrington and the glass industry at St Helens. But the most significant change was in the brewing of porter, a heavier, darker drink which was suitable for mass production. Brewing of ale was a temperamental process, and it was difficult to store: a large ale brewer such as Charrington's in London produced 15,900 barrels in 1800. By contrast, the largest London brewer of porter—Whitbreads—produced 137,000 barrels in 1800. These concerns entailed a considerable investment in fixed plant and machinery, and the brewers were amongst the first and largest users of steam power. Benjamin Truman's brewery in London, for example, was valued at £225,090 in 1790, which surpassed the largest factories in the north. Even more nportant was the working capital needed to purchase malt, hold stocks of porter s it matured, and supply credit to publicans who only paid after the porter was old. The circulating capital dwarfed the sizeable fixed investment in plant; at 'rumans in 1810, trade debts amounted to £222,225, stocks of raw material 101,204, and of porter £121,897.[8] The porter brewers had moved towards a fully ntegrated system of production and distribution, moving back into the provision f raw materials, and forward into the control of public houses. Their prosperity ested as much on marketing and the provision of credit as on production, and it s not surprising that they formed close connections with bankers, particularly in last Anglia, which was so heavily dependent on the trade in barley and malt. The artners in Truman's brewery included Sampson Hanbury, a leading malt factor, nd the Buxtons, who were important figures in country banking in East Anglia. hey were closely connected to their fellow Quakers, the Gurneys, who were artners in the brewers Barclay Perkins. There was a web of family and business onnection between London brewers and East Anglian bankers and merchants, vhich formed an integral feature in the movement of agricultural profits from last Anglia through the country banking system via London to Lancashire. 3arley, malt, and beer contributed to the financing of industrialization.

The marketing of grain had changed from the assumptions of the *Book of Orders* and legislation directed against forestallers and engrossers. Chartered narkets ceased to provide the link between areas of deficit and surplus, and pitched' markets to which farmers brought their carts of wheat or barley were of nerely local significance. Marketing was no longer so visible and regulated, and he bulk of grain was in the hands of a complex hierarchy of middlemen, nvolving large sums of working capital and investment in granaries, mills, nalt-houses, and breweries. What were the economic consequences of these changes in marketing for producers and consumers, and how far did the framework of public regulation change to take account of shifting patterns of marketing?

Moral Economy versus Political Economy?

Public policy started to shift in the later seventeenth century, when the government placed greater reliance on the creation of a free market which would, they hoped, remove the danger of monopoly and encourage production, which would prevent shortages and equalize prices. The aim was to maintain relatively stable prices, reducing fluctuations by establishing lower and upper prices which would provide a reasonable return to the producer, so creating an incentive to expand output and to maintain a steady supply at reasonable prices which would benefit the consumer. The new approach had three strands: most controls over internal trade were abolished in 1663; imports were regulated by a sliding scale of duty in 1670 designed to keep out foreign grain when prices were low and to permit entry when prices were high; and corn exports were assisted from 1673 by a bounty when prices fell below a given level. A minimum price was maintained by helping farmers to dispose of any surplus through exports and imposing high import duties on foreign supplies at times of low prices. The maximum was fixed by reducing the rate of duty as prices increased, and encouraging production through the expectation of a reasonable return. The policy would, it was hoped, protect consumers from famine and provide farmers with a stable market environment by ensuring that prices remained at an acceptable level. The role of the state was to influence the inflow and outflow of grain into the country through import duties and export bounties, and to leave the internal market to a free, unregulated market which would act in the best interests of consumers and producers. How far was this approach accepted?

A common complaint of farmers was that they were exploited by large merchants who were able to control the market more successfully than small, scattered, competing farmers. A Kentish farmer, for example, sold his corn to a small group of factors in a port such as Faversham, where the six largest 'hoymen' controlled 80 per cent of the trade. When the Kent hoymen arrived on the quays of London, they were submerged in a larger body of factors from other ports who were selling to the great London merchants. There was unequal power in the marketing system, which led Adam Smith to argue that export bounties were captured by corn merchants, who took the profit at the end of the chain of distribution, rather than by the farmers. However, the farmers were not simply victims of the merchants in an unequal relationship; they were beneficiaries. Merchants were making a market, not in the old sense of a physical point of sale but in the very different sense of a system of exchange relations stretching across the country. An integrated market allowed farmers and regions to specialize in the crops most suited to their land, which provides one explanation for the increased productivity of land in the later seventeenth and early eighteenth centuries, and the development of a more effective regional division of labour. The introduction of sale by sample rationalized the carriage of grain, which could be sent direct to the purchaser without a detour to a 'pitched' market. Consolidation of the trade in the hands of larger concerns, and the trend towards integration, meant that there were lower unit handling costs. Indeed, it could be argued that farmers and middlemen were mutually supportive rather than rivals: changes in the system of marketing and distribution reduced costs and gave farmers a better market for their produce; and middlemen benefited from changes in farming which gave them a larger output to handle in the market. The emergence of a national, integrated market therefore led to a more

fficient allocation of resources which maximized output, but it was not entirely
vithout friction. Specialization could benefit some groups in society at the
xpense of others: it could give landowners an incentive to renegotiate leases or
nclose land; it could allow larger farmers to consolidate at the expense of their
maller neighbours. There could be surplus labour in areas which shifted to
astoralism, freeing labour for industrial outwork; in areas which shifted to
rable cultivation, industrial by-employment could be reduced, or transformed
nto a sweated female sector. The benefits of specialization were appropriated in
lifferent ways, which were far more complicated than a simple matter of
roducers versus merchants.

How did consumers react to these changes in marketing? Of course, it was
mpossible to feed large cities such as London, or grain deficit areas such as
Devon and Lancashire, without an increasingly sophisticated marketing system.
Lower transaction costs and gains in productivity by specialization meant lower
rices for the consumer. But specialization also had its dangers, for it exposed
reas of grain deficit to serious problems in the event of a bad harvest or
lisruption to supplies, which resulted in spasmodic food riots. Despite a number
of bad harvests, the situation in the early eighteenth century was favourable to
he policy of free trade in grain: output was expanding faster than the population,
rices were falling, and there was a substantial export trade in grain between 1715
and a peak in 1750. There were greater problems in the second half of the
eighteenth century, as population growth started to outstrip the food supply,
rices rose, and exports dwindled. The agricultural policy which had worked so
well in the later seventeenth and first half of the eighteenth century was faltering.
Not only were the export bounties and import duties frequently suspended;
there were also spates of food riots in 1756–7, 1766–7, 1795, and 1800–1. How
should these riots be interpreted?

Food riots have been interpreted as an outbreak of popular frustration when
high food prices coincided with high unemployment, but E. P. Thompson has
rejected this 'crass economic reductionism'. He denies that these disturbances
were 'involuntary spasms' and argues that the actions of the crowd must be
understood in terms of the beliefs which provided legitimization. The 'moral
economy' of the poor was based upon 'a consistent traditional view of social
norms and obligations, of the proper economic functions of several parties
within the community'.[9] In the nineteenth century, social conflict was usually
over the issue of wages through the medium of the strike; in the eighteenth
century, he argues, it was usually over rising prices through the medium of the
food 'riot', which was, he suggests, a disciplined response with clear objectives.
The 'rioters', were striving to defend paternalistic controls over markets and
the regulation of the internal corn trade: marketing was to be transparent,

undertaken openly in public markets, with honest measures and fair prices; the hoarding of stocks, and sales by sample or in advance of the harvest, led to manipulation of the market, and should be stopped. The assumptions of the 'moral economy' of the crowd were underpinned by the paternalist model of the *Book of Orders*, which justified the crowds in taking enforcement into their own hands, visiting farmers to survey their stocks, or taking control of markets to require them to sell grain at a 'fair' price. The 'rioters' were not pilfering or looting grain; they were restrained and disciplined, setting the price and handing the proceeds to the farmer or merchant. Direct action was, of course, anathema to the paternalist model of the *Book of Orders*, but it did provide the crowd with a justification for their behaviour and placed the local magistrates in a dilemma. It was difficult to suppress public disorder, for they did not have a police force or regular army, and they were dependent on the local militia, which shared many of the sentiments of the rioters. The alternative was to reassert paternalistic control over the market, so containing the threat to social stability at the expense of legitimizing the principles on which the rioters were acting. Although regulations of the internal grain trade had fallen into disuse in the late seventeenth century, they could be reactivated. Even when legislation against forestalling was repealed in 1772, it was still possible to turn from statute law to other levels of the complex English legal system. Manorial lords or boroughs could be pressed to enforce charters which gave them a monopoly of trade at 'pitched' markets; and the Lord Chief Justice ruled that forestalling and engrossing remained offences at common law after the repeal of the statute in 1772. The legal system was not simply a device for imposing 'capitalist' relations; it offered a bargaining counter to the poor to assert rights and to pressurize the local authorities, who often shared the same assumptions. Consequently, local justices often reacted to riots by reviving the paternalist model, which had lapsed during years of moderate prices. The food riots, argues Thompson, were 'a pattern of social protest which derives from a consensus as to the moral economy of the commonweal in times of dearth',[10] which only dissolved in the French revolutionary and Napoleonic wars when fear of Jacobinism meant that popular unrest was treated less sympathetically. Paternalism and moral economy, argues Thompson, were displaced by political economy with its belief that the free market should set the price without intervention.

Food riots were certainly more than reactions to a coincidence of high food prices and unemployment: they involved cultural assumptions and beliefs. But is Thompson correct in his somewhat romantic view that they were a battle between two fundamentally different perceptions of social relations? On the one side, there was a traditional 'moral economy' which derived from self-sufficiency and the culture of an integrated community in which it was considered 'unnatural' to profit from others; on the other side, there was the ideology of political economy which was based upon a capitalist free market. In Thompson's view, the crowd was fighting to preserve the first, often with the support of the local justices, against the central government. But was the distinction so clear-cut? Regulation of markets was not necessarily paternalistic, for their property rights offered monopoly profit which could be defended on capitalist' grounds. When Sir John Mosley, the lord of the manor at Manchester, took legal action against dealers who sold flour in a 'private, secret and clandestine way', his concern was not to defend the 'moral economy' of a paternalist order; it was to protect his market tolls, which were eventually purchased by the town council in 1846 for £200,000.[11] And were food rioters protecting a long-established, traditionalist moral economy against the norms of the market? It is more realistic to interpret the riots within the context of the marketing system, rather than as an attempt to reject political economy as a new, disruptive, intrusion in a 'traditional' community.

The grain riots of 1766, for example, were concentrated in the rural cloth districts of Gloucestershire and Wiltshire, the central Midlands, and East Anglia, and particularly in a short period in September and October. The timing may be explained by the actions of the government, which had been expecting a reasonable harvest. Import duties were reintroduced to prevent any glut of foreign grain which would force down prices, and merchants were offered export bounties to absorb the anticipated surplus. However, the harvest proved to be poor, and prices soared at the very time that bounties were being paid for exports of grain to southern Europe. The riots were not a rejection of the incursion of 'political economy' into traditional areas, for they occurred in the areas which were most heavily dependent on the commercial market for provisions. The rioters were themselves part of a capitalist market economy, whose actions should be placed in the context of the marketing system and its specific problems. They were acting *within* rather than *against* a market economy.

The food rioters should not be romanticized as guardians of a co-operative commonwealth, and neither should the government be castigated as the demons of a harsh political economy. The central government felt that condemnation of the middleman was counter-productive, and stressed that free movement of grain was the best way of meeting specific shortages. They urged local authorities to provide protection for merchants and an unregulated trade in corn as 'absolutely and indispensably necessary to ensure a tolerable supply of the markets'.[12] The reduction of prices by control of markets was no solution. 'Whenever a scarcity of Provisions exists', argued the Home Secretary in 1800, '... the only means which can lead effectually to obviate it, and to prevent the Grain from rising to an excessive price, consists in holding out full security ... to

all Farmers and other lawful Dealers, who shall bring their corn to market and . .
to suppress ... every attempt to impede by open acts of violence, or b
intimidation, the regular business of the markets.'[13] The government argued tha
the continued supply of grain over long distances depended upon the mainter
ance of a sophisticated system of distribution, which did not imply that the poc
should be left to starve until the market could react. What was at issue was th
type of intervention. Rather than imposing an artificially low price of grain b
regulating the market, the poor should be relieved by subsidies of high prices
The Parish Relief Act of 1800 permitted parishes to acquire stocks of food for sal
to the poor at a loss; and up to a third of poor relief could be paid in substitutes fo
bread rather than cash. The basic shortcoming of this policy in the eyes of th
overseers was that it imposed a burden on the rates. The local authorities whe
responded to food riots by invoking the assumptions of the *Book of Orders* wer
not necessarily invoking a 'paternalistic' model to protect the poor agains
exploitation; they were adopting the easy option of blaming the middleman as .
scapegoat and avoiding the more costly and troublesome policy of restorin
public order, subsidizing the wages of the poor, and importing grain into th
region. The willingness of the local authorities to take effective rather than
symbolic action depended upon pressure from the Lord-Lieutenants of th
counties who represented the central government, the movement of troops to
restore public order, and a realization on their own part that the attack or
middlemen was counter-productive.

The Retail Trades

The service sector is one of the most difficult areas of the economy to analyse, fo
few concerns left any records and there is no physical output to measure
Consequently, most estimates of national income simply assume that the service
sector grew at the same rate as the rest of the economy, despite the fact that the
service sector absorbed a considerable part of the population released from
agriculture, and that the number of shopkeepers and traders expanded faster
than the economy as a whole. The problem is how to interpret the expansion of
services. In many societies, the service sector is a refuge for underemployed
labour, with a low level of wages, productivity, and output; an increase in the
proportion of the work-force can be seen as a sign of weakness. On the other
hand, an efficient service sector can be a means of extending markets, reducing
transaction costs, and allowing specialization to be carried to a new level. Which
interpretation applies to Britain in the eighteenth and early nineteenth centuries?

Markets ceased to be the hub of the wholesale trade, and local craftsmen and
farmers selling their own goods gave way to professional market traders who

ere attracted by a central location and the low overheads of renting a stall. Weekly markets continued to be held in villages and small towns, and itinerant traders set up their stalls on a regular round. In larger towns, permanent traders were based in street markets and enclosed market halls which were erected by local authorities. These markets were not simply a prior stage of development before the emergence of fixed retail shops, for they specialized in different types of goods. The market traders concentrated on goods which were perishable, less valuable, and did not require processing, such as fruit, vegetables, fish, and meat. More expensive goods which were not perishable, which needed to be held in considerable quantities, or involved processing were located in fixed shops. Grocers, for example, held large and varied stocks of tea, coffee, sugar, rice, and spices which were expensive and needed specialist knowledge and equipment for blending, roasting, and sorting. Similarly, suppliers of textiles and accessories to fashionable markets needed to hold a wide range of fabrics and designs to appeal to a discriminating consumer. A market stall could supply the basic needs of the labourer for a cheap length of cloth; the wife of a professional man or landed gentleman demanded a wide range of the latest designs in comfortable surroundings with a subservient staff.

Markets and shops were supplemented by hawkers, pedlars, or chapmen who carried goods to consumers for sale. They were not necessarily direct competitors, for economic growth in the late seventeenth and eighteenth centuries shifted to areas outside the medieval system of markets, and they concentrated on different types of goods from permanent shops. Chapmen specialized in textiles and small goods such as lace and ribbon, light cotton and linen fabrics, and buttons and buckles which they could carry in packs on their backs, and which could be made into shirts and shifts by the housewife at home. An Act of 1696/7 obliged chapmen to obtain a licence, and 2,559 licences were issued in the first year.[14] London, with 501 licences, was an important centre where pedlars could obtain goods and travel into the country. But above all they were concentrated in the textile districts and west Midlands metal district, where they obtained the bulk of their goods to be carried in a circuit of farms and villages in the course of the year. These hawkers became less important in distributing small metal goods and textiles in the course of the eighteenth century, as producers came to rely on trade circulars and permanent shops opened in more villages. Nevertheless, itinerant pedlars did not disappear, even in the largest towns where there were considerable numbers of shops and permanent markets. Perishable commodities which were needed regularly, such as bread and milk, were distributed by street sellers, who were based on permanent dairies and bakeries rather than competing with fixed shops. 'Scotchmen' or 'Manchester men' made regular visits to working-class districts to sell clothing and household goods on credit, calling on women at home and collecting weekly payments which was clearly a sensible strategy where there was little disposable income. I addition, tinkers, coopers, plumbers, and glaziers toured urban streets an country roads, to repair pots and pans, sharpen knives and implements, men pipes and cisterns, and replace window panes. Many of these men were skille craftsmen who had a regular round, but there was also a casual fringe c underemployed men who undertook odd jobs. However, it was predominantl in London that the service sector was open to criticism as a refuge for low productivity, underemployed workers, such as the poverty-stricken crossin sweepers and hawkers who populated Charles Dickens's and Henry Mayhew' descriptions of the capital. But the metropolis was not typical of even the larges provincial cities. Not only was London cursed with a large pool of casual labou it was also exceptional in its size, and in the early development of wholesal markets such as Covent Garden for fruit and flowers, Spitalfields for vegetables and Billingsgate for fish. It was possible for street vendors to obtain supplies from these markets, and to hire a costermonger's barrow to carry inferior goods int working-class districts. In provincial towns, the role of the hawker was les important, limited to dealing with an occasional glut or disposing of stale good left at the end of the day.

The development of permanent retail shops was one of the most striking features of eighteenth-century Britain. Of course, the most well-developed form of retailing in the eighteenth century was the inn and alehouse, which wer found in every village and neighbourhood, but shops were not far behind. When the excise collected data on the number of shops in England and Wales in 1759 there were 141,700 shops in England and Wales, or one per 43.3 population; eve this large total was an underestimate, for stalls were excluded and only one shop allowed per building.[15] Clearly, retail shops were well developed by 1759 including both genteel shops for the prosperous middle class and gentry, an 'back-street' and village shops used by workers for commodities such as tea sugar, salt, and basic consumer goods. By 1759 retail shops were ceasing to operate within the framework of fairs and markets. In the late seventeenth an early eighteenth centuries, shopkeepers were still operating in a way which wa not far removed from face-to-face contact at a fair or market. William Stout, who set up a shop at Lancaster in 1688, travelled on horse to London and Sheffield to obtain supplies, and his pattern of trade was still similar to a stallholder in a market or fair: his sales depended upon customers coming to town for the weekly market, and the annual fair determined the timing of his journeys for stock. The supply of goods started to change from 1709, when he obtained his Sheffield goods by paying a commission to an ironmaster, and he relied on a cousin who set up a shop in the metropolis for his London purchases. By the middle of the eighteenth century, the provision of goods to shopkeepers was more efficient with the emergence of pattern cards, circulars, and commercial travellers, which allowed goods to be ordered as needed, from a wider range of competing suppliers. Abraham Dent, a country shopkeeper in Kirkby Stephen, utilized about 190 suppliers between 1756 and 1777, drawing his supplies from a wide area stretching from Kendal, to Penrith, Lancaster, Manchester, Newcastle, London, and Norwich.[16] Not only was he purchasing goods from other areas; he was also purchasing hosiery from local knitters for sale to army contractors in London, which gave him access to funds to cover his purchases from the metropolis. The mundane, small-scale activities of country shopkeepers such as Stout and Dent helped to integrate the national economy.

Changes in retailing in the eighteenth and early nineteenth centuries led to greater efficiency in distribution and created a more continuous market. The shift from discontinuous fairs or markets and itinerant pedlars, to permanent shops supplied by circulars, pattern cards, and commercial travellers, helped to reduce transaction costs. There was, of course, still scope for considerable change in distribution in the later nineteenth century. There were no department stores by 1850; neither were there any multiple stores, which emerged in the later nineteenth century in food and clothing. Shoes and woollen clothes were still bought from producer-retailers, who increasingly obtained components from sweat-shops rather than making the entire article in their own workshop. In the later nineteenth century, these trades started to move into factories, and chain stores were opened by firms such as Burtons and Clarks to sell mass-produced items. The largest stores in the early nineteenth century were drapers and haberdashers, who sold lighter textiles and accessories which were made into clothing at home or by milliners who were employed by the customers; it was usually these concerns which formed the basis for the growth of department stores. Until 1850, shops were still overwhelmingly family concerns, and small corner shops in working-class districts were often run by the wife of a working man, who obtained goods on credit and relied on her knowledge of the local community to extend credit to her customers. The distinction between wholesalers and retailers was not clear-cut by 1850, with the partial exception of London, and larger shopkeepers often combined retailing for more affluent customers with supplying small shopkeepers. Specialist firms did emerge, in colonial products such as tea, tobacco, and sugar, and tea-dealers such as Twinings of London sent price lists to shopkeepers around the country. But most of these commodities were still supplied loose for packing by the retailer, and it was only in the later nineteenth century that suppliers moved to prepackaged, branded goods and mass advertising. There was, then, considerable scope for change in retailing after 1850, which led to further gains in efficiency and reduction in transaction costs. Nevertheless major changes took place in the eighteenth and early nineteenth centuries, which created a much more regular constant market for consumers throughout the country, and contributed to a fall in transaction costs.

Merchants and International Trade

The leading businessmen in the major towns and cities of eighteenth-century Britain were merchants, who were usually wealthier than industrialists, and had a higher social status. They were recruited from the families of landed gentry and the well-to-do middle class in town and country, whose families were willing to pay substantial premiums for a mercantile training, as did the father of Thomas Snedell, a landowner, who paid £450 in 1719 for a five-year apprenticeship to a merchant in Leeds.[17] Most merchants formed partnerships in order to spread risks and to obtain more capital, and it was usually necessary to contribute a sizeable sum to the firm. In Leeds, a partner would need to bring about £1,500 to the firm up to the 1780s, and more in the late eighteenth century as the scale of production increased and trade shifted to long-distance markets in North America. But the merchant class was not simply the product of landed and professional society within Britain: it was cosmopolitan. Merchant houses in European trading centres such as Hamburg, Amsterdam, and Frankfurt sent junior partners to British cities, to obtain supplies of manufactures and to purchase colonial products such as tea, tobacco, and sugar from the East and West Indies and North America. London, Liverpool, Hull, Bristol, Glasgow, and Leeds were dominated by an oligarchy of merchant families in the eighteenth century, whose position was being challenged by the early nineteenth century with the emergence of other commercial and professional groups, the growth of larger industrial concerns, and the development of a greater degree of specialization.

By 1700, it was no longer usual for merchants to travel with their goods, selling them to foreign customers and purchasing a return cargo with the proceeds. It was more normal to rely on a 'supercargo', often the ship's master, who received a commission for selling the cargo assembled by the merchant and purchasing the return cargo. By the eighteenth century, supercargoes were in turn giving way to factors or commission houses based in foreign ports, who had discretion to sell cargoes dispatched by British merchants, buy local commodities, handle insurance, and collect payment; they could also finance the trade by allowing the merchant to draw bills of exchange on the goods. Where the trade with an area was sufficiently large, the merchant might establish a branch house in a foreign port, under the control of a partner. In either case, the essential point was the ame: merchants traded on their own account, owning the goods which were old overseas and purchasing imports. They were the crucial figures, bearing the risks of trade.

Merchants obtained goods from British producers in a number of ways, which influenced the structure of industry and its development. The relationship between merchants and producers in the cloth industries of the West Country and the West Riding of Yorkshire, for example, differed in two important respects. In the West Country, the dominant figures were 'gentlemen clothiers', who put out raw materials to specialist workers, controlling the whole process from the processing of raw wool through to finishing and dyeing the cloth. The finished article was usually sold to merchants based at Blackwell Hall in London, who were outsiders without any direct say in the production of cloth in the West Country. The cloth industry in the West Country had the danger of inflexibility, for production was concentrated in the hands of a small group of 'gentlemen clothiers', with little opportunity for new men to emerge from the ranks of dependent specialists, and reliance on outside merchants made the industry less responsive to market changes. In the woollen textile industry of Yorkshire, the pattern was different. There was a group of 'gentlemen merchants' based within the region at Leeds, comprising seventy-three merchant houses in 1781 with a dominant inner circle of twenty-four firms.[18] They bought unfinished cloth from small artisan clothiers in the woollen trade and putters out in the worsted trade, who took their product for sale at cloth halls at Leeds or Wakefield, and the piece halls at Bradford and Halifax. Increasingly, merchants bypassed the halls and purchased directly from the producers, at first from the larger putters out in the worsted industry, and from the early nineteenth century in the woollen sector. The merchants were not directly involved with production, but they were concerned with finishing cloth for export. The merchants usually paid independent cloth-dressers to finish and dye the cloth in the early eighteenth century, but in the course of the century many acquired their own workshops. The 'gentlemen merchants', in other words, provided a more effective link between producers and consumers than the 'gentlemen clothiers' and Blackwell Hall merchants, for they were in closer contact with the producers of cloth, which they finished to meet the needs of export markets.

The capital accumulated by merchants was often not transferred into factory production; rather, merchants became more concerned with the provision of financial services than with trading in goods on their own account. Manufacturers were more likely to move into merchanting, taking a direct and active role in marketing. The shift in the pattern of trade could make the expertise of merchants redundant, such as in Leeds where merchants who specialized in European markets found it difficult to adjust to the Americas after 1793, and

gentlemen merchants who were accustomed to spend their time in count
society were not attracted by the prospects of building up businesses in Sout
America. The increase in the fixed capital of industrialists gave them a greate
incentive to maintain a high level of output in order to reduce unit costs an
cover overheads, especially when the impact of intense competition and fallin
prices at the end of the Napoleonic wars squeezed profit margins. Merchant
were reluctant to take risks in the difficult market environment, but industrialist
needed to maintain production, and had an incentive to push trade and captur
the profits of the merchants. It was a relatively simple matter for a producer c
cloth in the West Riding, for example, to take on the final stages of production
by using the services of independent dressers and dyers, or establishing his own
finishing department. By contrast, merchants were less inclined to integrat
backwards into manufacturing: it was one thing to arrange the finishing and
dyeing of cloth, which could be left to specialist contractors, but it was quite
another matter to take over production with its very different demands o
managing a large work-force and investment in fixed capital. Merchants were
more likely to remove their capital into land, government stocks, and transpor
securities than to invest in industry; those who did not become *rentiers* o
landowners were more likely to move into the professions, and the provision o
financial services to manufacturers who handled their own sales. The result wa
a shift in the social structure of provincial towns, as the mercantile oligarchy wa
remade.

A number of large industrialists were already taking an active role in market
ing by the later eighteenth century, before the squeeze on profits at the end of the
war. Matthew Boulton and Josiah Wedgwood entered into partnership with
merchants who travelled Europe looking for custom; Samuel Oldknow attended
the great European fairs; and Robert Peel employed agents and travellers in
North America and Europe. Low prices and profits in the early nineteenth
century led to a change in strategy, from direct control over distribution to
reliance on commission agents who were resident in foreign cities. The proportion of output sold overseas increased, markets were more dispersed, and it was
more difficult for small and medium firms than market leaders such as Boulton
and Wedgwood to assume the burden of marketing in foreign countries. Agents
were able to act for a large number of different British producers who dispatched
goods on their own account for sale on commission. Manufacturers had the
prospect of capturing the merchant's profit margin, but there was also a greater
market risk and they had to wait for payment until their goods were sold by the
agents, who were often obliged to offer extended credit to the customer. Most
manufacturers therefore continued to sell part of their output to middlemen in
order to reduce risks. John Foster, the West Riding producer of worsted, sold

inished and dyed cloth in the North American market through agents; by contrast, in European markets he sold unfinished cloth to merchants, such as Jacob Behrens from Hamburg who settled in Bradford in 1838, buying on commission for foreign customers, and undertaking finishing and dyeing to their specification. These changes in marketing were associated with the development of acceptance houses which provided manufacturers with credit. These specialists in the finance of foreign trade developed from the ranks of merchants who had previously bought and sold goods on their own account. They were transformed into merchant banks who were concerned with two tasks: providing finance for manufacturers to send their goods to commission agents; and floating loans on the London money market for foreign governments, railway companies, and other investments in an expanding world economy. Barings, for example, moved from direct involvement in importing raw cotton from the southern United States and exporting manufactures to the provision of trade finance and floating loans for Argentina.

A further set of specialists emerged in the early nineteenth century: brokers who acted on behalf of merchants and factors in the import trades. A merchant in London or Liverpool might receive a consignment of, say, raw cotton from the Levant or the southern United States which he wished to sell to a spinner in Derbyshire or Lancashire. Until about 1815, the importing merchant and manufacturer were linked by 'dealers' who bought cotton and took it to a warehouse in the manufacturing centre, and sold it to the spinners. From about 1815, dealers were increasingly replaced by selling and buying brokers, who acted for the importers and spinners. Unlike dealers, the brokers were not buying and selling on their own account, and made their profit from commissions and interest on credit. The brokers had detailed knowledge both of raw material supplies in the port and of the requirements of the cotton-spinners, who were no longer limited to the stocks in the dealer's warehouse, for they could purchase precisely what they needed at the port, at short notice. The brokers provided knowledge which helped in the creation of a market, and they also provided finance to merchants and spinners. The brokers often paid freight charges, import duties, and insurance of a cargo of cotton before it was sold, and they offered advances to merchants on the security of consignments; the spinners were allowed three months to pay for their purchases. Such brokers became increasingly important figures in London and Liverpool, making a market in a wide range of goods, and linking importers of raw materials and colonial goods to industrialists and distributors. The advances made by brokers on the security of goods consigned for sale in Britain were crucial to the expansion of foreign trade.

This pattern of marketing and finance has been criticized by historians of the later nineteenth century, who feel that it caused problems for British industry.

British exports, they suggest, suffered from reliance upon commission agents, which meant that there was little contact between the foreign consumer and the home producer. Above all, it is claimed that merchant bankers were more concerned with foreign loans and the finance of overseas trade, and neglected the needs of domestic industry for investment. The merchant bankers were socially distinct from provincial industrialists, and it is argued that they formed marriage alliances with the landed aristocracy and shaped economic policy in the interests of finance rather than industry. The validity of these criticisms is open to dispute in the late nineteenth century, and it would certainly be inappropriate to apply them to the period before 1850 when British industry was establishing an unrivalled dominance of world trade. The use of commission agents allowed manufacturers to penetrate new markets, and to escape from problems of declining profit and over-production; the provision of trade credit by acceptance houses freed industrialists to use their own capital in production. It is by no means obvious that the German or American pattern of investment by bankers in industrial concerns was preferable to the British pattern of provision of trade credit, which gave industrialists a greater degree of flexibility and autonomy.

Conclusion

Between 1700 and 1850, some of the most significant changes in the British economy were in marketing and distribution: goods were more easily moved around the country as a result of changes in the transport system; and the pattern of wholesale and retail trade was transformed. The consequent fall in transaction costs was as significant as changes in production: markets became more integrated, and competition less 'imperfect', which allowed specialization to develop, both in agriculture and in manufacturing. This in turn led to a fall in costs, as regional economies concentrated on goods in which they had the greatest comparative advantage; the division of labour could be carried further; there were internal economies in the firm and external economies as a result of the emergence of specialist services within regional networks of towns.

NOTES

1. W. D. Rubinstein, *Men of Property: The Very Wealthy in Britain since the Industrial Revolution* (1981), 44–5.
2. Quoted in E. P. Thompson, 'The Moral Economy of the English Crowd in the Eighteenth Century', *Past and Present*, 50 (1971), 132.
3. A. Smith, *An Inquiry into the Nature and Causes of the Wealth of Nations* (repr. 1937), 493 (book iv, ch. v).
4. R. Perren, 'Markets and Marketing', in J. Thirsk (ed.), *The Agrarian History of England and Wales*, vi: *1750–1950* (Cambridge, 1989), 223.

5. D. Defoe, *A Tour through the Whole Island of Great Britain* (1724–6), i. 80–5.

6. Ibid. i. 51.

7. J. Chartres, 'The Marketing of Agricultural Produce', in J. Thirsk (ed.), *The Agrarian History of England and Wales*, vii: *1650–1750: Agrarian Change* (Cambridge, 1985), 411.

8. P. Mathias, *The Brewing Industry in England, 1700–1830* (Cambridge, 1959), 12, 24, 26, 558.

9. Thompson, 'Moral Economy', 79.

0. Ibid. 126.

1. R. Scola, *Feeding the Victorian City: The Food Supply of Manchester, 1770–1870* (Manchester, 1992), 154, 161.

2. Quoted in W. Thwaites, 'Dearth and the Marketing of Agricultural Produce: Oxfordshire c.1750–1800', *Agricultural History Review*, 33 (1985), 128.

3. Quoted in R. Wells, 'The Revolt of the South-west, 1800–1801: A Study in English Popular Protest', *Social History*, 6 (1977), 716.

4. M. Spufford, *The Great Reclothing of Rural England: Petty Chapmen and their Wares in the Seventeenth Century* (1984), 18.

5. H.-C. Mui and L. H. Mui, *Shops and Shopkeeping in Eighteenth-Century England* (Kingston, 1989), 40.

6. T. S. Willan, *An Eighteenth-Century Shopkeeper: Abraham Dent of Kirkby Stephen* (Manchester, 1970), 28–41; J. D. Marshall (ed.), *The Autobiography of William Stout of Lancaster, 1665–1752* (Manchester, 1967), 89, 160.

7. R. G. Wilson, *Gentleman Merchants: The Merchant Community in Leeds, 1700–1830* (Manchester, 1971), 24.

8. Ibid., viii, 18–19, 239–40.

FURTHER READING

Alexander, D., *Retailing in England during the Industrial Revolution* (1970).

Baker, D., 'The Marketing of Corn in the First Half of the Eighteenth Century', *Agricultural History Review*, 18 (1970).

Blackman, J., 'The Food Supply of an Industrial Town: A Study of Sheffield's Public Markets, 1780–1900', *Business History*, 5 (1963).

Bohstedt, J., *Riot and Community Politics in England and Wales, 1790–1810* (Cambridge, Mass., 1983).

Booth, A., 'Food Riots in the North-West of England, 1790–1801', *Past and Present*, 77 (1977).

Buck, N. S., *The Development of the Organisation of Anglo-American Trade, 1800–50* (New Haven, Conn., 1925).

Chapman, S. D., 'British Marketing Enterprise: The Changing Role of Merchants, Manufacturers and Financiers, 1700–1860', *Business History Review*, 53 (1979).

——— *The Rise of Merchant Banking* (1984).

——— *Merchant Enterprise in Britain: From the Industrial Revolution to the First World War* (Cambridge, 1992).

Charlesworth, A., 'From the Moral Economy of Devon to the Political Economy of Manchester, 1790–1812', *Social History*, 18 (1993).

Chartres, J. A., *Internal Trade in England, 1500–1700* (1977).

—— 'The Marketing of Agricultural Produce', in J. Thirsk (ed.), *The Agrarian History* *England and Wales*, v: *1640–1740*, 2: *Agrarian Change* (Cambridge, 1985).

Edwards, M. M., *The Growth of the British Cotton Trade, 1780–1815* (Manchester, 1967).

Fisher, F. J., 'The Development of the London Food Market, 1540–1640', *Economic History Review*, 5 (1935).

Gatty, R., *Portrait of a Merchant Prince: James Morrison, 1789–1857* (Northallerton, 1976).

Gras, N. S. B., *The Evolution of the English Corn Market from the Twelfth to the Eighteenth Century* (Cambridge, Mass., 1915).

Hyde, F. E., Parkinson, B. B., and Marriner, S., 'The Cotton Broker and the Rise of the Liverpool Cotton Market', *Economic History Review*, 2nd ser. 8 (1955–6).

Jones, S. R. H., 'The Country Trade and the Marketing and Distribution of Birmingham Hardware, 1750–1810', *Business History*, 26 (1984).

Lee, C. H., 'Marketing Organisation and Policy in the Cotton Trade: M'Connel and Kennedy of Manchester, 1795–1835', *Business History*, 10 (1968).

McKendrick, N., 'Josiah Wedgwood: Eighteenth-Century Entrepreneur in Salesmanship and Marketing Techniques', *Economic History Review*, 2nd ser. 12 (1959–60).

Marshall, J.-D. (ed.), *The Autobiography of William Stout of Lancaster, 1665–1752* (Manchester 1967).

Mathias, P., *The Brewing Industry in England, 1700–1830* (Cambridge, 1959).

Minchinton, W. E., 'The Merchants in England in the Eighteenth Century', *Explorations in Entrepreneurial History*, 10 (1957–8).

Mui, H.-C. and L. H., *Shops and Shopkeeping in Eighteenth-Century England* (Kingston, 1989).

Perren, R., 'Markets and Marketing', in G. E. Mingay (ed.), *The Agrarian History of England and Wales*, vi: *1750–1850* (Cambridge, 1989).

Rowlands, M. B., *Masters and Men in the West Midland Metalware Trades before the Industrial Revolution* (Manchester, 1975).

Rubinstein, W. D., *Men of Property: The Very Wealthy in Britain since the Industrial Revolution* (1981).

Scola, R., *Feeding the Victorian City: The Food Supply of Manchester, 1770–1870* (Manchester 1992).

Sigsworth, E. M., *Black Dyke Mills: A History* (Liverpool, 1958).

Spufford, M., *The Great Reclothing of Rural England: Petty Chapmen and their Wares in the Seventeenth Century* (1984).

Thompson, E. P., 'The Moral Economy of the English Crowd in the Eighteenth Century', *Past and Present*, 50 (1971).

Thwaites, W., 'Dearth and the Marketing of Agricultural Produce: Oxfordshire c.1750–1800', *Agricultural History Review*, 33 (1985).

Wadsworth, A. P., and Mann, J. de L., *The Cotton Trade and Industrial Lancashire, 1600–1780* (Manchester, 1931).

Wells, R., 'The Revolt of the South-West, 1800–1801: A Study in English Popular Protest', *Social History*, 6 (1977).

—— *Wretched Faces: Famine in Wartime England, 1763–1803* (Gloucester, 1988).

Westerfield, R. B., *Middlemen in English Business, 1660–1760* (New Haven, Conn., 1915).

Willan, T. S., *An Eighteenth-Century Shopkeeper: Abraham Dent of Kirkby Stephen* (Manchester, 1970).

Williams, D. E., 'Were "Hunger" Rioters Really Hungry? Some Demographic Evidence', *Past and Present*, 71 (1976).

—— 'Morals, Markets and the English Crowd in 1766', *Past and Present*, 104 (1984).

Williams, D. M., 'Liverpool Merchants and the Cotton trade, 1820–50', in J. R. Harris (ed.), *Liverpool and Merseyside: Essays in the Economic and Social History of the Port and its Hinterland* (1969).

—— 'Merchanting in the First Half of the Nineteenth Century: The Liverpool Timber Trade', *Business History* (1966).

Wilson, R. G., *Gentlemen Merchants: The Merchant Community in Leeds, 1700–1830* (Manchester, 1971).

CHAPTER 13

Banks and Money

Britain developed two distinctive banking systems in the eighteenth and early nineteenth centuries, one in Scotland and the other in England and Wales, whose relative merits were debated by contemporaries and are contested by historians. Rondo Cameron, in his comparative analysis of banking and economic development, had no doubt which was the more efficient and conducive to economic growth. Scotland, he claimed, had 'the strongest, most competitive, most efficient banking system of the times', in contrast to England where there was a sorry tale of missed opportunities. 'At almost every point at which banking and monetary policy might have been used constructively to promote economic growth', he complains, 'the authorities either made the wrong decision or took no action at all.'[1] The result, if Cameron is to be believed, was that banks assisted the process of rapid industrialization in Scotland, whereas in England and Wales economic growth took place almost despite the banks.

There is a long tradition of criticism of the English banking system for neglecting the needs of industry, which argues that the City of London and the Bank of England were more interested in the needs of overseas lending and public finance. A contrast is often drawn with Germany, where banks were closely involved in the finance of industrial concerns in the later nineteenth century. But there is a danger of reading this criticism of British, and especially English, banks into the past. After all, the needs of industry for fixed capital were much less in the eighteenth and early nineteenth centuries than at later stages of industrialization, and the provision of circulating capital or credit could be much more crucial. British banks had less need to provide fixed capital than German banks; their main function was to meet short-term credit needs, improving the means of remittance and increasing the supply of money through the issue of notes. Consequently, British banks were 'credit banks' rather than industrial banks such as characterized Germany in the later nineteenth century. Arguably British banks were appropriate to the needs of the economy in general and industry in particular at the time of their emergence, but were unable to adapt to the needs of a mature industrial economy. Perhaps the British banking system can be redeemed before 1850, and damned after 1850 when it failed to adjust to changes in the needs of industry, continuing to concentrate on short-term credit rather than long-term funds.

Criticism extends beyond the banks themselves to the policy of the state, and in particular the development of monetary policy. Industrial capital, it is often argued, was subordinate to the interests of finance and the land which dominated the formulation of policy. The adoption of a 'hard' money policy based on the gold standard and a restriction of note issue has been portrayed as benefiting creditors at the expense of debtors, and the financial interests of the City against productive enterprise. Can monetary policy be interpreted as a triumph of the 'gentlemanly capitalists' of finance and landowners, or was it the outcome of a more complex process of debate?

Scottish Banks

The creation of the Bank of England in 1694 preceded the Act of Union of 1707 between England and Scotland, and its monopoly of joint-stock banking was not extended north of the border. Scotland did have its own privileged bank—the Bank of Scotland, which was granted a charter by an Act of the Scottish parliament in 1695—but its position was rather different from that of the Bank of England. It did not have the same monopoly rights and it was barred from lending to the state, so that it relied upon the issue of bank notes for its profits. Rivals soon emerged. The Bank of Scotland was Jacobite, and in 1727 a charter was granted to a rival Whig creation, the Royal Bank of Scotland. A third chartered company, the British Linen Co., which was formed in 1746 to encourage the development of the linen industry, increasingly moved into banking. These three Edinburgh-based 'public banks' co-operated with a number of private bankers, forming what their critics saw as a closed oligarchy. They were, however, soon challenged by the emergence of rival banking companies in the 1750s and 1760s in other Scottish cities, such as the Banking Company of Aberdeen in 1767. Scotland escaped the requirement which was imposed on English banks in 1708, that they should have no more than six partners, and the Aberdeen company had 197 partners on its formation.[2] Such banks brought together the leading businessmen of a town in order to mobilize savings for local lending, and to make a profit from note issues.

The initial response of the public banks to this competition was to bury their differences, and to seek a monopoly of the issue of notes. They failed, for freedom of issue was maintained by an Act of 1765 and the public banks had to learn to live with the banking companies. In 1771 the Bank of Scotland and Royal Bank agreed to accept the notes of ten of the strongest banks, who were admitted to the 'note exchange' at which banks settled their balances. The Edinburgh public banks' share of total liabilities declined from 77 to 54 per cent between 1744 and 1802, and the private banks fell even more from 23 to 9 per cent. Meanwhile, the banking companies rose from nothing to 37 per cent, and a dense network of banks was created across the country. In the early nineteenth century, the banking companies were themselves challenged by joint-stock banks, largely based in Glasgow, which aimed to create a national branch network. The first, the Commercial Bank of Scotland, was created in 1810 and had thirty-one branches by 1826. By 1850 there had been a fundamental shift: the public banks' share of total liabilities stood at 33 per cent, private banks had disappeared, banking companies had slumped to 3 per cent, and the joint-stock banks surged to 64 per cent.[3] The Glasgow banks became more dynamic and aggressive than their rivals in Edinburgh.

The proponents of the Scottish banking system stressed that its flexibility and dynamism contributed to the development of the Scottish economy. The Scottish banking system, so they claim, was the 'least inhibited in Europe', for the absence of legal impediments to entry fostered competition, encouraged the rapid development of banking services, and stimulated the creation of credit. The banks had a wide coverage: by 1845 there were 19 banks of issue and about 400 branches, which amounted to one office to 7,200 people or double the level in England. Bank assets per inhabitant grew faster than in England, moving from parity in the 1770s to a ratio of 5:2 in favour of Scotland by 1844.[4] The note exchange system was a guarantee of stability and solvency, for any bank which was tempted to over-issue would have a balance against it at settlement. The danger of a run on the banks was reduced by the existence of a branch network, and by the limited reliance on specie. Small denomination notes were issued, which removed problems in the supply of money, monetizing the economy and encouraging the use of banks by a large part of the population for savings and payment. Indeed, Adam Smith claimed that the Scottish economy largely dispensed with the use of specie: 'the business of the country is almost entirely carried on by means of the paper of these different banking companies. . . . Silver very seldom appears . . . and gold still seldomer.'[5] Scottish banks did not need to hold expensive gold reserves, and the ready acceptance of notes allowed them to use their own unissued notes as security, so making it possible to run small branches which would otherwise have been uneconomic. Not only did the low gold reserve contribute to the density of the banking network; it also made the acceptance of small accounts feasible and the payment of interest on deposits affordable, which stimulated the supply of savings. Small branches gathered in deposits in saving areas, moving them to branches in urban areas where they could be used by growing industries. Indeed, another distinctive feature of Scottish banking was its willingness to provide assistance to industry and trade through the 'cash credit' or 'running cash' system which was introduced by the Royal Bank of Scotland in 1728. A merchant or industrialist was allowed to draw up to a specified maximum sum in the bank's notes, such as the cash credit of £12,500 offered to the Carron Iron Co. by the Royal Bank in 1772; these loans did not have a fixed term and could be repaid when convenient. This system, it is argued by admirers of the Scottish system, contributed to the rapid industrialization of the Scottish economy. The Scottish banking system has, therefore, been seen as a paragon of efficiency and dynamism.

Admiration for the Scottish system should be moderated in a number of respects. The coincidence of the emergence of a banking system and the development of Scottish industry does not, after all, mean that the one caused the other. It is a moot point whether the absence of regulation led to a greater freedom of entry and competition at a local level than in England, for banking companies could be local monopolies created by the élite of a town, unlike England where the six-partner rule produced a number of competitors. The banking companies could become cautious, and many turned towards government securities at the end of the eighteenth century. Certainly, the Scottish banking system created a large amount of liquidity and was very successful in generating means of payment, but there was always the danger that it was at the expense of stability. Although there were fewer failures than amongst English country banks this was not necessarily a sign of the superiority of the Scottish banking system. The note exchange was not really a substitute for a central bank, and it is doubtful whether Scottish banking should be seen as an independent system: the Bank of England was always in the background, which allowed the Scots to operate on a low cash reserve.

The financial crisis of 1825 marked a widening of the divergence between Scottish and English banks. Rigid controls were imposed on the issue of notes in England, but Scottish banks were able to convince parliament that small notes were crucial to their operation. The freedom of the Scottish system was eventually curtailed by the Act of 1845, which required banks to hold a costly gold reserve, and controlled the note circulation. The Scottish banking system had already started to change as a few joint-stock banks became dominant and the Act of 1845, by checking the formation of new banks, contributed to the emergence of a cartel. The branch system meant that the price of money was more or less uniform across the country and it made sense, at a time of low profits, to agree rates for borrowing and lending in order to avoid destructive battles. The emerging cartel could not be easily challenged by a newcomer because of the cost of acquiring a branch network, and the Scottish banking system consequently shifted from being open and competitive to closed and controlled.

Banking in England

The English banking system has been criticized as inappropriate to industrialization. The Bank of England's monopoly of joint-stock banking and the six-partner rule of 1708, it has been argued, did 'much harm by depriving the country of a banking system commensurate with a period of rapid economic growth'.[6] But can this harsh judgement be sustained? Did the English banking system impose costs and constraints upon the development of the economy in the eighteenth and early nineteenth centuries, by limiting the supply of capital or creating barriers to monetizing the economy by restrictions on note issue?

The institutional form of English banks was different from that in Scotland, at least until the 1820s. There were two types of bank. The first were the London private bankers in the West End and in the City. The West End bankers developed in response to the need of aristocrats and gentry to transfer rents to London to cover periods of residence in the capital; they emerged from the ranks of scriveners, merchants, brokers, and goldsmiths, such as Hoare's and Child's. The West End bankers concentrated on the needs of landowners for mortgages, leaving the discounting of bills of exchange or loans to stockbrokers to specialist banks clustered on Lombard Street. These banks emerged from the industrial and commercial world of the City. In 1754, for example, the firm of Vere, Glyn and Hallifax opened in Lombard Street, bringing together Joseph Vere (a private banker), Richard Glyn (a supplier of dyestuffs to silk manufacturers), and Thomas Hallifax (a grocer from Yorkshire who had become a clerk in Vere's bank); in 1772, Glyn and Hallifax were joined by William and Charles Mills, leading merchants in the East India trade. In the late eighteenth century, these City banks increasingly came to act as the London agents for a second type of bank: the country banks.

The country banks were local banks, usually with a single branch. There were few barriers to entry, for there was no legal impediment to forming a bank, the capital requirement was low, and they were restricted to six partners. The country banks usually developed as an ancillary activity to the main business of the partners, and specialization was in many cases delayed until the emergence of joint-stock banks after 1826. Their origins were diverse. It was a short step for attorneys, who collected rents or held trust funds and acted as intermediaries in the mortgage market, to move into the provision of banking services. Traders needed to transfer money from the sale of goods, and collectors of government revenue to remit taxes and excise duties to London in the form of bills or drafts. Other recruits came from industry. Circulating capital was, of course, vital to most industries, and industrialists were consequently heavily involved in finance, especially in Lancashire where the bill of exchange was used extensively. Reliance on credit meant that any industrialist was obliged to become a banker of sorts, and the shortage of a local means of payment provided an incentive to move into the issue of notes. The country banks therefore emerged from the ranks of existing business, by slow stages and often without abandoning their initial activity. One of the earliest of the country banks, the Nottingham firm of Smith and Co., grew from Thomas Smith's involvement in the hosiery trade, which obliged him to remit funds to London. This led him to become a subcommissioner of the excise in 1671, which gave him a valuable source of funds to develop his business, and it was a natural step for other merchants and landowners in the east Midlands to use his services to remit their funds to London. Similarly, the Gurneys of Norwich, who became one of the major country bankers, were involved in the East Anglian cloth industry as worsted manufacturers and yarn and wool merchants, which gave them links throughout the region and with London. In 1775, John and Henry Gurney created a distinct banking firm—the Norfolk and Norwich Bank—which had an extensive network of twenty-one banks in East Anglia by 1830. The first bank in Manchester—Jones, Loyd and Co.—started as a tea-dealer, and the first bank in Birmingham—Taylor and Lloyd—was established in 1765 by John Taylor, a button manufacturer, and Sampson Lloyd II, an ironmaster.

The number of country banks increased in the second half of the eighteenth century, from something over 100 in the early 1780s to about 300 by 1800. Licences for the issue of bank notes stood at a peak of 783 in 1810, which included some branches as well as separate banking concerns, after which the number of country banks started a slow decline, with a recovery in the early 1820s before a sudden and permanent fall with the crash of 1825–6.[7] The crisis was also instrumental in convincing parliament of the virtues of joint-stock banking: in 1826 the formation of note-issuing joint stock banks was permitted outside a 65-mile radius of London; and in 1833 joint-stock banking was permitted within this area, without the right to issue notes. The legislation of 1826 and 1833 allowed English banks to operate, as the Huddersfield Banking Co. announced on its formation in 1827, 'on the system hitherto so successfully adopted in Scotland' and the company, not surprisingly, recruited its first manager from the Arbroath Banking Co. By 1850, there were 99 joint-stock banks in England and Wales with 576 offices, in comparison with 327 private banks with 518 offices.[8]

Despite the emergence of joint-stock banks, the English banking system for many years continued to be more fragmented than the Scottish, with a less

TABLE 13.1. *English note issue*

1775	Notes to be at least £1 denomination
1777	Notes to be at least £5 denomination
1797	Suspension of convertibility of Bank notes into cash. Notes of £1 denomination were permitted
1819	Resumption of convertibility from 1821
1826	No further notes of less than £5 to be issued and existing notes to be withdrawn in 1829. The Bank of England was empowered to open branches in the provinces in order to increase the circulation of its notes; and offered discount facilities to banks on condition they relinquished their own issues
1844	The Bank Charter Act prohibited banks which were not already issuers from issuing notes; and once issue was suspended for any reason, it could not be resumed. Existing issuers were not to increase their issue beyond the level of 1844. Any banks which combined and had more than six partners were to lose the right to issue.

developed branch network. Many English joint-stock banks were local, based upon an existing country bank with only a few branches in the immediate vicinity, such as Stuckey's Banking Co. The Stuckey family were involved in coastal trading in the Bristol Channel and emerged as country bankers at Langport in Somerset around 1770, with a few local branches. In 1826 Vincent Stuckey decided to convert the business into a joint-stock bank, and he acquired another country bank in Bristol. By 1837 his venture had a head office in Langport and eighteen branches in Somerset and the immediate vicinity. Other joint-stock banks were newcomers without roots in country banking, such as the West of England and South Wales District Bank, which was formed in 1834 with a head office in Bristol; by 1837 it had fifteen branches in the industrial towns of south Wales and the market towns of the West Country. These branch networks were, at best, regional and the majority of concerns were small. In 1850 the average number of branches was still only 5.8 per joint-stock bank in England and Wales, in comparison with 24 in Scotland.[9] The other major contrast between England and Scotland was in the restriction on small denomination bank notes. The Bank of England issued notes of a high denomination which were only payable in London, and other banks were increasingly constrained (see Table 13.1). Paper currency was effectively restricted by the amount of specie, with the exception of the period of 'suspension' from 1797 to 1821, and the monetary environment in England was much less liberal than in Scotland.

Whether economic growth was frustrated is an open question, for restrictive regulations may generate innovations to circumvent the intentions of legislators. Indeed, a strong case can be made that the English banking system was *not* a hindrance to economic growth, and that the slower development of a branch network had an economic rationale. In Scotland, most branches received more than they lent, operating as deposit-gatherers to feed lending branches in the urban, industrial districts in order to overcome the shortage of funds. Arguably, there was less need for an extensive deposit-gathering network of branches in England, where funds were more readily available. Neither did the limits to the geographical spread of branches matter, provided a mechanism was devised for transferring funds around the country from 'saving' to 'investing' areas. This was provided by the development of interconnections between provincial country banks and the private banks and bill brokers of London. The English banking system may be described as 'loose-jointed',[10] which is not the same as un-co-ordinated. Country bankers in some parts of the country received more money than could be invested within the locality. These 'saving' areas were usually agricultural districts or had declining industry where money was not being reinvested, such as East Anglia and the West Country. The Gurneys' branch network drew savings from East Anglia and directed them to the London money market, to which country bankers in industrial 'investing' areas such as Lancashire could look for assistance. Credit surpluses and deficiencies were adjusted in the London discount market, which equalized the demand and supply of funds between regional banks: surplus funds arriving in London from East Anglia were used to purchase bills of exchange from Lancashire and other deficit areas. Some large country bankers themselves acquired a London branch and joined the ranks of City bankers, such as Abel Smith of Nottingham who entered into partnership with John Payne of London in 1758, or Lloyds of Birmingham who opened a London office in 1770. Most country banks, however, relied upon City firms such as Glyn, Hallifax, Mills, who were agents for four country banks in 1790 and forty-nine in 1830.[11] By the end of the eighteenth century, specialist bill brokers or discount houses emerged in London who were the linchpin of the English banking system by the early nineteenth century. By judging the reliability of bills, brokers made large numbers of bills negotiable which would otherwise have been rejected; they bought from those with a surplus and sold them to bankers looking for an outlet for their funds.

Ultimately, the need for bill brokers was removed by the development of joint-stock banks with an integrated branch network straddling areas of saving and investing. At first, however, joint-stock banks were *more* reliant upon bill brokers than the country banks, not only because their branch networks were too limited to transfer funds internally, but also because they took deposits from customers in return for the payment of interest. They could only offer high interest rates to attract deposits by keeping their resources fully employed, so that they were heavily reliant upon bills of exchange, which they might need to rediscount when cash was required. The result was a great increase in the London discount business, and the bill market reached the peak of its importance for the local distribution of credit between the 1830s and 1860s. The connection between the joint-stock banks and the bill brokers was encouraged by the policy of the Bank of England. Although the Bank was the final source of funds for rediscounting bills, it refused facilities to any bill endorsed by a note-issuing joint-stock bank. This separation between commercial banks and the Bank of England encouraged the use of bill brokers or discount houses who played a vital role in stabilizing the system; they were admitted to rediscounting at the Bank in 1830. London private bankers, who did have access to the rediscounting at the Bank, also became more dependent on bill brokers. Until the financial crisis of 1825, they used their resources to the full to purchase bills, and rediscounted at the Bank to obtain cash. The experience of 1825 showed that the Bank might not be able to cope, and London bankers started to hold bills until redemption, ensuring liquidity by a second line of bills 'on call' (repayable on demand) with brokers. They no longer met an increased demand for cash by rediscounting at the Bank of England; rather, they called in loans from bill brokers, who sought funds from another bank and only in the last resort turned to the Bank of England for rediscount. The discount houses therefore acted as a regulator, and there was no need to turn to the central bank until it was absolutely necessary. The rise of joint-stock banking, the development of 'call loans', the end of rediscounting by London banks, and the admittance of brokers to discount facilities at the Bank, all contributed to the development of a highly efficient money market system around Lombard Street which meant that the slow spread of branches did not lead to serious problems in the movement of funds around the country.

A further charge against English banks is that they ignored the needs of industry, through their insistence upon short loans and their failure to develop 'cash credits'. The banks' main liabilities were notes and the deposits of the public, both of which were subject to immediate withdrawal, so that there was always the possibility of a run on banks as in 1825–6, when ninety-three banks in England and Wales suspended payment. Banks were vulnerable and needed liquid assets which could easily be called upon to meet demands. Bills of exchange met this requirement, unlike long-term loans to industrialists. The banks were consequently more concerned with credit than investment, but this is not necessarily a criticism at a time when circulating capital was more important than fixed capital. The banks had an important role in the 'credit matrix' and the provision of short-term capital, which allowed industrialists to free their own resources for long-term investment. If anything, the increase in fixed capital made industrialists more anxious about credit stability: a merchant could reduce the scale of his operations when credit was stringent, whereas a manufacturer had to keep his plant in operation to hold down unit costs.

The banks were more responsive to the needs of industry than was admitted by the authors of handbooks on banking principles. Country bankers were often drawn from the ranks of industrialists and after 1826 they were often directors of joint-stock banks, which remained local concerns dominated by local businessmen who saw banking as complementary to their other interests. There could even be a greater involvement of industrialists in joint-stock banks: although Manchester cotton interests were not closely involved in country banks, they controlled eight joint-stock banks formed between 1828 and 1836 in order to preserve a sound credit system and to sustain the bill system which was crucial to their operation. Although country banks and early joint-stock banks might restrict firms outside their circle of partners and directors to short-term credit, they offered greater flexibility to industrial concerns with which they had interlocking interests. Indeed, bank finance could be more important than self-finance, especially during periods of expansion. By receiving deposits from the public, and then employing the funds within the bankers' industrial venture, banks were in effect circumventing the law of partnership and restrictions on joint-stock organization. The capital of industrial concerns was increased beyond the means of the partners, without the depositor incurring the dangers of unlimited liability. Although English banking principles opposed overdraft facilities on the lines of Scottish cash credit, in practice they were common. Banks in Lancashire and Yorkshire were usually willing to allow an overdraft of 10 per cent of the annual turnover of an account. Loans were also made on the security of merchandise or property, such as a credit of £5,000 in 1828 from the Huddersfield Banking Co. to Joshua Lockwood and Co. which was backed by the lease of a factory.[12] Although banks were under pressure to maintain liquidity, they were not as reluctant to provide loans as their critics have claimed, and there does not seem to have been a serious shortage of industrial loans.

The reality of the English banking system differed from the principles which were laid down by the end of the nineteenth century. By discounting bills, banks were creating currency which was necessary for the growth of the economy; and their provision of 'external' credit financed the production, movement, and marketing of goods. They might well have introduced more instability than internal or 'open' credit, but it is difficult to see how the economy could have expanded without the banks to provide funds. Contrasts with German industrial banks are of little relevance to the early nineteenth century, for it was the merger movement of the late nineteenth century, with the shift from locally based country and joint-stock banks towards a more centralized system controlled in

London, which severed ties between bankers and industrialists, and led to an erosion of local discretion.

'Resumption' and Power

The debate over monetary policy was more than a dry, technical matter left to bankers: it was one of the crucial political issues of the early nineteenth century, involving fundamental issues of power. The intention, when the right to exchange notes into gold was suspended in 1797, was to resume convertibility six months after peace. However, at the end of the war in 1815, the circulation of paper money was large and prices were high, so that resumption would only be possible after a period of deflation which would bring the value of paper money into line with gold. Deflation threatened some groups in society, such as farmers and landowners who had invested in agricultural improvements at a time of high wartime prices, and the government decided in 1816 that resumption should be postponed for two years. In this interval, the Bank could gradually curtail issues and allow a smooth, controlled adjustment to a lower level of prices, costs, and rents which would protect existing investment, maintain the cultivation of land taken into use during the war, and expand output by inducing investment in 'high farming' which would sustain profits through high yields rather than high prices, so reconciling tenants to the higher level of rents attained during the war, and maintaining the supply of food to a growing industrial and urban population. By 1819, it seemed to the government that the process of adjustment had succeeded sufficiently for resumption to be feasible, with effect from 1821. Not everyone was convinced.

Resumption led to a virulent debate between 'hard' money bullionists who wished to tie currency to gold, and 'soft' money anti-bullionists who preferred a currency determined by the needs of trade. The social and economic alignments of the two positions were complex. Resumption had the effect of reducing prices by limiting the supply of money, and W. Cooke Taylor was convinced that it 'sacrificed the landed interest to the money power'.[13] Landowners and farmers, he assumed, borrowed money from the City to invest in improvements, so that a fall in the price of agricultural output increased the burden of interest payments and benefited creditors in the City. The earl of Carnarvon shared these concerns, claiming in 1821 that resumption would have the result

in a constitutional point of view, of destroying by its means the aristocracy of the country—the gentlemen and the yeomanry of England, on whose existence our institutions alone could rest. The monied interest had been formed by the calls of war finances; they could be removed; they were inhabitants of this or of any other country;

but the stability of our institutions, and the safety of the throne itself, depended on our agricultural population.[14]

Carnarvon was expressing a common 'country' hostility to a monied oligarchy which was corrupting society by credit and the national debt. The division, argued some commentators, was wider than a conflict of land and finance: it was between production, which included industry and commerce as well as land, and parasitical financiers and holders of the national debt. Deflation, these critics argued, increased the burden of taxes on those who produced goods or received rents which were falling in value, and would benefit investors in the national debt whose interest payments would be worth more in real terms. 'Our taxes are being still paid in the currency which is nominally the same, though really so different', claimed John Edye in 1817, 'the fundholder is wallowing in imaginary and unexpectedly doubled wealth, whilst the landed, manufacturing and commercial interests which alone support him, are groaning under the doubled pressure of an artificial debt.'[15]

Such claims make it easy to draw an analogy between resumption in 1819 and the return to gold in 1925 after the next period of suspension, when it is often suggested that the City wanted the restoration of gold in order to maintain its international role at the expense of the domestic economy. In fact the analogy between 1819 and 1925 is misleading, and the decision of 1819 in favour of resumption was not intended to assert the City against landed wealth or producers. Far from resumption being a policy pursued in the interests of the City, it was part of an attempt by the government to reduce the power of the Bank and loan contractors and win independence. There was a feeling that the Bank was usurping the power of parliament, exploiting a monopoly and benefiting from the profits of note issue during suspension. The automatic mechanism of the gold standard offered the prospect of liberation from the Bank's management of the currency. 'The nature of the relations existing between the government and the Bank', urged Robert Peel, 'should be changed', and resumption was 'a tactical blow against City and Bank in a constitutional battle for power and responsibility'.[16]

Most landed interests were, despite Carnarvon's fears, inclined to take a bullionist line. Landowners were not convinced that their economic position would be harmed by resumption and falling prices. Many believed that their economic position had suffered since 1797 as a result of a decline in the real value of rents, and they argued that resumption would shift the distribution of wealth in their favour: rents were likely to be 'sticky' and to fall less rapidly than prices. Their economic reasoning was suspect, for many landowners had increased the real value of rents during the French revolutionary and Napoleonic wars, and the real burden of mortgages fell as prices rose. However, landed support for bullion had less to do with an assessment of immediate economic self-interest than with a vision of the structure of society. A policy of 'hard money' and gold represented social stability; paper money represented social dislocation by newcomers who were subverting the social order by speculation. 'Merchants and manufacturers and those whose business it is to make their fortunes by a few years of speculation', claimed Edward Littleton in 1819, 'always require large discount and think the larger the circulating medium the better for them.'[17] The intention of resumption was, as Liverpool said, to end 'a system by which fictitious capitals might be ... created and extended', so preventing 'unsound' activity which upset the balance of social stability.[18]

Bullionists believed that convertibility, deflation, and dearer credit acted as a sieve to separate 'improvident and unreasonable speculations' from reputable traders, which would 'improve the quality; but diminish; the quantity of commerce'.[19] Resumption consequently appealed to established landlords, merchants, and industrialists who believed that easy credit and money had distorted and disrupted society. The debate over resumption was in part a continuation of the eighteenth-century antithesis of 'virtue' and commerce, with its hostility to monied corruption. But policy was largely shaped by pragmatic concerns: the prospects of growth, it was assumed, were limited and an over-expansion of trade, commerce, and industry threatened considerable dangers of unbalancing the currency and exceeding the ability of agriculture to feed the expanding population. The government's ambition was to return the economy to its 'natural' pre-war state, with no expectation that long-term growth would offer a solution. Such an approach received additional support from the emerging consensus amongst classical economics that resumption and the quantity of money did not affect the total volume of trade and employment. Full employment, argued Ricardo, was automatic and the amount of money in circulation merely affected the price level rather than the volume of activity. Resumption and a limited supply of money, he argued, would entail an automatic, frictionless adjustment in the money market which would not harm production.

Not surprisingly, opponents of resumption were likely to be merchants, manufacturers, bankers, bullion brokers, and financiers who feared the impact of monetary stringency and realized that the solvency of business concerns rested upon an easily disrupted and complex mutual dependence. A petition protesting against resumption was signed by over 400 City merchants and bankers; Manchester cotton interests were well aware that the immediate effect of resumption would be to over-value the pound against foreign currencies, and make it more difficult to export; Liverpool merchants, involved in unstable markets in primary commodities and heavily dependent upon bills of exchange, felt that the major

oncern should be the liquidity of the mercantile community. Monetary stringency and falling prices would, argued Alexander Baring, redistribute income
rom useful to less useful groups of society: harmful speculation would be
hecked, but so would legitimate commerce, and the beneficiaries would be idle
entiers whose real income would rise as prices fell. 'The effect', he remarked,
was that the industrious were obliged to labour under difficulties, that the
lrones might live in the greater affluence.'[20] Above all, the Ricardian position
vas challenged by the Birmingham economists, and especially the banker
Thomas Attwood, both at the time of resumption and in the subsequent debate
over monetary policy. He contended that the volume of trade and employment
vas conditional upon the *amount* of money. 'The issue of money *will* create
narkets', Attwood argued in 1817, 'and . . . it is upon the abundance or scarcity of
noney that the extent of all markets principally depends.' But there was a
problem, which he put in Malthusian language. 'Gold and silver', he remarked in
817, 'only increase in *arithmetical* ratio. Man increases in *geometrical* ratio.' The
answer, he argued, was to break the link between currency and gold, and to
expand the circulation in order to maintain demand and full employment. 'The
lisease', he remarked in 1843, 'is "under-consumption"', and the supply of
noney should be consciously managed as a cure. Gently rising prices would
stimulate enterprise, whereas falling prices shifted income in favour of non-
producers. 'If the scale of justice *must* lean at all to one side', he remarked in 1826,

or God's sake, let it be to the side of money. Let it be in favour of the weak against the
strong, of the Debtor against the Creditor, of the man struggling to raise his head above
he waters, and not of the man who already stands upon firm ground. Of all the cruel and
monstrous doctrines that ever were broached in political economy, the most cruel and
preposterous is that, which . . . pretends that the *raising of the value of money* is no greater
injury and injustice to Debtors than the *lowering of such value* is to the Creditors in a
Community.[21]

Attwood's approach was defeated by Ricardian orthodoxy, both during the
debate over resumption and in the policies devised in response to the financial
and commercial crises of the second quarter of the nineteenth century.

The distinction between 'real' bills based on legitimate trade and 'fictitious'
bills based on speculation was by no means as clear as the government and Bank
liked to believe, and the dangers became abundantly clear in the crisis of 1825–6
when the financial system was close to collapse under the weight of speculative
paper. The response of the government to the crisis was shaped by the assumption that business failure in peace was the responsibility of individuals, who
should bear the consequences of their own actions. William Huskisson argued in
1826 that any intervention by the government to rescue them or to offer limited

liability would be 'as much calculated to encourage speculation as the poor-law
were calculated to encourage vagrancy, and to discourage honest industry'.²
The crisis of 1825–6 was consequently welcomed as a corrective to the preten
sions of speculators and over-trading. Bullionism, it was believed, would driv
out speculation, sifting sound and unsound trade and selecting 'real bills', and th
correct response was to impose still further restrictions on paper money, with it
capacity for sudden expansion and contraction. Although notes were convertibl
into gold from 1821, banks retained a considerable degree of discretion i
deciding how many to issue in relation to their assets, on the assumption tha
holders of notes would not all demand payment of gold at the same time. Th
hard money 'currency school' argued that the discretion of banks should b
reduced, with the circulation of notes strictly tied to the Bank of England'
holding of specie.

Gold and convertibility, Huskisson was confident, would make the Bank 'th
great steam engine of the state, to keep the channel of the circulation alway
pressing full'.²³ Reality contradicted his hopes, for a restriction of the supply o
money and credit could harm legitimate trade and 'real' bills. The governmen
emphasized the dangers of over-issue and ignored the possibility of seriou
deflation; by offering justice to creditors who had suffered from inflation, it wa
threatening the interests of debtors and producers. The anti-bullionists had a
point: tight money and stringent credit disrupted the web of credit which wa
crucial to all industrialists and mercantile firms, whether they were net debtor
or creditors. The anti-bullionists such as Attwood had good reason to doub
whether reversion to gold would provide sufficient currency, fearing that th
supply of money was less than required by the economy. The 'soft' money
banking school tried to unite small traders and farmers in town and country
against the currency school, arguing for a greater degree of flexibility so that th
volume of money was left to the discretion of bankers according to the level o
prices, wages, and economic activity.

The Bank Charter Act of 1844 marked the defeat of the banking school by the
currency school, with its assumption of automatic equilibrium at full employ
ment, guaranteed by the gold standard. All notes issued by the Bank of Englanc
above £14 million were to be backed by bullion; existing private issues were
restricted; and new banks of issue prohibited. The Bank was, however, still free
to compete in the ordinary business of banking, which posed dangers fo
financial stability. The pursuit of an aggressive banking policy, with changes ir
discount policy and interest rates to compete for business, stimulated credi
during the railway mania of the mid-1840s. After the crash of 1847, the Bank
ceased to be a competitor in the money market and concentrated on regulating
and stabilizing the monetary system through its discounting and Bank rate. By

50, the gold standard and the Bank Charter Act were articles of faith for
mainstream economists, and part of the consensus of the mid-Victorian political
system. After all, most economic disturbances had arisen from an over-expansion
of credit rather than a deflation of commodity prices, and there were grounds for
distrust of a 'banking' policy which gave discretion to a private, monopolistic
bank composed of City merchants. The contrast drawn by the anti-bullionists
and banking school between productive debtors and parasitical creditors was too
neat and schematic; after all, some industrialists were net debtors and some net
creditors within the credit matrix; and some landowners were debtors who had
borrowed to improve their estates while others had invested in government
funds. Political mobilization was hampered because monetary policy did not
have an immediate and straightforward economic impact on clearly defined
groups, as the anti-bullionists and banking school liked to suggest. Even radical
critics of the currency school accepted the Ricardian assumption that monetary
policy could not affect the *volume* of income and employment, and they were
suspicious of Attwood's motives. Changes in monetary policy and rising prices
would relieve debtors at the expense of creditors, remarked the radical Henry
Hetherington, but this was no more than 'a mere transfer of plunder from one set
of schemers to another'.[24] Workers would not benefit, he felt, for prices of their
purchases would rise faster than their wages, and he did not accept Attwood's
argument that the volume of employment would increase. The gold standard
and Bank Charter Act was far from a simple pro-City policy: it was part of the
social contract of the Victorian, state which offered a rising standard of living to
the working class from stable or falling prices.

Conclusion

The stark contrast between Scottish banks facilitating and English banks hinder-
ing industrialization does not stand up to close scrutiny. Both English and
Scottish banks have been criticized as credit rather than investment banks, which
neglected the needs of industry for long-term funds, in contrast to Germany in
the late nineteenth century. This is to accept the principles espoused by bankers
at face value without asking whether they were implemented in practice. In the
eighteenth and early nineteenth centuries, there was a much closer connection
between banks and the local business community than in the late nineteenth
century when amalgamation led to a concentration of power in London.
Although banks certainly had an incentive to remain liquid and to concentrate on
short-term loans, this was not necessarily harmful to industry, which required
credit in order to function. Neither did banks shun medium- and long-term loans,
and there is little sign that industrial development was checked by an inadequate

or inappropriate banking structure. The debate over monetary policy is als
more complicated than a simple neglect of industry in order to benefit th
financial interests of the City. Resumption was intended, in fact, to check th
power of financiers and the Bank, and to benefit genuine trade and enterprise a
the expense of speculation and 'fictitious capital'. Of course, intention is not th
same as outcome, for the distinction between genuine and fictitious capital wa
never clear-cut. The debate over banking policy was part of a wider concern fo
economic policy after the Napoleonic wars which involved a complicate
interplay between monetary policy, taxation, and protection. The government'
policy was designed to maintain balance in the economy, in the belief tha
long-term growth was not feasible; it was concerned that the growing populatio
should be fed, and was worried about subsistence. The danger was that polic
might be pushed in the direction of supporting the class interests of landowner
against industry and workers, by sustaining high food prices through the cor
laws, and by rejecting the income tax in 1816, which made the fiscal regime muc
more regressive. The debate over these policies was at the heart of British politic
until the repeal of the corn laws in 1846, and the consensus on tax policy whic
emerged in the early 1850s.

NOTES

1. R. Cameron, 'England, 1750–1844', in R. Cameron (ed.), *Banking in the Early Stages c
   Industrialization: A Study in Comparative Economic History* (New York, 1967), 58; an
   'Scotland, 1750–1845', in ibid., 72.
2. S. G. Checkland, *Scottish Banking: A History, 1695–1973* (Glasgow, 1973), 115.
3. Ibid. 84, 240, 426.
4. R. Cameron, 'Banking and Industrialization in Britain in the Nineteenth Century', i
   A. Slaven and D. H. Aldcroft (eds.), *Business, Banking and Urban History* (Edinburgh
   1982), 106; R. Cameron, 'Scotland, 1750–1844', in Cameron (ed.), *Banking in the Earl
   Stages of Industrialization*, 75.
5. A. Smith, *An Inquiry into the Nature and Causes of the Wealth of Nations* (repr. 1937), 28
   (book ii, ch. ii).
6. L. S. Pressnell, *Country Banking in the Industrial Revolution* (Oxford, 1956), 6.
7. Ibid. 11.
8. C. Munn, 'The Development of Joint-Stock Banking in the British Isles in th
   Nineteenth Century: A Comarative Approach', unpublished paper presented t
   Economic History Society; M. Collins, *Banks and Industrial Finance in Britain, 1800–
   1939* (1997), 28.
9. P. Ollerenshaw, 'The Development of Banking in the Bristol Region, 1750–1914', ir
   C. E. Harvey and J. Press (eds.), *Studies in the Business History of Bristol* (Bristol, 1988)
   Collins, *Banks and Industrial Finance*, 28.
10. Presnell, *Country Banking*, 77.
11. R. Fulford, *Glyn's, 1753–1953: Six Generations in Lombard Street* (1953), 59.
12. M. Collins and P. Hudson, 'Provincial Bank Lending: Yorkshire and Merseyside
    1826–60', *Bulletin of Economic Research*, 31 (1979), 77.

3. B. Hilton, *Corn, Cash and Commerce: The Economic Policies of the Tory Governments, 1815–30* (Oxford, 1977), 56.

4. F. W. Fetter, *The Development of British Monetary Orthodoxy, 1797–1875* (Cambridge, Mass., 1965), 103.

5. Quoted ibid. 75.

6. Hilton, *Corn, Cash and Commerce*, 48.

7. Ibid. 59–60.

8. Ibid. 61.

9. Ibid. 62.

10. Fetter, *British Monetary Orthodoxy*, 102.

11. Ibid. 75: S. G. Checkland, 'The Birmingham Economists, 1815–50', *Economic History Review*, 2nd ser. 1 (1948), 1; Hilton, *Corn, Cash and Commerce*, 230.

12. Hilton, *Corn, Cash and Commerce*, 227.

13. Ibid. 65.

14. Quoted in Fetter, *British Monetary Orthodoxy*, 143.

FURTHER READING

Ashton, T. S., 'The Bill of Exchange and Private Banks in Lancashire, 1790–1830', *Economic History Review*, 15 (1945).

Black, I., 'Geography, Political Economy, and the Circulation of Finance Capital in Early Industrial England', *Journal of Historical Geography*, 15 (1989).

Cameron, R. (ed.), *Banking in the Early Stages of Industrialization: A Study in Comparative Economic History* (New York, 1967).

—— 'Banking and Industrialization in Britain in the Nineteenth Century', in A. Slaven and D. H. Aldcroft (eds.), *Business, Banking and Urban History: Essays in Honour of S. G. Checkland* (Edinburgh, 1982).

Checkland, S. G., *Scottish Banking: A History, 1695–1973* (Glasgow, 1975).

—— 'The Lancashire Bill System and its Liverpool Protagonists, 1810–27', *Economica*, NS 21 (1954).

—— 'The Birmingham Economists, 1815–50', *Economic History Review*, 2nd ser. 1 (1948–9).

Collins, M., *Banks and Industrial Finance in Britain, 1800–1939* (1991).

—— and Hudson, P., 'Provincial Bank Lending in Yorkshire and Merseyside', *Bulletin of Economics Research*, 31 (1979).

Davies, M. G., 'Country Gentry and Payments to London, 1650–1714', *Economic History Review*, 2nd ser. 24 (1971).

Fetter, F. W., *The Development of British Monetary Orthodoxy, 1797–1875* (Cambridge, Mass., 1965).

Fulford, R., *Glyn's, 1753–1953: Six Generations in Lombard Street* (1953).

Gershenkron, A., *Economic Backwardness in Historical Perspective: A Book of Essays* (Cambridge, Mass., 1962).

Hilton, B., *Corn, Cash and Commerce: The Economic Policies of the Tory Governments, 1815–30* (Oxford, 1977).

Horsefield, J. K., 'The Banks and the Bullionists in 1819', Journal of Political Economy, 57 (1949).

Hudson, P., 'The Role of Banks in the Finance of the West Yorkshire Wool Textile Industry, c.1780–1850', Business History Review, 55 (1981).

Jones, S., 'The Manchester Cotton Magnates' Move into Banking, 1826–50', Textile History, 9 (1978).

Joslin, D. M., 'London Bankers in Wartime, 1739–84', in L. S. Pressnell (ed.), Studies in the Industrial Revolution (1960).

—— 'London Private Bankers, 1720–85', Economic History Review, 2nd ser. 7 (1954–5).

King, W. T. C., History of the London Discount Market (1936).

Leighton-Boyce, J. A. S. L., Smiths the Bankers, 1658–1958 (1958).

Munn, C. W., 'The Development of Joint-Stock Banking in the British Isles in the Nineteenth Century: A Comparative Approach', paper to Economic History Society Conference, 1986.

—— The Scottish Provincial Banking Companies, 1747–1864 (Edinburgh, 1981).

—— 'The Development of Joint-Stock Banking in Scotland, 1810–1845', in A. Slaven and D. H. Aldcroft (eds.), Business, Banking and Urban History: Essays in Honour of S. G. Checkland (Edinburgh, 1982).

Ollerenshaw, P., 'The Development of Banking in the Bristol Region, 1750–1914', in C. E. Harvey and J. Press (eds.), Studies in the Business History of Bristol (Bristol, 1988).

Pollard, S., 'Rondo Cameron 20 Years On', in Y. Cassis (ed.), Finance and Financiers in Europe 1880–1960 (Cambridge, 1992).

Pressnell, L. S., Country Banking in the Industrial Revolution (Oxford, 1956).

Scammell, W. M., The London Discount Market (1968).

Taylor, A. M., Gilletts: Bankers at Banbury and Oxford: A Study in Local Economic History (Oxford, 1964).

CHAPTER 14

Demand, Supply, and Industrialization

n England the several ranks of men slide into each other almost imperceptibly, and a
pirit of equality runs through every part of their constitution. Hence arises a strong
mulation in all the several stations and conditions to vie with each other; and the
erpetual restless ambition in each of the inferior ranks to raise themselves to the level of
hose immediately above them. In such a state as this fashion must have uncontrolled
way. And a fashionable luxury must spread through it like a contagion.[1]

Nathaniel Forster's description of English society in 1767 has encouraged some historians to argue that there was a consumer revolution in the
eighteenth century, marked by 'an unprecedented propensity to consume:
unprecedented in the depth to which it penetrated the lower reaches of society
and unprecedented in its impact on the economy'.[2] But was Forster referring to
economic reality, or was he complaining of the demise of social order and
deference? The title of Forster's pamphlet should be borne in mind: *An Enquiry
into the Present High Price of Provisions*, with its suggestion that consumerism was
harmful because it drove up prices. Writers such as Forster did not necessarily
welcome the spirit of equality and emulation, and its expression in 'fashionable
luxury'. He was a critic of the governing oligarchy, which was, he believed, sunk
in materialism and insensitive to the poor. Far from leading to prosperity and
growth, many contemporaries feared that emulation and luxury were dangers to
society, undermining deference and social stability.

Luxury was at the centre of a debate in the eighteenth century which raised
fundamental issues about the nature of social order, the behaviour of the ruling
class, and the basis of national prosperity. In 1700, the dominant assumption was
still that prosperity was achieved through a strong balance of payments: luxuries
were criticized as exotic imports, and home demand was considered a necessary
evil competing with exports. Total demand was seen as inelastic, and it was not

anticipated that new wants at all levels of society could enhance purchasing power and break through traditional notions of consumption. Such notions were starting to be challenged by a few daring spirits from the 1690s, when Mandeville's *Fable of the Bees* indicated the gradual development of 'the idea of man as a consuming animal with boundless appetites, capable of driving the economy to new levels of prosperity'.[3] Mandeville was not simply suggesting that prosperity could be based upon an increase in domestic consumption; he argued that the private vices of vanity, avarice, and greed were public benefits which produced the possibility of economic progress. 'Every Part was full of Vice', ran his couplet, 'Yet the whole Mass a Paradise.'[4]

Such sentiments were by no means universally accepted during the eighteenth century. Luxury had led to the fall of Rome, and the existence of habits of luxury in the Church, Westminster, and among the people could indicate a deterioration of the national character. Henry Fielding in 1751 commented that

while the Noblemen will emulate the Grandeur of a Prince and the Gentleman will aspire to the proper state of a Nobleman, the Tradesman steps from behind his Counter into the vacant place of the Gentleman. Nor doth the confusion end here: It reaches the very Dregs of the People.[5]

An economic historian might seize on this passage as evidence of a widening domestic market, yet Fielding's pamphlet had an alarmist title: *An Enquiry into the Causes of the Late Increase of Robbers*. The 'vast Torrent of luxury' was, to Fielding, a sign that order had collapsed and had 'almost totally changed the Manners, Customs, and Habits of the People, more especially of the lower Sort'.[6] It seemed a threat to social discipline and order, leading to insubordination as plebeians insulted their betters. The idea that society was no more than an aggregation of self-interested individuals tied together by envy and competition alarmed commentators such as Fielding. It led Tory landowners in the early eighteenth century to urge the introduction of new sumptuary laws, a call which was repeated by the *London Magazine* in 1754 on the grounds that the 'reigning vice' of luxury 'not only enervates the people, and debauches their morals, but also destroys their substance'.[7] The attack on luxury appealed in particular to Jacobites, Tories and Catholics who were 'out' in Hanoverian society and resented the flaunting of opulence by Whig oligarchs, placemen, and monied wealth.

There was, however, a shift by the end of the eighteenth century which was most cogently expressed by Adam Smith in *The Wealth of Nations*, with his notion that the pursuit of private self-interest would be guided by the invisible hand of the market in order to produce growth and prosperity. 'Consumption', said Smith, 'is the sole end and purpose of all production; and the interest of the producer ought to be attended to, only so far as it may be necessary for promoting that of the consumer.'[8] Although writers such as Malthus and Ricardo were not convinced that it was possible to escape the limits set to consumption by the constraints of finite natural resources, they *were* inclined to give a positive role to emulation and the desire to purchase luxuries by the poor. It was the desire for a more comfortable existence which lay behind Malthus's stress upon the 'prudential restraint' on early marriage. The spread of consumption and luxury were viewed in a more positive light, and Adam Smith rejected the complaints of those who criticized the poor for ceasing to be content with their food, clothing, and accommodation. 'What improves the circumstances of the greater part can never be regarded as an inconveniency to the whole. No society can surely be flourishing and happy, of which the far greater part of the members are poor and miserable.'[9] Far from undermining social order, luxury could bind it more securely together. 'The greater the luxuries of every country, the more closely, politically speaking, is that country united,' argued Oliver Goldsmith, so that 'he who finds out a new pleasure is one of the most useful members of society'.[10]

The attack upon luxury continued, but its focus shifted. In the eighteenth century, the main criticism was directed at the poor and middle classes who emulated their betters and threatened the social hierarchy. It complemented 'civic humanism', with its notion that the leisured life of a landed gentleman was necessary for civic virtue, offering freedom from the narrow self-interest of tradesmen, merchants, and industrialists, and permitting arms to be born in defence of the nation. In the first half of the nineteenth century, criticism of luxury shifted to the idle and profligate life of the ruling class, and virtue now resided in being a man of business, not a man of leisure. The change is well expressed in Thackeray, who commented in 1856 'What could a great peer, with a great castle and park, and a great fortune, do but be splendid and idle? It is to the middle class we must look for the safety of England. ... Their minds were not debauched by excess, or effeminate with luxury.'[11] The idea of luxury and emulation is therefore linked with a profound shift in contemporaries' understanding of the nature of civic virtue and the basis of social order.

Such sentiments shaped economic and social policy, and are vital for an understanding of the formation of the British state. What is not clear is whether the pamphlets and books on luxury which poured from the presses may also be read as evidence of a shift in the market for goods. Demand has been seen as a crucial component of the industrial revolution. 'The factory could not become typical', Elizabeth Gilboy suggested, 'until demand had been extended ... throughout the entire population to consume the products of large-scale industry.'[12] A higher level of demand could place pressure upon the domestic system of production, creating bottle-necks which led to technological innovation and the coming of the factory. Demand, on such a view, was the motor of the industrial revolution; the problem is deciding whether the fuel was supplied by the domestic market or exports. There are a number of competing interpretations. One school of thought argues that the key was a fall in the price of agricultural goods relative to industrial goods, which released consumption from the narrow limits of subsistence and created a new set of expectations. A second approach follows the debate on luxury and stresses a *social* process of emulation and fashion which created a new attitude to goods. The social anthropologist Mary Douglas has argued that expenditure on goods is a means of communication or social participation. Expenditure on entertaining other people in the household was a way of showing how far the family was involved in social networks; it involved the purchase of new artefacts for the consumption of tea and coffee. Patterns of consumption were signs of social status and means of establishing social relationships. Goods were not simply 'objects of desire'; they were also 'threads of a veil that disguises the social relations under it'.[13] A shift in social attitudes could change attitudes to work: the desire to purchase goods could lead to an increase in the demand for money income, encouraging workers to abandon their high preference for leisure in favour of working to secure cash for consumption. A third possibility is that domestic demand was influenced by a shift in income distribution. The poor were more likely to spend their income on food, and the rich on personal services and conspicuous consumption; an increase in the proportion of income for 'middling' groups might increase the demand for industrial goods. Or was there simply an increase in the population which raised the demand for basic industrial goods? These explanations focus upon the nature of domestic demand, but there is another possibility, that the demand for industrial goods came from abroad. The domestic market was facing problems in the later eighteenth century, for growth of population eroded wages, increased food prices, and choked off demand. An increase in the price of food relative to industrial goods could shift income towards the landed aristocracy who spent their income on personal services and grandiose building schemes. In these circumstances, the crucial component of demand could possibly come from foreign markets, particularly with the growth of the empire in the Atlantic and Indies.

There is a final possibility, that neither domestic nor export demand was the crucial engine of change. Could developments on the side of supply be more significant?[14] A change in technology could reduce costs of manufacture; or improved systems of transport and marketing could lead to savings in transaction costs. Such improvements on the side of supply would bring consumption within the reach of a wider portion of society at home, and allow British manufacturers

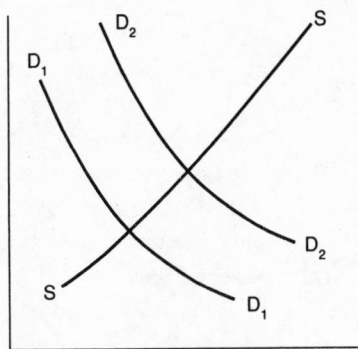

FIG. 14.1. Supremacy of demand

to capture foreign markets. A fall in costs could encourage the emulation which so horrified Nathaniel Foster, rather than emulation stimulating demand and producing cost-cutting innovations. Could it be that the ability of the lady's maid to wear printed Indian calicoes arose from the success of printers and dyers in London in cutting their costs, and increasing their market penetration? The figures show the differences in the two views. In Fig. 14.1, the demand curve shifts from D_1D_1 to D_2D_2, and puts pressure on the supply of goods; in Fig. 14.2, the supply curve shifts from S_1S_1 to S_2S_2, which shifts demand along the existing demand schedule, from a to b. Did domestic demand, exports, or changes in supply have the greatest impact on the development of the British economy?

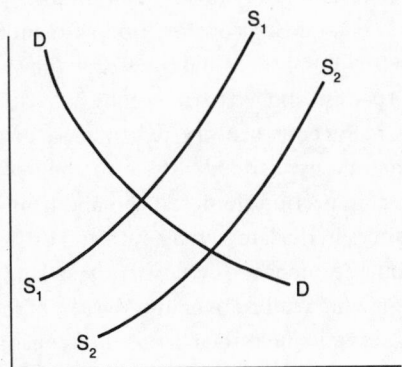

FIG. 14.2. Supremacy of supply

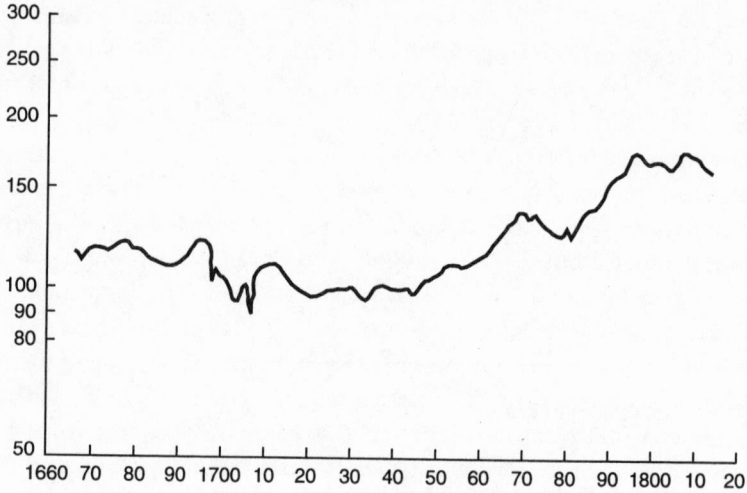

FIG. 14.3. Terms of trade between agriculture and industry, 1660–1820

Source: P. K. O'Brien, 'Agriculture and the Home Market for English Industry, 1660–1820', *English Historical Review*, 100 (1985), 776.

Domestic Demand

Changes in the agricultural economy were, in the opinion of some historians, the crucial variable which influenced the domestic market. A fall in agricultural prices relative to industrial prices would release consumption from food for the purchase of manufactures; at the same time, the income of agriculturalists would fall so that they were able to buy fewer manufactures. Such a pattern applied to the late seventeenth century and first half of the eighteenth century, when the terms of trade between industry and agriculture moved in favour of industry. By contrast, a rise in agricultural prices relative to industrial prices would increase expenditure on food and squeeze consumption of manufactures; at the same time, the income of agriculturalists would rise so that they were able to buy more manufactures. Such a pattern applied to the second half of the eighteenth century and opening of the nineteenth century, when food prices moved ahead of industrial prices. There were certainly shifts in the sectoral terms of trade (Fig. 14.3); their precise impact on domestic demand is more difficult to assess. Did the fall in food prices in the late seventeenth and early eighteenth centuries lead to a squeeze on the incomes of farmers and landowners, creating an agricultural depression which spilled over into the rest of the economy? Or did it permit urban consumers to adjust their pattern of consumption, so that they spent less on food and more on industrial commodities which gave a boost to industrial growth? When food prices rose in the second half of the eighteenth century, did prosperity for the agricultural community stimulate demand for industrial goods, or did it erode the demand from non-agricultural workers who had to spend more on food? The pattern of demand depended to a considerable extent upon which section of the agricultural economy benefited. Ricardo's analysis suggested that the bulk of the gains were taken by wealthy landowners through higher levels of rent. How would these landowners respond? Generally, the rich have a higher marginal propensity to consume, and a shift in income towards the landed élite could increase the savings ratio or encourage spending upon conspicuous consumption as a sign of status and authority. Could their increased rental income generate a demand for imported luxuries, urban services, lavish expenditure on houses in town and country, and land purchases? This could lead to prosperity for producers of high-value craft goods, yet make the producers of basic commodities such as cotton textiles turn to unstable foreign markets, which were susceptible to wide cyclical fluctuations. If there were an increase in savings and the availability of funds, much would depend upon whether the landowners simply lent money to the state to finance wars against France rather than productive industry.

The extent to which low agricultural prices up to 1750 increased the 'social depth' of consumption and stimulated the domestic market for cheap industrial goods such as pottery, linen, cotton, and ironwares depends upon the elasticity of demand for food. When the standard of living was relatively low, expenditure upon food would increase, with a switch from rye and oats to wheaten bread or a higher consumption of meat, dairy products, beer, and gin. It is therefore plausible to assume that the demand for food was relatively elastic, and that benefits for industry from falling food prices were consequently relatively slight. In any case, the shift in the intersectoral terms of trade between agriculture and industry was modest between 1666 and 1746, probably producing an increase in expenditure upon industrial goods of only between 3 and 8 per cent. Food prices rose after 1746 to a peak in the Napoleonic wars, and even after the fall in the early nineteenth century, prices remained twice as high as in the early eighteenth century. A basket of industrial goods in 1820 bought only 60 per cent of the primary products it had secured in 1745. The impact of this shift in the sectoral terms of trade depended upon the behaviour of consumers. It did not necessarily squeeze consumption of industrial goods, for consumers could respond to higher agricultural prices by spending less upon gin and more on cotton cloth whose relative price had fallen. Possibly, the era of low food prices in the early eighteenth century led to the emergence of new patterns of consumption which were maintained by workers who were willing to extend their hours of labour, forgoing leisure in order to gratify their new-found tastes. Of course, these tastes could be for imported luxuries such as tea, coffee, and tobacco rather than industrial goods; and it is difficult to see how a change in attitudes to work could explain *continued* economic growth. On balance, it is likely that the demand for industrial goods was checked as a result of higher prices for agricultural commodities after 1745: depending upon the assumptions which are made about elasticities, the increase in the price of food relative to manufactures reduced the demand for industrial goods by between 8 and 20 per cent. The favourable movement in the terms of trade in the later seventeenth and early eighteenth centuries was more than countermanded, and the long-term trend in intersectoral terms of trade cannot explain increased demand for industrial goods. 'It is difficult', Patrick O'Brien has concluded, 'to see increased agricultural productivity as the primary source behind the growth of domestic purchasing power for manufactures.'[15]

Agricultural prices did not only influence the purchasing power of consumers of food: they also determined the income of farmers and landlords, and their ability to buy industrial goods. Could agricultural depression in the early eighteenth century spill over into the rest of the economy as some historians have contended? This argument depends upon a sizeable fall in agricultural incomes, which is highly unlikely given that agricultural depression was regional and sectoral rather than universal. A diffusion of depression from agriculture to industry in the early eighteenth century is implausible, as is the suggestion that higher agricultural prices in the later eighteenth century provided a major boost to industrialization by allowing farmers, landlords, and agricultural labourers to purchase more industrial commodities. The impact of changes in agricultural incomes depended upon two factors: the income elasticity of demand for manufactures; and agriculture's share of total industrial demand, which was shrinking as the proportion of the population deriving its income from agriculture fell from about 60 per cent in 1700 to 30 per cent in 1815. A rough calculation suggests that the general order of magnitudes was something as follows: between 1700 and 1800, agricultural incomes increased by about 81 per cent, and comprised about 36 per cent of the total demand for industrial goods; on the assumption that the elasticity of demand from the agricultural sector was between 1.0 and 1.5, agriculture increased its consumption of industrial goods by somewhere between 29 and 44 per cent. The significance of this figure is put in perspective when it is noted that the total expenditure on industrial goods increased by something like 370 per cent between 1700 and 1800. The bulk of the gain in agricultural income in any case went to landlords rather than to farmers and labourers, so that a large part of the increased demand was for luxury goods, services, and building. It does not seem that demand for industrial goods from agriculture was an important factor in the process of industrialization.[16]

There is, however, a third way in which agriculture would contribute to increased demand: by releasing labour into higher-paid jobs in industry and services, where they could consume more industrial goods. The release of labour is calculated by a simple statistical exercise. The first task is to calculate a 'counterfactual': how many workers would be required to produce the farm output of 1800, at the level of output per worker in 1700? The difference between the 'counterfactual' figure and the *actual* number of workers who produced the output in 1800 is a measure of the number of workers released from English agriculture. The answer is 1,270,000. The economic consequences of this release of labour depend upon a further counterfactual: how would they have been employed if they had remained in agriculture? A shift from gross underemployment in agriculture into high-productivity industry would produce a considerable increase in consumption; on the other hand, the result would be more modest if labour moved from an agricultural sector where it could be profitably employed into urban underemployment. The calculation is rough and ready, but does at least provide upper and lower estimates. The upper bound estimate assumes that workers in agriculture had a low opportunity cost; that they received the average industrial or service wage when they left agriculture; and that they spent 30 per cent of their wage on manufactures. The application of these assumptions suggests that the release of labour from agriculture contributed at most a modest 24 per cent of the 370 per cent increase in expenditure upon industrial goods between 1700 and 1800. The lower bound assumptions are that they had a higher opportunity cost in agriculture, and that the effect of the release of labour was limited to the difference between industrial and agricultural wages. The contribution of the release of labour from agriculture is reduced to 6 per cent of the increase in expenditure upon industrial goods between 1700 and 1800.[17] These calculations suggest, even on the most generous assumptions, that the release of labour from agriculture was not a major factor in the increased consumption of industrial goods.

The contribution of agriculture to increased industrial demand was not decisive. Movements in the intersectoral terms of trade were at best neutral and at worst depressed industrial demand; the increase in agricultural incomes contributed somewhere between 29 and 44 per cent of the total increase of 370 per cent in industrial expenditure between 1700 and 1800; and the release of labour contributed a further 6 to 24 per cent. On the most optimistic assumption, improvements in agricultural productivity accounted for 68 per cent of the total increase of 370 per cent in expenditure on industrial goods. The key to increased demand for industrial goods must be found elsewhere.

Of course, the rate of population growth accelerated in the later eighteenth century, which created more consumers. Whether it generated much additional demand for industrial goods is doubtful, for population pressure was likely to lead to diminishing returns, a reduction in per capita incomes, and an increase in food prices which checked the demand for industrial goods. Perhaps what mattered more was the distribution of income, which shaped the *type* of demand. The economic consequences of emulation and luxury depend, in part, upon who was emulating whom. It might mean nabobs returning from India who indulged themselves in building magnificent new houses such as Sir Francis Sykes at Basildon Park; or *nouveaux riches* financiers such as the Hoares and their Arcadian gardens at Stourhead; or placemen who were spending their fees and perquisites on self-glorification, such as Lord Mansfield at Kenwood; or landowners who were commissioning Capability Brown, Humphrey Repton, and the Adams to provide a new setting for their life of opulence. Such men and their families might indulge in the dance of fashion, parading themselves at Bath or at court, and their consumption would generate demand for luxury products which affected a relatively narrow range of goods. But emulation could penetrate more deeply into society. One of the striking changes in the eighteenth century was the emergence of a whole range of centres of 'conspicuous consumption' around the country at which the local élite could meet at assembly rooms and balls. There was an 'urban renaissance' based upon leisure facilities for the middle and upper classes, consisting of assembly rooms and 'walks' where people could display themselves, town races, theatres, or music festivals. These developments were linked with the growth both of crafts producing high-value goods such as guns, jewellery, watches, furniture, books, and of service trades such as barbers, confectioners, grocers, tobacconists, innkeepers, lawyers. Specialized resorts such as Bath and Harrogate, and county towns with markets and assizes such as Preston, provided a forum in which social status could be pursued by newcomers who sought to transfer wealth into acceptance. The walks and assemblies were intensely competitive arenas for social emulation and snobbery, which also indicated the relative openness and fluidity of society. In the process, the political divisions of the seventeenth century could be healed, and the forces of social tension arising from economic change resolved. This led to diatribes against the vice of luxury which was dissolving the hierarchy of society—but what were the economic consequences?

Probate inventories which recorded possessions at death indicate that a new world of goods was emerging between 1675 and 1725, which was more marked in London and among families engaged in dealing and commerce than among higher-status gentry families (see Table 14.1). The process was not simply one of emulation, for gentry families were *less* likely to own certain goods than traders. It could, indeed, be argued that the crucial element in demand came from the 'middling sort'.

TABLE 14.1. *Ownership of 'new' goods, 1675 and 1725 (%)*

	England		London		Gentry (whole period)	Dealing trades (whole period)
	1675	1725	1675	1725		
Earthenware	27	57	64	88	39	49
China	0	9	4	80	6	10
Clocks	9	34	56	88	51	27
Cutlery	1	10	8	64	11	11
Window curtains	7	21	68	94	26	28

Source: L. Weatherill, *Consumer Behaviour and Material Culture in Britain, 1660–1769* (1988), 26, 27, 168, 184.

Josiah Tucker commented that the British manufactures

are more adapted for the demands of Peasants and Mechanics, in order to appear in warm circumstances, for Farmers, Freeholders, Tradesmen and Manufacturers in Middling Life; and for Wholesale Dealers, Merchants, and for all persons of Landed Estates to appear in genteel life; than for the Magnificence of Palaces or the Cabinets of Princes. Thus it is ... that the English of those several denominations have better Conveniences in their Houses, and affect to have more in Quantity of Clean, neat Furniture, and a greater variety, such as Carpets, Screens, Window Curtains, Chamber Bells, polished Brass Locks, Fenders etc (Things Hardly known abroad among Persons of such Rank) than are to be found in any other country of Europe.[18]

Britain was, claimed Arthur Young, unlike France where 'you go at once from beggary to profusion'; it had a more differentiated social hierarchy. The crucial point was the 'middling sort of people', who stood between the 'upper part of mankind' with independent means from land or investments, and the 'mechanick part of mankind' which worked with its hands.[19] Wedgwood realized the significance of the 'middling sort' in his marketing strategy, and Daniel Defoe praised them in *Robinson Crusoe* in 1719:

the middle state ... was the best state in the world, the most suited to human happiness; not exposed to the miseries and hardships, the labour and sufferings of the mechanic part of mankind and not embarrassed with the pride, luxury, ambition and envy of the upper part of mankind.[20]

They were the families engaged in commerce, industry, and the professions, whose numbers were growing with the development of inland and overseas trade, industry, and urbanization.

In early eighteenth-century London, as many as a fifth to a quarter of households, or 20,000 to 25,000, were in the middling station, with perhaps 3,000 to 5,000 gentry and upper middle-class families in the West End.[21] These families derived their income from a variety of sources. There were government officials lawyers who kept the courts in operation and advised landowners and busi nessmen; doctors, clergymen, and teachers who made London a major centre o learning despite the absence of a university; publishers, printers, stationers, anc copyists who produced their books, ledgers, bills, and documents; the bankers o Lombard Street and the West End, the stockbrokers and insurance brokers whc were emerging from the coffee houses of the City; the merchants trading overseas who clustered around the Royal Exchange, attending the sales of the East India Co. and exchanging news at the coffee houses; owners of barges, coastal and overseas shipping, stage-coaches, and wagons; merchants whc handled the trade in coal and corn and cattle, owners of inns which were the termini of coaches and centres of inland trade, master mariners who guided the ships on their voyages, and chandlers, instrument-makers, sail-makers, chart-makers, and myriad other trades which kept the merchant marine afloat. The great brewers and distillers slaked the thirst of the metropolis; the owners of theatres and pleasure gardens kept them amused. Haberdashers and milliners traded in clothing. In London, textiles were manufactured or finished, clothes stitched, metals worked, ships, coaches, and furniture made, beer brewed, gin distilled, leather tanned. The wealthiest men of London in the early eighteenth century included such unlikely figures as William Ladds, a manufacturer of bodices who had 11 tons of whalebone in stock at his death; or, less surprisingly, Robert Maddox, a distiller of Thames Street. This was the world entertained by the impresario Solomons who sponsored Haydn's London seasons, a culture based on a paying public which was far removed from aristocratic patronage in Austria or even Paris.

There was an emphasis upon self-reliance, on the virtues of Robinson Crusoe. 'The hand of the diligent maketh rich', Joseph Butler assured the Lord Mayor in a sermon in 1740, 'and, other circumstances being equal, in proportion to its diligence.'[22] This does not mean that they were necessarily self-made men. Many were recruited from the younger sons of country gentlemen, who paid for an apprenticeship of seven to eight years in London. Others came from the 'middling sort' of the country, such as millers and innkeepers. The accumulation of fortunes was less the product of spectacular windfalls than of modest profits over time, and as life expectancy increased, so did fortunes, which meant that fathers could leave larger sums to their sons. In earlier centuries, accumulation was checked by the scale of charitable bequests and the constraints of fraternal-ism; by the eighteenth century, there was greater freedom. London was a major centre of industry, finance, and trade; and what applied to London was applicable to smaller provincial centres.

The result was to generate demand for the works of silversmiths, cabinet-makers, milliners, and dressmakers. There was, however, a danger. The expenditure on conspicuous consumption in London could be a sign of a more unequal distribution of income. The success of the Whig grandees might be at the expense of other families who declined, or of small copy- and freeholders who lost out in the eighteenth century. The burden of taxation was regressive, shifting income from the poor to the better off and falling upon industry and commerce rather than land. The sharp rise in rent levels at the end of the eighteenth century accentuated the redistribution of income towards the landed élite, fuelling a massive spate of expenditure upon London town houses and the whirl of Society. In London and Bath, two central nodes of the 'economy of delight',[23] the standard of living of the working class in the later eighteenth century was stagnant, and it is possible to argue that such emulation and search for fashion was socially limited, producing a dependent service sector and the production of luxury goods by craftsmen. Certainly, the importance of this market for 'conspicuous consumption' was immense. A visit to any country house at once indicates the market for fine furnishings from the workshops of Thomas Chippendale or Gillows of Lancaster; for gilded picture frames, chandeliers, plasterwork, fine porcelain, and plate; and all the other goods which a landowner and gentleman required. Seddon and Son of London, for example, employed 400 gilders, mirror-makers, locksmiths, carvers, sawyers, and joiners in 1796. Matthew Boulton, who is better known for his partnership with Watt in the production of steam engines, was more interested in making fine bronze furnishings at his works at Soho in Birmingham in competition with Parisian producers for the London market. But the limits to the market should not be exaggerated. Boulton instructed his London agent that he should sell as widely as possible. 'We think it of far more consequence to supply the People than the nobility only; and though you speak contemptuously of Hawkers, Pedlars and those who supply *Petty shops*, yet we must own that we think they will do more towards supporting a great manufactory, than all the Lords in the Nation.'[24] Josiah Wedgwood pursued aristocratic patronage and sought a fashionable market at high prices by using social distinction to provide *cachet*. This was done by capturing the world of fashion, securing patronage from the nobility by uneconomical commissions or even gifts, pandering to their requirements, and indulging in flattery. Once he had the support of the court and aristocracy, he could sell goods at a high price, exploiting the seal of fashionable approval by advertisements, salerooms, exhibitions, and travelling salesmen. He was not aiming for a mass market so much as 'the *Middling class* of People, which class we know are vastly, I had almost said infinitely superior, in number to the Great'.[25] London had its private palaces and town houses of the aristocrats; it also had the residences of merchants, tradesmen, and professionals. The market was wider than in the cities of Europe, and production less constrained by the regulations of guilds or the privileged position of 'court artisans'.

The most plausible explanation for increased domestic demand for industrial goods is that it emerged from the urban-industrial sector rather than agriculture. At the start of the eighteenth century, food and raw materials accounted for an unusually low 40 per cent of the national product. Agriculture was able to sustain a large number of people off the land, and the potential for industrial growth was already present. All that was required for its release was the integration of domestic markets through improvements in transport and marketing, and a moderate investment in industry to realize the possibilities for growth. Agriculture had prepared the ground before 1700, and had retreated to the background; the significant agents of change in the eighteenth century were canals, turnpikes, merchants, and industrial entrepreneurs. The industrial revolution, as O'Brien remarks, was 'quintessentially industrial, commercial and urban'.[26]

Export Demand

In 1851 the products of British mills, workshops, and factories were exhibited at Crystal Palace for the admiration of the world. Free trade was vindicated, for Britain in 1851 was exporting vast quantities of manufactures to foreign consumers in return for primary products. Could it be argued that growth was export led, that the emergence of new markets overseas was more important than domestic demand? Such is the contention of Eric Hobsbawm, who asserted that 'home demand increased but foreign demand multiplied ... If a spark was needed, this is where it came from.'[27] The main changes in the level and structure of trade are indicated by data collected by the customs authorities, despite the problems of under-recording as a result of smuggling and evasion (Table 14.2–14.4); more problematical is an assessment of the importance of

TABLE 14.2. *Percentage of British manufactured exports by destination, 1699–1701 to 1854–1856*

	Europe	N. America, West Indies	Australia, Latin America, Africa, Near East, Asia
1699–1701	83.6	13.3	3.1
1772–4	45.0	46.9	8.1
1804–6	37.3	49.4	13.3
1834–6	36.3	34.7	29.0
1854–6	28.9	28.1	43.0

Source: N. F. R. Crafts, *British Economic Growth during the Industrial Revolution* (Oxford, 1985), 145.

TABLE 14.3. *Composition of British merchandise exports, 1700–1831* (%)

	Cottons	Woollens	Iron/steel
Composition of exports			
1700	0.5	68.7	—
1750	1.0	46.7	—
1801	39.6	16.5	9.3
1831	50.8	12.7	10.2
Percentage of gross output exported			
1760	50	46	—
1801	62	35	24
1831	56	19	23

Source: Crafts, *British Economic Growth*, 143.

overseas trade in total output and national income for which the statistics are much less reliable.

The geographical and commodity structure of exports changed over the period.[28] The major market in 1700 was Europe, which was overtaken during the eighteenth century by North America and the West Indies. In the early nineteenth century, there was a further change as other areas of the world increased in importance, and particularly India. These geographical shifts were associated with a change in the *type* of commodity. At the start of the eighteenth century, exports were predominantly woollen manufactures which were sold to north and north-west Europe in exchange for other textiles, and to south and east Europe in exchange for primary products. During the eighteenth century, British cloth faced increasing competition in European markets from German, Austrian, and French producers. Although producers in Yorkshire had more success with new and cheaper lines than the older established areas of the West Country and East Anglia, there was a striking reduction in the share of wool cloth in exports

TABLE 14.4. *Commodity composition of British exports, 1784–1786 to 1844–1846* (%)

	1784–6		1814–16		1844–6	
Cotton goods	6.0		42.1		44.2	
Woollen goods	29.2	45.8	17.7	68.0	14.2	69.3
Other textiles	10.6		8.2		10.9	
Other manufactures	38.3		17.5		18.7	
Food/raw materials	15.9		14.5		12.0	

Source: R. Davis, *The Industrial Revolution and British Overseas Trade* (Leicester, 1979), 15.

up to the 1770s. Between 1700 and the 1770s, exports diversified away from wool towards a wider range of textiles such as linen, cotton, and silk, and non-textile industrial goods such as pottery, glass, and small metal goods. European markets became less important, and exports went increasingly to North America and the West Indies in return for primary products. Particularly significant was the trade to America and Africa, which was based upon the notorious triangular trade: small metal goods were exchanged in west Africa for slaves, who were transported to the New World, where they produced colonial products such as sugar and cotton which were shipped to Britain. The slaving triangle was linked to trade within the New World, for colonists in North America supplied food and materials to the sugar plantations of the Caribbean, and exchanged tobacco, indigo, and ships' supplies for British manufactures. The colonists required a wide range of goods, and in particular metals and metalware which were produced by traditional handicraft methods. The economy of the Atlantic formed the basis of British export growth in the eighteenth century.

A further change started in the 1770s, with a rise in exports of cotton yarn and cloth, which were linked to new methods of production in factories and the use of power. Cotton goods accounted for 52.8 per cent of the increase in the current value of British exports between 1784–6 and 1814–16, and 45.9 per cent between 1814–16 and 1844–6. Textiles again dominated exports as in the heyday of wool in the early eighteenth century, reversing the eighteenth-century trend towards a more diversified structure. The change in the commodity composition of trade was linked with a further geographical shift. Initially, the most important sector of the cotton trade was the export of cloth to North America and the West Indies, but by the end of the eighteenth century Europe was the most important destination, particularly for cheap factory-produced yarn, which accounted for 1.6 per cent of cotton goods exported to Europe in 1794–6 and 55.8 per cent in 1844–6. The market for cotton subsequently shifted to Latin America and Asia, which accounted for over half of cotton exports by the early 1850s, increasingly of machine-made cloth. There was renewed diversification from textiles by the mid-nineteenth century. A modest export market in machinery and steam engines started from 1815, with a more significant trade in refined and semi-finished metal for construction, gas pipes, and railways. Although cotton still accounted for 27.4 per cent of the increase in the value of exports between 1844–6 and 1871–3, metals and metal manufactures closed the gap, with 22.4 per cent of the increase.

The expansion of British industry during the eighteenth century meant that manufactured imports became less significant, falling from about a third of all imports in 1700 to 10.5 per cent in 1784–6 and 1.1 per cent in 1814–16. The import of Asian silks and cotton, and of European linen and iron, collapsed, and the

emoval of trade restrictions produced only a modest increase in imports of
extiles. Imports were predominantly food, which accounted for 42.4 per cent of
imports in 1784–6, and raw materials which accounted for 47.1 per cent; by
844–6, the share of food had fallen to 33.4 per cent and that of raw materials had
isen to 62.3 per cent. Britain was largely self-sufficient in 'temperate' products
uch as grain, meat, and dairy produce, which accounted for about 10 per cent of
imports until the late 1830s, after which their share increased to reach 43 per cent
by 1854–6. Until the late 1830s, most food imports came from warmer areas, such
as sugar from the West Indies and tea from China, and their prices fell as a result
of lower freight rates and reduced costs of production. Raw material imports in
he eighteenth century were mainly timber, iron, hemp, flax, silk, oil, and dyes
from the Baltic and Mediterranean. Subsequently, the significance of European
aw materials declined, largely because of the increasing importance of raw
cotton imports which became the largest single commodity by the 1820s.
initially, cotton came from the Levant and West Indies, which encountered
supply problems and rising prices; the constraints were removed by the expansion of production in the southern United States in the nineteenth century. Raw
material supply shifted away from Europe, with wool coming from Australia
rather than Spain and Germany, silk from China rather than Italy, timber from
Canada rather than the Baltic, dyes from the Caribbean rather than the Mediterranean, and completely new materials such as jute from Bengal and palm oil
from Africa. Europe's share of raw material imports declined from two-thirds to
a third between the late eighteenth century and mid-nineteenth century. The
trading links of the British economy were fundamentally transformed.

Much more difficult is any estimate of the share of exports and imports in
national income or of the proportion of production of different industrial sectors
which was sold overseas. One estimate by Ralph Davis suggests that imports rose
from about 10 per cent of national income between 1700 and the 1770s to 15 per
cent in the early nineteenth century, as a result of imports of raw materials and
non-temperate foodstuffs, with a further increase to around 25 per cent of the
national income in the mid-nineteenth century as a result of imports of raw
materials and temperate food.[29] The share of exports in the output of wool
textiles fell, according to Crafts's estimate, from 46 per cent in 1760 to 19 per cent
in 1831.[30] Perhaps half of cotton output was exported in 1760, rising to 62 per cent
in 1801; the proportion fell to 56 per cent in 1831 as a result of the rapid fall in
prices, with a recovery to 61 per cent in 1851. Iron was the only other industry in
which exports were a significant share of output: Britain was a net importer in the
eighteenth century, but was exporting about a quarter of output in 1801. Exports
were heavily concentrated on a narrow range of goods, which suggests that
many important sectors of the economy were heavily reliant upon the domestic

TABLE 14.5. *Exports as a percentage of national and industrial output, 1700–1851*

	Exports as % of:		Increase in exports as % of increase in:	
	National output	Industrial output	National output	Gross industrial output
1700	8.4	24.4	—	—
1760	14.6	35.2	30.4	56.3
1780	9.4	21.8	5.1	2.5
1801	15.7	34.4	21.0	46.2
1831	14.3	21.9	11.3	11.0
1851	19.6	24.7	29.4	30.0

Source: Crafts, *British Economic Growth*, 131, 132.

market, such as furniture, clothing, small metal goods, cutlery, or coaches and carriages.

Any attempt to calculate exports as a percentage of total industrial output or, even more ambitiously, national output is extremely difficult because of limitations of the data. Some historians have argued that the share of exports in national output was stable until the late eighteenth century, when there was a marked increase.[31] This does not seem likely: Crafts's 'best guess' is that exports rose from 8.4 per cent of national output in 1700 to 19.6 per cent in 1851, and formed about a quarter of industrial output at both dates (see Table 14.5). He argues that the significance of exports was 'erratic', playing a major role in three subperiods from 1700 to 1760, 1780 to 1801, and 1831 to 1851.[32] Of course, much depends on the reliability of Crafts's measure of output, but this pattern is more plausible than a sudden spurt at the end of the eighteenth century.

One feature is beyond doubt: Britain was more dependent on overseas markets, exported a higher share of its industrial output, and had a much higher proportion of manufactures in total exports, than other countries at similar

TABLE 14.6. *Economic structures at US$550 (1970 prices)*

	Manufactures as % of exports	% of pop. in towns	% of work-force in:	
			Primary production	Industry
Britain 1840	90.5	48.3	25.0	47.3
France 1870	53.2	31.1	49.3	28.7
Germany 1870	52.5	36.1	50.0	n/a

Source: Crafts, *British Economic Growth*, 57–8, 60.

stages of development (Table 14.6). These features had important implications for the structure of the British economy, for production for export raised industry's share of output and the labour force in comparison with other countries. Exports were 13 per cent of British gross national product but only 6 per cent of French gross national product in 1840; a reduction in British trade to the French level would reduce the share of industry in output and the labour force to the European norm. Whether the peculiarities of Britain's economic structure were in the long-term interests of the country has been questioned. Britain's dominance of world trade in manufactures was narrowly based upon cotton and iron, which were the major users of steam power, and employed unskilled labour rather than skilled artisans. Structural transformation meant a low proportion of the work-force in agriculture and a high share in manufacturing industries with a low level of human capital formation and of investment in education and science. 'The new technology', argues Sanderson, 'could operate with an illiterate labour force which it had helped to produce, and economic growth was not impeded by educational retardation.'[33] The contrast between Britain and Europe was noted by W. S. Jevons. On the one hand, there was 'Great Britain, capable for the present of indefinitely producing all products depending on the use of coal'. On the other, there was Europe, 'capable of an indefinite production of artistic, luxurious, or semi-tropical products, but debarred by comparative want of coal from competition with us'.[34] The reliance upon exports contributed to a skewed pattern of industrialization based on a few trades with a low level of human capital formation, producing cheap cotton cloth for sale to relatively poor markets, and semi-finished iron goods. By redeploying a high proportion of its work-force from agriculture into staple industries with a high dependence upon exports and a low level of training and education, Britain became incapable of achieving higher growth rates offered by investment in education and science in the later nineteenth century. Britain was trapped by a pattern of growth which rested upon low levels of capital formation and of investment in education, and high levels of foreign investment. The artisan radicals of the early nineteenth century had warned of the dangers of relying on the sale of cheap goods at low profits to foreign markets, which led to cost-cutting and the erosion of craft skills; they urged that the home market should be encouraged by changes to the regressive fiscal regime. They were, it would seem, close to the mark.

Is this to say that manufacturing exports led to 'immiserating growth'? There was at least a danger that higher levels of domestic production could result in lower prices for exports; increased purchases of food and raw materials could force up their prices; and the outcome, if the fall in the price of British exports relative to imports was sufficiently large, would be a net reduction in national income. The welfare benefits of an increase in the export of industrial goods depended upon the terms of trade, which certainly moved against Britain in the early nineteenth century, the net barter terms of trade falling from 196 in 1799–1803 to 154 in 1819–23 and 108 in 1849–53. Export prices fell particularly heavily in the case of cotton, with a reduction in the price of 40s. count yarn from 16s. in 1779 to 7s. 6d. in 1799, 2s. 6d. in 1812, and 1s. 2½d. in 1830. The concentration of export growth in a few commodities where it was fuelled by a fall in prices meant that there was a real possibility that the terms of trade would deteriorate to such an extent that real income would fall.[35] The threat to real income from expansion of production at low prices was only removed when economic growth spread to other parts of the world from the 1820s, and provided a market which absorbed British goods without harmful price cuts. The genuine threat of 'immiserating growth' was avoided, largely because food imports were held down by the success of agriculture in feeding the population. The purchase of more food from abroad in the early nineteenth century might well have resulted in a further deterioration in the terms of trade, and Britain would have bought expensive food with cheap manufactures, with a fall in real income. This prospect of 'immiserating growth' meant that Liverpool, Huskisson, and Peel's policy of balanced growth, based on a prosperous agriculture and industry, was economically rational. The maintenance of agricultural self-sufficiency was not simply a selfish pursuit of landowners' self-interest; it prevented a further deterioration in the terms of trade and a fall in national income.

The Supremacy of Supply?

An increase in exports or in domestic sales does not mean that demand was the crucial factor: it could be that production and transaction costs fell, allowing British goods to replace foreign supplies, or permitting purchases by lower-income consumers. Could it be argued that changes on the supply side mattered more than an increase in demand, whether from home or abroad? 'Cost-reducing and factor-increasing changes occupy the center of the stage', Joel Mokyr has claimed; 'supply rules supreme'.[36] Such an argument rejects the view that technological change was induced by increased demand for the final good, either by creating 'bottle-necks' which had to be removed by new processes, or by offering economies of scale. Neither of these arguments for demand-induced innovation is overwhelming in the eighteenth and early nineteenth centuries. Bottle-necks could be overcome by reallocation of resources, by the use of more and better hand tools, or by organizational changes which led to the integration of markets. Could it even be argued that *reduced* demand led to increased efforts to improve technology? It is certainly possible that technological improvements and gains in productivity arose from an increased specialization of craft regions in particular commodities, which was not simply a response to increased demand, for the process was started by the easing of pressure on food supplies which allowed regions to concentrate on the goods in which they had comparative advantage. Specialization led to gains in productivity and encouraged technological change; and as production and transaction costs fell, the supply curve shifted from S, S, to S_2, S_2 (see Fig. 14.2).

Nevertheless, demand should not be ignored. Increased export demand was not simply the result of a fall in the supply price of British goods which captured foreign markets; it was also the result of investment in war which secured the empire against the French, and of the creation of London as the greatest entrepôt in Europe at the expense of the Dutch. A shift in demand was also crucial in preventing increased production and falling costs from eroding profit levels and squeezing wages, so producing a shift in the *internal* terms of trade in favour of landowners and away from industrialists and workers, which could threaten immiserating growth. This was certainly a danger at the end of the eighteenth and beginning of the nineteenth centuries when higher food prices threatened to depress the domestic market, and industrialists had to pay more for raw materials as the external terms of trade deteriorated. The return on industrial capital was reduced, industrialists were forced to sell more goods in volatile markets overseas, funds for reinvestment were cut, and risks were increased. On the other hand, incomes from agricultural production rose and in particular the rents of landowners, which provided the basis for the lavish expenditure of aristocrats on rebuilding their town houses in the West End. The Prince Regent set the tone with his lavish transformation of Carlton House, and he was followed by magnates such as the third duke of Northumberland who was reported to have spent £160,000 on refurbishing his town house around 1820. Here was the basis of the complaints of artisan radicals such as John Gast. Landowners were denounced as brigands who arrived with William the Conqueror to impose a 'Norman yoke' and subvert the free and democratic society of Anglo-Saxon England. The possessions of the landed aristocracy were, they claimed, based upon seizure, a process which started at the conquest, continued with the dissolution of the monasteries, and was completed by the enclosure movement. The French revolutionary and Napoleonic wars should not have been fought in order to protect Russian feudalism, and the high taxes needed to finance the army and navy were checking consumption, holding down the home market, and forcing exports towards volatile foreign markets, which placed pressure on wages, destroyed 'honourable trades', and created distress. The answer, argued the artisan radicals, was to remove the corn laws and shift taxes from the poor to a progressive income tax on the rich. Domestic consumption would consequently rise, and could be further boosted by legislation to maintain wages. Machinery should be controlled and the benefits directed to workers as well as employers, by imposing a tax on machines. Free trade and the growth of export markets were seen as threats which would lead to low wages and insecurity. The structure of demand, Gast realized, was a political matter which rested upon the power to determine the structure of taxation and regulation of the labour market. The failure of the demand schedule for industrial goods to shift at the end of the eighteenth and early nineteenth centuries, as a result of a redistribution of income within Britain and a deterioration in the terms of trade overseas, meant that the gloom of Malthus and Ricardo about the prospects of long-term growth is understandable. It was only after about 1820 that the dangers of a fall in the level of domestic demand were overcome, and real wages started to rise.

NOTES

1. N. McKendrick, 'The Consumer Revolution of Eighteenth-Century England', in N. McKendrick, J. Brewer, and J. H. Plumb, *The Birth of a Consumer Society: The Commercialisation of Eighteenth-Century England* (1982), 11.
2. Ibid.
3. J. Appleby, 'Ideology and Theory: The Tension between Political and Economic Liberalism in Seventeenth-Century England', *American Historical Review*, 81 (1976), 509.
4. Quoted in McKendrick, 'Consumer Revolution', 17.
5. *The Complete Works of Henry Fielding*, xiii: *Legal Writings* (repr. 1967), *An Inquiry into the Causes of the Late Increase of Robbers* (1751), 21–2.
6. J. Sekora, *Luxury: The Concept in Western Thought, Eden to Smollett* (Baltimore, 1977), 6.
7. Ibid. 65.
8. A. Smith, *An Inquiry into the Nature and Causes of the Wealth of Nations* (repr. 1937), 625 (book iv, ch. viii).
9. Ibid. 78–9 (book i, ch. viii).
10. Sekora, *Luxury*, 124.
11. Ibid. 18.
12. E. W. Gilboy, 'Demand as a Factor in the Industrial Revolution', in R. M. Hartwell (ed.), *The Causes of the Industrial Revolution in England* (1967), 122.
13. M. Douglas and B. Isherwood, *The World of Goods: Towards an Anthropology of Consumption* (1979), 202.
14. J. Mokyr, 'Demand versus Supply in the Industrial Revolution', *Journal of Economic History*, 37 (1977).
15. P. K. O'Brien, 'Agriculture and the Home Market for English Industry, 1660–1820', *English Historical Review*, 100 (1985), 783.
16. Ibid. 780.
17. Ibid. 781–2.

8. McKendrick, 'Consumer Revolution', 26.

9. Ibid. 20.

20. L. Weatherill, *Consumer Behaviour and Material Culture in Britain, 1660–1760* (1988), 1.

21. P. Earle, *The Making of the English Middle Class: Business, Society and Family Life in London, 1660–1730* (1989), 81.

22. Quoted ibid. 13.

23. The phrase of M. Sturmer, 'An Economy of Delight: Court Artisans of the Eighteenth Century', *Business History Review*, 53 (1979).

24. N. McKendrick, 'Commercialisation of Fashion', in McKendrick, Brewer, and Plumb (eds.), *Birth of a Consumer Society*, 77.

25. Quoted in Weatherill, *Consumer Behaviour*, 1.

26. O'Brien, 'Agriculture and the Home Market', 786.

27. E. J. Hobsbawm, *Industry and Empire* (1968), 32.

28. R. Davis, *The Industrial Revolution and British Overseas Trade* (Leicester, 1979); N. F. R. Crafts, *British Economic Growth during the Industrial Revolution* (Oxford, 1985), ch. 7.

29. Davis, *Industrial Revolution and British Overseas Trade*, 51.

30. Crafts, *British Economic Growth*, 143.

31. F. Crouzet, 'Towards an Export Economy: British Exports during the Industrial Revolution', *Explorations in Economic History*, 17 (1980).

32. Crafts, *British Economic Growth*, 131.

33. Quoted in ibid., 146.

34. Ibid.

35. Ibid. 147–51.

36. Mokyr, 'Demand versus Supply', 989.

FURTHER READING

Appleby, J., 'Ideology and Theory: The Tension between Political and Economic Liberalism in Seventeenth-Century England', *American Historical Review*, 81 (1976).

Borsay, P., 'The English Urban Renaissance: The Development of Provincial Urban Culture, c.1680–1760', *Social History*, 5 (1977).

Coats, A. W., 'Changing Attitudes to Labour in the Mid-Eighteenth Century', *Economic History Review*, 2nd ser. 11 (1958–9).

—— 'Economic Thought and Poor Law Policy in the Eighteenth Century', *Economic History Review*, 2nd ser. 13 (1960–1).

Crafts, N. F. R., *British Economic Growth during the Industrial Revolution* (Oxford, 1985).

Crouzet, F., 'Towards an Export Economy: British Exports during the Industrial Revolution', *Explorations in Economic History*, 17 (1980).

Davis, R., *The Industrial Revolution and British Overseas Trade* (Leicester, 1979).

Douglas, M., and Isherwood, B., *The World of Goods: Towards an Anthropology of Consumption* (1979).

Earle, P., *The Making of the English Middle Class: Business, Society and Family Life in London, 1660–1730* (1989).

Eversley, D. E. C., 'The Home Market and Economic Growth in England, 1750–80', in E. L. Jones and G. E. Mingay (eds.), *Land, Labour and Population in the Industrial Revolution: Essays Presented to J. D. Chambers* (1967).

Farnie, D. A., 'The Commercial Empire of the Atlantic, 1607–1783', *Economic History Review*, 2nd ser. 15 (1962–3).

Gilboy, E. W., 'Demand as a Factor in the Industrial Revolution', repr. in R. M. Hartwell (ed.), *The Causes of the Industrial Revolution in England* (1967).

Hatton, T. J., Lyons, J. S., and Satchell, S. E., 'Eighteenth-Century British Trade Homespun or Empire Made?', *Explorations in Economic History*, 20 (1983).

Hobsbawm, E. J., *Industry and Empire* (1968).

Holmes, G., *Augustan England: Professions, State and Society, 1680–1730* (1982).

Ippolito, R. A., 'The Effects of the "Agricultural Depression" on Industrial Demand in England, 1730–50', *Economica*, 42 (1975).

Jones, E. L., 'Agriculture and Economic Growth: Economic Change', in E. L. Jones *Agriculture and the Industrial Revolution* (Oxford, 1974).

McKendrick, N., Brewer, J., and Plumb, J. H., *The Birth of a Consumer Society: The Commercialization of Eighteenth-Century England* (1982).

Mokyr, J., 'Demand versus Supply in the Industrial Revolution', *Journal of Economic History*, 37 (1977).

O'Brien, P. K., 'Agriculture and the Home Market for English Industry, 1660–1820', *English Historical Review*, 100 (1985).

Pocock, J. G. A., *Virtue, Commerce and History: Essays on Political Thought and History, Chiefly in the Eighteenth Century* (Cambridge, 1985).

Prothero, I., *Artisans and Politics in Early Nineteenth-Century London: John Gast and his Times* (Folkestone, 1979).

Sekora, J., *Luxury: The Concept in Western Thought, Eden to Smollett* (Baltimore, 1977).

Sturmer, M., 'An Economy of Delight: Court Artisans of the Eighteenth Century', *Business History Review*, 53 (1979).

Weatherill, L., *Consumer Behaviour and Material Culture in Britain, 1660–1760* (1988).

PART IV

Poverty, Prosperity, and Population

....

CHAPTER 15

Births, Marriages, and Deaths

Malthus, in the 1826 edition of his *Essay on Population*, attempted to discover 'the only effectual mode of improving the condition of the poor'. He was certain that any attempt to increase output faster than population growth was bound to fail, for the powers of reproduction could always keep pace with the supply of commodities, and there would be no long-term improvement in the condition of the poor. The alternative was to concentrate on slowing down the growth of the population, so that there was more for everyone and the condition of the poor would improve. There was, he suggested, a race between the tortoise of output and the hare of population, and only one effective means of raising the standard of living: 'If we can persuade the hare to go to sleep, the tortoise may have some chance of overtaking her.'[1]

Was Malthus guilty of exaggerating the difference in the speed of the contestants? Perhaps the hare was less speedy than he assumed, for there were biological constraints on both births and deaths which set limits to the rate of population growth. The level of mortality was high, especially for infants, in an age before public health and medicine had conquered disease, and life expectancy was low. Although there was no effective birth control other than abstinence and celibacy, women could bear only a limited number of children between menarche and menopause, a period of at most thirty years which was reduced by the late age of marriage in European societies. The population in such circumstances was rarely capable of growing at more than about 1.5 per cent a year. Most estimates place the annual rate of growth of the gross national product in the eighteenth century at considerably below 1 per cent, so that population certainly had the *capacity* to outstrip production at least two- and probably threefold. Population growth much above 0.5 per cent a year would be likely to strain output and threaten the standard of living, and the major determinant of prosperity was society's ability to hold back or to release its full potential of population growth.

British agriculture was able to feed more people as a result of its high levels of productivity, which could lead to a wide range of outcomes. At one end of the spectrum, the existing population could consume more food at a lower price, so that the standard of living improved, more money was available for the purchase of industrial goods and services, and the agricultural surplus allowed people to move to industry and the towns. At the other end of the spectrum, it could allow more people to be fed without any gain in the standard of living, so that improved agricultural productivity resulted in 'agricultural involution', permitting holdings to be subdivided and the rural population to increase. The growth of the Irish population in response to the potato well illustrated the danger of 'agricultural involution': the population was highly susceptible to any fall in agricultural yields, such as the failure of the Irish potato crop in the 1840s. One of the most important issues in the economic and social history of Britain is where it should be placed on this spectrum, and what determined the response to improvements in agricultural productivity. Did gains in agricultural productivity in the seventeenth and early eighteenth centuries produce a higher standard of living and alter expectations; or did they lead to an acceleration in the rate of population growth, pressure on the land, decreasing marginal returns, mounting prices, and a decline in the standard of living to a long-run equilibrium? In the late eighteenth century, did the slower rate of growth of agricultural output mean that population growth surged ahead of food supplies, so causing a sharp drop in the standard of living?

An answer to these questions depends on measuring population growth, which is no easy task, for the first census was not taken until 1801. Measuring the rate of population growth is difficult enough, but the task cannot stop there: it is also necessary to establish the mechanism which controlled growth. Malthus believed that the hare of population was regulated by the age and rate of marriage, which provided the key to the demographic history of eighteenth- and early nineteenth-century Britain. Such a view implies that young men and women carefully analysed their prospects before marriage, obeying the injunction of the *Book of Common Prayer* that matrimony 'is not to be enterprised nor taken in hand unadvisedly, lightly or wantonly, to satisfy man's carnal lusts and appetites, like brute beasts that have no understanding; but reverently, discreetly, advisedly, soberly, and in the fear of God'. The argument rests upon measuring systematic fluctuations in the age and rate of marriage, and establishing that these variations were the most important influences on population growth rather than the birth rate within marriage or the death rate. Unfortunately, civil registration of births, marriages, and deaths only came in 1837, so that any measure of the relative importance of the age of marriage and death rates rests upon considerable ingenuity in interpreting available data.

Reconstructing English Population

*emographic history reached a new level of sophistication with the publication f E. A. Wrigley and R. S. Schofield's *The Population History of England, 1541–1871: A econstruction* in 1981, which forms the basis of all subsequent discussion. Their nalysis rested on 404 parish registers in which parish priests from 1538 recorded very wedding, christening and burying'. These were religious rites rather than direct observation of demographic events, which can lead to distortions. Many ifants died before they could be christened by the parish priest, so that their irths are missing, and neither were their burials recorded so that the crucial ariable of infant mortality was under-recorded. It was also possible for couples) start their lives together without a formal ceremony. These problems were ompounded by the incompetence or absence of clergymen, and by the rise of Jonconformity, which meant that part of the population escaped registration by .nglican clergy. The task facing Wrigley and Schofield was formidable: to inflate ie aggregate data of marriages, christenings and baptisms recorded in 404 egisters to produce annual national totals for all 10,000 or so parishes in England, orrected to allow for late baptism, the growth of Nonconformity, and emigra- ion. The difficulty is not only that data in the parish registers need considerable orrection; there are also problems with the structure of the sample. The egisters were selected for their usefulness in another research project on 'family econstitution'. The ages of a couple at marriage may be established by searching he registers to find the date of their baptism; the birth of their children may be toted from the baptismal records; and the age of death of the parents calculated rom the registration of burials. Reconstitution provides detailed evidence on lemographic behaviour, and requires registers meeting high standards of re- iability over an extended period, which are likely to be found in rural parishes vhere there was a reasonable chance of locating individuals over time. There is, onsequently, a conflict between the needs of the reconstruction project and the •roduction of national aggregate data on births, marriages, and deaths, which equire a balanced coverage of different areas. Rapidly growing provincial towns .nd industrial districts are excluded, such as Birmingham, Manchester, Bristol, .nd Leeds, which were increasing their share of the population in the eighteenth .nd early nineteenth centuries, and had a higher death rate than the country. \lthough the research effort is impressive and the technical sophistication emarkable, the whole exercise rests upon very large assumptions that the data in :ach register are reasonably accurate, that under-recording may be corrected, .nd that the sample of 404 parishes may be converted into the much greater total)f English parishes.

The national aggregates produced from the parish registers (Fig. 15.1 and

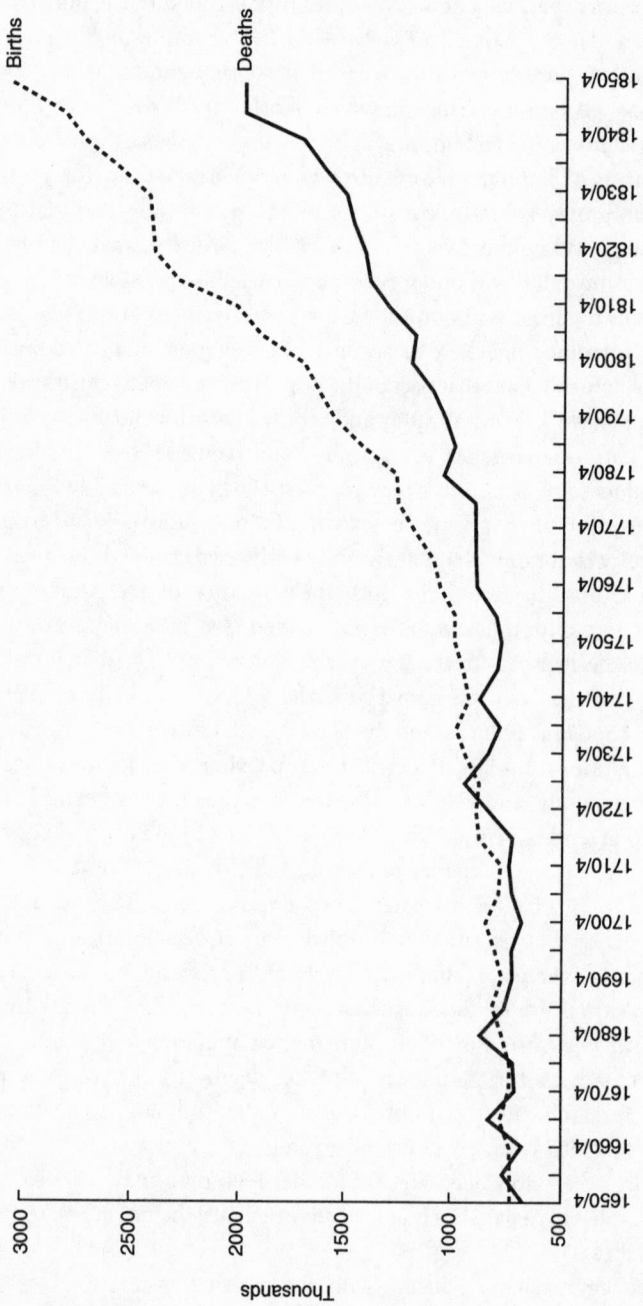

FIG. 15.1. Quinquennial totals of births and deaths, England, 1650–4 to 1850–4

Source: E. A. Wrigley and R. S. Schofield, *The Population History of England, 1541–1871* (1981), table A2.2, 495.

Appendix) suggest that births and deaths roughly balanced in the later seventeenth century, with small surpluses of births interspersed with deficits when deaths soared as a result of sudden calamities such as the plague in 1665. The pattern started to change in the late 1690s when the surplus of births rose, but population increase was held at a low level by a fall in the number of births between 1704 and 1710, and by a rise in the number of deaths in 1719–24, 1727–31, and 1740–2. It was not until the mid-1740s that births consistently pulled ahead of deaths, and they rose to unprecedented levels in the nineteenth century. The aggregate annual series of births and deaths pinpoint some major changes, but information on the *rate* of births, marriages, and deaths per 1,000 population is essential for an understanding of the process of demographic change.

Conversion of the aggregate numbers of marriages, christenings, and burials into the rates of nuptuality, fertility, and mortality requires estimates of the total population, which rely upon 'back projection'. The census of 1871 provides information on the age structure of the population, which is projected back to 1866 by making everyone five years younger, adding those who died or migrated between 1866 and 1871, and subtracting those not born in 1866. The aggregate data of births and deaths from the parish registers were used to project the population back into the past at five-yearly intervals (Fig. 15.2 and Appendix). The population of England, it emerges, grew rapidly in the later sixteenth and first half of the seventeenth centuries, followed by a period of decline or stagnation in the second half of the seventeenth century; growth in the first half of the

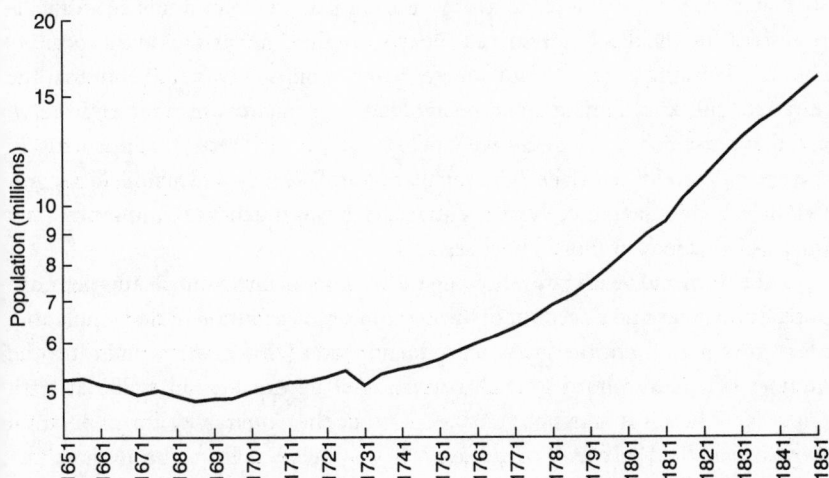

FIG. 15.2. Population of England, 1651–1851

Source: Wrigley and Schofield, *Population History*, table 7.8, pp. 208–9.

eighteenth century was modest, with acceleration from the middle of the century, and particularly after 1786. These back-projection estimates of the total population are then used to convert the aggregate figures of births, deaths, and marriages into rates of fertility and mortality upon which any explanation of the process of population growth must rely.

The results depend upon the statistical techniques used to refine the raw data from the parish registers, which actually show a fall in the birth rate in the second half of the eighteenth century before the adjustments are made. The great virtue of *The Population History* is that its methods are rigorous and open to scrutiny, allowing others to replicate the calculations and to apply different assumptions. The results have been generally accepted, for not only have Wrigley and Schofield's methods survived scrutiny, but the results have a high level of internal consistency, and are in agreement with other trends in the economy. More contentious than their estimate of the population of England is their explanation of trends in the rate of growth.

Accounting for Nuptuality

What demographic mechanism allowed the achievement of an unprecedented rate of growth at the end of the eighteenth and beginning of the nineteenth centuries? Some historians have placed their faith in changes in the death rate, arguing that pre-industrial societies had a fairly constant level of fertility, which was determined by inflexible social rules concerning marriage and child-bearing, so that population grew at a steady rate until it met the limits of available resources and the death rate soared. They place the emphasis upon the 'positive checks' of Malthus's model.[2] Of course, Malthus himself was confident that the 'ultimate check' of famine could be avoided by prudential restraint of fertility, and that pre-industrial societies were able to vary births through adjustments in the age and rate of marriage. The calculations of Wrigley and Schofield suggest that he was right, and that the preventive check was much more important than the positive check of mortality crises.

Crude birth and death rates showing the number of births and deaths per 1,000 population do not take account of the age and sex distribution of the population. More meaningful are the gross reproduction rate (GRR), which indicates the number of children born to each couple, and the expectation of life at birth (Fig. 15.3). The GRR was not constant, so that the potentiality for population growth was held in check or released: it was below 2 from the 1650s to the mid-1680s so that the population was not replacing itself; in the later eighteenth century, it rose to a peak of 3.06 in 1816. The expectation of life at birth increased from 32 or 33 in the 1670s and 1680s to about 39 in the 1810s and 1820s, apart from a

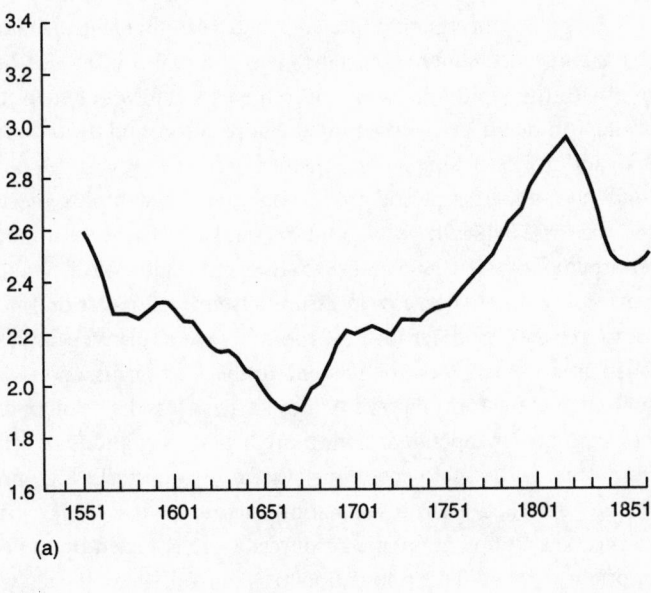

(a)

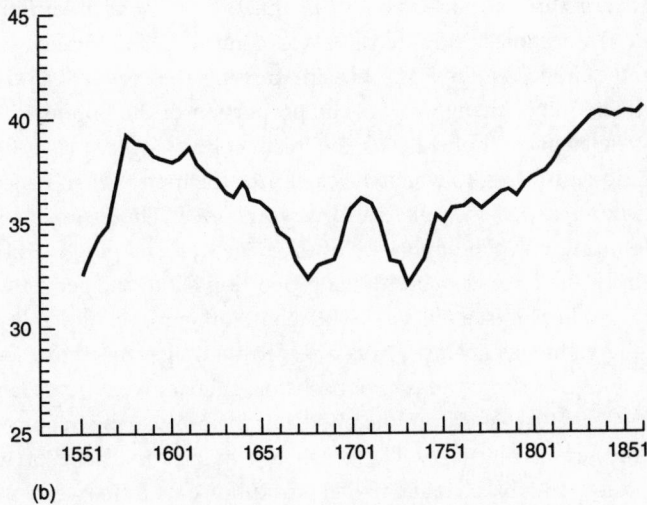

(b)

FIG. 15.3. (*a*) Gross reproduction rate, and, (*b*) life expectation at birth, England, 1551–1861

Note: Five-point moving average of quinquennial rates.

Source: Wrigley and Schofield, *Population History*, 235.

period of high death rates between 1727 and 1731. Clearly, the increase in population in the eighteenth and early nineteenth centuries was the product of both a rise in the gross reproduction rate and an increase in life expectation, but their relative significance shifted. Mortality was the major influence between 1691 and 1751, with the rapid improvement in life expectancy between 1691 and 1706 accounting for the bulk of recovery in the population, and the deterioration between 1726 and 1731 imposing a check. After 1751, fertility was the dominant influence and it was in this period that population growth was most rapid. Consequently, the rise in fertility was about two-and-a-half times as important as the fall in mortality between 1680 and 1820. England, claim Wrigley and Schofield, had 'a fertility-dominated low pressure system'.[3] Population was small relative to resources, and both fertility and mortality were relatively low; growth was controlled predominantly by the preventive check on births, and food crises were unusual. Changes in mortality were, they suggest, less the result of pressure on resources than the 'independent and unpredictable visitations of infectious disease'[4] from outside the socio-economic system. By contrast, 'high-pressure' demographic systems had a large population relative to resources, with high fertility and mortality; population and resources were adjusted by the positive check of mortality crises. The population of England, they argue, was not adjusted by mortality so much as by 'wide, quiet fluctuations in fertility'.[5]

The crucial question is how fertility was controlled and varied, and here Wrigley and Schofield follow Malthus in stressing the 'prudential check' of nuptuality. The initial change was in the proportion of the population which married. Wrigley and Schofield took the 'birth cohort' (aged 0 to 5) from the back-projection estimates, to which they allocated the marriages recorded in the parish registers between fifteen and forty years later. The estimates show a remarkable increase in the popularity of marriage, for 24.9 per cent of people aged 40–4 in 1701 had never married; the proportion fell to 11.2 per cent in 1741 and 6.8 per cent in 1801 (see Fig. 15.4). The major influence on nuptuality to the middle of the eighteenth century was *access* to marriage, the choice between matrimony and remaining a spinster or bachelor. Celibacy went out of fashion in the eighteenth century, and from the middle of the century the major determinant was the *age* at marriage. The mean age at first marriage of women according to estimates based on family reconstitution data from twelve parishes was 26.5 in 1650–99, falling to 24.9 in 1750–99 and 23.4 in 1800–49.[6] This reduction in the age of marriage by three years was sufficient to produce an extra child before the onset of menopause, and earlier marriage alone could account for more than half of the increase in the gross reproduction rate between the late seventeenth and the early nineteenth centuries.

The stress on nuptuality as the regulator of births implies that there were few

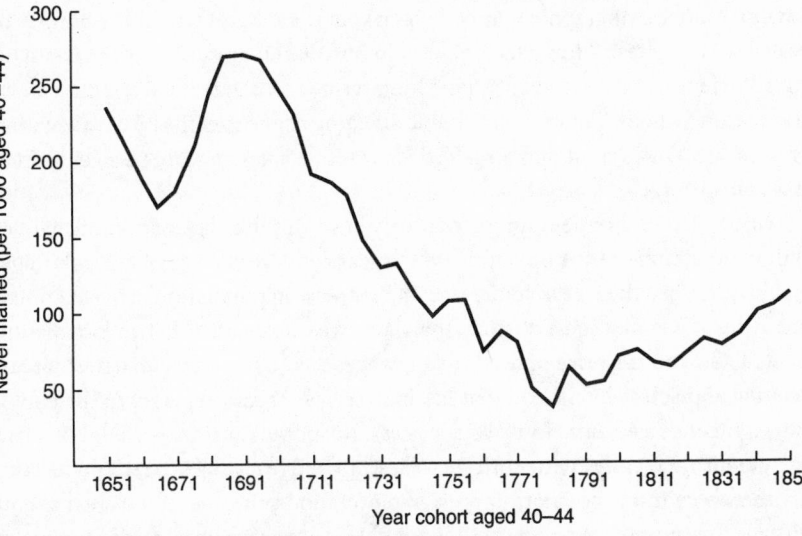

Fɪɢ. 15.4. Proportion of people never marrying in England, 1551–1851

Note: Per 1,000 aged 40–4; five-point centred moving average.

Source: Wrigley and Schofield, *Population History*, 260.

restrictions upon fertility within marriage, and that the crucial determinant of the birth rate was the number of years women were married between menarche and menopause. There was a regime of 'natural fertility', in which births were spread over the whole child-bearing period from marriage to menopause, rather than concentrated on part of the period; and the behaviour of couples did not depend upon the number of children already born, with a sharp fall once a desired family size was reached. The average age of women at the birth of their last child was high in eighteenth-century England, at around 40, and there is no sign that births were limited to part of a woman's productive years until the late nineteenth century. Natural fertility does not mean that women bore as many children as was biologically possible between marriage and menopause, for the gap between pregnancies could vary. At Colyton, for example, the interval was wider in the later seventeenth and early eighteenth centuries, presumably as part of a strategy of adjusting births to the resources of the parish. Reconstitution data suggest that English women generally had fewer children over their child-bearing years than their European counterparts because of longer gaps between pregnancies, which were influenced by variations in the level of sexual activity, the use of coitus interruptus, and by breast-feeding, which determined the return of menstruation after a pregnancy. Natural fertility in England was consequently relatively modest, and behaviour within marriage helps to explain the existence of a 'low-pressure demographic regime' which kept population within the bounds of available resources.[7] However, changes in birth intervals within marriage were not sufficiently marked to explain the long-term trends in fertility and the rate of population growth. The crucial variable affecting changes in the birth rate within a regime of 'low-pressure' natural fertility was the fact that more people married at a younger age.

The key to English demographic history becomes the explanation of changes in the proportion of the population which married, and the age of first marriage. Malthus stressed the role of food prices: an increase in population drove up prices and forced down wages, so that marriage was delayed; a fall in population growth allowed the price of food to fall, wages rose, and people married earlier. Wrigley and Schofield believe that his analysis was broadly correct to the end of the eighteenth century: low food prices and population growth in the late seventeenth and early eighteenth centuries allowed real wages to rise; in the later eighteenth century, population grew rapidly, food prices rose, and real wages fell. At this point, one part of the Malthusian system was overturned: the connection between population increases and price movements. Prices fell from the end of the Napoleonic wars despite continued population growth, and real wages started to improve. But Wrigley and Schofield argue that another part persisted until about 1870: fertility was controlled by nuptiality which was related to trends in real wages. They claim that movements in real wages and the marriage rate were correlated, with a thirty-year lag, from the middle of the sixteenth century to the middle of the nineteenth century. An improvement in real wages at the end of the seventeenth and early eighteenth centuries, they contend, led to a reduction in the age of marriage and an increase in the rate of marriage in the late eighteenth century; a fall in real wages in the late eighteenth century reduced the rate of marriage in the early nineteenth century; and the recovery of real wages in the early nineteenth century produced a higher rate of nuptiality in the mid-nineteenth century. 'As each generation grew up and crossed the threshold into adult life', suggest Wrigley and Schofield,

the marriage conventions of society, reflecting its underlying conditions, acted like a filter. At times young men and women were allowed to pass relatively freely into the married state, but at other times the mesh tightened, ponding back the flow so that many had long to wait before they passed through, while others spilled round, moving forward into middle life single and excluded from marriage.[8]

This attempt to explain changes in the rate and age of marriage by a lagged response to prices and real wages is far too simple and mechanistic. Is it likely that movements in real wages can explain both a fall in the level of celibacy in the early eighteenth century as well as a fall in the mean age at first marriage? Is it lausible that high real incomes thirty years earlier mattered more in making a ecision to marry than low current incomes? The indices used by Wrigley and chofield are flawed, but even if acceptable indices could be devised, the problem vould still remain that correlation is not the same as causation. An increase in rices could, after all, have different effects upon different people. For some, it vould mean a fall in their standard of living which could lead to a variety of esponses. Some would delay marriage in the face of extreme poverty; others ould be forced into the labour market which would increase the likelihood of narriage; still others might be reluctant to leave their village, tying them to the and and delaying marriage. For others, rising prices led to increased incomes, vhich could either allow them to marry earlier or change their reference group o a higher social status with later marriage.

A serious weakness of Wrigley and Schofield's argument is that they do not lirectly analyse the social behaviour of specific groups, in conditions of major tructural change. The wide range of variation between localities is clear from ivil registration data at the end of the period: to take one example, between 1838 nd 1841, only 8 per cent of women in London married under the age of 21, and 25 er cent in Bedfordshire.[9] It is not feasible to explain this divergence by variations n real wages, and the more likely explanation is structural: a high proportion of ;irls in London spent some time in service before marriage, whereas Bed-ordshire had few opportunities for domestic or farm service, and little chance of mployment in factories which could offer independence outside marriage. A hift in the proportion of the population in different types of community would learly affect nuptiality, yet Wrigley and Schofield proceed from national .ggregates of demographic behaviour and trends in real wages. These are meaningless means' which are produced by lumping together a number of liverse patterns, which cannot explain the experience of any social group or ocality.

The underlying assumption in Wrigley and Schofield's model is of a society in vhich sons and daughters entered service or apprenticeship until they could hemselves become farmers or self-employed craftsmen; they saved resources or marriage from their earnings, so that the age of marriage rose when wages ell. The timing of marriage was 'welfare dependent', determined by the ac-:umulation of the resources needed to win a livelihood which was responsive to he level of real income. There is, however, an alternative model: marriage could >e 'density dependent', relying upon the availability of land or some other asset vhich could support a family. Marriage would depend upon 'dead men's shoes', .nd the crucial variable would be periods of mortality which created an opening n the agricultural or trading community, rather than income levels. There was, n this model, a tendency to return to a relatively stable equilibrium between population and available 'openings', or 'homoeostasis'. In Worcestershire, fo example, the epidemic of 1725–9 was followed by a surge of marriages in 1730– and baptisms in 1735–40, with a further peak of marriages in 1760–5 as the earlie 'bulge' of births moved into adulthood.[10] The 'density' model most obvious applies to societies with a strict limit to resources, and a finite number o smallholdings and trading opportunities; it became less applicable with th expansion of waged employment, where marriage depended upon securing a jo and renting a house rather than on a limited number of openings. A major facto in the decline of 'homoeostasis' was the erosion of service in husbandry, whic maintained equilibrium by balancing families with 'surplus' and 'deficit' childrer Servants in husbandry who lived in the households of their employers could nc marry without leaving their positions, and districts dominated by service had higher age of marriage than areas which relied upon day labourers. The labou market at Mitford in Norfolk, for example, was dependent upon day, wage labour with only 5.0 per cent of men and 28.9 per cent of women aged 15 to 29 i domestic or farm service in 1861. The mean age of first marriage was 26.9 for me and 24.9 for women, and the proportion married by age 30 was 75 per cent fo men and 81 per cent for women. At Atcham in Shropshire, service was sti important in 1861, with 34.3 per cent of men aged 15 to 29 and 41.9 per cent c women in domestic or farm service. The mean age of first marriage wa considerably higher, at 29.4 for men and 28.4 for women, and the proportio married by age 30 much lower, at 54 per cent for men and 65 per cent fo women.[11] Clearly, a decline in the proportion of communities dominated b service would reduce the age of marriage and increase potential marital fertility

Transition from service to day labour was more likely at a time of rising price which altered the comparative costs of the two labour systems. Farmers had an incentive to employ day labourers when money wages lagged behind rising prices, such as in the late eighteenth century. A fall in real wages therefore encouraged a shift from service in husbandry to the employment of day labour ers, which led to *earlier* marriage, so contradicting Wrigley and Schofield' contention that falling real wages *delayed* marriage. There was, however, nc simple mechanistic connection between displacement of service in husbandry and price trends, for there were considerable variations across the country according to the nature of the labour market and the agrarian structure (see Fig. 15.5). Where industrial employment placed pressure on the supply of agricul tural labour, service offered the advantage of securing a work-force over the year. Service accordingly persisted in Lancashire and in the north-east o England, where it was no longer part of a 'homoeostatic' regime. Servants were no longer waiting for openings to become farmers as part of their life-cycle, and it could evolve into a permanent status of married farm servants as a means of

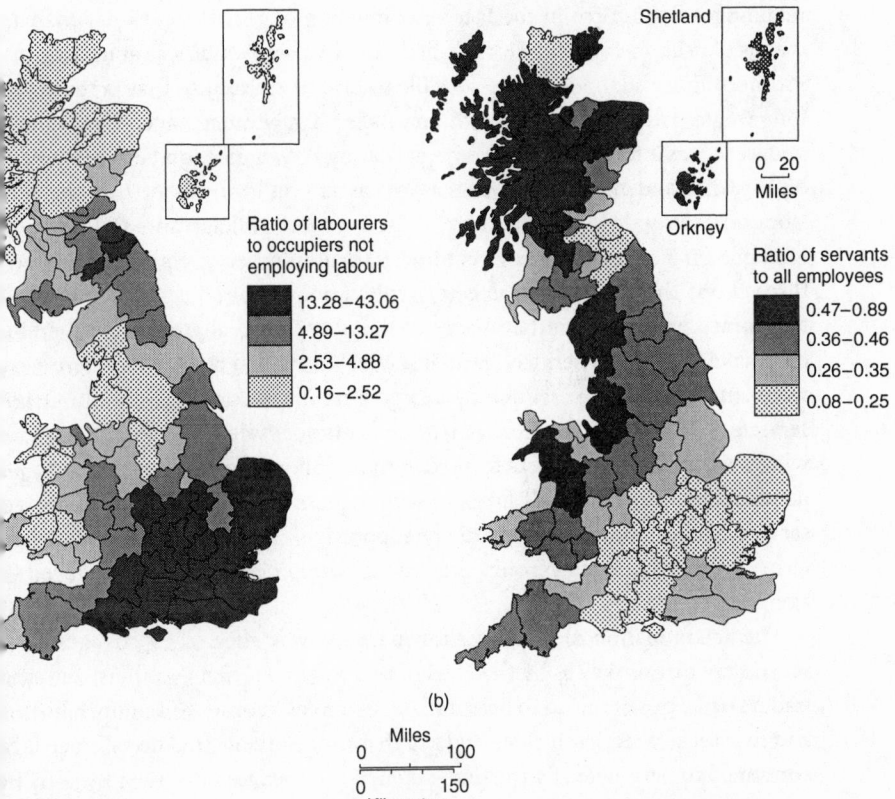

(b)

FIG. 15.5. Agricultural labour force, 1831. (*a*) Ratio of labourers to occupiers not employing labour. The lower the ratio, the more family farms which did not employ waged labour; the higher the ratio, the more 'capitalist' farms with a waged work-force. (*b*) Composition of hired agricultural labour force: ratio of farm servants to all hired workers

Source: M. Overton, 'Agriculture', in J. Langton and R. J. Morris (eds.), *Atlas of Industrialising Britain, 1740–1914* (1986), 45, using PP 1833, xxxvi, *Census Enumeration Abstract, 1831*; (*b*) utilizes the technique of A. Kussmaul, *Servants in Husbandry in Early Modern England* (Cambridge, 1981), app. 8.

retaining a work-force in the face of competing opportunities rather than a٤ means of fitting people into established slots. Where labour was abundant, as southern England, it was more sensible to hire day labour so that in these cas low wages were associated with marriage at a younger age. The agrari structure was a further influence complicating the connection between areas high wages and the survival of service: as late as 1851, about half the hir٠ labourers in the low-wage county of Devon were still servants in husband٠ Reliance on livestock farming required a small number of permanent worke throughout the year, whereas cereal cultivation required a larger number ٠ temporary workers at certain times of the year. Pastoral areas were therefo٠ more likely to retain service, particularly in areas such as Devon where farr٠ were small and were sustained by a large amount of common land. In Devo٠ service continued to function as part of a homoeostatic demographic regin٠ which allowed small farmers to shed surplus children in order for them to jo the families of other small farmers where there were gaps. Small farms ar service in husbandry were mutually supportive, and the emergence of lar٤ farms in the eighteenth century therefore undermined service and reduced t١ age of marriage.[12]

The accumulation of resources for marriage was affected by changes in t١ social structure as well as by the level of real wages. Farmers, artisans, and sm٠ traders had a greater need to accumulate resources in order to acquire a holdir and livestock, or to learn skills and purchase tools; their 'traditional' marriag٠ continued to be affected by the time taken to accumulate resources. By contras wage labourers simply needed a reasonable chance of employment, and tende to marry young. A decline in the proportion of 'traditional' marriages and a ri٤ in 'proletarian' occupations and young marriages would consequently weake constraints on the age of marriage. Family reconstitution data from thirtee parishes suggests an increase in the proportion of 'young marriers': 25.3 per ce٠ of first marriages of men were at age 19–23 in 1650–99, rising to 45.1 per cent ٠ 1750–99.[13] It was not simply that higher incomes permitted 'traditional' marrie٠ to accumulate resources for earlier marriage; there was also an increase in th number of people who had no reason for delay. Prudential restraints were n٠ attractive when there were few prospects for advancement or independence, s٠ that a decline in smallholdings and an expansion of waged employment reduce the age at marriage. The expansion of waged employment could also explain th٠ fall in the level of celibacy in the early eighteenth century, by suggesting tha waged employment initially absorbed underemployed labourers who wer prevented from marrying at all because they fell below the necessary threshold ٠ income. Arguably, the number of underemployed 'non-marriers' increase during the sixteenth and seventeenth centuries as population growth outstrippe the opportunities for waged labour; a lower rate of population growth then allowed the glut of underemployed labour to be absorbed, permitting more people to marry and reducing the number of celibates. Subsequently, expansion of waged employment might have been at the expense of artisans and small farmers, which increased the proportion of young marriers. The argument has a certain plausibility, but it needs to be tested against data on changes in the labour market, and to be developed through analyses of particular locations with different economic structures. Certainly, the connection between 'proletarian' waged labour and the age of marriage was not simple and linear, for it was affected by women's employment. Women in mining villages and centres of heavy industry were less likely to be employed, which meant that they were under greater pressure to marry early than in textile towns where they could obtain paid work. Marriage could also be affected by earnings over the life-cycle, for men in mining and heavy industry were likely to secure relatively well-paid jobs in their early 20s, whereas in textile trades the adult rate was often achieved later. The result could be marked contrasts in the age and rate of marriage between industrial centres dependent on 'proletarian' waged employment. In Sheffield, a town based on steel and cutlery manufacture, 85 per cent of women were married by the age of 30 in 1861; in Keighley, a wool textile town, only 69 per cent of women were married by age 30.[14]

A single explanation operating over the entire period and country is not realistic at a time of major social change when communities and social groups were so divergent. The same rate and age of marriage could be produced by widely different social processes, which are obscured by a crude statistical correlation between an inadequate national index of real wages and a national aggregate pattern of marriage. Wrigley and Schofield's approach is *demographic*, treating the age and rate of marriage as social facts in themselves, largely isolated from the wider social structure. Crucially, the selection of communities for analysis was determined by the quality of demographic data and not by their ability to verify hypotheses. Aggregation masks the processes which were at work, and a single aggregate figure of changes in the age of marriage is less useful than an analysis of why marriage rates varied between communities or social groups, and how their proportions changed. Such an analysis awaits the completion of family reconstitutions for a larger number of parishes with different occupational structures, carefully selected to test the impact of various social variables. Problems will still remain, for the coverage of parishes is heavily biased against urban and industrial areas, which are crucial to an understanding of demographic change. Further, the procedure can only yield results for the 'reconstitutable minority' of the population which, at a time of high permanent and temporary migration, stayed in a parish to be baptized, married, and buried.

It is not likely that the demographic behaviour of the 'persistent' population was similar to that of migrants. Neither do parish registers record occupations, so that it is not possible to specify the marriage patterns of particular trades; the best that can be done is a broad comparison between parishes with fundamentally different economic systems. Nevertheless, the family reconstitution data are useful within broad limits and can permit a more subtle analysis of the determinants of nuptiality.

The use of parish registers and family reconstitution to understand marriage patterns at a local level turns from a mechanistic correlation of population with national statistics of real wages, and stresses the nature of the household economy in different types of community. This approach introduces its own set of preconceptions. The most ambitious comparison between parishes has been undertaken by David Levine, who argues that there were wide divergences in demographic behaviour between Colyton in Devon, Shepshed in Leicestershire, and Terling in Essex.[15] In Colyton, production of woollen textiles declined, threatening the viability of small farms and leading to fragmented holdings. The result was that women had a high age of first marriage of 29.4 in the period 1650–99, and fertility was further limited by a wider interval between births within marriage. The age of first marriage for women fell in the later eighteenth and early nineteenth centuries, to 24.4 between 1800 and 1849. The change, so Levine contends, was the result of greater prosperity with the extension of the market for butter and the spread of lace-making among women, which gave them a dowry and made men willing to choose younger brides. Shepshed, on the edge of Charnwood Forest, did not have a dominant landowner who could exclude residents; its chronology of industrial development was different, for it became an important centre of domestic industry with the emergence of framework knitting in the early eighteenth century. The age of marriage fell for both men and women: in the seventeenth century, the mean age at first marriage was 29.4 for men and 28.1 for women; by 1750–1824, it was 24.0 and 24.1. The explanation proposed by Levine is that knitters required help in the household unit of production, so creating an incentive to marry early; the couple had children immediately in order to get over the 'dependency hump' during which they were a drain on the household economy. An intensification of the work of women and children encouraged early marriage, made children an asset, and produced rapid population growth which removed the need to improve techniques and led to industrial 'involution'. At the end of the Napoleonic wars, wages came under pressure as a result of competition from Saxony, and knitters did not respond by delaying marriage. Maximum earnings were achieved early in life, and they needed assistance; the age of first marriage of women actually *fell* to 22.6 between 1825 and 1851. Terling was very different from both Colyton and

Shepshed: it was an area of commercial grain production for the London market, dominated by a large landowner and a few tenant farmers, with a mass of agricultural labourers. The age of first marriage was already low in the seventeenth century at 25.2 for men and 23.8 for women between 1625 and 1699. There was no prudential motivation to accumulate assets for a smallholding or trade, and the peak of an agricultural labourer's income was in young adulthood, which encouraged early marriage.

Levine's analysis of the three parishes relies upon 'household economics', which suffers from some of the same problems as the demographic approach. Essentially, it assumes a similar Malthusian balancing of population and resources, which concentrates on local structural factors rather than national aggregate variables. There is a danger that the small size of communities and the constraints of reconstitution mean that some of the variations in the age of marriage are random, and that slender data have to bear a heavy burden of interpretation. More serious are the questionable and untested assumptions made by both the demographic and household economics approaches. Above all, the family is seen as pursuing a strategy to maximize income. In Shepshed, it would seem, husband and wife made a conscious calculation of the 'dependency hump' in framework knitting and planned their sexual behaviour accordingly; and the household is seen as co-operative and consensual, pursuing conscious strategies towards an agreed end. These assumptions are not directly tested, and social meaning is simply inferred from the statistics without an analysis of the social context of decisions to marry and the structure of family relations. How plausible is the argument that couples in Shepshed would marry early to produce children to assist in production, with its implication that parents could see beyond the 'dependency hump' which lasted for ten years or more? Could it be that conflict rather than consensus marked the family unit of production? Levine's analysis hints at a divergence of interests, for parents in Shepshed had an incentive to keep their children at home to assist in production, while children had an incentive to start their own production unit at an early age. There were, presumably, generational tensions within the household and it is not clear how the competing needs of parents and children were settled. The household economy approach suggests an instrumental attitude to children as means of augmenting the family economy, which was possibly true of areas of domestic industry where there was a demand for children. However, population growth was also apparent in towns and in the south and east of England where there were few opportunities for child employment, and the question of what to do with the glut of children was an acute social issue.

The transition from childhood to adulthood was handled in a variety of ways, with complex implications for the family economy and the pattern of marriages.

When children left to serve a period in service or apprenticeship, they migh expect to return to the family farm or workshop or, more likely, lose contact witl their family of origin and make their own way in the world. When daughter moved to a town to work as domestic servants, they could retain contact witl the community of origin and return to marry, or start a family in the new location. When daughters stayed at home and worked in domestic industry outside a household unit of production, such as in lace-making in Colyton, wha were the consequences for the balance of power in the family? If the income o daughters was absorbed into the family budget, parents would be reluctant tc lose the supplementary income and marriage would be delayed. Alternatively the income could be retained by the daughter, which could either provide ; nest-egg to allow early marriage and offer an inducement to prospective hus bands (as Levine suggests), or it could make her financially more independen and remove the need to marry. In the cotton and wool textile towns with a large proportion of women working, the result was to delay marriage, for the women had no need to become dependent on the wage of a husband. Levine's sugges tion that men in Colyton were able to select younger wives because they had a dowry from their earnings in the lace trade implies a particular patterr of courtship, and assumes that the power to make decisions rested with men who chose women according to their financial resources. Why should a young woman with assets not choose to marry a man of her own age, or tc remain single?

The underlying assumption of the demographic and household economics approaches is that marriage was instrumental, under the control of the groom rather than the bride, and monitored by the parents. The model is inferred from demographic data rather than tested. It is not self-evident that marriage was a co-operative enterprise, with symmetrical relationships, and changes in the economic structure could affect the balance of power between men and women, both in the marriage market and within marriage. It is necessary to analyse attitudes and behaviour, which reflected shifts in courtship patterns and in the role of the family in selecting spouses, avoiding the over-determined and materialistic interpretations of the demographic and household economics ap- proaches. Many conundrums remain for future social historians to tackle; the work of Wrigley and Schofield and family reconstitution has not so much closed as refocused the debate.

Was Scotland Different?

The debate over the population history of eighteenth-century England has shifted from the relative significance of changes in the birth and death rates to the age and rate of marriage in a 'low-pressure' demographic regime. Just how distinctive was the English pattern? Generally, western Europe had low-pressure demographic regimes with a late age of marriage and a benign environment, and they differed in degree rather than kind, with some countries such as England at the bottom end of the spectrum, and others such as France at the top end. In France, fertility and mortality rates were higher and population growth slower than in England, as a result of reaching or passing the limit of resources. This is not necessarily to argue that the population of France was adjusted mainly by the positive check of famine and disease, for tension between agricultural production and reproduction made the positive check of marriage in France more sensitive to 'shocks' than in England, where greater success in adjusting production and reproduction reduced the need for short-run adjustments to marriage patterns.[16] Where does Scotland fit on this spectrum?

It would be easy to assume that Scotland's harsher climate and the slower commercialization of agriculture meant that the population pressed hard on resources, with a greater likelihood of famine and disease. Scotland was certainly more susceptible to harvest failures than England, with serious crises in the late 1690s, 1739–41, and 1782, in part because there were few winter-sown crops to compensate for a failure of spring-sown crops. Indeed, the major survey of Scottish demographic history by Flinn and his collaborators emphasized trends in mortality, arguing that population growth only became possible with a reduction in crisis mortality in the eighteenth century, when harvest failures merely created periods of scarcity rather than famine and mortality crisis.[17] The change was not, so it was argued, the result of improvements in agricultural techniques so much as of the growth of internal trade and the spread of a commercial economy which raised incomes and allowed food to be purchased outside an area of deficit. Economic change was complemented by the political response of famine relief by the poor law authorities, by the central government in the Highlands, and by landlords, which meant that crop failures such as in Aberdeenshire in 1782 did not produce a famine or mortality crisis on the scale of the 1690s when as many as a fifth of the population in the county perished. But can this emphasis on mortality be accepted? The major study of Scottish population pre-dates Wrigley and Schofield, and reflects an older historiographic tradition in which population growth was periodically cut back by violent fluctuations in the death rate. The implication is that Scotland had a 'high-pressure' demographic regime in which fertility was not held in check by controls over nuptuality, so allowing a serious imbalance between population and resources. Whether the demographic history of Scotland was radically different from England, or was simply the product of difficulties with the sources, remains a nagging conundrum in British demographic history.

The argument that population growth was controlled by short-run fluctu ations in mortality is not plausible, for a crisis usually lasted for a few years, did not affect all areas, and could easily be made good by releasing the reserve of fertility. The underlying *levels* of mortality and fertility are more significant than short-term fluctuations. Unfortunately, reconstruction of Scottish population is hampered by inadequacies of the records. There is not a single Scottish parish register suitable for family reconstitution, and even extraction of the total number of baptisms and burials is fraught with difficulties. Absence of aggregate data on births and deaths makes it impossible to utilize 'back projection' and to calculate fertility and mortality rates. Neither is it possible to make definite statements on the age and rate of marriage, because of bad record keeping and the peculiarities of Scottish law and customs. The Scottish Church did not consider marriage a sacrament, and was concerned mainly with good order Registers merely record the proclamation of banns, which required the deposit of 'conscription money' to be returned if the marriage was celebrated in a suitable manner and the first child was not born within nine months. 'Irregular' marriages without proclamation were valid, provided the two parties consented which could be proved by a verbal promise, or presumed from the act of sexual intercourse or 'cohabitation and repute'.

In the absence of reliable data from parish registers, Scottish historians have been obliged to rely on estimates from the hearth tax of 1691 and a private census of 1755 (see Table 15.1). These figures suggest that the population in the first half of the eighteenth century at best grew by 13 per cent and at worst merely recovered

TABLE 15.1. *Population of Scotland, 1691–1861*

	Population	Growth rate %
1691[a]	766,000	
1691[b]	862,000	
1755	866,000	
1801	1,625,002	
1811	1,824,434	12.3
1821	2,099,945	15.1
1831	2,373,561	13.0
1841	2,620,184	10.4
1851	2,822,742	10.3
1861	3,062,294	6.0

Notes: [a] Assuming 4 persons per head; [b] assuming 4.5 persons per head.

Source: M. W. Flinn *et al.*, *Scottish Population History from the Seventeenth Century to the 1930s* (Cambridge, 1977), table 3.2.6, pp. 192–9; table 5.1.1, p. 302.

from the mortality crisis of the late 1690s; by contrast, the population of England grew by 22 per cent between 1691 and 1756. Scottish population grew by a relatively modest 28 per cent between 1755 and the census of 1801, when growth in England was 45 per cent.

There is some scrappy and impressionistic evidence that the lower rate of population growth arose from a regime of high mortality and low fertility. The age structure of the Scottish population in the census of 1755 implies a life expectancy at birth of 31 or 32, in comparison with 36 to 37 in England, and the crude death rate in Scotland in the 1750s was about 31 per 1,000 in comparison with 26 per 1,000 in England, with a high level of infant mortality at over 220 per 1,000 births in Scotland compared with 170–190 in England in the first half of the eighteenth century.[18] Mortality is not the only factor, for it is at least arguable that Scottish fertility was held in check for a longer period than in England by a high level of celibacy and a high age of marriage. Personal details provided by women when they gave evidence in court offer a rough guide to age at first marriage: the mean age at first marriage of women in the Lowlands between 1660 and 1770 was 26 to 27, with 11 per cent remaining single at the end of their fertile period. Similar figures have been found in partial family reconstitutions, and the fertility of the Scottish population was clearly constrained. A reserve of births was available which could be released by a fall in the level of celibacy and the age of marriage, and Scotland probably differed from England because the constraints on nuptiality were not removed during the eighteenth century. It has been suggested, on the basis of the shreds of available evidence, that the mean age at first marriage of Scottish women remained around 26 to 27 in the late eighteenth and early nineteenth centuries, and that the level of celibacy remained high.[19] A tentative explanation for stable nuptiality is that there was less room for manœuvre and less opportunity for economic independence, which led to greater caution in marrying. Grain yields were low, with a high annual variation in the amount of food for human consumption, and a large annual and decadal variation in real wages; there was also less non-agricultural employment than in England. These constraints were intensified by the less generous provision of poor relief in Scotland. If the few scraps of evidence are anywhere close to the truth, the marriage pattern was a crucial component of the Scottish demographic regime. It held the Scottish population below its potential level of growth, preventing more serious subsistence and mortality crises: the apparently greater relative importance of mortality depended upon stability of nuptiality.

Unfortunately, Scottish demographic history remains an area of considerable uncertainty. Of course, there were likely to be considerable divergences between the Lowlands and Highlands, and major changes over time as the agrarian structure was transformed. The change in the pattern of tenancies and the decline of cottars or subtenants, the demise of clans, and clearance of the Highlands would presumably affect the pattern of marriage. In many ways, it is misleading to refer to a monolithic 'Scottish' or 'English' demographic system; the reality is that they formed a collection of regional systems, which shaded into each other along the border.

Restoring Mortality

The new-found importance of nuptuality has led to an over-reaction against the role of mortality in England; it may not provide the key to population growth, but it does need to be integrated into the demographic process and social structure. Deaths could affect the decision to marry through the creation of 'openings', and obviously determined the duration of marriage. The disruption of marriage by death had major social consequences, for approximately 30 per cent of children in Bristol in the 1690s had lost one or both parents, and bereavement was one reason for children leaving home to seek work or to live with kin. Single parents and their children formed a large proportion of the dependent poor, with 19.1 per cent of households in Bristol in the 1690s headed by widows and a further 4.2 per cent by widowers; the poor law was to a large extent concerned with relatively generous income support for these families.[20] Of course, widows and widowers could remarry, and remarriages accounted for 25 to 30 per cent of all marriages in the late sixteenth century. The proportion fell to 10 per cent in the mid-nineteenth century, only in part as a result of a lower level of mortality. A widow was an attractive marital proposition where she had inherited land or a business, and she might welcome remarriage if she needed assistance; on the other hand, a widow with dependent children and no assets was less attractive and might have to rely upon the poor law or taking in lodgers or laundry to maintain herself and her children. Changes in the economy during the eighteenth century led to a relative decline in the former and an increase in the latter type of widow. Children who were orphaned or whose surviving parent could not cope might be left in the care of a relative or passed to the poor law authorities who had a continuing problem of how to handle their charges. Many apprenticed pauper children to learn a trade, paying a premium to the employer who would find board and lodgings. The child might learn a trade, but could equally well be treated as cheap labour in cotton-mills or as a domestic servant. The pattern of mortality clearly had major consequences for the bereaved and for social policy.

Life expectancy affected the transmission of landed estates in landed society, influencing the flow of land on to the market and the prospects of maintaining strict settlement. The demographic lottery did not affect only the landed élite, for the timing of a father's death determined whether a child would obtain the family holding or business at a young age, or be forced to wait before inheriting any family asset. By the 1770s, the eldest child was, on average, about 35 at the time of his father's death. The life experience of women was profoundly affected by changes in the relationship between ages of marriage, birth of last child, and death. In the eighteenth and early nineteenth centuries, the median age of women at the birth of their last child was 39, and a woman born in 1711 would have a life expectancy of 65 once she had survived the dangers of childhood. Her first child would be likely to marry when she was about 48 and her last child when she was about 62, around the same time as the death of her husband. She would only survive the marriage of her last child by three years, and would die about thirteen years before the birth of her last grandchild. The age of marriage fell in the late eighteenth century, which meant that the first grandchild arrived soon after the birth of her last child. Many women therefore spent their adult lives caring for their own children and assisting in the care of grandchildren. When natural fertility was abandoned in the later nineteenth century, the median age of women at the birth of their last child fell, and increased life expectancy meant that many had a long period free of child care when they could return to work. Mortality and life expectancy need to be integrated with the age of marriage and the timing of births in order to understand the changing shape of the family life-cycle.[21]

Mortality, argue Wrigley and Schofield, ceased to be the most significant variable after 1750, and was a reflection of 'independent and unpredictable visitations of infectious diseases' coming from outside rather than within the socio-economic system. Social and economic variables are, in their analysis, confined to the explanation of nuptuality and births. This is to overlook marked regional variations within the national trend in mortality, and especially the shift of population towards towns and industrial districts which had a considerably higher mortality rate, particularly for infants and children. In Whickham, a mining village on Tyneside, mortality was 'disastrously high'[22] and the population could only grow by constant migration. Even in the small market town of Gainsborough in Lincolnshire, infant mortality was 272 per 1,000 births in 1700–49, or three times the level of the rural parish of Hartland in Devon where there were 85 infant deaths per 1,000 births. In 1811, the expectation of life at birth in London and towns in England and Wales with a population of 100,000 was 30; in the country, it was 41.[23] Clearly, the release of labour from agriculture would, other things being equal, produce a rise in the death rate and a fall in life expectancy. In reality, the death rate fell and life expectancy improved, which indicates a considerable improvement in the death rate in order to compensate for urbanization and industrialization, and to allow a modest increase in life expectancy. Why was the curse of mortality not so much worse?

Mortality crises caused by famine and epidemic disease certainly disappeared. Wrigley and Schofield calculated twenty-five-year moving averages of deaths and isolated years with markedly higher mortality. The last mortality crises in England with a death rate 30 per cent above the twenty-five-year moving average were in the late 1720s and 1741–2; there was no crisis with a death rate 20 per cent above the moving average after 1762–3. One sign of famine conditions is a rise in *all* grain prices; in England, a failure in one crop did not drive up all prices with the possible exception of 1728. Subsistence crises on a major scale disappeared earlier than in France, where the last serious crisis was in 1817. England, unlike France and Scotland, had a balance between spring- and winter-sown crops so that a failure in one set of crops was less likely to cause a subsistence crisis, and improvements in distribution meant that local food shortages could be rectified. There was, however, a cost: improved transport and integration provided pathways for the transmission of diseases between regions, which helps to explain a shift in the location of English mortality crises. Southern England was worst affected in the seventeenth century, when well-developed markets and communications reduced the impact of harvest failures, but dense settlement and economic integration allowed the rapid spread of infectious disease; it escaped lightly in the eighteenth century. The remote, pastoral north-west was little affected in the seventeenth century, but was seriously affected in the eighteenth when integration into the national economy initially imposed strains on the marketing of food, and facilitated the spread of disease. Increased mortality was a perverse sign of economic growth, and it took some time for the distribution of food to adjust and the population to come to terms with a new disease environment.[24]

England certainly became less prone to crises of famine and epidemic disease, but more significant were changes in the underlying level of mortality, where a striking feature of the second half of the eighteenth century was the reduction in urban mortality. Although the death rate remained higher than in the country-side until the end of the nineteenth century, towns ceased to be 'devourers' of population with more deaths than births. In Nottingham, for example, the 'age of massacre by epidemic'[25] was over by the 1740s and, despite a deterioration at the end of the eighteenth century, towns did not again become areas of natural population decline. The experience of London is particularly important, for it accounted for 10 per cent of the total English population, and during the seventeenth and eighteenth centuries, when it had a deficit of births over deaths, it was only able to sustain itself by absorbing as much as half the population growth of England. The relationship between the metropolis and the rest of the country could be crucial for spreading disease. The great metropolises of pre-industrial Europe had high levels of mortality which were stable in the short term. Smallpox and measles were endemic in the metropolis, and on occasion spilled into the rest of the country as an epidemic: provincial mortality was less severe in the long term, but was subject to short-term fluctuations. Any understanding of the mortality patterns of the eighteenth and early nineteenth centuries needs to take account of London's demography, rather than concentrating on national aggregate figures which are a composite of distinct patterns of rural and urban, metropolitan and provincial mortality.

London was a devourer of population in the eighteenth century (see Fig. 15.6).[26] The London Bills of Mortality record an average of 5,400 more burials than baptisms a year in 1700–9, or an excess of burials of 25.7 per cent; the situation subsequently deteriorated, and in the 1740s there were 11,600 more burials a year, or an excess of 44.4 per cent. By the 1790s mortality was in retreat,

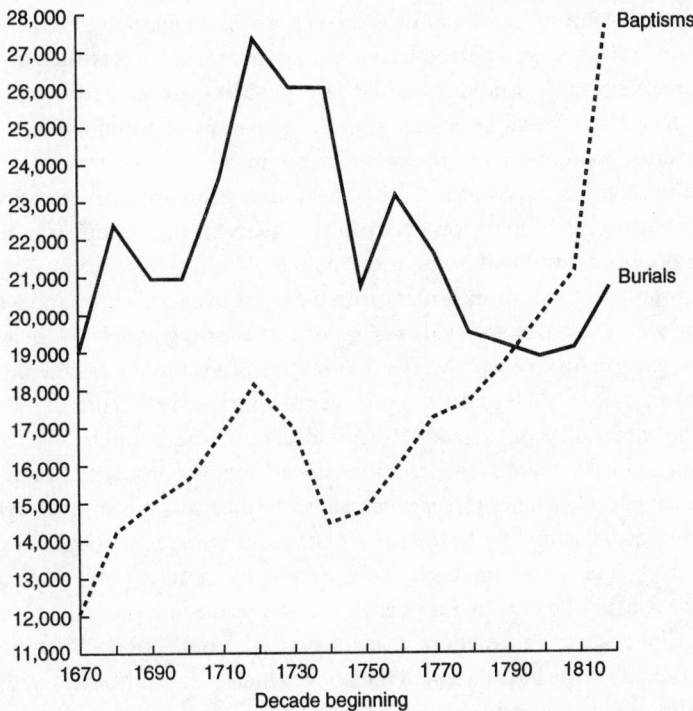

FIG. 15.6. London Bills of Mortality: annual average of baptisms and burials per decade, 1670–1820

Source: J. Landers, 'Mortality and Metropolis: The Case of London, 1675–1825', *Population Studies*, 41 (1987), 63.

for there were only 500 more burials than baptisms a year, an excess of 2.6 per cent; and by the 1820s, there were 7,000 more baptisms than burials, or an excess of baptisms over burials of 33.8 per cent. The decline in mortality in late eighteenth- and early nineteenth-century London is confirmed by data kept by the London Quakers, whose infant mortality rate fell from 341 per 1,000 births in 1725–49 to 151 per 1,000 by 1825–49. The high level of mortality in eighteenth-century London can be explained without too much difficulty: it was largely a result of 'crowd diseases' such as smallpox, measles, and tuberculosis. Children, whether born in London or migrants, lacked immunity and had a high death rate; London-born adolescents and young adults acquired immunity and had a low mortality; immigrants to London lacked immunity and had a higher death rate. The presence of a large number of migrants consequently contributed to the high mortality of London, and provided the means of spreading diseases to the rest of the country. The sharp fall in London's mortality at the end of the eighteenth century is more difficult to explain, and may best be understood through analysing the process of 'conduction' of infectious diseases along 'pathways', which were affected by social and structural factors such as social segregation, housing conditions, child-care practices, or drainage and water supply. Mortality should be inserted into the analysis of social and economic change rather than pushed to the margins: the micro-biological world was not autonomous, for it was mediated by social and economic structures which influenced patterns of infection between the reservoir of metropolitan disease and the provinces, and within the metropolis.

Unfortunately, accurate information on the cause of death is rare, and without knowing which diseases declined, it is impossible to know which 'pathway' was relevant. Historians are left to infer the nature of visitations of disease from indirect indications, such as the time of year at which death occurred: influenza hits in the winter, diseases spread by flies and faeces in the summer. The scourge of the plague certainly disappeared after its last major outbreak in London in 1665, but a variety of killer diseases remained: typhus was transmitted by body lice; dysentery was carried by flies; influenza and whooping cough were airborne; chicken-pox and smallpox were caught by contact; and cholera was spread by water. The only disease which was amenable to medical intervention was smallpox, after inoculation was introduced from Turkey in 1720, and overseers paid for the inoculation of the poor in their parishes from the 1750s and 1760s. Although some historians claim that the effects were dramatic, it is not certain that smallpox was the major killer in the first half of the eighteenth century, and inoculation was by no means comprehensive or effective against the various strains of the virus. A major component of the decline in mortality was a fall in the level of infant mortality, particularly in the first month of life. The

London Quaker data, for example, indicate a fall from 112 deaths per 1,000 births in the first month in 1725–49, to 33 in 1825–49. The explanation is probably to be found in child-rearing practices and improved housing with better heating, which led to a reduction in deaths from respiratory infections. The construction of houses with brick; the availability of coal for domestic fuel; the spread of cheap, easily washed cotton clothing; the improvement of street paving and cleaning; the movement of the better off to separate areas of towns, could all help to explain a fall in mortality. Of course, micro-organisms could still wreak havoc in the absence of effective therapies, and the arrival of cholera from Asia in the 1830s and typhus in the 1840s led to high death rates. In Glasgow, for example, the death rate rose from 24.8 per 1,000 in 1821–4 to 49 in 1832 as a result of cholera, and to 56 in 1847 as a result of typhus.[27] These diseases were transmitted by the contamination of drinking water by sewage, which was essentially a political problem of the provision of adequate finance and administrative structures to supply pure water and effective drainage. Many European cities remained susceptible to visitations of cholera to the end of the nineteenth century; British cities had their last significant epidemic in 1866, and never returned to the high levels of urban mortality of the eighteenth century.

Migration

Britain did not have a single, homogeneous demographic regime which can be analysed through national aggregates. It is more realistic to construct a national population history from 'a series of distinctive regional demographic processes that are linked together by migration'.[28] There was, indeed, a high level of mobility in seventeenth- and eighteenth-century Britain, both within Britain and to other countries.

Movement was in part contained within the regional demographic system, as children of one family moved a short distance to spend a period as a farm servant in a nearby parish, or to a nearby town to learn a trade. Such migration was circular and short distance, largely confined to adolescents and young adults. Indeed, there was a contraction of longer-distance 'subsistence' migration which led the poor to wander in search of casual work. Such 'vagrancy' had troubled the authorities in the sixteenth and seventeenth centuries, leading to strict regulations to control movement. Subsequently, a slackening of population growth and lessening of famine meant that long-distance migration ceased to be a feature of the very poor, and was predominantly for betterment. Much more significant in connecting regions in the eighteenth century was 'ripple' migration. A town or industrial parish acted like a stone thrown into a pond, sending out ripples to the bank: the town attracted migrants from the immediate hinterland, whose places were filled by incomers from neighbouring parishes. These ripples of migration connected different demographic systems, and gradually shifted population from regions with surplus population to those with a demand for labour in trade and industry. Migration was endemic, but it was not uniform throughout the country. It was affected by social policy, for parishes were concerned that newcomers would impose a charge when they were unemployed or old, and they tried to balance their need for labour against the possible costs. The extent of migration was also affected by the social structure of the community. The northern and western Highlands of Scotland, for example, were poorer and more vulnerable to famine than the southern and eastern Highlands but fewer migrants left the north and west where crofting and subdivision of holdings by cottars gave access to a small plot, which was supplemented by temporary migration to the Lowlands as seasonal workers. In the southern and western Highlands, the right to land was curtailed by the rise of direct tenancies, and permanent migration to the Lowlands was more attractive.

Migration within Britain did not affect the overall growth of the population; migration overseas reduced the size of the population and limited future births. About 20 per cent of the natural population increase of England between 1695 and 1801 was absorbed by emigration, which contributed to the fall in the population in the late seventeenth century. Emigrants were, on the whole, not drawn from the poorest members of society, with the exception of 37,000 convicts who were transported to North America between 1718 and 1775. Generally, emigrants fell into two broad types. The first was similar to service in husbandry or apprenticeship: it consisted of indentured servants who agreed to work for a master for a fixed period, usually of four years, in return for a passage and board and lodging on arrival. Between 1650 and 1780, about 300,000 to 400,000 indentured servants left, predominantly single young men from the south of England, usually craftsmen who had served at least part of an apprenticeship or acquired a skill. They were in great demand in America to supply affluent consumers: bookbinders, engravers, gilders, carpenters, masons, wheelwrights were eagerly sought in expanding and prosperous towns such as Philadelphia, Boston, and New York. Of course, servants had an incentive to break their indentures in order to earn high wages or buy land; and masters had an incentive to impose controls to enforce the contract, or to sell the indenture for a profit. The system became adversarial, ceasing to be like service in husbandry and becoming more like chattel slavery. The second, and smaller, stream of emigrants consisted of families, who were mainly drawn from Scotland and the north of England. Most came from farming families which sold their assets to start a new holding in America, attracted by land speculation rather than the flourishing urban labour market. Yeomen and 'tacksmen' were in decline in

Britain; they were reborn on the American frontier. The history of British agrarian society and demographic structures continued across the Atlantic, among the craftsmen of Boston, New York, and Philadelphia and the small farmers of New England. The craftsmen of the Atlantic seaboard shared with the craftsmen in London, from whom so many were drawn, the same attitudes to the maintenance of their 'honourable' trades and their property in skill. On the frontier, settlers developed the country ideology of hostility to monied corruption and aristocratic privilege which was a commonplace in the county associations of England. Britain was, indeed, part of a wider Atlantic demographic and political system.[29]

NOTES

1. Quoted in E. A. Wrigley, *Continuity, Chance and Change: The Character of the Industrial Revolution in England* (Cambridge, 1988), 33.

2. e.g. P. E. Razzell, 'Population Change in Eighteenth-Century England: A Reinterpretation', *Economic History Review*, 2nd ser 18. (1965), and, more generally, T. McKeown, *The Modern Rise of Population* (1976), ch. 2.

3. E. A. Wrigley and R. S. Schofield, *The Population History of England, 1541–1871: A Reconstruction* (1981), 451.

4. Ibid. 453.

5. Ibid. 451.

6. Ibid. 257–65; see also D. R. Weir, 'Rather Never than Late: Celibacy and Age at Marriage in English Cohort Fertility, 1541–1871', *Journal of Family History*, 9 (1990).

7. E. A. Wrigley, 'Family Limitation in Pre-industrial England', *Economic History Review*, 2nd ser. 29 (1966); and C. Wilson, 'Natural Fertility in Pre-industrial England, 1600–1799', *Population Studies*, 38 (1984).

8. Wrigley and Schofield, *Population History*, 435.

9. R. B. Outhwaite, 'Age at Marriage in England from the Late Seventeenth to the Nineteenth Century', *Transactions of the Royal Historical Society*, 5th ser. 23 (1975), 59.

10. D. E. C. Eversley, 'A Survey of Population in an Area of Worcestershire from 1660–1750 on the Basis of Parish Registers', in D. V. Glass and D. E. C. Eversley (eds.), *Population in History: Essays in Historical Demography* (1965), 403, 406, 408–9.

11. P. R. A. Hinde, 'Household Structure, Marriage and the Institution of Service in Nineteenth-Century Rural England', *Local Population Studies*, 35 (1985); and 'The Marriage Market in the Nineteenth-Century English Countryside', *Journal of European Economic History*, 18 (1989).

12. A. Kussmaul, *Servants in Husbandry in Early Modern England* (Cambridge, 1981).

13. J. A. Goldstone, 'The Demographic Revolution in England: A Re-examination', *Population Studies*, 39 (1986), 19.

14. R. I. Woods and P. R. A. Hinde, 'Nuptiality and Age at Marriage in Nineteenth-Century England', *Journal of Family History*, 10 (1985), 125.

15. D. Levine, *Family Formation in an Age of Nascent Capitalism* (New York, 1977).

16. D. R. Weir, 'Life under Pressure: France and England, 1670–1870', *Journal of Economic History*, 44 (1984).

17. M. W. Flinn et al., *Scottish Population History from the Seventeenth Century to the 1930s* (Cambridge, 1977).

18. R. Mitchison, 'Webster Revisited: A Re-examination of the 1775 Census of Scotland', in T. M. Devine (ed.), *Improvement and Enlightenment* (Edinburgh, 1989), 71.

19. R. A. Houston, 'The Demographic Regime, 1760–1830', in T. M. Devine and R. Mitchison (eds.), *People and Society in Scotland*, i (Edinburgh, 1988), 19–20; and 'Age at Marriage of Scottish Women, c.1660–1770', *Local Population Studies*, 43 (1990).

20. P. Laslett, 'Parental Deprivation in the Past: A Note on the History of Orphans in England', *Local Population Studies*, 13 (1974); J. R. Holman, 'Orphans in Pre-industrial Towns: The Case of Bristol in the late Seventeenth Century', *Local Population Studies*, 15 (1975).

21. M. Anderson, 'The Emergence of the Modern Life-Cycle in Britain', *Social History*, 10 (1985), 74, 76.

22. D. Levine and K. Wrightson, *The Making of an Industrial Society: Whickham, 1560–1765* (Oxford, 1991), 179.

23. E. A. Wrigley and R. S. Schofield, 'English Population History from Family Reconstitution: Summary Results, 1600–1799', *Population Studies*, 37 (1983), 179; R. Woods, 'The Effect of Population Redistribution on the Level of Mortality in Nineteenth-Century England and Wales', *Journal of Economic History*, 45 (1985), 650.

24. Wrigley and Schofield, *Population History*, 334 and app. 10.

25. J. D. Chambers, 'Population Change in a Provincial Town: Nottingham, 1700–1800', in L. S. Pressnell (ed.), *Studies in the Industrial Revolution* (1960), 110.

26. J. Landers, 'Mortality and Metropolis: The Case of London, 1675–1825', *Population Studies*, 41 (1987).

27. Flinn et al., *Scottish Population History*, 377.

28. R. A. Houston, *The Population History of Britain and Ireland 1500–1750* (1992), 60, quoting J. de Vries on Holland.

29. B. Bailyn, *The Peopling of British North America: An Introduction* (Cambridge, Mass., 1985); D. Galenson, *White Servitude in Colonial America: An Economic Analysis* (Cambridge, 1981).

FURTHER READING

Anderson, M., 'The Emergence of the Modern Life-Cycle in Britain', *Social History*, 10 (1985).

—— 'The Social Position of Spinsters in Mid-Victorian Britain', *Journal of Family History*, 9 (1984).

—— 'Marriage Patterns in Victorian Britain: An Analysis Based on Registration District Data for England and Wales, 1861', *Journal of Family History*, 1 (1976).

—— 'Historical Demography after *The Population History of England*', *Journal of Historical Demography*, 4 (1984–5).

—— *Approaches to the History of the Western Family, 1500–1914* (1980).

Appleby, A. P., 'Grain Prices and Subsistence Crises in England and France, 1690–1740', *Journal of Economic History*, 39 (1979).

Armstrong, W. A., 'The Trend of Mortality in Carlisle between the 1780s and the 1840s: A Demographic Contribution to the Standard of Living Debate', *Economic History Review*, 2nd ser. 34 (1981).

Bailyn, B., *The Peopling of British North America: An Introduction* (Cambridge, Mass., 1985).

Baker, D., *The Inhabitants of Cardington in 1782*, Publications of the Bedfordshire Historical Records Society 52 (1973).

Chambers, J. D., 'Population Change in a Provincial Town: Nottingham, 1700–1800', in L. S. Presnell (ed.), *Studies in the Industrial Revolution* (1960).

——*Population, Economy and Society in Pre-industrial England*, ed. W. A. Armstrong (Oxford, 1972).

Clark, P., 'Migration in England during the Late Seventeenth and Early Eighteenth Centuries', *Past and Present*, 83 (1979).

Cunningham, H., 'The Employment and Unemployment of Children in England, c.1680–1851', *Past and Present*, 126 (1990).

Devine, T. M., 'Highland Migration to Lowland Scotland, 1760–1860', *Scottish Historical Review*, 62 (1983).

Eversley, D. E. C., 'A Survey of Population in an Area of Worcestershire from 1660 to 1750 on the Basis of Parish Registers', in D. V. Glass and D. E. C. Eversley (eds.), *Population in History: Essays in Historical Demography* (1965).

——'Population, Economy and Society', in D. V. Glass and D. E. C. Eversley (eds.), *Population in History: Essays in Historical Demography* (1965).

Flinn, M. W., *British Population Growth, 1700–1850* (1970).

——et al., *Scottish Population History from the Seventeenth Century to the 1930s* (Cambridge, 1977).

Galenson, D., *White Servitude in Colonial America: An Economic Analysis* (Cambridge, 1981).

Goldstone, J. A., 'The Demographic Revolution in England: A Re-examination', *Population Studies*, 49 (1986).

Gooder, A., 'The Population Crisis of 1727–30 in Warwickshire', *Midland History*, 1 (1971–2).

Habakkuk, H. J., 'The Economic History of Modern Britain', *Journal of Economic History*, 18 (1958).

——'English Population in the Eighteenth Century', *Economic History Review*, 2nd ser. 6 (1953–4).

Hajnal, J., 'European Marriage Patterns in Perspective', in D. V. Glass and D. E. C. Eversley (eds.), *Population in History: Essays in Historical Demography* (1965).

Hinde, P. R. A., 'Household Structure, Marriage and the Institution of Service in Nineteenth-Century Rural England', *Local Population Studies*, 35 (1985).

——'The Marriage Market in the Nineteenth-Century English Countryside', *Journal of European Economic History*, 18 (1989).

Holman, J. R., 'Orphans in Pre-industrial Towns: The Case of Bristol in the Late Seventeenth Century', *Local Population Studies*, 15 (1975).

Houston, R. A., 'Geographical Mobility in Scotland, 1652–1811: The Evidence of Testi monials', *Journal of Historical Geography*, 11 (1985).

—— 'The Demographic Regime, 1760–1830', in T. M. Devine and R. Mitchison (eds.) *People and Society in Scotland*, i (Edinburgh, 1988).

—— 'Age at Marriage of Scottish Women, c.1660–1770', *Local Population Studies*, 43 (1990)

—— *The Population History of Britain and Ireland, 1500–1750* (1992).

Jackson, S., 'Population Change in the Somerset–Wiltshire Border Area, 1701–1800: A Regional Demographic Study', *Southern History*, 7 (1985).

Jones, R. E., 'Further Evidence on the Decline in Infant Mortality in Pre-industrial England: North Shropshire, 1561–1810', *Population Studies*, 34 (1980).

Krause, J. T., 'The Changing Adequacy of English Registration, 1690–1837', in D. V. Glass and D. E. C. Eversley (eds.), *Population in History: Essays in Historical Demography* (1965)

—— 'Changes in English Fertility and Mortality, 1781–1850', *Economic History Review*, 2nd ser. 11 (1958–9).

Kussmaul, A., *Servants in Husbandry in Early Modern England* (Cambridge, 1981).

—— *A General View of the Rural Economy of England, 1538–1840* (Cambridge, 1990).

Landers, J., 'Mortality and Metropolis: The Case of London, 1675–1825', *Population Studies* 41 (1987).

—— 'Age Patterns of Mortality in London during the "Long Eighteenth Century": A Test of the "High Potential" Model of Metro-mortality', *Social History of Medicine*, 3 (1990)

Laslett, P., 'Parental Deprivation in the Past: A Note on the History of Orphans in England', *Local Population Studies*, 13 (1974).

—— *Family Life and Illicit Love in Past Generations* (Cambridge, 1977).

Levine, D., *Family Formation in an Age of Nascent Capitalism* (New York, 1977).

—— 'Some Competing Models of Population Growth during the First Industrial Revolution', *Journal of European Economic History*, 7 (1978).

—— 'Industrialisation and the Proletarian Family in England', *Past and Present*, 107 (1985).

—— and Wrightson, K., *The Making of an Industrial Society: Whickham, 1560–1765* (Oxford, 1991).

McKeown, T., *The Modern Rise of Population* (1976).

Malthus, T. R., *An Essay on the Principle of Population* (1803 edn.), ed. with variora by Patricia James (Cambridge, 1989).

Martin, J. M., 'Marriage and Economic Stress in the Felden of Warwickshire during the Eighteenth Century', *Population Studies*, 31 (1977).

Mitchison, R., 'Webster Revisited: A Re-examination of the 1775 Census of Scotland', in T. M. Devine (ed.), *Improvement and Enlightenment* (Edinburgh, 1989).

Outhwaite, R. B., 'Age of Marriage in England from the Late Seventeenth to the Nineteenth Century', *Transactions of the Royal Historical Society*, 5th ser. 23 (1975).

Razzell, P. E., 'Population Change in Eighteenth-Century England: A Reinterpretation', *Economic History Review*, 2nd ser. 18 (1965).

Schofield, R., 'English Marriage Patterns Revisited', *Journal of Family History*, 10 (1985).

Sharpe, P., 'Literally Spinsters: A New Interpretation of Local Economy and Demography in Colyton in the Seventeenth and Eighteenth Centuries', *Economic History Review*, 2nd ser. 44 (1991).

Smith, R. M., 'Fertility, Economy and Household Formation in England over Three Centuries', *Population and Development Review*, 7 (1981).

—— 'Some Issues Concerning Families and their Property in Rural England, 1520–1800', in R. M. Smith (ed.), *Land, Kinship and the Life Cycle* (Cambridge, 1984).

Smout, T. C., 'Scottish Marriage, Regular and Irregular, 1500–1940', in R. B. Outhwaite (ed.), *Marriage and Society* (1981).

Snell, K. D. M., *Annals of the Labouring Poor: Social Change and Agrarian England, 1660–1900* (Cambridge, 1985).

Tucker, G. S. L., 'English Pre-industrial Population Trends', *Economic History Review*, 2nd ser. 16 (1963–4).

Tyson, R. E., 'The Population of Aberdeenshire, 1695–1755: A New Approach', *Northern Scotland*, 6 (1985).

Wall, R., 'The Age at Leaving Home', *Journal of Family History*, 3 (1978).

—— 'Leaving Home and the Process of Household Formation in Pre-industrial England', *Continuity and Change*, 2 (1987).

Weir, D. R., 'Life under Pressure: France and England, 1670–1870', *Journal of Economic History*, 44 (1984).

—— 'Rather Never than Late: Celibacy and Age at Marriage in English Cohort Fertility, 1541–1871', *Journal of Family History*, 9 (1990).

Wilson, C., 'Natural Fertility in Pre-industrial England, 1600–1799', *Population Studies*, 38 (1984).

Woods, R., 'The Effects of Population Redistribution on the Level of Mortality in Nineteenth-Century England and Wales', *Journal of Economic History*, 45 (1985).

—— 'The Structure of Mortality in Mid-nineteenth Century England and Wales', *Journal of Historical Geography*, 8 (1982).

—— and Hinde, P. R. A., 'Nuptiality and Age at Marriage in Nineteenth-Century England', *Journal of Family History*, 10 (1985).

Wrigley, E. A., 'The Growth of Population in Eighteenth-Century England: A Conundrum Resolved', *Past and Present*, 98 (1983).

—— 'Family Limitation in Pre-industrial England', *Economic History Review*, 2nd ser. 19 (1966).

—— and Schofield, R. S., 'English Population History from Family Reconstitution: Summary Results, 1600–1799', *Population Studies*, 37 (1983).

—— —— *The Population History of England, 1541–1871: A Reconstruction* (1981).

CHAPTER 16

The Standard of Living and the Social History of Wages

'I was reading a work the other day', said Egremont, 'that statistically proved that the general condition of the people was much better at the moment than it had been at any known period of history.'

'Oh! Yes, I know that style of speculation', said Gerard; 'your gentleman who reminds you that a working man now has a pair of stockings, and that Henry the Eighth himself was not so well off. At any rate, the condition of classes must be judged of by the age, and by their relations with each other. One need not dwell on that. I deny the premises. I deny that the condition of the man today is better now than at any other period of our history that it is as good as it has been at several. I say, for instance, that the people were better clothed, better lodged, and better fed just before the War of the Roses than they are at the moment. We know how an English peasant lived in those times; he ate flesh every day, he never drank water, was well housed, and clothed in stout woollens.'[1]

The dialogue between Egremont the optimist, and Gerard the pessimist, has run through British history since *Sybil* appeared during the debate over the condition of England in the 1830s and 1840s. They were disagreeing over trends in real wages, an absolute measure of prosperity or poverty, and the clash continued, with social historians such as the Hammonds who argued for decline being challenged by T. S. Ashton who suggested that 'for the majority the gain in real wages was substantial' between 1790 and 1830.[2] Although Gerard was confident that the standard of living was declining in *absolute* terms, he was also aware of a second, *relative*, definition of prosperity. Workers could feel worse off when their improvement lagged behind other classes. Relative deprivation was central to the case made by a Chartist delegate in *Sybil*, who argued that, in comparison with the aristocrats who formed 'the most prosperous class that the history of the world can furnish', British workers were 'the most miserable people on the face of the globe ... for they are not only degraded, but conscious of the degradation ... compared with the privileged classes of their own land

hey are in a lower state than any other population compared with its privileged
lass. All is relative ...'[3] It is difficult enough to measure the standard of living
over time; it is even more difficult to establish trends in the distribution of
ncome and wealth; and consciousness of degradation is a highly subjective
natter, for an artisan who was materially better off could feel that he was losing
his independence, being reduced to a wage labourer with little control over his
work. Degradation involved personal identity and status, and was not simply a
natter of material loss. 'People may consume more goods and become less
happy or less free at the same time', remarked E. P. Thompson, suffering 'a
catastrophic experience' of 'intensified exploitation, greater insecurity, and increasing human misery'.[4]

Money Wages and Exchange Entitlements

Much of the debate consists of optimists and pessimists exchanging indices of
money wages and real wages in various localities. There are grave problems in
compiling data to construct these indices and serious doubts whether they
provide meaningful measures of the standard of living, for they can obscure
some of the most significant features of British economy and society between
1700 and 1850. The real wage index is constructed by deflating money wages by a
cost of living index based upon the price of traded commodities, which assumes
remuneration through a cash wage. This may be anachronistic, for many people
received cash as part of a wider bundle of entitlements, whether payment in kind,
the right to various perquisites, or the provision of public relief and private
charity. Between 1700 and 1850, there was an increase in the proportion of
income paid in cash which was used to buy commodities on the open market, a
significant change with implications for social relationships and behaviour. A
social history of the wage is therefore required before statistical series of money
and real wages are too readily accepted.

Movements in wages cannot be calculated with any certainty for many
occupations because of the method of payment. Lead-miners, for example,
negotiated a 'bingtale' rate which varied according to the quality of the ore in
each seam, and earnings depended upon the number of tons of ore produced.
They received an annual 'pay', with a subsistence allowance in the interim which
was deducted from the 'pay' along with a charge for candles and washing the ore.
Where there was a deficit at the end of the year, it was carried forward to the next
pay. Such patterns of payment make it difficult to produce meaningful series of
money wages, and there were similar problems with domestic outworkers such
as tailors or weavers. They worked for small concerns which did not leave
systematic records and paid a piece-rate which can only be converted into weekly

wages when it is known how much the worker produced. Consequently estimates of trends in money wage rates have frequently relied upon building craftsmen, for the simple reason that a significant number were paid by the day and employed by record-keeping institutions such as churches and colleges. Care is needed in using these rates, for building may be a misleading guide to the local economy, reflecting the specific circumstances of the construction industry. The rates of institutional workers may not be representative of the building trades as whole, for they are 'custom-based' contract hire rates'[5] rather than the more responsive rate paid to jobbing builders. Neither did the daily wage rate of building workers necessarily reflect their entire remuneration. Craftsmen benefited from the employment of other workers and the supply of raw materials and often took part in small speculations by building a few houses or sub contracting for work, which mixed the payment of wage and profit. They could combine a variety of occupations, engaging in agriculture for subsistence and the market, making or repairing furniture and carts. Daily wage rates of building craftsmen drawn from institutional records apply only to regularly employed workers who received no share of profits, supplied no materials or labourers, and had no ancillary occupation. Such workers were far from typical of the labour market of the eighteenth and early nineteenth centuries, at a time when there were a large number of self-employed artisans and 'the small unit of production and the small unit of ownership and control prevailed in most trades'.[6] It is a very large assumption to take trends in the daily money wage rates of building workers employed by institutions as a guide to trends in total remuneration for the work-force as a whole, yet this is the basis of the wage series which was used by Wrigley and Schofield in their analysis of marriage rates.

Wage *rates* are not the same as *earnings*, and the common practice of multiplying the time rate by a constant figure to arrive at weekly or annual earnings is dubious, for a major influence on earnings was the level of unemployment or underemployment, so that income could fluctuate even when the rate remained stable. Demand fluctuated over the year and the trade cycle and work was at the mercy of the weather and seasons, most obviously in agriculture but also in industry, where water power was affected by ice or drought, and the supply of materials could be disrupted by the state of roads. Workers responded to seasonality and irregularity by engaging in several occupations, so that their income depended upon the precise mix of employment over the year. The relationship between wage rates and earnings was also influenced by 'leisure preference', the extent to which workers preferred to take a higher wage rate by working fewer hours rather than by an increase in earnings. The response depended in part upon whether there was an expanding range of goods to purchase, and whether they could escape from a conventionlly defined pattern of consumption. Where the range of goods was limited, workers would be likely to increase consumption upon traditional items of expenditure such as drink, and then stop work rather than redefining the pattern of consumption, so that higher wage rates did not lead to a proportional increase in earnings. In other cases, workers purchased new commodities and were anxious to increase their earnings in order to participate in a consumer society. A further complication is that time rates were often conventional. An employer might prefer to keep the nominal daily rate at the same level, and adjust earnings by offering payment for three days in return for two days of actual work. Stability of the wage rate can obscure changes in the level of earnings.

Money income was only part of a wider package of entitlements, a notion which pervaded all levels of eighteenth-century society. Measurement of the cash element of earnings alone ignores changes in the structure of remuneration, for the proportion of income received in cash and kind was not constant. Entitlements came from employers, gleaning after harvest, foraging on commons and woods, the Church, charity, poor law, friends, and neighbours. Nominal daily or piece-rates were mediated by a whole range of devices which make them a highly suspect guide to effective wages, and a greater understanding of the realities of working-class life can be gained from an analysis of the social history of the wage than from simply charting changes in wage rates. These exchange entitlements should not be viewed as part of a 'moral economy' or custom which was distinct from the market, for they were often the crucial arena of bargaining. The entitlement was influenced by the monetary economy, for employers shifted the proportion of remuneration in beer or food according to movement in price levels. An institutional employer, who had access to beer, bread, and fuel produced within the organization or purchased on favourable terms, might find it cheaper to supply workers with goods at a time of inflation, rather than to increase their money wages for the purchase of equivalent amounts on the open market. 'Exchange entitlements' were often at the heart of disputes between employers and labour, as one side tested the other and tried to shift the limits of what was accepted, for example by redefining the line between a legitimate 'perquisite' and illegitimate 'embezzlement'. In some cases, entitlements were formally incorporated into the wage bargain, such as the right of miners in the north-east of England to rent-free accommodation and coal. A large part of the negotiation over remuneration was consequently concerned with the nature of entitlements rather than the level of the money wage.

Workers' entitlements were legion. At the gunpowder mill at Hounslow in the 1760s, workers had the right to dip wood into the brimstone to make matches for sale. Carpenters in the naval dockyards could keep 'chips', in theory for use as firewood but in reality for sale as tree-nails. Dockers engaged in unloading ships on the Thames in the eighteenth century had low money wages, supplemented by the right to collect sugar, tobacco, coffee, tea, and other commodities spilled in the hold or on the quay which were sold to produce a cash income, or bartered for other goods. 'Accidents' could, of course, often be encouraged by the dockers. In outwork industries, workers retained part of the materials which were 'put out'. A shoemaker might be able to substitute cheap leather for a more expensive grade, and weavers might keep the weft ends which were left in the loom when the cloth was removed. It was possible to claim that more cloth had been made or yarn spun by wetting the fabric to increase its weight or by 'false reeling' the yarn. Of course, manipulation of weights and measures was open to the putter out as well as the outworker. He could give short weight in materials by supplying damp yarn or by stating that a pound would be counted as 17 rather than 16 ounces; an 'unfair' manipulation by employers was countered by an increase in the level of 'embezzlement' by workers. Although the piece-rate nominally remained constant, the employer could make arbitrary deductions in times of depression, by withholding payment or imposing fines for 'bad' work much more strictly or unfairly. The worker might, indeed, be tied to the putter out in a form of debt bondage. Some outworkers were paid cash in advance, and remained in debt when the account was settled; others were paid in arrears and were obliged to live on credit. The putter out was less able to use such devices when trade was buoyant, and might be obliged to make extra payments for tasks such as repairing or edging cloth. Much of the bargaining over the remuneration of workers accordingly took place through these strategies rather than adjustment of the money wage rate, which remained relatively stable.

The line between perquisites and theft was contested, and the employer's attitude ranged from public recognition of 'perquisites' through tacit approval to passive hostility and active repression of 'embezzlement'. Much depended on the state of trade: what an employer condoned in a period of buoyancy, he tried to stop in a period of depression by dismissing or prosecuting workers in order to redefine the limits of entitlement. Workers, for their part, had more incentive to exploit 'perquisites' to maintain their income in times of slack trade. In some cases, formal agreements were reached between workers and employers over what was permissible, such as in the naval dockyards in 1753 when it was agreed that carpenters should only remove as much wood as they could carry untied under one arm. The boundary between 'perquisites' and 'embezzlement' was drawn by a mutual testing of limits, which turned to the courts for a legal definition. In the London docks, for example, employers brought a charge against workers when they felt that the removal of goods was not justified by the performance of a particular task. Employers could also establish mechanisms to police the boundary between 'perquisites' and 'embezzlement', such as in

orkshire where the Worsted Acts of 1777 set up an inspectorate under the charge
of a committee of employers in an attempt to check the removal of materials.

At some point, there was a more fundamental change from a shifting balance
within the structure of entitlements to a rejection of the system and the
replacement of non-monetary entitlements by a monetized wage. Some historians have located a sharp break in the treatment of embezzlement and
perquisites in the Act of 1749 which redefined embezzlement as a criminal act
punished by imprisonment or whipping, rather than a civil breach of contract
which was remedied by restitution. The notion that worker and employer were
equal partners in a contract was replaced, so the argument runs, by the assumption that the worker was a wage labourer with different, and inferior, rights; the
law is seen as the agent of capitalists against the workers, imposing absolute
property rights, a monetized wage, and capitalist social relations.[7] In reality, the
trend was gradual and patchy rather than the result of a sudden break created by
a deliberate criminalization of embezzlement by a specific Act of Parliament.
Embezzlement had been punished in practice by imprisonment and corporal
punishment before 1749, and financial restitution continued after 1749. The
legislation reflected an attempt to *control* employers by creating more scrupulous
procedures, rather than a crude use of law to redefine property in the interests of
capitalist production. Certainly, there was no once and for all transformation in
attitudes towards entitlements. The creation of committees of worsted manufacturers in 1777 to detect embezzlement of yarn was part of a succession of
campaigns in 1764–5, 1770, 1812, and 1819—and the problem still existed in 1837.[8]
Rather than a sudden transformation to a monetized economy and absolute
property rights, a series of intermittent campaigns gradually rolled back the
significance of entitlements. In the naval dockyards, for example, a monetary
allowance was substituted for the right to remove a certain amount of wood. On
the London waterfront, there was a shift at the end of the eighteenth century
from negotiation of the limits of legitimate perquisites to cash payment and the
criminalization of all perquisites. The construction of enclosed docks with walls,
gates, and police made it easier to enforce a stricter definition, which was
possibly encouraged by a rise in the value of colonial goods. Remuneration was
becoming much more a matter of wages paid by the employer, eroding the
importance of perquisites which were open to manipulation by the workers; the
fringe benefits which survived were under the control of the employers, as a
reward for loyalty and a means of creating deference rather than an arena of
dispute.

More significant than the criminalization of embezzlement and perquisites by
parliament in the interests of a new capitalist mode of production was the ability
of employers to pay wages in cash. Shortages of small coins meant that non-

monetized wages could survive the demise of outwork and the emergence of industrial capitalism. Small coins were minted from copper which, unlike silver and gold, had many uses and fluctuated sharply in price so that there was an incentive to melt coins when the price of copper rose. The Mint made little attempt to produce small coins, and the high cost of transport of copper coin around the country resulted in regional shortages. The result, as Lord Liverpool remarked in 1805, was that 'many principal manufacturers are obliged to make coins or Tokens to enable them to pay their workmen and for the convenience of the poor employed by them'.[9] The nominal money wage was a very different matter from the value of these tokens when they were spent, for they were not legal tender which meant that they incurred a discount or were accepted by few shops, which could charge high prices. In 1817 the issue of tokens was made illegal and in 1821 the Mint at last began to produce large amounts of small coin. But employers were still faced with a second potential constraint on the payment of cash wages: liquidity.

The amount of ready cash needed to meet the wage bill could be reduced by paying workers in 'truck' or goods. The wage was expressed in monetary terms but workers did not receive cash and instead drew their income in goods from a truck or 'tommy' shop which was run directly by the employer or specified by him. At least some employers used company stores as a means of avoiding wage disputes by holding down prices, such as the Dowlais Iron Co., which sold flour at its shops in 1821 for 40s. per sack when the price elsewhere was 75s. But the motivation in most cases was blatantly exploitative. John Foster and Co., for example, assigned a credit to the account of each hand-loom weaver at the beginning of each month, which was drawn upon to buy goods from the firm. Prices were set at a high level, and most of Foster's weavers fell into debt, which limited their mobility. Truck was a device to obtain credit from the work-force, and it increased in the early nineteenth century despite the improved supply of coin, for it allowed employers to save perhaps 10 to 15 per cent of their wage bill by purchasing goods on credit and making a profit on their sale. As late as 1846, an ironmaster at Merthyr Tydfil complained about the behaviour of competitors in Monmouthshire 'where full 10 per cent of the wages were regained to the Masters thro' the "*Tommy Shops*"... . Now that the men can get work when and where they please, the *truck* works *must* pay higher wages. They have had their day during the bad times, when men were obliged to put up with what they could get.'[10] Large employers with adequate capital and liquidity opposed the misuse of truck, complaining that it was exploited by small, marginal masters with inadequate liquidity as a means of reducing their wage costs.

A further shortcoming of indices of money wages is that they adopt a chronological approach, taking the wage rate of, say, a London building worker and indicating how it changed over the period. Such an approach obscures one of the most significant changes between 1700 and 1850: a shift in regional wage differentials. In 1765, the daily wage rate for carpenters in Exeter was 2s., which was higher than in the north of England (1s. 11d. in Manchester) and Scotland (1s. 3d. in Edinburgh). Manchester moved ahead of Exeter by the end of the eighteenth century, and Edinburgh caught up by the mid-nineteenth century, and by 1886 the daily wage rate for carpenters was only 4s. 1½d. in Exeter, compared with 6s. in Manchester and 4s. 10½d. in Edinburgh. A similar regional shift occurred in agricultural wage rates. In the mid-eighteenth century, wages were low in the north and high in the south; by the nineteenth century, this pattern was reversed (Table 16.1).

The shift in regional wage differentials has considerable implications for the debate over the standard of living. Regional differentials initially narrowed as the north caught up with the south, and subsequently widened as the north pulled ahead of a stagnant south. The differential was maintained despite migration and more rapid population growth in the north, because industrializing districts had higher productivity in factories and workshops, exploited water power and coal, developed transport and services, gained from economies of scale, and benefited from ancillary industries and trades such as the cotton brokers of Manchester and the machine-builders in Oldham. In the north, there was a virtuous upward spiral of growth, whereas in the south there was a vicious downward circle as capital accumulated in protoindustrialization was exported or moved into non-industrial sectors such as innkeeping or land. Labour was abundant, and the problem was to find something for men to do, sharing out available work at low levels of productivity and pay which led to a poor diet, lethargy, and underachievement. Employment in the south declined with the fall in the production of woollens, silk, lace, pins, gloves, footwear, and there were few expanding occupations to

TABLE 16.1. *Weekly wage rate for agricultural labourers, 1767–1770 to 1867–1870*

	1767–70	1794–5	1833–45	1867–70
Buckinghamshire	8s. 0d.	7s. 4d.	9s. 10d.	14s. 3d.
Norfolk	8s. 0d.	8s. 1d.	10s. 7d.	14s. 9d.
Dorset	6s. 9d.	8s. 3d.	7s. 10d.	11s. 6d.
Lancashire	6s. 6d.	10s. 1d.	12s. 5d.	17s. 9d.
Northumberland	6s. 0d.	10s. 3d.	11s. 9d.	17s. 6d.
Dunbartonshire	—	7s. 0d.	10s. 6d.	16s. 6d.
Aberdeenshire	—	6s. 0d.	9s. 6d.	13s. 0d.

Source: E. H. Hunt, 'Industrialisation and Regional Inequality: Wages in Britain, 1760–1914', *Journal of Economic History*, 46 (1986), 965–6.

absorb displaced handworkers. The transformation of regional wage differentials suggests that there is no single answer to the question of whether living standards improved or deteriorated during industrialization.

The Family Wage

A further crucial flaw in the measurement of money wage rates or earnings is that they refer to individuals and predominantly men. Of course, relatively few people were self-supporting individuals or dependent upon a male bread-winner, and the yearly income of the family is more significant than the daily wage rate of an individual man. At Corfe Castle in 1790, for example, 30 per cent of the budget of labourers' families was contributed by women and children, and in the London parish of St Georges in the East End, the proportion in 1848 was 23 per cent.[11] Even when women did not work for a wage, they undertook tasks such as making clothes for the family, which reduced the need to buy commodities and saved cash earnings. The relationship between the wages of men, women and children varied over time and between areas, so that indices based upon male wage rates are inadequate guides to the standard of living. Unfortunately, historians have paid little attention to variations in the rate of labour-force participation, which mediated between male wages and family earnings. At first sight the relationship might appear simple: an increase in the male wage rate would lower the rate of labour-force participation, allowing children to be sent to school or women to remain at home; a fall in the male wage rate would increase the participation of women and children and raise their contribution to family earnings. Reality was more complicated.

Some of the possible variations have been highlighted by a typology which distinguishes between a 'family economy', a 'family wage economy', and a 'family-consumer economy'.[12] The first treated the family as the unit of both production and consumption, and members were retained to provide labour or left to find work elsewhere if they were surplus to requirements. This would apply to small farmers and craftsmen who shed or engaged adolescents as servants in husbandry and apprentices. The assumption of the 'family economy' model is that production was undertaken by a family unit, with the implication that the rise of rural industry increased female participation and gave women a larger role than in agriculture and urban trades. In a family wage economy, each member was in receipt of a money wage from an employer, which broke any link with the productive needs of the household and removed limits to the number of wage-earners. In a 'family-consumer economy', members depended upon the paid labour of the husband/father and the unpaid work of the wife/mother in domestic tasks; the family became a private sphere excluded from commerce and industry. The retreat of protoindustrial trades which utilized all members of the family is assumed to have led to a fall in the level of female participation, severing the connection between production and reproduction and banishing women to a purely domestic sphere. The typology is too neat and schematic, but it does point to some areas of change.

It is unlikely that the rise and retreat of rural protoindustry was the main driving force behind women's participation in the labour market, for many women were employed on the land and in crafts outside the family unit of production. Women were apprenticed to a wide range of crafts in the eighteenth century such as gilders, stonemasons, furniture-makers, blacksmiths, butchers, and dentists, and there were many cases in which women worked alongside their husbands without a formal apprenticeship. In the late eighteenth century, these possibilities of female artisan activity started to decline quite apart from the contraction of rural industry, and women were increasingly confined to specifically 'female' work which was poorly paid and exploited. The explanation was in part demographic. In the late seventeenth and early eighteenth centuries, the level of population growth was low, and there were many single women as a result of the high age of first marriage and celibacy. Men did not see apprenticeship of women as a threat, and knowledge of a trade provided support for single women. The situation changed in the later eighteenth century, with a restriction in the range of trades open to women and a fall in the number of female apprentices. The Spitalfields silk-weavers, for example, barred women from better-paid work in 1769, and bookbinders expelled women from their union in 1779. Population pressure, the intensification of competition, and the challenge to artisan skills in many trades led men to fear women as a threat to the 'honourable trades' and wage rates. Women were, in any case, marrying younger and fewer remained single, so that there was less need to learn a trade. There was a similar pattern in agriculture in southern England, where women were excluded from work in the fields as the position of men in the labour market deteriorated. Low wages were in these cases reducing the participation of women in the labour market.

Although domestic production in rural industries offered employment for women, it is doubtful that it led to higher status or wages. Women did not necessarily have more opportunities within a 'family economy' in which they were able to combine housework and child care in a household unit of production. In many cases, it entailed work for very low wages unconnected with the employment of other members of the family. Domestic trades such as lace-making or straw-plaiting in the country and tailoring in the towns employed women because they were cheap; the piece-rate was driven below subsistence levels, for the women were supplementing family income. Putting out trades did not necessarily involve a family unit of production or allow the integration of production and reproduction, for a weaver needed yarn from a number of female spinners who formed 'an unorganised mass of sweated labour',[13] many of whom were married to men employed in other trades. The wives of agricultural labourers or coal-miners might be employed in spinning wool or cotton, and they were seriously affected by the spinning-jenny, which reduced the number of spinners needed to sustain a weaver. In 1790, for example, a magistrate in Somerset was called to protect spinning machinery 'from the Depredations of a lawless Banditi of colliers and their wives, for the wives had lost their work to spinning engines'.[14] Of course, where spinning-jennies were used *within* the household unit of production, they allowed the wife to supply a larger proportion of the yarn needed by the husband, and the family stood to gain.

Employment outside the home offered many women more opportunities at higher wages. Women domestic spinners, for example, earned only from 1s. 6d. to 3s. a week in 1797, in comparison with 4s. to 5s. a week in factories in Yorkshire.[15] Indeed, the best-paid women workers in the eighteenth century were not employed at home, but in workshops in calico-printing, pottery, and hardware. Calico-printing entailed tapping pins into wooden blocks to produce a pattern, or painting cloth by hand; both techniques were delicate and women could obtain good wages. These were labour-intensive methods, which allowed employers to circumvent highly paid and organized men who engraved copper plates. In the metal trades, women were similarly employed in delicate, intricate work such as button-making, painting designs, lacquering, and japanning. The incentive for the employment of women was usually to undermine male wage rates and control technology, so that high male wage rates could lead to an increase in labour-force participation, providing an incentive to industrialists to develop techniques which utilized the cheaper labour of women and children. Gender influenced the development of technology in textiles, where many new machines employed women and children. A survey of textile factories in 1833 found that only 25.5 per cent of the workers consisted of males aged 18 and above; 15.9 per cent were children between the ages of 8 and 12, 12.2 per cent boys between the ages of 13 and 17, and 47.3 per cent girls and women aged 13 and above. The proportion of children in the mills started to fall before the Factory Act of 1833 banned the employment of children under the age of 9 and limited the hours of children aged 9 to 12, for there was less need to employ children in steam mills in towns than in the isolated water-powered mills, and rising real incomes allowed families to withdraw children from the labour market. The replacement of adults by children had stopped by 1833; what the Act did achieve was a replacement of children by women.[16]

Children were by no means an economic asset in all areas of the country, and

ere was as much concern about their *under*employment as about their employ-
ent in factories and coal-mines. The provision of schools was less an attempt to
move children from exploitation than a measure to fill idle time. In 1851 boys
ged 10 to 14 had few opportunities for work in agricultural districts in the east
nd south; in Suffolk, for example, only 32.4 per cent were employed. Urban
reas such as Middlesex, with an economy based on workshops, had little child
mployment: only 18.0 per cent of boys aged 10 to 14 were at work compared
ith 57.5 per cent at school. Factory towns had a higher level of employment,
ith 51.6 per cent of boys aged 10 to 14 in employment in the West Riding.[17] The
ontribution of children to the family budget did not simply depend upon the
umber at work; it was also influenced by the extent to which sons and daughters
ayed within their family of origin until marriage. A striking feature of British
ociety is the extent to which adolescence meant an exodus from the family
ome. This is clear from the parish censuses at Cardington in Bedfordshire in
782 and at Binfield in Berkshire in 1801, which listed resident and non-resident
hildren. At Cardington, 82 per cent of sons aged between 10 and 14 lived with
heir parents, which fell to 22 per cent of sons aged 15 to 19; daughters were more
kely to remain at home, with a slight fall from 88 per cent aged 10 to 14 to 71 per
ent aged 15 to 19, probably because they could contribute to the domestic
conomy by lace-making. At Binfield, the exodus of sons and daughters was
nore even, with a fall in the proportion of sons residing with their parents from
4 per cent to 54 per cent, and of daughters from 97 per cent to 50 per cent. These
ariations clearly affected the structure of family earnings.[18]

In the eighteenth century, 'living-in' as an apprentice, servant in husbandry, or
lomestic servant was often a stage in the life-cycle for unmarried adolescents and
oung adults between leaving the parental home and forming a new household.
armers, tradesmen, and craftsmen would retain some children to help run the
usiness or learn a skill, and would adjust supplies of family labour to the needs of
roduction by shedding or absorbing 'surplus' children through living-in.
abourers' children were even more likely to leave home, unless there was a
uoyant labour market in the parish. The standard of living of 'living-in' workers
vas protected, at least in the short term, during periods of inflation for they were
argely paid through board and lodging. However, in the longer term mounting
osts of upkeep forced employers to reconsider the provision of board and
odgings, and encouraged a shift to waged day labourers who themselves bore
he costs of buying food and accommodation. The proportion of the work-force
vhich was living in fell in the later eighteenth century, as a combined result of
ising prices and structural changes leading to a decline in apprenticeship and the
growth of industries which did not use labour resident in the house of employers.
n some cases, children remained in their family of origin and were employed in

local industry, but a large number of adolescents continued to leave home befor
they became household heads. In 1851, the census found that 49 per cent of me
and 46 per cent of women aged 20 were neither resident with their parents, no
themselves heads of household. The proportion living in had fallen, largel
consisting of domestic servants, of whom two-thirds were women. Male se
vants were still mainly in farm service, with some resident as shopmen an
apprentices, and a low proportion working as domestic servants, grooms, an
gardeners. A major change from the eighteenth century was the large number o
adolescents and young adults who left their family of origin and depended on
money wage away from their employer's household. In 1851, between 20 and 2
per cent of adolescents and young adults who were in the intermediate stag
between leaving their family of origin and marriage were living with relative
and a further third of men and fifth of women were lodgers.[19]

The 'family economy' and a 'family wage economy' were by no mean
successive stages, for adolescents could often make a choice between joining
family unit of production or entering waged employment. A more realisti
definition would be an 'adaptive family economy',[20] which stresses the flexibilit
of families in selecting from a range of opportunities, whether protoindustria
occupations in the parental home, a period of service in another household, o
waged labour. A son could leave the family to spend a period in service: he coul
stay at home to work for wages as a ploughboy or errand boy; or he could serv
an apprenticeship with a local tradesman. In Cardington, the family was not ar
integrated production unit for there was a mix of household production and
waged labour: daughters worked in the family home as lace-makers, their father
worked as agricultural labourers, and their mothers often had other occupations
A similar pattern applied to workers on the London waterfront in the later
nineteenth century, where dockers' wives and daughters took domestic work ir
tailoring. Many communities in eighteenth- and early nineteenth-century Britair
fitted into neither the family nor the family wage economy: members of the
household selected from a range of opportunities which reflected 'a diversified
more flexible attitude to employment'.[21] Factory towns also differed from each
other. Textile factories offered jobs for men, women, and children, and a family
could well have a number of wage-earners. On the other hand, towns based on
mining, heavy engineering, and shipbuilding offered fewer jobs for women and
families were more dependent upon the income of a male bread-winner.
However, women who stayed at home could still contribute to the family
income by taking in washing, child-minding, or providing lodgings. Where the
distinction between the family and family wage economies has the greatest
applicability is in the middle class. Until the early nineteenth century, it was
common for wives to assist their husbands in running the dairy on a farm, or

eeping the accounts in an urban business. By the mid-nineteenth century, many
rmers' wives had retreated from the dairy into the parlour, and in towns the
eparation of the place of business from suburban residence removed middle-
lass women from the sphere of commerce. Middle-class women were in-
reasingly confined to domesticity and child care.

The Cost of Living and Real Wages

Money wage rates or income must be converted into real wage rates or income
y the use of a cost of living index. There is broad agreement on the main trends
n prices (see Fig. 16.1): they rose from about 1750, with rapid inflation of 65 to 85
er cent between 1790 and 1815; prices then fell by 25–35 per cent by the early
820s, and more slowly by about 10–20 per cent to the late 1840s. However, the
way in which the price series are constructed can influence the calculation of the
tandard of living. Price data are often drawn from the records of large insti-
utional purchasers, predominantly in the south, who usually bought in bulk
with long contracts on terms which were more favourable than for working
eople who bought small quantities from a local supplier as needed. Workers
ould not purchase in bulk when prices were low, so that they felt the full force of
easonal fluctuations, and they often needed credit from the local shopkeeper,
which was reflected in the price. Data based on wholesale prices are open to
imilar criticisms, for it is not clear how the mark-up varied over time, between
reas, or for different types of consumer. Indices based upon local *retail* prices are
o be preferred, but are not easily compiled. The choice of index certainly has a
major influence on results, for Silberling's price index (based on London whole-
ale prices) suggests that the real wages of a bricklayer in Glasgow rose by 64 per
ent between 1810 and 1831, whereas an index of local retail prices suggests a more
modest rise of 20 per cent.[22]

A cost of living index requires reliable price data for a range of commodities
which must be 'weighted' according to their share of consumption. Unfortunately, it is not certain how much working-class families spent on various items
nd how the pattern of consumption changed over time. Budgets are scarce,
usually referring to the poorest labourers in periods of distress when high
agricultural prices reduced consumption on non-essentials. Consumption pat-
erns varied by region, with a greater expenditure on oats in Scotland and the
north than in the south, and there is little information on the influence of family
ize, income levels, or the age of the head of household. Clearly, a family with a
arge number of children had a different pattern of consumption from a family
with an older head of household, where children had left home or were
contributing to the budget. Poorer members of society would assign a greater

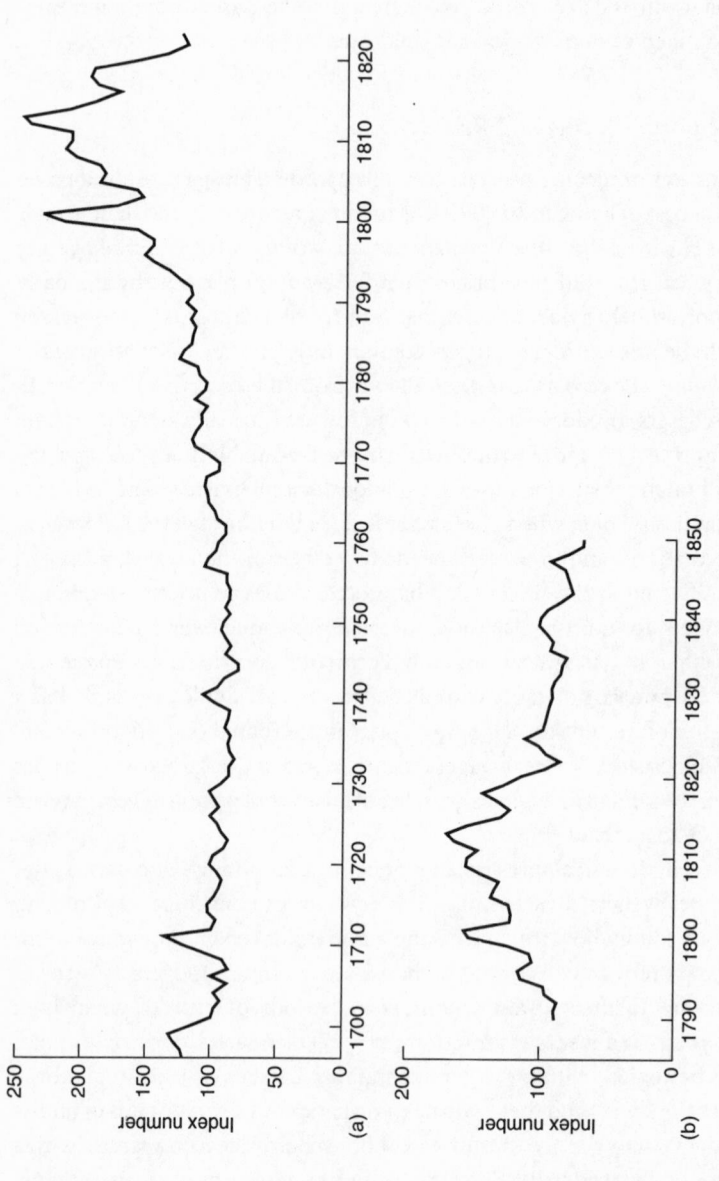

Fig. 16.1.

(a) Schumpeter–Gilboy index of consumer goods prices, 1696–1823 (1701=100)

(b) Gayer–Rostow–Schwartz index of British commodity prices (imported and domestic), 1790–1850 (monthly average of 1821–5=100)

Source: B. R. Mitchell, *British Historical Statistics* (Cambridge 1988), 721

weight to basic foodstuffs than the better off, who spent more on manufactures. A price rise could lead to the substitution of 'inferior' goods, so that more was spent on bread and less on meat; equally, a fall in prices or a rise in wages could lead to a switch from oats to wheat, and an increase in expenditure upon meat and dairy products. Workers with a high leisure preference simply earned enough to purchase a conventionally defined collection of goods, often supplemented by increased expenditure upon drink. Brewing and distilling were amongst the largest and most capital-intensive industries of the eighteenth and nineteenth centuries, and it was only after 1880, when a rapid fall in food prices produced an unprecedented and sustained increase in working-class living standards, that per capita consumption of alcohol started to fall. There was also increased expenditure upon new items of consumption such as colonial products (tea, sugar, tobacco), cloth (linen, fustian, and cotton), and cheap pottery and metal goods whose weight needs to be increased over time. A major weakness is the lack of satisfactory data on rent. Some working-class families lived rent free in tied property which presumably led to lower money wages; others had their own cottage; or they offset rent by subletting to another family. Not surprisingly, the weightings used by historians vary widely and can have considerable influence on the index of real wages.

Calculation of real wages is highly problematical, and can at best provide a crude indication of the main trends within wide margins of error. A single national figure is certainly not realistic, as is apparent from a comparison between London and the Potteries. Daily wage rates for building craftsmen in London are suspiciously stable for long periods of time, and there were many mediating devices between rates and earnings which cannot be captured. For what the figures are worth, there was an increase from 2s. 6d. in 1700 to 3s. in 1743, followed by stability until the 1790s when rates rose to a peak of 5s. 9d. between 1813 and 1815; the rate subsequently fell back to 5s. between 1819 and 1852. Conversion into real wages varies according to the price index which is used. The Phelps Brown and Hopkins index (PBH) produces an increase in the early eighteenth century to a plateau between the late 1720s and early 1750s, followed by a precipitous fall to 1801; recovery then started without regaining the level of the mid-eighteenth century until 1850. Use of Crafts's 'best-guess' price index produces a somewhat different pattern, with a less serious deterioration in real wages from 1750 to 1800, followed by recovery to the level of the mid-eighteenth century by the 1820s, and a considerable improvement by 1850. What is agreed is that the London labour market, in common with much of the south, was depressed in the late eighteenth century, with improvement in the early nineteenth century marking a return to an earlier standard of living rather than the onset of unprecedented prosperity.[23] A different pattern emerges in the Potteries of north Staffordshire, where there were major gains for building workers in the second half of the eighteenth century. The money wage index of bricklayers in the Potteries rose by 75 per cent between 1752 and 1790 (see Table 16.2) application of local prices and consumption patterns produces an increase of real wages of 13.8 per cent.[24] Possibly, the relative gains of the north were even greater, for family earnings probably rose as a result of demand for women's and children's labour, and the greater likelihood of moving from a low- to a high-wage job. In the south, the employment of women and their relative wage declined, and many high-wage jobs were lost.

Any search for a single answer to the question of what happened to the standard of living between 1700 and 1850 is unrealistic, obscuring major structural shifts in the economy. A regional approach is more helpful, which leaves the question of how many areas experienced a pattern similar to London, and how

TABLE 16.2. *Real wage rates of bricklayers, 1700–1850*

	London		Potteries	
	PBH	Crafts	Botham/Hunt	Crafts
1700	108	—	—	—
1710	97	—	—	—
1720	137	—	—	—
1730	145	—	—	—
1740	128	—	—	—
1750	148	68.1	86.2[a]	34.2[a]
1760	135	63.4	76.7	30.4
1770	122	54.2	99.1[b]	27.2[b]
1780	119	55.4	114.6	34.8
1790	100	54.5	100.0	42.2
1800	74	47.5	—	—
1810	96	55.7	—	—
1820	107	67.3	—	—
1830	127	75.8	—	—
1840	113	75.0	—	—
1850	150	100.0	—	—

[a] Figures for 1752.
[b] Figures for 1775.

Sources: N. F. R. Crafts, 'Real Wages Inequality and Economic Growth in Britain, 1750–1850', in P. Scholliers (ed.), *Real Wages in Nineteenth and Twentieth Century Europe: Historical and Comparative Perspectives* (Oxford, 1989); 81–2; L. D. Schwarz, 'The Standard of Living in the Long Run', *Economic History Review*, 2nd ser. 38 (1985), 39–41; F. W. Botham and E. H. Hunt, 'Wages in Britain during the Industrial Revolution', *Economic History Review*, 2nd ser. 40 (1987), 392.

many were closer to trends in the Potteries. Should the picture of slow growth which has come to dominate the literature on the industrial revolution be rejected in favour of a stress upon areas where the standard of living was rising? Crafts argues that the emphasis on slow growth and constraints on the standard of living remains reasonable. He assigns a weight of 75 per cent to the south and 25 per cent to the north, and allows building craftsmen in London and the Potteries to stand proxy for the two regions; the result is that the national standard of living was static between 1760 and 1780, followed by a modest growth of 0.6 per cent per annum between 1780 and 1820, and 1.3 per cent between 1820 and 1850.[25] There was, it would seem, no major breakthrough in the standard of living until the 1820s, at least on these assumptions.

Could it be that skill differentials altered as well as regional differentials in the process of industrialization? Simon Kuznets suggested that industrialization used capital and skill in place of unskilled labour, which placed a premium on skills and led to a widening of the differential between skilled and unskilled labour. It has been argued by Williamson that in Britain this widening of differentials was delayed until the end of the Napoleonic wars by the 'crowding out' of investment by government expenditure, and that the premium for skill subsequently rose to the middle of the nineteenth century. Although the case for 'crowding out' is suspect, and the statistics provided by Williamson for a surge in inequality of pay are deeply flawed,[26] the Kuznets hypothesis does have a plausibility and might well be confirmed when more data has been collected for a wider variety of occupations in various parts of the country. In Glasgow, for example, real wages of building labourers rose by a modest 8.2 per cent between 1810 and 1831, whereas the real wage of bricklayers rose by 20.2 per cent.[27] It does seem likely that the distribution of wages was 'stretched' by structural change in the economy, for wages in trade and commerce were higher than in agriculture. An increase in the differential between skilled and unskilled wages might also account for the desire of employers to substitute women in processes such as calico-printing, not least because women's work was defined as 'unskilled' and cheaper. Differentials by skill should therefore be considered alongside changes in labour-force participation, in order to provide a firmer understanding of the standard of living.

Macroeconomics: Per Capita Consumption and Equality

The bottom-up approach of estimating the standard of living from wages may be complemented by a macroeconomic, top-down approach. This starts from the gross national product, and deducts gross investment and the balance of payments to arrive at total consumption, which is divided by the population to

TABLE 16.3. Index of real per capita consumption, 1700–1851 (1851=100)

	Consumption
1700	59.4
1760	57.2
1770	67.4
1780	57.3
1801	63.0
1821	69.1
1831	76.6
1841	88.2
1851	100.0

Source: N. F. R. Crafts, British Economic Growth during the Industrial Revolution (Oxford, 1985), 95.

produce a figure of per capita consumption. The result is approximate, to say the least. Estimates of English population are reasonably secure, but calculations of GNP are subject to extremely wide margins of error and exclude non-monetized entitlements which were significant elements in the working-class standard of living. Crafts's figures (Table 16.3) suggest that real per capita consumption rose from 1700 to 1770, and that the subsequent fall was not made good until 1821 when rapid growth commenced and the working class started to share in the benefits of industrialization. Crafts's estimates of GNP have been challenged, but the broad chronology is consistent with other trends in the economy. The standard of living probably rose most rapidly in the earlier eighteenth century, for food output grew faster than population, allowing food prices to fall and real incomes to rise. A period of faster population growth followed, coinciding with slower expansion of agricultural output, which put pressure on food prices. Many workers found that their wages did not keep pace because of the increased supply of labour, and real per capita income grew more slowly or even fell. The rate of growth of per capita income accelerated in the second quarter of the nineteenth century as coal and steam power were applied to a greater number of processes, permitting an increase in productivity. Food prices fell despite continued population growth, and working-class standards of living improved. The existence of restraints on living standards and consumption is confirmed by a simple exercise. The statistical relationship between increases in real wages in the second half of the nineteenth century and the consumption of imported consumers' goods such as sugar, tea, tobacco, and coffee can be applied to data for imports of these goods between 1790 and 1850.[28] Of course, import data were distorted by smuggling, and consumption was affected by changes in tariffs nd tastes as well as by movements in real wages, but the result that the standard of living was static until the late 1840s does offer further confirmation of constraints on the standard of living until the end of the period. Despite flaws in each separate calculation, they do tell a consistent story.

A simple division of total consumption by total population is complicated by changes in the distribution of income, for a shift of income towards better-off members of society in the late eighteenth and early nineteenth centuries would mean a drop in the consumption of the poor. Income tax data suggest that there may well have been a shift in favour of the rich. In 1801 there were 26,366 people in Britain or 0.24 per cent of the population who paid tax on over £500 a year; in 1867 there were 49,500 people in England and Wales, again 0.24 per cent of the population, who paid tax on over £1,000 a year. The share of national income taken by this group had increased by as much as 10 per cent, and their average income by 120 per cent. Estimates of the national income of England and Wales made by Thomas Colquhoun for 1803 and Dudley Baxter for 1867 suggest that there was a 'stretching' of the distribution of incomes. In 1803, the top 2 per cent of families had about a fifth of income, and in 1867 about two-fifths; in 1803 the top 10 per cent had about two-fifths of income, and in 1867 over half.[29] If these figures are accurate, it would appear that the rich were getting richer at a faster rate than the poor, and that inequalities were increasing. The classical economists believed that the distribution of the national income shifted from labour and profit towards rent, and their supposition is confirmed by the increase in rent levels in the late eighteenth century and opening years of the nineteenth century. It can also be argued that taxation was regressive, falling more heavily on the poor than the rich and on industry rather than land. The burden of taxation could, as the artisan radicals argued, skew the market by reducing domestic consumption, shifting sales to risky overseas markets, and reducing profit margins; and deterioration in the terms of trade meant that more exports were needed to pay for a constant level of imports so that many of the benefits of industrialization were captured by foreign consumers rather than British workers or industrialists. The case for the pessimists during the late eighteenth and early nineteenth centuries is strong.

'Well-Being'

Calculation of the standard of living is fraught with difficulties, whether bottom up through wage rates or top down through per capita consumption. On balance, a pessimistic interpretation of the period from about 1770 to 1820 seems plausible, with gains in the north not fully compensating for losses in the south. Only in the second quarter of the nineteenth century can it be argued with any certainty that working-class living standards as a whole started to rise. But these statistical calculations of the purchasing power of money income are only part of the story, for there is also the question of the quality of life or 'well-being'. At one time, when the 'optimists' were in the ascendant, this was a fall-back position of predominantly left-wing 'pessimists'; now the importance of environmental factors is generally accepted.

Of course, it is impossible to know how much weight contemporaries themselves placed upon money income in comparison with a broader definition of the quality of life. How did they judge the change from rural domestic work to waged factory work and urban residence? 'The Lancashire workman probably preferred his big coal fires and hot water with air pollution', remarks Boyson, 'to the scenic views with few coal fires, few hot meals and rare hot water under the domestic system.'[30] Not many historians are so confident that they have privileged access to the feelings of workers. What is certain is that urban residents who were breathing polluted air and drinking contaminated water were more likely to die at a younger age than their rural counterparts. Migration to the town offered higher weekly wages, but was the gain sufficient to offset urban disamenities and a reduction in life expectancy? Williamson's calculation of wage differences between small market towns with a high quality of life and 'large, industrial, dark satanic mill towns' with their pollution and congestion produces an 'urban disamenities provision' of 10 to 24 per cent in the 1830s, and he is confident that this was a reasonable compensation for any environmental deterioration in cities. Urban disamenities were, he suggests, accepted by workers who 'placed a far greater weight on high-wage city jobs than they did on low-quality city environments',[31] and put up with a pall of coal smoke for cheap fuel, warmer homes, cooked food, and hot water. Indeed, investment in improvements to the urban environment would simply have increased taxes and rates which were regressive and would therefore have eroded levels of consumption. 'The pessimists' "Dark Satanic Mills" view of the Industrial Revolution', he concludes, 'simply will not wash.'[32] Not everyone would be so confident.

He assumes that urban workers in large factory towns were able to demand 'compensation', but did they in fact have such a degree of power in the labour market? An alternative measure of 'well-being' is to take height as a proxy for the standard of living. Nutrition and the environment affect stature, which can be taken as the summation of all influences on economic welfare. The hand-loom weavers, it was remarked in 1840, 'are decayed in their bodies; the whole race of them is rapidly descending to the size of Lilliputians. You could not raise a grenadier company amongst them all.'[33] The height of military recruits provides one source of data, indicating that the average height of recruits initially rose from 163.91 cm. for men born in 1752 to 171.42 cm. for men born in 1822, before falling to a puny 163.47 cm. for men born in 1852. The height data suggest, argues

Floud, that gains in real wages in the second quarter of the nineteenth century 'were bought at a very high price', producing a stunted population in an unhealthy environment.[34] The data could, however, be read differently: Britain had a volunteer army which tended to be an employer of last resort, so that it could be that workers were better able to obtain well-paid jobs without being forced to join the colours. The debate over 'well-being' remains inconclusive.

It is possible that workers experienced a psychological decline even if 'economic welfare' improved, after taking account of the cost of urban disamenities. The attack on common rights, the erosion of entitlements, the decay of artisan production, and political repression could make workers feel that they were losing their rights as free-born Englishmen:

It is quite possible for statistical averages and human experiences to run in opposite directions. A *per capita* increase in quantitative factors may take place at the same time as a great qualitative disturbance in people's way of life, traditional relationships, and sanctions. People may consume more goods and become less happy or less free at the same time.[35]

Factory employment could, for example, reduce the amount of leisure, so that higher per capita consumption was at the expense of free time. But did workers consider this to be a rise or fall in their standard of living? Much depends on whether leisure time in the eighteenth century was 'worthless' or valued. Perhaps the more limited and defined time for leisure in the early nineteenth century was valued more highly because towns offered greater facilities for recreation. Work discipline in the factory was more onerous, but was compensated by freedom from the supervision of squire and parson, and the ability to form independent clubs and chapels. Neither should politics be excluded from the assessment of workers' 'well-being'. They could, during the revolutionary and Napoleonic wars, feel powerless as legislation on apprenticeship or wage regulation was abrogated, and the Combination Laws challenged their right to organize. Social change coincided with the French Revolution and the attack on Jacobinism and 'it is the political context as much as the steam engine, which had most influence upon the shaping consciousness and institutions of the working class'.[36] In the end, purely statistical measures of real wages, per capita consumption, economic well-being or height must be integrated with social and cultural behaviour and attitudes in the growing towns.

NOTES

1. B. Disraeli, *Sybil; or, The Two Nations* (1845), 198–9.
2. T. S. Ashton, 'The Treatment of Capitalism by Historians', in F. A. Hayek (ed.), *Capitalism and the Historians* (1954), 41.
3. Disrael, *Sybil*, 261–2.

4. E. P. Thompson, *The Making of the English Working Class* (1964), 211.

5. G. N. von Tunzelmann, 'Trends in Real Wages, 1750–1850, Revisited', *Economic History Review*, 2nd ser. 32 (1979), 36.

6. D. Woodward, 'Wage Rates and Living Standards in Pre-industrial England', *Past and Present*, 91 (1981), 45.

7. E. P. Thompson, *Whigs and Hunters* (1975), 207.

8. J. Styles, 'Embezzlement, Industry and the Law in England, 1500–1800', in M. Berg, P. Hudson, and M. Sonenscher (eds.), *Manufacture in Town and Country before the Factory* (Cambridge, 1983).

9. Quoted in P. Mathias, *The Transformation of England: Essays in the Economic and Social History of England in the Eighteenth Century* (1979), 198.

10. M. Elsas (ed.), *Iron in the Making: Dowlais Iron Company Letters, 1782–1860* (Cardiff, 1960), 78.

11. R. Wall, 'The Place of the Unskilled Male Worker in the Economy of a Nation: A Comment', in P. Scholliers (ed.), *Real Wages in Nineteenth and Twentieth Century Europe: Historical and Comparative Perspectives* (Oxford, 1989), 68.

12. L. A. Tilly and J. W. Scott, *Women, Work and the Family* (New York, 1978).

13. J. de L. Mann, quoted in M. Berg, *The Age of Manufactures* (Oxford, 1985), 140.

14. Ibid. 143.

15. Francis Eden, quoted ibid. 140.

16. C. Nardinelli, 'Child Labour and the Factory Acts', *Journal of Economic History*, 40 (1980).

17. H. Cunningham, 'The Employment and Unemployment of Children in England, c.1680–1851', *Past and Present*, 126 (1990).

18. R. Wall, 'The Age at Leaving Home', *Journal of Family History*, 3 (1978), 190.

19. M. Anderson, 'The Emergence of the Modern Life-Cycle in Britain', *Social History*, 10 (1985), 83–4.

20. R. Wall, 'Work, Welfare and the Family: An Illustration of the Adaptive Family Economy', in L. Bonfield, R. M. Smith, and K. Wrightson (eds.), *The World We Have Gained* (Oxford, 1986).

21. Ibid. 279.

22. T. R. Gourvish, 'The Cost of Living in Glasgow in the Early Nineteenth Century', *Economic History Review*, 2nd ser. 25 (1972), 74.

23. L. D. Schwarz, 'The Standard of Living in the Long Run: London, 1700–1860', *Economic History Review*, 2nd ser. 38 (1985).

24. F. W. Botham and E. H. Hunt, 'Wages in Britain during the Industrial Revolution', *Economic History Review*, 2nd ser. 40 (1987).

25. N. F. R. Crafts, 'Real Wages, Inequality and Economic Growth in Britain, 1750–1850: A Review of Recent Research', in Scholliers (ed.), *Real Wages*, 83.

26. J. G. Williamson, *Did British Capitalism Breed Inequality?* (Cambridge, 1985), and the critique in R. V. Jackson, 'The Structure of Pay in Nineteenth-Century Britain', *Economic History Review*, 2nd ser. 40 (1987), and C. Feinstein, 'The Rise and Fall of the Williamson Curve', *Journal of Economic History*, 48 (1988).

27. Gourvish, 'Cost of Living', 76.

28. J. Mokyr, 'Is There Still Life in the Pessimist Case? Consumption during the Industrial Revolution, 1790–1850', *Journal of Economic History*, 48 (1988).

29. H. Perkin, *The Origins of Modern English Society, 1780–1880* (1969), 135–6, 419.

30. R. Boyson, 'Industrialisation and the Life of the Lancashire Factory Worker', in Institute of Economic Affairs, *The Long Debate on Poverty* (1972), 77.

31. J. G. Williamson, *Coping with City Growth during the British Industrial Revolution* (Cambridge, 1990), 260.

32. J. G. Williamson, 'Urban Disamenities, Dark Satanic Mills and the British Standard of Living Debate', *Journal of Economic History*, 41 (1981), 83.

33. Quoted in R. Floud, K. Wachter, and A. Gregory, *Height, Health and History: Nutritional Status in the United Kingdom, 1750–1980* (Cambridge, 1990), 2.

34. Ibid. 305.

35. Thompson, *Making*, 211.

36. Ibid. 197.

FURTHER READING

Anderson, M., 'The Emergence of the Modern Life-Cycle in Britain', *Social History*, 10 (1985).

Ashton, T. S., 'The Standard of Life of the Workers in England', *Journal of Economic History* (1949).

—— 'The Treatment of Capitalism by Historians', in F. A. Hayek (ed.), *Capitalism and the Historians* (1954).

Berg, M., 'Revisions and Revolutions: Technology and Productivity Change in Manufacture in Eighteenth-Century England', in J. A. Davis and P. Mathias (eds.), *Innovation and Technology in Europe from the Eighteenth Century to the Present Day* (Oxford, 1991).

Berg, M., *The Age of Manufactures: Industry, Innovation and Work in Britain, 1700–1820* (Oxford, 1985).

Borsay, P., *The English Urban Renaissance: Culture and Society in the Provincial Town, 1660–1770* (Oxford, 1989).

—— 'The English Urban Renaissance: The Development of Provincial Urban Culture, c.1680–c.1760', *Social History*, 5 (1977).

Botham, F. W., and Hunt, E. H., 'Wages in Britain during the Industrial Revolution', *Economic History Review*, 2nd ser. 40 (1987).

Boyson, R., 'Industrialisation and the Life of the Lancashire Factory Worker', in Institute of Economic Affairs, *The Long Debate on Poverty* (1972).

Burley, K. H., 'A Note on a Labour Dispute in Early Eighteenth-Century Colchester', *Bulletin of the Institute of Historical Research*, 29 (1956).

Cage, R. A., 'The Standard of Living Debate: Glasgow, 1800–50', *Journal of Economic History*, 43 (1983).

Chalklin, C. W., *The Provincial Towns of Georgian England: A Study of the Building Process, 1740–1820* (1974).

Clarke, L., *Building Capitalism: Historical Change and the Labour Process in the Production of the Built Environment* (1992).

Coleman, D. C., 'Labour in the English Economy of the Seventeenth Century', *Economic History Review*, 2nd ser. 8 (1955–6).

Crafts, N. F. R., 'Real Wages, Inequality and Economic Growth in Britain, 1750–1850: A Review of Recent Research', in P. Scholliers (ed.), *Real Wages in Nineteenth and Twentieth Century Europe: Historical and Comparative Perspectives* (Oxford, 1989).

—— 'Regional Price Variations in England in 1843: An Aspect of the Standard of Living Debate', *Explorations in Economic History*, 19 (1982).

Cunningham, H., 'The Employment and Unemployment of Children in England, c.1680–1851', *Past and Present*, 126 (1990).

Davidoff, L., and Hall, C., *Family Fortunes: Men and Women of the English Middle Class, 1780–1850* (1987).

d'Sena, P., 'Perquisites and Casual Labour on the London Wharfside in the Eighteenth Century', *London Journal*, 14 (1989).

Elsas, M. (ed.), *Iron in the Making: Dowlais Iron Company Letters, 1782–1860* (Cardiff, 1960).

Feinstein, C., 'The Rise and Fall of the Williamson Curve', *Journal of Economic History*, 48 (1988).

Flinn, M. W., 'Trends in Real Wages, 1750–1850', *Economic History Review*, 2nd ser. 27 (1974).

Floud, R., Wachter, K., and Gregory, A., *Height, Health and History: Nutritional Status in the United Kingdom, 1750–1980* (Cambridge, 1990).

Gibson, A., and Smout, T. C., *Prices, Food and Wages in Scotland, c.1550–1780* (Cambridge, 1994).

Gilboy, E. W., *Wages in Eighteenth-Century England* (Cambridge, Mass., 1934).

—— 'The Cost of Living and Real Wages in Eighteenth-Century England', *Review of Economic Statistics* (1936).

Gourvish, T. R., 'The Cost of Living in Glasgow in the Early Nineteenth Century', *Economic History Review*, 2nd ser. 25 (1972).

Hartwell, R. M., 'The Standard of Living during the Industrial Revolution: A Discussion II', *Economic History Review*, 2nd ser. 16 (1963–4).

Hilton, G. W., *The Truck System, Including a History of the British Truck Acts, 1465–1960* (Cambridge, 1960).

Hobsbawm, E. J., 'The Standard of Living during the Industrial Revolution: A Discussion I', *Economic History Review*, 2nd ser. 16 (1963–4).

—— 'The British Standard of Living, 1790–1850', *Economic History Review*, 2nd ser. 10 (1957–8).

Hudson, P., *The Genesis of Industrial Capital: A Study of the West Riding Wool Textile Industry, c.1750–1850* (Cambridge, 1986).

Hunt, C. J., *The Lead Miners of the Northern Pennines in the Eighteenth and Nineteenth Centuries* (Manchester, 1970).

Hunt, E. H., 'Industrialization and Regional Inequality: Wages in Britain, 1760–1914', *Journal of Economic History*, 46 (1986).

Jackson, R. V., 'The Structure of Pay in Nineteenth-Century Britain', *Economic History Review*, 2nd ser. 40 (1987).

Lindert, P. H., and Williamson, J. G., 'English Workers' Living Standards during the Industrial Revolution: A New Look', *Economic History Review*, 2nd ser. 36 (1983).

Linebaugh, P., *The London Hanged: Crime and Civil Society in the Eighteenth Century* (Cambridge, 1992).

Mathias, P., 'The People's Money in the Eighteenth Century: The Royal Mint, Trade Tokens and the Economy' and 'Leisure and Wages in Theory and Practice', in *The Transformation of England: Essays in the Economic and Social History of England in the Eighteenth Century* (1979).

—— 'The Brewing Industry, Temperance and Politics', *Historical Journal*, 1 (1958).

Millward, R., 'The Emergence of Wage Labour in Early Modern England', *Explorations in Economic History*, 18 (1981).

Mokyr, J., 'Is there Still Life in the Pessimist Case? Consumption during the Industrial Revolution 1790–1850', *Journal of Economic History*, 48 (1988).

Moras, D., 'Is it Justified to Use Real Wages as a Standard of Living Index?', in P. Scholliers (ed.), *Real Wages in Nineteenth and Twentieth Century Europe: Historical and Comparative Perspectives* (Oxford, 1989).

Morgan, V., 'Agricultural Wage Rates in Late Eighteenth-Century Scotland', *Economic History Review*, 2nd ser. 24 (1971).

Nardinelli, C., 'Child Labor and the Factory Acts', *Journal of Economic History*, 40 (1980).

Neale, R. S., 'The Standard of Living, 1780–1844: A Regional and Class Study', *Economic History Review*, 2nd ser. 19 (1966).

Perkin, H., *The Origins of Modern English Society, 1780–1880* (1969).

Pollard, S., *The Genesis of Modern Management: A Study of the Industrial Revolution in Britain* (1965).

Randall, A. J., 'Peculiar Perquisites and Pernicious Practices: Embezzlement in the West of England Woollen Industry, c.1750–1840', *International Review of Social History*, 35 (1990).

Rule, J., *The Experience of Labour in Eighteenth-Century Industry* (1981).

Saito, O., 'Who Worked When: Life-Time Profiles of Labour Force Participation in Cardington and Corfe Castle in the late Eighteenth and Early Nineteenth Centuries', *Local Population Studies* (1979).

—— 'Labour Supply Behaviour of the Poor in the English Industrial Revolution', *Journal of European Economic History*, 10 (1981).

Schwarz, L. D., 'The Standard of Living in the Long Run: London, 1700–1860', *Economic History Review*, 2nd ser. 38 (1985).

—— 'The Formation of the Wage: Some Problems', in P. Scholliers (ed.), *Real Wages in Nineteenth and Twentieth Century Europe: Historical and Comparative Perspectives* (Oxford, 1989).

Snell, K. D. M., *Annals of the Labouring Poor: Social Change and Agrarian England, 1660–1900* (Cambridge, 1985).

—— and Millar, J., 'Lone-Parent Families and the Welfare State: Past and Present', *Continuity and Change*, 2 (1987).

Styles, J., 'Embezzlement, Industry and the Law in England, 1500–1800', in M. Berg,

P. Hudson, and M. Sonenscher (eds.), *Manufacture in Town and Country before the Factory* (Cambridge, 1983).

—— ' "Our Traitorous Money Makers": The Yorkshire Coiners and the Law, 1760–83', in J. Brewer and J. Styles (eds.), *An Ungovernable People: The English and Their Law in the Seventeenth and Eighteenth Centuries* (1980).

Taylor, A. J., 'Progress and Poverty in Britain, 1780–1850: A Reappraisal', *History*, 45 (1960).

Thompson, E. P., 'Time, Work-Discipline and Industrial Capitalism', *Past and Present*, 38 (1967).

—— *The Making of the English Working Class* (1963).

—— *Whigs and Hunters* (1975).

Thomson, D., 'The Decline of Social Security: Falling State Support for the Elderly since Early Victorian Times', *Ageing and Society*, 4 (1984).

Tilly, L. A., and Scott, J. W., *Women, Work and the Family* (New York, 1978).

von Tunzelmann, G. N., 'Trends in Real Wages, 1750–1850: Revisited', *Economic History Review*, 2nd ser. 32 (1979).

Wall, R., 'The Place of the Unskilled Male Worker in the Economy of a Nation: A Comment', in P. Scholliers (ed.), *Real Wages in Nineteenth and Twentieth Century Europe: Historical and Comparative Perspectives* (Oxford, 1989).

—— 'Work, Welfare and the Family: An Illustration of the Adaptive Family Economy', in L. Bonfield, R. M. Smith, and K. Wrightson (eds.), *The World We Have Gained: Histories of Population and Social Structure* (Oxford, 1986).

—— 'The Age at Leaving Home', *Journal of Family History*, 3 (1978).

—— 'Leaving Home and the Process of Household Formation in Pre-industrial England', *Continuity and Change*, 2 (1987).

Williams, J. E., 'The British Standard of Living, 1750–1850', *Economic History Review*, 2nd ser. 19 (1966).

Williamson, J. G., *Did British Capitalism Breed Inequality?* (Cambridge, 1985).

—— 'Urban Disamenities, Dark Satanic Mills, and the British Standard of Living Debate', *Journal of Economic History*, 41 (1981).

—— *Coping with City Growth during the British Industrial Revolution* (Cambridge, 1990).

—— 'Was the Industrial Revolution Worth it? Disamenities and Death in Nineteenth-Century British Towns', *Explanations in Economic History*, 19 (1982).

Woodward, D., 'Wage Rates and Living Standards in Pre-industrial England', *Past and Present*, 91 (1981).

....

CHAPTER 17

Poor Relief and Charity

There is no Nation I ever read of who by a Compulsory Law, raiseth so much Money for the Poor as *England* doth; That of *Holland* is voluntary . . .; but our Charity is become a Nuisance, and may be thought the greatest Mistake of that Blessed Reign, in which that Law passed, which is the Idle and Improvident Man's Charter.[1]

Sir Francis Brewster's complaint of 1695 was directed against the poor law legislation of 1598–1601 which came into effect at the end of the 'Blessed Reign' of Elizabeth and survived until the creation of the new poor law of 1834. The Elizabethan legislation made it a mandatory responsibility of each parish to maintain the 'impotent' and to provide work for the able-bodied under the supervision of the overseers of the poor. Finance was raised by the church-wardens, who increasingly relied upon an annual poor rate. England was the only country in Europe with a system of poor relief financed from taxation: Brewster could equally well have drawn a contrast *within* Britain, for tax-funded poor relief was by no means the norm in Scotland.

How significant were the payments of poor relief in England and Scotland in supporting the income of the poor? Brewster's fear was that relatively generous relief was false charity, which made people feckless, allowing them to live in idleness without regard for the future, secure in the knowledge that the parish would maintain them in old age or sickness. His complaint was repeated a century later by Malthus, who urged the abandonment of the poor law, at least for support of the able-bodied poor. It was, Malthus feared, weakening the prudential restraint on marriages and births by offering support to family income. There was also concern about the effect of poor relief on the pattern of migration. The availability of poor relief in England for the elderly, ill, and unemployed could act in one of two ways. Would it remove the incentive to move in search of opportunities elsewhere and tie people to their parish; or would knowledge that support was available in times of necessity encourage people to leave their family of origin and seek jobs which offered a higher marginal productivity than staying on the family holding? The answer depended on whether parishes were willing to accept immigrants and offer them relief, or attempted to restrict newcomers who might impose a financial burden on the parish.

Brewster attacked *compulsory* charity, fearing that the provision of poor relief as a right would undermine social order and deference, creating a dependent class and removing self-sufficiency. The virtue of *voluntary* charity in the eyes of its proponents was that it could preserve social order and encourage self-sufficiency: it was not a right so much as a privilege, which could foster a sense of obligation and reward 'correct' social behaviour. The exact relationship between tax-funded poor relief and voluntary charity remained a matter of debate, with periodic attempts to tighten up the provision of public relief and to make voluntary charity more discriminating in providing assistance to deserving cases. There was, then, a shifting boundary between public and private provision of welfare, and in the organization of both the poor law and philanthropy.

Poor Relief in England

Brewster feared that the cost of poor relief had reached ruinous levels by 1695; it rose still further in the eighteenth century. The absolute level of expenditure was affected by trends in population growth and in price levels, and a more meaningful figure is relief per capita in real terms, which can be indicated by the amount of wheat purchased. This doubled in the first half of the eighteenth century and then stabilized until the turn of the eighteenth and nineteenth centuries. Expenditure on poor relief also increased as a share of national income and relative to central government taxation, particularly in the early and mid-eighteenth century (Table 17.1).

TABLE 17.1. *Poor relief expenditure in England and Wales, 1696 to 1802–1803*

	Total (£)	Expenditure per head		% of:	
		Shillings	Quarters wheat	National income	Central govt. revenue from direct/excise
1696	400,000	1.5	0.04	0.8	11
1748–50 (av.)	689,971	2.3	0.08	1.0	12
1776	1,529,780	4.4	0.10	1.6	19
1783–5 (av.)	2,004,238	5.3	0.11	2.0	19
1802–3	4,267,965	9.5	0.15	1.9	21

Source: P. Slack, *The English Poor Law, 1531–1782* (1990), 30, 34.

The legislation of 1598–1601 established a clear legal obligation to deal with two broad classes of applicants for relief: the impotent poor who were unable to support themselves, such as orphans, widows, the sick, and the elderly; and the able-bodied poor who were fit and capable of working, but unable to find a job or earn enough to support their family. Although the debate on policy was dominated by relief of the able-bodied poor, in practice the operation of the poor law was dominated by relief of the impotent poor. An enumeration of Lichfield in 1695 found that 47.3 per cent of paupers were children under the age of 15, and a further 17 per cent were aged over 60. This pattern was confirmed by a muddled national survey of 1802–3: 1,040,716 people in England and Wales (excluding London) received relief, of whom 29.4 per cent had only occasional assistance; children under the age of 14 accounted for 30.3 per cent; and the old or infirm for 16.0 per cent.[2] The finances of the poor law in the later seventeenth and eighteenth centuries were dominated by relief of the impotent poor, and the increasing level of real expenditure on poor relief in the late seventeenth and early eighteenth centuries was largely the result of more generous payments to them. Payments to the able-bodied poor only became a pressing concern at the turn of the eighteenth and nineteenth centuries.

The overseers of the poor throughout England and Wales relieved parishioners on an individual basis according to the circumstances of each case, without any nationally determined standard. The most common response to hardship was the simple expedient of exemption from payment of the poor rate, which could well apply to 30 per cent of households at any time. The elderly and infirm, and widows supporting children, were usually granted a weekly parish pay or pension; the parish might rent or own a few cottages for the poor; grants were given for the purchase of clothing and fuel; payments were made to cover periods of ill-health and to provide treatment by the local 'goodwife' or doctor; families were paid to look after orphans, illegitimate, and deserted children; and heads of household with large families were given a family allowance. Parish records contain thousands of individual cases rather than statements of policy, but they do offer some clue to the underlying assumptions which guided decisions.

Poor relief from the end of the seventeenth century generally made up income almost to the level of a non-dependent agricultural worker with a family. In Norfolk, for example, the usual payment to an individual impotent pauper in the early seventeenth century was about 6*d.* a week, rising to about 1*s.* at the end of the century, which was probably enough to live on. The relative generosity of relief meant that it was not necessary to fall into extreme poverty before turning to the parish for assistance, and the level of relief under the old poor law was, indeed, high relative to wages. Poor law support for lone-parent families in the

early nineteenth century represented 78 per cent of the average income from
employment of two-parent families; similarly, the old received between 70 and
90 per cent of the average income of a manual worker in 1837–8. These transfer
payments were a significant element in working-class income, with payments to
single parents amounting to 5 per cent and to the elderly to 4.6 per cent of the
total income of wage-earners. It has, indeed, been argued that poor law 'pen
sions' in the eighteenth and early nineteenth centuries were considerably more
generous relative to the income of non-beneficiaries than in either the 'new' poor
law or the modern welfare state. Poor law payments to the elderly in 1887–9
were only 25 to 38 per cent of the average income of a manual worker and in 1978
40 per cent.³ But the generosity of the old poor law should not be overdrawn.
Generous relief was offered to the elderly and lone parents who could sustain a
claim and had a 'settlement', but there were also a considerable number who
were treated more harshly. Deterioration of welfare payments relative to
manual wages is less meaningful than comparison with the income needed for
subsistence: manual wages in the eighteenth and early nineteenth centuries were
close to subsistence level and the parish was simply offering enough for survival;
by the later nineteenth century, manual wages had risen and poor relief was
more generous in real terms. The figures do, nevertheless, have an important
implication: there was no great discrepancy between the standard of living of
those receiving welfare and those dependent on earnings from the late seventeenth to the early nineteenth centuries.

One reason for the increase in the level of relief in the later seventeenth and
early eighteenth centuries was the nature of the English state and the political
structure of poor law administration. A tax-funded poor law on the English
model was only possible because there was a relatively strong central state
providing a general framework within which 15,000 separate parishes could
operate, and ensuring that landowners paid their contributions. At the same
time, there had to be a willingness to leave the administration of the tax and the
payment of relief in local hands in order to secure wide support, drawing upon
the existing community structures of authority and power based on church-
wardens and overseers. The ability of large landowners and ratepayers to impose
economy, and to restrict the granting of relief, was consequently limited. The
daily control of the poor law rested with an unpaid overseer of the poor, under
the general supervision of the vestry meeting of ratepayers, which approved the
rate and heard petitions against the overseer's decisions. The local justices of the
peace, who were drawn from the gentry and clergy, had oversight of the
accounts of the parish, and could attempt to shape the general policy of the
county, particularly during the inflationary period at the turn of the eighteenth
and nineteenth centuries. There was, however, no need for the parish to accept

heir advice, and the justices usually preferred to leave the operation of the poor
aw to the overseers and vestries. Individual paupers had the right of appeal to
any justice in the county against a refusal of relief, so that the legal role of justices
was more often to protect the rights of applicants than to impose economy.

The administration of the poor law was, in the eyes of reformers, chaotic and
inefficient, dominated by small units, and loaded against ratepayers in favour of
applicants. Expenditure was given an advantage over economy, for vestry
meetings were open to all parishioners rather than limited to larger landowners;
and overseers who were drawn from the ranks of the village were susceptible to
pressure from their neighbours and to being overruled by any justice in the
county. In 1764 Thomas Gilbert proposed one means of imposing stricter
controls: the discretion of the overseers should be removed and they should be
brought under the control of Guardians drawn from larger landowners, clergy,
and justices. His bill failed to gain support in 1765, and he returned to the task in
1782, when an Act gave parishes the option of grouping together into unions in
which the overseers were simply collectors of the rates, and Guardians were
appointed by justices. This was simply a permissive measure at the discretion of
parishes; in 1786, he failed to secure support for a comprehensive scheme which
would divide the whole country into districts and transfer relief to salaried
officials, independent of the overseers. There was considerable hostility to a
measure which would undermine local structures of power and increase central
government control, particularly given the reliance of public order and social
stability upon patronage. Strictly enforced, bureaucratic rules would require a
shift of public order to a salaried police force, which many members of the local
landed élite opposed as a threat to their power. Some larger parishes did adopt
'select' vestries, removing power from open meetings to a committee drawn
from the larger ratepayers, which was given legislative sanction by the Sturges
Bourne Acts of 1818–19. But even in select vestries, any two justices in the county
could still overturn a decision and one justice could order relief to any 'industrious poor person' in urgent need. The administration of the old poor law,
therefore, gave considerable discretion to individual parishes where the ability of
large landowners to dominate decisions was limited, and the rights of the poor to
relief were protected by appeal to any justice in the county. In Scotland,
however, the pattern was very different. The ability of the central government to
shape policy was weaker and large landowners were able to impose a much
stricter control over the administration of the poor law in the localities.

The explanation for the emergence of a relatively generous, state-funded
system in England is not simply political. There is also a functional or economic
explanation. Parish relief possibly became more generous because other sources
such as begging and informal charity were replaced by tax-funded support. There

was also a degree of slack in the system as a result of the reduction in subsistenc
crises and the need to pay emergency relief: rather than reducing the rate.
pensions were increased. Such an outcome was only possible because there was
broad identity between ratepayers and the recipients of relief: the fundament.
point about relief to the impotent poor is that most families would at some tim
turn to the parish for assistance. Perhaps as many as 25 per cent of households ha
some relief in the course of the year, accounting for about 15 per cent of th
population; and 10 per cent of households and 5 per cent of the population ha
regular relief.[4] These recipients were not a separate, marginal group in society
for old age and ill-health or widowhood were ever-present threats to everyone
The ratepayers, churchwardens, and overseers of the poor were not providing
system of relief for a distinct and despised class; they were themselves likely t
turn to the parish at some stage in their life-cycle, and generosity and self-interes
were one and the same. The poor law was largely concerned with 'life-cycl
poverty' as part of a demographic regime which made it a crucial part of the lif
of most people. The high death rate resulted in a large number of lone-paren
families and orphans. At St Mary-le-Bow in the East End of London in 1695 singl
parents headed 17 per cent of family households with children, and the figure a
Stoke-on-Trent in 1701 was as high as 24.5 per cent. The elderly (those aged 60 an
above) comprised about 9 per cent of the population in the early eighteenth
century, and they often needed communal support as a result of the Englis
pattern of marriage. Most couples married in their middle to late twenties, an
the birth of children pushed them into a deficit phase of their life-cycle betweer
the ages of 35 and 45; it was precisely at this point that their own parents move
into a period of poverty as a result of old age, with its threat of declining earning
and widowhood. The nuptuality regime in England was not suited to direc
support of the old by their own children; and this was intensified by the Englis
pattern of forming a separate household at marriage. The difficulty of relyin
upon transfers of income between generations within families led to greate
reliance upon extra-familial institutions. In effect, parents paid the cost of rearing
their children and were supported in their old age by other people's children
through the transfer payments of the poor law. Poor law support of the elderly
was therefore a central feature of the pattern of late marriage, which meant that
some form of extra-familial support was necessary.[5] Much the same problem
arose elsewhere in north-west Europe, with its late age of marriage; the genera
demographic requirement for non-familial support is in many ways more
important than the divergence in the institutional form between countries.
England solved the problem by a tax-funded poor law, but it was equally possible
to rely upon guilds or almshouses.

A distinction is often drawn between support of the impotent poor, which was ccepted, and support of the able-bodied poor, which was contentious. The ifference should not, however, be overdrawn, for relief of the able-bodied poor vas in many cases a product of the life-cycle and demographic regime. The ncome of the nuclear family came under pressure with the birth of more hildren, and entered a period of deficit until children could contribute or left iome: the deficit was most severe for couples in their late thirties and forties. The iarish was usually willing to provide some assistance to families during this first ieriod of deficit in the life-cycle, which coincided with the deficit in their parents' ife-cycle. A balance had to be struck between support of families with young hildren and the elderly, which was shaped by fluctuations within the demo- raphic system, for in periods of high population growth there were larger iumbers of dependent children than in periods of low population growth. In the 590s, population growth was rapid and there were something between 850 and 100 children under the age of 14 for every 1,000 productive adults aged 25 to 59. In he later seventeenth and early eighteenth centuries, the number of dependent hildren under the age of 14 fell to about 700 for every 1,000 adults. The demands of young dependents on the poor law were reduced, and there were more esources for elderly couples and widows. The pattern shifted again in the later ighteenth and early nineteenth centuries, when the number of young depen- dents increased and absorbed a greater proportion of resources: in 1831, there were 1,086 children under the age of 14 for every 1,000 adults. There was, herefore, a variation over time in the relative significance of various stages of the ife-cycle, and the poor law authorities had to strike a balance between compet- ng demands on their limited resources: a low proportion of children allowed hem to be generous to the elderly; a high proportion of young dependents might lead them to greater strictness and a demand for the family to take more responsibility (see Fig. 17.1).[6]

The cost of relief fell entirely on the individual parish, which led church- wardens and ratepayers to limit claims by controlling residence, and imposing tests which restricted relief to the needy and encouraged self-reliance. Brewster's complaint of 1695 was one expression of a belief that stringency was needed to prevent the exploitation of ratepayers by the 'idle and improvident' who should be encouraged to seek work. The threat of entry into a workhouse, it was argued, would deter the work-shy, encourage labour discipline, and reform morals. Between 1696 and 1715, fourteen provincial towns and the City of London established new, city-wide Corporations of the Poor. These opened workhouses which would, it was hoped, discipline vagrants and teach children 'honest *Labour* and *Industry*'.[7] These local initiatives were recognized by the Workhouse Test Acts of 1722 and 1723 which allowed parishes to form unions, construct work- houses and apply a labour test as a condition of relief. The threat of the

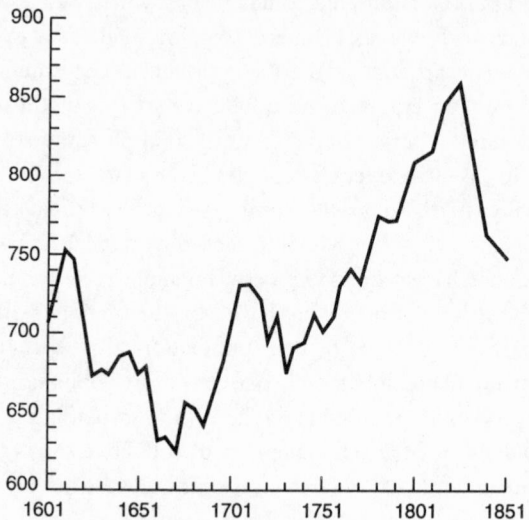

FIG. 17.1. Dependency ratio, England, 1601–1851 (number aged 0–14 and 60 and over per 1,000 aged 15–59)

Source: E. A. Wrigley and R. S. Schofield, The Population History of England, 1541–1871 (1981), 444.

workhouse certainly discouraged applications for relief: at Stepney, the completion of the workhouse in 1725 encouraged sixty-four of seventy pensioners in the parish 'to subsist by their own industry'.[8] But the use of the workhouse test was not without its problems.

There were thorny issues of political control and social order. In London, for example, the Corporation of the Poor was formed in 1698 and was dominated by Whigs associated with leading institutions such as the Bank of England and East India Co., who argued that social order should be based upon the imposition of an automatic and impersonal workhouse test. It collapsed in 1713, largely because individual parishes resented loss of control over their funds, and stressed the importance of personal patronage as the basis of order and deference. Stringency also flew in the face of the demographic system, without delivering the financial savings which were anticipated. Workhouses were expensive to build and operate, and the expectation that they would be self-supporting by setting the poor to work was not realized. Indeed, they were more likely to complement than to replace outdoor relief. By 1802–3, 3,765 parishes in England and Wales (excluding London) used workhouses to accommodate 83,468 paupers or about 11 per cent of the long-term recipients of relief.[9] In part they were used as houses of correction to punish 'Rogues, Vagrants, Sturdy Beggars, or other idle or isorderly persons', but more often they provided institutional care for the lderly and young who were not capable of supporting themselves. In Ormskirk, was explained in 1821, 'none but houseless and impotent have been placed within [the workhouse's] walls and ... they have looked to it rather as a omfortable asylum for those really distressed and without comfort of a home han for the Idle and Disorderly'.[10] Such a use of workhouses as specialist nstitutions was recognized by Gilbert's Act of 1782, which permitted parishes to orm unions in order to build separate houses for the care of the elderly and hildren, and to support the able-bodied poor outside the workhouse; the Act was adopted by a total of 924 parishes by 1834, mainly in towns and industrial districts. Clearly, workhouses were viewed very differently in the legislation of 722–3, with its emphasis on deterrence, and in 1782, with its stress on institutional care.

It has been argued that legislation of 1722–3 was based on the assumption that high wages led to more leisure, and that people would not work unless they were forced to by low wages; workhouses were part of a strategy of imposing labour discipline. But in the later eighteenth century, so the argument runs, there was a growing acceptance that higher wages provided an incentive to work and improved productivity, and workhouses were no longer needed as a deterrent.[11] Such a distinction between the early and late eighteenth century is, in fact, too neat and schematic. The 'reformation of manners' was as much a matter of concern in the late eighteenth century as in the early eighteenth century, and the reformers of the early nineteenth century stressed the deterrent role of the workhouse. Rather than a simple shift in attitudes over the century from an economy of low wages to high wages, there was a continuing debate over the role of individual or family responsibility and collective provision. The outcome was shaped in part by concern for economy and in part by demographic constraints. It was also shaped by the conflict of ideology and changing perceptions of the role of institutions in remaking character which affected policy towards prisons, asylums, hospitals, and schools.

Outdoor relief to the able-bodied poor had long existed as a means of covering the deficit phase of the life-cycle, but in the late eighteenth and early nineteenth centuries it dominated the debate over the poor law to an unprecedented degree. Rapid population growth and inflation were causing serious problems, leading to the payment of subsidies in aid of wages. The most notorious was the so-called Speenhamland scale of 1795: relief was paid to men who were in work, according to the price of bread and the number of their dependants. When the price of a loaf was 1s., the income for a single man was made up to 3s.; for a man and wife to 4s. 6d.; for a man, wife, and one child to 6s.; and so on up to 15s. for a couple with seven children. The attacks on the Speenhamland system give the impression that such 'bread scales' were commonplace, but they were less frequent than allowances paid according to the number of children (see Table 17.2), whic usually applied only to large families. Less common were wage allowances, flat-rate payment regardless of the size of the family. There were also schemes t encourage the employment of labour. The 'labour rate' assigned a price t able-bodied unemployed men, and farmer-ratepayers were given the choice o employing the men at this wage or paying the poor rate to the parish; any me left over were allocated to the ratepayers in proportion to their rates. Th scheme was more likely to be favoured by large farmers than by small farmers o tradesmen who would have little use for the labour assigned to them. In th roundsman system, an applicant for relief took a ticket to a farmer, who coul employ him for as long as he liked, for whatever he wished to pay; the farme signed the ticket, which was taken back to the overseer who made up the wag out of parish funds. The result of these systems was that farmers employe surplus labour at less than the market rate, often below their marginal pro ductivity. These strategies were to form the basis of the attack on the old poo law at the end of the eighteenth century and beginning of the nineteenth.

Malthus feared that allowances in aid of wages were creating misery rathe than relieving poverty. By offering support to families according to the numbe of children, the poor law was weakening 'prudential checks' and encouragin early marriages; the outcome would be a faster rate of population growth, lowe wages, and higher food prices. The 'first obvious tendency' of allowances, he argued,

TABLE 17.2. *Patterns of relief in aid of wages, 1832*

	Percentage of parishes				
	Allowances in aid of wages	Children's allowances	Bread scale	Roundsman system	Labour rate
'Speenhamland' counties					
Sussex	6	82	22	4	14
Buckinghamshire	17	71	9	11	17
Berkshire	3	73	63	13	27
All Speenhamland	11	61	27	8	17
Non-'Speenhamland' counties					
Kent	21	49	2	2	12
Westmorland	0	24	0	0	0
Durham	3	5	0	11	11
All non-Speenhamland	7	31	7	6	10

Source: M. Blaug, 'The Poor Law Report Re-examined', *Journal of Economic History*, 24 (1964), 236–7.

s to increase population without increasing the food for its support. A poor man may marry with little or no prospect of being able to support a family without parish assistance. They may be said, therefore, to create the poor which they maintain; and as the provisions of the country must, in consequence of the increased population, be distributed to every man in smaller proportions, it is evident that the labour of those who are not supported by parish assistance will purchase a smaller quantity of provisions than before, and consequently more of them must be driven to apply for assistance.

It was only, he believed, the shame of dependence which prevented more people from marrying, and it was essential for the 'happiness of the great mass of mankind' that 'dependent poverty ought to be held disgraceful'. Unfortunately, the operation of the poor law was driving more and more people to apply for relief, so weakening the disgrace and making the problem still worse. His conclusion was inescapable: 'if the poor laws had never existed in this country, though there might have been a few more instances of very severe distress, the aggregate mass of happiness among the common people would have been much greater than it is at present.'[12]

Malthus was more cautious than many commentators, for he realized that the outcome 'depends mainly upon the feelings and habits of the labouring classes of society and can only be determined by experience'. The incentive to early marriage offered by allowances might, he accepted, be offset by the 'desire of bettering our condition, and the fear of making it worse ... [which] is continually counteracting the disorder arising from narrow human institutions'.[13] Others were less hesitant. The Select Committee on Labourers' Wages of 1824, for example, concluded that 'a surplus population is encouraged; men who receive but a small pittance know that they have only to marry, and that pittance will be augmented in proportion to the number of their children'.[14] Malthus's caution was in fact more realistic than these prophecies of doom. The incentive to abandon prudence was, after all, not huge: in Kent, for example, most parishes offered allowances only on the birth of the fourth child, and they did not usually rise in proportion to family size. There is no sign that parishes in Kent which paid allowances had earlier marriages than those without allowances, or that the birth rate was higher in parishes which gave allowances to the first child. This conclusion is confirmed by data from parishes in southern England which abandoned allowances in the 1820s, when their marriage and birth rates actually rose. Population growth was, after all, the outcome of a wide range of variables, and it is unlikely that allowances were sufficient to make a major difference; it is, indeed, more plausible that allowances were a consequence rather than a cause of rural underemployment and low wages, and were necessary in order to maintain a minimal standard of living.

If the gloomier expectations of the demographic consequences of allowances in aid of wages had been fulfilled, the cost of poor relief would have steadily mounted as more and more dependants were created. In fact, there was not an inexorable upward trend. The most rapid development of the allowance system in the southern counties was in response to high prices and poor harvests at the end of the eighteenth and start of the nineteenth centuries, with poor relief expenditure per capita in the south rising to a peak between 1795 and 1801. The real level of relief remained fairly stable until 1814, and then rose until the early 1820s as prices fell. At this point, expenditure on poor relief was determined less by the level of food prices, and more by underemployment and low wages as a result of structural features of the southern economy. This is reflected in the shifting incidence of poor relief. In the seventeenth and early eighteenth centuries, the highest level of relief per capita was found in towns and industrial areas; by the late eighteenth century, it was highest in the arable farming districts of the south and east. The payment of allowances was much less common in the pastoral or industrial counties of the west and north, where there was a steady demand for labour over the year, and surplus labour was more likely to be absorbed into domestic industry or attracted into the towns or coalfields. In the south, the income of labourers' families was under strain as a result of rising prices and population pressure, with a reduction in income from domestic industry and an erosion of contingent property rights. Agricultural labourers' families were becoming more dependent on the wages of the male head of household as women were forced out of the labour market; and wages were highly seasonal in grain-producing areas. The payment of allowances was a rational economic response for grain farmers who needed a large number of seasonal harvest-workers, for allowances passed part of the cost of maintenance on to the parish and ratepayers without a direct interest in the employment of seasonal workers. Such a strategy was possible because large farmers were more able to dominate the decisions of the vestry in arable than in pastoral or protoindustrial districts with more small farmers and traders, especially where the adoption of Gilbert's Act and the creation of a 'select vestry' increased the power of large ratepayers. (See Fig. 17.2.)

Although allowances arose from structural features of the economy of southern England, the architects of the new poor law of 1834 were more inclined to the view that poor relief was the cause of the problem, and they aimed to destroy allowances in aid of wages, and to restrict the payment of poor relief by a deterrent workhouse test. Their strategy rested upon a major shift in the structure of power, through the creation of a national system of unions, increased central direction, and the removal of discretion from overseers to Guardians who were elected on a franchise which gave more power to larger ratepayers. The new poor law of 1834 attempted to overturn the administrative

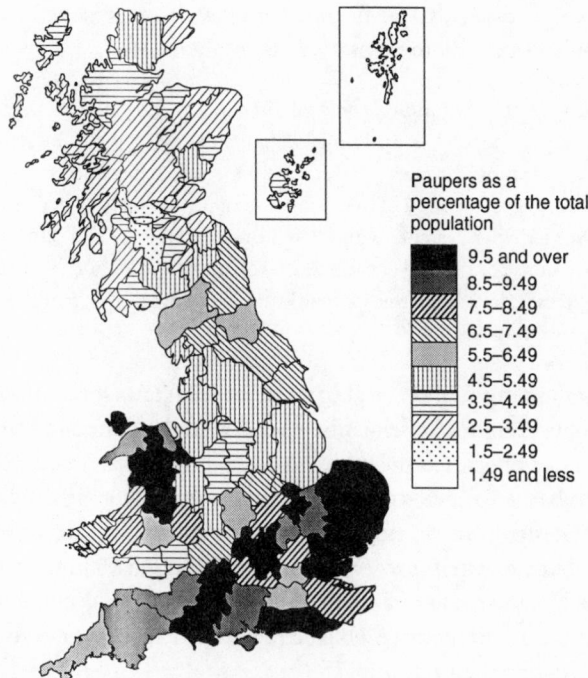

FIG. 17.2. Paupers in Britain, by county, 1837–1839

Paupers as a
percentage of the total
population

■	9.5 and over
	8.5–9.49
	7.5–8.49
	6.5–7.49
	5.5–6.49
	4.5–5.49
	3.5–4.49
	2.5–3.49
	1.5–2.49
	1.49 and less

Source: I. Levitt, 'Poor Law and Pauperism', in J. Langton and R. J. Morris (eds.), *Atlas of Industrialising Britain, 1780–1914* (1986), 161, using data from PP 1839, xx, *Report by a Committee of the General Assembly on the Management of the Poor in Scotland*, and PP 1841, xi, *A Return Showing the Number of Paupers in England and Wales, 1839 and 1840*.

and political system which had permitted the development of a relatively generous pattern of relief in the later seventeenth and eighteenth centuries. However, it misunderstood the nature of poverty in the southern agricultural counties, and ignored the pattern of cyclical unemployment which had emerged in the industrial towns of the Midlands and the north. The new poor law of 1834 marked the triumph of ideology over social reality.

Settlement

The parochial administration of the poor law meant that local ratepayers were concerned to control who had a claim for relief, which led to regulation of 'settlement'. 'There is scarce a poor man in England of forty years of age', claimed Adam Smith in 1776, '. . . who has not in some part of his life felt himself

most cruelly oppressed by this ill-contrived law of settlement.'[15] Malthus de
nounced the laws of settlement as a threat to liberty:

the whole class of the common people of England is subjected to a set of gratin
inconvenient and tyrannical laws, totally inconsistent with the genuine spirit of th
constitution. The whole business of settlements ... is contradictory to all ideas (
freedom. The parish persecution of men whose families are likely to become chargeabl
and of poor women who are near lying-in, is a most disgraceful and disgusting tyrann
And the obstructions continually occasioned in the market of labour, by these laws, hav
a constant tendency to add to the difficulties of those who are struggling to suppo
themselves without assistance.[16]

But Malthus was not simply critical of the settlement laws for limiting migratio
in search of opportunities for self-sufficiency, for he also admitted that they coul
have a beneficial effect. Complete freedom of migration would allow surplu
population to be transferred to other districts, so removing the need for pruder
tial restraint; restrictions on migration might reduce the rate of marriage b
limiting the ability to export excess population. Although Malthus feared that th
payment of allowances encouraged population growth, he also noted a counter
influence: because 'each parish is obliged to maintain its own poor, it is naturall
fearful of increasing their number'.[17]

   A settlement was originally created by the place of birth, but it was extended i
1503–4 to anyone who lived in a parish for three years, and in 1597 for one yea
However, there was not an absolute right to move into a parish and obtain
settlement, for the Elizabethan poor law restricted the movement of 'rogues an
vagabonds', who were defined as 'wandering persons and common labourer
being persons able in body using loitering and refusing to work for sucl
reasonable wages as is taxed or commonly given in such parts'.[18] Such person
could be seized, whipped, and sent back to their place of settlement, so tha
migration would be restricted to people with work who would not be a drai
upon the parish. Of course, many people who did not fall into the category o
'rogues and vagabonds' could nevertheless be a drain upon the parish througl
claims in old age or ill-health, by access to communal resources such as commoi
land, and through competition with established artisans. Consequently, a rang
of devices was developed by towns and parishes to control the influx o
'strangers', which included regulations on the housing stock by banning new
construction or subdivision; and taking a bond of indemnity against becoming a
charge, especially from those who were setting up in trade.

   These local regulations threatened the common law right of mobility fo
everyone who was not a rogue or vagabond, and the position was regularized by
the Settlement Act of 1662. On the one hand, the Act liberalized the law o

ettlement by reducing the period of residence and adding further methods of
cquisition. On the other hand, the Act established procedures for removing
otential claimants. The parish could make a complaint, within forty days, to
wo JPs for the removal of anyone who paid a rent of less than £10 a year and was
kely to become chargeable, unless sufficient security was given to discharge the
arish from any expense. When the complaint was upheld, the migrant was not
ecessarily physically expelled from the parish, but it was impossible to obtain a
ettlement and claim relief. The Act discriminated between valuable or self-
ufficient and harmful migration. It gave stringent powers to the parish to
emove newcomers who were a potential burden, or to deny them relief; at the
ame time, it was easier for others to obtain a settlement by renting property of
nore than £10 a year, giving a bond, or living in the parish undisturbed for forty
lays. Provision was also made for migratory, seasonal workers who did not wish
o change their residence permanently and would return to their parish when
hey needed relief. They could obtain a settlement certificate, stating that they
ıad left their house and wife or children in another parish which would be
esponsible for their relief.

The phrase 'likely to be chargeable' was vague and it could be defined by
ɔarishes and justices more or less as they pleased. 'Too great a scope', com-
ɔlained *Dalton's Country Justice* in 1682, 'is given to any person, although never so
ust and prudent, to inspect and to determine of another Man's livelihood and
:ondition.'[19] But at least the act of 1662 placed the onus on the parish to discover
ıny new residents and to take action within forty days; this ceased to be the case
when the law was amended in 1685 and 1692. The onus was shifted to the migrant
to give notice in writing, after which the parish had forty days to make a
complaint; failure to give notice meant that a settlement could not be obtained.
Parish officers had every incentive to make a complaint in order to reduce their
liability, and many migrants neglected to give notice because they were illiterate
or because they preferred not to take the risk of expulsion. The Act made it
harder for 'undesirable' migrants to obtain a settlement, and easier for 'desirable'
migrants to obtain a settlement by 'merit'. A number of categories of migrants
were granted exemption from the need to give written notice: those who paid
rates in the parish; served a year in a public office; completed an apprenticeship
with settlement determined by the last forty days' residence; or had an annual
hiring if the person was unmarried and without children. This ability to 'sift'
migrants protected parishes against undesirable migrants, but there was a danger
that potential claimants would be forced to remain in their home parish where
they might already be in receipt of relief, rather than move to an expanding area
of the economy where they might lose the right to relief. Clearly, this was in the
interest neither of areas with surplus population nor of areas which required

labour. The solution adopted in 1697 was to extend settlement certificates from single temporary migrants to workmen and their families who wished to move permanently to a new parish. The parish of settlement accepted a permanent obligation to support the members of the family when they became chargeable in their parish of residence, which extended even to children born in the new parish. Claimants could be issued with a 'removal' order to return to their parish of settlement, which clearly reduced the incentive to apply for relief; and the parish of settlement usually preferred to reimburse the parish of residence for relief rather than take back people. The result, so it was claimed, was to increase freedom of movement, for without such provisions men and women were 'confined to live in their owne Parishes Townshipps or Places and not permitted to inhabitt elsewhere though their Labour is wanted in many other Places where the Increase of Manufactures would imploy more Handes'.[20] It was hoped that parishes would provide certificates in order to encourage claimants to find work in areas of economic growth where they could become self-supporting, and so reduce the burden on the poor rates. Such was the expectation, but there was no obligation to issue a certificate, and parish officers could argue that greater opportunities elsewhere were sufficiently attractive without making any commitment. Overseers, advised one clergyman, should insist that anyone *entering* the parish should have a certificate, but they should refuse to issue certificates to their own poor when *leaving*, 'for it is far more than an equal chance, but they will have them again, and in a worse condition'.[21]

Parishes varied in their application of the law of settlement. Expanding industrial districts with a high demand for labour obviously stood to gain if migrants had certificates, for their labour was available without the threat of a burden on the rates. They might, however, not enforce certificates strictly, for their demand for labour might be paramount, and parish government was in any case likely to be under strain in rapidly growing industrial towns so that control was difficult. Other parishes were more inclined to enforce the law. Where a large landowner dominated a parish, he might be able to restrict residence by controlling the housing stock, and ensuring that the law of settlement was strictly enforced. Apart from these 'closed' estate villages, many parishes had an incentive to prevent competition for jobs and trade, especially where there was little economic growth; or to protect their communal resources against an influx of migrants. In some cases, they attempted to restrict the number of migrants before there was any threat of a claim, by refusing a settlement to those who were 'likely to be chargeable' and did not have certificates. This made sense where there was a desire to prevent the over-exploitation of resources such as commons, waste, woods, and charitable bequests, which were open to all residents whether or not they had a settlement. The strategy became less significant in the course of the eighteenth century, with the erosion of contingent property rights and the development of individual control over resources. Attention turned from the regulation of entry to removal when a claim was made on the rates, which was confirmed in 1795 when the distinction between certificated and uncertificated poor was ended. A parish could no longer refuse residence to a family without a certificate on the grounds that it might become chargeable in future; removal could only be required when there was a claim for relief, with the exception of unmarried women. Barriers against labour mobility were further weakened, with an emphasis on the control of paupers who made claims on the rates rather than on restrictions on the movement of the respectable poor.

The law of settlement certainly had the potential to cause hardships and difficulties. Men and women who needed support in old age could be threatened with removal to a parish where they had never lived; they could be forced to claim from a parish where they had served an apprenticeship or undertaken a year's service in husbandry many years previously. But in many cases, the system's apparent harshness was moderated because the parish of settlement would prefer to send money—an 'out-parish allowance'—to the parish of residence. The law of settlements could in fact reduce the risks of labour mobility. Relief based upon individual parishes had the potential for frustrating mobility, by making people unwilling to surrender their rights; the thrust of revisions in the law of settlement in the seventeenth and eighteenth centuries was to reduce the dangers of migration for both the individual and the parish. The overall result was a transfer of income from rural to industrial parishes, for areas which were growing and attracting migrants could benefit from their labour and pass the cost of maintenance in sickness and old age to the parish of settlement. The poor law provided a safety-net which allowed people to leave their family of origin, and was essential to a demographic system based on late marriage and a high level of labour mobility; it was not an inducement to feckless early marriage. The English poor law was shaped both by the demographic system, and by the political structure, which created a delicate balance between the autonomy of the parish and the provision of a general framework under the guidance of the central state.

The Poor Law in Scotland

In England ... recognition of a legal right in the able-bodied poor ... led ... to most of the evils to which the English system has given birth. In Scotland, on the contrary, a legal right in the able-bodied poor was never acknowledged ... and hence those evils, so oppressive ... have, in this part of the island, been avoided.[22]

This comment of 1838 suggests that Sir Francis Brewster's complaint about the generosity of the poor law in England could not apply north of the border. When the poor law in England was criticized in the early nineteenth century, Scotland was held up as a model. The able-bodied poor, it was claimed, had no right to relief and even the impotent poor were offered 'a miserable and uncertain pittance'.[23] The levying of a poor rate or assessment was much rarer in Scotland than in England, so that funds to relieve the poor were raised by voluntary contributions, usually through church collections. 'The people in general are persuaded of its expedience', remarked the General Assembly in 1838, 'and with very few exceptions, are anxious to preserve it.'[24]

The contrast drawn between the destructive generosity of England and the constructive harshness of Scotland says much about thinking on social policy in the 1830s, with its stress on deterrence and 'less eligibility'. But was it an accurate picture of the Scottish poor law, or were commentators exaggerating its harshness for ideological reasons? Was the divergence as wide in reality as the early nineteenth-century commentators liked to believe? And if there was a divergence, why did it arise? Contemporary commentators took it for granted that the Scottish poor law was superior, creating a greater degree of self-sufficiency. A modern historian is more likely to be puzzled by the contrast with England, where the poor law was a crucial part of the demographic system in dealing with life-cycle poverty. Could it be that the demographic system in Scotland placed less strain on the transfer of income between the generations within a family? Or did the poor law, contrary to the assertions of the early nineteenth-century commentators, in fact provide relief to the impotent and able-bodied poor in much the same way as in England?

The Scottish poor law act of 1579 referred to relief of the 'poor, aged and impotent', a phrase which was contested by lawyers in the early nineteenth century. The assertion that the Scottish poor law precluded relief of the able-bodied poor rested upon an interpretation of these words to mean people who were either poor *and* aged or poor *and* impotent, but not merely poor. Not all lawyers agreed with this definition, and it was ruled in the case of *Pollock* v. *Darling* in 1804 that it was permissible to grant relief to the able-bodied poor. The matter nevertheless remained confused. During the depression of 1819–21, unemployed workers in Paisley were refused relief, and Whig lawyers were able to dismiss the decision in *Pollock* v. *Darling* as an aberration. It arose, they claimed, from a mistaken belief that people would starve unless supported by 'compulsory provision'; this had been undermined 'by the greater knowledge which has been acquired, as to the true causes and remedies of pauperism'.[25] Such an assertion owed more to a reading of Malthus than to an understanding of Scottish law and history. In fact, legislation of the Scottish parliament in 1649,

663, and 1672 permitted able-bodied paupers to be returned to their home parish where they were to be set to work in houses of correction; and parishes were allowed to raise compulsory 'assessments' to complement voluntary contributions. Further, proclamations of the Privy Council in Scotland urged parishes to raise assessments, particularly in the famine of the 1690s. Clearly, lawyers and commentators in the 1830s who asserted that the Scottish poor law had never recognized the rights of the able-bodied poor and relied on voluntary contributions were on doubtful ground.

There were certainly signs that parishes were starting to move towards the English pattern of relief at the end of the seventeenth and early eighteenth centuries. Although tax-funded relief was less general than in England, it was not unknown at least in the south of the country. About a fifth of parishes for which records survive made compulsory assessments during the famine of the 1690s, and assessments were certainly levied in the early nineteenth century. There were also cases of relief to the able-bodied poor, and of generous payments to the impotent. At Chirnside in 1699, for example, £12 was granted to Robert Dunbar to buy a horse to maintain a family of small Children',[26] and at Cambulsang in 1750 £8 was given to a widower to employ a home help. The historical experience of the poor law was more varied than commentators in the 1830s assumed, and restriction of the Scottish poor law was contested. What needs to be explained is why the intentions of the legislation of 1649–72 and the proclamations of the Privy Council were contained, so that convergence with the English pattern did not go further. Compulsory assessments were more contentious than the poor rate in England; it was obviously more difficult for the able-bodied poor in Scotland to claim a right to relief; and there was nothing akin to the Speenhamland system of wage subsidies in the late eighteenth and early nineteenth centuries. This divergence must be explained, rather than accepted as an intrinsic feature of Scottish legislation.

The development of the poor law in the two countries was shaped by the structure of government, which affected the balance of power between social groups. In England, the poor law was implemented by parish authorities within a framework created by a relatively strong central state. The parish was a unit of civil government which coincided with the ecclesiastical parish of the Church of England but was in many respects separate, with its own funds and officers. The vestry was open to all ratepayers, and the power of large landowners was constrained. In Scotland, the Calvinist Presbyterian kirk did not act as a unit of civil government in the same way. It collected voluntary contributions which were not kept apart from other church funds, and decisions about the granting of relief were made by the kirk session, a local church court drawn from the congregation. The decisions of the kirk session were less open to challenge and supervision than in England, for justices of the peace were less influential than in England, in part because a more concentrated pattern of landownership meant that the gentry class was less significant, with a survival of 'heritable jurisdictions' and military power of clan chieftains into the eighteenth century. The influence of central government through the Privy Council in Scotland was also weak until the later seventeenth century, so that it was difficult to create a national system such as emerged in England. When the kirk did decide to make a compulsory assessment, problems arose from the structure of local government. The 'heritors' or landowners who were liable to pay the assessment demanded a greater say in the administration of the poor law, which resulted in the removal of compulsory assessments from the kirk sessions. Administration passed to a joint committee drawn from the kirk and the 'heritors', and it was not long before the heritors intervened in the administration of parishes where contributions were still voluntary, and claimed the right to manage all parish funds. The heritors argued that mismanagement of voluntary funds would make a compulsory assessment necessary, which they would have to pay; they were also concerned to remove power from the non-landed and control religious fervour, which they feared as a threat to social order. Legal decisions in 1751 and 1752 gave them the right of joint administration of all parish funds, with the poor fund being run separately. Consequently, a parish could only impose a compulsory assessment with the consent of the landowners, who had no interest in allowing costs to rise. Rural society was considerably more polarized than in England, so that large landowners were able to dominate the administration of the poor law and impose their desire for economy against the concern of smallholders or occupiers for support in periods of poverty. Essentially, control over the poor law was removed from the bulk of the inhabitants of the parish and placed in the hands of the great landowners at an earlier date than in England, where the transfer of power from the parish community to the large ratepayers was only achieved by the 'new' poor law of 1834. The relative strictness of the Scottish poor law was, at least in part, the result of a struggle for control in the mid-eighteenth century which allowed large landowners to assert their will over the community.

Such an interpretation assumes that the Scottish poor law would, in the absence of control by great landowners, have developed in the same way as in England. Much depends upon whether 'collective' relief was necessary. In England, the poor law was an integral feature of the demographic system which allowed families to cope with life-cycle poverty, and the absence of 'collective' assistance would have caused serious problems. Does this mean that the relatively narrow limits which were set to poor relief in Scotland created difficulties, and that the power of the landowners ignored the requirements of the demographic system; or were the needs for poor relief in Scotland different as a result f the divergence in agrarian social structure? Unfortunately, information on emographic history is not as good in Scotland as in England, but a plausible case an be made to suggest that generous 'collective' provision was less necessary. he survival of the clan system in the Highlands until the early eighteenth entury provided an alternative method of support; and a lower level of ommercialization and greater reliance on subsistence agriculture removed ome of the needs for poor relief which were apparent in England. Fermetouns vith subtenants and cottars arguably provided the means for subsistence and nade poor relief less necessary. They were replaced by a regular, married vork-force on annual contracts which meant that the agricultural labour force vas utilized more intensively over the year than in southern England so that here was little need to adopt 'Speenhamland' methods of subsidizing wages. .arge landowners who consolidated their farms into single tenancies were able o displace population from the land, so that there was no glut of rural labour as n southern England, and their attempt to exclude the able-bodied poor from elief was part of a general strategy of 'clearing' their estates of surplus population. There might, in other words, have been a congruence between the ›olitical constraints on the poor law and the agrarian system.

Compulsory assessments could not be avoided in some parishes, particularly n the south. People who were not members of the kirk resisted making voluntary contributions, but they were nevertheless permitted to make claims or relief: compulsory assessments dealt with the problem of 'free riders'. The 'eduction in the number of cottars, increased reliance on waged labour, and the ;rowth of rural industry meant that a larger proportion of the population was ikely to turn to the poor law for support. Above all, reliance on voluntary :ontributions, and exclusion of the able-bodied poor from relief, were under ;reatest challenge in the expanding industrial towns. It was difficult for voluntary :ontributions to cope with the problems of large towns and it was not realistic to :xclude able-bodied workers from relief in periods of mass unemployment luring trade depressions, as at Paisley. The insistence of commentators in the ₁830s that relief was not available to the able-bodied poor was a rearguard action, ɑ desperate attempt to hold the line against the pressures of social and economic :hange.

Charity

The development of a tax-funded poor law in England in the later sixteenth century may, all too easily, be interpreted as an attempt to fill a vacuum left by the dissolution of the monasteries and other religious foundations. But this is far too simple an interpretation. The Calvinist reformation in Holland and Scotland swept away monasteries and other religious foundations, yet there was a continued reliance upon voluntary contributions rather than compulsory taxation. Charity and voluntary organizations of various types remained significant in both Protestant and Catholic countries, in societies with and without a state system of welfare. Catholics and Protestants continued to debate the proper role of charity, in much the same terms as they were discussed before the Reformation. One view of charity was that it was an expression of the virtue of mercy which would offer eternal life to the donor; it could even be argued that a greater degree of mercy was shown in giving to the unjust than to the righteous. Another view was that charity should be used selectively, directed to those who were 'deserving' as a reward for correct social behaviour, and as an incentive to self-sufficiency, taking care that charity did not 'demoralize' recipients by making them dependent on hand-outs and undermining their character. The proponents of this view of charity felt that relief by poor law authorities should be harsh and punitive, confined to those who were 'undeserving'; and they opposed 'indiscriminate' charity to people in need. Others saw charity as a way of remaking character, rescuing people from sin, and converting them to the religious views of the donors: charity should therefore be directed to saving prostitutes or 'ragged' children or drunkards. Charity should be offered to the wicked, but in a way which would produce a moral transformation. Not only did charities differ in their objects, but also in their forms of organization. Bequests established at death could be used to set up an almshouse, school, or a fund to relieve the poor, which obviously could not entail the active participation of donors, who left the administration to executors or a corporate body. Other charities stressed the need for personal service in ministering to the poor, or active involvement by subscribers during their lives in the administration of hospitals or schools. Charity did not disappear in eighteenth- and early nineteenth-century Britain, but there were shifts in emphasis between these approaches and patterns of organization.

In sixteenth- and seventeenth-century England, wealthy merchants, clothiers, or landowners often made a charitable bequest in their will. The purpose of the bequest changed after the Reformation, from predominantly religious to largely secular concerns. Between 1480 and 1490, religious bequests accounted for 60.6 per cent of the total, but between 1651 and 1660 only 11.6 per cent; chantries to say masses for the souls of the dead gave way to the creation of almshouses for the care of the elderly, schools for the education of the young, or funds to distribute fuel, clothing, or money to the needy. Although the total value of bequests fell in real terms, the shift in their composition meant that the real value of *secular* bequests doubled between the 1480s and 1650s, and the yield of income from the accumulated private benefactions devoted to the poor probably rose in real value er capita. Private charitable bequests did not collapse with the Reformation: their income in 1660 was probably about the same as the poor rates, at something around £100,000. The sharp decline in their importance came in the eighteenth century. A government return of 1788 placed the income of charitable trusts at £258,700, which was only 10 per cent of the sum raised by poor rates; even when allowance is made for omissions in the return, a wide gap had opened between the sums raised by charitable bequests and taxation.[27]

This does not necessarily mean that there was a decline in the overall importance of charity. Rather, there was a change in its nature. Bequests at death declined in importance, and there was a growth of 'associated philanthropy' which depended on the collection of money from a large number of subscribers who played an active role in the administration of voluntary organizations. 'Associated philanthropy' concentrated on a number of areas. Charity schools were established, and the Society for Promoting Christian Knowledge aimed to spread literacy in order to stimulate reading the Bible and to teach morality. The Foundling Hospital established by Thomas Coram in 1740 took in abandoned children; the Marine Society created by Jonas Hanway apprenticed pauper boys to the merchant navy; and the Magdalen Hospital aimed to reform 'poor, young, thoughtless females'. A number of hospitals were created for the sick poor, such as the Westminster in 1720 and the London in 1740. The aim of these organizations was not simply to be benevolent, without thought of return; there had to be 'beneficence', an improvement in the lot of the recipient and the nation. Bequests given at death usually offered relief without any attempt to shape the behaviour of the recipient, and were open to misuse by incompetent or corrupt managers. Charity, it was argued, should be given during life and incorporate active involvement by the donors in management, with a concern to moralize the recipients and create a more efficient nation. The charity schools would provide a Christian education for the poor; the Marine Society and Magdalen Hospital would transform boys and fallen women from threats to society into productive members of the nation; the hospitals would return the sick to work, allowing them to support their families rather than to impose a drain on the state. Associated philanthropy was, so its supporters argued, more efficient than the poor law, for subscriptions would only continue so long as the management showed 'honesty, skill and integrity'.[28] The blessings of associated philanthropy were obvious to John Masie in 1759: 'Thus might CHARITY, HUMANITY, PATRIOTISM AND OECONOMY be made to go Hand-in-Hand; and the ways to form this quadruple Alliance are so obviously proper and so easily practicable that one can scarcely help wondering how so much Good can be obtained from such simple means.'[29]

Associated charities often entailed the provision of institutional care as a means of reshaping character. Such an approach was not confined to the hospitals and schools of 'associated charities', but was carried through into the debate on prisons, asylums, and workhouses, which were given a new role in the later eighteenth and early nineteenth centuries. There was also a concern with moral reform in society at large. The Societies for the Reformation of Manners in the 1690s urged the need to suppress vice and immorality, to stamp out prostitution, blasphemy, gambling, and drunkenness, through the imposition of the existing legal code. This depended in the first place upon convincing justice of the peace and town councils of their moral duty to civilize and reform society by controlling fairs or enforcing sobriety and order. This approach revived with new force in the 1780s and 1790s when the choice facing British society seemed, in the phrase of John Bowdler, to be 'reform or ruin'. The loss of the American colonies suggested national decay; the outbreak of the French Revolution was a warning of the dire consequences of social dissolution; the increase of population and the slide into dependence on the poor law raised fears about the future of the country. What was needed, it seemed to leading evangelicals such as William Wilberforce and Samuel Thornton, was a moral regeneration of society. Such was the ambition of the Proclamation Society, formed by Wilberforce in 1787 and the Society for the Suppression of Vice founded in 1807. The well-to-do had to teach by their own behaviour, eschewing the vices of gambling, pleasure gardens, and theatres by adopting a disciplined and austere life-style. Their moral example was complemented by the creation of charities designed to encourage self-sufficiency and providence amongst the poor. The Society for the Support and Encouragement of Sunday Schools was established in 1785, sponsored by the Society for the Propagation of Christian Knowledge, which had been active in the charity school movement in the early eighteenth century. Mechanics Institutes were created to educate working men, and savings banks to receive their small deposits. Public amusements were attacked and 'rational recreation' urged, which should, in the words of Patrick Colquhoun, be 'rendered subservient to the improvement of morals, and to the means of infusing into the mind a love of the Constitution, and a reverence and respect for the Laws'.[30] The ambition was explained by the *Philanthropist*:

to encourage and stimulate their habits of industry, sobriety and economy; to furnish them with such knowledge as may be useful in their pursuits and in their station of life as well as to confirm in their minds the importance of fulfilling their religious and moral duties; to connect them with the higher orders by the ties of kindness and gratitude, without that sense of dependence which diminishes a just confidence in their own exertions, is to confer intrinsic and lasting benefits which do not terminate with our lives but form a useful example to be transmitted to our posterity.[31]

The evangelicals' ambition of 'moralizing' the poor coincided with Malthus's fear that relief in aid of wages was undermining self-sufficiency: reform of the poor law in order to deter fecklessness was associated with the regeneration of the character of the poor through education, rational recreation, and thrift. Voluntary organizations formed an essential element in the response to social change in the late eighteenth and early nineteenth centuries, a crucial feature in the attempt of the middle class to stabilize an increasingly urban and industrial society which involved a major shift in the nature of social order and the state.

NOTES

1. Quoted in S. Macfarlane, 'Social Policy and the Poor in the later Seventeenth Century', in A. L. Beier and R. Finlay (eds.), *London, 1500–1700: The Making of a Metropolis* (1986), 253.

2. D. C. Coleman, 'Labour in the English Economy of the Seventeenth Century', *Economic History Review*, 2nd ser. 9 (1955–6), 285–6. Parliamentary Papers 1803–4, xiii, *Abstract of Answers and Returns*, 715.

3. K. D. M. Snell and I. Millar, 'Lone Parent Families and the Welfare State: Past and Present', *Continuity and Change*, 2 (1987); D. Thomson, 'The Decline of Social Welfare: Falling State Support for the Elderly since Early Victorian Times', *Ageing and Society*, 4 (1984).

4. T. Arkell, 'The Incidence of Poverty in England in the Later Seventeenth Century', *Social History*, 12 (1987), 46–7.

5. T. Wales, 'Poverty, Poor Relief and the Life Cycle: Some Evidence from Seventeenth-Century Norfolk', in R. M. Smith (ed.), *Land, Kinship and the Life Cycle* (Cambridge, 1984), 352–3, 386; Snell and Millar, 'Lone Parent Families', 415.

6. R. M. Smith, 'Transfer Incomes, Risk and Security: The Roles of the Family and the Collectivity in Recent Theories of Fertility Change', in D. A. Coleman and R. S. Schofield (eds.), *The State of Population Theory* (Oxford, 1986), 201–2.

7. Macfarlane, 'Social Policy', 252, 263.

8. D. Marshall, *The English Poor in the Eighteenth Century* (1926), 152.

9. There were fewer workhouses, for one parish might rely on another: in 1776 there were 1,970 workhouses in England and Wales, excluding London, capable of accommodating 89,775 persons. PP 1804 xiii, *Abstract of Answers and Returns*, 716.

10. G. W. Oxley, 'The Permanent Poor in South-west Lancashire under the Old Poor Law', in J. R. Harris (ed.), *Liverpool and Merseyside* (1969), 35.

11. A. W. Coats, 'Changing Attitudes to Labour in the Mid-Eighteenth Century', *Economic History Review*, 2nd ser. 11 (1958–9); 'Economic Thought and Poor Law Policy in the Eighteenth Century', *Economic History Review*, 2nd ser. 13 (1960–1).

12. T. R. Malthus, *An Essay on the Principle of Population*, ed. Patricia James (Cambridge, 1989), 361.

13. Ibid. 363; Smith, 'Transfer Incomes', 192.

14. Quoted in J. P. Huzel, 'Malthus, the Poor Law, and Population in Early Nineteenth Century England', *Economic History Review*, 2nd ser. 22 (1969), 434.

15. A. Smith, *An Inquiry into the Nature and Causes of the Wealth of Nations* (repr. 1937), 14 (book i, ch. x).
16. Malthus, *Essay*, 360.
17. Ibid. 363.
18. See P. Slack, *Poverty and Policy in Tudor and Stuart England* (1988), 28–9 and 91–100 on its practical impact.
19. Quoted in P. Styles, 'The Evolution of the Law of Settlement', *University of Birmingham Historical Journal*, 9 (1963–4), 46.
20. Ibid. 50.
21. Quoted in N. Landau, 'The Regulation of Immigration, Economic Structures and Definitions of the Poor in Eighteenth-Century England', *Historical Journal*, 33 (1990) 560.
22. General Assembly 1838, quoted in R. Mitchison, 'The Making of the Old Scottish Poor Law', *Past and Present*, 63 (1974), 68.
23. The phrase of the General Assembly in 1838: see ibid. 58.
24. Ibid.
25. Quoted in R. Mitchison, 'The Poor Law', in T. Devine and R. Mitchison (eds.), *People and Society in Scotland*, i (1988), 262.
26. Mitchison, 'Making of the Old Scottish Poor Law', 72–3.
27. W. G. Bittle and R. T. Lane, 'Inflation and Philanthropy in England: A Reassessment of W. K. Jordan's Data', *Economic History Review*, 2nd ser. 29 (1976); P. Slack, *The English Poor Law 1531–1782* (1990), 52.
28. Thomas Alcock in 1753, quoted in D. T. Andrew, *Philanthropy and Police: London Charity in the Eighteenth Century* (Princeton, NJ, 1989), 102.
29. Ibid.
30. Ibid. 173.
31. Ibid. 201–2.

FURTHER READING

Andrew, D. T., *Philanthropy and Police: London Charity in the Eighteenth Century* (Princeton, NJ, 1989).
Arkell, T., 'The Incidence of Poverty in England in the Later Seventeenth Century', *Social History*, 12 (1987).
Bittle, W. G., and Lane, R. T., 'Inflation and Philanthropy in England: A Reassessment of W. K. Jordan's Data', *Economic History Review*, 2nd ser. 29 (1976).
Blaug, M., 'The Myth of the Old Poor Law and the Making of the New', *Journal of Economic History*, 23 (1963).
—— 'The Poor Law Report Re-examined', *Journal of Economic History*, 24 (1964).
Boyer, G. R., 'The Old Poor Law and the Agricultural Labor Market in Southern England: An Empirical Analysis', *Journal of Economic History*, 46 (1986).
—— *An Economic History of the English Poor Law, 1750–1850* (Cambridge, 1990).
—— 'An Economic Model of the English Poor Law, c.1780–1834', *Explorations in Economic History*, 22 (1985).
Brown, F. K., *Fathers of the Victorians: The Age of Wilberforce* (Cambridge, 1961).

Cage, R. A., *The Scottish Poor Law, 1745–1845* (Edinburgh, 1981).

Coats, A. W., 'Changing Attitudes to Labour in the Mid-Eighteenth Century', *Economic History Review*, 2nd ser. 11 (1958–9).

—— 'Economic Thought and Poor Law Policy in the Eighteenth Century', *Economic History Review*, 2nd ser. 13 (1960–1).

—— 'The Relief of Poverty, Attitudes to Labour, and Economic Change in England, 1660–1782', *International Review of Social History*, 21 (1976).

Coleman, D. C., 'Labour in the English Economy of the Seventeenth Century', *Economic History Review*, 2nd ser. 8 (1955–6).

—— 'Philanthropy Deflated: A Comment', *Economic History Review*, 2nd ser. 31 (1978).

Hadwin, J. F., 'Deflating Philanthropy', *Economic History Review*, 2nd ser. 31 (1978).

Huzel, J. P., 'The Demographic Impact of the Old Poor Law: More Reflexions on Malthus', *Economic History Review*, 2nd ser. 33 (1980).

—— 'Malthus, the Poor Law, and Population in Early Nineteenth-Century England', *Economic History Review*, 2nd ser. 22 (1969).

Landau, N., 'The Regulation of Immigration, Economic Structures and Definitions of the Poor in Eighteenth-Century England', *Historical Journal*, 33 (1990).

—— 'The Laws of Settlement and the Surveillance of Immigration in Eighteenth-Century Kent', *Continuity and Change*, 3 (1988).

McClure, R. K., *Coram's Children: The London Foundling Hospital in the Eighteenth Century* (New Haven, Conn., 1981).

Macfarlane, S., 'Social Policy and the Poor in the Later Seventeenth Century', in A. L. Beier and R. Finlay (eds.), *London, 1500–1700: The Making of the Metropolis* (1986).

Malthus, T. R., *An Essay on the Principle of Population* (1803 edn.), ed. with variora by Patricia James (Cambridge, 1986).

Marshall, D., *The English Poor in the Eighteenth Century* (1926).

Marshall, J. D., *The Old Poor Law, 1795–1834* (1968).

Mitchison, R., 'The Making of the Old Scottish Poor Law', *Past and Present*, 63 (1974).

—— 'North and South: The Development of the Gulf in Poor Law Practice', in R. A. Houston and I. D. Whyte (eds.), *Scottish Society, 1500–1800* (Cambridge, 1989).

—— 'The Poor Law', in T. Devine and R. Mitchison (eds.), *People and Society in Scotland*, i (Edinburgh, 1988).

Nash, S., 'Prostitution and Charity: The Magdalen Hospital, a Case Study', *Journal of Social History*, 17 (1984).

Newman Brown, W., 'The Receipt of Poor Relief and Family Situation: Aldenham, Hertfordshire, 1630–90', in R. M. Smith (ed.), *Land, Kinship and Life Cycle* (Cambridge, 1984).

Owen, D., *English Philanthropy, 1660–1960* (Cambridge, Mass., 1964).

Oxley, G. W., 'The Permanent Poor in South-West Lancashire under the Old Poor Law', in J. R. Harris (ed.), *Liverpool and Merseyside: Essays in the Economic and Social History of the Port and its Hinterland* (1969).

—— *Poor Relief in England and Wales, 1601–1834* (Newton Abbot, 1974).

Pullan, B., 'Catholics and the Poor in Early Modern Europe', *Transactions of the Royal Historical Society*, 5th ser. 26 (1976).

Roberts, M. J. D., 'The Society for the Suppression of Vice and its Early Critics', *Historical Journal*, 26 (1983).

Slack, P., *The English Poor Law, 1531–1782* (1990).

—— *Poverty and Policy in Tudor and Stuart England* (1988).

Smith, R. M., 'The Structured Dependence of the Elderly as a Recent Development: Some Sceptical Historical Thoughts', *Ageing and Society*, 4 (1984).

—— 'Transfer Incomes, Risk and Security: The Roles of the Family and the Collectivity in Recent Theories of Fertility Change', in D. A. Coleman and R. S. Schofield (eds.), *The State of Population Theory* (Oxford, 1986).

—— 'Welfare and Management of Demographic Uncertainty', in M. Keynes, D. A. Coleman, and N. H. Dimsdale (eds.), *The Political Economy of Health and Welfare* (1986).

Snell, K. D. M., and Millar, J., 'Lone-Parent Families and the Welfare State: Past and Present', *Continuity and Change*, 2 (1987).

Styles, P., 'The Evolution of the Law of Settlement', *University of Birmingham Historical Journal*, 9 (1963–4).

Taylor, J. S., 'The Impact of Pauper Settlement, 1691–1834', *Past and Present*, 73 (1976).

—— *Jonas Hanway, Founder of the Marine Society: Charity and Policy in Eighteenth-Century Britain* (1985).

—— 'The Mythology of the Old Poor Law', *Journal of Economic History*, 29 (1969).

Thomas, E. G., 'The Old Poor Law and Medicine', *Medical History*, 24 (1984).

Thomson, D., 'The Decline of Social Welfare: Falling State Support for the Elderly since Early Victorian Times', *Ageing and Society*, 4 (1984).

—— 'Welfare and the Historians', in L. Bonfield *et al.*, *The World We Have Gained: Histories of Population and Social Structure* (Oxford, 1986).

Wales, T., 'Poverty, Poor Relief and the Life-Cycle: Some Evidence from Seventeenth-Century Norfolk', in R. M. Smith (ed.), *Land, Kinship and the Life-Cycle* (Cambridge, 1984).

Woodward, J., *To Do the Sick No Harm: A Study of the British Voluntary Hospital System to 1875* (1974).

PART V

Public Policy and the State

CHAPTER 18

The Visible Hand:
The State and the Economy

Britain in the eighteenth century, it was sometimes suggested, had a 'Venetian constitution', with a small, closed group of landowners dominating the state like the élite of Venice. Britain, contended Benjamin Disraeli, suffered from a combination of 'Venetian politics, Dutch finance and French wars'[1] by which Whig aristocratic landowners controlled the state, raising loans in London to finance war on the lines established by Dutch financiers who had been introduced into England by William of Orange. The 'triumph of the Venetian oligarchy' has been linked, above all, to the political career of Robert Walpole who, according to his modern biographer, 'fused the interests of aristocracy, high finance, and executive government':

The Revolution of 1688 and all that followed were retrogressive from the point of view of the emergence of the middle class into political power. Socially and economically they continued to thrive, but not politically. The power of the land and of commerce fused to create a paradise for gentlemen, for the aristocracy of birth; it thus became much easier for England to adopt an imperial authority, to rule alien peoples, and to train its ruling class for that purpose, rather than to adjust its institutions and its social system to the needs of an industrial society.[2]

The outcome, so it is argued, was 'gentlemanly capitalism', an alliance between a prosperous agrarian capitalism and the power of commerce and finance in pursuit of empire, which subordinated industrial capitalism and excluded the industrial middle class from power and influence.

The proponents of 'Venetian oligarchy' or 'gentlemanly capitalism' can make a strong case. General elections became less frequent with the increase in the life of parliament from five to seven years in 1716; and only about a third of constituencies were contested when an election *was* called. The franchise was limited and became more restricted, and the distribution of seats was full of anomalies, allowing decayed boroughs to elect members and failing to recognize new industrial and commercial centres such as Birmingham or Manchester. Voting was, in the opinion of Lewis Namier, a sham; he suggested that large landowners were able to decide elections in thirty-nine of forty English counties through their influence on tenants, and 'probably not more than one in every twenty voters at county elections could freely exercise their statutory rights'.[3] Similarly, he calculated that about half the boroughs were controlled by patrons through the influence of property, donations to charities, offers of patronage, and outright bribery. In the eyes of some leading historians, eighteenth-century politics amounted to inducing a narrow electorate to vote for candidates supported by the landed élite and the government. Such an interpretation has little role for issues or ideas, and sees politics as a mindless search for seats through manipulation of a passive electorate which was simply not capable of comprehending problems of national importance.[4]

The growth of oligarchy could be interpreted as the survival of an outmoded political system which was increasingly in tension with a new middle class and industrial-urban society, but some historians have suggested that it *complemented* Britain's socio-economic structure. Oligarchy and patronage, they argue, created political stability, which suited merchants and industrialists whose main concern was a secure environment for business.[5] Dominance by a landed oligarchy was not surprising, for the rise of large estates allowed landed magnates to impose a firmer grip on the counties. Meanwhile, the 'financial revolution' in London created a wealthy élite of loan contractors and merchants who were allied to the state and its pursuit of war and empire, so bolstering rather than challenging the old élite. Industry, they suggest, posed little threat to the political order, for growth was concentrated in workshops and outwork which were based on the household, and relied on traditional, low-productivity technology rather than 'revolutionized' factories. Indeed, J. C. D. Clark has gone so far as to suggest that the real problem is explaining *why* the electoral system was reformed in 1832, for 'it is by no means clear that the sort of material changes witnessed by the vast majority before 1832 were enough in themselves to necessitate or effect immediate and basic transformations of outlook or belief'.[6]

The explanation favoured by Clark replaces the 'mindless' pursuit of electoral influence by the vital role of ideology. Full participation in political life, he argues, was based upon membership of the Church of England, which created a 'confessional state' whose authority was underwritten by theology. Christ exercised divine authority and instituted a priesthood with divine right; the Anglican clergy acted as agents of the state in their parishes, and the monarch was the head of both the Church and the state. Monarchy, hierarchy, and aristocracy were justified in theological terms as a divinely ordained order. Theology was,

Clark argues, supported by personal allegiance and patriarchalism, for 'service' was common, and most concerns were based on the family. The major threat, according to Clark, was not economic change or class conflict: it was religion. The confessional state and the theological legitimacy of the established order were challenged by Dissenters who denied the divine right of the priesthood, and by Irish Catholics who demanded 'emancipation'. The growth of dissent, argues Clark, had not gone far enough by the late 1820s to overturn the existing order: its dissolving power was reinforced by high political calculations. The Whigs resented their exclusion from power, and 'their eventual response, Samson-like, was to pull down around their ears the late eighteenth-century constitution'.[7] The Reform Act, on this interpretation, was a coup by one group of aristocrats against another.

The attempt to put the mind back into eighteenth-century politics is an important corrective to the simple pursuit of electoral influence. Nevertheless, there is significant common ground between the two interpretations: both deny the importance of economic and social change; they emphasize the aristocratic nature of the state, which was guaranteed either by electoral management or by ideology; and they assume the exclusion of the 'middling sort' from an active political role. These interpretations give little weight to economic and social change in challenging the political system; similarly, the writings of 'new' economic historians ignore the role of the state in the functioning of the economy. It is, in fact, more plausible to argue that the state had an active role in shaping the development of the economy; that the unreformed electoral system was responsive to the demands of the electorate rather than the plaything of patrons; and that parliament was providing an effective legislative service for the economy. It is also possible to argue that the impact of economic change has been underestimated. There was, after all, massive structural transformation with the release of labour from land into industry, services, and towns. It is true that only a small proportion of the population moved into factories and was immediately affected by the adoption of powered machinery, but hand labour was not necessarily family-based patriarchalism. Workers in putting out trades were dependent wage labourers, and there were many opportunities for conflict with merchant-manufacturers over the definition of perquisites or embezzlement, so that social conflict existed in the absence of large-scale factory production. The impact of mechanization and centralization was not confined simply to those workers who were directly affected, for 'revolutionizing' one stage could destabilize other sectors which continued to rely on hand labour. Social relations in eighteenth-century Britain cannot be reduced to the survival of patriarchalism and a 'confessional' state.

Elections and Political Life

The unreformed electoral system of the late eighteenth and early nineteenth centuries may easily be portrayed as corrupt and anachronistic, in need of rationalization to meet the changing distribution of the population and to extend the vote to a wider section of society. There is, however, a danger in viewing the unreformed electoral system through the eyes of radical critics at the time or in terms of the electoral system which emerged in Victorian Britain, with its stress on the direct representation of a community by its member and the vote as a civil right. Rather, the electoral system of the eighteenth century should be treated on its own terms in order to establish how it responded to the needs of a society undergoing major structural change and economic development.

The electorate of eighteenth-century Britain is usually portrayed as passive raw material for patrons to manipulate, which is to ignore the possibility that the electorate could influence patrons. The electors' local concerns are also dismissed as indicating a lack of interest in important national issues. Such an interpretation is implausible. Awareness of national political issues was fostered by an increasing level of literacy, the development of an active press, better channels of communication with London, and the growth of religious dissent which raised major issues of civil rights. Above all, a rigid distinction between national and local politics overlooks their interpenetration, which was a fundamental feature of eighteenth-century politics. The creation of a nationally integrated market depended upon parliamentary approval of local turnpikes, waterways, bridges, and harbours. The shaping of the poor law and settlement, which affected the majority of the population, relied upon local initiatives rather than the imposition of uniform national policies. Concern with labour discipline led employers in specific trades to urge the repeal of Tudor regulations of wages and apprenticeships and to advocate legislation against 'embezzlement'; their workers petitioned parliament to maintain the Tudor code. Similarly, the challenge to 'contingent property rights' involved members of rural parishes in seeking private bills and petitioning parliament. Particular trades and industries campaigned for the adjustment of customs and excise duties to protect their interests against rivals at home and abroad. Lobbies became more common and sophisticated, with organizations such as the Society of West India Merchants, the Midland Association of Ironmasters, and the West Riding Committee of Worsted Manufacturers monitoring government policy and making representations to shape legislation. There was no homogeneous business interest, for these trade and industrial groups were divided amongst themselves rather than a cohesive force against landed or monied interests, which meant that national bodies such as the General Chamber of Manufacturers of 1785–7 were short lived.

But industrialists and merchants were far from being subordinate to aristocratic patrons: these special interest groups operated in an open and accountable political system which was responsive to their needs.

Interest in the political process was intense, involving an interplay between local concerns and national policies, and creating an active, participatory political life. The electorate in many eighteenth-century constituencies was able to exert influence upon patrons in a process of bargaining. Neither should the theological underpinnings of a 'confessional state' be exaggerated. Rather than providing the dominant ideology of the governing élite, it appealed to particular social group-ings such as Anglican clergymen and bishops with large stipends and properties, fellows of Oxford colleges, and more old-fashioned rural squires. Certainly, emphasis upon the advance of dissent in dissolving the basis of order rests upon too rigid a distinction between social and religious explanations. The growth of dissent in towns and industrial districts was itself a reflection of social and economic change, and it is necessary to ask why dissent flourished when it did, and why it appealed to certain social groupings. Englishmen might possibly criticize the political system because they were opposed to the Trinity; but it is just as likely that they became dissenters because their concern for civil and religious rights made them hostile to the established order and led to an attack on the privileges of the Anglican Church. In any case, the differences between Anglicans and other sects should not be overdrawn. All could agree on notions of political obligation and social restraint, which allowed Anglicans and Dissenters to co-operate in prison reform, hospital provision, and the repression of vice. At other times, reconciliation gave way to conflict between separate philanthropic ventures, or to a tussle for control of bodies such as the town council, vestry, or improvement commission. The important point is the circumstances which generated co-operation or conflict, rather than a reduction of eighteenth-century politics to a tussle between Anglicans and Dissenters. Indeed, pressure for reform was by no means confined to alienated heretics, for it drew upon the 'country' ideology of gentry and freeholders which often coincided with the grievances of urban artisans, merchants, industrialists, and shopkeepers. The association movement of the early 1780s, for example, was initiated by Christopher Wyvill, an Anglican clergyman, and gained support from urban interests in Middlesex. The demand for parliamentary reform had a far longer tradition than a reaction by disaffected Anglicans to Catholic emancipation in 1829.

The 'confessional state' passed long before the Reform Bill crisis. By no means all offices were affected by the Test and Corporation Acts which required membership of the Church of England. Municipal corporations were covered, but not manorial offices, which allowed Nonconformists to secure a large measure of power in towns such as Birmingham which did not have a corporation. Dissenters could hold offices which *were* covered by religious tests, by occasional conformity to the Church of England or by payment of an indemnity. Above all, there was a massive expansion of new public bodies with the sanction of parliament, such as turnpike trusts, commissions for waterways and harbours, canal companies, improvement commissions to provide street lighting and paving, or Corporations of the Poor and unions to run the poor law. They rejected tests of religious conformity, and based membership upon the payment of a subscription; participation in the administration of these bodies allowed a large number of the 'middling sort' to become involved in civil society. In 1783 alone, 280 trustees were appointed for the Wetherby–Knaresbrough turnpike; 108 commissioners were elected by the ratepayers of Birmingham to administer the poor law; the Trent navigation was undertaken by a company of 88 members with powers of arbitration given to 800 commissioners; and the Leeds–Liverpool Canal Act gave powers to every owner of property in Lancashire and the West Riding worth £100 a year.[8] Participation in public bodies was extended to a wider circle of small property owners, with scant regard for the dictates of a 'confessional state'.

At the same time as participation in civil society was extended to small property owners, the franchise was restricted by excluding non-property owners from the parliamentary electorate. About 24 per cent of adult males had the vote in England and Wales in 1715, falling to 14 per cent in 1831.[9] The process was more interesting than a simple imposition of oligarchy: there was both restriction and expansion in order to construct a political nation based upon modest amounts of property, broadly defined. The Reform Act of 1832 can be read as a continuation of this trend, for it merely increased the proportion of the adult male population with the vote to 18 per cent, which was within the limits of the eighteenth-century electoral system, and reduced the proportion of electors drawn from the ranks of craftsmen and labourers. A less democratic franchise was created, with a closer connection between property and the vote. This outcome was the result of a tussle between two different notions of property and political legitimacy. The first argued that land was the basis of 'civic virtue', providing independence, leisure, and liberty for an involvement in public life. Landed property was equated with morality and full citizenship, unlike industrial and commercial wealth, which was too narrowly specialized and time-consuming. This contrast between landed virtue and moneyed corruption was challenged in the course of the eighteenth century by a commercial definition of citizenship. Commerce, it was contended, led to the growth of refinement and politeness, and the replacement of barbarism by the rule of law. The basis of political legitimacy shifted from a public to a private definition of civic virtue, a belief that the citizen 'does good to [Mankind] by gratifying himself'.[10] Property and political power ontinued to be connected, but the definition of property was widened and legal ecurity was extended to forms of property such as bills of exchange and nortgages which relied upon credit. Rights were increasingly viewed in terms of n individual's property, and public affairs seen as an expression of propertied nterests rather than in terms of allegiance based on religious oaths and tests. Far om dominating until the 1820s, the ideology of the 'confessional state' and 'civic irtue' was challenged in the course of the eighteenth century; political debate vas characterized by a rights-based rhetoric which emphasized the rule of law nd contract.

Although full participation in national government and membership of parlia- nent remained the preserve of a narrow élite of landowners, the political system vas responsive to the concerns of a wider propertied and commercial society. atrons could not take control for granted, and had to show concern for the nterests of local trade and the expectations of the community. Holders of long eases or copyholds in the county constituencies were proudly independent, and ubstantial tenant farmers were not likely to respond favourably to heavy- anded intimidation. Similarly, most urban constituencies were dominated by mall retailers and craftsmen who stressed their rights as 'free-born Englishmen', nd asserted the dignity given by freedom of their trade or borough. They could ppeal to high constitutional principles against aristocratic patrons, stressing the ndependence of the Commons from interference by members of the House of .ords and insisting on the rights of their chartered borough. Economic change vorked in the same direction, for there was a growing urban middling class of rtisans, shopkeepers, and professionals which was less dependent on a 'client conomy' servicing the needs of the aristocracy, and more attuned to a broadly ased domestic market for goods and services. These artisans and shopkeepers lid not simply follow the political wishes of the borough patrons; on the ontrary, they developed a critique of the distribution of government contracts nd loans to hangers-on of the court and government, and complained of the urden of taxes which they paid to subsidize the court and aristocracy. Patrons ad to work with the culture and attitudes of the 'middling sort', stressing nterdependence rather than subordination, and negotiating with a participatory lectorate rather than imposing deference upon subservient voters. Boroughs ad an active associational life with clubs and societies of all types, to protect nembers against social insecurity, to co-operate in urban improvement, to nitiate charities, or to organize cultural and social events. These bodies were sually dominated by tradesmen and professional men, creating a sense of mutuality amongst the 'middling sort', giving them access to their own sources of patronage in dispensing charity and appointing teachers, hospital staff, night- watchmen, and toll-collectors. These bodies weakened patrician power, and the activities of these clubs carried over to politics. Members of parliament were called before meetings to justify their actions; election committees organized canvasses and produced leaflets; political clubs flourished; and petitions to parliament were frequent. Political life in eighteenth-century Britain was more than a subordination of the electorate to oligarchy; landed aristocrats held power through the involvement of the 'middling sort' of professional men, merchants and industrialists.

Critics of the 'unreformed' parliament complained that it failed to provide direct representation of growing towns and interests, so that it was not an expression of the national community. This is to make anachronistic assumptions about eighteenth-century parliaments, which had the less heroic purpose of providing a legislative service and acting as an umpire between conflicting interests. Parliamentary sessions became more frequent from the early eighteenth century, and most sittings were devoted to consideration of a mass of small-scale, local legislation which overturned settlements, enclosed open fields, established turnpike trusts, authorized poor law unions, or created improvement commissions. These measures often led to disputes between communities, such as the Ribble Bridge Bill in 1751 which aimed to impose a tax on the entire county of Lancashire for a bridge which would benefit a few parishes; or set interests against each other, as in enclosure Acts. The role of parliament was to arbitrate, providing legal authority for reshaping property rights and imposing taxes to finance the schemes. It did not really matter that Birmingham lacked its own member of parliament, for it was able to submit five bills for consideration between 1773 and 1782, and its leading industrialists were adept at lobbying parliament and the government. Matthew Boulton, for example, appealed to leading politicians in order to secure a new assay office: he succeeded in 1773, with the support of aristocrats and gentry who felt they were under some obligation to promote the interests of the Midlands, and often themselves had significant business interests. 'These old country families', remarked Samuel Garbett, another successful Birmingham lobbyist, in 1766, 'look upon themselves as the Patrons of the Trade of the Neighbourhood and really have great inclination to serve us when they distinctly understand the subject.'[11] It is often claimed that Britain had a weak state between the early seventeenth century, when the Privy Council played an important role in shaping policy, and the reforms of the early nineteenth century. In reality, Britain had an effective state, in terms both of its ability to raise finance for warfare and the role of parliament in directing social and economic policy.

The existence of a 'Venetian oligarchy' is to be explained less by the power of patrons to manipulate the electorate than by a high level of public participation which legitimized the political system. The situation changed when tensions

ould no longer be contained *within* the existing oligarchic system, and spilled
▪ver into hostility *against* the electoral system, which the 'middling sort' of
maller property owners came to see as unrepresentative, corrupt, and lacking in
egitimacy. The explanation for this change was not simply a growth in religious
dissent and a high political calculation by the Whigs to bring the system crashing
down. Economic and social change cannot be pushed to the margin in explaining
vhy the urban middle class found its relationship with an aristocratic state
increasingly unsatisfactory from the 1790s. A growing sense of unease arose in
part from changes in the agricultural economy at the end of the eighteenth
century, when rent was taking an increasing share of the national income and the
anded élite was becoming more stable. Critics of the aristocratic state could
plausibly argue that it was behaving in a more self-interested manner during the
French revolutionary and Napoleonic wars and in the period of post-war
adjustment. The depredations of 'pluralists, placemen, pensioners and sinecu-
ists' or 'old corruption' formed the common currency of radical attacks, which
culminated in John Wade's *Extraordinary Black Book* of 1831. The most notorious
example was Lord Eldon, the son of the owner of a Tyne coal keel, who built up a
personal fortune of £707,000 and extensive landholdings from his career in law
and his long tenure of the Lord Chancellorship.[12] Although some historians
suggest that 'old corruption' was an endemic or structural feature of the British
state of the eighteenth century, it is more plausible to argue that there were strict
imits to venality during the eighteenth century, which were weakened by the
unprecedented scale and cost of the French revolutionary and Napoleonic wars.
The wartime suspicion that the landed aristocracy was exploiting the state to the
detriment of other social groups was confirmed by post-war policy. The corn
laws were criticized by middle-class radicals as a device to maintain high wartime
rents and food prices, which increased the costs of industry and eroded the
domestic market. Similarly, the abandonment of the income tax in 1816 led to a
high level of indirect taxation which fell on domestic production and working-
class consumers. The landed aristocracy was, it seemed, failing to pay its 'fair'
share of taxation.

There was a growing sense of alienation of the urban middle class from the
aristocratic state. The Peterloo massacre of 1819, when the militia attacked a
political rally at Manchester, indicated to the northern middle class that the state
was not able to negotiate stable class relations; distaste for the extravagant and
dissolute court of the Prince Regent came to a head in the 'Queen Caroline affair'
in 1820; and the slumps of 1826 and 1830–1 called into question the ability of the
state to provide economic prosperity. The legitimacy of the oligarchic or
aristocratic state was being undermined in the 1820s and 1830s, and the demand
for direct representation was growing. In Birmingham, for example, the *Argus*

newspaper remarked in 1829 that 'The very serious losses to which the trade (Birmingham has been exposed ... might have been greatly diminished, if nc entirely prevented, had we been so fortunate as to have possessed two FAITHFUI REPRESENTATIVES IN PARLIAMENT.'[13] Such sentiments did not mean that th middling sort were previously subservient. The survival of oligarchy was th result of a negotiated compromise, as much on the terms of the 'middling sort' a of the aristocracy. Legitimacy did not, in any case, rest primarily on the role (theology: one of the characteristic features of the British state in the eighteent century was the importance of law.

Law, Economy, and Social Order

Law had a central role in eighteenth-century England. Parliamentary politic were dominated by debates over jurisprudence, and most people 'experience government and understood politics through their dealings with the law'.[1] Rioters protesting against high food prices appealed to justices to enforce law against forestallers; landowners and tenants tussled over the interpretation o copyhold and customary tenure; employers disputed the limits of perquisites workers sought the enforcement of apprenticeship and wage assessments; th rural poor challenged farmers over their right to glean or graze on the open field The legal system was at the centre of the debate over the nature of property an social relations. Should recognition be removed from contingent property right and customary tenures in order to create unfettered property rights more suite to a capitalist economy? Should recognition be granted to new devices such a: bills of exchange and mortgages, and how should commercial contracts b regulated and enforced? And the legal code was central to public order and socia relations. A 'bloody' legal code with a large number of capital offences provide the opportunity for the exercise of discretion, as part of a social system based or patronage and local structures of power; a legal code based upon the certainty o impersonal bureaucratic processes and a paid police force had very differen social and political implications.

The law, according to some historians, was crucial in remaking British society in a capitalist mould, by converting customary perquisites into criminal theft an destroying contingent property rights in order to allow the unfettered exploi tation of land.[15] Should this interpretation be accepted, or did courts protec rights, offering a means by which customary tenants or industrial workers could battle *against* the forces of change? The legal system has, indeed, been criticized on the grounds that it was slow to adapt, and held back the march of capitalism. 'Parliament's failure to sweep away a penumbra of obsolete statutes and to push the courts towards an assertion of free market principles', complains O'Brien, maintained a climate of uncertainty surrounding businessmen and traders and gave a semblance of legality to the actions of disorderly crowds and combinations of workers seeking to use collective forms of organisation, intimidation and violence, to change prices and wages in their favour.'[16] The courts, he suggests, did not provide an efficient and speedy system for settling breaches of contract between firms, handling disputes between debtors and creditors, or providing an environment for integrated markets and specialization. The legal system 'continued to be unpredictable and expensive to procure and was suffused with considerations of custom, equity and other anachronistic obstacles to the diffusion of competitive markets'.[17] And when parliament did interfere, he complains that it was not always to produce efficiency: the ban on corporate enterprise in the Bubble Act of 1720, for example, led to a lower rate of investment and sustained family-based business organization.[18] Such an interpretation criticizes the law for its *failure* to serve the needs of a capitalist economy, rather than for destroying long-established rights in the interests of capitalism.

William Blackstone, the leading writer on English law in the eighteenth century, suggested that the legal code was like an old Gothic castle. On the outside, it presented a forbidding front of moats and towers designed to repel invaders; the legal system was similarly based on medieval forms and feudal tenures. Inside, the castle had been adapted and modernized, and the rooms were cheerful and homely; in the same way, the law had been adjusted over time to meet the needs of 'a commercial mode of property'. The result was complex technicalities which were, in Blackstone's opinion, unavoidable and beneficial. Legal simplicity was, he claimed, a feature of despotism. The complex English system protected liberty and allowed a flexible response to economic and social conditions; it was mistaken to 'require the same paucity of laws, the same conciseness of practice, in a nation of freemen, a polite and commercial people, and a populous extent of empire'.[19] Was Blackstone simply an 'indiscriminate apologist'[20] who was protecting the legal profession from reform, or did he have a case?

The law consisted of three elements: statutes passed by parliament, which had sovereignty in making law; common law, which was based upon historical precedents and practices interpreted by common law judges; and the law of equity, which accepted that general laws cannot foresee all eventualities and must be adapted in the light of circumstances. Equity was exercised by the Court of Chancery, which dealt with matters such as trusts, mortgages, and contracts, and the development of these legal forms made it possible to circumvent difficulties created by parliament. It is doubtful that the rate of investment was depressed by the Bubble Act, for the law of trusts offered business ventures most of the benefits of limited liability, and mortgages and bills of exchange gave increased access to credit. The common law, for its part, was not simply a fixed body of historical precedents. Some judges heeded Blackstone's argument that their judgements should take account of reason and be 'adapted to the convenience of the time'. Above all, Lord Mansfield, the Chief Justice of King's Bench between 1756 and 1788, undertook a major revision of commercial law, laying down general rules so that 'all questions of mercantile law should be fully settled and ascertained'. England was, consequently, able to devise legal rules which satisfied 'the concerns of a trading population'[21] without the need for regulation by parliament.

Is this to say that the legal system was a tool for the creation of a capitalist economy? A connected point is the question of how legal authority was wielded. Eighteenth-century law, it is often suggested, was a 'bloody code' with punishment directed against the body, through exposure in the stocks, whipping, branding, and death by hanging. This 'bloody code' was, in the opinion of some historians, a crucial component of social order in the eighteenth century, with an increase in the number of capital statutes from about 50 in 1688 to more than 200 by 1820, particularly directed at offences against property. Most notorious was the 'Black Act' of 1723 which contained at least 50 different capital offences against hunting deer, poaching hare, cutting down trees, or maiming cattle: the intention was to control the resources of forests, redefining as theft what farmers and squatters saw as an exercise of their rights. The law, it seems to some historians, was an agent of capitalist transformation, imposing absolute property rights by striking terror into the population. Yet at the same time that statutes were becoming more 'bloody', the proportion of sentences which were actually carried out fell. These two trends, it has been suggested, were complementary: terror and mercy were two prongs of a single strategy of social order. The increased threat of death gave the élite more opportunity to exercise discretion in granting mercy, and hence allowed them to extract deference. The power to punish *and* to forgive helped to maintain a fabric of obedience and gratitude, reinforcing a social order based on patronage and favour, sustaining the power of the ruling class, and allowing England to be governed without a standing army or police force. A legal system based on rational, bureaucratic decisions and a police force would subvert the existing basis of authority, and was consequently opposed by most members of landed society.

Such an interpretation is too simple, for the courts were more than tools of class power. Judges defended customary tenure and did not unequivocally destroy rights such as gleaning. Discretion was not entirely in the hands of the élite as part of a strategy of deference; it was also available to the poor as a 'negotiative process'.[22] Criminal prosecutions were brought privately, and the

ictim could decide on the charge. Victims were often of the same social status as
he defendants, and the criminal law was used by one member of a village to take
ction against a neighbour as much as by the landed élite against the poor. In
.ssex, for example, 21.5 per cent of prosecutions for felony between 1760 and 1800
vere brought by 'husbandmen' and labourers, and 33 per cent by tradesmen and
rtisans.[23] The power of the élite was limited by juries which reached well down
he social scale, and exercised a large amount of discretion in returning verdicts
.ccording to their assessment of the circumstances of the crime and the character
»f the defendant. The poor were not simply passive victims of legal processes, for
hey could play one court and set of legal principles against another, appealing to
.ustom and tradition in order to test the legality of the actions of the rich and
»owerful. The law was the arena within which the debate over property rights
vas fought out and conflict mediated, rather than a simple instrument of class
.uthority.

This gave the law a more subtle role in legitimizing power, for it was idealized
.s applying with equal fairness and justice to all Englishmen, whose liberties had
»een secured in earlier generations by a struggle against despotism. The auth-
)rity of the ruling class did not rest upon the coercive power of a standing army
)r police, which most landowners opposed as symbols of an over-mighty
:xecutive which threatened their local autonomy. An emphasis upon the rule of
aw helped to preserve their own position against the central government and
egitimized their power over the localities. But at the same time, the appeal to the
ustness of the legal system limited their unmediated exercise of power, for a
)latantly coercive use of the law would undermine the legitimizing rhetoric of
:he 'rule of law'. Accordingly, social conflict was to a large extent fought out
:hrough the courts, with the notion that all men were equal before the law.
Resistance was justified on the grounds that those in authority were accountable
to the law, and were in dereliction of their duty to enforce apprenticeship clauses,
assess wages, or control forestallers. Although the room for manœuvre was
limited, it was exploited to the full: the ideology of the law served to constrain
authority, even if it did not permit an explicit challenge to authority.

English law in the eighteenth century was developing a wider range of
non-capital punishments, and was not simply becoming more 'bloody'. The
escalation of capital offences was more apparent than real. In part, it arose from
the character of English legislation, which proceeded by particularities, applying
the death sentence for attacks on this bridge or that type of property; and in part,
it was a response to 'benefit of clergy', a device which gave exemption from the
death penalty. 'Benefit' applied only to a first offence, and convicted criminals
were branded on their thumb with a letter M or T (murderer or thief) which
served as a lesser form of punishment as well as a means of checking repeat

offences. Initially it applied only to churchmen, but it was extended to any man who proved his literacy by reading a verse from the psalms; and in 1706 this test was formally abandoned. The extension of benefit to larger groups of the population was offset by the exclusion of various categories of crime: in the sixteenth century, the most serious classes of murder and robbery were excluded, and after 1689, it was withdrawn from a long list of less serious crimes either because of the character of the offenders (attacks by servants on their masters) or because of the place from which goods were stolen (shops, warehouses, ships, and mines). What was at stake was less the creation of a 'bloodier code than a retreat from the high-water mark of benefit. The stress on capital punishment also misses the addition of two non-capital punishments: transportation and imprisonment. Until the end of the seventeenth century, judges had very little choice in their sentences: for most felonies it was death, whipping, or branding. Punishment seemed to be too inflexible, with branding too lenient for many 'clergyable' offences and the death sentence too draconian for many crimes which were removed from the scope of benefit. The solution was transportation, which was put on a regular basis in 1718, when a sentence of seven years' transportation could be imposed for non-capital felonies or fourteen years for capital offences. The change is striking: in Surrey between 1663 and 1715, 57.8 per cent of men convicted of non-capital felonies against property were allowed 'clergy', branded, and discharged; 4.5 per cent were transported; and 37.7 per cent whipped. Between 1763 and 1771, the proportion sentenced to transportation rose to 63.6 per cent. The policy was called into question even before it was halted by the War of American Independence in 1776, for the proportion of men convicted of non-capital offences against property in Surrey who were transported fell to 37.2 per cent between 1772 and 1775, and it never had the same importance when transportation to Australia started in 1787. Transportation was less of a deterrent by mid-century when many people were voluntarily migrating to the prosperous colonies, and there was a desire to create a morally healthy, hard-working population which was expressed in the establishment of the Marine Society and Foundling Hospital. What was needed, it seemed, was a more effective penalty for non-capital property crimes. Attention turned to imprisonment: the proportion of men convicted of non-capital property offences in Surrey who were imprisoned rose from 6.1 per cent in 1763–71 to 26.2 per cent in 1772–5, and 39.7 per cent in 1783–1802 (with a further 12.7 per cent sentenced to imprisonment and whipping).[24]

In the 1750s, the need to rescue minor offenders through imprisonment and hard labour was stressed in the same way as the idle poor would be made productive through the workhouse. A leading advocate of such a policy was Henry Fielding, the magistrate for Middlesex. He urged that the terror of the death sentence should be increased, by carrying it out with greater dispatch, removing the long drawn out process of petitioning for pardon, and destroying the carnival atmosphere in which the condemned could play a heroic role. Punishment should be appropriate to the crime: a system which required the same punishment for murder as for shoplifting was a deterrent to the prosecutor rather than the offender. The certainty of death for serious offences should be complemented by a change in the punishment of petty crime by using imprisonment to convert the offender into a productive member of society. The assumption was that minor offences such as embezzlement and petty thieving arose from the habits of the working poor, which could be cured by 'correction of the mind' rather than the body, so that men would be put back on to an 'honest course of life' and saved from the gallows.[25] Moderate and reformative punishment based on imprisonment, rigid time discipline, hard labour, and separate confinement would allow prisoners to spend their time 'in solitude and silence' which was 'favourable to reflection and may possibly lead them to repentance'.[26] Public and violent punishment which attacked the body by branding, whipping, and hanging was giving way to reformation of the mind of the criminal by breaking his spirit, and encouraging him to reflect on his shame, before labour and religion transformed his character.

Fundamental changes were needed in order to make prisons fit their new role of teaching repentance and inculcating work discipline and religious duty. The existing prisons were, claimed the reformers, breeding grounds of corruption. Debtors were mixed with defendants awaiting trial for criminal offences, and those condemned to execution or transportation, as well as the relatively small number sentenced to a term of imprisonment. Keepers were largely free of state control, making their living from fees and perquisites, running coffee shops, and letting rooms. There was little control over access from outside and discipline was largely left to the residents. The Penitentiary Act of 1779 aimed to implement changes, but it was some time before resources were available to construct expensive, large prisons on new lines, and before the political will was mobilized to impose greater uniformity on a legal system marked by discretion and popular participation. The Gaols Act of 1823 started the process of standardizing prison discipline; it was complemented in 1829 by the creation of the first full-time, paid police force in London in order to secure a higher rate of detection and prosecution. Magistrates were also given greater powers of summary conviction without jury trial, which removed the element of uncertainty and discretion. The opening of Pentonville prison in London in 1842 symbolized the triumph of the new order.

Men, it seemed, could be remade by institutions. The evangelicals believed that men could be made aware of their state of sin in order to be reborn; Bentham and the utilitarians argued that men had to be made aware that short-term gratification was at the cost of pain, which would make them control their passions in a rational way. Both viewed men as essentially malleable, accepting that men's minds could be reshaped by discipline within an orderly environment. The same approach was extended from prisons to other institutions, whether factories, mental hospitals, or workhouses: criminality, laziness, madness, and pauperism were all seen as the result of loss of self-control and abandonment of reason which could be rectified through surveillance, hard labour, and obedience to rules. Such an approach was adopted in the new prisons; by the asylum for the insane which was opened at York in 1813; and by the new workhouses erected after the Poor Law Amendment Act of 1834. Social order was shifting to a new basis. An absence of a standing army or full-time police force and toleration of public demonstrations had been sanctioned so long as tension could be contained within a framework provided by the rule of law, with its stress upon mutuality and reciprocity between different levels of the social hierarchy. Such an approach had the virtue of limiting the power of the central executive within the locality but by the late eighteenth and early nineteenth centuries there were mounting doubts about the fragile nature of social order in an increasingly urbanized industrialized society.

These different conceptions of social order came into conflict in the poor law. One approach, urged by Malthus at the end of the Napoleonic wars, was to abolish the poor law: if the poor knew that they had to rely on their own efforts to support their family, their passions would be brought under the control of reason, and population growth would be checked. Reform of the poor law also involved the question of who held power, and on what basis: at the end of the Napoleonic wars at a time of distress and unrest it was politically dangerous to question the system of relief which underwrote a social order based on local influence and patronage. Attitudes changed when the poor law was seen as a threat rather than a prop to social order during the 'Swing' riots of 1830, with its spate of rick-burning and machine-breaking in the low-wage, cereal districts of southern and eastern England. The initial response to the 'Swing' riots was to offer more generous relief as in earlier outbreaks of rural unrest in the mid-1790s, with the expectation that it would purchase order and deference. In fact, it seemed merely to stimulate further pressure for more concessions. The emergence of a starker divide between large tenant farmers and waged labourers was stretching the organic conception of society which underpinned the old order. Perhaps more importantly there was a change in the perceptions of significant groups of rulers. The ability of magistrates and parish officials to grant relief was seen as the problem rather than the cure of social tensions, providing an incentive for riot and disorder to win concessions from local rulers who shared

ıe labourers' conception of the moral basis of wages and were open to pressure.
Vhat was needed, it seemed, was the adjustment of wages by the invisible hand
f the market. 'The riots, and still more the fires, of 1830', argued Nassau Senior,

rere a practical lesson on the rights of the poor and the means of enforcing them. . . . That
rages are not a matter of contract but a matter of right, that they depend, not on the
alue of the labourer's services, but on the extent of his wants, or of his expectations . . . all
ıese monstrous and anarchical doctrines were repeated not only by the rioters them-
elves but by the farmers, the clergy, the magistrates, in short by all the ignorant and timid
ıroughout the country.[27]

ı 1832, Senior was appointed one of the Poor Law Commissioners and their
eport of 1834 resulted in the passing of the Poor Law Amendment Act.

Although the Commissioners agreed with Malthus on the demographic
onsequences of the allowance system of the old poor law, they departed from
ıim in other respects. Senior was more optimistic, arguing that the means of
ubsistence were outstripping the growth of population, and that the economy
ould absorb additional labour and increase productivity, provided that a free
narket was created. By withdrawing relief in aid of wages, the Commissioners
ırgued, labourers would become 'more steady and diligent', so giving farmers a
ıigher return on capital which would enable them to pay higher wages. This
/irtuous cycle would be set in motion by 'less eligibility', a concept which was
'ormulated by Jeremy Bentham in 1796. The aim was to make relief conditional
ıpon entry into a workhouse, where conditions were to be worse or 'less eligible'
ıhan experienced by the lowest class of independent labourer. The 'frugal habits'
)f the poor would be strengthened, so restoring their industry, increasing the
demand for labour, and raising their wages. Of course, there had been earlier
ıttempts to use the workhouse as a deterrent, but the Report of the Poor Law
Commission and the Poor Law Amendment Act of 1834 were based on a changed
conception of society. They rejected the notion that society was reciprocal and
organic, with social order based upon custom, mutuality, patronage, and deference, and substituted a view of society based on an interdependent market
economy resting on self-interest, competition, and contract. This was, of course,
part of a wider change which was expressed in the enclosure movement, the
replacement of coincidental use-rights by unitary property rights, the repeal of
measures such as the statute of apprentices and the assize of bread, and changes
in patterns of law enforcement. The Poor Law Amendment Act marked the
culmination of these trends, and was particularly significant because it involved
major administrative changes which modified the basis of government and social
relations.

The Elizabethan poor law was based upon the individual parish, with the granting of relief in the hands of overseers drawn from the community. The justices of the peace provided some oversight, but this was limited and they were just as likely to order additional relief as to impose strict controls: they were visible and their behaviour was judged against expectations of mutuality. Earlier attempts to change the basis of administration rested upon local initiatives, and there was resistance to proposals for general reform imposed from the centre which threatened the local power of the justices and challenged the existing basis of social order. In 1834, the government *was* willing to impose change throughout the country, redefining the nature of power and authority. The parish was superseded by unions; the division between local overseers and county magistrates was ended, for the poor law was in future administered by a Board of Guardians with the magistrates as ex officio members; and the power to elect Guardians was concentrated in the hands of larger property owners.

The change is open to various interpretations. One is to suggest that the landed élite was losing its authority by containment within the Board of Guardians, which was implementing a middle-class ideology of free competition and individualism. At the other extreme, it has been argued that the landowners were reasserting their power through membership of the Board and a property-based franchise; the result, it has been suggested, was that large landowners could dominate a union and use deference as the basis of social cohesion. It is true that the landowners were not simply deposed, but the intention was not to re-establish an older form of landed control through paternalism. Rather, the aim of the new poor law was to replace paternalism by an ideology of free competition within the market, which entailed replacing the discretion of individual justices by the corporate decision of the Board; preventing divergence between overseers and magistrates; transferring administration from members of the community to salaried workhouse masters and relieving officers; and removing appeals from personal considerations to a central authority in London. The aim was to create national uniformity based upon the principle of 'less eligibility' enforced by indoor relief in a deterrent workhouse, removing local discretion in granting relief and replacing the nexus of paternalism by a mechanical, impersonal process. This leads to a third, more realistic, interpretation: what was at stake was neither the reassertion of deference by landowners nor the rejection of landed paternalism, so much as the creation of a new form of social order at the behest of 'modernizing' members of the landed élite, who wished to bring their more traditionalist colleagues to heel and limit their power of discretionary paternalism.

Of course, the change in the operation of the poor law fitted with the restructuring of rural society with the virtual completion of the enclosure movement and the reduction of customary rights. It was of a piece with the

peal of the corn laws in 1846, which aimed to create a high-productivity
gricultural system as an alternative to protection. It fitted with changes in the
system of public order with the emergence of a full-time police force and the
mphasis upon systematic, regularized punishment; and it complemented the
moval of regulation of wages and bread prices. These changes had been taking
lace in piecemeal fashion over a century or more, with revivals of older notions
f paternalism at times of social tension. The new poor law marked the triumph
f a new conception of order, which was now embedded in the administrative
ructure of the country. It confirmed the hegemony of an ideology which saw
ie economy as a natural order in which it was wrong to meddle, a view which
was justified by the 'invisible hand' of political economy and by evangelical
ideology. Although the ideology had changed, the social composition of the
iling élite remained remarkably stable, for the landowners 'had integrated
narket logic into their way of thinking, and used it to consolidate their own
osition as the linchpin of the English governing class'.[28] A new ideology had
ained hegemony, without displacing the landed aristocracy from control of the
entral state.

The Survival of Patriarchy?

New economic historians' have stressed the slow rate of economic growth and
he continued dominance of non-'revolutionized' sectors based on workshops
nd outwork, which gives some credence to the argument that British society in
he eighteenth century was characterized by the survival of patriarchy. This is,
.owever, to ignore major structural transformations as a result of an increase in
he proportion of the population in industry and service occupations. It also
leglects the impact of centralized production on other stages of a process. The
listinction between 'revolutionized' and 'traditional' industries is far too simple:
he important point is how their relationship changed.

A small firm could become more dependent upon a larger, centralized
:oncern which bought its product for assembly, and supplied credit and market-
ng facilities. In the Birmingham metal trades, for example, the small artisan
masters of the mid-eighteenth century had become *petit bourgeois* small manufac-
urers by the 1830s, which involved a change of identity. A workshop run by a
small master was seen as an 'artisan republic' with a close relationship between
employer and employee, which cannot be reduced to patriarchy. Rather, the
workshop was a working community which followed the 'rules of the trade' and
had a shared set of collective values. There was pride in the social utility of
abour, a sense of social worth and equality as a result of having a stake in society
:hrough the property of skill and the rights in a job, purchased by the time taken

to master a skill which was valuable to the community. This would be main
tained by restricting the number of apprentices, preventing deskilling by contro
ling machinery, adhering to agreed prices, taking common action against 'illega
masters who ignored the customs of the trade, supporting societies to find wor
and provide benefits, and the rejection of excessive rivalry for work. A collectiv
co-operative ethic was combined with a stress on the role of small artisa
employers within the working community, with individual efforts regulated b
the well-being of the trade and an expectation that journeymen would them
selves become small masters. Artisans stressed their respectability and indeper
dence, based on thrift, hard work, and independence from charity: they pride
themselves on supporting their families by their labour, and providing for the
old age. In 'honourable' trades, masters and men shared this ethos and co
operated in honest industry. The problem, as the artisans saw it, was the rise o
'dishonourable' trades in which the masters rejected the notion of the worksho
as a world of mutual obligation.

These assumptions were challenged in the early nineteenth century. I
London, trades such as shoemaking, silk-weaving, or tailoring led to an in
tensification of competition and a subdivision of labour and 'sweating'. I
Birmingham, small artisan producers gave way to *petit bourgeois* small manufac
turers. On the surface, there was a continued reliance upon hand labour an
small units, but differences in organization and assumptions altered the nature o
social relationships and created tensions. The small manufacturer ceased to
operate as part of the working community and to share its values; rather, he
accepted the logic of the market and the primacy of capital in deskilling
production, challenging apprenticeship, and cutting prices. The small manufac
turer was following the lead of larger firms which had emerged in Birmingham
which supplied credit and marketing, and could exert control over the way smal
firms were run. The owner of a capital-intensive brass foundry or wire-mil
would distribute metal to small workshops, collect the goods for assembly o
finishing, and handle their sale: he was able to determine prices and force the
small producer to cut wages or deskill. Clearly, there was no need for the
majority of the work-force to move into factories for a major change to take place
in the nature of work. Indeed, 'there was nothing inherently cohesive about the
small unit of production'.[29] Tension between employer and employee could be
greater in small manufacturers' workshops than in larger units, for the challenge
to established artisan traditions meant that workers were more likely to support
radicalism. Social mobility was also redefined. The artisan workshop offered
journeymen the prospect of mobility within the working community, which
confirmed the mutual identity of small master and artisan. In the early nineteenth century, the emphasis was instead placed on mobility from worker to

mall producer to large industrialist within an open, competitive market. This was, in reality, unlikely; but the meaning of mobility was being redefined by the arger manufacturers in a way which justified their own dominance of production.

'Traditional' industry was not static, and social tension did not depend upon the creation of a factory proletariat. Outwork and hand production were far from a simple patriarchy; what is needed is a close analysis of how various sectors were organized, and how they were affected by growth and the introduction of machinery in particular stages of production. The impact of machinery, it has been shown, depended upon the existing structure of work, which determined whether it was accepted or generated social conflict. In the woollen industry in the West Country, for example, resistance to machinery was intense: master clothiers co-ordinated specialists who handled each stage of production, so that the introduction of machinery into one occupation threatened technological unemployment. By contrast, machinery was more readily accepted in the woollen industry in the West Riding, which was based upon artisan production: the introduction of mechanization in one stage freed the workshop to spend more time on other tasks (see Fig. 6.1).

The ability to sustain resistance was also influenced by the character of the manufacturing community. In some cases, a strong craft consciousness, community cohesion, and a tradition of protest existed *before* the coming of machinery, and workers were able to defend their customary controls over the work-place and practices. In the textile districts of the West Country, for example, full-time industrial development with a reliance upon the market for food meant there was a strong craft culture and a tradition of food riots. By contrast, parishes on the fringe of the West Country textile district were more agrarian, with less tradition of protest and a weaker craft culture, so that there was little protest despite the serious impact of the spinning-jenny on employment. In the West Riding of Yorkshire, the involvement of artisan producers in the agricultural sector lessened the impact of fluctuations, and the lower level of dependence on the market for food meant there were fewer food riots. This emphasis upon the strength of the culture of the craft and community suggests that action against machinery cannot be understood as a blind reaction to distress, a sign of weakness, and the inability to form trade unions. Machine-breaking was usually very selective, directed against specific targets which were considered to be in breach of trade customs or statute law. Industrial sabotage was not necessarily a despairing gesture, but could be the 'pre-emptive, calculated choice of a powerful labour élite'.[30] The attacks of the Wiltshire shearmen on cloth-finishing machinery in 1802 was complemented by an appeal to the courts to declare machines illegal, and by pleas to parliamentary inquiries in 1803 and 1806 to introduce regulations, as well as by strike action. Industrial violence in the West Country was most apparent where organization was strongest, rather than a sign of inability to sustain unions.

Machine-breaking or 'Luddism' is often castigated as mere 'throwbacks' to 'disorganized activities' which were not the forerunner of 'modern collective bargaining'.[31] This is to overlook its rationale, for attacks on machinery could be a protest against technological redundancy, or part of a strategy of purposeful intimidation. When Newcastle miners destroyed the winding gear of their pit in 1765, they were not attacking machinery which threatened their jobs, for it was essential to their employment. It was a means of pressuring their employers. Similarly, they might intimidate employers and fellow workers by threatening letters, ritual humiliation of strike-breakers, or marches against the houses of men who ignored the wishes of the trade. Workers invented fictive, powerful leaders who threatened dire retribution on those who ignored their wishes: the machinery-breakers of 1811 and 1812 were servants of Ned Ludd; miners in south Wales blackened their faces and intimidated employers as 'Scotch cattle'; agricultural labourers in southern England in 1830 were led by the astute and cunning 'Captain Swing'. It is impossible to comprehend such movements by regretting that they were not unions on the model of the later nineteenth century. These movements had their own form of organization and discipline; the significant point was the ability of workers to mobilize in order to defend work regulation and trade practices, using whatever strategies seemed appropriate. It was difficult to create permanent organizations and a formally constituted movement, but there was a recurrent pattern of behaviour and continuous association.

Workers did create more formal links through their 'box' clubs, to provide sick pay and funeral benefits; they organized 'tramping' funds to pay men to seek work in other towns, which were based on the 'houses of call' or public houses where men were hired and paid. These clubs could form the basis of a wider organization, such as in London where forty tailors' box clubs federated, with a 'House of Representatives' and executive committee which was active in the strike of 1764. Similar organizations were found in other trades, both helping workers to cope with social insecurity and providing a means of organizing within the legal restraints. It was a common law offence to conspire in restraint of trade, and employers in specific trades obtained legislation against combinations which aimed to raise wages or shorten hours, such as in London tailoring in 1721. There were more than forty such acts when the Combination Acts of 1799–1800 introduced more summary procedures to make the common law ban more effective. But the law did not cover petitions to parliament or appeals to secure the regulation of wages and apprenticeships, which reinforced the workers' strategy of appeals for the enforcement of fair wages and prices.

The response of workers should not be interpreted in terms of disorder and ineffectuality, but as part of a well-developed and articulate 'corporate discourse' which stressed stability, regulation, and the need to observe strict limits to innovation which threatened independence and responsibility. Workers threatened by the rise of 'dishonourable trades' appealed for the state to protect their property in skill in the same way as other property, and to recognize their social value. The rejection of legislative support for this set of assumptions was political, and workers continued to press for its restoration. Luddites who continued to urge the implementation of laws which no longer existed were, according to some historians, not adjusting to new realities. This fails to comprehend their attitudes and assumptions, and gives priority to the ideology of their opponents. A political defeat could, after all, be reversed. The government, argued artisan radicals such as John Gast of the London shipwrights, was failing to protect their property, infringing their rights, and imposing higher taxes and food prices through the removal of income tax and the introduction of the corn laws. Land was not worthy of protection: the artisans grouped landowners with office holders and financiers as parasites who expropriated their property through political power, unlike the useful, valuable labour of artisans. Taxes, they contended, were distorting the home market, forcing employers to cut costs, which threatened the 'honourable' trades, and encouraging exports which, generated insecurity. The answer was to make the government more accountable, by extending the franchise to include the property of skill. Political reform would, argued the artisans, lead to more equitable taxes and reduce the depredations of a corrupt oligarchy with its pensions and places. Wage agreements could be given legal support, hours of work reduced, and taxes placed on machinery so that the benefits went to both workers and masters. The aim was to maintain the 'fair and proper value' of their 'superior talent and industry' which allowed them 'that decent and respectable appearance in society as becomes valuable members'.[32]

Such attitudes fed into Chartism. The six points of the People's Charter of 1838 demanded the implementation of a system of universal male suffrage supported by secret ballots, equal electoral districts, annual parliamentary elections, payment of MPs, and abolition of the property qualification for MPs. Many commentators have been puzzled by a reaction to economic depression and hardship in the form of apparently unrealistic political demands, and have criticized the Chartists for a lack of connection between means and ends. There has been a tendency to minimize the political expression of Chartism as at worst a distraction from the economic roots of distress and at best a vain attempt to provide a 'symbol of unity' which failed in its purpose.[33] Instead, historians have concentrated on analysing underlying social phenomena, to establish the connection between support for Chartism and distress, or to link it with declining protoindustrial areas or growing factory towns. But the *form* taken by Chartism did matter, and the political content of the Charter should be considered on its own terms, rather than dismissed as irrelevant to the 'real' concerns of the movement. The political reasoning of the Charter was based upon clearly articulated assumptions which had a wide purchase in decaying *and* expanding areas. It was easy to argue that the roots of distress and hardship were political. The 'country' ideology of the eighteenth century stressed that the people or nation were being exploited by financiers and hangers-on of the government, which could be rectified by reforming the franchise and purifying the system. Although dread of the revolution in France resulted in repression of radicalism, it revived after Waterloo with a new stress upon the inequities of the tax system, the self-interest of the corn laws, the burden of the national debt, and the misuse of patronage. The 'Queen Caroline affair' in 1820–1 brought together London artisans and members of the middle class against the government and court by exploiting the estranged wife of George IV as a symbol of opposition. In the 1830s and 1840s this alliance dissolved. The Reform Act of 1832 had extended the vote to members of the propertied middle class, but removed it from many artisans and workers. The franchise was redefined in terms of real property, and justified by claiming that anyone could join through their efforts and enterprise, so that there was therefore no division of interests between large and small producers, or between workmen and employers. This marked the defeat of 'artisan republicanism' with its stress upon participation in a communal pattern of production and an emphasis upon rights. The Charter was a challenge to this redefinition of the franchise, which had—so it seemed—permitted the implementation of measures ignoring the interests of working men and women. There was a large element of continuity with the language of radicalism, and its attack on political origins of distress; the change was in the definition of the 'people'. The Reform Act had, it seemed, separated the middle class from the people, making them part of the system of oppression.

It is not surprising that Chartism took a political form, for the 1830s were marked by major political changes from the decentralized system of public and social order which characterized the eighteenth century. The reform of the poor law, the creation of a police force, the Coercion Act in Ireland in 1833 which suppressed political activity, the transportation of the 'Tolpuddle martyrs' in 1834 and the leaders of the Glasgow spinners' strike in 1837 caused disquiet. 'What have we had since the Whigs passed the Reform bill?', asked a workman in Yorkshire in 1833. 'We have had nothing but cruelty and hypocrisy.'[34] Chartism was a response to the changing nature of the state, which was now perceived less as the seat of 'old corruption' than as an oppressive device of capitalists to create a coercive, bureaucratic framework for social order and free competition. What was needed—so it seemed to the Chartists - was a change in the basis of political representation in order to adjust policies which caused hardship, for it was the unrepresentative political system which allowed the aristocracy and the middle class to deprive workers of the product of their labour. Why did the state protect other forms of property but allow machinery to destroy workers' property in their labour and skill? Wealth, it seemed, was the creation of a political and legal system which allowed landowners to maintain their rents through the corn laws, the fundholders to prosper from specie resumption, and the poor to be ground down by a deterrent poor law and high taxes. There was a continuing emphasis upon the need for 'fair' wages and for the limitation of destructive competition. Such an approach emphasized divisions between represented and unrepresented rather than between workers and employers, or between the working and middle classes; it located oppression in the political rather than the economic sphere. Poverty, argued Bronterre O'Brien, 'is the result not the cause of your being unrepresented'.[35]

The British state in the eighteenth and early nineteenth centuries was considerably more complex than many historians have suggested. It cannot be reduced to the power of a 'Venetian oligarchy' and 'old corruption' or a stable *ancien régime* held together by the power of theology and patriarchy. Neither can it be reduced to 'gentlemanly capitalism' through an alliance between capitalistic landowners and financial interests in the City of London. It would be more realistic to portray British politics in the eighteenth century in terms of an active middling order, whose interests and attitudes increasingly permeated politics. Social conflict was more than a matter of religious dissent, and was fought out through the law, which was much more than a tool of capitalist oppression. The continued existence of small workshops and outwork, and the slow spread of factories and powered machinery, by no means precluded social conflict. Above all, there was a long tussle between different definitions of social order, between locally based paternalism which was expressed in the old poor law, the *Book of Orders*, and a legal code based on discretion; and a more centralized, bureaucratic system supported by a professional police force, the new poor law, and prisons. The shift in the basis of public order was only finally completed in the 1830s and 1840s, and was still denied by the opponents of the new poor law and the Chartists.

In the course of the eighteenth and early nineteenth centuries, the British economy underwent a major transformation, and it has often been assumed that the state was not an active participant, and that it might even have slowed down economic development. On such an account, the state was affected by economic change rather than an active agent in the process of change. But is this a reasonable interpretation? A strong case may be made that the legal system was able to respond to the changing needs of the economy, and that the British state in the eighteenth century was remarkably effective and strong. Could it be argued that the British state had an active role in the development of the British economy, encouraging the growth of new industries such as cotton, providing a protected home market, and wielding military power to secure foreign markets against the French and Dutch? Perhaps the development of the British economy was a political rather than a merely economic phenomenon.

NOTES

1. B. Disraeli, *Sybil; or, The Two Nations* (1845), 25.
2. Ibid. 187.
3. L. Namier, *The Structure of Politics on the Accession of George III* (2nd edn., 1957), 68–9, 73.
4. Ibid. 133–4.
5. J. H. Plumb, *The Growth of Political Stability in England, 1675–1725* (1967), 5.
6. J. C. D. Clark, *English Society 1688–1832* (Cambridge, 1985), 65.
7. Ibid. 36.
8. P. Langford, *Public Life and the Propertied Englishman, 1689–1798* (Oxford, 1991), 208.
9. F. O'Gorman, *Voters, Patrons and Parties: The Unreformed Electoral System of Hanoverian England, 1734–1832* (Oxford, 1989), table 4.3, p. 179.
10. Cato, quoted in S. Burtt, *Virtue Transformed: Political Argument in England 1688–1740* (Cambridge, 1992), 74.
11. Quoted in E. Robinson, 'Matthew Boulton and the Art of Parliamentary Lobbying', *Historical Journal*, 7 (1974), 221.
12. W. D. Rubinstein, *Men of Property: The Very Wealthy in Britain since the Industrial Revolution* (1981), 71.
13. Quoted in J. R. Dinwiddy, *From Luddism to the First Reform Bill: Reform in England, 1810–32* (Oxford, 1986), 13.
14. J. Brewer, 'The Wilkites and the Law', in J. Brewer and J. Styles (eds.), *An Ungovernable People: The English and their Law in the Seventeenth and Eighteenth Centuries* (1980), 133.
15. D. Hay, 'Property, Authority and the Criminal Law', in D. Hay *et al.* (eds.), *Albion's Fatal Tree: Crime and Society in Eighteenth-Century England* (1975).
16. P. K. O'Brien, *Power without Profit: The State and the Economy, 1688–1815* (1991), 9.
17. Ibid. 10.
18. Ibid. 11.
19. Quoted in D. Lieberman, *The Province of Legislation Determined: Legal Theory in Eighteenth-Century Britain* (Cambridge, 1989), 48.
20. The phrase is Bentham's, quoted ibid. 67.
21. Quoted ibid. 121.
22. J. Brewer and J. Styles, 'Introduction', in Brewer and Styles (eds.), *Ungovernable People*, 17.

23. P. King, 'Decision Makers and Decision Making in the English Criminal Law, 1750–1800', *Historical Journal*, 27 (1984), 29.

24. J. Beattie, *Crime and the Courts in England, 1660–1800* (Princeton, NJ, 1986), 507.

25. The phrase of J. Massie, quoted ibid. 553.

26. John Howard, quoted ibid. 572.

27. Quoted in P. Dunkley, *The Crisis of the Old Poor Law in England, 1795–1834* (New York, 1982), 99.

28. P. Mandler, 'The Making of the New Poor Law Redivivus', *Past and Present*, 117 (1987), 157.

29. C. Behagg, *Politics and Production in the Early Nineteenth Century* (1990), 6.

30. A. Randall, *Before the Luddites: Custom, Community and Machinery in the English Woollen Industry, 1776–1809* (Cambridge, 1991), 183.

31. The phrases are from D. Bythell, *The Handloom Weavers* (Cambridge, 1969), 180.

32. I. Prothero, *Artisans and Politics in Early Nineteenth-Century London: John Gast and his Times* (Folkestone, 1979), 68.

33. A. Briggs, 'The Local Background to Chartism,', in A. Briggs (ed.), *Chartist Studies* (1959), 26.

34. Quoted in Dinwiddy, *From Luddism to the First Reform Bill*, 73.

35. G. Stedman Jones, *Language of Class: Studies in English Working-Class History, 1832–1982* (Cambridge, 1983) 16.

FURTHER READING

Apfel, W., and Dunkley, P., 'English Rural Society and the New Poor Law: Bedfordshire, 1834–47', *Social History*, 10 (1985).

Aspinall, A., *The Early English Trade Unions* (1949).

Beattie, J., *Crime and the Courts in England, 1660–1800* (Princeton, NJ, 1986).

—— 'The Pattern of Crime in England, 1660–1800', *Past and Present*, 62 (1974).

Behagg, C., *Politics and Production in the Early Nineteenth Century* (1990).

Blaug, M., 'The Myth of the Old Poor Law and the Making of the New', *Journal of Economic History*, 23 (1963).

—— 'The Poor Law Report Re-examined', *Journal of Economic History*, 24 (1964).

Brewer, J., 'Commercialization and Politics', in N. McKendrick, J. Brewer, and J. H. Plumb, *The Birth of a Consumer Society: The Commercialization of Eighteenth-Century England* (1982).

—— *The Sinews of Power: War, Money and the English State, 1688–1783* (1989).

—— and Styles, J. (eds.), *An Ungovernable People: The English and their Law in the Seventeenth and Eighteenth Centuries* (1980).

Briggs, A. (ed.), *Chartist Studies* (1959).

Brock, M., *The Great Reform Act* (1973).

Brundage, A., 'The English Poor Law of 1834 and the Cohesion of Agricultural Society', *Agricultural History*, 48 (1974).

—— 'The Landed Interest and the New Poor Law: A Reply', *English Historical Review*, 90 (1975).

—— Eastwood, D., Mandler, P., 'Debate: The Making of the New Poor Law Redivivus' *Past and Present*, 127 (1990).

Burtt, S., *Virtue Transformed: Political Argument in England, 1688–1740* (Cambridge, 1992).

Bythell, D., *The Handloom Weavers* (Cambridge, 1969).

Christie, I. R., *The End of North's Ministry* (1958).

Clark, J. C. D., *English Society, 1688–1832: Ideology, Social Structure and Political Practice during the Ancien Regime* (Cambridge, 1985).

Coleman, D. C., 'Technology and Economic History, 1500–1750', *Economic History Review*, 2nd ser. 11 (1958–9).

—— 'Industrial Growth and Industrial Revolutions', *Economica*, NS 23 (1956).

Crafts, N. F. R., *British Economic Growth during the Industrial Revolution* (Oxford, 1985).

Dinwiddy, J. R., *From Luddism to the First Reform Bill: Reform in England, 1810–32* (Oxford, 1986).

Dunkley, P., 'The Landed Interest and the New Poor Law: A Critical Note', *English Historical Review*, 88 (1973).

—— 'Whigs and Paupers', *Journal of British Studies*, 20 (1981).

—— 'Paternalism, the Magistracy and Poor Relief in England, 1795–1834', *International Review of Social History*, 24 (1979).

—— *The Crisis of the Old Poor Law in England, 1795–1834: An Interpretative Essay* (New York, 1982).

Goodway, D., *London Chartism, 1838–48* (Cambridge, 1982).

Gray, R., 'The Languages of Factory Reform in Britain, c.1830–60', in P. Joyce (ed.), *The Historical Meanings of Work* (Cambridge, 1987).

Hay, D., 'War, Dearth and Theft in the Eighteenth Century: The Record of the English Courts', *Past and Present*, 95 (1982).

—— 'Property, Authority and the Criminal Law', in D. Hay et al., *Albion's Fatal Tree: Crime and Society in Eighteenth-Century England* (1975).

Hobsbawm, E. J., 'The Machine Breakers', in *Labouring Men: Studies in the History of Labour* (1968).

—— and Rudé, G., *Captain Swing* (1969).

Hole, R., *Pulpits, Politics and Public Order in England, 1760–1832* (Cambridge, 1989).

Ignatieff, M., *A Just Measure of Pain: The Penitentiary in the Industrial Revolution, 1750–1850* (New York, 1978).

Innes, J., 'Jonathan Clark, Social History, and England's "Ancien Regime"', *Past and Present*, 115 (1987).

—— 'Parliament and the Shaping of Eighteenth-Century English Social Policy', *Transactions of the Royal Historical Society*, 5th ser. 40 (1990).

Jones, D. J. V., *Before Rebecca: Popular Protests in Wales, 1792–1835* (1973).

King, P., 'Decision Makers and Decision Making in the English Criminal Law, 1750–1800', *Historical Journal*, 27 (1984).

Landau, N., *The Justices of the Peace, 1679–1760* (Berkeley, Calif., 1984).

Langbein, J. H., 'Albion's Fatal Flaws', *Past and Present*, 98 (1983).

Langford, P., *Public Life and the Propertied Englishman, 1689–1798* (Oxford, 1991).

Lieberman, D., *The Province of Legislation Determined: Legal Theory in Eighteenth-Century Britain* (Cambridge, 1989).

Mandler, P., 'The Making of the New Poor Law Redivivus', *Past and Present*, 117 (1987).

——*Aristocratic Government in the Age of Reform: Whigs and Liberals, 1830–1852* (Oxford, 1990).

——'Cain and Abel: Two Aristocrats and the Early Victorian Factory Acts', *Historical Journal*, 27 (1984).

Mather, F. C., *Public Order in the Age of the Chartists* (1959).

Morris, R. J., *Class and Class Consciousness in the Industrial Revolution, 1780–1850* (1979).

Namier, L., *The Structure of Politics at the Accession of George III* (2nd edn. 1957).

Norris, J. M., 'Samuel Garbett and the Early Development of Industrial Lobbying in Great Britain', *Economic History Review*, 2nd ser. 10 (1957–8).

O'Brien, P. K., *Power without Profit: The State and the Economy, 1688–1815* (1991).

O'Gorman, F., *Voters, Patrons and Parties: The Unreformed Electoral System of Hanoverian England, 1734–1832* (Oxford, 1989).

Plumb, J. H., *The Growth of Political Stability in England, 1675–1725* (1967).

Pocock, J. G. A., *Virtue, Commerce and History: Essays on Political Thought and History, Chiefly in the Eighteenth Century* (Cambridge, 1985).

——*The Machiavellian Moment* (Princeton, NJ, 1975).

Porter, R., *Mind-Forg'd Manacles: A History of Madness in England from the Restoration to the Regency* (1987).

Poynter, J. R., *Society and Pauperism: English Ideas on Poor Relief, 1795–1834* (1969).

Prothero, I., *Artisans and Politics in Early Nineteenth-Century London: John Gast and his Times* (Folkestone, 1979).

Randall, A. J., 'Work, Culture and Resistance to Machinery in the West of England Woollen Industry', in P. Hudson (ed.), *Regions and Industries: A Perspective on the Industrial Revolution in Britain* (Cambridge, 1989).

——*Before the Luddites: Custom, Community and Machinery in the English Woollen Industry, 1776–1809* (Cambridge, 1991).

——'The Shearmen and the Wiltshire Outrages of 1802: Trade Unionism and Industrial Violence', *Social History*, 7 (1982).

——'New Languages or Old? Labour, Capital and Discourse in the Industrial Revolution', *Social History*, 15 (1990).

Robinson, E., 'Matthew Boulton and the Art of Parliamentary Lobbying', *Historical Journal*, 7 (1964).

Rogers, N., *Whigs and Cities: Popular Politics in the Age of Walpole and Pitt* (Oxford, 1989).

——'Aristocratic Clientage, Trade and Dependency: Popular Politics in Pre-radical Westminster', *Past and Present*, 61 (1973).

Rubinstein, W. D., *Men of Property: The Very Wealthy in Britain since the Industrial Revolution* (1981).

Rule, J., *The Experience of Labour in Eighteenth-Century Industry* (1981).

Schultz R., 'The Small-Producer Tradition and the Moral Origins of Artisan Radicalism in Philadelphia, 1720–1810', *Past and Present*, 127 (1990).

Seed, J., 'Unitarianism, Political Economy and the Antinomies of Liberal Culture in Manchester, 1830–50', *Social History*, 7 (1982).

Stedman Jones, G., 'The Language of Chartism', in G. Stedman Jones, *Languages of Class: Studies in English Working-Class History, 1832–1982* (Cambridge, 1983).

Thomis, M. I., *The Luddites: Machine Breaking in Regency England* (1970).

Thompson, D., *The Chartists: Popular Politics in the Industrial Revolution* (Hounslow, 1984).

Thompson, E. P., *The Making of the English Working Class* (1963).

—— *Whigs and Hunters: The Origins of the Black Act* (1975).

....

CHAPTER 19

Taxation and Public Finance

Britain in the eighteenth century was a nation at war, locked in a world-wide struggle with the French which ended with the battle of Waterloo in 1815. The clash of empires may be charted through military and naval campaigns; less stirring, though no less important, is the question of finance. Money provided the sinews of war, to provision and pay the army, to finance the fleets which straddled the world, and to operate the massive naval dockyards which built and maintained the ships. The navy was the largest business of the eighteenth century. A first-class naval vessel with a crew of 900 exceeded the work-force of the largest factory; it involved large fixed capital in dockyards; and demanded a massive provisioning system to supply food, munitions, ropes, sails, and myriad pieces of iron, brass, and copper. Britain in the eighteenth century was a 'fiscal-military state',[1] and governments were dominated by the needs of the army and, above all, the navy for money to wage war. The outcome was an efficient system of tax collection and public finance which allowed Britain to bear a heavier financial burden than France, yet without a political crisis threatening the state.

Land Taxes and the Excise Duties

When William accepted the throne in 1688, commented Benjamin Disraeli, he 'did not disguise his motives; he said "Nothing but such a constitution as you have in England can have the credit that is necessary to raise such sums as a great war requires". The prince came, and used our constitution for his purpose: he introduced into England the system of Dutch finance.'[2] William's need was above all for money to pursue his campaign against Louis XIV, and government expenditure tripled from less than £2 million a year before 1688 to £5–6 million between 1689 and 1702. The government faced difficulties in raising such large sums at a time when the power of the crown and its finances were under discussion. Many MPs were cautious about William's policy, fearing that he was obtaining too much power, and doubting whether a land war against the French was in English interests. William wished to have financial independence, with a revenue settled on him for life, but he had to concede power to parliament in order to obtain money. The result was the constitutional compromise of 1697, which gave the crown a permanent 'civil list' for its upkeep, household expenses, and for the payment of salaries and pensions for judges, officials, and courtiers. Parliament did not, however, grant the king a permanent revenue to pay for a standing army, and kept control over the funds for war.

The king therefore had to turn to parliament for money for his wars, which led to political problems. There were two main methods of raising taxes. The monthly assessment placed a quota on each county and borough, which was theoretically a rate in the pound on income from real and personal property and office; in practice it fell on land. The quotas were not determined by the ability of the county or borough to pay, and the pound rate which was needed to collect the contribution varied widely across the country. The alternative was an 'aid' based on a standard national rate in the pound, such as in 1694 when a tax of 4s. in the pound was imposed on real and personal property and office. There was much scope for regional interests to clash, for counties and boroughs with high quotas preferred a uniform national pound rate, whereas areas with low quotas wished to preserve the monthly assessment. The outcome was a compromise in 1698, which formed the basis of the land tax. Nominally, a national rate of 1s., 2s., 3s., or 4s. in the pound was levied each year, on the lines of the aid. In reality, these rates produced a fixed sum varying from £500,000 to £2 million, divided among counties and boroughs according to their payments of 1693, so preserving the principle of the assessment. A similar system was applied to Scotland by the Act of Union of 1707, which fixed the Scottish land tax or 'cess' at £48,000, the equivalent of a 4s. tax in England and Wales.

The political compromise removed the immediate problem of tax collection, at the expense of longer-term difficulties. The burden of the land tax varied widely between and within counties, and it reflected neither the major changes in the geography of economic growth in the eighteenth century, nor the increase in land values and rents. Clearly, a genuine tax of 4s. in the pound should have produced considerably more revenue as time passed than a fixed £2 million. The tax became stereotyped, reflecting historic land values rather than current realities, under the control of local landowners who paid the tax. The attempt to raise a form of income tax on real and personal estate and the profits of office had failed, and was not revived for another hundred years. A parliament of landowners agreed to tax itself during the wars of 1688–97, exploiting the financial strains on the crown in order to secure control over taxes and to stabilize the contribution of land to the public revenue. The settlement of 1698 survived until 1799, when the financial needs of the revolutionary war with France led to the taxation of incomes.

Although the land tax made a considerable contribution to the wars of William III, it became increasingly inflexible over the eighteenth century and the government had to turn to other sources of taxation. Some were short-term expedients, such as the tax of 1695 on bachelors and on births, marriages, and deaths. More important were assessed taxes, stamp duties, customs, and excise. Assessed taxes fell on conspicuous or visible expenditure such as houses, windows, male servants, hair powder, carriages, and pleasure horses. They were, strictly speaking, an indirect tax, but were designed to fall on the rich and it is more realistic to group them with land tax as a direct tax on income. They were, like the land tax, collected locally by amateur administrators drawn from the county community, and any attempt to check their assessments by salaried supervisors raised a thorny constitutional issue of executive power. Stamp duties were levied on legal documents, newspapers, and financial instruments such as bills of exchange, and were no more than a useful supplement to government revenues. Customs duties proved unsuitable as a means of increasing revenue, for the customs office was inefficient. Officers were appointed by the Treasury, often for reasons of political patronage, and many held their position with a patent and life freehold which allowed them to turn it into a sinecure. They were often paid a small salary, deriving the bulk of their income from fees and paying a deputy to undertake the work. The imposition of duties was complex, and merchants often employed customs officials to calculate their liability, a practice which was clearly open to abuse. Smuggling was endemic, and the yield was further affected by the changing structure of trade. Tariffs were designed to favour food and raw materials, with a bias towards the empire, and placed higher duties on luxuries than on necessities. During the eighteenth century, imports shifted from manufactures to food and raw materials, from foreign countries to the colonies, and from luxuries to necessities. Customs duties were also constrained by a variety of strategic considerations, for the fiscal-military state needed to maintain British shipping and shipbuilding, and to provide seamen for the navy. Further, tariffs were politically sensitive, and any change was likely to inspire lobbies of interest groups. The government's room for manœuvre was highly constrained, and almost by default the most important additional source of revenue was excise duties, which rose from 26.1 per cent of total taxes in 1696–1700 to 50.6 per cent in 1751–5.

The government's ambition of introducing a general excise in the 1690s was guaranteed to produce 'country' outrage against the threat of an over-mighty executive. The result was a succession of specific duties which were adjusted in a piecemeal fashion, such as doubling the excise on drink in 1691, and the introduction of new duties on malt and leather in 1697. The government had to take care not to push excise duties too far, which would create fears of an increase in executive powers and a threat to the constitution, such as were apparent in response to Walpole's scheme of 1733. He proposed to replace customs duties on wine and tobacco by excise duties, which were less easily evaded and would produce a larger income. This seemed modest and uncontentious, merely taking further his extension of the excise to tea, coffee, and chocolate in 1723, and he also hoped that the revenue would hold down the land tax, so defusing the complaints of the gentry. It seemed an attractive political ruse, but led to a considerable political crisis in 1733–4. The proposals of 1733 created greater commercial and urban opposition than the measures of 1723. Chocolate and coffee were minor commodities, and tea was controlled by the monopoly of the East India Co.; by contrast, an excise on wine and tobacco affected small trades throughout the country as well as great merchants in London. Walpole also miscalculated the reactions of the small gentry and yeomen farmers. Although they stood to gain from an excise which promised effective taxation of commerce and a reduction of the land tax, they co-operated with merchants against the scheme. The excises on wine and tobacco were seen as a further step towards a 'general excise' which would tax all commodities as in France or Holland. The country gentry, who exercised control over the counties, were wary of strong central government and feared measures which would undermine their local power and offer greater authority to a strong executive. The apparently modest proposal of 1733 was, on this view, a threat to the settlement of 1697. The excise crisis was a major political event because it united the economic interests of major commercial groups with the entrenched localism of the gentry and their dread of an over-mighty executive. The events of 1733–4 established the broad limits of the tax system which persisted until the French revolutionary wars: a mix of land tax, customs, and excise which was based upon a sensitive balancing of economic interest groups and political principles.

Excise duties had a number of advantages. The revenue reflected increases in consumption and economic growth, unlike the land tax. They were collected in a much more efficient manner than the land tax and customs, by salaried officers rather than amateurs drawn from the ranks of taxpayers or sinecurists. The country was divided by the Commissioners for England and Wales and for Scotland into a hierarchy of areas which were toured by Gaugers; producers made monthly returns which were checked by the Gaugers, who were themselves subject to scrutiny by Surveyors. The excise service was organized bureaucratically, with salaries rather than fees, a career ladder, promotion on merit, and the prospect of a pension on retirement. The hold of patronage and the possibility of creating a personal fiefdom were weakened by control through a Board of Commissioners rather than a single officer. Administration of the excise was, unlike the customs, capable of reform from within. Professional administrators who were paid a salary had every incentive to create efficient methods of operation, for their work-load was likely to increase without recompense, unlike their counterparts in the customs who were paid fees and had every incentive to cling to outmoded methods. The excise was the antithesis of the customs service and land tax in its effectiveness, and it was integral to the 'fiscal-military state'. Although it was not politically feasible to reform or abolish the 'inefficient' parts of the fiscal machinery run by the customs or amateurs in the counties, the relative importance of the 'efficient' excise and its professional state officials increased during the eighteenth century.

Funding the National Debt

The British state developed an efficient tax system upon which an edifice of borrowing could be erected. Taxes could not meet the massive and sudden costs of war, but they could offer the security for loans. Initially, borrowing was short term, for tax revenue came in irregularly during the year, and the Treasury borrowed in anticipation. Government departments also needed short-term credit, especially for the payment of military and naval wages and supplies. Over-reliance on the short-term capital market caused problems of securing sufficient funds at a reasonable rate and Godolphin, the Lord Treasurer between 1702 and 1710, turned to long-term loans which made it easier to borrow at a lower rate of interest. These became increasingly important in providing the additional revenue for wars; the share of taxes fell from 49 per cent of the extra revenue needed for war in 1689–97 to 21 per cent in 1739–58. The policy was reversed by Pitt in 1799, and taxes accounted for 58 per cent of the extra revenue needed during the revolutionary and Napoleonic wars of 1793–1815.

The crucial role of long-term loans in the wars of the eighteenth century does not mean that the tax system was inadequate. On the contrary: long-term loans and the capacity to levy taxes were intimately related, for investors were only willing to subscribe to large loans because they were backed by a highly efficient tax regime which guaranteed the payment of interest. The 'funding system' linked the repayment of loans to a specific tax which served as the security or 'fund' for each loan, and the limit of borrowing was set by tax revenues, which left the government with the delicate task of selecting the tax to back each loan. The system of 'funded' loans led to complex negotiations between the government and interest groups over taxes, such as in 1759 when a proposed tax on sugar was opposed by West Indian planters and merchants, and chocolate and coffee were selected instead. The Treasury also had to consult the City on the interest rate and amount of loan which could be absorbed. During the Seven Years War, for example, the Treasury sought advice from Sir John Barnard who represented English financiers of moderate means, from spokesmen of Dutch capital such as Sir Joshua Vanneck, and from Jewish financiers such as Samson Gideon. The system of 'funded' loans created a political process of negotiation over taxes and the placing of loans which was central to the formation of the British state.

The form of loans changed during the eighteenth century. In the early eighteenth century, annuities offered an annual payment for a number of lives or years in return for a loan. They were popular, but expensive for the government. Loans could also be raised from privileged companies, such as the Bank of England, which loaned £1.2 million to the government at 8 per cent in return for a charter for twelve years. The government turned to the South Sea Company as a way of freeing itself from the burden of annuities, by transferring them into stock of the South Sea Co. and increasing the government's debt to the Company. The government's cost of borrowing would fall, for the Company would take a lower rate than the annuitants. Of course, the holders of annuities would only be attracted by conversion so long as there was the chance of a speculative gain from an increase in the price of South Sea stock, and the scheme proved a disaster for annuitants when the 'bubble' broke in 1720 and they were left with worthless stock. The government had secured a large reduction in the scale of the national debt, but confidence in loans had been jeopardized by the fiasco.

It made more sense to escape from reliance on companies, and to tap a larger pool of savings by widening the holding of government stock. The government came to rely upon a group of intermediaries or underwriters such as Samson Gideon, who agreed to take the whole loan at a discount and to sell it to the public, with the expectation of making a profit by securing a higher price. The underwriters were taking the risk from the government, and creating a wider market. The number of public creditors increased from 10,000 in 1709 to at least 60,000 in 1756, and the actual number was considerably larger because banks and other bodies held stock for clients. Since the loans were permanent rather than for a fixed term, there was a further requirement: an active market so that holders of stock could sell when they needed cash. This was the basis of the Stock Exchange, which emerged by the 1770s as a market to create liquidity for the individual fundholder. The administration of the entire system of issuing loans, paying dividends to the holders of the stock, and keeping records of ownership was undertaken by the Bank of England, which allowed the government to bypass the cumbersome and antiquated machinery of the Exchequer. The market in public loans was at the heart of the financial development of the City of London, and crucial to the success of the fiscal-military state.

Virtue, Corruption, and 'Economical Reform'

The social impact of the tax regime greatly exercised contemporaries, many of whom feared that the national debt distorted the social hierarchy. Critics argued that the stockholders and great chartered monopolies of the Bank of England, the East India Co., and the South Sea Co. waxed fat on the backs of a high land tax. In the eyes of the country party, whose members were hit by the land tax, the formation of the Bank of England in 1694 was anti-agrarian, a sign of the shift of power from the land to money and commerce. The ability of the Bank to provide loans was also seen as a device to weaken parliamentary control over the purse. The country party consequently pressed for a National Land Bank which would provide cheap mortgages, and would be more independent of the City. It failed, not least because the country party was hostile to a general excise which offered an alternative to the land tax, and most landed gentry came to the conclusion that the Bank and long-term borrowing were the lesser of two evils. Concern that landed virtue was being threatened by monied corruption nevertheless continued as an important theme in the discourse on politics in eighteenth-century Britain.

The monied interest of the City was seen as a threat to productive interests, and as a malign political pressure group. The result, claimed Swift in 1710, was that 'Power, which according to the old Maxim, was used to follow *Land*, is now gone over to *Money*'.[3] The sentiment was shared by many in the City, and opposition to 'monied power' was not simply a rallying cry of rural backwoodsmen. The use of underwriters such as Samson Gideon led to complaints from Sir John Barnard that a small, powerful group of cosmopolitan financiers was gaining at the expense not only of land but also of 'legitimate' commerce which was 'real' and national. The national debt also meant, according to the critics, a flourishing system of patronage and corruption. The military and naval establishment offered places to favoured men of the ruling oligarchy, and opportunities for lucrative contracts. Here, claimed Bishop Burnet of Salisbury, was the means for 'artful Men in Office and Credit' to 'raise vast Wealth for themselves'.[4] The national debt, it was argued, was a political device designed to buy the loyalty of powerful interests involved in government loans, which was essential because the landed gentry were hostile to the land tax. 'Whoever were Lenders to the Government', claimed Burnet, 'would by the surest Principle be obliged to support it. Besides, the Men of Estates could not be persuaded without Time and Difficulty to have those Taxes laid on their Lands . . .: and it was the Business of such as were then in Power to cultivate a money'd interest.'[5]

The standard Tory complaint was that funding created a sinister monied interest acting against land which was synonymous with virtue. 'The landed men', asserted Bolingbroke in 1749, 'are the true owners of our political vessel, the moneyd men as such, are no more than passengers in it.'[6] Bolingbroke's ideal social and political personality was epitomized by 'virtue', the possession of property, which gave leisure and liberty to engage in public affairs and to bear arms in defence of the public, and assured independence from narrow vested interests. By contrast, monied wealth was seen as self-interested and incompatible with citizenship, which connected with criticism of the demoralizing impact of luxury. 'The Publick Debts', argued Sir John Barnard in 1737, 'encourage IDLENESS, the *Mother* of *Luxury*.'[7] Taxes placed on land to service the national debt meant, so the critics claimed, a fall in the price of land and a diversion of income towards the *rentier* class which held the funds and did not contribute to the wealth of the country. Savings were diverted into government loans and war, which depressed the land market, creating a credit shortage, and driving up interest rates on mortgages and loans for productive enterprise. It was a view with which many merchants and industrialists could make common cause. The burden on land and trade, so it was argued, limited employment and increased costs, pricing British goods out of markets, and leading to unemployment and high poor rates. Here was the rationale for Barnard's call for a reduction in interest on the national debt to 3 per cent, in order to reduce taxes and interest rates, which would lead to lower costs of production and stimulate trade.

The national debt was not without its defenders. Of course, it permitted the defeat of the French and Catholicism. 'The *national Debt*', argued an apologist in 1733, 'was contracted in Defence of our *Liberties* and *Properties*, and for the Preservation of our most excellent *Constitution* from *Popery* and *Slavery*. This encouraged the best subjects at the *Revolution* to venture their *Lives* and *Fortunes* in maintaining a long and expensive *War*.'[8] Some defenders were willing to go further, arguing that it encouraged the development of the economy. Rather than 'crowding out' investment in agriculture and industry, it could have the effect of 'crowding in' by attracting idle balances which would help to finance productive enterprise. 'The regular influx of money into the hands of the bankers (and lenders)', one commentator noted in 1784, 'naturally produced a decrease in the rate of interest.'[9] The debate between these two perceptions of the national debt is of immense importance. The tussle between the critics and beneficiaries of the national debt and the fiscal-military state was a crucial theme in eighteenth-century politics, which continued into the early nineteenth century when the bloated system which emerged from the Napoleonic wars came under attack as 'old corruption'.

The system of funded loans worked during the Seven Years War of 1756–63, and the government could avoid the political tensions which would be produced by changes to the structure of taxation until the American War of Independence, hen pressures on finance and military failures led to a searching debate. Should ne war be stopped; the excise and assessed taxes increased yet again; the land tax eassessed to increase the yield; or 'economical reform' introduced? Economical eform became a crucial political issue, a cry which had contested meanings for ifferent groups. It was urged by Christopher Wyvill and the Yorkshire Associ-tion in 1779, and spread to the rest of the country, drawing on the long-stablished country ideology with its hostility to the corruption of politicians and .angers-on at court, and its fear of an over-mighty executive and dominance by a mall clique of magnates. These concerns were apparent in the excise crisis of 733–4, and could go a stage further to a demand for parliamentary reform and a lesire to make the government more accountable. Politicians at Westminster, in •oth government and opposition, were fearful of these implications and pre-erred to draw a line between parliamentary reform and economical reform. Although the opposition could turn criticism of waste and corruption against the .dministration, both had a pragmatic interest in an efficient revenue system.

Edmund Burke focused upon the 'civil list', which was, in his opinion, the root •f political corruption. In 1780 he proposed the abolition of offices which were reated simply to secure support for the administration, developing the country omplaint against placemen financed by the civil list, which was unaccountable o parliament. Economical reform was also, in Burke's eyes, a means of defusing he challenge to the existing order posed by parliamentary reform, which he saw ıs overturning the balance of the constitution. His case was exaggerated, a trategy of opposition which was far from solving the financial problems of the government. Payments to the royal family and household had risen above the ʻivil list granted to George III on his accession in 1760, and pensions and ›erquisites were awarded to support court factions and clients. However, ncreased expenditure by the crown was not simply a sign of extravagance and political corruption. Prices were rising, and the civil list paid for government ʻunctions such as the diplomatic service, the Board of Works, and judges' salaries, as well as allowing the administration to make payments which it preferred not to place before parliament. The mixed purposes of the civil list led to muddle and confusion, without doing much in practice to bolster the ınfluence of the crown or ministry; it was scarcely a vast machine of 'old corruption', for expenditure was strictly limited and a defining feature of the eighteenth-century state was less the scale of peculation and favours than the tight controls on depredations of revenue. Burke's experience in government after the fall of North in 1782 led to a different and more pragmatic policy.

Burke's attack on the civil list and the influence of the crown was a diversion from the more fundamental problems which emerged in office, of how to tackle the issues of finance and secure the public credit. The emphasis on economical reform shifted to the need to control expenditure and prevent waste of money especially in the finance of the army. Criticism was directed against the management of public finance rather than the crown, and the solution was the appointment of a parliamentary committee of accounts to examine expenditure and methods of accounting in 1782, 1786, and 1792. This programme of economical reform built upon work already started by North, who accepted the justice of complaints and appointed a Commission for Examining the Public Accounts in 1780. It was a conservative strategy of containing opposition, isolating the campaign for economic reform from parliamentary reform and from criticism of the influence of the crown. Neither did he want to threaten the Treasury: the commissioners were to co-operate with the Treasury, which was placed in charge of 'economical reform'. The commissioners produced detailed recommendations to make administration more efficient and economical, by tightening up the accounting system, paying salaries instead of fees, removing sinecures and deputies, and generally separating the public business of office from private profit. The ethos and practices of the excise were extended, creating full-time, salaried, accountable officials with career advancement. The emphasis was on office as a public trust, which had precedence over vested interests and perquisites. The ministerial need for efficiency made common ground with the association movement's ideology of public trust, which had developed in professional societies, turnpike trusts, paving and lighting commissions, and the associated charities which ran hospitals and schools. The association movement was not simply a reactionary 'country' attack on corruption and ostentation at court, for it also drew on the ideology of professionalization and commercial probity which was reflected by the election of the evangelical bankers William Wilberforce and Samuel Thornton in 1784 with the support of the Yorkshire Association. These sentiments were shared by the Commissioners for Examining Public Accounts, who aimed to foster a rational, professional, bureaucratic style of administration while shoring up public credit and circumventing parliamentary reform.

At the end of the war with the American colonies, William Pitt the younger continued the strategy of economical reform, aiming to reduce the cost of servicing the national debt, which was taking a large part of the government's revenue. He revived a device which had been introduced by Walpole in 1717: the payment of money into a sinking fund to redeem the national debt. Walpole suspended payment into the fund in 1733 in order to avoid the unpopularity of additional taxation to fund a new loan. His decision was politically expedient but also made financial sense, for there was little point in redeeming loans which paid 3 per cent while incurring new ones at a higher rate of interest. The ambition of paying off the national debt was revived in 1783, when the Commissioners for examining the Public Accounts urged the creation of an inviolate sinking fund, to be financed by a revenue surplus. The aim was to increase revenues by encouraging foreign trade and home industry, which would increase the income from customs and excise duties; and expenditure should be held down by more economical administration. Pitt responded by creating the 'old sinking fund' of 1786, into which an annual sum was paid to redeem existing loans, and by establishing the 'new sinking fund' in 1792 which ensured that future debts were redeemed by an annual payment into the fund of 1 per cent of any loan. Pitt pursued a cautious policy of financial management, based on the redemption of debts by creating a budgetary surplus. He adopted the strategy outlined in 1783 in order to increase the revenue: he made a commercial treaty with France, and paid bounties to shipping; he reduced the level of the tea duties to make smuggling less attractive and to increase the yield; he replaced customs duties on imported wine, tobacco, and spirits by excise duties; and he reformed import duties in 1787.

Pitt was not able to carry administrative reform as far as he wished, and in 1792 he failed to remove sinecures in the customs. Here was the difference between Pitt's economical reform and the politics of the 1830s, when sinecures *were* overturned. In the eighteenth century, a compromise had to be made between efficiency and spoils. The explanation was not simply the power of vested interests, for the use of statutes to abolish posts whose holders were appointed by the monarch raised a serious constitutional issue: the ability of a ministry to dismiss officials appointed by its predecessors threatened the independence of civil servants as officers of the crown. Burke was able to prune the civil list when constitutional concerns and the self-interest of officers were overcome by the immediate problem of a deficit on the civil list. In 1792, Pitt was unable to abolish posts, and he instead proceeded by the simple device of leaving them vacant when the holder died or retired. The Whigs in the 1830s were in many ways completing the work of Burke and Pitt rather than embarking on a new radical attack to destroy 'old corruption'. A strict limit was set to 'old corruption', by the country ideology and the pragmatic needs of the government. Burke and Pitt aimed to remove abuses and inefficiencies, showing the responsibility and efficiency of the existing system so that economical reform would make a more fundamental measure of political reform unnecessary. The fiscal-military state rested on the excise, and the aim was to extend its efficient procedures to the rest of the administration. Ultimate success had to wait until the nineteenth century, but this did not entail a sudden rejection of an *ancien régime* permeated by 'old corruption'. Standards of bureaucratic efficiency had long existed, and 'old corruption' was not a defining structural feature of the British state. Efficiency was needed to maintain the credit-worthiness of the fiscal-military state, and to contain the threat to the constitution from those who wanted more fundamenta parliamentary reform.

The Coming of Income Tax

Pitt's strategy of redeeming the debt was flawed, for payment was made into the sinking fund whether or not there was a budgetary surplus or war. The outbreak of war with France in 1793 made it difficult to continue payments, and Pitt wa reluctant to commit himself to all-out war, which would mean sacrificing the sinking fund. By 1797, crisis loomed: the level of borrowing increased, the flood of loans depressed the price of government stock, interest rates rose, the nationa debt mounted, and the government was forced to suspend convertibility after run on the banks. After the crisis of 1797, Pitt's aim was to prevent the nationa debt from growing any bigger, even if it could not be reduced in the course of the war, by holding down interest rates, reducing borrowing, and increasing taxes

In the budget of 1798, assessed taxes became a form of income tax by sleight of hand. A graduated scale was introduced, so that a person who paid £20 of assessed taxes would be liable for £60, and someone who paid £100 would be liable for £400. Taxpayers were also given the option of substituting a declaration of income, and paying tax on a scale graduated from 0.8 to 10 per cent. This simply made it easy to evade the increase in assessed taxes, which were known and inescapable; self-assessment of annual income was open to manipulation. Another innovation in 1798 was designed to reduce the national debt: the land tax could be removed by paying sufficient stock into the sinking fund to produce a fifth more interest than the annual land tax. Few landowners found the terms attractive. Pitt's strategy of 1798 failed, and the outcome was the introduction of income tax in 1799, which placed a graduated tax on all incomes above £60. The income tax was a novel means to Pitt's unchanging end of preserving the sinking fund and redeeming the national debt. It was, in Pitt's eyes, a temporary measure to allow redemption of the wartime debt, after which the sinking fund would deal with the debt which existed before 1798.

The income tax was due to expire at the end of the war, but in 1816 the government felt that it should continue for a further two years. The intention was frustrated by an alliance of urban and rural taxpayers, who formed a common front against the beneficiaries of the post-war fall in prices. Creditors gained, for the real value of their loans increased; debtors had to find repayments out of shrinking incomes. Fundholders in receipt of high wartime interest rates benefited from lower prices, but the real burden of taxes needed to maintain interest payments rose. Taxpayers grumbled that they were being drained by the holders of the national debt. The result, claimed indebted owners of real

roperty in their more paranoid moments, was the subversion of the social
rder, a transfer of estates from landholders to stockholders, 'from those, in fact,
vho paid taxes to those who received them'.[10] Land, industry, and merchants
ould unite in urging the government to reduce salaries, taxes, and public
xpenditure to the level of 1792, and their refusal to sanction the extension of the
ncome tax was a means to achieve such an end. It was a view of taxation as a
vertical' conflict between the 'real' activities of land and honest production, and
rtificial 'monied' interests and speculation, rather than a 'horizontal' divide
etween rich and poor.

There was, however, a new concern at the end of the war for the 'horizontal'
ncidence of taxation. The government was worried about post-war social
anrest, and felt that it should abandon the malt tax as a means of reconciling the
population to the 'selfish' removal of the income tax. The result would be
cheaper beer, but it was at the same time a further concession to agriculture
which created political problems. In 1819, at a time of social discontent, the
government again wished to reintroduce the income tax, partly on fiscal grounds
put also for social reasons. The secretary to the Treasury explained to the Prime
Minister, Lord Liverpool, that an income tax would

arrest the progress of those sentiments which if not arrested, must inevitably overturn the
constitution and government. . . . A *modified* Property Tax upon the Income of all *realized*
Capital only to such an extent or percentage as might enable a Reduction of other Taxes
to a corresponding amount, which may bear hardly or inconveniently upon the Income
of labour.—Such a measure would be the best practical *Refutation* of the Calumnies of the
Demagogues against the Rich.[11]

This strategy of concessions was dropped, for the government needed to obtain
votes in parliament to pass the repressive measures of the Six Acts. The
government's desire to restore the income tax as a means of defusing social
conflict was prevented by the exigencies of parliamentary politics, and tariffs
were left to bear the main burden of the revenue.

The income tax and free trade were to form complementary strands of the
mid-Victorian fiscal regime, with the revenue from the income tax allowing the
reduction of tariffs. This connection between free trade and the income tax was,
however, not accepted immediately in the 1820s. Canning, a free trader, opposed
the reintroduction of the income tax, urging that direct taxes should be cut as a
concession to the parliamentary electorate. By contrast, Liverpool—a supporter
of protection—argued in 1824 that direct taxes should be increased and indirect
taxes reduced in the hope that 'we should considerably increase the wealth and
resources of the country, by the relief which might be afforded to commerce'.[12]
This was a fiscal and economic case for a shift to direct taxes: an income tax

would raise revenue and reduce the burdens on trade and industry. Peel als
stressed a second, social, motivation: the income tax would reduce class antag
onism. Peel rejected the 'vertical' debate over the incidence of taxation an
adopted a 'horizontal' or class approach which urged the need to reduce taxatio
on the poor who were the source of both wealth and revolution.

Peel's concern in the 1820s differed from his approach in 1842, when th
reintroduction of income tax was a means of introducing free trade. Indeed
liberal economists were likely to *oppose* income tax, arguing that all taxes reduce
production and that the income tax in particular discouraged investment an
reduced the demand for labour. Consequently, they preferred indirect taxes
Similarly, many radicals viewed the rejection of income tax in 1816 as a triumph
over 'corruption', a sentiment which was shared by Richard Cobden, the apostl
of free trade. Income taxes, he feared, were a military weapon designed t
support an expensive foreign policy, and his interpretation did contain a
element of truth. In 1842 Peel saw the income tax as a means of putting th
country on a war footing by rescuing state finances, increasing private wealth
and allowing war without debt. Free traders only came to accept the virtues o
income tax when Gladstone showed that it could be used to control foreign
policy and militarism. In the 1820s, income tax was designed to permit wa
without loans; in the 1850s, Gladstone made income tax an agent of a pacific
cosmopolitan free trade policy. Electors would, he argued, be less bellicose wher
their own pockets were hit by the costs of war, rather than these being passed t
their descendants through loans. The unpopularity of income tax, and the close
connection between paying the tax and the parliamentary franchise, created an
incentive to reduce expenditure, removing the threat of foreign military adven
tures and keeping expenditure at a low level which permitted money 'to fructify
in the pockets of the people'. The income tax could be reconciled with in
vestment and production.

Taxes and Distribution

The debate over the tax system and funded debt was concerned with their impact
on the distribution of wealth and income between landed and monied power,
between the rich and poor. What is the evidence for the impact of the fiscal
regime on British society? Certainly, in periods of peace, a large part of tax
revenues went to holders of the national debt, which could mean a 'vertical'
transfer between sectors of the economy. But a considerable amount of stock
was purchased by foreigners: in 1723–4, 14.2 per cent of Bank stock was owned by
foreigners, rising to 35.3 per cent by 1750. Above all, the United Netherlands were
major investors, for the rate of interest in Holland was low, British securities had

e great merit of being tax free, and the Dutch had a surplus on their payments ith Britain. In 1750, the United Netherlands held 79.5 per cent of foreign-owned ock, and Amsterdam merchants were increasingly supplemented by the *rentier* lass of provincial towns.[13] Of course, the availability of foreign funds reduced e possibility of 'crowding out', but the role of Dutch holders of government ecurities declined in the late eighteenth century: their investment in govern-nent securities did not increase during the American War of Independence, and was rapidly liquidated after 1783. There was, however, a renewed inflow of unds during the French revolutionary and Napoleonic wars, when leading nanciers and merchants relocated in London from centres such as Amsterdam nd Hamburg, and wealth fled from the advancing French armies. The funds to lefeat Napoleon were, to some extent, provided by an influx of European noney, rather than a drain on British resources.

The frequent complaint of Tories such as Bolingbroke was that domestic olders of funds were men 'who, borne to serve and obey, have been bred to ommand even government itself'.[14] An analysis of the ownership of five stocks around 1750 confirms some of his fears that the social order was subverted by a nonied plutocracy.[15] The landed aristocracy accounted for only 2 per cent of the tock, with a few large owners such as the Marlborough family with £276,154; in addition, some non-aristocratic landed magnates had sizeable holdings, such as Sir James Lowther of Whitehaven with £108,400. Above all, 93 per cent of holders of stock lived in London and the home counties, and the largest London-based nolders of stock give some credence to Bolingbroke's picture of a plutocracy of successful office holders, naval and military men, and monied interest battening on the country. There were the great merchants and financiers such as the merchant Francis Craiesteyn (£131,053), Samson Gideon (£76,450), and the banker Samuel Child (£49,500). Military and naval men reinvested the wealth they had derived from the fiscal-military state, such as Admiral Anson who held £30,000. Yet Bolingbroke was guilty of exaggeration, for most London stockholders were far from the world of cosmopolitan monied interests. They were doctors, shopkeepers, artisans, and even domestic servants, with a considerable number of charities and corporate bodies such as the Churchwardens of Hampstead and the Society for the Propagation of the Gospel. The national debt appealed to the small investors of London and the home counties who wanted a safe, secure outlet for moderate sums. The national debt could be interpreted in a very different way from Bolingbroke's somewhat paranoid account of a conspiracy against the social order: it had reached down the social scale, allowing a wide range of middling people to become involved with the state, and providing a sign of confidence and social stability.

The impact of the tax regime does not depend simply on who owned the

TABLE 19.1. *Central government taxation in Britain, 1715–1812*

	Tax revenue in £m.		Index of 'real' taxes 1715=100	Per capita real taxes	
	Current	Constant		£	Index 1715=100
1715	5.76	5.82	100	0.82	100
1740	5.93	5.70	98	0.62	100
1765	10.04	8.52	146	1.05	128
1790	17.51	13.21	227	1.36	166
1803–12	54.70	24.61	423	2.12	259

Source: P. Mathias and P. K. O'Brien, 'Taxation in Britain and France, 1715–1810', *Journal of European Economic History*, 5 (1976), 605.

national debt; it was also influenced by the incidence of taxes and the share of the national income appropriated by the government. Were taxes merely increasing in line with the development of the economy so that the government was taking a stable or even falling share of the national income; or was the government increasing its share of the national income? Both the 'real' revenue of the central government at constant prices and the real tax burden per head were stable until the 1740s, when a rapid increase started which accelerated in the 1790s (see Table 19.1). It is more difficult to calculate taxation as a proportion of national income or production, not least because so many statistics of production and national income are themselves based on the excise figures. On balance, it does appear that taxation took an increasing share of both output and the national income. One crude estimate suggests that the share of commodity output taken in taxes rose from about 17 per cent at the beginning of the eighteenth century to about a quarter at the end, and 35 per cent in the first decade of the nineteenth century. 'Economic expansion in Britain', conclude Mathias and O'Brien, 'was not off-setting the rising real burden of taxes during the early decades of the Industrial Revolution.'[16] The tax burden was increasing; is this to say, as country critics claimed, that it fell disproportionately on landowners to the advantage of the monied interest? The country ideology could be viewed as selfish special pleading, for the tax regime in the eighteenth century allowed land to escape relatively lightly. The proportion of revenue raised from direct taxes (land and assessed) fell from the 1690s to the 1790s (Table 19.2). Although the introduction of income tax reversed this trend against direct taxes, they were still less significant in the Napoleonic wars than in the late seventeenth and early eighteenth centuries. The break in trend was also a short-run phenomenon, for the abolition of the income tax meant that the share of revenue from direct taxes fell to a mere 10 per cent. The British tax regime was more reliant upon indirect

TABLE 19.2. *Direct and indirect taxes as a share of total tax revenue in Britain,
1696–1700 to 1831–1835*

| | Direct taxes on wealth and income (land and assessed) | Indirect taxes on commodities | | | |
		Customs	Excise	Total	Other
1696–1700	36.3	26.5	26.1	52.6	11.1
1711–15	31.1	26.4	35.9	62.3	6.6
1731–5	17.0	27.3	50.1	77.4	5.6
1751–5	21.9	23.8	50.6	74.4	3.7
1771–5	17.2	24.4	46.1	70.5	12.3
1791–5	16.0	20.9	47.3	68.2	15.8
1811–15	29.2[a]	19.2	37.7	56.9	13.9
1831–5	10.0	36.6	34.7	71.3	18.7

Note: Net income to 1791–5; thereafter gross.

Including property and income tax.

Source: B. R. Mitchell and P. Deane, *Abstract of British Historical Statistics* (Cambridge, 1962), 386–8, 392–3.

taxes between 1816 and the restoration of the income tax in 1842 than at any point since 1688. A simple breakdown of taxes by their method of collection therefore suggests that landowners escaped relatively lightly in the eighteenth century as taxation shifted to excise duties on consumption.

Unfortunately, it is very difficult to assess where the economic incidence of taxes ultimately rested, which affects both the vertical and horizontal distribution of taxes, and the extent to which the fiscal regime was regressive or progressive. Contemporaries were uncertain whether excises fell on consumers or merchants, or were shifted back to the landowner: a tax on malt and beer could reduce the price which farmers and maltsters could charge for their barley, so cutting agricultural profits and rents. Historians are not much clearer than contemporaries, for the ultimate incidence of taxes on consumption depends upon the price elasticities of demand and supply, which are very difficult to establish. At first sight, the increased reliance on indirect taxes shifted the fiscal regime in a regressive direction, particularly after the Napoleonic wars. But it should not be assumed that indirect taxes were always regressive, for a tax on wine and foreign spirits (brandy) consumed by the affluent had a different impact from a tax on malt, beer, salt, and domestic spirits (gin and whisky) consumed by the poor. Other taxes are more problematical, for the social composition of consumption shifted. Colonial goods such as sugar, tea, and tobacco were luxuries of the rich at the beginning of the eighteenth century, and necessities of the poor by the end. One benign interpretation of eighteenth-century taxation

argues that the government placed taxes on commodities which were mor
likely to be consumed by the rich, and exempted the necessities of the poor out o
concern for the 'horizontal' impact of taxes. Certainly, duties on basic necessitie
were varied so that more expensive varieties (soft soap, wax candles) paid
higher level than cheap varieties (hard soap, tallow candles), and taxes o
necessities rose less than those on other commodities. It was, remarked Willia
Pitt the younger, 'justice to tax the wealthier in preference to the more indiger
part of the population'.[17] The government had an incentive to select goods an
services with an income-elastic demand, for increases in consumption as income
rose would allow the government to tap increased prosperity. This applied, fo
example, to duties on fine textiles, male servants, windows, carriages, an
pleasure horses. Governments were always looking for items of visible an
conspicuous consumption to tax, and Pitt extended the range of dutiable luxurie
to include hair powder and armorial bearings. Yet these points should not b
exaggerated: they at most mitigated a trend towards a much more regressive ta
regime.

The impact of the land tax became less onerous between 1698 and 1798, an
the introduction of excise duties in the 1690s overturned earlier assumptions tha
the poor should not be taxed. The sentiments of William Pitt the younger wer
not so much evidence of a deep-seated belief that the poor should not b
burdened, as a realization that a limit had been reached in taxing working-clas
consumption. The duke of Newcastle in 1759 took a different line, preferring t
raise revenue by a higher duty on malt, on the grounds that taxes should fall or
everyone rather than on a small part of the population, such as the land tax. Th
malt tax, he argued, 'is a duty upon universal consumption at home; which by a
the rules for levying taxes ... is the best, and fairest'.[18] There was a clea
administrative rationale in taxing items of mass consumption, for taxes or
luxuries were levied either by the customs, which was inefficient and liable t
evasion by smuggling, or by assessed duties, which were collected by an amateu
administration under the control of the country gentry. Duties on domestic
consumption were, by contrast, collected by an efficient excise service, and were
less easily evaded where goods were produced in centralized plant. There wa
also a fiscal incentive to tax goods which were price inelastic, for the yield would
not fall as the tax rose. Taxation policy was not based upon social equity so much
as the search for goods whose demand was price inelastic. Above all, this meant
taxes on widely consumed goods for which there were no substitutes, such as
malt, beer, domestic spirits, salt, and coal, and, by the end of the eighteenth
century, tea and sugar. It is difficult to see how the tax regime could be anything
other than regressive, for taxes on price-inelastic goods by far outweighed the
contribution of taxes on income-elastic goods and services. The annual average

.eld on malt, hops, and beer alone amounted to £3.9 million between 1788 and '92, which fell on a staple item of working-class consumption; taxes on price-elastic consumption as a whole amounted to £6.9 million or 45 per cent of :venue. By contrast, land and assessed taxes amounted to £3.4 million or 22 per :nt and on income-elastic consumption to £2.9 million or 19 per cent. Between 598 and 1798, the trend was towards taxes on goods and services rather than on ´ealth and income, and the tax regime became more regressive. This trend was :versed to some extent by Pitt, and about 63 per cent of extra taxation during the ´ars of 1793–1815 fell on the incomes and consumption of the rich. Even so, the 1ift should not be exaggerated, for the wartime changes merely moderated the ighteenth-century trend towards a regressive tax system, and were reversed in 316 with the abolition of income tax. The years from 1799 to 1816 were a short 1terlude in a long period during which taxes fell increasingly on working-class onsumption.[19]

The complaints of the landed interest were special pleading of doubtful alidity, for they resisted a reassessment of the land tax and their tax burden fell ver the eighteenth century. A rough calculation suggests that direct taxes (land 1d assessed) fell from about 10 per cent of agricultural income at constant prices 1 1700 to 8 per cent in 1780; they then increased from 7 per cent of agricultural 1come at current prices in 1795 to 20 per cent in 1810 as a result of income tax, efore reverting to the pre-war level after 1816.[20] Not only did landowners pay a maller proportion of taxes; they also derived considerable benefits from wars hrough the profits of office in the armed forces and government. The fiscal-military state between the end of the war in 1698 and the outbreak of war in 1793 vas, contrary to the 'country' ideology, a massive transfer payment in favour of he landed interest, rather than imposing an inequitable burden to support an edifice which was hostile to land. It has even been argued that the landed élite 1ad a common interest with the monied class as 'gentlemanly capitalists', and hat, if anything, the tax regime was hostile to industry. This is suggested by a eclassification of taxes into three categories: retained imports, consisting of :ustoms duties and any excise levied on imports, which largely fell on inter-1ational trade; domestic production and services, consisting of excise and stamp luties; and income and wealth, consisting of land tax, assessed duties, and 1come tax, which largely fell on rent. The rough and ready figures in Table 19.3 lo hint at some broad patterns. Not only did landed income escape taxation to he 1790s; international trade also paid a declining share of taxation between the early eighteenth century and the wars of 1793–1815, and the Exchequer benefited only to a limited extent from the commercial revolution of the eighteenth century. Most of the burden fell on domestically produced goods and services. Excise revenue rose from 11 per cent of domestic production of industrial goods

TABLE 19.3. *Source of taxation, 1695–1810* (%)

5-year average centred on:	Domestic production/services	Retained imports	Wealth/income
1695	27	27	47
1720	46	28	26
1745	48	20	32
1770	57	25	18
1795	44	36	20
1810	36	30	34

Source: P. K. O'Brien, 'The Political Economy of British Taxation, 1660–1815', *Economic History Review*, 2n ser. 41 (1985), 9.

at constant prices in 1700 to 23 per cent in 1780, before stabilizing or falling during the wars of 1793–1815.[21] Industrialization in the eighteenth century took place in a harsh fiscal climate.

Nevertheless, the contention that industry was sacrificed to 'gentlemanly capitalism' is, like the country ideology, overdrawn. Not all industry suffered, for many sectors escaped the imposition of excise duties, including cotton, wool pottery, and iron, which were amongst the most dynamic sectors of the economy. Many industries were protected by tariffs, such as iron, glass, paper, and soap, which could compensate for the impact of excise duties. Industrialists were organized, and the government had to take account of their demands as well as the East and West Indian lobbies. The fiscal-military state was not necessarily harmful to industry, for wars extended markets in the Americas and the national debt was at the heart of the financial revolution of the eighteenth century. The rise of public borrowing created a range of securities which gave merchants, brokers, insurance offices, banks, and trading companies a more varied and flexible outlet for funds than land. 'Without these facilities', claims Peter Dickson, 'it is at least arguable that the City's complex structure of services could not have been built up by the mid-eighteenth century, for there was no industrial sector whose bonds could be used for the same purpose. Delay in the emergence of the City as a financial centre would, like failure to hold existing overseas markets and win new ones, have put back England's industrialisation, and thus changed the course of European history.'[22]

An assessment of the impact of the tax regime of the eighteenth century on industry depends upon what is considered to be the major constraint on growth. One view is that the constraint was from the side of demand, in which case the fiscal system was probably harmful. The wars of the eighteenth century did, it is true, widen overseas markets, and expenditure on the army and navy stimulated me sectors of industry by creating demand for munitions and supplies. Yet the xes which financed war were regressive, and depressed the standard of living d reduced the level of effective demand at home. Part of the government's val and military expenditure was incurred abroad, and the interest payments the national debt went to better-off individuals who were more likely to save. he regressive tax system reduced demand, and consequently hampered indus-ial growth if this was the major constraint. Alternatively, growth might have en constrained by the savings ratio, in which case the tax regime was eneficial: taxes on high-income groups declined, and they had a higher propen-ty to save. Clearly, much depends upon whether demand or investment is nsidered to have been the crucial constraint on growth.

The argument that the tax system led to increased investment conflicts with e contention that government loans 'crowded out' investment in the private ctor, so delaying the development of capital-intensive technology until the 20s when government borrowing fell. Public finance and taxation, according to ich an interpretation, explains slow economic growth during the industrial volution; far from loosening constraints, war finance and taxes created bar-ers. It has already been argued, however, that 'crowding out' rests on a number f questionable assumptions. It assumes full employment of resources; more alistically, government borrowing 'crowded in' underemployed resources, imulating the economy by injecting demand. It also assumes a single pool of sources which could be drawn upon by private business or by government; ore realistically, labour and capital markets were segmented. The government cruited adult male soldiers, and industry turned to women and children; the ational debt attracted southern *rentiers*, while industry obtained funds from kin nd retained profits, under the influence of market expansion and the creation of family firm rather than the rate of interest on government loans. The 'crowding ut' hypothesis does not seem plausible.

The tax system was more likely to have stimulated savings by shifting income owards the better off and to have depressed demand. Whether this was eneficial or harmful depends on the view which is taken of savings. The eynesian argument is that investment demand for savings was crucial, which epended upon the expected rate of expansion in the market; savings would espond to the level of demand. Consequently, the tax system led to a low level f investment and savings, by holding down the demand for goods. Alterna-ively, neo-classical economists assume that the supply of savings was itself a onstraint, so that taxation policy would increase the supply of funds for nvestment by shifting income towards savers. On balance, the Keynesian pproach seems more realistic in the eighteenth century. Savings were more ikely to be a consequence of growth rather than a constraint, for a major source

of capital formation in industry was ploughed-back profits and the movement
funds from domestic production. Consequently, the reduction of demand as
result of regressive taxation was likely to hold back growth and reduce the lev
of investment. Public finance could therefore help to explain slow growt
through constraints on the market rather than 'crowding out'. There is,
course, still a possibility that the short-run disadvantages of lower growth wei
compensated by longer-term economic prosperity as a result of securing marke
and raw materials overseas. 'War and taxation in the eighteenth century may, i
the long run', remark Beckett and Turner, 'have been what made Britain great.'

Taxes and State Formation

The tax burden of eighteenth-century Britain was both increasing and shifting i
a regressive direction. Yet it was in France, where the level of taxation was lowe
and the tax regime more progressive, that the state's demand for financ
contributed to revolution. In 1700–25 the English paid something over twice th
amount of taxes per capita, and by the 1780s the discrepancy had widened to 2.
times.[24] Although war finance led to episodic problems in Britain, it neve
produced a fundamental challenge to the social and political order. It was not th
actual burden of taxation which threatened the state, so much as the impact o
political and social relationships.

In part, the success of British governments in extracting high levels of taxatio
rested upon the constitutional settlement of the 1690s, which led to parlia
mentary control over the choice of taxes and created wide support for the fisca
system, unlike in France where the calling of the estates general after a lon,
period contributed to the collapse of the political system. In Britain, there wer
no exemptions from direct taxes; in France, there were many exemptions fo
peers and the Church. In Britain, direct taxes were collected by unpaid loca
commissioners drawn from the class which was liable, rather than by a stat
bureaucracy or subcontractor. The land tax was granted by a parliament o
landowners, and was administered by them in the localities, rather than by
royal bureaucracy. This was both its weakness and its strength. Amateu
administration meant that assessments were not equal and the level of the ta
was frozen. However, the yield was known and secure, and collection wa
relatively uncontentious. The British government avoided any attempt at usin
the land tax as a more realistic means of taxation, which would have inflamed the
'country' party against the crown and ministry. Under-assessment was tolerate
because it was preferable to non-payment, and the tax was administered locally
by the consent of those who were liable; it underlined local social patterns

drawing the localities into the central administration, unlike in France where the local community was set against the central government and the Intendant.

The political acceptability of taxes rested less on their level than on their visibility. The fact that the land tax fell on landowners rather than farmers and labourers made it 'invisible' to most people. Neither did indirect taxes cause so much hostility as in France, despite the fact that their incidence was greater. Import duties were seen as taxes on foreigners, and were paid at the port, ceasing to be visible when the goods entered internal trade. Excise duties were mainly collected from a few large producers who owned centralized plants, so that tax collectors dealt with a few manufacturers rather than the mass of the population. Again, the excise ceased to be visible to the consumer. Although the excise was resented as an incursion of executive power, the possibilities of conflict were less than in France. The collection of customs and excise duties was in the hands of centrally appointed government officials rather than private tax farmers, and the absence of internal tax boundaries such as existed in France meant there was no need for a paramilitary presence in internal trade. The excise relied on the routines of quantifying output, and was uniform across Britain. The result was that taxes in France were lighter and less regressive, but also more visible and contentious.

Britain lacked an institutionalized system of purchase of hereditary office, which had considerable influence on the French state. The efficiency of the excise system meant that the extent of venality was limited, and Britain was characterized by 'the absence of a sprawling, tentacular state apparatus made up of venal office-holders'.[25] Partly, it was a matter of timing, for England was only marginally involved in Continental wars in the seventeenth century, during which France raised money by the sale of office, so creating an enormous administration with fiscal exemptions. Crucially, the fiscal-military state emerged in Britain after the Dutch had developed an alternative means of raising money through funded loans. The capacity of the British state to expropriate a rising share of the national income rested upon flexible administration, the tolerance of evasion, and the prudent selection of groups and commodities to bear the increased burden of taxation. By these means, the British state was able to raise revenue without recourse to autocracy. The scope of government was limited, and there was an endemic distrust of a strong state, army power over civilians, and a centralized bureaucracy. Paradoxically, the constrained executive was able to raise high levels of taxation by fully exercising its authority. Public accountability and parliamentary consent made resistance more difficult; government action was legitimized; and peculation was reduced. The fiscal-military state was contained, with the result that it was slimmer and more effective.

NOTES

1. J. Brewer, *The Sinews of Power: War, Money and the English State, 1688–1783* (1989) p. xvii.
2. B. Disraeli, *Sybil; or, The Two Nations* (1845), 23–4.
3. Quoted in J. Hoppit, 'Attitudes to Credit, 1680–1790', *Historical Journal*, 33 (1990), 310
4. P. G. M. Dickson, *The Financial Revolution in England: A Study in the Development of Public Credit, 1688–1756* (1967), 17.
5. Ibid.
6. H. Bolingbroke, *Some Reflections on the Present State of the Nation* (1749), in *The Works of Henry St John Bolingbroke*, iv (1809), 388.
7. Hoppit, 'Attitudes to Credit', 311.
8. Ibid. 316–17.
9. Ibid. 317.
10. B. Hilton, *Corn, Cash and Commerce: The Economic Policies of the Tory Governments 1815–30* (Oxford, 1977), 32.
11. Quoted ibid. 82.
12. Quoted ibid. 260.
13. Dickson, *Financial Revolution*, 312, 321, 324.
14. Quoted ibid. 292.
15. Ibid. 284–300.
16. P. Mathias and P. K. O'Brien, 'Taxation in Britain and France, 1715–1810: A Comparison of the Social and Economic Incidence of Taxes Collected for the Central Governments', *Journal of European Economic History*, 5 (1976), 610.
17. P. K. O'Brien, 'The Political Economy of British Taxation, 1660–1815', *Economic History Review*, 2nd ser. 41 (1985), 12.
18. Quoted in R. Browning, 'The Duke of Newcastle and the Financing of the Seven Years War', *Journal of Economic History*, 31 (1971), 358.
19. O'Brien, 'Political Economy of British Taxation', 10, 11, 13, 16–17.
20. Ibid. 15.
21. Ibid.
22. Dickson, *Financial Revolution*, 11–12.
23. J. V. Beckett and M. Turner, 'Taxation and Economic Growth in Eighteenth-Century England', *Economic History Review*, 2nd ser. 43 (1990), 401.
24. Brewer, *Sinews of Power*, 89.
25. Ibid. 15.

FURTHER READING

Anderson, J. L., 'A Measure of the Effect of British Public Finance, 1793–1815', *Economic History Review*, 2nd ser. 27 (1974).
Beckett, J. V., 'Land Tax or Excise: The Levying of Taxation in Seventeenth- and Eighteenth-Century England', *English Historical Review*, 100 (1985).
—— and Turner, M., 'Taxation and Economic Growth in Eighteenth-Century England', *Economic History Review*, 2nd ser. 43 (1990).

Binney, J. E. D., *British Public Finance and Administration, 1774–92* (Oxford, 1958).

Brewer, J., *The Sinews of Power: War, Money and the English State, 1688–1783* (1989).

Brooks, C., 'Public Finance and Political Stability: The Administration of the Land Tax, 1688–1720', *Historical Journal*, 17 (1974).

Browning, R., 'The Duke of Newcastle and the Financing of the Seven Years War', *Journal of Economic History*, 31 (1971).

Cain, P. J., and Hopkins, A. G., 'Gentlemanly Capitalism and British Overseas Expansion, i: The Old Colonial System, 1688–1850', *Economic History Review*, 2nd ser. 39 (1986).

Cooper, R., 'William Pitt, Taxation, and the Needs of War', *Journal of British Studies*, 22 (1982–3).

Dickinson, W. C., 'The Sword of Gold: Sidney Godolphin and War Finance, 1702–10', *Albion*, 6 (1974).

Dickson, P. G. M., *The Financial Revolution in England: A Study in the Development of Public Credit, 1688–1756* (1967).

Hausman, W. J., and Neufeld, J. L., 'Excise Anatomized: The Political Economy of Walpole's 1733 Tax Scheme', *Journal of Economic History*, 10 (1981).

Hill, B. W., 'The Change of Government and the "Loss of the City", 1710–11', *Economic History Review*, 2nd ser. 24 (1971).

Hilton, B., *Corn, Cash and Commerce: The Economic Policies of the Tory Governments, 1815–30* (Oxford, 1977).

Hoppit, J., 'Attitudes to Credit in Britain, 1680–1790', *Historical Journal*, 33 (1990).

Langford, P., *The Excise Crisis: Society and Politics in the Age of Walpole* (Oxford, 1975).

McCloskey, D., 'A Mismeasurement of the Incidence of Taxation in Britain and France, 1715–1810', *Journal of European Economic History*, 7 (1978).

Mathias, P., and O'Brien, P., 'Taxation in Britain and France, 1715–1810: A Comparison of the Social and Economic Incidence of Taxes Collected for the Central Governments', *Journal of European Economic History*, 5 (1976).

—— 'The Incidence of Taxes and the Burden of Proof', *Journal of European Economic History*, 7 (1978).

Mui, H.-C. and L. H., 'The Commutation Act and the Tea Trade in Britain, 1784–93', *Economic History Review*, 2nd ser. 16 (1963–4).

Neal, L. S., *The Rise of Financial Capitalism: International Capital Markets in the Age of Reason* (Cambridge, 1990).

O'Brien, P. K., 'The Political Economy of British Taxation, 1660–1815', *Economic History Review*, 2nd ser. 41 (1988).

Reitan, E. A., 'From Revenue to Civil List, 1688–1702: The Revolution Settlement and the "Mixed and Balanced" Constitution', *Historical Journal*, 13 (1970).

—— 'Edmund Burke and Economical Reform, 1779–83', *Studies in Eighteenth Century Culture*, 14 (1985).

—— 'The Civil List, 1761–77: Problems of Finance and Administration', *Bulletin of the Institute of Historical Research*, 47 (1974).

Rubini, D., 'Politics and the Battle for the Banks, 1688–97', *English Historical Review*, 85 (1970).

Torrance, J., 'Social Class and Bureaucratic Innovation: The Commissioners for Examining the Public Accounts, 1780–87', *Past and Present*, 78 (1978).

Ward, W. R., *The English Land Tax in the Eighteenth Century* (Oxford, 1963).

Wilson, G. J., 'The Land Tax Problem', *Economic History Review*, 2nd ser. 35 (1982).

....

CHAPTER 20

Mercantilism and Free Trade

In January 1846 Richard Cobden addressed a great rally at the Free Trade Hall in Manchester, at the heart of the cotton district. The Hall was built by the Anti-Corn Law League which, under the leadership of Cobden, protested against protective duties on imported corn; more generally, the 'Manchester school' preached the virtues of free competition and unfettered trade. The introduction of free trade, Cobden assured the audience which packed the Free Trade Hall, would lead to peace and prosperity:

the physical gain will be the smallest gain to humanity from the success of this principle. I look further; I see in the Free Trade principle that which shall act on the moral world as the principle of gravitation in the universe—drawing men together, thrusting aside the antagonism of race, and creed, and language, and uniting us in the bands of eternal peace. . . . I believe that the desire and the motive for large and mighty empires; for gigantic armies and great navies—for those materials which are used for the destruction of life and the desolation of the rewards of labour—will die away; I believe that such things will cease to be necessary, or to be used, when man becomes one family, and freely exchanges the fruits of his labour with his brother man.[1]

Free trade would remove the possibility of war by creating mutual dependence between nations. Cobden denied that prosperity rested upon protection and a drive for empire, which merely led to high taxes, sinecures, government contracts, and privileges which distorted both the economy and the political system. Free trade would, argued Cobden, destroy the basis of a corrupt political system, undermining the fiscal-military state.

An article of faith of the Manchester School was that free trade led to prosperity through the operation of 'comparative advantage', a concept developed by Adam Smith in *The Wealth of Nations*. No family would make at home what it could buy more cheaply; and 'What is prudence in the conduct of every private family, can scarce be folly in that of a great kingdom.'[2] Unfortunately, a policy of protection or 'mercantilism' prevented this desirable outcome. It would be absurd, suggested Smith, to ban the import of French claret and burgundy into Britain in order to encourage the production of Scottish wine from grapes grown in hothouses at thirty times the cost, and there was a similar absurdity in encouraging the production of goods which required the employment of a thirtieth or even a three-hundredth more labour and capital than a foreign competitor. The result, he argued, was a waste of resources and a reduction of welfare. Although Smith was confident that free trade led to prosperity, he feared that its implementation was as implausible as the creation of Utopia. Many producers had made investments within a system of protection, and they formed a formidable block which could intimidate parliament. The 'clamorous importunity of partial interests',[3] Smith believed, prevented the dismemberment of the system of protection for the common good.

Free trade was introduced by the 1840s, and utopia—at least in the eyes of Cobden—was achieved. Peace, prosperity, and reform would, he believed, follow. But should the defeat of protection by free trade be viewed through the eyes of Smith and Cobden? The consensus in the second half of the nineteenth century was that mercantilism held back economic development and fostered political corruption and warfare. Protection could, however, have been less harmful than Smith and Cobden believed, and could have fostered the development of new sectors of the economy. Cobden in 1846 focused upon the corn laws, which favoured the landed aristocracy against the industrialists, and it was convenient to reduce the debate over protection to a simple divide between 'feudalism' and industrial growth. In reality, the lines of division were more complex, and protection was not simply in the interests of land and imperialism. The cotton industry, which was such an assiduous supporter of free trade in the 1840s, was itself the product of protection.

The shift in policy in the second quarter of the nineteenth century needs to be explained. Was it the result of the cogent criticism of the system of protection by Smith and his followers? Or were political decisions taken by government ministers for pragmatic reasons? Tariffs and duties produced revenue, and ministers needed to raise money in different ways: much depended upon the ability of government to reintroduce the income tax in 1842, and to create a more secure and less socially divisive fiscal regime. Structural change in society could induce governments to reconsider agricultural protection: at some point it was less politically expedient to conciliate the landed interests than to secure foreign supplies of grain to feed the growing urban population, which was a potential source of social unrest in the depression of 1837–42. The arrival of free trade could confirm Smith's cynicism: could it be the outcome of the 'clamorous importunity' of industrialists with a vested interest in free trade rather than protection, as economic growth shifted the balance between interests which benefited from protection or that flourished in an environment of free trade? Smith feared that protection would create a vested interest in the continuation of tariffs; what he had not foreseen was the possibility that industries could secure dominance in international competition and adopt a policy of free trade as a means of securing hegemony in trade. By the early nineteenth century, the cotton industry did not need protection against foreign competitors; what it desired above all was liberty to export to other countries without the constraint of tariffs—a policy which could be secured in part through the use of state power as in India and China, and in part through the propagation of a liberal ideology. Cobden's rhetoric of free trade was as much a product of self-interest as the protectionism he derided.

Defining 'Mercantilism'

The trade restrictions which were dismantled in the second quarter of the nineteenth century are often characterized as 'mercantilism', a term which has caused considerable confusion. It was not used by the creators of tariffs, but emerged as a concept in later debates over free trade, creating a spurious impression of a systematic policy. The definition of mercantilism varied. To Adam Smith, it was a system devised by merchants and manufacturers for mercantile ends, with the aim of accumulating reserves of bullion. Mercantilists, he complained, fell into the error of supposing that 'all wealth consists in gold and silver, and that to multiply those metals is the great object of national industry and commerce'.[4] Trade policy therefore rested on the prohibition of exports of gold and silver, and the attraction of bullion by creating a balance of payments surplus. Bounties would encourage exports of manufactures, colonies would provide captive markets, and imports of manufactures and exports of domestic raw materials were limited by restrictive duties. Mercantilism was, in Smith's view, against the national interest: it was a narrow, sectional policy which sacrificed the consumer to the producer, fostering monopolies and creating inefficiencies.

In the later nineteenth century, a positive definition of mercantilism emerged amongst some economists who favoured the replacement of free trade by tariffs. Mercantilism, argued Cunningham, was concerned with 'the power of the country' rather than a narrow sectional interest. It was a commendable attempt to build a mutually beneficial state and national economy which subordinated private interests to the state in order to produce power and wealth. Here, claimed some commentators, was the key to Britain's rise to greatness. The Dutch were displaced from the world's carrying and entrepôt trades, the French were defeated in the world-wide tussle for empire, and a strong national economy emerged securely based on a flourishing merchant marine, on

London's role as a centre of world trade and finance, and on access to colonial markets for British industrial goods. Their opponents in the debate over tariffs in the late nineteenth and early twentieth centuries were not convinced, arguing that such policies led to a misallocation of economic resources, and resulted in high taxes for war which fell on production, and a powerful class of financiers and placemen who corrupted the state for their own ends.

The concept of 'mercantilism', and the controversy over its economic and political impact, emerged from later political controversies rather than from disinterested analysis of economic policy in the eighteenth century. The word 'mercantilism' suggests a systematic and coherent policy; the word gives a false unity to a 'jumble of devices' which was assembled over time for particular reasons in order to meet the needs of state finance, power politics, and sectional interests. It is necessary to understand the particular circumstances which produced any measure. The favourable balance of trade, which Smith saw as the defining feature of mercantilism, for example, was propounded by Thomas Mun in 1622 at a time of trade depression, and policies were developed to alleviate distress and stimulate the economy by import substitution and an attack upon Dutch dominance of the carrying and finishing trades. Smith felt that wealth and money were confused, but he was writing at a time when paper money and bank credit reduced the fear that a shortage of coin would lead to depression. A preoccupation with bullion was more rational in the seventeenth century when it was needed to settle the adverse balance of trade to the Baltic and East Indies. The attempt to secure bullion was not necessarily a narrow policy favouring the producer against the consumer, for a strong balance of payments could produce an inflow of gold, which would hold up prices, reduce interest rates, increase the prosperity of the domestic economy, and curb unemployment. There was a concern for the 'real' economy and wealth which was more sophisticated than Smith allowed in his dismissal of crude bullionism. The classical economists, remarked Keynes, committed a 'presumptuous error in treating as a puerile obsession what for centuries had been a prime object of practical statecraft'.[5]

The Dutch, remarked Defoe in 1728, were 'the Carryers of the World, the middle persons in trade, the factors and brokers of Europe'.[6] The shipping industry produced lucrative freights, fostered a shipbuilding industry, and created a market in marine insurance; processing and storing goods created major industries and generated profits from warehousing and commissions. Any weakening of the Dutch entrepôt trades was likely to benefit the English economy in general and London in particular, and this ambition lay behind the navigation laws of 1651, 1660, 1662, and 1663. The intention was to cripple the Dutch carrying and entrepôt trade by excluding them from England's import trades and the growing empire in the Atlantic and Asia, which were increasingly important suppliers of commodities to European markets. The coastal trade was limited to English-owned ships; imports from Europe of 'enumerated' articles such as flax and wine had to be carried in ships owned in England or the producing country, which cut out Dutch carriers; there was a ban on the import of goods such as timber and tobacco through Holland or Germany; and long-distance import trades from Asia, Africa, and America were confined to English ships which came directly from the country of growth or port of first shipment. The trade of the expanding colonies was limited to English shipping, and exports of an ever-expanding list of 'enumerated' colonial products had to be sent to England before they were re-exported to Europe. Initially, duties were imposed when the goods arrived in England, and a refund or 'drawback' was allowed when they were re-exported. This imposed a burden on merchants, and in the 1730s they were allowed to store goods free of duty, provided they gave a deposit or 'bond'. The entrepôt trade was liberalized by the Warehousing Act of 1803, which transferred responsibility for the bond to the owner of the warehouse, and allowed merchants to deposit goods for up to fifteen months free of duty. Similar regulations were imposed on goods sent to the colonies, to ensure that their trade was channelled through England. A major motivation for the navigation laws, therefore, was the attempt to remove the Dutch from the carrying and entrepôt trades, to build up a strong merchant marine, which was crucial to the naval strategy of Britain, and to earn foreign exchange by providing commercial and financial services.

Trade regulations also allowed the government to raise revenue to finance its world-wide strategic commitment. Although the inefficiency of the customs office and widespread smuggling meant that the weight of new taxation shifted to excise duties in the eighteenth century, customs duties still contributed 20.9 per cent of revenue in 1791–5, and the abandonment of income tax in 1816 meant that their significance subsequently increased to 36.6 per cent of revenue in 1831–5 (see Table 19.2). Although the government's motivation was to raise money, this was not necessarily incompatible with the use of tariffs as a means of protecting industry. How far was this a conscious aim of government policy?

The tariff system of 1690 was not protective in intention or in practice. There was a general tariff of 5 per cent on the 'official' value of both imports and exports, and the highest rate of duty on specific items fell on goods such as sugar and wine which could not be grown in England. The incentive was fiscal: they were income-elastic luxuries. Subsequently, duties were increased to finance the French wars, and at the same time there was a shift towards protection. Exemption from the general export duty was granted to woollen textiles in 1700; and in 1722 the general duty on exports was abolished. Meanwhile, the general import duty was raised in stages to reach 25 per cent of 'official' values by 1759.

Protection was offered to the woollen industry, with a duty of 20 per cent on imports of cotton and silk textiles from India and China in 1690, and a complete ban on the import of silk cloth and printed and dyed calicoes in 1701. Between 1763 and 1776, there was a spurt of protective legislation which resulted in a ban on the import of silk goods, and increased duties on linen and paper. Import duties were also removed from essential industrial inputs, such as dyestuffs in 1714, flax in 1732, and raw silk in 1765. Further, industrialists secured export bounties, for silk goods in 1722, sailcloth in 1732, and linen in 1742 and 1756. The system of 'drawbacks' was modified to offer more protection to British producers. In 1705, for example, it was no longer possible to claim back import duties paid by Swedish bar iron or Dutch nails when they were re-exported to the colonies, which gave a competitive edge to English producers. Clearly, the tariff system was becoming more protective in the course of the eighteenth century.

The shift towards protection was an incidental result of the government's search for revenue rather than a conscious act of policy. The tariff structure was shaped by an interplay between the government and the interest groups seeking special treatment. The government was anxious to make duties acceptable to these interests, which would ease the task of enforcement and collection, and also attach them to the state. Indeed, the complex negotiation of duties was part of the process of state formation. The British state depended upon an open process of power-broking between interests such as West Indian sugar-planters, ironmasters, and West Country clothiers, unlike in France where tax farmers and the sale of offices created a different state structure. Protectionism was less the result of a conscious 'mercantilist' policy than the outcome of endemic conflict between interest groups eager to secure their own ends—including industries such as cotton which were later to be advocates of free trade. Reality was far removed from the rhetoric of free traders who imagined a coherent, homogeneous mercantilist block with the ear of the government, which forced them to bear a burden of heavy taxes to support a bloated state and its hangers-on. In fact, there was not a single protectionist interest. A ban on the import of silk cloth and printed and dyed calicoes from Asia protected the woollen textile industry, but threatened the East India Co., which urged the virtues of free trade in textiles—a contention which sat uneasily with its own monopoly of trade to the east. The campaign of the linen and iron producers against 'drawbacks' on foreign goods brought them into conflict with London merchants, and with the government's desire to foster an entrepôt. Shipowners who were protected against foreign competition in long-distance trades resented the need to buy ships from British builders, who in turn complained that the navigation laws made it difficult to sell to foreign owners.

There was no single 'mercantilist' interest, and when the campaign for free trade started, it was another weapon in the tussle between interest groups rather than an altruistic desire for the common good. The Petition of the London Merchants of 1820 is often taken as the beginning of the demand for free trade. Its author, Thomas Tooke, was an associate of leading classical economists such as Ricardo, and the Petition utilized the rhetoric of comparative advantage. But the Petition was less a united commercial plea for free trade than a traditional complaint by particular interests for favour. North European merchants were protesting against preference to Canadian timber; the East India Co. was urging free trade in sugar against West Indian interests while defending its own monopoly of tea from China. Free trade was another weapon to be used by commercial and industrial interests in a battle to shape policy for their own ends.

The state was not simply an umpire, adjudicating between interests: it had concerns of its own. It wished to raise revenue in the most efficient way, which would secure the support and co-operation of interest groups. It was concerned with public order, social stability, and poor law expenditure, which meant that it was anxious to prevent serious depression and unemployment in major industries: the title of the measure of 1701 which banned the import of silk cloth and printed and dyed calicoes was 'an act for the more effective employing the poor by encouraging the manufactures of the kingdom'. The government was concerned about the deficit in trade with the East for silk and cotton, and with Europe for linens. The linen industry in Scotland and Ireland was an antidote to Jacobitism and rebellion, leading to the establishment of the Board of Trustees for the Linen and Hempen Manufacturers in Ireland in 1711 and the Board of Trustees for Manufacturers in Scotland in 1727, and making the government careful that tariffs did not threaten the industry and provoke unrest. The structure of tariffs was also influenced by strategic considerations, which altered the balance between interest groups. Britain was heavily dependent upon imports of bar iron from Sweden, but diplomatic relations were strained, leading to war between 1756 and 1763. The result was to encourage the substitution of American iron, a policy which had previously been blocked by the owners of British furnaces and forges who feared competition, despite the pleas of nailmakers and smiths who were eager for cheap supplies of iron. The British state, therefore, was pursuing its own concerns for revenue, social order, and strategic advantage, as well as placating and balancing a wide range of industrial, commercial, and regional interests. The result was far from coherent: duties were highly contingent, shaped by a range of considerations which were often contradictory; and the process of negotiation and compromise was a crucial element in the formation of the British state.

The advocates of free trade argued that tariffs and the navigation laws led to inefficiency and waste, preventing the optimal allocation of resources. Were they correct, or could it be argued that these regulations and duties led to the development of London as an entrepôt, the growth of a British merchant marine and shipbuilding, the emergence of financial and commercial services, and the development of industries such as linen, cotton, and iron? Obviously, there were major structural changes in the British economy in the eighteenth century, and it might be wondered what role was played by tariffs and trade regulations. Did they distort and delay the process of economic development; were they irrelevant; or did they encourage the transformation of the economy and provide the basis of British hegemony in the world economy?

Navigation Laws, Tariffs, and Economic Development

What was the impact of these duties and regulations on the British economy? The ban on the import of dyed and printed calicoes in 1701, for example, did not extend to plain calicoes, which encouraged the development of a printing and dyeing industry in London. Should this be interpreted as a misallocation of resources, a breach of the principle of comparative advantage; or as the creation of a necessary foundation for the emergence of new industries? And were the costs of the system of regulation worthwhile? The navigation laws and regulations of trade required the colonies of North America to send their goods to London, and to buy their imports from Britain; the development of their own industries was constrained. These regulations needed to be enforced, which led to expenditure on the navy and army: was this money well spent, or would the colonies have used the services of London anyway? Critics of the system of imperial trade regulation such as Josiah Tucker argued that it was unnecessary to pay for the defence of the empire in order to direct colonial trade to the mother country, when the free market would produce the same result at no cost. America, he remarked in 1782, 'were always from first to last a heavy weight upon us; a weight which we ourselves ought to have thrown off if they had not done it for us'.[7] Tucker was part of a tradition which ran through the nineteenth century that the empire imposed costs upon the metropole and distorted the social and economic structure.

The navigation laws aimed to direct trade with the colonies into British ships, and to route their goods through Britain for re-export. In 1660, the Dutch offered cheaper freights, and Amsterdam was the dominant entrepôt for sugar and tobacco, and the major centre for financial and commercial services. By the end of the eighteenth century, London had captured a large part of the role of Amsterdam, and British shipowners had driven the Dutch from many trades. There is no doubt that a change took place, but was it the result of the navigation laws or of other factors? Could it be that the regulation of trade distorted trade patterns, which increased costs, and gave British shipowners the opportunity to charge higher freight rates than would have been possible within a competitive international market? The Navigation Law of 1651 and the wars with the Dutch limited Dutch ships' involvement in the major short carrying trades which used the bulk of tonnage. In the case of coal, a higher duty was paid if it was shipped in foreign vessels; and the export bounty on grain was paid only to British ships. The capture of about a thousand Dutch ships between 1652 and 1654 was also significant, doubling the size of the fleet and changing its character with the addition of cheaply operated 'fly boats'. There are two possible interpretations of these changes. One is to argue that the navigation laws and naval victories broke the dominance of the Dutch shipbuilders and owners, and allowed the development of English shipowning and building, which were highly efficient and low cost. The alternative interpretation is that English shipowners and builders were high cost, or were able to take monopoly profits within a sheltered market.

A good case could be made for the first interpretation, that the navigation laws allowed English owners and yards to escape from the dominance of the Dutch, and to achieve a high level of productivity and efficiency. It is unlikely that they were able to take monopoly profits, despite the exclusion of foreign-built and -owned ships from many trades. There was still a high level of competition both in the construction of ships and in the freight market. The construction of cheap vessels for the bulk cargoes of coal, timber, grain, and flax, shifted from the Thames and East Anglia to the north-east of England. It was difficult for these shipyards to charge high prices, for they competed with each other and with American builders, particularly in New England, whose ships counted as British for the purposes of the navigation laws. Similarly, shipowners were part of a highly competitive trade, as a result both of ease of entry produced by the pattern of ownership and of the development of a market in freights. Shipowners achieved considerable improvements in productivity during the eighteenth century, and there is little sign that freight rates were higher as a result of the navigation laws. Indeed, British shipbuilders and owners had a great advantage over their foreign rivals for purely economic reasons: the availability of bulk cargoes of coal on the eastern coast, grain exports to Europe in the first half of the eighteenth century, and the growth of long-distance trades particularly to the Americas.

One way of measuring the impact of the navigation laws is to compare the situation before and after their repeal in 1849. Certainly, there was an increase in the proportion of foreign-owned ships entering and leaving British ports from 29 per cent in 1848 to almost 40 per cent in the late 1850s. Possibly, British shipowners found it difficult to compete with American and Scandinavian owners in a free market, particularly as crew costs increased. The navigation laws might, therefore, have resulted in somewhat higher freight rates in the second quarter of the nineteenth century, but this was slight and short term. A large part of the increase in the proportion of foreign ships was simply the result of substitution of native for British vessels, rather than a wide price differential: it was possible for Scandinavian owners to send timber to Britain, or American owners to carry cotton. By contrast, shipbuilders gained from repeal. They were internationally competitive under the navigation laws, which had served to limit their exports rather than protecting them from cheaper foreign competitors, for foreign ships trading with Britain had to be owned and *built* in the country. On balance, it does not seem that the navigation laws led to high costs and inefficiencies on the part of either shipowners or builders. They allowed England to escape from the shadow of the Dutch in the mid-seventeenth century, and do not seem to have led to any major inefficiencies or monopoly prices.

The navigation laws played a role in redirecting trade from Amsterdam to London and the provincial ports of Liverpool, Bristol, and Glasgow. However, the navigation laws were not enough to produce a major restructuring of trade, and there were other important factors. The expansion of the British empire in the East and West Indies and north America meant that European merchants were more likely to find sugar, tobacco, tea, silk and cotton textiles in London, on better terms. The development of the protoindustrial trades in ironwares along the Severn valley provided the export goods which could be exchanged for slaves in West Africa, which were used to grow sugar in the West Indies. And London was able to develop processing industries, and to escape from the constraints on the growth of cities in 'organic' economies because it had access to coal from Newcastle. There were certainly other factors at work than the navigation laws, and it may be argued that the development of the commercial and financial services of an entrepôt were as much the result of competitive strength as of trade regulations. But it should also be remembered that the expansion of British control over supplies of sugar, tobacco, tea, spices, textiles, and other commodities was largely the result of the successful prosecution of war with Holland and France, leading to the development of loan finance which formed the basis of the London money market. Although the pursuit of strategic ambitions was not the only reason for the emergence of London to domination in the world economy, it was certainly important.

The growth of London and leading provincial ports as major centres of commerce and finance produced considerable invisible earnings from freights, insurance, trade credit, and warehousing, and led to the development of major trades such as sugar-processing or dyeing and printing textiles. But to some contemporary commentators and modern historians, the outcome was beneficial to financial and mercantile interests, particularly in the City of London, which provided loans for the national debt and developed the entrepôt services, and harmful to industrialists. Policy, it has been argued, was shaped by the interests of 'gentlemanly capitalism', an amalgam of aristocratic landowners who gained from the expansion of the empire and positions in the armed forces and government, and financiers and merchants.[8] However, such an analysis is difficult to sustain.

The development of tariffs and trade regulations was considerably more complex than support for 'gentlemanly' versus industrial capitalists, and it was possible for industry to obtain support for its demands against the wishes of financiers and merchants. In 1701, for example, the woollen and silk industries defeated the East India Co. over the importation of dyed and printed calicoes and silk cloth, which marked a significant divergence from the pattern in Holland where commercial interests were able to dominate policy at the expense of industry. In Holland, the market remained open to dyed and printed Asian textiles, and the local bleaching, dyeing, and printing industries declined. By contrast, the Act of 1701 fostered the development of print and dye shops in London to finish the plain calicoes which were allowed entry. The characteristic feature of public policy in Britain was less the fact that it gave priority to commercial and financial interests, than the aim of governments to maintain a balance between interests, and to take care that no group was alienated from the state. Robert Walpole was castigated as an ally of great Whig landowners and 'cosmopolitan' financiers, but his policy was more balanced than his critics allowed. He was conscious that he needed the support of landowners who controlled parliament, and the City of London which was crucial to the issue of long-term loans. Yet he did not neglect industry, and he pursued policies which were sufficiently neutral to secure the support of a wide range of groups. Political stability, it has been seen, was not the result of dominance by a narrow landed oligarchy using electoral influence. On the contrary, there was an active political life within towns and counties, with interest groups placing pressure on representatives drawn from local landowners. Political stability arose from policies which balanced these interests. Protection of markets would increase Britain's share of world trade, which would clearly benefit the mercantile interests of the City and shipowners, but would also reduce the level of underemployment and the burden of poor relief. Buoyant trade and production would increase revenue from customs and excise duties, which would allow the repayment of part of the national debt; a reduction in the supply of government stock would increase the market price of fixed interest securities, interest rates would fall, and private investment would be stimulated. Walpole's economic and social policy was designed to create a broad-based prosperity, in an attempt to generate political unity through social and economic progress. The British state rested upon a strategy of *inclusion* of pluralistic interests to produce *balanced* growth, rather than the pursuit of narrow class interests. Of course, the strategy was placed under strain by the pressures of war finance, which could force an increase in excise duties on industrial goods, and there were serious strains after the Napoleonic wars when the abolition of the income tax led to a regressive fiscal regime, and the continuation of the corn laws seemed a blatant attempt to support landowners against other classes. But it would be wrong to extrapolate from the early nineteenth century to the whole of the eighteenth century, and even in the early nineteenth century the government was more concerned to maintain balance in the economy and between interests than the radical advocates of free trade were prepared to admit.

The emergence of the cotton industry in the eighteenth century can only be fully understood in the context of government policy, which was shaped by a tussle between different textile trades. The woollen industry was concerned to limit competition from new cotton textiles from the East, and the Act of 1701 was merely the start of a long campaign. Import duties were imposed on plain calicoes in 1701 and were increased in 1704 and 1708, and an excise duty was placed on domestically printed calicoes in 1712 and 1714. The woollen trade pressed for a total ban on calicoes, which was granted in 1721: the Calico Act made it illegal to wear any calico cloth on penalty of a fine paid to the informer. The government was willing to support the woollen industry against Asian textiles, in order to check the drain of bullion to the east, to prevent unemployment and social unrest, and to raise revenue from the duties on calicoes. But the victory of the woollen industry against Asian competition was Pyrrhic, for it was also facing competition from the domestic linen, industry, which the government was eager to encourage in place of European imports. Duties were increased on imports of linen, which were doubled in 1704 and again by 1779. The initial motivation was to raise revenue, but the structure of tariffs increasingly moved towards protection: the duty on exports was abolished in 1717 and export bounties were paid in 1743; import duties on flax and yarn were removed in 1731 and 1756; and bounties were paid for growing hemp and flax in 1781. A considerable industry emerged, not only in Ireland and Scotland but also in the West Country, Yorkshire/Co. Durham, and the lowlands of Lancashire. The government was not willing to accede to the demand of the woollen industry that linen should be banned from the home market, which threatened unrest in Scotland and Ireland, and led to protests from dyers and printers in London. Crucially, the Act of 1721 took no action against the production of linen cloth and permitted the wearing of fustians woven from a mix of cotton and linen which was explicitly legalized by the 'Manchester Act' of 1736. The result was very different from the expectations of the woollen industry, for the ban on Asian textiles did not so much protect wool as stimulate the domestic cotton and linen industries to fill the gap. Not only did the structure of duties encourage the development of the fustian industry in Lancashire; high duties on linen imports also stimulated the substitution of goods made entirely from cotton for such uses as table cloths, napkins, towelling, and sheets. The growth of the fustian and cotton industry threatened the linen industry, but the government was less concerned about the possibilities of unrest in Ireland and Scotland by the 1770s. In 1774, the wearing of all-cotton cloth was legalized. Clearly, the visible hand of government shaped the development of the textile industries, and the cotton industry—the heart of the demand for free trade in the 1830s and 1840s—was itself the product of protection against Asian calicoes and European linen.

Industrialization was a political process, and policy had an important role to play in shaping the structure of the economy. There is little sign that commerce and finance were given a privileged position, and industry ignored. On the contrary, commercial interests were sometimes defeated by industry. The outcome was influenced by the concerns of the state at any time, whether for social unrest or revenue. Public policy was not, of course, the only factor which shaped the development of the textile industries. The rise of cotton in place of linen owed much to the fact that supplies of raw cotton could be increased more readily than flax, and to the existence of fewer technical difficulties in spinning cotton than flax. Similarly, the growth of the iron industry was less the result of an increase in import duties from 10s. a ton in 1688 to 48s. 6d. in 1759 than of the application of cheap coal. The result of higher duties could simply be an increase in the costs of bar iron for producers of metal goods, and advocates of free trade could argue that it was more efficient to purchase bar iron from Sweden. But there are two arguments on the other side. The first is economic: would it have been possible for the owners of British furnaces to develop the techniques which allowed them to use coal unless they had been protected from cheap foreign producers? The second is political: was it practical to adopt a free trade strategy in the eighteenth century? The government needed to raise revenue from import duties, and there were strategic problems with dependence on Sweden. The introduction of free trade was no less a political decision than tariffs and the navigation laws, which only become possible in very precise circumstances in the second quarter of the nineteenth century.

The Corn Laws and Agricultural Protection

No element of the system of trade regulation generated more controversy than the corn laws, and posed more of a threat to the strategy of inclusion of interests. Here, it seemed to Cobden and the Anti-Corn Law League, was a policy designed to maintain food prices and land rents against the interests of industrialists and workers. The corn law of 1815 was, according to one historian, 'one of the most naked pieces of class legislation in English history',[9] and it was denounced at the time by radicals, manufacturers, and the urban poor as a 'pact of famine' between the landed aristocracy and the government of Lord Liverpool to maintain high wartime rents and the position of the landed aristocracy. These criticisms of the corn law were a crucial element in British politics between 1815 and 1846, but was it so obviously a class-based measure, or could it be justified as an economically rational response to post-war adjustments and the uncertainties of the food supply? The emphasis on the last thirty years of the corn law should, in any case not obscure its earlier history. What precisely was the rationale of the corn law from the late seventeenth century to the early nineteenth century?

The corn law of 1670 established a sliding scale, imposing a high duty of 16s. a quarter when the price of wheat was less than 53s. 3d. a quarter, falling to 8s. when the price was between 53s. 4d. and 80s., and to 4d. when it was above 80s. In 1689 the sliding scale on imports was complemented by an export bounty of 5s. a quarter when the price of wheat was 48s. or less. The rational was to reduce fluctuation of prices and to create a stable market, by encouraging exports when prices were low and imports when prices were high. The aim was to protect the consumer from famine and to ensure that prices were fair; and to offer a decent return to producers in order to encourage production. The policy was un contentious up to 1750, for agricultural output was rising faster than the popu lation, prices were falling, and there was a large export of grain. But from 1750 it came under increasing criticism as the fundamental change in the relationship between food supply and population started to call the policy into question Exports of grain dwindled to a negligible amount by 1765, and export bounties were often suspended and grain allowed into the country duty free. Agricultural policy was faltering under the strain of population growth and the declining rate of increase in productivity.

In the opinion of some critics, the policy had always been misconceived Bounties, it was argued, simply provided foreigners with cheap food, allowing them to cut their wages and compete with British manufacturers. The structure of tariffs should, it was suggested, be altered so that high import duties were placed on fully manufactured goods and low duties on commodities to which labour could be added; similarly, exports of corn and commodities to which foreigners could add value should be forbidden. This was a policy based in the free import of food in order to sustain the largest number of industrial workers, and Adam Smith adopted a similar position. He argued that government policy harmed the consumer in two ways. On the one hand, the export bounty increased the price level by holding up prices in years of surplus and removing the surpluses which could be used in years of scarcity. On the other hand, the consumer was faced with higher taxes to pay the bounty, which, Smith claimed, went to the export merchant in higher profits rather than to the farmer as an incentive to increase production. Despite such criticisms, it was still generally assumed in the 1770s that the maintenance of regular prices encouraged agricultural output and resulted in lower prices.

What was needed, it seemed to the government, was an adjustment in the light of changed circumstances rather than a fundamental change in policy. Import duties and export bounties had been suspended on an annual basis, as a result of pressure from consumers and government's concern for public order. These demands for suspension led to political tension, with the danger that the state of the harvest could be misjudged with disastrous consequences if bounties were restored at a time of shortages, as in 1766. In 1773, it was hoped to take the corn laws out of contention by formalizing the payment of export bounties and import duties in line with current practice: export bounties would be paid when the price of wheat fell below 44s., with a complete ban on exports when the price was higher; and import duties started at 22s. when prices were 44s. or less a quarter, falling to a nominal level when prices were 48s. or more. At the same time, stocks of grain to counter future shortages were encouraged by allowing imports to be landed free of duty and stored, for either re-export or domestic sale on payment of duty. Merchants would, it was assumed, purchase foreign grain when the price was low, and hold it for sale on the domestic market when prices rose and the import duty was lower. The government's policy was to encourage the free market as a means of overcoming shortages of grain and preventing high prices, which was linked with the repeal of legislation controlling the domestic market in 1772. The government's priority was to ensure food supplies for the growing population, and to prevent unrest in response to high prices, and the readjustment of bounties and import duties was more in the interest of consumers than landowners. In 1773, the landowners took a pragmatic view that they were not surrendering anything which they enjoyed in practice, with the benefit of removing constant political challenge through pressure for temporary suspensions of the corn law.

The landed interest was soon disappointed, for the price of grain rose in the late eighteenth century, and the thresholds of 1773 meant that exports were usually banned and the import duty at the nominal level of 6d. per quarter. The corn law was now, argued the landed interest, favouring the *consumer* by encouraging imports, discouraging exports, and creating large stores of grain which prevented farmers from securing a reasonable price. The corn law, they contended, was no longer encouraging farmers to grow more grain so as to maintain steady prices which were fair to the consumer and the producer; rather, it was discouraging the cultivation of grain because prices were held down by stockpiles held in the ports, and by the low level of import duties. The corn law, they argued, should be revised in order to encourage production by allowing export bounties and applying the nominal level of import duties at a higher price threshold. In 1791 and 1804, the landed interest were able to secure such an adjustment to the corn law. Should these revisions be interpreted as blatant class legislation which sacrificed urban and industrial interests? There were certainly signs of unease amongst industrialists who felt that there should be free export and import of grain without the payment of bounties or import duties. Britain, they argued, was no longer able to feed itself so it was pointless to encourage exports by the payment of bounties, and high import duties merely increased food prices and drove up wages. A free trade in grain would, they claimed, allow Britain to become the granary of Europe, holding stocks of grain to meet shortages in other countries, which would produce profits for merchants and increase the demand for shipping. But this was a high-risk strategy, which placed the population at the risk of disruptions in the international grain market. The government was not simply acting in the class interests of landowners, for its main motivation was to ensure self-sufficiency in grain as an insurance against famine and social unrest. In any case, benefits to landowners from the revisions of 1791 and 1804 should not be exaggerated. The adjustment of price bands did not increase the real level of protection, for they did no more than take account of inflation, and the government allowed imports duty free between 1796 and 1801, and paid bounties on *imports* in 1797, 1800, and 1801. The landowners were certainly securing higher rents and taking an increased share of the national income, but this was the result of population pressure rather than government policy, which was designed to secure an assured supply of food rather than to favour landowners against other groups in society.

A stronger case can be made for interpreting the corn law of 1815 as 'naked class legislation'. Grain prices started to fall in 1813, and it has been argued that landowners and farmers were able to use the corn law to prevent prices falling to their natural, market level: there was an outright ban on imports when the price fell below 80s., and duty-free imports were allowed when prices were 80s. or more. Legislation was used, so the critics claimed, to maintain high wartime prices and rents, and to preserve the shift of national income in favour of the landed interest. There was, they suggested, a fundamental change in the nature of the corn law. In the eighteenth century, the aim was to keep prices within limits which were fair to both consumers and producers; by contrast, the law of 1815 was a one-sided attempt by landowners to retain their wartime gains and to preserve the dominance of agriculture over commerce and industry. Should this interpretation be accepted, or was reality more complicated?

The corn law of 1815 was more than a simple use of state power in the interest of landowners against industry and consumers. It was, in part, an *Irish* policy, designed to remove their European competitors in British markets. It also involved internal competition within agriculture rather than a united front by domestic grain-growers versus foreign imports. Marginal soils brought into production during the war were only profitable when prices were high. Farmers and landowners on good soils with higher yields could make a profit at a lower price level, and were less concerned about foreign competition; they might even welcome a reduction of cultivation on marginal soils as a means of keeping up prices and securing a larger profit. The government was not simply siding with a selfish aristocracy to maintain high rents and prices, for the Prime Minister, Lord Liverpool, and his Home Secretary, Lord Castlereagh, were aware of the dangers of alienating industrial districts which were already facing disruption at the end of the war. But could they allow over-capitalized farmers on marginal soil to bear the brunt of lower prices, and was it sensible to rely upon imports to feed the growing urban and industrial population? Malthus expressed the reservations. 'It is', he suggested, 'our wisest policy to grow our own average supply of corn.'[10] Imports would, he believed, be unfair to those who had invested capital in agriculture and inferior land during the war; there was a danger that agricultural labourers would be thrown out of work when low prices forced farmers to give up their leases; labourers would suffer from greater fluctuations in corn prices and their wages would fall, in line with food prices; and traders and manufacturers would face a reduction in the income of customers. The only beneficiaries of low corn prices, claimed Malthus, would be people who lived on fixed incomes and grain merchants. Such arguments were far more than a justification for the class interest of landowners, for ministers at the end of the war were concerned to ensure an adequate food supply. The experience of France before the Revolution was a warning of the consequences of pressure on food supplies, and the dangers of harvest failure were confirmed by a subsistence crisis in large parts of Europe in 1817. Disruptions to the food supply posed a serious threat to political and social stability, and a sharp fall in food prices which forced marginal land out of cultivation would give the consumer a short-term gain with harmful long-term consequences. 'If one quarter of the wheat land of the kingdom was thrown out of cultivation', remarked Liverpool in 1815, 'no foreign supply would possibly make up the deficiency in the quantity of food.'[11] The government's policy was autarky, maintaining domestic production as a guarantee against famine and ensuring 'a sufficiency of supply at *steady* and *moderate* prices'.[12] The corn laws would, it was hoped, be needed only for a short time as farmers and landowners gradually adjusted to a lower price level, and increased their efficiency so that they could make profits, even on the poorest soils, from high yields and large sales. There was, indeed, a continuity of ministerial policy from the late eighteenth century to Liverpool and Peel who at length abolished the corn law, based on an attempt to set prices at a level which was fair to consumers and producers rather than to support landowners against industry and the working class.

Ministers were aware of the need to balance interests in society, and the corn laws were part of a complex balancing act at the end of the war, for Liverpool was anxious to retain the income tax as an equitable way of spreading the costs of the national debt between classes, and he realized that a concession was needed to secure backing in parliament. But his offer of the corn law as a political 'bribe' for the continuation of the income tax failed: the corn law was accepted and the income tax rejected, not only by the landowners but also by commercial and industrial interests concerned about a tax on enterprise. The difficulty of securing support for the income tax was to be a major constraint on the adoption of free trade, and the line of division was not simply between landowners and industrialists. One important constraint, therefore, was the budget. The government's ambition that the corn law should be a short-term expedient was also frustrated by the attitude of landowners in parliament, who preferred to see it as a long-term attempt to maintain prices. Ministerial policy was not intended as 'blatant class legislation'; landowners tried to ensure that it was. The government had great difficulties in convincing landowners that the period of transition had ended, particularly as food prices fell in the early 1820s.

The government welcomed lower food prices as a solution to the problems of working-class unrest, and its main concern continued to be the maintenance of the food supply. By the early 1820s, it was less clear that Ireland was a reliable source of grain, and the corn laws, it was becoming obvious, were necessary to secure a decent return from marginal land rather than a transitional measure to allow farmers to increase their productivity. A more reliable food supply, it now seemed to ministers such as William Huskisson, could be obtained from European suppliers rather than by pursuing autarky, and a regular demand was more likely to encourage foreign farmers to increase output than an intermittent demand when prices were high. The end remained the same, to maintain steady prices and ensure a food supply as an antidote to social unrest and famine; the means changed to free trade. The shift in ministerial policy was pragmatic rather than ideological, and there was a basic continuity of purpose. It did, nevertheless, have unsettling consequences. Advocacy of free trade assumed that Britain should specialize in the production of manufactured goods to exchange for food, and the government was not surprisingly threatened by a country revolt against any reduction in import duties. Attempts to buy off opposition by cheaper money, tax cuts, and loans to agriculture failed, and duties were, indeed, increased in 1822 against the wishes of the government. The country victory was

Mercantilism and Free Trade · 551

1 empty gesture of defiance: wheat prices never reached the level of 80s. a
uarter which would trigger the new duties. The government remained commit-
d to a policy of free trade in corn, and the only question was when ministers
ould be able to get the measure through parliament. The 'great object',
ommented Londonderry in 1822, was 'substituting a more extended commerce
a grain instead of a monopoly, and then prospectively the removal of re-
rictions'.[13] Extra-parliamentary pressure from Cobden and the Anti-Corn Law
eague was not needed to explain the virtues of free trade to ministers. Sir Robert
eel, the heir to the economic liberalism of Huskisson, did not need convincing;
that he needed was the right moment. When did this appear, and was it the
sult of 'high political' manœuvres, extra-parliamentary pressure, and the threat
f social unrest, or a pragmatic response to changes in the supply of grain and the
alance of economic interests?

The Coming of Free Trade

'he introduction of free trade was conditioned by other elements of government
olicy, and liberalization of trade was more feasible in the mid-1820s. One
onstraint was fiscal policy, for the abolition of duties was not possible unless
here was a revenue surplus as in 1824 and 1825. A second influence was monetary
olicy, for liberalization of trade complemented convertibility. A gold-based
urrency was more susceptible to fluctuations in imports and exports, which
ffected the flow of bullion. Stability of monetary policy, the government
rgued, made regular trade essential. Greater freedom of trade would, it was
elieved, allow imports and exports to find their natural level by 'purifying'
rade, which complemented the use of monetary policy to separate 'real' and
artificial' or speculative trade. Trade liberalization was linked with concern that
nass unemployment in periods of trade depression threatened public order. Free
rade was, of course, connected with agricultural policy and the government's
ealization that the food supply could not be guaranteed by autarky. Freer trade,
t was also expected, would mean more trade: by reducing trade barriers, foreign
ountries would be able to sell more to Britain, and hence increase their income
or purchasing British manufactures. This was the policy advocated by the
oreign Trade Committee of 1820–4, which Huskisson started to implement
etween 1822 and 1826. He revised the navigation laws in 1822, negotiated
ommercial treaties with newly independent countries in Latin America, and
offered a reduction in duties on goods carried on foreign ships to countries which
offered reciprocal rights. 'The means', remarked Huskisson in 1825, 'which lead
o increased consumption, and which are the foundation ... of our prosperity,
will be most effectually promoted by an unrestrained competition not only

between the capital and industry of different classes in the same country, but als
by extending that competition, as much as possible to all other countries.'[14] Th
reduction on protection for shipping and industry would, it was hoped, lead to
greater volume of trade to pay for imports of food; it would also placat
agriculturalists before revising the corn laws. Duties on grain imports wer
reduced in 1828, marking the first step in the policy of freer trade.

The trend towards economic liberalism was halted in the 1830s. Although th
navigation laws were revised in 1822, they were only abolished in 1849; th
import duties on corn were reduced in 1828 but only removed in 1846. Th
explanation was not a change in policy, so much as a change in politica
circumstances and, above all, disagreement over finance. When there was
surplus, should priority be given to the repayment of the national debt or, a
Huskisson preferred, to the reduction of taxes in order to remove the burden o
industry? And should the income tax be reintroduced in order to make good
loss of revenue from lower customs and excise duties? Both the Whigs and th
Tories were divided, and it was impossible to secure a majority for a reform o
the fiscal system. In 1830, the Tories proposed a reduction in duties on beer
leather, and sugar, and the introduction of an income tax. 'It was expedient'
remarked Peel, 'to reconcile the lower with the higher classes, and to diminis
the burthen of taxation on the poor man.'[15] The attempt failed, and the Whig
were no more successful in 1831 when they aimed to use a surplus to reduce taxe
on a range of commodities and to challenge the system of colonial preference
This offended a large number of vested interests, which was compounded by th
government's attempt to impose alternative taxes. The Whigs were reduced to
hand-to-mouth financial policy, attempting to cut expenditure and to reduce
unpopular taxes as trade expanded. The government preferred to avoid change
to the tax system which would alienate powerful vested interests, at a time wher
the political agenda was dominated by the highly controversial reform of th
franchise, poor law, and municipal corporations.

By 1837, the political context had changed. Government finance moved into
deficit, and the Whigs' parliamentary position was weaker, forcing them to rel
on support from the radicals who were pressing for a reduction in duties and the
introduction of free trade. In 1841, the Whigs consequently tried to reform the tax
system in a way which would both balance the budget and attract support from
free traders by adopting the proposals developed in the 1830s at the Board o
Trade and on the Select Committee on Import Duties. The reduction of high
taxes, it was suggested, would not threaten revenue, for consumption would
rise. The strategy did not work, for the revision of duties offended a number of
powerful vested interests by making foreign goods more competitive with
colonial products, and it did not satisfy the Anti-Corn Law League, which wished

o *abolish* tariffs as a source of revenue. Whig financial policy had reached an mpasse, for they could not agree on an income tax as an alternative source of evenue, since it was, to free traders such as Cobden, an imposition on enterprise and a means of financing an extravagant foreign policy.

It was left to Peel and the Conservatives to tackle the same problems after their victory in 1842. Peel's solution was to reintroduce the income tax in 1842 for an initial period of three years in order to remove the immediate budget deficit and to raise additional revenue. His strategy differed from that of the Whigs in 1841, who saw tariff reform as a device to stimulate the revenue; by contrast, Peel intended to use the revenue from income tax as a means of tackling poverty, social unrest, and trade depression. His aim was to secure support for the income tax by offering tariff reform and a new corn law to the advocates of free trade, while preserving a fair level of protection for agriculture. Above all, he argued that economic prosperity and social stability would be secured by increasing the purchasing power of the masses through a reduction in the price of food and consumer goods by reducing the burden of customs and excise duties and adjusting the corn law. This would, he claimed, lead to full employment and rising consumption to the benefit of all classes in society. The aim was to strike a balance, between a sound commercial policy, a reasonable level of protection for agriculture, and social justice to the working class. By 1845 the strategy was vindicated by the recovery of the economy and a budget surplus. Although Peel could have used the surplus to allow the income tax to lapse, he preferred to invoke the prosperity of the economy as evidence of the success of his policy, and to renew the income tax for a further period. The revenue was used to reduce a large number of duties which 'press more onerously on the community than the income tax',[16] with the ambition of resolving the 'condition of England' question by removing grievances against high, regressive taxes and by stimulating the economy to provide steady employment.

By 1845, the future of the corn laws was in doubt, and their abolition was the next stage in Peel's strategy of reducing food prices in order to increase purchasing power, mitigate poverty, and stimulate the economy. Maintenance of the corn laws was, he believed, harmful to the landed interest and repeal was a necessary step of self-preservation. Agriculture was a target of hostility as the only major industry with protection, and Peel stressed that the aristocracy would place itself in an invidious position by linking its interests to the corn laws, which could only be retained at the cost of class conflict. Repeal would reconcile the masses to aristocratic government by removing the sense of injustice and showing concern for the conditions of the people. Abolition of the corn laws was a necessary *conservative* measure. 'My earnest wish has been', Peel told the Commons, to impress the people of this country with a belief that the legislature was animated with a sincere desire to frame its legislation upon the principle of equity and justice ... the greatest object which we or any other government can contemplate should be to elevate the social condition of that class of the people with whom we are brought into no direct relationship by the exercise of the elective franchise.[17]

Agriculture and land ownership would, Peel argued, remain profitable and prosperous by pursuing low costs and high productivity in an expanding market rather than clinging to protection which would simply create hostility and class conflict. In 1846, he resolved on the repeal of the corn laws.

Not every one agreed with his assessment, and the immediate effect of repeal was a split within the Conservative party. What was the point of a policy of free trade which allowed the silk industry of Lyons to destroy its rivals in Coventry, so that the cotton trade of Manchester could destroy its rivals in Rouen? Free trade would, the critics argued, sever the ties which held society together, undermining the values of landed society which led to stability and integrity. Industrialists, with their precarious capital, were selfish and unreliable; the landed gentry with their broad view of the national interest would foster stability. The old notions of landed virtue versus commercial corruption continued to inform the debate over trade policy. Free trade, commented the *Quarterly Review* in 1849,

is in its very essence a mercenary, unsocial, democratising system, opposed to all generous actions, all kindly feelings. Based on selfishness—the most pervading as well as the most powerful of our vicious propensities—it directs that impulse into the lowest of all channels, the mere sordid pursuit of wealth. It teaches competition and isolation, instead of co-operation and brotherhood; it substitutes a vague and impracticable cosmopolitanism for a lofty and enabling patriotism; it disregards the claims of the poor. ... Wealth is its end and Mammon its divinity.[18]

But the worst predictions were confounded. Agriculture remained prosperous as Peel had assumed; the standard of living of the working class rose and the worst alarms of the 1830s and 1840s receded; and British merchants and industrialists secured an unparalleled dominance of world trade. By the early 1850s, free trade was widely accepted as the linchpin of British prosperity and it was not challenged for another half-century.

The decision of Peel to repeal the corn laws was not the result of the pressure of the Anti-Corn Law League or the crisis of the famine in Ireland, which was the occasion rather than the explanation for his announcement. Rather, Peel was implementing the ministerial policy which had been devised in the 1820s by the government of Lord Liverpool, and which had continuities with the policies of Pitt and his attempt to foster an entrepôt trade. The timing of repeal after the delays of the 1830s may be explained by the political constraints on the actions of ministers, and the difficulties of reforming the fiscal system. But is this to say that he repeal of the corn laws and the coming of free trade were simply a matter of igh politics? One possible explanation of the repeal of the corn laws was that it eflected changing supply conditions in Europe. In the 1820s and 1830s there was a urplus of grain in Europe and prices were lower than in Britain; the corn laws herefore had a crucial role in preventing cheap corn from undermining British griculture. By the 1840s supply conditions had changed as a result of population rowth in Europe, and prices had converged with the British level so that the orn laws were no longer necessary to protect British agriculture. Changes in upply made it possible for Peel to repeal the corn laws with confidence that he vould not be endangering the landed interest, but it is too reductionist to explain he change in policy as a simple response to conditions in the grain market. The onversion of ministers such as Huskisson and Peel to freer trade *preceded* the lisappearance of the European surplus in the 1840s, and was based upon a policy •f making foreign grain an integral part of Britain's food supply. The basic oncern of ministers was a steady supply of food and a reasonable price in order o prevent famine and social unrest. By the early 1820s, ministers realized that a)olicy of autarky could no longer guarantee an adequate food supply, and they urned to a strategy of holding domestic production below the average level of lemand and importing the balance, which would offer a steady demand to :ncourage foreign producers. The reduction in the European grain surplus was a *hreat* to this strategy by throwing Britain back on domestic supplies.

Policy was influenced by the changing economic and social structure of 3ritain, largely through a concern for the supply of food and its connection with ocial unrest and the threat of famine. Ministers did not need the campaigns of he Anti-Corn Law League to convince them that Britain was an increasingly urban and industrial society, and that it was necessary to face the facts of :conomic and social change. 'If you had to constitute new societies', Peel nformed a correspondent in 1842, 'you might on moral or social grounds prefer :ornfields to cotton factories, an agricultural to a manufacturing population. But)ur lot is cast and we cannot recede.'[19] They were aware, above all, that)opulation growth might outstrip the supply of food, and that rising prices would provoke hardship and social unrest, which was changing from the food riots of the eighteenth century to trade unions and Chartism. What they had to decide was how to respond to these economic and social changes. One solution was to maintain a balance, ensuring that the growth of industry and population did not outstrip the ability of agriculture to provide food. The alternative was to accept that Britain could not feed itself, and to encourage specialization in trade and industry in order to purchase food from abroad. The propaganda of the Anti-Corn Law League, by threatening landed interests and alarming them with the prospects of repeal, might well have made it *more* difficult for ministers to introduce free trade.

The clash over protection was far more than a simple division of land versus trade and industry. Many industries and merchants clung tenaciously to protection. West Indian sugar-planters dreaded competition from lower-cost producers who would emerge with the equalization of duties on foreign and colonial sugar in 1846. The planters were already in difficulties as a result of the abolition of slavery, and many were in debt to London merchants, who feared a loss of their money. Sir John Rae Reid, a director of the Bank of England from 1820 to 1847 and a leading West Indian merchant, voted for the repeal of the corn laws but opposed the equalization of sugar duties: his firm was bankrupt in October 1847 for £1.5 million. Similarly, the East India Co. fought to preserve its profitable control of the tea trade to the East, which it lost in 1833. Free trade divided shipowners, for some stood to gain from the removal of restrictions and the extension of trade; others such as the great London shipowner Joseph Somes and the members of the General Shipowners' Society feared that competition from foreign owners and the diversion of trade into new channels would destroy their business. In the Commons, Alderman William Thompson defended the navigation laws, and was converted from a critic to a supporter of the corn laws in 1841. He was a leading figure in the City, where he was at some point Lord Mayor, member of parliament, alderman, director of the Bank of England, and chairman of Lloyd's, as well as owning a large ironworks in south Wales and serving as a director of several railway companies. Free trade had little attraction to City merchants and shipowners whose prosperity rested upon imperfect competition. 'The City', remarked an Anti-Corn Law League orator in 1840, 'are a heap of rascally monopolists themselves and they are somewhat fearful of loosening the wedge that holds all the rotten rubbish of corruption together.'[20] It was not so much that the commercial interests of the City made free trade; it was the adoption of free trade which helped to remake the City. Merchants and shipowners who had flourished in the world of imperfect competition were weakened in the commercial crisis of 1847, and firms with a commitment to free trade emerged. The world of the East India Co. gave way to new concerns such as Jardine Matheson which flourished in a new environment.

The Anti-Corn Law League attracted support, above all, from Lancashire and the cotton industry, which was heavily dependent on export markets and the purchase of raw material from foreign countries. The policy also appealed to industries such as iron, heavy engineering, and shipbuilding which were internationally competitive and export oriented. Free trade was, for them, a sound proposition which they could advocate from a dominant position in world trade. Their hegemony was, however, the result of protection and political

tervention to a greater extent than Cobden cared to admit. The cotton industry
ad developed within a system of protection against Asian textiles, and its
arkets in Asia were secured by Britain's ability to shape trade policy in India.
obden supported free trade as a means towards international peace and
nderstanding, as the benefits of comparative advantage increased prosperity; it
ould, he hoped, lead to a reduction in expenditure on the armed forces.
owever, British hegemony in trade and the liberal economy of the nineteenth
entury were political creations as a result of investment in war and empire in the
ighteenth and early nineteenth centuries. Free trade was, at least in part, the
esult of the success of the 'fiscal-military state'.

NOTES

1. Quoted in N. McCord, *Free Trade: Theory and Practice from Adam Smith to Keynes* (Newton Abbot, 1970), 73–4.

2. A. Smith, *An Inquiry into the Nature and Causes of the Wealth of Nations* (repr. 1937), 424 (book iv, ch. ii).

3. Ibid. 438 (book iv, ch. ii).

4. Ibid. 418 (book iv, ch. i).

5. J. M. Keynes, *The General Theory of Employment, Interest and Money* (1936), 333, 339.

6. L. Gomes, *Foreign Trade and the National Economy: Mercantilist and National Perspectives* (Basingstoke, 1987), 29.

7. Quoted in W. E. Clark, *Josiah Tucker, Economist: A Study in the History of Economics* (New York, 1903), 190.

8. P. J. Cain and A. G. Hopkins, *British Imperialism: Innovation and Expansion, 1688–1914* (1993), which is an expansion of 'Gentlemanly Capitalism and British Expansion Overseas, I: The Old Colonial System, 1688–1850', *Economic History Review*, 2nd ser. 39 (1986).

9. R. Blake, *The Conservative Party from Peel to Churchill* (1970), 15.

10. *The Works of T. R. Malthus*, vii: *Essays in Political Economy*, ed. E. A. Wrigley and D. Souden (1986), *The Grounds of an Opinion on the Policy of Restricting the Importation of Foreign Corn* (1815), 174.

11. B. Hilton, *Corn, Cash and Commerce: The Economic Policies of the Tory Governments, 1815–30* (Oxford, 1977), 21.

12. Ibid. 20.

13. Ibid. 156.

14. J. Blow Williams, *British Commercial Policy and Trade Expansion, 1750–1850* (Oxford, 1972), 458.

15. L. Brown, *The Board of Trade and the Free-Trade Movement, 1830–42* (1958), 9.

16. McCord, *Free Trade*, 84.

17. N. Gash, *Sir Robert Peel: The Life of Sir Robert Peel after 1830* (1972), 590.

18. R. Stewart, *The Politics of Protection: Lord Derby and the Protectionist Party, 1841–52* (Cambridge, 1971), 46.

19. L. J. Jennings (ed.), *The Correspondence and Diaries of J. W. Croker*, ii (1985), 381.
20. Quoted in A. C. Howe, 'Free Trade and the City of London, c.1820–1870', *History*, :
    (1992), 396.

FURTHER READING

Barnes, D. G., *A History of the English Corn Laws from 1660–1846* (1930).

Blake, R., *The Conservative Party from Peel to Churchill* (1970).

Blaug, M., 'Economic Theory and Economic History in Great Britain, 1650–1776', *Past an Present*, 28 (1964).

Brown, L., *The Board of Trade and the Free-Trade Movement, 1830–42* (Oxford, 1958).

Cain, P. J., and Hopkins, A. G., 'Gentlemanly Capitalism and British Overseas Expansion i: The Old Colonial System, 1688–1850', *Economic History Review*, 2nd ser. 39 (1986).

—— *British Imperialism: Innovation and Expansion, 1688–1914* (1993).

Coleman, D. C., 'Eli Heckscher and the Idea of Mercantilism', *Scandinavian Economi History Review*, 5 (1957).

Davis, R., 'The Rise of Protection in England, 1689–1786', *Economic History Review*, 2nd se 19 (1966).

—— *The Rise of the English Shipping Industry in the Seventeenth and Eighteenth Centurie* (1962).

Dickson, P. G. M., *The Financial Revolution in England: A Study in the Development of Publi Credit, 1688–1756* (1967).

Fairlie, S., 'The Nineteenth-Century Corn Law Reconsidered', *Economic History Review* 2nd ser. 18 (1965).

—— 'The Corn Laws and British Wheat Production, 1829–76', *Economic History Review* 2nd ser. 22 (1969).

Gash, N., *Sir Robert Peel: The Life of Sir Robert Peel after 1830* (2nd edn. 1986).

Gomes, L., *Foreign Trade and the National Economy: Mercantilist and Classical Perspective* (Basingstoke, 1987).

Grampp, W. D., 'The Liberal Elements in English Mercantilism', *Quarterly Journal o Economics* (1952).

—— 'How Britain Turned to Free Trade', *Business History Review*, 61 (1987).

Harper, L. A., *The English Navigation Laws: A Seventeenth-Century Experiment in Socia Engineering* (New York, 1939).

Harte, N. B., 'The Rise of Protection and the English Linen Trade, 1690–1790', in N. B Harte and K. G. Ponting (eds.), *Textile History and Economic History* (Manchester, 1973).

Hilton, B., *Corn, Cash and Commerce: The Economic Policies of the Tory Governments, 1815–30* (Oxford, 1977).

Howe, A. C., 'Free Trade and the City of London, c.1820–1870', *History*, 77 (1992).

McCord, N., *Free Trade: Theory and Practice from Adam Smith to Keynes* (Newton Abbot, 1970).

—— *The Anti-Corn Law League, 1838–46* (1958).

Macintyre, A. D., 'Lord George Bentinck and the Protectionists: A Lost Cause?', *Transactions of the Royal Historical Society*, 5th ser. 39 (1989).

O'Brien, P. K., Griffiths, T., and Hunt, P., 'Political Components of the Industrial Revolution: Parliament and the English Cotton Textile Industry, 1660–1774', *Economic History Review*, 2nd ser. 44 (1991).

Palmer, S., *Politics, Shipping and the Repeal of the Navigation Laws* (Manchester, 1990).

Smith, A., *An Inquiry into the Nature and Causes of the Wealth of Nations* (1776), ed. E. Cannan (1904; repr. in 1 vol. New York, 1937).

Stewart, R., *The Politics of Protection: Lord Derby and the Protectionist Party, 1841–52* (Cambridge, 1971).

Walton, G. M., 'The New Economic History and the Burdens of the Navigation Acts', *Economic History Review*, 2nd ser. 24 (1971).

Webster, A., 'The Political Economy of Trade Liberalisation: The East India Co. Charter Act of 1813', *Economic History Review*, 2nd ser. 43 (1990).

Williams, J. B., *British Commercial Policy and Trade Expansion, 1750–1850* (Oxford, 1972).

Wilson, C., 'Mercantilism: Some Vicissitudes of an Idea', *Economic History Review*, 2nd ser. 10 (1957–8).

——*Mercantilism* (1958).

....

CHAPTER 21

Conclusion

Many commentators in the 1840s were alarmed at the future prospects of Britain. In 1844, Engels confidently predicted the onset of revolution in *The Condition of the Working Class in England*. In the northern factory towns, argued Engels, the victory of machine work was creating an industrial proletariat which faced a wealthy group of factory owners. The population was 'reduced to the two opposing elements, workers and capitalists'.[1] The result, claimed Engels, was

the deep wrath of the whole working-class, from Glasgow to London, against the rich, by whom they are systematically plundered and mercilessly left to their fate, a wrath which before too long a time goes by, a time almost within the power of man to predict, must break out into a Revolution in comparison with which the French Revolution, and the year 1794, will prove to have been child's play.[2]

Engels was not alone in his prophecies. Disraeli, in his novel *Sybil; or, The Two Nations* (1845), expressed similar views. Queen Victoria, remarked one character, reigned over two nations rather than one:

Two nations; between whom there is no intercourse and no sympathy; who are as ignorant of each other's habits, thoughts, and feelings, as if they were dwellers in different zones, or inhabitants of different planets; who are formed by a different breeding, are fed by a different food, are ordered by different manners, and are not governed by the same laws ... THE RICH AND THE POOR.[3]

Engels looked forward to the onset of the revolution which would sweep away oppression, and his compatriot and collaborator Marx set about explaining the process by which capitalism would collapse through its internal contradictions. Disraeli, of course, had a different approach, urging that the gulf between rich and poor could and should be bridged by paternalism on the part of the ruling class in order to create one nation.

The fears of the 1840s were to dissolve in the 1850s, as British society moved to n 'age of equipoise' and stability. Engels's prophecy was disappointed, and Marx's analysis of the inevitable demise of capitalism was contradicted by events. Marxist historians were left with a problem: why did the revolution not happen? They turned to the notion of the 'labour aristocracy', the separation of an upper stratum of workers which was paid from the proceeds of large firms or the spoils of imperialism, to become 'the real agents of the bourgeoisie in the working-class movement'.[4] The concept has a number of problems. The extent of social polarization should not be exaggerated even in the largest and most 'advanced' factory towns, where there were many intermediate groups rather than a simple division into a small capitalist class and an industrial proletariat. Neither were 'labour aristocratic' groups of workers entirely the creation of capitalists eager to stabilize society after the alarms of the 1830s and 1840s. Many had a longer existence, such as the puddlers in the iron industry, where there was a clear technological base for their position as skilled workers. Indeed, employers in the 1830s and 1840s might well wish to *destroy* the bargaining position of powerful groups of workers, rather than to build them up as allies against the labouring class. This was certainly the case in the cotton industry, which was central to Engels's case. The problem faced by the owners of spinning mills in the 1820s was that male spinners were able to control the semi-automated mule spinning process. The ambition of the owners was to introduce fully automated machinery in order to displace the men and substitute cheaper and more amenable women. They failed, and the emergence—or, more accurately, survival—of the labour aristocracy in the cotton industry was not the result of manipulation by the employers. Rather, the 'minders' took control of the self-acting mules through their ability to organize, and to exploit the competitive divisions among the owners. The labour aristocracy was, at least in this case, created in opposition to the employers. Certainly, their institutions such as friendly societies or co-operative shops cannot simply be understood as succumbing to the embrace of the middle class; they could be seen as the development of distinctive working-class organizations which stressed their autonomy, and which relied upon collective insurance against hardship.[5]

The explanation for mid-century stabilization may more plausibly be found within the political analysis of Chartism, and in the changing nature of the state. Once the economy recovered, the political system could no longer be seen as the cause of oppression, and 'there was no independent rationale within radical ideology for antagonism towards the middle class as such'.[6] On this account, the emergence of a more stable society is to be explained by the failure of Chartism as a system of beliefs: the political system could, so it appeared by 1850, deliver increasing prosperity, which undermined the radical critique with nothing to put in its place. The governments did not make any direct concessions to Chartism, but the policies pursued by the Whig governments between 1830 and 1852 aimed to protect the welfare of the people, demonstrating that the state was responsible and considerate. The answer, in the eyes of men such as Lord Ashley, was to return to paternalism in order to protect workers against mill-owners through Factory Acts. By contrast, aristocratic Whigs such as Lord John Russell argued that their natural role was to govern at Westminster for the welfare of the people rather than narrow interests, and that they should ensure that the people would be 'cemented and bound up with the institutions and welfare of the country' through a policy of enlightened and popular intervention by the central government. Such an approach fitted the attitudes of the aristocratic Whigs, who operated on a national rather than local stage and were suspicious of local government. They concentrated on social reform: the introduction of state support for education in 1833; the Ten Hour Act in 1847; controls on employment in mines in 1842; and measures to improve public health. The strategy pursued by Peel was different in means but similar in outcome: rather than social reform, he adopted free trade with the abolition of the corn laws in 1846 and readjusted the tax burden away from consumption by reducing duties and through the reintroduction of income tax in 1842. The outcome was to sustain rather than challenge the institutions of the state, in order to convert the 'people to a belief in the neutrality of political institutions. The result of both strategies was that popular confidence in political institutions was restored.[8]

In 1845 Disraeli adopted a romantic Tory paternalism, on the lines of Ashley, and in 1846 he was instrumental in splitting the Tory party over the repeal of the corn laws. By the 1850s his attitude was changing as he came to accept that free trade was electorally expedient. His aim was to construct a more popular Conservatism which could not be viewed as special pleading for landed society. He offered social reform to the working class, including legal recognition of trade unions; and mobilized the appeal of patriotism around the empire and the queen. The Liberals, for their part, forged alliances with unions, temperance societies, Nonconformists, and friendly societies which mobilized behind the banner of retrenchment, self-determination, thrift, and independence. The result was very different from Germany, where unions were opposed by the state and the power of the elected Reichstag strictly limited. The British state, it seemed, was 'fair' rather than a means of oppression. The structure of the state, and the character of British political parties, had a significant role to play in stabilizing class society.

The process of stabilization also had a local dimension, by the action of the middle classes through 'associational voluntarism' of organizations such as poor relief funds, Mechanics Institutes, educational societies, hospitals, temperance societies, philosophical and literary societies, and so on. These societies played a dual role, in forging the identity of the middle class and negotiating relations with

he working class. The middle class was divided by religion, between Noncon-
ormists and Anglicans; by party, between Whigs and Tories; and by status,
ɛtween wealthy merchants, manufacturers, and tradesmen. The voluntary
ocieties helped these groups to work together in the 1830s and 1840s, containing
he divisions within the middle class in two ways. In the case of education, the
onflict between religious groups threatened the stability of the state, which
ɔreferred to leave the provision of schools for the workers to competing
Nonconformist and Anglican voluntary societies, to whom grants would be paid.
Although the societies were rivals, they took the same institutional form and
created a common pattern of behaviour for middle-class members; they had the
ame motivation of bargaining with the working class; and a highly divisive issue
was removed from the state. There was not only competition between two
ɔarallel sectarian groups, for voluntary societies also created a neutral arena by
excluding religion and politics, such as in the provision of hospitals. The
voluntary societies provided a means of overcoming the intense division of
religion and party within the middle class, as well as providing venues for
negotiation with the working class. Further, the middle class was led by its élite:
the merchants and professionals provided the officers for the societies whose
members were drawn from manufacturers and traders. Rather than the mercantile middle class merging with the landed aristocracy, it was providing leadership
for the urban middle class, and creating a civic culture within the industrial
towns. Although the public culture of the large industrial towns was shaped by
men who were often not directly involved in daily contact with waged labour,
they were well aware that prosperity rested upon the stabilization of relations
between capital and labour. They were not adopting an anti-industrial gentry
culture so much as overcoming fragmentation within the middle class. The
aristocracy was drawn into the process as patrons and supporters of voluntary
societies rather than by wielding the power of clientage; they were subscribing to
an ideology of respectability and responsibility which was not aristocratic in
origin. British society was being remade in the image of the middle class and the
voluntary society, 'inviting everyone, aristocrats and working class to join,
providing of course they obeyed the rules and paid their subscriptions'.[9]

The emergence of mid-Victorian social stability may also be explained by a
change in the character of the economy. Engels, Marx, and Disraeli were writing
at a time when the constraints of an organic economy, and the limits of a
Malthusian world, had not been fully loosened. By the early nineteenth century,
one part of the Malthusian system had stopped functioning: food prices no longer
rose as a result of an increase in the population, and there was greater confidence
by the 1830s that the economy could absorb more labour. In other respects, the
Malthusian system continued. The birth rate was still determined by the age of

marriage. The Malthusian system was finally rejected in the 1870s, when the ke determinant of the birth rate ceased to be the age of marriage and became th control of births within marriage. In the last quarter of the nineteenth century the standard of living of the working class improved at an unprecedented rate; a the same time, there was a significant fall in the birth rate. This demographi revolution was one of the most striking changes in the last century, marking fundamental break with the Malthusian world. It helped to remove the prospec of immiseration which Engels and Marx believed would fuel revolution.

The slackening of the pressure of population on resources initially came abou by removing the constraints of the organic economy, which preceded th slackening of population growth. Marx's model was based on Ricardo's notion c the labour theory of value and of rent: capitalists were expropriating the surplu value of labour beyond what the workers needed in order to live and reproduc their labour power; there was no outlet for accumulated profits, for the marke for goods was limited by the low standard of living of the proletariat; an capitalism was therefore doomed. Ricardo believed that the economy woul reach a stationary state as a result of the accumulation of rent in the hands o landowners; Marx believed that it would grind to a halt as a result of th accumulation of surplus value in the hands of capitalists, which would produce a revolution. Both predictions proved to be wrong, for they had not allowed fo the large gains in productivity which became possible with the application o mineral fuel and powered machinery. Improvements to productivity as a resul of specialization and division of labour were overwhelmed by the gains produce by the application of steam power to industry and to transport which made cheap food and raw materials available from the rest of the world.

Britain was at the peak of its comparative advantage in 1850, which wa symbolized by the Great Exhibition in the Crystal Palace and reflected in Britain's share of world trade in manufactures. Britain had a well-developed system of handicraft production, which rested upon abundant credit, and a favourable institutional environment. It was also the world's major user of steam power and producer of coal. In the next half-century, this comparative advantage was eroded as other countries—Belgium, Germany, and the United States— applied steam power to their industry. Britain's comparative advantage was whittled away, for it was relatively easy to transfer the technology of steam and coal to other countries; and it could be argued that the institutional structure which had been so well adapted to handicraft production and the early stages of factory development was increasingly inappropriate. Arguably, a gap was open- ing up between the production *institutions* which were developed in Britain— small family firms, a reliance on subcontracting between and within firms, a highly formalized system of collective bargaining—and the needs of production

echnology. By the end of the nineteenth century there was a new mood of
anxiety, which was reflected in political debate. The rise of foreign competition
ed some to doubt the value of free trade, and to urge the return of protection.
There was deep unease that the slower rate of population growth was a source of
weakness, particularly because the birth rate of the middle class and 'respectable'
workers was lower than that of the poor. The result, it was feared by some
commentators, would be a deterioration in the racial stock and degeneration.
Others shared the concern, but felt that the consequences could be overcome by
improvement in the environment, health, and education in order to increase
efficiency and productivity. Perhaps the experience of Germany and America
showed the virtues of improved technical education and the application of
science to industry, which led some politicians to urge a reform of the education
system, which was strongly opposed by others who stressed the value of a liberal,
non-vocational education. Until 1914, these debates took place from a position of
strength, for Britain was still highly prosperous, with a dominant role in world
trade in manufactures and financial markets. After the First World War, there
were far deeper problems: the position of London was challenged by the rise of
New York, the world economy on which Britain was so dependent was unstable,
the staple industries of coal, cotton, and shipbuilding were in decline, and the
costs of defending the extended British empire were straining the domestic
economy.

NOTES

1. F. Engels, *The Condition of the Working Class in England*, ed. with an introd. by E. J. Hobsbawm (1969), 51.
2. Ibid. 53.
3. B. Disraeli, *Sybil; or, The Two Nations* (1845), 76–7.
4. V. I. Lenin, *Imperialism: The Highest Stage of Capitalism*, preface to the French and German edns. (Peking edn., 1975), 9–10.
5. See Ch. 8.
6. G. Stedman Jones, *Languages of Class: Studies in English Working-Class History, 1832–1982* (Cambridge, 1983), 107.
7. The comment of Lord John Russell, quoted in P. Mandler, *Aristocratic Government in the Age of Reform: Whigs and Liberals, 1830–52* (Oxford, 1990), 41.
8. On this, see E. Biagini, *Liberty, Retrenchment and Reform: Popular Liberalism in the Age of Gladstone, 1860–80* (Cambridge, 1992); and R. McKibbin, 'Why Was there no Marxism in Great Britain?', in his *The Ideologies of Class: Social Relations in Britain 1880–1950* (Oxford, 1990).
9. R. J. Morris, *Class, Sect and Party: The Making of the British Middle Class: Leeds, 1780–1850* (Manchester, 1990), 331.

FURTHER READING

Biagini, E., *Liberty, Retrenchment and Reform: Popular Liberalism in the Age of Gladstone* *1860–80* (Cambridge, 1992).

Engels, F., *The Condition of the Working Class in England*, ed. with introd. by E. J. Hobsbawm (1969).

Foster, J., 'Nineteenth-Century Towns: A Class Dimension', in H. J. Dyos (ed.), *The Study of Urban History* (1971).

—— *Class Struggle and the Industrial Revolution: Early Industrial Capitalism in Three English Towns* (1974).

Koditschek, T., *Class Formation and Urban Industrial Society: Bradford, 1750–1850* (Cambridge, 1990).

Lenin, V. I., *Imperialism, the Highest Stage of Capitalism* (Peking edn., 1975).

McKibbin, R., 'Why Was there no Marxism in Great Britain?', in *The Ideologies of Class: Social Relations in Britain, 1880–1950* (Oxford, 1990).

Mandler, P., *Aristocratic Governments in the Age of Reform: Whigs and Liberals, 1830–52* (Oxford, 1990).

Morris, R. J., *Class, Sect and Party: The Making of the British Middle Class, Leeds, 1780–1850* (Manchester, 1990).

—— 'Voluntary Societies and British Urban Elites, 1780–1850: An Analysis', *Historical Journal*, 26 (1983).

Stedman Jones, G. S., *Languages of Class: Studies in English Working-Class History, 1832–1982* (Cambridge, 1983).

CHRONOLOGY

1651		Navigation Act
1662		JPs given powers to raise rates for roads
		Settlement Act
1663		abolition of controls on internal grain trade
		first turnpike
1670		corn law
1673		bounty on corn exports
1689	William and Mary Nine Years War starts	export bounty on corn
1694		Bank of England formed
1695		Bank of Scotland Commonty and Runrig Acts
1697	Nine Years War ends	civil list extension of settlement certificates Scottish famine (also 1698 and 1699)
1698		Savery's patent for a steam engine land tax London Corporation of the Poor
1701		ban on import of silk cloth, printed and dyed calico
1702	Anne; War of Spanish Succession starts	
1706		honest bankrupts protected
1707	Act of Union between England and Scotland	
1708		six-partner rule in English banks United East India Company
1709		Abraham Darby smelted iron with coke
1710		Sun Fire formed
1712		Thomas Newcomen's steam engine
1713	War of Spanish Succession ends	Collapse of Corporation of the Poor

1714	George I	
1715	Jacobite rebellion	first enclosed dock at Liverpool
1716	septennial parliaments	
1717		sinking fund
1718		transportation regularized
		Thomas Lombe's silk mill, Derby
1720		South Sea Bubble
		Bubble Act imposed limits on joint-stock companies
		Westminster Hospital formed
		Royal Exchange Assurance formed (marine insurance)
1721		Calico Act banned wearing of, calico
1722		Workhouse Test Act (and 1723)
1723		'Black Act' against poaching etc.
1725		first improvement commission in London
1726		Grand Alliance in the coal trade
1727	George II	Royal Bank of Scotland
1733		Kay's flying shuttle
		excise crisis
1739	War of Jenkins's Ear	
1740	War of Austrian Succession starts	Foundling and London Hospitals formed
1745	Jacobite rebellion	
1748	War of Austrian Succession ends	
1749		embezzlement defined as criminal
1754		start of construction of Sankey navigation
1756	Seven Years War starts	food riots (and 1757)
1757		Sankey navigation completed
1759		Act for construction of Bridgewater canal
		Wedgwood's Burslem pottery
1760	George III	
1761		Bridgewater canal opens
1762		Westminster Paving Commission
1763	Seven Years War ends	
1765		free note issue maintained in Scotland

1766		food riots (and 1767)
		Soho ironworks, Birmingham
1769		patents on Hargreaves's spinning-jenny; Watt's separate condenser; Arkwright's water-frame
		Wedgwood's Etruria factory
1772		repeal of legislation on forestalling
		Staffordshire and Worcestershire canal linked the Severn and Mersey
1773		New Stock Exchange
		revised corn law
		Spitalfields Act regulated wages in silk
1775	War of American Independence starts	English bank notes to be at least £1
		Boulton and Watt partnership
		start of abolition of colliery serfdom
1776		publication of Adam Smith's *Wealth of Nations*
1777		Worsted Act: inspectors to check on removal of materials
		English bank notes to be at least £5
1779	Wyvill's Association	Penitentiary Act
1780		patent for crankshaft in steam engine
		Commission for Examining the Public Accounts
		Samuel Crompton's 'mule'
1781		Watt's patent for sun and planet gear
1782		Gilbert's Act permitting Unions of parishes
1783	War of American Independence ends	Henry Cort's patent on puddling (also 1784)
1784		first mail coach from London to Bristol
		Watt's patent for parallel motion
		Cartwright's power loom (patented 1786)
1785		General Chamber of Manufactures
		Society for the Support and Encouragement of Sunday Schools
		Arkwright's patent overturned
1786		old sinking fund
		commercial treaty with France
1787		transportation to Australia
		Proclamation Society
1791		revised corn law
		ordnance survey
1792		new sinking fund
1793	French revolutionary war starts	

1795		food riots
		Speenhamland scale
		end of distinction between certificated
		and uncertificated poor
1797		suspension of convertibility
		£1 bank notes permitted
1798		publication of Malthus's *Essay on Population*
		revision of assessed taxes as a form of income tax
1799		income tax introduced
		West India Dock Act
		Combination Act (and 1800)
1800		Parish Relief Act: parishes to acquire food stocks
		Trevithick's high-pressure steam engine
		food riots (and 1801)
1801	Union with Ireland	first census
1802	French revolutionary	Patriotic Fund
	war ends	opening of first stage of West India dock
1803	Napoleonic war starts	Warehousing Act
		East India Dock Act
1804		revised corn law
		Trevithick's locomotive
1806		opening of East India dock
1807		Society for the Suppression of Vice
1810		first Scottish joint-stock bank
1811		Luddism (and 1812)
1812	war with USA	cotton weavers' petition for wage assessment
		Gas Light and Coke Co. formed in London
1813		abolition of East India Co. monopoly in Indian trade
		repeal of wage clauses of statute of artificers
		York asylum opened
		Horrock's power loom
1814		repeal of statute of artificers
1815	Napoleonic wars end	corn law
1816		income tax expires
		safety lamps in mines
1817		publication of Ricardo's *Principles*
		issue of tokens made illegal
1818		Sturges Bourne Act for select vestries (and 1819)

1819		resumption agreed
		Peterloo massacre
1820	George IV	Queen Caroline affair
		petition of London merchants
		Rainhill trials for locomotives
1821		resumption of convertibility
1822		revision of navigation laws
		patent on Roberts's power loom
1823		Gaols Act
		Reciprocity of Duties Act
1824		common standard of weights and measures
		repeal of Combination Acts against trade unions
1825		first patent on Roberts's self-acting mule
		Stockton–Darlington railway
		financial mania: Latin American loans
		penalties imposed on anyone using threats to promote strikes or enforce union membership
1826		financial panic
		ban on bank notes below £5 in England
		joint-stock banks permitted outside a 65-mile radius of London
		Metropolis Roads Act
1829		Catholic emancipation
		Metropolitan Police
1830	William IV	completion of self-acting mule
		Swing riots
		Manchester–Liverpool railway
1831		arrival of cholera (epidemic 1832)
		Truck Act prohibited payment of wages in goods
1832	Reform Act	defeat of north-east miners' strike
1833		joint-stock banks permitted in London
		end of East India Co.'s monopoly in tea
		Coercion Act
		state support for education
		Factory Act prohibited employment of children under 9 in factories and restricted children aged 9 to 13 to 48 hours a week
1834		slavery abolished in the empire
		Tolpuddle martyrs transported
		Grand National Consolidated Trade Union formed
		'new' poor law

1835	Municipal Corporations Act
1836	railway mania (and 1837)
1837 Victoria	
1838	Anti-Corn Law League People's Charter
1840	Penny Post
1842	restoration of income tax Coalmines Act Pentonville prison opened
1844	Rochdale pioneers (co-operative society) Bank Charter Act registration of unincorporated societies miner's strike broken Factory Act limited children under 13 to 6½ hours a day and women and persons under 18 to 12 hours railway mania (and 1845–6)
1845	controls on Scottish banks final collapse of Limitation of the Vend McNaught's patent on compounding
1846	repeal of the corn laws
1847	Ten Hour Act imposed a 10-hour day for women and children in factories
1848	cholera (and 1849) Public Health Act
1849	repeal of the navigation laws
1851	Great Exhibition
1852	Industrial and Provident Societies Act
1855	introduction of limited liability

STATISTICAL APPENDIX

I. POPULATION

*(a) Quinquennial totals of births and deaths, England,
1650–1654 to 1845–1849*

	Births	Deaths	Natural increase
1650–4	722,863	657,292	+65,571
1655–9	722,100	756,613	−34,513
1660–4	725,134	662,715	+62,419
1665–9	757,619	822,664	−65,045
1670–4	734,112	705,561	+28,551
1675–9	737,001	729,525	+7,476
1680–4	762,127	851,065	−88,938
1685–9	802,180	750,580	+51,600
1690–4	758,591	705,579	+53,012
1695–9	799,681	708,393	+91,288
1700–4	846,128	670,076	+176,052
1705–9	792,543	706,666	+85,877
1710–14	766,531	727,826	+38,705
1715–19	866,106	716,736	+149,370
1720–4	886,596	831,009	+55,587
1725–9	867,767	936,734	−68,967
1730–4	933,746	821,067	+112,679
1735–9	971,105	769,099	+202,006
1740–4	906,323	866,795	+39,528
1745–9	942,251	774,822	+167,429
1750–4	986,021	752,181	+233,840
1755–9	989,242	792,215	+197,027
1760–4	1,054,513	884,810	+169,703
1765–9	1,084,216	885,479	+198,737
1770–4	1,160,571	880,876	+279,695
1775–9	1,248,719	889,260	+359,459
1780–4	1,249,260	1,023,918	+225,342
1785–9	1,403,446	975,264	+428,182

1790–4	1,533,071	1,037,722	+495,349
1795–9	1,601,298	1,089,716	+511,582
1800–4	1,686,800	1,180,010	+506,790
1805–9	1,876,520	1,163,298	+713,222
1810–14	1,995,505	1,293,635	+701,870
1815–19	2,263,182	1,368,617	+894,565
1820–4	2,375,157	1,398,994	+976,163
1825–9	2,395,181	1,447,103	+948,078
1830–4	2,401,836	1,482,274	+919,562
1835–9	2,544,581	1,591,372	+953,209
1840–4	2,709,272	1,681,559	+1,027,713
1845–9	2,804,848	1,902,153	+902,695

Source: E. A. Wrigley and R. S. Schofield, *The Population History of England, 1541–1871: A Reconstruction* (1981), 177, 495.

(b) *Quinquennial English population totals and annual growth rates, 1651–1851*

	Population	Compound growth (% p.a.)		Population	Compound growth (% p.a.)
1651	5,228,481	0.20	1756	5,993,415	0.75
1656	5,281,347	0.20	1761	6,146,857	0.51
1661	5,140,743	−0.54	1766	6,277,076	0.42
1666	5,067,047	−0.29	1771	6,447,813	0.54
1671	4,982,687	−0.34	1776	6,740,370	0.89
1676	5,003,488	0.08	1781	7,042,140	0.88
1681	4,930,385	−0.29	1786	7,289,039	0.69
1686	4,864,762	−0.27	1791	7,739,889	1.21
1691	4,930,502	0.27	1796	8,198,445	1.16
1696	4,961,692	0.13	1801	8,664,490	1.11
1701	5,057,790	0.38	1806	9,267,570	1.35
1706	5,182,007	0.49	1811	9,885,690	1.30
1711	5,230,371	0.19	1816	10,651,629	1.50
1716	5,275,978	0.17	1821	11,491,850	1.53
1721	5,350,465	0.28	1826	12,410,995	1.55
1726	5,449,957	0.37	1831	13,283,882	1.37
1731	5,263,374	−0.69	1836	14,105,979	1.21
1736	5,450,392	0.70	1841	14,970,372	1.20
1741	5,576,197	0.46	1846	15,933,803	1.26
1746	5,634,781	0.21	1851	16,736,084	0.99
1751	5,772,415	0.48			

Source: Wrigley and Schofield, *Population History of England*, table 7.8, 208–9.

(*c*) *Gross reproduction rate (GRR) and life expectancy at birth, England, 1651–1851* (five-year periods centred on the year indicated)

	GRR	Expectancy		GRR	Expectancy
1651	1.85	37.8	1756	2.32	37.3
1656	2.01	34.1	1761	2.37	34.2
1661	1.81	35.7	1766	2.39	35.0
1666	1.98	31.8	1771	2.50	35.6
1671	1.90	33.2	1776	2.53	38.2
1676	1.91	36.4	1781	2.49	34.7
1681	1.94	28.5	1786	2.62	35.9
1686	2.17	31.8	1791	2.77	37.3
1691	2.16	34.9	1796	2.76	36.8
1696	2.18	34.1	1801	2.69	35.9
1701	2.34	37.1	1806	2.93	38.7
1706	2.25	36.4	1811	2.87	37.6
1711	2.05	35.9	1816	3.06	37.9
1716	2.25	37.1	1821	2.98	39.2
1721	2.27	32.5	1826	2.86	39.9
1726	2.21	32.4	1831	2.59	40.8
1731	2.20	27.9	1836	2.53	40.2
1736	2.37	35.6	1841	2.49	40.3
1741	2.22	31.7	1846	2.37	39.6
1746	2.27	35.3	1851	2.40	39.5
1751	2.34	36.6			

Source: Wrigley and Schofield, *Population History of England*, 230.

(*d*) *Proportion of people never marrying per 1,000 aged 40–44, England, 1651–1851*

	Proportion never marrying		Proportion never marrying
1651	236	1691	270
1656	214	1696	267
1661	188	1701	249
1666	171	1706	230
1671	181	1711	191
1676	208	1716	185
1681	241	1721	176
1686	270	1726	147

1731	128		1796	52
1736	131		1801	68
1741	112		1806	72
1746	96		1811	65
1751	107		1816	63
1756	107		1821	71
1761	73		1826	78
1766	86		1831	75
1771	77		1836	82
1776	46		1841	96
1781	36		1846	102
1786	62		1851	110
1791	49			

Note: Data refer to the year each cohort was aged 40–44.

Source: Wrigley and Schofield, *Population History of England*, 260.

(e) London Bills of Mortality: annual averages of recorded events per decade

Decade beginning	Burials	Baptisms	Burials surplus (%)
1670	19,000	12,200	35.8
1680	22,400	14,200	36.6
1690	21,000	15,000	28.6
1700	21,000	15,600	25.7
1710	23,800	16,900	29.0
1720	27,400	18,200	33.6
1730	26,100	17,000	34.9
1740	26,100	14,500	44.4
1750	20,800	14,800	28.8
1760	23,200	16,000	31.0
1770	21,700	17,300	20.3
1780	19,500	17,700	9.2
1790	19,200	18,700	2.6
1800	18,900	19,900	−5.3
1810	19,100	22,100	−15.7
1820	20,700	27,700	−33.8

Source: J. Landers, 'Mortality and Metropolis: The Case of London, 1675–1825', *Population Studies*, 41 (1987), table 1, 63.

2. PRICES

a) *Price of wheat, in shillings per Winchester quarter, at Winchester College,
1690–1817*

	Price of wheat			Price of wheat			Price of wheat
1690	23.40		1727	44.37		1764	39.12
1691	37.18		1728	44.22		1765	38.35
1692	45.92		1729	30.22		1766	51.60
1693	57.67		1730	26.96		1767	51.46
1694	34.59		1731	22.74		1768	40.72
1695	53.98		1732	22.94		1769	35.00
1696	49.24		1733	24.68		1770	43.37
1697	56.74		1734	31.10		1771	49.79
1698	55.55		1735	33.19		1772	54.94
1699	37.53		1736	26.91		1773	49.37
1700	32.59		1737	25.94		1774	56.34
1701	24.87		1738	26.50		1775	37.37
1702	26.52		1739	36.39		1776	40.79
1703	38.49		1740	50.20		1777	46.54
1704	26.52		1741	26.64		1778	34.62
1705	22.29		1742	20.92		1779	34.34
1706	23.03		1743	18.13		1780	49.78
1707	26.91		1744	18.55		1781	48.07
1708	48.36		1745	26.22		1782	51.73
1709	69.52		1746	28.03		1783	48.59
1710	44.98		1747	26.98		1784	44.45
1711	40.81		1748	28.58		1785	39.56
1712	35.26		1749	26.78		1786	39.42
1713	48.89		1750	27.61		1787	46.76
1714	31.11		1751	34.93		1788	48.13
1715	43.56		1752	34.59		1789	56.48
1716	38.07		1753	33.19		1790	52.33
1717	34.96		1754	25.94		1791	42.22
1718	25.04		1755	30.40		1792	51.85
1719	31.55		1756	49.92		1793	51.17
1720	31.55		1757	42.12		1794	63.08
1721	25.81		1758	31.24		1795	99.83
1722	28.77		1759	29.00		1796	57.25
1723	27.99		1760	28.50		1797	64.75
1724	36.15		1761	28.59		1798	56.83
1725	38.07		1762	30.54		1799	112.00
1726	29.55		1763	37.93		1800	148.50

1801	83.75	1807	76.50	1813	84.08
1802	61.75	1808	96.00	1814	75.00
1803	57.04	1809	119.00	1815	69.00
1804	100.50	1810	104.50	1816	122.00
1805	82.50	1811	134.50	1817	96.00
1806	86.21	1812	128.25		

Source: W. Beveridge *et al., Prices and Wages in England* (1939), i. 81–4.

(b) *Average price of domestic wheat per imperial quarter, England and Wales,*
1771–1850

	Price of wheat		Price of wheat		Price of wheat
1771	48s. 7d.	1798	51s. 10d.	1825	68s. 6d.
1772	52s. 3d.	1799	69s. 0d.	1826	58s. 8d.
1773	52s. 7d.	1800	113s. 10d.	1827	58s. 6d.
1774	54s. 3d.	1801	119s. 6d.	1828	60s. 5d.
1775	49s. 10d.	1802	69s. 10d.	1829	66s. 3d.
1776	39s. 4d.	1803	58s. 10d.	1830	64s. 3d.
1777	46s. 11d.	1804	62s. 3d.	1831	66s. 4d.
1778	43s. 3d.	1805	89s. 9d.	1832	58s. 8d.
1779	34s. 8d.	1806	79s. 1d.	1833	52s. 11d.
1780	36s. 9d.	1807	75s. 4d.	1834	46s. 2d.
1781	46s. 0d.	1808	81s. 4d.	1835	39s. 4d.
1782	49s. 3d.	1809	97s. 4d.	1836	48s. 6d.
1783	54s. 3d.	1810	106s. 5d.	1837	55s. 10d.
1784	50s. 4d.	1811	95s. 3d.	1838	64s. 7d.
1785	43s. 1d.	1812	126s. 6d.	1839	70s. 8d.
1786	40s. 0d.	1813	109s. 9d.	1840	66s. 4d.
1787	42s. 5d.	1814	74s. 4d.	1841	64s. 4d.
1788	46s. 4d.	1815	65s. 7d.	1842	57s. 3d.
1789	52s. 9d.	1816	78s. 6d.	1843	50s. 1d.
1790	54s. 9d.	1817	96s. 11d.	1844	51s. 3d.
1791	48s. 7d.	1818	86s. 3d.	1845	50s. 10d.
1792	43s. 0d.	1819	74s. 6d.	1846	54s. 8d.
1793	49s. 3d.	1820	67s. 10d.	1847	69s. 9d.
1794	52s. 3d.	1821	56s. 1d.	1848	50s. 6d.
1795	75s. 2d.	1822	44s. 7d.	1849	44s. 3d.
1796	78s. 7d.	1823	53s. 4d.	1850	40s. 3d.
1797	53s. 9d.	1824	63s. 11d.		

Source: B. R. Mitchell, *British Historical Statistics* (1988), 756.

(c) *Schumpeter–Gilboy price index, 1696–1823: consumers' goods* (1701 = 100)

	Price index		Price index		Price index
1696	121	1735	89	1774	116
1697	122	1736	87	1775	113
1698	128	1737	93	1776	114
1699	132	1738	91	1777	108
1700	115	1739	89	1778	117
1701	100	1740	100	1779	111
1702	99	1741	108	1780	110
1703	94	1742	99	1781	115
1704	98	1743	94	1782	116
1705	89	1744	84	1783	129
1706	101	1745	85	1784	126
1707	88	1746	93	1785	120
1708	92	1747	90	1786	119
1709	107	1748	94	1787	117
1710	122	1749	96	1788	121
1711	135	1750	95	1789	117
1712	101	1751	90	1790	124
1713	97	1752	93	1791	121
1714	103	1753	90	1792	122
1715	104	1754	90	1793	129
1716	99	1755	92	1794	136
1717	95	1756	92	1795	147
1718	93	1757	109	1796	154
1719	97	1758	106	1797	148
1720	102	1759	100	1798	148
1721	100	1760	98	1799	160
1722	92	1761	94	1800	212
1723	89	1762	94	1801	228
1724	94	1763	100	1802	174
1725	97	1764	102	1803	156
1726	102	1765	106	1804	161
1727	96	1766	107	1805	187
1728	99	1767	109	1806	184
1729	104	1768	108	1807	186
1730	95	1769	99	1808	204
1731	88	1770	100	1809	212
1732	89	1771	107	1810	207
1733	85	1772	117	1811	206
1734	88	1773	119	1812	237

1813	243	1817	189	1821	139
1814	209	1818	194	1822	125
1815	191	1819	192	1823	128
1816	172	1820	162		

Source: Mitchell, *British Historical Statistics*, 719–20.

(*d*) *Gayer–Rostow–Schwartz index of British commodity prices (domestic and imported), 1790–1850*

	Price index		Price index		Price index
1790	89.3	1811	145.4	1832	91.5
1791	89.7	1812	163.7	1833	88.6
1792	88.1	1813	168.9	1834	86.5
1793	96.6	1814	153.7	1835	84.5
1794	98.5	1815	129.9	1836	95.2
1795	114.9	1816	118.6	1837	94.3
1796	116.1	1817	131.9	1838	97.8
1797	106.2	1818	138.7	1839	104.3
1798	107.9	1819	128.1	1840	102.5
1799	124.6	1820	115.4	1841	97.7
1800	151.0	1821	99.7	1842	88.8
1801	155.7	1822	87.9	1843	79.7
1802	122.2	1823	97.6	1844	81.1
1803	123.6	1824	101.9	1845	83.3
1804	124.3	1825	113.0	1846	86.0
1805	136.2	1826	100.0	1847	96.8
1806	134.5	1827	99.3	1848	81.8
1807	131.2	1828	96.4	1849	73.9
1808	144.5	1829	95.8	1850	73.5
1809	155.0	1830	94.5		
1810	153.4	1831	95.3		

Source: Mitchell, *British Historical Statistics*, 721.

e) *Index of coal prices, England 1700–1830 (1770–9 = 100)*

	Price index		Price index		Price index
700	74.8	1740	87.4	1780	108.5
701	85.8	1741	85.7	1781	111.5
702	98.2	1742	85.0	1782	101.7
703	94.9	1743	89.6	1783	94.3
704	92.1	1744	89.2	1784	100.7
705	83.7	1745	90.1	1785	100.9
706	78.7	1746	88.2	1786	99.0
707	88.1	1747	86.0	1787	99.7
708	91.1	1748	84.6	1788	98.2
709	91.7	1749	82.9	1789	104.7
710	91.8	1750	80.9	1790	105.5
1711	77.1	1751	83.2	1791	106.5
1712	77.9	1752	84.9	1792	110.6
1713	78.7	1753	85.0	1793	115.2
1714	77.3	1754	92.3	1794	123.7
1715	74.4	1755	102.5	1795	108.8
1716	79.1	1756	104.3	1796	107.3
1717	82.2	1757	101.0	1797	108.9
1718	83.3	1758	100.6	1798	128.1
1719	81.1	1759	97.8	1799	136.5
1720	80.2	1760	99.4	1800	122.6
1721	78.1	1761	100.7	1801	121.1
1722	77.1	1762	96.9	1802	128.6
1723	76.9	1763	99.6	1803	138.6
1724	78.1	1764	99.1	1804	142.4
1725	80.6	1765	92.3	1805	146.2
1726	79.0	1766	91.0	1806	145.4
1727	77.4	1767	90.3	1807	148.1
1728	81.5	1768	89.5	1808	151.3
1729	78.5	1769	91.3	1809	167.7
1730	84.7	1770	98.5	1810	152.9
1731	79.0	1771	98.8	1811	162.6
1732	79.3	1772	93.0	1812	159.3
1733	80.2	1773	91.5	1813	171.9
1734	78.6	1774	93.8	1814	172.6
1735	79.5	1775	100.9	1815	158.0
1736	78.2	1776	103.5	1816	146.1
1737	80.1	1777	107.1	1817	143.6
1738	80.4	1778	106.4	1818	141.0
1739	93.1	1779	109.4	1819	138.7

1820	140.3	1824	136.9	1828	131.6
1821	141.7	1825	131.7	1829	127.0
1822	139.1	1826	125.6	1830	127.5
1823	141.6	1827	129.3		

Source: M. W. Flinn, *The History of the British Coal Industry*, ii: *The Industrial Revolution* (Oxford, 1984), table 9.4.

(*f*) *Terms of trade between agriculture and industry, 1690–1820*

	Agricultural prices/ industrial prices		Agricultural prices/ industrial prices		Agricultural prices/ industrial prices
1690	99	1719	102	1748	107
1691	105	1720	99	1749	106
1692	124	1721	90	1750	104
1693	135	1722	88	1751	112
1694	113	1723	90	1752	107
1695	124	1724	92	1753	106
1696	113	1725	100	1754	99
1697	123	1726	95	1755	103
1698	128	1727	108	1756	126
1699	117	1728	115	1757	126
1700	100	1729	105	1758	112
1701	96	1730	101	1759	102
1702	86	1731	91	1760	102
1703	93	1732	88	1761	100
1704	94	1733	92	1762	109
1705	93	1734	97	1763	120
1706	87	1735	100	1764	124
1707	92	1736	97	1765	127
1708	110	1737	96	1766	134
1709	138	1738	94	1767	140
1710	120	1739	103	1768	122
1711	109	1740	122	1769	117
1712	103	1741	104	1770	131
1713	113	1742	96	1771	139
1714	100	1743	87	1772	144
1715	103	1744	92	1773	145
1716	106	1745	95	1774	146
1717	99	1746	100	1775	133
1718	99	1747	98	1776	125

777	129	1792	149	1807	174
778	116	1793	146	1808	180
779	111	1794	161	1809	165
780	120	1795	188	1810	179
781	118	1796	162	1811	184
782	137	1797	160	1812	204
783	131	1798	152	1813	167
784	128	1799	206	1814	154
785	133	1800	212	1815	141
786	121	1801	178	1816	161
787	144	1802	150	1817	153
788	142	1803	150	1818	169
789	151	1804	133	1819	141
790	150	1805	166	1820	132
791	134	1806	165		

Source: P. K. O'Brien, 'Agriculture and the Home Market for English Industry, 1660–1820', *English Historical Review*, 100 (1985), app. A.

3. OUTPUT

(a) *Trade in wheat and wheaten flour, Great Britain, 1697–1842: net import (−) and net export (+)* (thousands of quarters)

	Net import/export		Net import/export		Net import/export
1697	+15	1707	+174	1717	+26
1698	+5	1708	+84	1718	+74
1699	+1	1709	+70	1719	+131
1700	+49	1710	+17	1720	+84
1701	+98	1711	+81	1721	+83
1702	+90	1712	+149	1722	+179
1703	+107	1713	+180	1723	+158
1704	+90	1714	+181	1724	+247
1705	+96	1715	+173	1725	+211
1706	+188	1716	+76	1726	+144

1727	+31	1766	+154	1805	−843
1728	−71	1767	−493	1806	−280
1729	−21	1768	−342	1807	−380
1730	+95	1769	+46	1808	+13
1731	+131	1770	+75	1809	−425
1732	+203	1771	+7	1810	−1,491
1733	+427	1772	−18	1811	−238
1734	+499	1773	−49	1812	−245
1735	+155	1774	−273	1813	−559
1736	+118	1775	−470	1814	−742
1737	+466	1776	+190	1815	−156
1738	+588	1777	−145	1816	−210
1739	+285	1778	+35	1817	−772
1740	+49	1779	+217	1818	−1,635
1741	+37	1780	+220	1819	−581
1742	+296	1781	−57	1820	−901
1743	+376	1782	+64	1821	−507
1744	+234	1783	−532	1822	−351
1745	+325	1784	−128	1823	−278
1746	+131	1785	+22	1824	−380
1747	+270	1786	+154	1825	−749
1748	+545	1787	+62	1826	−877
1749	+631	1788	−66	1827	−655
1750	+950	1789	+27	1828	−1,334
1751	+663	1790	−192	1829	−2,115
1752	+430	1791	−398	1830	−2,169
1753	+301	1792	+278	1831	−2,802
1754	+357	1793	−413	1832	−964
1755	+237	1794	−173	1833	−1,070
1756	+103	1795	−295	1834	−822
1757	−130	1796	−854	1835	−617
1758	−11	1797	−407	1836	−604
1759	+228	1798	−337	1837	−801
1760	+394	1799	−424	1838	−1,764
1761	+442	1800	−1,243	1839	−3,068
1762	+295	1801	−1,397	1840	−2,440
1763	+430	1802	−499	1841	−2,880
1764	+397	1803	−297	1842	−3,043
1765	−598	1804	−398		

Source: Calculated from Mitchell, *British Historical Statistics*, 221.

b) Coal output, Britain, 1700 to 1850–1854

	Thousands of tons		Quinquennial averages, millions of tons
1700	2,985	1830–4	32.0
1750	5,230	1835–9	37.8
1775	8,850	1840–4	44.7
1800	15,045	1845–9	55.9
1815	22,265	1850–4	68.4
1830	30.861		

Source: Flinn, *History of the British Coal Industry,* ii, table 1.2, and R. A. Church, *History of the British Coal Industry,* iii (1986), table 1.1.

c) Pig iron output, 1720–1724 to 1850 (in thousands of tons)

	Output (000 tons)		Output (000 tons)		Output (000 tons)
1720–4	27	1801	200	1826	520
1725–9	29	1802	220	1827	690
1730–4	28	1803	230	1828	700
1735–9	27	1804	240	1829	690
1740–4	26	1805	250	1830	680
1745–9	27	1806	270	1831	600
1750–4	28	1807	290	1832	630
1755–9	31	1808	300	1833	780
1760–4	34	1809	350	1834	790
1765–9	40	1810	400	1835	930
1770–4	40	1811	360	1836	970
1775–9	48	1812	360	1837	1,030
1780–4	62	1813	370	1838	1,120
1785–9	80	1814	400	1839	1,250
1790	90	1815	340	1840	1,400
1791	100	1816	270	1841	1,330
1792	100	1817	260	1842	1,080
1793	110	1818	280	1843	1,220
1794	110	1819	280	1844	1,560
1795	120	1820	320	1845	2,200
1796	120	1821	390	1846	2,210
1797	140	1822	360	1847	2,000
1798	160	1823	450	1848	2,090
1799	170	1824	550	1849	2,170
1800	180	1825	580	1850	2,250

Source: P. Riden, 'The Output of the British Iron Industry before 1870', *Economic History Review,* 2nd ser. 30 (1977).

(d) (i) Retained imports of raw cotton, Britain, 1697–1810 (000 lb.)

	Cotton imports		Cotton imports		Cotton import
1697–8	862	1736	1,836	1774	5,400
1699	1,289	1737	1,526	1775	6,077
1700	1,083	1738	2,368	1776	5,844
1701	1,768	1739	2,164	1777	6,372
1702	1,380	1740	1,464	1778	5,896
1703	584	1741	1,571	1779	5,468
1704	1,026	1742	1,764	1780	6,553
1705	—	1743	1,203	1781	5,102
1706	366	1744	2,015	1782	11,407
1707	472	1745	1,549	1783	9,558
1708	2,784	1746	2,375	1784	11,280
1709	872	1747	2,290	1785	17,993
1710	663	1748	4,873	1786	19,152
1711	613	1749	1,480	1787	22,177
1712	—	1750	2,254	1788	19,614
1713	949	1751	2,903	1789	32,278
1714	1,284	1752	3,410	1790	30,604
1715	1,661	1753	4,102	1791	28,344
1716	1,956	1754	3,036	1792	33,422
1717	1,714	1755	3,665	1793	17,869
1718	1,957	1756	2,714	1794	23,009
1719	1,342	1757	1,818	1795	25,207
1720	1,809	1758	1,988	1796	31,431
1721	1,442	1759	2,209	1797	22,745
1722	2,005	1760	1,741	1798	31,280
1723	2,042	1761	2,627	1799	42,534
1724	901	1762	2,873	1800	51,594
1725	1,738	1763	2,457	1801	54,143
1726	1,408	1764	3,647	1802	56,616
1727	—	1765	3,699	1803	52,251
1728	1,474	1766	6,853	1804	61,364
1729	1,088	1767	3,425	1805	58,878
1730	1,468	1768	3,945	1806	57,524
1731	1,301	1769	4,045	1807	7,748
1732	1,406	1770	3,246	1808	41,961
1733	1,784	1771	2,328	1809	88,461
1734	1,308	1772	4,951	1810	123,702
1735	2,021	1773	2,388		

Source: A. P. Wadsworth and J. de L. Mann, *The Cotton Trade and Industrial Lancashire, 1660–1780* (1931), 520–1, and E. Baines, *History of the Cotton Manufacture* (1835), 347.

d) (ii) Raw cotton consumption, United Kingdom, 1800–1850 (million lb.)

	Cotton consumption		Cotton consumption		Cotton consumption
1800	52	1817	107	1834	303
1801	54	1818	110	1835	318
1802	56	1819	109	1836	347
1803	52	1820	120	1837	366
1804	61	1821	129	1838	417
1805	59	1822	145	1839	382
1806	57	1823	154	1840	459
1807	73	1824	165	1841	438
1808	42	1825	167	1842	435
1809	88	1826	150	1843	518
1810	124	1827	197	1844	544
1811	89	1828	218	1845	607
1812	73	1829	219	1846	614
1813	78	1830	248	1847	441
1814	74	1831	263	1848	577
1815	81	1832	277	1849	630
1816	89	1833	287	1850	588

Source: T. Ellison, *A Handbook of the Cotton Trade* (1858) and *The Cotton Trade of Great Britain* (1886).

e) Index of industrial production and rate of growth, 1730–1830 (% p.a.)

	Industrial production		Industrial production per head	
	Index no.	Rate of growth	Index no.	Rate of growth
1730	63		83	
1740	65	0.3	82	−0.1
1750	71	0.9	87	0.5
1760	78	0.9	89	0.3
1770	89	1.3	97	0.8
1780	100	1.2	100	0.3
1790	126	2.3	115	1.4
1800	153	1.9	124	0.8
1810	200	2.7	143	1.4
1820	242	1.9	149	0.4
1830	361	4.1	192	2.6

Source: R. V. Jackson, 'Rates of Industrial Growth during the Industrial Revolution', *Economic History Review*, 2nd ser. 45 (1992), 19.

4. TRADE

(a) *Computed values at current prices of external trade, Great Britain, 1784–1786 to 1854–1856* (annual averages, £m)

	Imports	Exports	Re-exports
1784–6	22.8	13.6	3.6
1794–6	37.9	24.0	8.3
1804–6	55.6	41.2	9.8
1814–16	71.8	48.0	17.7
1824–6	66.4	39.9	9.6
1834–6	70.3	46.2	10.2
1844–6	82.0	58.4	10.8
1854–6	151.6	102.5	21.0

Source: R. Davis, *The Industrial Revolution and British Overseas Trade* (Leicester, 1979), table 37, p. 86.

(b) *Terms of trade*

(i) *Gross barter terms of trade, England and Wales* (three-yearly moving average)

	Terms of trade		Terms of trade		Terms of trade
1700	100	1725	119	1750	190
1705	129	1730	110	1755	154
1710	158	1735	129	1760	171
1715	145	1740	124	1765	149
1720	133	1745	178	1770	126

(ii) *Gross barter terms of trade, Great Britain* (three-yearly moving average)

	Terms of trade		Terms of trade		Terms of trade
1775	119	1785	100	1795	127
1780	106	1790	114	1800	141

Source: P. Deane and W. A. Cole, *British Economic Growth 1688–1955* (Cambridge, 1962).

(ii) *Net barter terms of trade, United Kingdom*

	Terms of trade		Terms of trade		Terms of trade
1800	176.5	1820	156.5	1840	105.1
1805	191.1	1825	147.0	1845	119.6
1810	158.5	1830	149.8	1850	110.1
1815	138.2	1835	122.4		

Source: A. H. Imlah, *Economic Elements in the Pax Britannica* (Cambridge, Mass., 1958), 94–8.

INDEX

DATE DUE